T0334057

This textbook is dedicated to our families who have been very supportive with our academic endeavours.

ISLAMIC BANKING AND FINANCE

AN INTRODUCTION

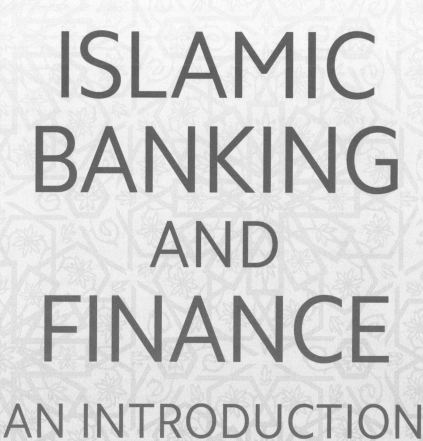

ROSZAINI HANIFFA

MOHAMMAD HUDAIB

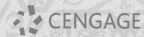

Australia • Brazil • Mexico • Singapore • United Kingdom • United States

Islamic Banking and Finance:
An Introduction, **1st EMEA Edition**
Roszaini Haniffa and Mohammad Hudaib

Publisher: Annabel Ainscow

List Manager: Jennifer Grene

Development Editor: Hannah Close

Marketing Manager: Sophie Clarke

Senior Content Project Manager:
Sue Povey

Manufacturing Buyer: Eyvett Davis

Typesetter: Lumina Datamatics, Inc.

Text Design: Lumina Datamatics, Inc.

Cover Design: Design Deluxe Ltd

Cover Image(s): Shutterstock/Absent A

For product information and technology assistance, contact us at
emea.info@cengage.com

For permission to use material from this text or product and for permission queries, email **emea.permissions@cengage.com**

British Library Cataloguing-in-Publication Data

A catalogue record for this book is available from the British Library.

ISBN: 978-1-4737-3460-9

Cengage Learning EMEA
Cheriton House, North Way
Andover, Hampshire, SP10 5BE
United Kingdom

Cengage Learning is a leading provider of customized learning solutions with employees residing in nearly 40 different countries and sales in more than 125 countries around the world. Find your local representative at: **www.cengage.co.uk.**

Cengage Learning products are represented in Canada by Nelson Education, Ltd.

For your course and learning solutions, visit **www.cengage.co.uk.**

Purchase any of our products at your local college store or at our preferred online store **www.cengagebrain.com.**

Printed in Singapore by Seng Lee Press
Print Number: 01   Print Year: 2018

Brief contents

Contents

Preface

This is the first edition of our book *Islamic Banking and Finance: An Introduction*. We have written this book to provide an introductory grounding to the Islamic theoretical viewpoint and the practice of Islamic banking and finance. We hope it will serve as a useful guide for anyone studying Islamic banking and finance at final year undergraduate and postgraduate levels and for those who are perhaps considering a career in the Islamic banking, finance and insurance services sectors.

While there have been a number of books written on Islamic banking and finance, there are only a few textbooks that combine the Islamic worldview on economics and finance with the development and performance of Islamic financial institutions in a way that is suitable for delivery to the European educational market. Furthermore, most textbooks present only the Islamic perspective of finance and banking, while such courses are often offered as an elective to students, who may not necessarily have prior knowledge in conventional finance, banking and accounting and as such will struggle to understand the more complex concepts and mechanics of Islamic banking and finance. Hence, we start every chapter with some background on the conventional aspect in a manner that will help students to have a good grasp of the underlying principles, before presenting the Islamic aspect.

Features of the text

- *Objectives* – a bulleted list at the beginning of each chapter identifies the key issues covered in the chapter.
- *Examples* – provided to reinforce understanding.
- *Summary* – recaptures the major issues discussed in the chapter.
- *Key concepts* – refer to concepts students are expected to know in each chapter and they can also refer to the glossary to refresh their memory.
- *Questions* – this section at the end of each chapter tests students' understanding of the key concepts and may serve as tutorial or seminar assignments.
- *Cases/Applications* – available in some chapters to test students' ability to apply the concepts as well as their computational skills.
- *Readings* – provide relevant additional sources that students can use to enhance their further understanding on the topic.

Supplements to the text

- *Instructor's manual* – contains a chapter outline for each chapter and a summary of key concepts for discussions, as well as answers to the end of chapter Questions. Suggestions on topics for individual essays and group coursework are also provided.
- *PowerPoint slides* – the slides clarify content and provide a solid guide for student note taking.

Organization of the text

We divide the chapters into three parts. The first part will help readers to have a good grasp on the elements of worldview and their implications on thoughts and economic behaviour. The Islamic worldview, founded on *shari'ah*, emphasizes socioeconomic justice in society, which can be achieved through two central ideas: profit and risk sharing and interest free business dealings. Hence, the first three chapters (*Chapters 1–3*) lay the foundations in understanding the Islamic economic and financial systems and introduce readers to various basic concepts that will be encountered throughout the book.

The second part covers Islamic financial instruments and financial institutions and markets. *Chapter 4* introduces the importance of contract in business transactions between two or more parties in a just and equitable way. The reader will notice that all contemporary Islamic financial transactions and products have their own underlying contracts designed to suit different needs and circumstances. Hence, it is not surprising that besides the classical types of contracts developed by early Muslim scholars, there have been many innovations in developing new contracts and products that comply with Islamic principles to meet the demands of the fast developing Islamic finance industry beyond the Muslim world. *Chapters 5 & 6* introduce readers to financial instruments offered in the Islamic financial markets such as Islamic equity (shares or stocks), *sukuk* (Islamic bonds) and Islamic derivatives. Readers will be able to see how the innovation of *sukuk* in finance has changed the dynamics of the global financial industry that enable the flow of funds beyond domestic borders. The natural expansion of Islamic financial markets and products leads to more risk exposure for both individuals and businesses. Therefore, this creates demand for Islamic insurance, widely known as *takaful*, where policyholders jointly guarantee among themselves against any hazard or loss incurred during the insurance period. The development of *takaful* and the various business models are covered in *Chapter 7*. Not everyone in society will have access to funds needed for their business operations, especially those entrepreneurs who have no tangible collateral to access the conventional banks, and this is especially prevalent in many Muslim dominated countries. Thus, Islamic microfinance is deemed as a valuable and novel tool for development and poverty alleviation, which is the subject matter in *Chapter 8*.

The third part of the book provides readers with a better understanding of the management and governance of Islamic financial institutions. *Chapters 9 & 10* focus on Islamic banking and reporting by introducing readers to accounting concepts and the various financial statements that Islamic financial institutions are expected to produce and report as well as the five important aspects in Islamic bank management: asset management, liabilities management, liquidity management, capital management and off balance sheet management, in ensuring the sustainability of the institution. While all businesses involved risks, there are risks that are unique to only Islamic financial institutions and *Chapter 11* highlights the various types of risks and techniques to mitigate them. Finally, *Chapter 12* explores how the integration of the roles played by various regulatory and supervisory bodies, such as the Islamic Financial Services Board (IFSB), the Accounting and Auditing Organization for Islamic Financial Institutions (AAOIFI), and the Bank of England, have supported the expansion and contributed to the resilience and sustainability of the global Islamic banking and finance sector.

We hope you enjoy reading the book and we welcome any feedback on omissions or recommendations to further improve the content of the book. Finally, we apologize for any mistakes that may have gone unnoticed when writing the text.

Roszaini Haniffa (Heriot-Watt University)
Mohammad Hudaib (University of Glasgow)

About the authors

Roszaini Haniffa is currently Professor of Accountancy at Heriot-Watt University, Edinburgh. She received her BSc from Northern Illinois University, her MSc from the University of Stirling and a PhD from Exeter University where she started her teaching career in the UK. She then moved to Bradford University School of Management and was the Head of Department of Accounting and Finance before joining Hull University Business School and Heriot-Watt.

Professor Haniffa's research interests are in the areas of auditing, business ethics, corporate governance, corporate social responsibility and sustainability, financial reporting, international accounting, and Islamic accounting and finance. Ros has published articles in scholarly journals such as *Journal of Business Ethics, Journal of Accounting & Public Policy, Accounting Forum, ABACUS, Accounting, Auditing & Accountability Journal, Accounting & Business Research,* and *Journal of International Accounting, Auditing & Taxation.* She has also written chapters in books, such as *Handbook of Islamic Accounting, Oxford Handbook in Economics and Finance: Islam and the Economy,* and *QFinance.*

Ros is the founder and chief editor of *Journal of Islamic Accounting and Business Research* (JIABR). She serves on various editorial boards and has been regularly invited to speak on Islamic accounting, finance and banking. She was included in the UK Muslim Women Power List 2010 by the Equality and Human Rights Commission.

Mohammad Hudaib is Reader of Accounting at Adam Smith Business School, the University of Glasgow. He received his BSc from King Saud University (Saudi Arabia), a MSc from the University of Stirling and a PhD from the University of Essex. He has previously taught at Exeter University, Bradford University School of Management, Essex University Business School and Nottingham University.

His research interests are in the areas of business ethics, auditing and accountability, corporate governance, and Islamic accounting and finance. His works have been published in reputable journals such as *Journal of Business Ethics, International Journal of Auditing, Accounting Forum, British Accounting Review, Journal of Business Finance & Accounting, Accounting, Auditing & Accountability Journal,* and *Journal of International Accounting, Auditing & Taxation.* Mohammad is editor of *Journal of Islamic Accounting and Business Research* (JIABR).

Acknowledgements

The authors and publishers would like to thank the following for their help in reviews and guidance on this text:

Adriana van Cruysen, Zuyd Hogeschool

Hugh McBride, Galway-Mayo Institute of Technology

Messaoud Mehafdi, University of Huddersfield

Philip Molyneux, Bangor University

Vasileios Pappas, University of Bath

Asif Zaman, Cardiff Metropolitan University

We thank Hannah Close, Development Editor for getting us involved in this book project, Susan Povey for her excellent editorial support and the editorial team at Cengage.

—Roszaini Haniffa and Mohammad Hudaib

Teaching & Learning Support Resources

Cengage's peer reviewed content for higher and further education courses is accompanied by a range of digital teaching and learning support resources. The resources are carefully tailored to the specific needs of the instructor, student and the course. Examples of the kind of resources provided include:

- A password protected area for instructors with, for example, a testbank, PowerPoint slides and an instructor's manual.

- An open-access area for students including, for example, useful weblinks and glossary terms.

Lecturers: to discover the dedicated lecturer digital support resources accompanying this textbook please register here for access: login.cengage.com.

Students: to discover the dedicated student digital support resources accompanying this textbook, please search for **Islamic Banking and Finance: An Introduction** on: cengagebrain.com.

BE UNSTOPPABLE

Overview of Islamic economics and finance

PART I

1 Islamic worldview

Learning Objectives

Upon completion of this chapter you should be able to:

- explain the meaning of worldview

- describe the broad classification of worldviews

- explain the seven elements of worldview and their implications on thoughts and actions

- discuss the foundations of the Islamic worldview and its link to *shari'ah*

- describe the objectives, source and dimensions of *shari'ah*

- explain the concept of *maqasid al-shari'ah* (ultimate objectives)

- discuss the implications of *shari'ah* on political, social and economic institutions

- describe the implications of the Islamic worldview on business activities

- distinguish between Islamic and other worldviews

1.1 Introduction

Islam is the second most widely spread religion across the world after Christianity. According to demographic analysis by the Pew Research Center (2017), the number of Muslims globally is about 1.8 billion people, or 24 per cent of the world's population. However, the number of Muslims is expected to increase by 70 per cent – from 1.8 billion in 2015 to nearly 3 billion in 2060. If the projection is correct, Muslims will surpass Christians as the largest religious group. There are currently 57 Muslim majority states (based on membership of the Organisation of Islamic Cooperation, OIC), and it is estimated that one out of five Muslims live in a Muslim minority country (160 million in India, 38 million in Europe and 5 million in the USA). Hence, Muslims are an important part of the world economy, and they are constantly seeking alternative economic solutions that are in line with *shari'ah* or Islamic law.

The word *shari'ah* has received substantial attention in the media for various reasons. One of the reasons is related to the growth of the Islamic finance industry worldwide. According to the Islamic Financial Services Board, or IFSB (2015), the Islamic finance industry is currently estimated at US\$ 1.88 trillion to US\$ 2.1 trillion with the expectation that the market size would reach US\$ 3.4 trillion by the end of 2018. This new phenomenon in the financial world came with the religious imperative to provide alternative financial services in accordance with the principles and teachings of Islam, which demands the preservation of ethics that include the ban on interest (*riba*) and other exploitative and speculative activities and transactions, promotion of risk-sharing methods as well as innovation and entrepreneurship (Warde, 2010; Iqbal & Mirakhor, 2007).

Before going straight into the subject matter of Islamic economics and its sub-area of specialization–Islamic banking and finance, which will be discussed in the remaining chapters – it is important to first understand the foundations of the Islamic worldview and how it differs from other worldviews. This will in turn help us in appreciating how worldviews influence the various institutions, particularly the economic and financial systems and their approach to capital allocation and mobilization as well as the conduct of business. This will be the focus of this chapter.

1.2   The meaning of worldview

The term *worldview,* or *Weltanschauung,* i.e. image of the world, introduced by the famous German philosopher Emmanuel Kant, epitomizes how man perceives this world and commits to a particular way of life based on some system of value-principles. Chapra (1992, p. 1) recognizes a worldview as:

> *a set of implicit or explicit beliefs or assumptions about the origin of the universe and the nature of human life.*

Hence, the way we act and live our day to day lives are guided by our particular worldview on some significant aspects of our lives such as the existence of the Creator or God, the cosmos, knowledge, purpose of life in this world and the hereafter, morals and values and destiny. Our worldview or belief system determines what we think is possible, which in turn influences the results that we create or allow in life. For instance, if we believe in equality of mankind and appreciate diversity, then we are compelled to be compassionate to others and will find ways to combat political and economic injustice in the world. On the other hand, if we accept certain races or social classes to be more superior and do not appreciate diversity, then we may not feel guilty in showing our hatred and oppressing others. In the same vein, if we believe in the connections in the ecosystem and its impact on our lives, then we will be obliged to take more care of our environment by taking actions to reduce pollution and waste, conserve energy and land, etc. In short, our worldview serves as a road map in guiding our decisions on how to live our lives in this world.

The notion of a worldview is contextual, dynamic and constructive. It is *contextual* because the distinctive spiritual and material aspects of the society in which we live and the various institutions, such as religion, media, schools, etc., may shape our worldview. A worldview is *dynamic* and may evolve over time as a result of the interactions between changing realities of life that we experience. As knowledge expands, there is a tendency to shape one's worldview in a certain path in life, and, therefore, worldview is *constructed and reconstructed* over time as it undergoes a continuous process of change around some particular elements.

1.3   Classification of worldviews

Worldviews can be distinguished based solely on the fundamental aspects of reality. Figure 1.1 illustrates the common classification of worldviews. Using this aspect as the basis, we can broadly classify worldviews into two types: religious and secular. *Religious worldview* is related to a notion of a deity, divine entity or God who has

Figure 1.1   Broad classification of worldviews

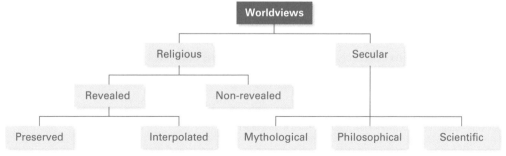

set up an eternal structure of morality that must be followed, as they have long term significance for humans. In contrast, a *secular worldview* is based on a materialistic and naturalistic standpoint that rejects the supernatural and the immortality of the Creator, and the cosmos being God's creation. The religious worldview can be further distinguished into revealed and non-revealed, while secular worldview can be further divided into mythological, philosophical and scientific. Each has its own assumptions and views on various aspects in life.

A religious worldview is intrinsically associated with the belief in a Supreme Being or God(s) as the basis and determinant of reality. The belief system may rely on sacred *revealed* text that has either been preserved (e.g. the *Qur'an*, the sacred book for Muslims) or interpolated (e.g. the *Old Testament* and *New Testament*, which are the holy books for the Jews and Christians), or on *non-revealed* text in the form of human wisdom (e.g. *Tipitaka* and *Vedas*, which are the holy books for Buddhists and Hindus, respectively).

As mentioned earlier, the secular worldview can be further classified into mythological, philosophical and scientific. A *mythological worldview* is based on collected myths that are deemed as being true by a particular culture, and the supernatural is often used to explain natural incidents and to explicate the nature of humanity and the universe. A *philosophical worldview* addresses all areas of existence, i.e. metaphysics, epistemology and ethics, thus recognizing both idealistic and materialistic aspects of reality. On the other hand, a *scientific worldview* is based solely on ideas that can be tested with empirical observation, and therefore conforms to the highest level of objectivity, but it detests the idea of creationism and postulates evolutionism as the foundation of reality.

1.4   Elements of worldview and their implications on thoughts and actions

Another way of understanding worldviews is by considering the seven elements of worldview that hint at how one will approach life. They are highly interrelated and affect all aspects of the others. Table 1.1 presents a summary of these seven elements of beliefs and their implications on one's thoughts and choice of actions.[1]

The first element, *epistemology*, is about the nature of knowledge, the rationality of belief and justification. For some, knowledge is derived solely on observation and reasoning, and as such, relies heavily on the senses and the brain or intellect. For others, besides accepting knowledge in the form of revelation, including divine revelation, which is driven by intuition controlled by some external source, they also trust in the message communicated even if there is no clear evidence.

The second element, *metaphysics*, deals with the ultimate nature of reality. To some, the universe is created and is controlled by a supernatural power, while others believe that the universe exists as a natural phenomenon devoid of control by any supernatural power.

The third and fourth elements, i.e. cosmology and teleology, address the core questions related to the origin and the end purpose of the universe and man. In terms of *cosmology*, some believe that the universe exists by chance, while others believe that it came into being via explosion of an initial matter of a certain density and temperature, i.e. the 'big bang', and yet others believe that an omnipotent (all powerful) and omnipresent (all knowing and all seeing) being was solely responsible for creating the universe. With regards to *teleology*, some believe that the end purpose of our universe is unknown, while others believe that they are signs to make inhabitants conscious of God, and yet others believe it is about making the inhabitants happy.

The fifth element, *theology*, is related to the beliefs on the existence and nature of God, as well as His relationship with man. Regarding the existence of God, some believe in His existence and His sacred texts, while others do not. To those who believe in His existence, some believe that there is only one God (monotheism) and that God is most benevolent, omnipotent and omniscient, while others believe in more than one God (polytheism)

---

[1]This classification is based on Hunter Mead's book, *Types and Problems of Philosophy*. Also see Funk, K. (2001), What is a worldview?, web.engr.oregonstate.edu/~funkk/Personal/worldview.html, accessed 6 November 2017.

Table 1.1 Elements of worldview and their implications

Elements	Related questions regarding:	Implications
1. Epistemology beliefs on the nature, basis and validation of knowledge	Knowledge	• if knowledge is associated with *brain state*, then beliefs and acts are dependent on neural mechanisms in corresponding to reality • if knowledge is associated with *cosmic mind*, then beliefs and acts correspond directly to revelation as fundamental truth
	Basis for knowledge	• if *empirical evidence* is the basis of knowledge, then *sensory mechanisms* will influence thoughts and actions • if *intuition and revelation* are recognized as basis of knowledge, then need to recognize that *some external source* control thoughts and actions
	Difference between knowledge and faith	• acceptance of validity of knowledge is through *logic of verification* • acceptance of faith is through the nominal *trust of the source delivering the message*
	Certainty: validated or absolute	• certainty can be achieved for some knowledge and/or faith up to an absolute degree of confidence as the highest level of validity
2. Metaphysics beliefs regarding the ultimate nature of reality	Ultimate nature of reality	• a *naturalist or materialist* ultimately believes that the universe exists, but it is mechanistic and indifferent and there is no mind or God or spirit that created, guides or considers it. Anything that cannot be apprehended by senses does not exist • an *idealist* believes that reality is ultimately spiritual in nature. The universe is created by a supernatural above it and has a part in guiding it. This universe has a moral order that inevitably has to be achieved
	Truth	According to Funk (2001), the theory of truth is of three types: • the *correspondence* theory of truth: you believe that truth corresponds to what your mind or brain comprehends of what actually exists outside yourself • the *consistency* theory of truth: you believe that truth is merely that knowledge which is internally consistent in mathematical logic as a necessary condition for any proposition to be considered valid • the *pragmatic* theory of truth: you believe that truth is what is valued by you, what works for you, what is true for you, though it might not be true for someone else
	Ultimate test of truth	• an *empiricist* holds that only empirical inquiry can lead to discovery of truth, which is validated *through inductive or deductive reasoning* • a *constructionist* holds that truth is acquired *directly through either revelation or intuition*
3. Cosmology beliefs regarding the origin of the universe and origin of life and man	Origin of the universe	• by *chance*: the universe exists due to the 'big bang', i.e. collision of matter and energy based on random events and law of physics • by *the acts of a supernatural Creator*: universe is formed through a big bang in a precise and controlled way, based on the command of the Creator
	Origin of life and man	• by *chance*: life and the human race are the result of natural selection (Darwinism) • by *supernatural Creator*: life and man are created from non-living matter and gradually evolved towards a desired end
4. Teleology beliefs about purpose	Purpose of the universe	• unknown and remains unknown • too complex to comprehend due to interdependence of its elements • becoming more self-conscious of its inhabitants and the universe itself • bring happiness to its conscious occupants • make conscious inhabitants to know God

(continued)

Table 1.1 Elements of worldview and their implications *(continued)*

Elements	Related questions regarding:	Implications
5. Theology beliefs about God	Existence of God	• a *theist* believes that God exists and governs, although the number of Gods may differ: monotheists (Judaism, Islam and Christianity) believe in one God, while polytheists (Hinduism, Zoroastrianism) believe in multiple Gods • an *atheist* does not at all believe in the existence of God • an *agnostic* is unsure whether God exists
	Nature of God(s)	• exists outside of and above nature • transcends localized person(s) or personhood(s) • opposite dispositions: can be benevolent or tyrannical, loving or indifferent, omnipotent or limited in power, or only partly knowledgeable of what is going on in the universe
	Relationship between God and man	• a loving parent or an immature tyrant • a lawgiver, judge and executioner who is caring and just • indifferent to man's activities or desires of an intimate relationship with each one of them • speaks to man and leaves them to reason things out themselves
6. Anthropology beliefs about man	Man's position in the universe	• an infinite and insignificant part of the universe, but evolved towards new and better beings • as part of earth's global ecosystem, having stewardship responsibility in ensuring the wellbeing of other creations • a unique position as a moral agent who always thinks and acts to realize the good
	Free will in man	• man has no free will as he is just a mechanism, a slave to his instinct, conditions and events that are beyond his control • man has no free will, and is nothing more than God's puppet who acts based on what has been written without his involvement • man is given the intellect to think and act: despite the constraints imposed by the laws of physics and biology or the guidance of God, man is still given free will to make choices
	Expectation from man	• no obligation to anyone or anything beyond himself • responsible for the wellbeing of other fellow human beings and the universe in general • to believe, love, obey and enter into communion with God
	Nature of man	• western thought, which is predominantly grounded in Christian teachings, believes in the sinful nature of man who always has to strive to fight his evil nature • others believe that man is basically good and always looking to express that goodness in everything he does • others believe that man is born morally neutral and it is the external influences and strength of will that direct him towards a path of good or evil
7. Axiology beliefs on values that drive behaviours	Types of value	• non-moral values include economic and aesthetic values, and simple goodness • moral value encompasses the extent to which a thought or act is morally right or wrong
	Source of value	• may be imposed by the self, or decided by a society or culture, or by nature of the universe, or by God or the gods
	Value: objective or relative	Four possible positions: • value is absolute and objective: applicable under all circumstances (absolute) to all people (objective) • value is absolute and subjective: applicable under all circumstances (absolute) to some people (subjective) • value is relative and objective: applicable based on varying circumstances (relative) to all people (objective) • value is relative and subjective: applicable based on varying circumstances (relative) to some people (subjective)

Source: Adapted from Funk, K. (2001), *What is a worldview?*, web.engr.oregonstate.edu/~funkk/Personal/worldview.html, accessed 6 November 2017.

and that each God has different powers. Nevertheless, they all worship their God(s) and live life as prescribed in some sacred texts, which may be either through revelation or human wisdom.

The sixth and seventh elements, anthropology and axiology, address beliefs about man and the values that drive man's behaviour, respectively. In terms of *anthropology*, beliefs about man include his purpose in the universe, expectations in this life as well as whether man has a free will. Some believe that man has a unique place in the universe and ecosystem created by God and is expected to play an important role as trustee and moral agent to realize the goodness, while others perceive man as nothing more than part of the universe with no specific purpose or at best as stewards to care for its wellbeing. In relation to *axiology* and concept of free will, some believe that man has no free will and is driven solely by instincts beyond his control while others believe in partial free will whereby man can use his intellect to make choices despite some physical, biological and religious constraints.

As for the last element, which is related to behaviours, some recognize values as defined by God(s) to be the best source of good behaviour, while others recognize values imposed by the self or decided by society as more important sources of good behaviour. These values can be absolute or relative and objective or subjective. An *absolute value* is one that is applicable under all circumstances: it may be objective, i.e. applicable to everyone, such as justice and happiness, or subjective, whereby it is only applicable to certain people, such as smoking or drinking alcohol. On the other hand, a *relative value* is dependent on varying circumstances and can be objective, i.e. applicable to everyone, such as smoking in public places or drink driving, or subjective, i.e. applicable to some people, such as the provision of controlled therapeutic medication for individuals seeking rehabilitation.

In short, beliefs or assumptions in the worldview will affect one's thoughts and actions. This includes economic activities and the conceptions on ultimate possession and disposal of wealth, rights and responsibilities, efficiency and equity, etc. Therefore, different worldviews give rise to different systems that lead to dissimilar end means of human life and behaviour.

1.5   The Islamic worldview

Islam, literally meaning 'peace' and 'submission' (or obedience), has a worldview. According to Al-Attas (1994, p. 26), the *Islamic worldview* is a vision of reality and truth as it involves:

> *a metaphysical survey of the visible as well as the invisible worlds including the perspective of life as a whole…*

Hence, the Islamic worldview encompasses both religious and worldly aspects, with the latter being the ultimate and most significant aspect in helping to achieve *al-falah*, a comprehensive human success, wellbeing and happiness in this world and the hereafter. The Islamic ontology (nature of reality) is concerned with both this universe (world) and the hereafter (i.e. Day of Judgement). Therefore, man should strive to fulfil his purpose in this life as well as prepare for the hereafter, as this world is only a transit to the perpetual life where man will be held accountable for every action in this world.

Iqbal and Mirakhor (2007) identify three fundamental axioms in the Islamic worldview which lay the foundation of Islam's political, social and economic systems:

(i) *Unity and oneness of the Creator (tawhid)*
The concept of *tawhid* is central to the Muslim belief system. It is the unqualified belief that all creation has only one omniscient and omnipresent Creator that is Allah, who has created and placed man in this earth as His vicegerent (*khalifa*) or trustee.[2] This means that as a trustee on this earth, man has to act as guardian or steward in dealing with the environment, wealth and rules governing the possession and

---

[2]The *Qur'an* states: 'Behold, thy Lord said to the angels; "I will create a vicegerent on earth" (Al-Baqarah, 2:30). www.wright-house.com/religions/islam/Quran/2-cow.php, accessed 6 June 2018.

disposal of wealth. Man has the right to own wealth but the right is not absolute, as Allah is the ultimate owner of all wealth. Since man has willingly accepted nature as a trust[3] from Allah, he must be willing to serve His purpose in this life. This requires man's unconditional surrender to Allah by making his desires, ambitions and actions subservient to His command.[4] Muslims view human creation and life as having a meaningful and sublime purpose beyond the physical needs and material activities of man and that the orbit of a man's life is much longer, broader and deeper than the material dimension in this world (Haniffa and Hudaib, 2011). This is in accordance with one's covenant with Allah, which is to worship Him alone in every aspect of life (Haniffa and Hudaib, 2011).

(ii) *Prophethood (nubuwwa)*

Muslims believe in all the prophets sent to mankind and recognized the Prophet Muhammad as the last and final messenger of Allah, bringing to mankind the most perfect set of rules of conduct or *risalah*[5] to aid man in fulfilling a perfect life in this world. It is also the belief that the actions and words of the Prophet Muhammad are personified as a model of the perfect man for all mankind to strive for.

(iii) *Ultimate return to the Creator (ma'ad)*

Muslims believe that there is a point in the cycle of life when Allah will call forth all mankind to a final destination. This axiom highlights the concept of the hereafter (*akhirah*) and by implication, acknowledges continuity of life beyond death that is eternal and that there is a system of accountability based on Divine Law, where complete accounts will be rendered and judged; good deeds rewarded with paradise and bad deeds with hell-fire. Therefore, the short span of life in this world must not be consumed by worldly matters alone, but must be used to prepare for the afterlife by observing Allah's rules in private and public affairs. The final judgement on actions has two dimensions, one at the individual level and the other as a member of society.

Besides the concepts of unity of God and Prophethood (*theology*) and the concept of the universe (*cosmology*), the Islamic worldview also addresses the concept of man and society (*anthropology*). Man secures a unique position among all creations as he has been designated a purpose in life (*teleology*) as a trustee on earth, which entails fulfilling specific responsibilities in creating a just and moral social order based on God's law. In discharging these responsibilities, man has been endowed with powers of cognition and intellectual volition that enables him to distinguish between right and wrong, just and unjust, true and false and the real and illusory (*axiology*). Furthermore, man is also provided with the criteria by which the Creator will judge all actions and is constantly reminded in His books that there will come a day of reckoning where deeds and misdeeds in this life will be judged and that there will be retributions for transgressions and rewards for efforts and obedience to His law.

To perform those responsibilities, man can tap on his intelligence to discover the knowledge that is necessary in utilizing the natural resources to the fullest potential. Thus, the Islamic worldview provides the recipe for the model of a successful man, as the purpose in life is clearly defined, responsibilities and the means for discharging the responsibilities are provided, the judgement criteria and the outcomes are made known, and guidance and reminders are clearly spelt out in His book of guidance. It is left to man's free will and choice to determine the path to follow.

To establish a just, moral and viable social order requires collective efforts in a united way in the form of an Islamic community or brotherhood (*ummah*) which is not founded on race, nationality, locality, occupation,

---

[3] Man's willingness to accept responsibility and trust is stated in the *Qur'an*: 'We did indeed offer the Trust to the Heavens and the Earth and the Mountains, but they refused to undertake it, being afraid thereof, but man undertook it' (Al-Ahzab, 33:72). www.wright-house.com/religions/islam/Quran/33-clans.php, accessed 6 June 2018.

[4] The *Qur'an* states: 'Say: "Truly, my prayer and my service of sacrifice, my life and my death, are (all) for Allah, the Cherisher of the Worlds"' (Al-An'am, 6:162). www.wright-house.com/religions/islam/Quran/6-cattle.php, accessed 6 June 2018.

[5] *Al-Risalah* is the channel of communication between God and mankind through His Prophets, His Angels and His Divine Books.

kinship or special interests. The central function of this community is to command the good and forbid the evil as part of their moral consciousness in fulfilling obligations to society in general. Adhering to Divine guidance and taking lessons from the fates of prior communities and civilisations that have risen and fallen,[6] should help in the development of behaviour which will lead to the existence of a justly balanced community that will be an example to all nations.

In short, in accepting the Islamic worldview, the individual as well as the community will simultaneously agree to observe the Divine Law (*shari'ah*), which represents the covenant between man and Allah to submit and worship Him alone. These rules are comprehensive and they govern all aspects of man's decisions and actions. Compliance with these rules will lead to unity of human society while failure to refrain from all the prohibitions in Islam may lead to disunity and social disintegration.

1.6   Islamic law – *shari'ah*

In Arabic, the word *shari'ah* literally means 'the way' or 'path to the water source'. In the context of Islam, *shari'ah* refers to the clear and straight path that leads humans to happiness in this world and hereafter. The linguistic meaning of *shari'ah* resonates in its '…technical usage: just as water is vital to human life, so the clarity and uprightness of *shari'ah* is the means of life for souls and minds' (Rabbani, 2011).

Figure 1.2 provides an illustration and summary of the various key concepts that will be discussed in this section. We will consider the links between the objectives, sources and the three dimensions of *shari'ah*.

Figure 1.2   Objectives, sources and dimensions of *shari'ah*

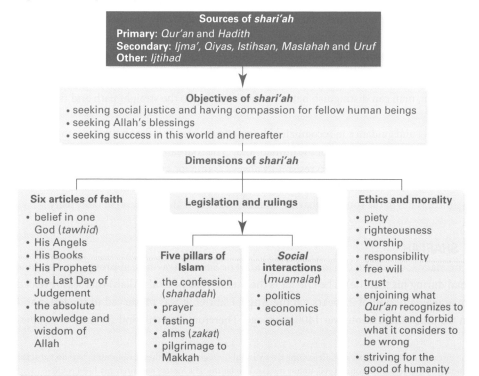

---

[6]The *Qur'an* states: 'Before thee We sent (apostles) to many nations, and We afflicted the nations with suffering and adversity, that they might learn humility' (Al-An'am, 6:42). www.wright-house.com/religions/islam/Quran/6-cattle.php, accessed 6 June 2018. For other examples, also see Al-Baqarah, 2:141-143; Al-Ma'idah, 5:66; Al-An'am, 6:108, and Al-A'raf, 7:164.

They are interrelated and not fragmented; only believing in the six articles of faith is not good enough, as one also needs to observe the five pillars of Islam, and conform to the Islamic code of ethics including aspects related to social interactions.

1.6.1 OBJECTIVES OF *SHARI'AH* (*MAQASID-AL SHARI'AH*)

According to Kamali (1989), the main objectives of *shari'ah* are to educate the individual, establish justice and realize benefits to the people in this world and in the hereafter. It governs every aspect of a Muslim's life, be it relationship with Allah or with others, including the political, economic and social institutions. In the words of al-Ghazali (cited in Islahi, 2014, p. 25):

> The obligation of the Shari'ah *is to provide for the well-being of all humankind, which lies in safeguarding their faith (din), their human self (nafs), their intellect ('aql), their progeny (nasl) and their wealth (mal).*

Ibn Al Qayim Al-Jawziyyah (cited in Abdalati, 1975) states that the basis of *shari'ah* is wisdom and welfare of the people in this world as well as the hereafter. As such, everything departing from justice to oppression, mercy to harshness, welfare to misery and wisdom to folly, runs counter to the tenets of *shari'ah* (Chapra, 1992). In other words, the goals of *shari'ah* are to establish justice and welfare in society and to seek Allah's blessings by setting the basic foundations for its moral, social, political and economic philosophy to achieve *al-falah* (Haniffa and Hudaib, 2011).

In order to achieve its objectives, *shari'ah* provides a scale by which all human actions are valued based on the weight of their merits and demerits, which are classified into five categories:

- obligatory actions, such as the daily five prayers
- recommended actions, such as supererogatory fasting beyond the month of Ramadan
- indifferent actions, such as preference for a particular permissible food (*halal*) over another
- reprehensible actions, such as smoking, which is not expressly forbidden like drinking alcohol but is discouraged as it is harmful and of no benefit
- forbidden actions (*haram*), such as committing any of the major sins like adultery, murder, etc.

Through such scales of valuation, man can distinguish between those leading to the straight path and those that will lead him astray.

Although man is given intellect and guidance in recognizing the right path based on the above scale, the actions taken may be influenced by the state of development of the human soul.[7] The soul can be one which is prone to evil, or one which consciously feels the evil and attempts to resist it by always asking for grace and pardon after repentance, or one where the soul achieves full satisfaction after the intellect has checked the evil tendencies of man. The interactions between these three states of the soul in behaving ethically will determine the level of one's piety.

1.6.2 SOURCES OF *SHARI'AH*

Shari'ah is based on two primary sources: the *Qur'an* and the *Hadith* or *Sunnah* (sayings, approvals and actions of the Prophet Muhammad during his lifetime). The *Qur'an* is the literal word of God (Allah) that was revealed to the Prophet Muhammad over a period of 23 years via the Angel Gabriel. It was preserved to the letter and remains unchanged from the time of revelation over 1400 years ago. Therefore, you will find that any two copies

---

[7]The *Qur'an* mentions about the three states of the human soul. Regarding the evil soul (*nafs ammarah*), the *Qur'an* states: 'Nor do I absolve my own self (of blame): the (human) soul is certainly prone to evil, unless my Lord do bestow His Mercy: but surely my Lord is Oft-forgiving, Most Merciful' (Yusuf, 12.53). www.wright-house.com/religions/islam/Quran/12-joseph.php, accessed 21 May 2018.

   As for the resisting soul (*nafs lawwammah*), the *Qur'an* states: 'And I do call to witness the self-reproaching spirit: (Eschew Evil)' (Al-Qiyamah, 75:2). www.wright-house.com/religions/islam/Quran/75-rising-of-dead.php, accessed 21 May 2018. With regards to the content soul (*nafs mutma'innah*), the *Qur'an* states: 'To the righteous soul will be said: "O (thou) soul, in (complete) rest and satisfaction!"' (Al-Fajr, 89:27). www.wright-house.com/religions/islam/Quran/89-dawn.php, accessed 21 May 2018.

of the *Qur'an* from anywhere in the world will have identical Arabic text. Furthermore, there are many Muslims, including those who do not speak Arabic, who have memorized the entire *Qur'an*. Although the *Qur'an* includes all the constitutive rules as guidance for mankind, it contains many universal statements that needed further clarification before they could become specific guides for human action. Hence, the principles enunciated in the *Qur'an* were explained, amplified, practiced and exemplified by the Prophet Muhammad, in the *Hadith*.

Although the two primary sources remain as key sources, *ijtihad* (independent reasoning), which refers to the efforts of individual jurists in providing solutions to problems on rules of behaviour which have not been addressed explicitly in the *Qur'an* and *Ahadith* that arise as human societies evolve, plays a crucial role. *Ijtihad* is exercised through the other secondary sources. These secondary sources of *shari'ah*, as long as the rule introduced is not in conflict with the main tenets of Islam, include the following (Iqbal and Mirakhor, 2007):

(i) *Ijma'*, which is a consensus of Muslim scholars sharing the same opinion and is applied only in the absence of an explicit answer to the issue in question.
(ii) *Qiyas*, which is represented in the analogical deductions from the other three sources for contemporary issues that are not directly mentioned in those sources but have similar characteristics with another or earlier situation or incident in the past which is clearly based on those sources.
(iii) *Istihsan*, which is a juristic preference where a scholar or knowledge seeker (*mujtahid*) prefers one alternative to another, although the former may not have an explicit argument in its favour.
(iv) *Maslahah*, which literally means to bring about utility and fend off damage or injury for public interest.
(v) *Urf*, based on customs.

1.6.3 DIMENSIONS OF *SHARI'AH*

Shari'ah provides the blueprint of an ideal life and is a much wider concept than Islamic law. It addresses three dimensions that are vital in achieving success and happiness in this world and the hereafter. According to Al-Qardawi (2007), the shari'ah covers three dimensions. The first dimension is related to all aspects of the creed and belief system or faith, the second is related to legislation and rulings which encompass the core relationship between man and his Creator in the form of worship and the relationship among human beings (*muamalat*), and the last dimension covers the system of ethics or morality:

(a) Faith

The six articles of the Islamic faith are the belief in the unity of one God (*tawhid*), His Angels, His Books, His Prophets, the Last Day of Judgement, and in His absolute knowledge and wisdom. As described earlier, the central belief of the Islamic faith is that there is only one God (monotheism). Muslims refer to God as Allah, which is Arabic for 'the' (*al*) and 'God' (*Ilah*). Accepting the unity of Allah also means accepting that He has no children, no parents and no partners, was not created by a being and there is none equal or superior to Him. Muslims believe in the nature of Allah being eternal, i.e. has always existed and will forever exist; omniscient, i.e. knows everything that can be known; and omnipotent, i.e. can do anything and everything; that He has no shape or form, has no gender and cannot be seen and heard; and that He is just and merciful.

In Islam, angels are recognized as spiritual creatures that are given various responsibilities in serving the purposes of Allah; the most significant among them is the Angel Gabriel, who relays communication to the prophets. Muslims believe in the holy books or scriptures revealed by Allah to a number of His Prophets: Scrolls (given to Prophet Ibrahim or Abraham); Torah (given to Prophet Musa or Moses); Psalms (given to Prophet Dawud or David); Gospel (given to Prophet Isa or Jesus Christ); with the *Qur'an* being the final and complete book for mankind being sent to the Prophet Muhammad. Muslims also believe that Allah has revealed to mankind His guidance through appointed messengers or prophets throughout history, beginning with the Prophet Adam and ending with the last of them all, the Prophet Muhammad. Twenty-five prophets are specifically mentioned by their name in the *Qur'an*, including Noah, Abraham, Joseph, Moses, Jesus and Muhammad, the last in this line of prophethood, sent for all humankind.

The afterlife is an important aspect in the Islamic worldview. Muslims believe that the soul continues to exist after death. On the Day of Judgement, all humans, depending on the weight of their deeds and misdeeds, will be destined eternally to either paradise or hell. Islam teaches that Allah not only foreknows but also foreordains all that happens in this world and the lives of individuals. However, this does not mean that humans have to be fatalistic because they have been given the intellect to think and act, which means that they do have choice of freedom.

(b) *Legislation and rulings*

This dimension deals with the transformation and manifestation of the faith and beliefs into actions and daily practices. This covers relationship between the Creator and man in the form of rites and rituals and also between human interactions (*muamalat*).

(i)   *Rites and rituals*

Rites and rituals of worship deals with ways to perform acts of worship in connecting man with his Creator as constituted in the five pillars of Islamic worship: declaration of belief in the Islamic faith, performance of daily prayers, paying alms and tithe (*zakat*), observing fasting in the month of Ramadan and performing the pilgrimage to Makkah. The central act of worship is the declaration of the Islamic faith (*shahadah*), 'There is no deity except Allah and that the Prophet Muhammad is the messenger of Allah', which is repeated many times in a day during prayers. Muslims perform ablution before making their five daily obligatory prayers (at dawn, noon, late afternoon, sunset and night) facing the direction of Makkah. The prayers can be done alone or in congregation in any clean location and not necessarily in the mosque (Muslim place of worship). The third act of worship is giving obligatory alms (*zakat*) annually based on two and a half per cent of one's income and wealth to the seven groups of beneficiaries mentioned in the *Qur'an*, in addition to other acts of charity throughout the year. During the month of Ramadan (ninth month of the lunar calendar), Muslims are required to fast from dawn to sunset. The fifth act of worship requires every Muslim, if financially and physically able, to make the pilgrimage to Makkah at least once in their lifetime, to the first house of worship of Allah (the *Kaaba*) built by the Prophet Abraham and his son Ishmael.

(ii)   *Human interactions*

Human interactions deals with worldly matters such as politics, economics and commercial transactions as well as social interactions between an individual and others such as marriage, inheritance and other human activities. Figure 1.3 illustrates the main concepts underlying three important aspects of human interactions: politics, social and economics.

Figure 1.3   Human interactions and their underlying concepts

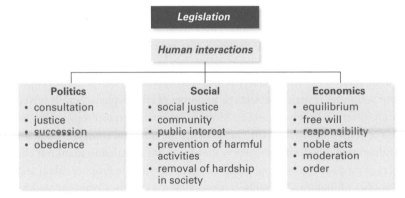

The *political* aspect of Islam is founded on the concepts of consultation, justice, succession and obedience. The belief in the unity (*tawhid*) of Allah means accepting that neither the rulers nor the people themselves have sovereignty, as it only belongs to Allah[8] and man's role is that of His vicegerent on earth. Free consultation at all levels[9] enables the ruler or leader with room to handle common affairs with the aim of achieving justice, providing security and protection to all citizens, and promoting their welfare regardless of colour, race or belief, in conformity with the stipulations of Allah's constitution.[10] In return, the ruler is entitled to obedience from the community as long as that role is performed in accordance with Allah's Law.[11] Thus, each citizen is enjoined to supervise the conduct of the governing administration and question its handling of public affairs and is also entitled to enjoy freedom of belief, thought and expression, etc. However, this freedom is not in the absolute sense as that may lead to chaos and anarchy. In short, the ruler has dual responsibility, to Allah and to society, and must act only as an executive chosen by the people to serve according to Allah's Law.

The *social* aspect of Islam is based on the concepts of justice, brotherhood and prioritizing benefit for the people. The belief in the unity of Allah means accepting everyone is equal in His sight, to whom there is direct access (Abdalati, 1975). Based on this concept of equality of mankind by nature and origin, the role of society as well as every individual is to be the true embodiment of the virtuous, the wholesome and the noble (Abdalati, 1975). By promoting equality, justice and virtues in society will guarantee the achievement of a comprehensive human welfare in this world and the hereafter.

The concept of brotherhood or community is founded on the principle of submission to the will of Allah, obedience to His law and commitment to His cause by advocating what is good, demand what is right and eradicate what is wrong.[12] The *Qur'an* also mentioned that the Muslim community must play an exemplary role[13] in striving for the truth by removing hardship and preventing the forbidden and harmful. The pursuance of benefit for the people is a commendable goal, concerned with the subsistence of human life, the completion of man's livelihood, and the acquisition of what his emotional and intellectual qualities require of him, i.e. protection of interests (Masood, 1989).

Islamic economics is founded on the concepts of equilibrium, free will and responsibility, as asserted in the *Qur'an* and *Ahadith* (Naqvi, 1994). The belief in the unity of Allah also means accepting that the ultimate ownership of all wealth belongs to Him. Man has only been given trust to use them in the ways prescribed by *shari'ah*. *Shari'ah* specifies eight rules governing private ownership and use of property: continuous utilization, payment of *zakat* according to market value, beneficial use of resources, care not to harm others when utilizing the resources, possession is in

---

[8]The *Qur'an* states: 'Blessed be He in Whose hands is Dominion; and He over all things hath Power' (Al-Mulk, 67:1). www.wright-house.com/religions/islam/Quran/67-sovereignty.php, accessed 21 May 2018.

[9]The *Qur'an* states: 'And consult them in affairs (of moment). Then, when thou hast Taken a decision put thy trust in Allah. For Allah loves those who put their trust (in Him)' (Al-Imran, 3:159). www.wright-house.com/religions/islam/Quran/3-family-of-imran.php, accessed 21 May 2018. Also see Ash-Shura, 42:38.

[10]The *Qur'an* states: 'O ye who believe! stand out firmly for justice, as witnesses to Allah, even as against yourselves, or your parents, or your kin, and whether it be (against) rich or poor: for Allah can best protect both. Follow not the lusts (of your hearts), lest ye swerve, and if ye distort (justice) or decline to do justice, verily Allah is well-acquainted with all that ye do' (An-Nisaa, 4:135). www.wright-house.com/religions/islam/Quran/4-women.php, accessed 21 May 2018. Also see An-Nisaa, 4:58.

[11]The *Qur'an* states: 'O ye who believe! Obey Allah, and obey the Messenger, and those charged with authority among you' (An-Nisaa, 4:59). www.wright-house.com/religions/islam/Quran/4-women.php, accessed 21 May 2018.

[12]The *Qur'an* states: 'Let there arise out of you a band of people inviting to all that is good, enjoining what is right, and forbidding what is wrong: They are the ones to attain felicity' (Al-Imran, 3:104). www.wright-house.com/religions/islam/Quran/3-family-of-imran.php, accessed 21 May 2018. Also see Al-Imran, 3:110.

[13]The *Qur'an* states: 'Thus, have We made of you an Ummat justly balanced, that ye might be witnesses over the nations, and the Messenger a witness over yourselves' (Al-Baqarah, 2:143). www.wright-house.com/religions/islam/Quran/2-cow.php, accessed 21 May 2018.

compliance with *shari'ah*, use must neither be parsimonious nor prodigal, self-due benefits to owners are permitted and property transfers are subject to Islamic inheritance laws (Mannan, 1986). The notion of equilibrium in Islam is based on the normative concept of justice as opposed to injustice, which denotes social disequilibrium whereby the resources of the society flow from the poor to the rich, and this is strongly forbidden in the *Qur'an*.[14] Free will indicates that man has the ability to make choices in various conflicting situations. Responsibility in Islam emphasizes two important concepts. The first is related to man's vicegerent role on earth, and the second is basically voluntary in nature, i.e. making sacrifices, but not to the extent of causing hardship to oneself.[15] In addition, Islamic economics encourage Muslims to engage in noble as opposed to corrupt actions when conducting economic activities. They are also expected to exercise moderation in consumption of resources to achieve order in society.

Accordingly, economic or business activities in Islam require Muslims to earn a living through lawful (*halal*) means. They must also avoid usury (*riba al-Fadl*) or interest *(riba al-Nasi'ah)*[16] by participating in profit sharing activities. *Riba al-Fadl* (usury and tampering with the freedom of the market) includes monopoly and monopsony, price control, taxation, imposed medium of exchange and exclusive rights of authors (copyrights) and inventors (patents) while *riba al-Nasi'ah* (unequal advantage) includes renting of money, uncertainty in transactions and unfair advantages in transactions (Vadillo and Khalid, 1992). In addition, they are expected to honour all their contracts, keep proper accounts, avoid extravagance, exercise moderation in consumption and fulfil obligations to society by paying *zakat*,[17] other form of taxes required by the state, as well as giving charity. They must avoid fraudulent practices, dishonesty, collusion, gambling and all forms of speculative (*gharar*) activities in any business transactions. These are all aimed at achieving economic justice based on equality and fairness.

(c) Ethical and moral behaviour

This third dimension of *shari'ah* relates to the moral aspects of Islam which are interrelated. Piety or love of Allah demands that man 'acts in obedience to Allah, and hopes in His mercy, upon a light from Him; and leaving acts of disobedience to Allah out of fear of Him, upon a light from Him' (Ibn Abee Shaybah cited in Al-Uthaymeen, 1998, p. 9). The *Qur'an* describes some obvious benefits of piety, of which achieving Allah's blessings is one. Some of the blessings mentioned in the *Qur'an* include making general affairs of mankind easier, protecting mankind from evil harm, attaining guardianship from Allah, distinguishing truth from falsehood and having knowledge of each one of them, preventing injustice in matters of wealth, providing the means of attaining Allah's mercy in this life and the hereafter as well as attaining knowledge.

Righteousness comprises all kinds of good and perfection expected in man, i.e. his faith should be true and sincere, he must be prepared to show kindness to his fellow man and to give charity and support charitable institutions and social organizations, he must be a good citizen and stay steadfast and unshakeable in all circumstances.[18] Besides believing in the truth of Allah and life, and making proper use of wealth by spending it

---

[14]The *Qur'an* states: 'In order that it may not (merely) make a circuit between the wealthy among you' (Al-Hashr, 59:7). www.wright-house.com/religions/islam/Quran/59-exile.php, accessed 21 May 2018.

[15]The *Qur'an* states: 'Those who spend their wealth for increase in self-purification' (Al-Lail, 92:18). www.wright-house.com/religions/islam/Quran/92-night.php, accessed 21 May 2018.

[16]Also see El-Ashker (1987) regarding different types of *riba*.

[17]*Zakat* is a religious duty and type of worship levied on Muslim individuals only. The spending of the proceeds and the beneficiaries are specified in the *Qur'an* (At-Tawbah, 9:60) and the rate is dependent on the type of economic activities (see El-Ashker, 1987; pp. 48-49).

[18]The *Qur'an* states: 'But it is righteousness – To believe in *Allah* and the last day, and the angels, and the book, and the messengers; to spend of your substance, out of love for Him, for your kin, for orphans, for the needy, for the wayfarer, for those who ask, and for the ransom of slaves; to be steadfast in prayer, and give *Zakat*, to fulfil the contracts which ye have made; and to be firm and patient, in pain (or suffering) and adversity, and throughout all periods of panic. Such are the people of truth, the God-fearing' (Al-Baqarah, 2:177). www.wright-house.com/religions/islam/Quran/2-cow.php, accessed 21 May 2018.

in accordance with *shari'ah*,[19] the righteous man will also make proper use of his spiritual and physical abilities by observing prayer, controlling his anger and emotions as well as having moral capacity for forgiveness and patience, and a conscious urge to regret and repent when he sins.[20] If such forms of righteousness can be established and sustained, then the individual and society will experience peace and security in all circumstances. Both concepts of piety and righteousness are founded on strong faith and constant practice, and not just convenient claims and oral confessions. Accordingly, Muslims use these concepts to define good and the source of happiness in life.

Man cannot escape from carrying out his responsibility, as Allah has provided him assistance in the form of *shari'ah*, intelligence and also free will, which serve as powerful tools in choosing one's course of conduct.[21] Furthermore, man has voluntarily accepted nature as trust from Allah and as such must be willing to serve His purpose (Haniffa and Hudaib, 2011). In short, three qualities as signs of sound faith and moral rectitude in Islam are believing in Allah, enjoining what *Qur'an* recognizes to be right and forbidding what it considers to be wrong, striving for the good of humanity and resenting and resisting returning to disbelief.

1.7 Differences between Islamic and other worldviews

The previous sections have presented the concept of worldview in general and the Islamic worldview in particular. In order to appreciate the differences between Islamic worldview from other worldviews, the seven elements of worldview identified in Table 1.1 will be used as the template in distinguishing the different worldviews. Since there are many worldviews, we will only highlight the Islamic worldview versus the Christian and secular worldviews. Table 1.2 presents a comparison between the three worldviews.

From the table, we can clearly see that the secular, Christian and Islamic worldviews centre around the issues concerning the reason–revelation interface: existence and nature of God, purpose and objectives in life, the method of valuing success and happiness, the relationship between God and man as well as between man with fellow man, which will all subsequently influence the approach to activities in life.

The secular worldview, which denies the existence of God and the hereafter, does not believe in the existence of an accountability system where actions in this world will be judged and denies the existence of the sacred texts that may provide a unifying guidance to man, and may have implications on one's behaviour. The notion of success, measured by visible materials and power based on the doctrine of the survival of the fittest, may lead to various types of injustice, with the weak in society getting weaker while the strong get stronger. Similarly, the lack of believe in the hereafter and the judgement system in the afterlife will motivate actions in seeking utmost pleasure and happiness in this world that may lead to disharmony within oneself which may spread to the various institutions and society.

On the other hand, the Islamic worldview, which is grounded in the belief in one God who has handed down *shari'ah* as a comprehensive guidance on every aspect of life including providing reminders on the consequences for failing to follow, will have implications on one's choice of actions. Furthermore, the believe that life in this

---

[19]Issues regarding wealth are given considerable attention and are mentioned 46 times in different verses in the *Qur'an*.

[20]The *Qur'an* states: 'Who believe in the unseen, are steadfast in prayer, and spend out of what We have provided for them; and who believe in the revelation sent to thee, and sent before thy time, and (in their hearts) have the assurance of the hereafter. They are on (true guidance), from their Lord, and it is these who will prosper' (Al-Baqarah, 2:3-5). www.wright-house.com/religions/islam/Quran/2-cow.php, accessed 21 May 2018. And 'And those who, having done something to be ashamed of, or wronged their own souls, earnestly bring Allah to mind, and ask for forgiveness for their sins, – and who can forgive sins except Allah. – and are never obstinate in persisting knowingly in (the wrong) they have done' (Al-'Imran, 3:135). www.wright-house.com/religions/islam/Quran/3-family-of-imran.php, accessed 21 May 2018.

[21]Islam views man as having a special status in the hierarchy of all known creatures, as man alone is gifted with rational faculties, spiritual aspirations as well as powers of action. Man is *Ashraful-Makhlooqat*.

Table 1.2 Differences between the Islamic, Christian and secular worldviews

Elements	Islamic worldview	Christian worldview	Secular worldview
1. Epistemology nature of knowledge	• reality is determined through a combination of methods: rational, empirical, intuition and revelation, as human has limited capacity	• reality is determined through God's word about truth and knowledge, and that the universe behaves in an orderly and rational fashion	• reality is based solely on rational and empirical evidence
2. Metaphysics beliefs regarding the ultimate nature of reality	• concerned with both this world and the hereafter • there is continuity of life beyond death that is eternal and where complete accounts will be rendered and judged, good deeds rewarded with paradise and bad deeds with hell-fire	• also concerned with both worlds • there is continuity of life beyond death that is eternal; those who behaved well go to heaven and others to hell-fire. Catholics believe in purgatory, but Protestants do not • sinners can confess their sins to Catholic priests and those sins are forgiven forever	• concerned only with this world • there is no other world or life after death and there is no system of judgement.
3. Cosmology beliefs about the origin of the universe and origin of life and man	• the universe is created by Allah upon His command and it has an end • all creations are planned with a purpose based on Allah's wisdom	• the universe is created and its existence is maintained by a transcendent and sovereign God • existence of the world is due to ultimate and supernatural cause	• the universe is created by chance through random events following laws of physics
4. Teleology beliefs about purpose	• the purpose of the universe is for the inhabitants to be conscious of Allah and to worship Him alone	• need to act with the best interests of one's brothers in mind and to obey God	• the purpose of the universe is unknown
5. Theology beliefs about God	• believe in the unity of God (*tawhid*) that is eternal, omniscient, omnipotent, the most gracious and the most merciful • Allah revealed holy books or scriptures to a number of His messengers with *Qur'an* being the last and perfect for mankind	• believe in the trinity of God • believe that God sent his only son, Jesus, to save them from sin. Those who believe in the Father, Son and Holy Spirit will have eternal life	• either disbelieves in or is unsure of the existence and/or nature of God • does not believe in the sacred texts
6. Anthropology beliefs about man	• man as Allah's vicegerent on earth to help realize the good • man born with free will and has ability to make choices	• man's fallen nature is redeemed through salvation • Jesus is the saviour who transformed man to a completely new person	• man is part of the evolution process in the ecosystem • man has no free will and is slave to his instincts
7. Axiology beliefs about values that drive behaviours	• Allah has provided man with *shari'ah*, intelligence and also free will to choose one's course of conduct • *shari'ah* provides a scale by which all human actions are valued based on the weight of their merits and demerits	• values are determined by one's nature, and that nature has a spiritual dimension • man are spiritual as well as physical beings	• behaviour is driven by self-imposed values or values decided by society or culture • there is no clear scale upon which human actions are judged

world is transitional with a purpose to act as moral agents and that there is an eternal life with judgement and reward system should lead to seeking ways in achieving success and happiness in this world and the hereafter by following the Divine guidance. This will in turn lead to a harmonious social and economic system that puts societal interest above self-interest.

Summary

A worldview is the lens through which we see the world and our choice of a particular lifestyle. Our worldview is constructed and reconstructed based on the situations or circumstances we are in (contextual) and may change over time (dynamic) as a result of changes in our experiences. Worldview may be broadly classified into religious and secular. The former may be further categorized into those based on Divine revelation and those based on human wisdom, while the latter further comprises mythology, philosophy and science. Each of these worldviews has its own assumptions of various aspects in life which can be distinguished based on seven elements of worldview: (i) epistemology (nature of knowledge), (ii) metaphysics (nature of reality), (iii) cosmology (origin of the universe and man), (iv) teleology (purpose of the universe), (v) theology (existence and nature of God), (vi) anthropology (purpose and expectations of man in this life) and (vii) axiology (values that drive man's behaviour).

The Islamic worldview is centred on the concept of unity of God (*tawhid*). Accepting the belief in one God also means accepting His last and perfect Divine book, the *Qur'an*, which was revealed to His last messenger, Prophet Muhammad, as guidance for all mankind in achieving success and happiness in this life and hereafter (*al-falah*), and that there is a Day of Judgement where all deeds and misdeeds committed in this world will be accounted for, which will consequently determine the final abode in either paradise or hell-fire.

The Islamic worldview recognizes that man has a purpose in this world, i.e. as vicegerent and trustee in ensuring social order based on prescriptions in *shari'ah*, which is comprehensive, as it covers three dimensions of *shari'ah*: (i) creed and belief system or faith; (ii) legislation and rulings, which encompasses the core relationship between man and the Creator in the form of worship and the relationship between man and his fellow beings as part of society; and (iii) system of ethics or morality.

In short, Islam is not just a religion but a complete and comprehensive way of life where there is no separation between the sacred and the profane. It teaches man about his relationship with God, with the universe and with other human beings. It provides a set of doctrines on how to build society and the important systems in life for family, social, political and economic issues in order to achieve happiness for oneself and mankind.

Key terms and concepts

absolute value	Islamic worldview	relative value
anthropology	*istihsan*	religious worldview
axiology	*maqasid al-shari'ah*	scientific worldview
cosmology	*maslahah*	secular worldview
epistemology	metaphysics	*shari'ah*
Hadith	*muamalat*	*tawhid*
halal	mythological worldview	teleology
haram	philosophical worldview	theology
ijma'	*qiyas*	*ummah*
ijtihad	*Qur'an*	worldview

Questions

1. Define worldview and explain why it is considered contextual, dynamic and constructive.

2. Identify and discuss the classifications of worldview.

3. Explain the seven elements of worldview and their implications on thoughts and actions.

4. Discuss the foundations of the Islamic worldview and its link to *shari'ah*.

5. Elaborate on the *maqasid al-shari'ah*.

6. Discuss the dimensions of *shari'ah* and their implications on political, social and economic institutions.

7. Distinguish between Islamic, Christian and secular worldviews.

References and further readings

Abdalati, H. (1975), *Islam in Focus*, American Trust Publications, Indiana, USA.

Addas, W.A.J. (2008), *Methodology of Economics: Secular vs Islamic*, IIUM Press, Malaysia.

Al-Attas, S.S. (1994), *Islam and the Challenge of Modernity*: Proceeding of the Inaugural Symposium on Islam and the Challenge of Modernity: Historical and Contemporary Contexts, Kuala Lumpur: The International Institute of Islamic Thought and Civilisation, International Islamic University, Malaysia.

Al-Qaradawi, Y. (2007), *The Lawful and the Prohibited in Islam*, Islamic Book Trust, Malaysia.

Al-Uthaymeen, M. (1998), *From the Fruits of Taqwaa*, Al-Hidaayah Publishing & Distribution, Birmingham, UK.

Beekun, R.I. (1997), *Islamic Business Ethics*, The International Institute of Islamic Thought, Virginia, USA.

Campanini, M. (2004), *An Introduction to Islamic Philosophy*, Edinburgh University Press, UK.

Chapra, U. (1992), *Islam and the Economic Challenge*, The Islamic Foundation, Leicester, UK.

El-Ashker, A.A. (1987), *The Islamic Business Enterprise*, Croom Helm, UK.

Funk, K. (2001), What is a worldview?, web.engr.oregonstate.edu/~funkk/Personal/worldview.html, accessed 6 November 2017.

Haniffa, R. and Hudaib, M. (2011), 'Conceptual framework for Islamic accounting', in Napier, C. and Haniffa, R. (eds), *Islamic Accounting*, Edward Elgar, Cheltenham, UK, pp. 43-113.

IFSB (2015), *Islamic financial services industry: Stability report 2015*, Islamic Financial Services Board, Kuala Lumpur.

Iqbal, Z. and Mirakhor, A. (2007), *An Introduction to Islamic Finance: Theory and Practice*. Asia: John Wiley & Sons, London.

Islahi, A.A. (2014), 'Muslim contributions to economic science', in Hassan, K. and Lewis, M. (eds), *Handbook on Islam and Economic Life*, Edward Elgar, Cheltenham, UK, pp. 21-44.

Kamali, M.H. (1989), 'Source, nature and objectives of Shari'ah', *The Islamic Quarterly*, 33(4), pp. 215-235.

Laldin, M.A. and Furqani, H. (2012), 'Maqasid al-Shari'ah and the foundational requirements in developing Islamic banking and finance', *ISRA International Journal of Islamic Finance*, 4(1), June, pp. 183-190.

Mannan, M.A. (1986), *Islamic Economics: Theory and Practice*, Hodder and Stoughton, London.

Masood, M.K. (1989), *Islamic Legal Philosophy*, International Islamic Publishers, New Delhi.

Mead, H. (1959), *Types and Problems of Philosophy*, Irvington Publishers; 3rd revised edition, Stratford.

Morgan, P. and Lawton, C.A. (2007), *Ethical Issues in Six Religious Traditions*, Edinburgh University Press, UK.

Naqvi, S.N.H. (1994), *Islam, Economics, and Society*, Kegan Paul International, London.

Pew Research Center (2017), Why Muslims are the world's fastest-growing religious group, www.pewresearch.org/fact-tank/2017/04/06/why-muslims-are-the-worlds-fastest-growing-religious-group/, accessed 6 November 2017.

Rabbani, F. (2011), What is the shariah? A path to God, a path to good, seekershub.org/blog/2011/03/what-is-the-shariah-a-path-to-god-a-path-to-good-faraz-rabbani, accessed 17 April 2018.

Vadillo, U.I. and Khalid, F. (1992), 'Trade and Commerce in Islam', in Khalid, F. and O'Brien, J. (eds), *Islam and Ecology*, Cassell, UK, pp. 74-78.

Warde, I. (2010), *Islamic Finance in the Global Economy*. Edinburgh University Press, UK.

2 Introduction to Islamic economics

Learning Objectives

Upon completion of this chapter you should be able to:

- explain the meaning of economics

- describe the different types of economic system

- define Islamic economics

- discuss Islamic economic theory

- distinguish between western and Islamic economic theories

- define Islamic economic system

- explain the goals of the Islamic economic system

- describe the features of an Islamic economic system

- distinguish between western and Islamic economic systems

2.1 Introduction

Islam is not just a religion but an entire way of life. There is no distinction between the sacred and the secular in the daily life of a Muslim. All activities, be it politics, economics, religious and social affairs, fall under the jurisdiction of the divine law of Islam the *shari'ah*. As we have seen in the last chapter, *shari'ah* provides comprehensive ethics governing economic activities and the operations of the relationships between man and God and man with man.

While western economics is normally dated to the time Adam Smith wrote his *Wealth of Nations* in 1776, there were many Muslim scholars who had also made valuable novel contributions to economic theory (macro and microeconomics) starting from the advent of Islam in the 7th century till the 16th century. Among them are Abu Yusuf (729-798) who is known for his work on taxation in a book called *Kitab al-Kharaj*, Al-Mawardi (974-1058) who is the first to talk about borrowing by the state and the idea of sustainable development, Ibn Tayyimah (1263-1328) who introduced the price volatility theory, and Ibn Khaldun (1332-1406), the 'father of modern economics', whose work covers almost every foundation of modern economics thought, ranging from microeconomics to international trade (Islahi, 2014).

However, Islamic economics as an independent discipline only took shape during the second half of the 20th century. Intellectuals in Muslim majority countries, especially in India and Egypt, began to reflect on alternative modes of postcolonial social organization, as the prevailing secular models of the economic system, communism and capitalism, do not fit the Islamic ethos (Hassan and Lewis, 2014). However, Islamic economics became virtually synonymous with Islamic finance when both bankers and academics paid more attention to banking and financial issues from the mid-1980s onwards. Other important areas, such as economic methodology, problems of the consumers and the firms, market structures, factor markets, public finance, poverty and economic development, which all deserve due attention, have been significantly sidelined until more recently.

In this chapter, we will look at the core principles of Islamic economic theory and to what extent they differ from western economics. To help us better appreciate the differences, we will briefly introduced the basic concepts of economics before looking in more detail at the Islamic economic system, its goals and the salient features of the system.

2.2   What is economics?

The word *economy* comes from the Greek words *oikos* meaning household and *nomos* meaning management: hence, *oikonomikos* means 'household management'. In every household, decisions must be made among members, for example, on who should work and who should stay at home, who should pay the bills, who should prepare food, who should plan family savings, who gets to go for a holiday, etc. These decisions have to be made due to limited resources in the household which may take the form of limited finance or wealth, abilities and capabilities, and/or time. Therefore, every household needs to decide how to allocate the limited resources to achieve the best outcome for everyone. Similarly, every society and country will have to manage their resources. Due to the limited nature of societal resources, it is vital for the resources to be efficiently managed so that each individual in society can attain the highest standard of living to which he aspires. When allocating the limited resources, choices have to be made based on some measures that will maximize the benefits to the decision maker.

Hence, *economics* is defined as the study of how society manages its scarce resources or how society makes choices. It encompasses three interrelated aspects: *how people as individuals make decisions, how people interact, and how the economy works as a whole*. The first two aspects are related to what is known as *microeconomics*, which studies how people and businesses make decisions regarding the allocation of resources, as well as prices of goods and services. The last aspect is related to *macroeconomics*, which studies the behaviour of the economy as a whole. It considers economy-wide phenomena, such as how gross domestic product (GDP) is affected by changes in factors such as unemployment, national income, rate of growth and price levels.

Let us look at the first aspect, i.e. *how individuals make decisions*. In our everyday life, we have to make many decisions, because we cannot achieve everything that our heart desires for various reasons arising from limited resources and/or restrictions. For instance, you have one hour (limited resource) between now and your next class and you have to decide between having coffee with your friend whom you have not seen for a while or to go to the library to revise for the test next week, as you need to get good grades. If you choose to chat with your friend, you have to give up your revision and vice versa. Hence, you are faced with what is known as a *trade-off*, which is you need to sacrifice or give up one goal against another. In making your decision on the trade-off that you face, you will compare the costs and benefits of alternative actions. If you have coffee with your friend, you will spend money for the coffee (cost) but will feel good as you enjoy his company (benefit); and if you revise for the test, you may not be able to enjoy his company (cost) but you know that the spare hour you spent on revision can help you achieve the grade that you wanted (benefit) and you do not have to spend money on the coffee (benefit). Therefore, whatever action you decide to give up is called the *opportunity cost*. It is assumed that in making your choice or decision, you have acted as a *rational person* and systematically and purposefully thought through what is the best action that will make you better off, after taking into account the marginal costs and benefits. The choice of action that you take is further induced by the *incentives*, i.e. the prospect of rewards or punishments.

From this simple example, we can deduce that when making decisions, individuals face trade-offs among alternative goals. As rational human beings, they make their decisions by comparing the marginal costs and benefits. The cost of any action that they make is measured based on the opportunities foregone. Their behaviour may also be influenced by the incentives they face. Thus, the behaviour of the individuals will collectively reflect the behaviour of the economy.

We now turn our attention to the second aspect in economics, *how people interact*. An economy is said to exist when there are interactions between groups of people for the purpose of trading or exchanging goods and services. Their interdependence on each other for goods and services will be mutually beneficial for everyone if they are able to meet the demand for and supply of goods and services. Since there are many suppliers and consumers of products and services, such economic activities can be coordinated through a market where price acts as the instrument to direct economic activities. In an efficient market, the demand for and supply of goods and services reflects the price. But this does not always work, resulting in *market failures* which will have significant impact on the wellbeing of society due to inequality and inefficiency in allocating the resources or due to a party having more power in controlling the market price. Hence, the government can help improve market outcomes by remedying market failures through enforcement of rules or regulations on institutions that are key to a market economy, or alternatively promoting greater economic equality through public policies.

The last aspect in economics is related to *how the economy works as a whole*. The ability of a country to produce goods or services, i.e. its *productivity*, affects the standard of living of its people. When the growth rate of productivity is high, the growth rate of income will also be high. When there is a high quantity of money in circulation in the economy, policymakers will have to intervene to control *inflation*.

From the preceding discussion, we can see that the study of economics involves understanding the behaviour of members of a society and how they organize themselves in making choices to fulfil their individual's and society's unlimited needs and desires from limited resources at hand. If the limited resources fall short in meeting the unlimited wants of society, this will eventually create scarcity. Hence, *scarcity* is seen as the basic and central western economic problem confronting every society.

2.3   Types of economic systems

There are various ways of allocating resources to meet human needs. In some societies, customs and traditional beliefs formed the basis when allocating societal wealth and resources. In some other societies, decisions on allocating resources are made by planning boards based on societal objectives and political orientations. However, the basis for allocation of resources in most societies today is the price or market mechanism. The different ways of organizing economic activities lead to different economic systems. So what is an economic system? An *economic system* is a network of organizations used by a society to resolve the basic problems of what to produce (type of product), how much to produce (quantity of production), how to produce the product (method of production) and for whom to produce (type of consumer). The economic systems in existence today include four main types: *traditional, command, free market*, and *socialist*.

2.3.1   TRADITIONAL ECONOMY

A subsistence economy is where a family produces goods only for its own consumption and normally without any surplus. In a traditional economic system, decisions on what, how, how much and for whom to produce are often made by the family or tribe head, according to their traditional means of production. A traditional economy is also where development of goods and services is dominated by the customs, traditions and beliefs in that area. Hence, a traditional economy is built around the way a particular society lives and the nature of goods and services are determined by their livelihood. Therefore, it comes as no surprise that the economy is often based on agriculture, hunting, fishing and gathering. In some traditional economies, barter trade is used instead of money. Examples of traditional economies are the Aborigines of Australia, Mbuti of Central Africa and Inuit of Canada.

Advantages and disadvantages of a traditional economy

You may wonder why such economies still exist in some parts of the world and what are their benefits? Well, for a start, every person in this type of economy understands their responsibility and job in that community. They also know the resources available and the way this will be distributed to the various groups in the community. Furthermore, each person in a traditional economy is aware of the return they will get from participating and doing their jobs. In these traditional economies, destruction of the environment is less as they use the land and resources in a positive manner.

While traditional economies have their advantages, there are also disadvantages. Since they rely heavily on farming, hunting, fishing and gathering, a change in the weather may affect their livelihood. Similarly, they may starve if they are unable to find animals to hunt, or fish to catch or suitable land to farm to produce food needed for survival.

2.3.2   COMMAND ECONOMY (COMMUNISM)

The word *command* simply means giving orders. Therefore a command economy is one where the government gives orders or has ultimate power over the financial management of the state. In this system, all economic activities are administered by the central planning agency of the state. The government not only determines what is produced, how it is produced and how it is distributed, but also controls the pricing of goods and services. All workers in such an economy are employed by the government, which not only assigns people to their jobs but also determines their wages. In a command economy, almost all entities are state owned, and only a few privately owned entities are allowed to operate. In short, all resources in the state are under the control of the government. Examples of countries having this type of economy are Cuba and North Korea.

Advantages and disadvantages of a command economy

It may seem strange, but a command economy does have some advantages. Everyone enjoys a minimum standard of living, such that the gap is very narrow between the rich and the poor in the country. Everyone has equal access to health care services and other essential services to live decently, usually for free or with a minimal fee. There is price stability, as the government controls the prices of goods and services. Consumer exploitation is rare, as the government provides essential goods and services to all its citizens. Also, there are low unemployment rates, as the government assigns and regulates all jobs. Since all economic activities are under the state, decisions can be made quickly by government officials to resolve any issues.

However, there are also disadvantages in this system. While everyone in the command economic system is ensured a minimum standard of living, they are collectively of low or minimal standard. Moreover, since the government dictates the production of goods and services, consumers' choices are restricted and the products are often of substandard quality. Similarly, innovation opportunities are limited and useless since what is required for the economy is determined by the government. Furthermore, the economy is often inefficient, as there is a tendency for officials to be corrupt and resources are wasted. Division of labour is also minimal, as the government decides on the jobs available. Lastly, since this economy is closely related to the political ideology of the government, it is difficult for such an economy to engage in international trade.

2.3.3   FREE MARKET ECONOMY (CAPITALISM)

The capitalist economic system ranges from *laissez-faire* with minimal government regulation and state enterprise, to regulated and social market systems which aim to reduce market failures or supplement the private market place with social policies to promote equal opportunities. In this economic system, individuals and firms are allowed to own and control resources or factors of production privately. They are also free to produce goods and services to fulfil the demand of consumers who, in turn, are also free to choose goods based on their own needs and desires. Hence decisions regarding production and investment are determined by private owners in the capital markets. Since economic activities are left to market forces with minimal intervention by the government, there is high competition among individuals vying for economic gain in maximizing their wealth. Examples of countries that employ this system include the USA, Canada and Australia.

Advantages and disadvantages of a free market economy

This type of economy is adopted by many countries due to the many foreseen advantages. Individuals and private firms can decide, with little government intervention, on the best options in utilizing the resources that they own and control to maximize their economic interest. Second, the existence of many firms and individuals in the market means that they have to compete, and competition between the firms leads them to produce as efficiently as possible so that the price of goods or services that they offer can be as low as possible to attract consumers to buy from them. This drive towards efficiency means that resources will not be wasted. Furthermore, given the highly competitive market, innovation is vital for capturing and/or staying in the market. Similarly, competition not only provides consumers with more choices of products and services that they need or desire but also drives their quality to be better. Firms will respond to the demands for goods and services that consumers want, and those that are not in demand will disappear from the market. Another advantage of this type of economy is that the price is determined by the demand and supply in the market (assuming that the market is efficient) instead of being controlled by the government.

There are several disadvantages of the free market system. Firstly, the freedom to own and control resources with little government intervention may widen the gap between the rich and poor in society. Since profit is the dominating objective for firms, they may try to reduce their costs surreptitiously with little consideration for damage to the environment, employees welfare and product safety. Similarly, only goods and services that are profitable will be made available with little consideration for those who still need such goods or services. Another disadvantage is that firms, without government intervention on diversity employment policy, may disregard employing certain members of society, e.g. the elderly and the disabled, or discriminate based on race and gender. Although competition is expected to disallow dominance or monopoly in the market, some firms may still be able to dominate and maximize their profits by exploiting suppliers, squeezing their prices down, and exploiting consumers by charging them higher selling prices.

2.3.4 SOCIALIST ECONOMY (SOCIALISM)

Socialism is an economic system that emphasizes equitable distribution of income and wealth. It is considered as an economic system that lies in between capitalism at one end and communism on the other hand. In socialist economic systems, decisions regarding the use of the means of production are adjusted to satisfy economic demand, and investment is determined through economic planning procedures. Like communism, the socialist system involves wide-ranging planning procedures and ownership structures, with the most common feature being social ownership of the means of production. This might take the form of either public ownership or cooperative ownership by employees. Like capitalism, this economic system recognizes private ownership with only some key enterprises being owned by the state. In this system, the state has no control over a large portion of capital assets and is only generally responsible for production and distribution of important goods. A sub-category of the socialist economic system is market socialism, whereby socially owned enterprises accumulate and utilize the capital markets to allocate their capital goods.

Advantages and disadvantages of a socialist economy

Socialism has the greatest goal of common wealth based on public benefits. Since the government still controls most of society's functions, it encourages better use of resources, labours and lands. Furthermore, excessive or insufficient production can be avoided and prices can be controlled to some extent through the government's policies. Socialism reduces disparity not only in wealth but also in all societal ranks and classes. For instance, those who suffer from illnesses, are too old to work or have been made redundant will receive social security benefits from the government. Government policy on minimum wage ensures that workers get fair wages and trade union recognition by the government helps protect employment rights for the benefit of workers.

Despite the benefits of a socialist economic system, there are also disadvantages. Social security benefits schemes may cause people to lose initiative to work and enthusiasm to study, as doing so may be less rewarding for them. Firms may be unable to get the maximum profit from the use of resources, labour and land, as economic activities are still under the government's control.

2.4 Islamic economic theory

Having reminded ourselves of the basics of economics, let us now turn our attention to Islamic teachings regarding economics. It is important at the outset to note that in Islam, economic activities are not considered as a distinct domain because there is no separation between the sacred and the profane in the daily life of Muslim societies. Hence, it should not come as a surprise that the specific word for economics is absent in classical Arabic. The nearest translation of the modern term *economics* in Arabic is *iqtisad* and *ilm-ul-iqtisad* (economics study), which refers to knowledge of discovering suitable ways to produce wealth and spend it in the right ways, as well as the causes for its destruction and waste. In classical Arabic, *iqtisad* is defined by Al-Ghazali in his famous book, *Iyha Ulum-id-din*, as the principle of moderation (Gazzali, 1971).

2.4.1 DEFINITION OF ISLAMIC ECONOMICS

As mentioned in the introduction, the term *Islamic economics* has often been associated with Islamic finance and banking as a result of undue emphasis on the issues of *riba* (usury), *gharar* (uncertainty) and *halal* (permissible), outlined in the Islamic commercial jurisprudence (*fiqh al-mu'amalat*). However, Islamic economics as an ideology has far-reaching meanings beyond simply following the immutable rules defined by *shari'ah*. In fact, it does not only study, analyse and understand economic behaviour and outcomes, but also attempt to operationalize the moral vision by offering solutions to the challenges facing our planet and matters jeopardizing the felicity of mankind. However, unlike conventional economics, there is no consensus on the definition of Islamic economics. Some of the definitions offered in the literature include the following:

> …*it is a social science that studies the economic problems of the people who were inspired by Islamic values* (Mannan, 1970).
>
> …*the knowledge and applications and rules of the* shari'ah *that prevent injustice in the requisition and disposal of material resources in order to provide satisfaction to human beings and enable them to perform their obligations to God and the society* (Zaman, 1984).
>
> …*a systematic effort to try to understand the economic problems and human behaviour in relation to these issues from an Islamic perspective* (Ahmad, 1992).
>
> …*an ideological construct developed by 20th century Islamists taking basic prescriptions from sharia (Islamic law), and systematizing and conceptualizing them to construct a coherent and functional ensemble offering a middle ground between the two systems of the twentieth century, Marxism and capitalism* (Roy, 1994).
>
> …*study of the process and the suspension of human activities related to production, distribution and consumption in Muslim society* (Kahf, 2014).
>
> …*is the subject that studies human behaviour in relation to multiplicity of wants and scarcity of resources with alternative uses so as to maximize falah that is the well-being both in the present world and in the hereafter* (Hasan, 2015).

All the preceding definitions, with the exception of Roy (1994) and Hasan (2015), share a similar idea on Islamic economics being related to studies on economic problems and man's behaviour from an Islamic perspective. In contrast, Roy (1994) perceives Islamic economics as a middle ground ideology constructed by 20th-century Muslim thinkers using prescriptions in *shari'ah* to address some mainstream economic concepts such as resource scarcity, pursuit of self-interest and maximizing behaviour. The definition offered by Hasan (2015) is perhaps by far the most comprehensive, as he not only highlights about human behaviours related to scarcity, wants and choices but also the goal of *al-falah* (more details of this in the following section), which is to achieve wellbeing both in this world and the hereafter.

2.4.2 PRINCIPLES OF ISLAMIC ECONOMICS

Every discipline has its underlying principles. It is important to know these principles as it provides us with an understanding of the world around us and how and why things are the way they are. *Economic principles* refer to the fundamental law of economics that serves to guide the decision making of consumers, producers, investors, employees and government. In mainstream economics they are seen as the product of the intellect alone, with scientific method being used to support the tests before they are accepted as economic principles. Islamic economics also acknowledges the important role of the intellect and sense making. However, it is Divine guidance or revelation that becomes the primary source of principles (theory) with the latter (intellect and sense) embodied in the economic system. Thus, the *Qur'an* and *Ahadith* (plural form of *Hadith*) serve as the premise of Islamic economic principles, while *ijtihad* (human reasoning) is used in operationalizing and finding solutions to economic problems. The following are some of the principles laid down in the *Qur'an* and *Ahadith* related to economic activities.

a) Principle of justice

Islam places the principle of justice at the core of all aspects governing economic activities, i.e. production, distribution, consumption and exchange. Fairness for all and maintaining a balance are critical to achieving this principle. A number of verses in the *Qur'an* drive this point:

> *O ye who believe! stand out firmly for justice, as witnesses to Allah, even as against yourselves, or your parents, or your kin, and whether it be (against) rich or poor* (An-Nisaa, 4:135).[1]
>
> *And do not eat up your property among yourselves for vanities, nor use it as bait for the judges, with intent that ye may eat up wrongfully and knowingly a little of (other) people's property* (Al-Baqarah, 2:188).[2]
>
> *O ye who believe! stand out firmly for Allah, as witnesses to fair dealing, and let not the hatred of others to you make you swerve to wrong and depart from justice. Be just: that is next to piety: and fear Allah. For Allah is well-acquainted with all that ye do* (Al-Ma'idah, 5:8).[3]

In terms of production, *justice* means nobody should be exploited by others in any way or form and nobody should acquire wealth by unfair, unlawful and fraudulent means. In order to achieve *justice in distribution*, all economic resources and wealth must be shared or distributed within the community in a way that everyone is provided with basic necessities of life and the gulf between the rich and the poor is narrowed. *Justice in consumption* means not consuming or using resources excessively to the extent of depriving others of their rights. *Justice in exchange* demands transparency, honesty and accountability between two parties involved in the exchange. Islam offers two mechanisms for achieving socio-economic justice: the redistribution system of wealth through *zakat*, and the prohibition of interest.

---

[1] www.wright-house.com/religions/islam/Quran/4-women.php, accessed 21 May 2018.

[2] www.wright-house.com/religions/islam/Quran/2-cow.php, accessed 21 May 2018.

[3] www.wright-house.com/religions/islam/Quran/5-table.php, accessed 21 May 2018.

(I) ZAKAT *Zakat* is an obligatory religious tax and its importance is signified by being the third pillar of Islam, after the confession of the Islamic faith (*shahadah*) and prayer. It is levied on the wealth of every Muslim and Islamic institution. The amount is 2.5 per cent beyond the wealth threshold. The purpose of *zakat* is as an act of worship to please Allah by purifying wealth and enhancing its redistribution within society, as well as preventing hoarding. The *Qur'an* emphasizes the importance of giving *zakat* and provides guidance on the recipients of *zakat* as stated in the following verses:

> *And be steadfast in prayer; practise regular charity (Zakat); and bow down your heads with those who bow down (in worship)* (Al-Baqarah, 2:43).[4]
>
> *Alms are for the poor and the needy, and those employed to administer the (funds); for those whose hearts have been (recently) reconciled (to Truth); for those in bondage and in debt; in the cause of Allah. and for the wayfarer: (thus is it) ordained by Allah, and Allah is full of knowledge and wisdom* (At-Tawbah, 9:60).[5]

(II) PROHIBITION OF *RIBA*, OR INTEREST   The prohibition of *riba* can be traced back approximately four thousand years ago (Iqbal and Mirakhor, 2007)[6] and it is not only confined to Islam but also to the other two Abrahamic religions, Judaism[7] and Christianity. The word *riba* literally means 'increase'. In the context of money lending, *riba* refers to any surplus or excess over the principal amount, irrespective of the purpose for which the loans have been raised. It also extends to exchange of goods. There are a number of verses in the *Qur'an* and also in the *Hadith* condemning *riba*:

> *Those who devour usury will not stand except as stand one whom the Evil one by his touch Hath driven to madness. That is because they say: 'Trade is like usury,' but Allah hath permitted trade and forbidden usury. Those who after receiving direction from their Lord, desist, shall be pardoned for the past; their case is for Allah (to judge); but those who repeat (The offence) are companions of the Fire: They will abide therein (forever)* (Al-Baqarah, 2:275).[8]
>
> *That they took usury, though they were forbidden; and that they devoured men's substance wrongfully; we have prepared for those among them who reject faith a grievous punishment* (An-Nisaa, 4:161).[9]
>
> *O ye who believe! Fear Allah, and give up what remains of your demand for usury, if ye are indeed believers* (Al-Baqarah, 2:278).[10]
>
> *Abu Hurayrah (ra) narrated that the Prophet (saw), said: 'Riba has seventy segments, the least serious is equivalent to a man committing incest with his own mother'* (Ibn Majah).[11]
>
> *Abu Hurayrah (ra) narrated that the Prophet (saw) said: 'There will come a time when there will be no one left who does not consume usury (interest), and whoever does not consume it will nevertheless be affected by it'* (Ibn Majah).[12]

Muslim jurists have classified *riba* into two types: *riba al-nasi'ah* and *riba al-fadl*. The word *nasi'ah* means to postpone or to wait. Hence, *riba al-nasi'ah* (interest on loan) refers to the time period that is allowed for the

---

[4]www.wright-house.com/religions/islam/Quran/2-cow.php, accessed 21 May 2018.

[5]www.wright-house.com/religions/islam/Quran/9-repentance.php

[6]See Iqbal and Mirakhor (2007) for a detailed discussion on the prohibition of interest or usury throughout history and in different religions.

[7]Judaism disallows interest as mentioned in the Old Testament: Exodus 22:25, Leviticus 25:35-36, Deutronomy 23:20, Psalms 15:5, Proverbs 28:8, Nehemiah 5:7.

[8]www.wright-house.com/religions/islam/Quran/2-cow.php, accessed 21 May 2018.

[9]www.wright-house.com/religions/islam/Quran/4-women.php, accessed 21 May 2018.

[10]www.wright-house.com/religions/islam/Quran/2-cow.php, accessed 21 May 2018.

[11]Vol. 3, Book 12, Hadith 2274 sunnah.com/ibnmajah/12, accessed 21 May 2018.

[12]Vol. 3, Book 12, Hadith 2278 sunnah.com/ibnmajah/12, accessed 21 May 2018.

borrower to repay the loan in return for additional reward (premium) above the principal amount borrowed, i.e. the interest on loans. Fixing in advance of a positive return on a loan as a reward for waiting is prohibited because it is considered unjust since money was not created to be sought for its own sake (money-to-money exchange) but for other objects. *Riba an-nasi'ah* is also known as *riba al-duyun* (interest on loans), *riba al-jali* (obvious interest), *riba al-mubashir* (direct interest), and *riba al-jahiliyyah/al-Qur'an* (interest prohibited by the *Qur'an*).

The word *fadl* means increase or growth. Thus, *riba al-fadl* (interest on excess in counter value) is the increase when two things that are the same are exchanged unequally. Such prohibition is derived from the narration in the *Hadith* whereby commodities are required to be exchanged for cash instead of barter due to difficulty in getting commodity of the same quality. The relevance of this *riba* has diminished, as these days exchange occurs through the medium of money. Nevertheless, the concept remains applicable to similar situations. *Riba al-fadl* is also known as *riba al-buyu'u* (interest in trade), *riba ghayr al-mubashir* (indirect interest), or *riba al-khafi* (hidden interest).

To conclude, *riba* is condemned as it is against the Islamic spirit of justice and equity. Easy access to loans may encourage individuals to live beyond their means and possibly spend on things that are not essential. Those who default on their loans or mortgages may risk losing their homes if they have used them as collateral. *Riba* may cause companies to be declared bankrupt when they cannot service interest on their loans, which leads to loss of employment for their employees and loss of productive prospects for society as a whole. High interest rates may cause businessmen to be unable or even reluctant to borrow from banks, thus hindering the growth and productivity of the business sector. *Riba* stifles innovation by small businesses, as they may be reluctant to take up loans and get charged high interest rate for new projects which are often perceived as having higher risk. Easy access to global financial institutions may cause governments to borrow, resulting in an accentuation of macroeconomic factors like inflation and external imbalances in addition to squeezing the resources available for development. This leads some poorer countries to over-exploit their earth's resources, and subsequently to the destruction of their ecological systems. The heavy debt burden held by some countries makes it difficult for them to recover from a depressed economy, causing further suffering to the whole society.

b) Principle of wealth

Islam encourages man to utilize all the resources that Allah has created and entrusted to man for his use. According to the *Qur'an*, the entire universe has been consciously designed, created and controlled by Allah. He has granted human beings the opportunity and authority to make use of the means and resources that He has specifically created for man's survival, as stated in following verses:

> *It is He Who hath created for you all things that are on earth* (Al-Baqarah, 2:29).[13]
>
> *It is He Who has made the earth manageable for you, so traverse ye through its tracts and enjoy of the Sustenance which He furnishes: but unto Him is the Resurrection* (Al-Mulk, 67:15).[14]
>
> *It is We Who have placed you with authority on earth, and provided you therein with means for the fulfilment of your life* (Al-A'raf, 7:10).[15]

Thus, this implies that wealth is an important means for the attainment of man's ultimate objective and not an end in itself. It is considered good as it is an object of delight and pleasure, but more wealth does not always guarantee more happiness if it is not spent in the manner ordained by Allah. But if it is spent for good causes as an act of obedience to Allah, wealth will be a blessing; if wealth increases disobedience to Allah, then it becomes a punishment.

---

[13] www.wright-house.com/religions/islam/Quran/2-cow.php, accessed 21 May 2018.

[14] www.wright-house.com/religions/islam/Quran/67-sovereignty.php, accessed 21 May 2018.

[15] www.wright-house.com/religions/islam/Quran/7-heights.php, accessed 21 May 2018.

Furthermore, wealth must be earned through productive and beneficial effort and *shari'ah* specifies lawful methods of earning them and types of economic activities that are prohibited. Similarly, *shari'ah* has laid down rules related to the disposal of wealth, which includes never using it to harm others, to acquire power, to corrupt the system or to indulge in extravagance, opulence and waste. The *Qur'an* reminds man of his role as vicegerent of Allah on earth and is accountable for the resources entrusted to him as revealed in the *Qur'an*:

> *It is He Who hath made you (His) agents, inheritors of the earth: He hath raised you in ranks, some above others: that He may try you in the gifts He hath given you* (Al-An'am, 6:165).[16]

In short, wealth and poverty are trials from Allah. It has a dual nature. It can either bring happiness or sorrow, it can be a blessing or a punishment, and it can either increase love of material goods and promote greed or weaken love of material goods and promote generosity. It is up to man to make the choice, as Allah has provided man with the intellect to understand the guidance that has been provided.

c) Principle of ownership

The *Qur'an* makes it clear that the universe and everything within it belongs to Allah alone. He is the real owner of everything and man only holds the resources in a trust for which he will be held accountable to Him, as stated in the following verses:

> *To Allah belongeth all that is in the heavens and on earth …* (Al-Baqarah, 2:284).[17]
> *To Allah belongeth the dominion of the heavens and the earth; and Allah hath power over all things.* (Al-'Imran, 3:189).[18]

Since absolute ownership belongs to Allah, this implies that all resources are collectively owned by man as everyone is His vicegerent and everyone has the right to make good use of them according to His guidance. Three parallel forms of ownerships are recognized in *shari'ah*: individual, public and state. However, their respective scopes are left wide, to be determined according to needs and circumstances. Similarly, the acquisition, use and disposal of property are subject to the principles and limits as defined by Islamic teaching. Individuals can obtain rights to property and resources either through their own creative work or effort, or inheritance, and/or through transfer via exchange of contract with another individual who has title to the property through their own effort. The importance of work is stressed in the *Qur'an* in over 360 verses. Hence, work or effort forms the basis in the acquisition of any asset or resources as stated in the *Qur'an* and *Hadith*:

> *And when the Prayer is finished, then may ye disperse through the land, and seek of the Bounty of Allah and celebrate the Praises of Allah often (and without stint): that ye may prosper* (Al-Jumu'ah, 62, 10).[19]
> *Abu Hurayrah (ra) narrated that the Prophet (saw), said: 'When an employee fulfils obligations of Allah and obligations of his employer he has two rewards for him'* (Muslim).[20]

It is a duty and obligation to put one's best effort into carrying out the responsibility that one is given. Islam considers laziness, idleness and socially unproductive work as manifestation of a lack of faith.

Similarly, Islam allows state ownership and public ownership for some kinds of wealth and property. *State property* encompasses certain natural resources and other property that cannot be immediately privatized. State property can be movable or immovable, and it can be acquired via conquest or peaceful means. Similarly, unclaimed, unoccupied and heirless properties, including uncultivated land, can be considered as state property. *Public property* in Islam includes natural resources such as water, minerals, forest, pastures, etc., under the

---

[16]www.wright-house.com/religions/islam/Quran/6-cattle.php, accessed 21 May 2018.

[17]www.wright-house.com/religions/islam/Quran/2-cow.php, accessed 21 May 2018.

[18]www.wright-house.com/religions/islam/Quran/3-family-of-imran.php, accessed 21 May 2018.

[19]www.wright-house.com/religions/islam/Quran/62-congregation.php, accessed 21 May 2018.

[20]Sahih Muslim Book 27, Hadith 70 sunnah.com/muslim/27, accessed 21 May 2018.

guardianship and control of the state. They are considered as collective property of the community where everyone in the state shares equal rights. They can be used by members of society as long as they do not undermine the rights of other citizens.

d) Principle of economic freedom

According to Islam, every individual will be held accountable for her or his actions in this world. Their actions will be judged as good or evil in the hereafter. Hence, Islam provides individuals freedom of action in every aspect of human activity, including economic freedom. This means that individuals are permitted freedom by Allah to earn, own, enjoy and spend their wealth as they like. However, the economic freedom is not unlimited and is confined within the boundaries of Islamic spiritual and moral values. Hence, Islam distinguishes between lawful (*halal*) and unlawful (*haram*) activities.[21] Everything else is considered lawful unless the activity is in the grey or doubtful zones, in which case it is better to avoid the activity, as stated in the following *Hadith:*

> *That which is lawful is clear and that which is unlawful is clear and between the two of them are doubtful [or ambiguous] matters about which not many people are knowledgeable. Thus, he who avoids these doubtful matters certainly clears himself in regard to his religion and his honour. But he who falls into the doubtful matters falls into that which is unlawful like the shepherd who pastures around a sanctuary, all but grazing therein. Verily every king has a sanctuary and Allah's sanctuary is His prohibition. In the body there is a morsel of flesh which, if it be sound, all the body is sound and which, if it be diseased, all the body is diseased. This part of the body is the heart* (Bukhari, Muslim).[22]

Unlawful ways of obtaining livelihood and wealth include bribery, gambling, speculation, interest and other business malpractices. In terms of consumption, the items of food considered as unlawful include wine, pork, animals not slaughtered in the name of Allah, and drugs. Similarly, it is unlawful to pay for any services and entertainments that endorse obscenity, lotteries and narcotics, etc.

Thus, Islam recognizes the role of organizations, capital, labour and market forces in economic activities in addition to human initiative, free enterprise and individuals' potential. Besides constraints in the form of *halal* and *haram*, other constraints are less common unless they are required for safeguarding society's common interest. Islamic law places responsibilities on the state to supervise general activities and to intervene in order to protect public interest by limiting the freedom of individuals in their actions.

e) Principle of moderation

Islam emphasizes moderation in everything an individual does and this is closely related to the issue of balance and justice. A moderate approach in balancing various concerns in any given situation and seeking the middle ground between them will often lead to the best correct action. This includes being moderate when it comes to balancing the duties of religion and of worldly affairs. Islam explicitly discourages its followers from crossing the boundaries and following extreme limits in any activities. This is emphasized in the *Qur'an:*

> *Thus, have We made of you an Ummat justly balanced, that ye might be witnesses over the nations, and the Messenger a witness over yourselves* (Al-Baqarah, 2:143).[23]

The principle of moderation is of supreme importance in economic matters relating to production, consumption, distribution and spending. Although Islam allows individuals to produce and acquire wealth by lawful means, it also demands the piety to exercise restraint in amassing wealth, especially if the individual would be so busy with worldly matters that responsibilities to Allah, religion and other fellow beings were forgotten. The same applies in terms of consumption and spending. Islam forbids miserliness such that the individual is reluctant to spend on his family and himself, let alone on noble causes and charities. Similarly, Islam forbids the

---

[21]For more details on what constitute halal and haram in Islamic teachings, see Al-Qardawi, Y. (1999).

[22]40hadithnawawi.com/index.php/the-hadiths/hadith-6, accessed 1 June 2018.

[23]www.wright-house.com/religions/islam/Quran/2-cow.php, accessed 21 May 2018.

individual from being extravagant in spending on luxuries for himself and family and forgetting others who are in need. The *Qur'an* values those who exercise moderation in spending when it states:

> *Those who, when they spend, are not extravagant and not niggardly, but hold a just (balance) between those (extremes)* (Al-Furqan, 25:67).[24]
>
> *Make not thy hand tied (like a niggard's) to thy neck, nor stretch it forth to its utmost reach, so that thou become blameworthy and destitute* (Al-Isra, 17:29).[25]

f) Principle of consumption

Allah has created all things for man's use and service. Man is allowed to fully enjoy his wealth as long as it is within the bounds of lawful (*halal*) and unlawful (*haram*) as prescribed by Allah and in keeping within the rules of moderation and prudence. The *Qur'an* states:

> *O ye people! Eat of what is on earth, Lawful and good; and do not follow the footsteps of the evil one, for he is to you an avowed enemy* (Al-Baqarah, 2:168).[26]

Similarly, the *Qur'an* clearly prohibits restraining of oneself or forbidding others from relishing lawful resources, products or services, as this renounces the blessings and favours of Allah:

> *O ye who believe! make not unlawful the good things which Allah hath made lawful for you, but commit no excess: for Allah loveth not those given to excess* (Al-Ma'idah, 5:87).[27]

Moreover, the *Qur'an* disapproves of those who impose restrictions on certain things which are not forbidden and also to choose to live a life of asceticism, as stated in the following verse:

> *Say: Who hath forbidden the beautiful (gifts) of Allah, which He hath produced for His servants, and the things, clean and pure, (which He hath provided) for sustenance?* (Al-A'raf, 7:32).[28]

2.5   Comparison between neoclassical and Islamic economics theory

Based on earlier discussions on neoclassical and Islamic economics theory, we can now compare between the two on a number of underlying principles as discussed in this section and also in the summary presented in Table 2.1.

Table 2.1 Comparison of neoclassical economics and Islamic economics

Principles	Neoclassical economics	Islamic economics
Scarcity	There are not enough resources on the planet to satisfy everyone, and therefore we must work on increasing production.	There are more than enough resources to fulfil everyone's legitimate needs as stated in the Qur'an. *"There is no moving creature on earth but its sustenance dependeth on Allah (11:6)."*
Needs and wants	Acquiring sufficient wealth will lead to a utopia where everyone is free from want and people will become kind and just.	Pursuit of wealth will lead people to desire even more, instead of contentment with the needs.

---

[24]www.wright-house.com/religions/islam/Quran/25-criterion.php, accessed 21 May 2018.

[25]www.wright-house.com/religions/islam/Quran/17-isra.php, accessed 21 May 2018.

[26]www.wright-house.com/religions/islam/Quran/17-isra.php, accessed 21 May 2018.

[27]www.wright-house.com/religions/islam/Quran/5-table.php, accessed 21 May 2018.

[28]www.wright-house.com/religions/islam/Quran/7-heights.php, accessed 21 May 2018.

Principles	Neoclassical economics	Islamic economics
Choices and accumulation of capital	Accumulation of capital and pursuit of increased productivity by industrialization, technology, etc. will remove problems of scarcity and want, and lead to development.	Human beings are the best of the creation and focusing on developing them morally, spiritually and in all dimensions will lead to development in all other dimensions.
Optimality and ethical neutrality	Economic theory is positive and makes no value judgements. Any redistribution of wealth requires value judgements, and hence is not part of positive economic theory.	To fail to redistribute wealth is as much a value judgement as redistribution. When required to save lives, redistribution of wealth is required by Islam.
Consumer behaviour and utility maximization	Consumer sovereignty or the equivalent assumption that interpersonal utility comparisons are not scientific means that wants and needs are on par. Furthermore, it is descriptively accurate (positive economics) to state that people are primarily motivated by self-interest in economic affairs.	The *Qur'an* encourages people to spend on their own needs and also to spend excess above their needs on needs of others. "…*They ask thee how much they are to spend; Say: 'What is beyond your needs' (2:219)."* It strongly discourages pursuit of idle desires, luxuries and conspicuous consumption and following the Qur'an prescriptions will lead to economics based on simple lifestyles, hospitality and cooperation.
Firm behaviour and profit maximization	Morality and ethics are subordinate to the pursuit of profits. Firms are only responsible for their immediate actions, and not for long term consequences or how consumers use/abuse goods sold to them. It is only actions, good or bad, which matter and not the intention behind them.	Morality and ethics are primary, and pursuit of profits is permissible only when it does not conflict with moral goals. Producers have responsibility for everything which occurs directly or indirectly as a result of their actions. Charitable or socially responsible acts done in pursuit of profits will not yield good results in this world or the next.
Use of mathematics to predict economic outcomes and behaviour	Individual and social behaviour, and economic outcomes are all subject to mathematical laws.	The *Qur'an* states: "*Lo! This is a Reminder. Let him who will, then, choose a way unto his Lord. Individuals can choose their path, and their choices cannot be predicted by mathematical law (73:19)."*
Selfishness as sole motivation in economic realm	Individuals are naturally selfish and this motivation is the best predictor of human behaviour in economics.	The process of encouraging towards the good and preventing the bad will lead to a transformation in society to being more cooperative, generous and trustworthy and overcome desires to be greedy, acquisitive and competitive.
Moral justification of selfishness	Individually selfish behaviour leads to good social outcomes.	Individually selfish behaviour leads to corruption on the earth as stated in the Qur'an: "*Corruption doth appear on land and sea because of (the evil) which men's hands have done, that He may make them taste a part of that which they have done, in order that they may return (30:41)."*
Justice in economic development	Providing money and power to capitalists and keeping wages low will lead to rapid investment and growth, the benefits of which will eventually trickle down to the poor, after an initial period of increasing inequality.	Supporting the poor and protecting the weak from exploitation will provide economic justice and equal opportunities to all. This will allow all to participate in the process of development which will lead to robust growth on all fronts.
Supply and demand	Operations of a free market determine the equilibrium prices, which decentralize production and consumption decisions, which will lead to socially optimal outcomes.	Free market mechanisms fail to provide justice in many instances and can only be corrected if individuals behave ethically and with social regulations.
Perfect competition versus cooperation	Removal of obstacles to free market operation will lead to higher efficiency that will enrich society via the mechanism of perfect competition.	Building integrity of character, trust and cooperation in a society will lead to societies which are rich spiritually, morally and materially that will help to reduce the gulf between the rich and the poor.

Source: Adapted from Zaman, A. (2012), An Islamic critique of neoclassical economics, *Pakistan Business Review*, April, pp. 9–58.

2.5.1 SCARCITY OF RESOURCES

This is a fundamental principle in the study of economics. For western economists, scarcity is said to arise because the available resources are not sufficient to fulfil human wants. This is based on two general assumptions about the universe (limited resources) and about man (unlimited wants). According to Ahmed (2014), Islamic economists have different views on the issue of scarcity of resources.[29] One view is similar to neoclassical economists, that scarcity of resources and unlimited wants coexist, except that in the case of Islamic economics, the focus is towards fulfilling needs and not wants (Khan, 2012). This view distinguishes between *relative and absolute scarcity*. In contrast, the second view perceives scarcity as purely a problem of injustice and maldistribution and not about relative and absolute scarcity. The third view takes the middle ground, asserting that Allah has provided sufficient resources (see the verses of the *Qur'an* mentioned earlier under the principle of wealth) but it is the system created by man that prevents the satisfaction of all of his needs and wants (Khan, 2012).

In short, there is no absolute scarcity in Islam. While organization of the economic system can help improve the equity problem, the scarcity problem may still exist as a natural process due to limited knowledge to exploit the resources and/or due to natural phenomenon that may drive the prices. Hence, in Islamic economics, both consumers and producers are bounded not only by resource constraints but also by ethical or moral restraints.

2.5.2 NEEDS AND WANTS

Neoclassical economics is founded on 'consumer sovereignty' which is embodied in two separate assumptions: (i) man knows what is best for him and will make the choice in accordance to that knowledge; and (ii) drawing distinctions between needs and wants is unnecessary, as the task of the economist is to fulfil all demands. Regarding the first assumption, the *Qur'an* clearly states the limited knowledge of man:

> But it is possible that ye dislike a thing which is good for you, and that ye love a thing which is bad for you. But Allah knoweth, and ye know not (Al-Baqarah, 2:216).[30]

As for the second assumption, the *Qur'an* emphasizes fulfilling needs and warns against gratifying idle desires:

> Then seest thou such a one as takes as his god his own vain desire? Allah has, knowing (him as such), left him astray, and sealed his hearing and his heart (and understanding), and put a cover on his sight. Who, then, will guide him after Allah (has withdrawn Guidance)? Will ye not then receive admonition? (Al-Jathiyah, 45:23).[31]

Furthermore, fulfilment of all needs and wants is near impossible, as wants are insatiable and keep increasing with increase in wealth, as informed by the following *Hadith*:

> Anas bin Malik reported that The Prophet (pbuh) said: 'If Adam's son had a valley of gold, he would like to have two valleys, for nothing fills his mouth except dust [of the grave]. And Allah forgives him who repents to Him' (Bukhari).[32]

Thus, Islamic economics recognized man's limited knowledge in making the best choice and course of actions to solve an economic problem. Furthermore, the scarcity problem can never be solved by neoclassical economics as there is no end to what man wants, whereas Islam teaches man to restrain from pursuing idle desires.

---

[29] For more discussion on the topic, also see Nomani, F. and Rahnema, A. (1995), *Islamic economic system*, S. Abdul Majeed, Kuala Lumpur.

[30] www.wright-house.com/religions/islam/Quran/2-cow.php, accessed 21 May 2018.

[31] www.wright-house.com/religions/islam/Quran/45-crouching.php, accessed 21 May 2018.

[32] abuaminaelias.com/dailyhadithonline/2011/05/21/nothing-can-satisfy-the-greed-of-mankind/, accessed 6 June 2018.

2.5.3 CHOICES

Due to scarce resources, choices need to be made from the feasible allocations. In western economics, the process of making choice involves comparing the costs and benefits. As long as the benefits exceed the marginal costs, the action will be chosen. Similarly, Islamic economics use the same criterion of weighing between costs and benefits. For instance, the injunction in the *Qur'an* concerning banning of intoxicants and gambling states:

> *They ask thee concerning wine and gambling. Say: 'In them is great sin, and some profit, for men; but the sin is greater than the profit'* (Al-Baqarah, 2:219).[33]

Hence, it can be deduced that the reason for prohibiting intoxicants and gambling is due to the cost (sin or harm) outweighing the benefits (profit). While Islamic economics includes the mundane features of costs and benefits in making choices, it also takes into account the subjective spiritual qualities such as sin and righteousness, rewards and punishment, etc.

2.5.4 RATIONAL ECONOMIC MAN

One of the distinctive features of Islamic economics compared to neoclassical economics is that the former is value laden. Therefore, the rationality of an individual as an economic man (*homo economicus*) will be different from that of a God-fearing Muslim man (*homo Islamicus*). A rational economic man's objective is based on self-interest, which is to optimize utilization and maximize profit. In contrast, a rational God-fearing man's objective will have both self-interest and altruistic features. In Islam, life in this world is a temporary phase and the permanent life is in the hereafter, where man will be rewarded or punished. Hence, the objective of economic agents in an Islamic economy will be that of balancing rather than optimizing since the goal of a Muslim is to achieve *al-falah*, i.e. happiness in this world and in the hereafter.

As explained by Ahmad (1992), a Muslim individual operates at two levels. At one level, the individual's action is driven by his self-interest just like any rational economic man. There is nothing wrong with this, as Islam encourages an individual to exploit his creativity and knowledge as well as effort to maximize his wealth. But at another level, the same individual acts as an instrument or agent (vicegerent), where his choice of actions is driven by his religious belief, which has far-reaching consequences. For instance, choosing to trade-off self-interest for collective interest may not seem to benefit much in this world, but the rewards may be higher in the hereafter. In short, a Muslim individual is not only *homo economicus* but also *homo Islamicus*, balancing between the material and spiritual needs to accomplish his economic goals.

2.5.5 INCENTIVES

Economics deal with incentives. People make choices and undertake actions based on incentives. 'What is in for me?' is a typical question that goes in one's head when making decisions, partly driven by selfishness. In neoclassical economics, incentives are often based on tangible things or something in the form that can be measured. In Islam, the incentives are not driven entirely by tangible things but by altruism and contentment with the blessings showered.

2.5.6 FREE MARKET

In Islamic economic history, the market plays a vital role as a distinctive place for transactions. These markets are regulated by price mechanisms whereby the forces of supply and demand will help the market to achieve equilibrium. In other words, people are free to transact and exchange goods and services, and intervention by

---

[33]www.wright-house.com/religions/islam/Quran/2-cow.php, accessed 21 May 2018.

the state authority is only needed to stop unjust or illegal acts that cause grievance to other stakeholders. *Shari'ah* provides guidance for fair and free trading, and price controls are meant to avoid monopoly and fight corruption. Islam prohibits market players from harming societal wellbeing through hoarding and profiteering from people's urgent needs for particular commodities.

2.6   Islamic economic system

Before delving into discussion on Islamic economic system, it is important to first define the word *system*. A system is defined as the 'functional components that together make certain sectors of the ethico-economic order work' (Choudhury and Malik, 1992, p. 15), and therefore refers to an integrated whole as part of an order. In other words, economic activities operate in a broad organizational framework called an economic system. An *economic system* consists of a collection of economic entities like households, business firms, public institutions and markets set up by society to deal with the allocation of resources, production and exchange of goods and services, and distribution of the resulting income and wealth. They are constituted and operated according to a set of rules of conduct governed by a certain doctrine or societal worldview (Mirakhor and Askari, 2017).

Every economic system has its own unique features. As we have seen in the earlier section, capitalism favours individual liberties in the pursuit of wealth, with no or very limited intervention of the state in economic affairs. The exceptional human advancement in science and technology contributed to the innovation and rapid industrialization that is needed for the operation of a free market economy. Moreover, financial institutions and markets facilitated the movement of capital from the surplus sector to the deficit sector, with interest playing a significant part in decision making. To counter capitalism, communism and socialism favour the communitarian spirit and support the role of the state in having complete or significant control on the economy and full ownership of means of production. While the social welfare scheme provides some assurance on the welfare of vulnerable groups in society, the downside of it is that people will have less incentive to work. Similarly, restrictions on private ownership may limit productivity.

On the other hand, an *Islamic economic system* is marked by a number of distinguishing features that set it apart from those conventional economic systems. Iqbal and Mirakhor (2007, p. 32) define an Islamic economic system as:

> *…a collection of institution, i.e., formal and informal rules of conduct and their enforcement characteristics, designed by the Law-giver, i.e. Allah (swt) through the rules prescribed in the Qur'an, operationalised by the Sunnah of the Prophet (pbuh) and extended to new situations by ijtihad – to deal with allocation of scarce resources, production and exchange of goods and services and distribution of resulting income and wealth.*

From the definition, what makes the Islamic economic system different is the origin of the rules of conduct: the divine law in the form of *shari'ah*, as opposed to human law which is the basis for the other economic systems. Since the law-giver is Allah, the system must be perfect, as Allah knows what is best for humans, and any imperfections that we see in the system may be attributed to man's own weaknesses.

2.6.1   OBJECTIVES OF AN ISLAMIC ECONOMIC SYSTEM

Discussion of any type of system is incomplete without addressing the goals and objectives of the system. Since an Islamic economic system is founded on guidance by Allah, the ultimate objective of any human activity, economic or otherwise, must be directed towards the Day of Judgement and earning the pleasure of Allah. Similarly, decisions on the best ways to organize economic affairs cannot be made without first understanding or specifying the purpose of human life. These aspects are related to the vertical relationship between man and his Creator. An economic system can also have objectives that require a tangible assessment process on the effectiveness and accomplishments directly related to the worldly activities among man, thus addressing the horizontal relationship between man and his fellow beings.

Al-falah is a comprehensive concept encompassing the moral, spiritual and socio-economic wellbeing in this world and success in the hereafter. The Islamic call for prayer (*azan*) that can be heard from mosques in Islamic countries five times a day includes the call 'Let us pray and seek *al-falah*'. The *Qur'an* also emphasizes the importance of seeking *al-falah*:

> *And there are men who say: 'Our Lord! Give us good in this world and good in the Hereafter, and defend us from the torment of the Fire'* (Al-Baqarah, 2:201).[34]

At the individual, or micro, level, *falah* refers to fulfilment of an individual's basic needs and enjoyment of freedom and leisure that are necessary for his or her spiritual and material advancement. At the macro level, *falah* refers to happiness of society as a whole through the provision of clean environment, freedom and equal opportunities for its members to progress in religious and socio-political affairs. The achievement of economic wellbeing and improvement in the welfare of the people through fair distribution of material resources and establishment of social justice is the economic aim of *al-falah*, as stated in the *Qur'an*:

> *But seek, with the (wealth) which Allah has bestowed on thee, the Home of the Hereafter, nor forget thy portion in this world: but do thou good, as Allah has been good to thee, and seek not (occasions for) mischief in the land: for Allah loves not those who do mischief* (Al-Qasas, 28:77).[35]

The second most important aim of the Islamic economic system is to establish *socio-economic justice* such that economic disparities that lead to social segmentation and divisiveness as well as exploitation in any form are absent. Iqbal and Mirakhor (2007) identify three elements of justice which can be accomplished based on the *shari'ah* framework: equality of liberty and opportunity on utilization of resources, justice in exchange and distributive justice. *Equal liberty and opportunity on utilization of resources* refers to the right of a person to have freedom and opportunity to combine creativity and knowledge with natural resources to generate products and services. Consequently, this will enable the person to offer goods and services and participate in the exchange market. To ensure *justice in exchange*, *shari'ah* has provided a network of ethical and moral rules of behaviour for all participants engaged in the market. The rules on demand and supply, for instance, only allow the exchange of products and services that are *shari'ah* compliant as they are not harmful to society. Similarly, a just price will be achieved as a result of interactions between buyers and sellers who abide by the *shari'ah* rules of being transparent and honest regarding the quantity, quality, weight, etc. Behaviours such as fraud, cheating, speculation, etc. are forbidden in *shari'ah* as they lead to injustice. *Distributive justice* refers to fair distribution of wealth, income and economic resources and this is possible because Allah has placed sufficient sustenance and provisions on the earth to cater for all human needs. However, Islam also recognizes unequal distribution of wealth that caused some to possess wealth more than their needs while others possess nothing or very little to meet their basic necessities of life. This may arise due to various reasons and also as a natural part of the Divine scheme of world order as mentioned in the *Qur'an*:

> *Allah has bestowed His gifts of sustenance more freely on some of you than on others: those more favoured are not going to throw back their gifts to those whom their right hands possess, so as to be equal in that respect. Will they then deny the favours of Allah?* (An-Nahl, 16:71).[36]

However, to help the poor and unfortunate members of the community, Islam overcomes the challenge of unequal division of wealth by making it an obligation upon the rich to surrender a part of their wealth to the institutions of *zakat* and *sadaqat* (alms and charity). Furthermore, Islam has made the circulation of wealth

---

[34]www.wright-house.com/religions/islam/Quran/2-cow.php, accessed 21 May 2018.

[35]www.wright-house.com/religions/islam/Quran/28-story.php, accessed 21 May 2018.

[36]www.wright-house.com/religions/islam/Quran/16-bee.php, accessed 21 May 2018.

between all citizens an obligation and has forbidden the restriction of such circulation to a certain group of people to the exclusion of others, as mentioned in the *Qur'an*:

> What Allah has bestowed on His Messenger (and taken away) from the people of the townships, – belongs to Allah, – to His Messenger and to kindred and orphans, the needy and the wayfarer; In order that it may not (merely) make a circuit between the wealthy among you (Al-Hashr, 59:7).[37]

Hence, the primary objective of the Islamic economic system is to bridge the gulf between the rich and the poor by altering the distribution of wealth and economic resources for the benefit of the less fortunate. Fair and equitable distribution of wealth can be achieved through positive and negative measures, such as through the institution of alms and charity, establishment of inheritance and will laws, prohibition of interest, hoarding and earnings of wealth by unlawful means, etc. An Islamic economic system discourages hoarding to ensure that there is constant circulation of wealth. The *Qur'an* clearly warned about the consequences of hoarding wealth:

> And there are those who bury gold and silver and spend it not in the way of Allah, announce unto them a most grievous penalty – On the Day when heat will be produced out of that (wealth) in the fire of Hell, and with it will be branded their foreheads, their flanks, and their backs, - 'This is the (treasure) which ye buried for yourselves: taste ye, then, the (treasures) ye buried!' (At-Tawbah, 9:34-35).[38]

The *zakat* system is a great intervention mechanism for hoarding. If *zakat* is paid regularly on the hoarded wealth, it will simply decline over the years with little benefit. Thus, the owner is encouraged to spend it or offer it for investment so as the wealth will be in circulation to benefit the economy.

The Islamic economic system has another important objective, which is to ensure that everyone has their basic necessities fulfilled. What constitutes basic needs is defined in this *Hadith*:

> The son of Adam has no better right than that he would have a house wherein he may live, and a piece of cloth whereby he may hide his nakedness, and a piece of bread and some water (Tirmidhi).[39]

Thus, having access to the basic necessities of life, such as food for survival and maintenance of health, a house to live in and clothing, is one of the fundamental rights of every human being. In Islam, fulfilment of such rights falls under the responsibility of the state, as mentioned in this *Hadith*:

> The government is the guardian of anyone who has no other guardian (Tirmidhi).[40]

Through a comprehensive system of social security, the Islamic economic system ensures the fulfilment of the basic needs of every needy person.

A further objective of the Islamic economic system is to enable man to manifest his role as a *khalifa* (vicegerent) of Allah by fulfilling the mission of "promoting what is good, forbidding what is wrong, establishing justice ('*adl*) and promoting beneficence (*ihsan*), resulting in attaining high levels of good life (*hayat al-tayyebah*), both individually and collectively" (Ahmad, 2003, p. 193). The role given to humans as vicegerent on earth to fulfil Allah's mission is an honour, as we are trusted to be capable of receiving the mandate and living up to the responsibilities associated with that mandate. The *Qur'an* states:

> Behold, thy Lord said to the angels: 'I will create a vicegerent on earth.' They said: 'Wilt Thou place therein one who will make mischief therein and shed blood? – whilst we do celebrate Thy praises and glorify Thy holy (name)?' He said: 'I know what ye know not' (Al-Baqarah, 2:30).[41]

---

[37]www.wright-house.com/religions/islam/Quran/59-exile.php, accessed 21 May 2018.

[38]www.wright-house.com/religions/islam/Quran/9-repentance.php, accessed 21 May 2018.

[39]Vol. 4, Book 10, Hadith 2341 sunnah.com/tirmidhi/36, accessed 21 May 2018.

[40]Vol. 2, Book 6, Hadith 1102 sunnah.com/tirmidhi/11, accessed 21 May 2018.

[41]www.wright-house.com/religions/islam/Quran/2-cow.php, accessed 21 May 2018.

The characteristics that made humans trustworthy in carrying out the mandate are represented by our ability to learn, to develop and to choose. Thus, in developing an Islamic economic system, man should take into account the guidelines in *shari'ah* on matters such as avoiding activities that are prohibited (i.e. *riba*), advocating equity and justice in the accumulation and allocation of wealth, and promoting innovations and entrepreneurship to provide beneficial goods and services. The two-dimensional utility function of an Islamic economic system is unique in the sense that the more one commits in doing social good in the temporal world, the more glad tidings one hopes to receive in the hereafter.

A further objective of the Islamic economic system is the promotion of the *ummah* (creation of unity among Muslims) and universal brotherhood. In a caring and cooperative society, everyone can count on the help of others in their time of need. It is the responsibility of every Muslim society to serve all mankind by inviting others to do good and work against injustice and evil, and also to collectively take care of basic needs including health, education, food, housing, employment opportunities, etc. The *Qur'an* states:

> *Help ye one another in righteousness and piety, but help ye not one another in sin and rancour: fear Allah. for Allah is strict in punishment* (Al-Ma'idah, 5:2).[42]

Hence, to help achieve social harmony and promote brotherhood between different sections of society, an Islamic economic system endorses the institutions of *zakat*, charity and other means of helping the poor. Despite the imbalance of wealth, this should not cause divisions in society between the rich and poor and between social classes if everyone respects and plays their social role.

The Islamic economic system also helps in achieving material and moral development of the community. For instance, wealth circulation through spending and investment creates a multiplier effect on the nation's income growth. The tax collection from the rich will increase when people earn higher incomes, and this enables the government to distribute money to the poor in the form of social security or benefit, which in turn helps strengthened their purchasing power, and subsequently increases the demand for products and services. Thus, industrialization and full-employment will increase, leading to full utilization of human and material resources, which subsequently boost growth in national income. A system of *zakat* and charity also promotes spiritual and moral development of society, as payment of *zakat* cleanses the human soul of negative values such as miserliness, greed, selfishness, etc. By making it obligatory for a person to pay *zakat* and part with his wealth, Islam elevates sentiments of love, sacrifice, kindness and mutual cooperation. The *Qur'an* states:

> *And likeness of those who spend their wealth, seeking to please Allah and to strengthen their souls, is as a garden, high and fertile* (Al-Baqarah, 2:265).[43]

Closely related to the objective of moral development, an Islamic economic system is able to eliminate abuse of one individual over the other. Islam provides many effective measures to eliminate the abuse. First of such measures is the prohibition of usury or interest, considered as the worst exploitation instrument on humans. The *Qur'an* declares *riba*, or interest, as one of the heinous crimes which amounts to war against God and God's messenger:

> *O ye who believe! Observe your duty to Allah, and give up what remaineth (due to you) from usury, if ye are (in truth) believers. And if ye do not, then be warned of war (against you) from Allah and His messenger. And if ye repent then ye have your principal (without interest). Wrong not and ye shall not be wronged* (Al-Baqarah, 2:278-279).[44]

---

[42]www.wright-house.com/religions/islam/Quran/5-table.php, accessed 6 June 2018.

[43]www.wright-house.com/religions/islam/Quran/2-cow.php, accessed 21 May 2018.

[44]www.wright-house.com/religions/islam/Quran/2-cow.php, accessed 21 May 2018.

Debtors are a group that are subject to exploitation. To help this group, Islam has not only outlawed interest but also encouraged the creditor to provide more time for the debtor to make debt repayment. To eliminate abuse of employees by the employer, Islam set a number of measures including paying employees their fair wages promptly.

2.6.2 SALIENT FEATURES OF AN ISLAMIC ECONOMIC SYSTEM

We have seen earlier the features of the various economic systems. We will now look at some of the features of an Islamic economic system in order to appreciate any similarities and differences.

First, unlike capitalism, which favours individual liberties, and socialism, which favours communitarian spirit, the Islamic economic system does not favour individual freedom over those of the collective, nor does it favour collective rights over those of the individual. Instead, it seeks the common welfare of the collective and the individual concurrently, such that the individual can exercise his or her liberty without harming and transgressing the welfare of the public. In other words, private property rights are established to fulfil the psychological inclination in human beings for ownership, while concurrently restricting the demands of the public wealth in order to gain a sense of balance that will lead to the realization of social progress as well as the feeling of stability and fulfilment.

Second, unlike capitalism, with its minimal intervention, and socialism with its almost total intervention by the state in economic activities, the Islamic economic system recognizes the duty of the state to intervene in some aspects of economic activity to prevent monopoly, exploitation, corruption and other actions that may be harmful to public interest. Similarly, Islamic economics distinguishes between private and public property and makes the state accountable to its citizens. The latter refers to natural resources such as forests, pastures, uncultivated land, water, oil and minerals, oceanic resources, etc., to which society has an equal right. These resources must be placed under the guardianship and control of the state to be used by any citizen as long as the use does not undermine the rights of other citizens. Similar to socialism, an Islamic economic system places responsibility on the state to provide social security for the unemployed and vulnerable groups in society that need financial and non-financial support to help them live with dignity.

Third, unlike capitalism, which allows individuals to maximize their self-interest in pursuing wealth, an Islamic economic system places restrictions on the expansion of individual wealth through various mechanisms. For instance, wealth must be pursued through lawful means by way of efforts and involvements in activities that are permissible, free from any form of abuse or harm to others. Furthermore, the state has the duty to block any potential harm that may arise when the accumulated wealth of an individual provides him or her with the financial power to alter the currency rates, corrupt officials in the state institutions, engage in speculations in the markets, or any other activities that is harmful to the state and society. Also, a wealthy individual has an obligation to fulfil his financial duties such as paying the *zakat* and other duties of social solidarity, in addition to tax.

Next, closely related to the earlier point, an Islamic economic system encourages economic activities and exhorts individuals to engage in work that is productive and profitable, and it strongly opposed idleness, dependency and unemployment. While the system of *zakat* and charity ensures fair distribution of wealth, it does not condone spending on the poor who are capable of working but prefer to stay idle and dependent on the donations. Islamic economic systems prohibit wealth hoarding and instead promote wealth circulation among all sections of society. The Islamic inheritance law helps in preventing wealth concentration in a few hands and also helps in avoiding disputes and injustice among families. The purchasing power of the poor can be enhanced through the circulation of wealth in productive channels.

Fifth, the foundation of capitalism is interest, and despite its harmful effects on society and the state, even socialism has not been able to eliminate it. However, in an Islamic economic system, this can be totally abolished, as the *Qur'an* clearly prohibited it. In Islamic teaching, the meaning of interest does not only pertain to financial debts but it also includes anything that is related to exploitation. Hence, interest (*riba*) is said to exist when the seller abuses the need of the customer by selling a product or service at an exorbitant price, and the employer exploits his employee by paying below minimum wage, as well as any exploitation on debt or sale.

Summary

Economics in its simplest form involves making decisions on how to allocate and utilize resources to fulfil human needs. Economic activities can be organized in different ways leading to different economic systems such as *traditional, command, capitalism* and *socialism*. Each system has its own advantages and disadvantages. *Islamic economics* is perceived as a middle ground ideology related to scarcity, wants and choices with the aim of achieving wellbeing both in this world and in the hereafter, or *al-falah*. Islamic economics theory is founded on six principles as laid down by the *Qur'an* and *Ahadith*: *justice, wealth, ownership, economic freedom, moderation* and *consumption*, as explained in an earlier section. Socio-economic justice can be achieved through redistribution of wealth through obligatory almsgiving (*zakat*) and prohibition of interest. Islam strongly condemns interest for a number of reasons, as explained earlier. There are 11 aspects that distinguish between neoclassical and Islamic economics, as presented in Table 2.1: *scarcity, needs and wants, choices and accumulation of capital, optimality and ethical neutrality, consumer behaviour and utility maximization, firm behaviour and profit maximization, use of mathematics to predict outcomes and behaviour, selfishness as sole motivation in economic realm, moral justification for selfishness, justice in economic development, supply and demand* and *perfect competition versus cooperation*. With *shari'ah* as the guiding force, an Islamic economic system would be able to overcome the defects in many of the existing economic systems.

Key terms and concepts

al-falah	Islamic principle of consumption	productivity
capitalist economy	Islamic principle of economic freedom	public property
command economy	Islamic principle of moderation	rational economic man
distributive justice	Islamic principle of ownership	rational person
economic principles	Islamic principle of wealth	relative and absolute scarcity
economics	justice in consumption	*riba al-fadl*
economic system	justice in distribution	*riba al-nasi'ah*
equal liberty and opportunity	justice in exchange	scarcity
halal and *haram*	justice in production	socialist economy
homo economicus	*khalifa*	socio-economic justice
homo Islamicus	macroeconomics	state property
incentives	market failures	trade-off
inflation	microeconomics	traditional economy
Islamic economic principles	needs and wants	*ummah*
Islamic economic system	opportunity cost	*zakat*

Questions

1. Define and explain the meaning of economics.

2. Discuss the four main types of economic systems and their advantages and disadvantages.

3. What is Islamic economics?

4. Discuss the six principles of Islamic economics and their components.

5. Why is *riba* condemned in Islam?

6. Distinguish between *riba al-nasi'ah* and *riba al-fadl*.

7. What is the Islamic view on wealth and poverty?

8. What is the meaning of *halal* and *haram* and explain giving examples.

9. Compare and contrast between neoclassical and Islamic economic theory.

10. Explain what is meant by an Islamic economic system.

11. Discuss the objectives of an Islamic economic system.

12. Distinguish the features between the four common economic systems and the Islamic economic system.

References and further readings

Ahmad, K. (1992), 'Nature and significance of Islamic economics', in Ahmad, A. and Awan, K.R. (eds), *Lectures on Islamic Economics*, IRTI, IDB, Jeddah, p. 473.

Ahmad, K. (2003), 'The challenge of global capitalism', in J.H. Dunning (ed.), *Making Globalization Good: The Moral Challenges of Global Capitalism*. Oxford University Press, UK, pp. 181-209.

Ahmed, H. (2014), 'Analytical tools of Islamic economics: choice and the equi-marginal principle', in Hassan, K. and Lewis, M. (eds), *Handbook on Islam and Economic Life*, Edward Elgar, UK, pp. 90-112.

Al-Qardawi, Y. (1999), *The Lawful and the Prohibited in Islam (Al-Halal Wal Haram Fil Islam)*, American Trust Publications, USA.

Choudhury, M.A. and Malik, U.A. (1992), *The Foundations of Islamic Political Economy*, Macmillan, London.

Gazzali, I.M. (1971), *Ihya Ulum-id-din*, English Translation by Al-Haj Maulaana Fazlur Karim, Sind Sagar Academy, Lahore, Pakistan.

Hasan, Z. (2015), *Economics with Islamic Orientation*, Oxford University Press (South-East Asia) Kuala Lumpur, Malaysia.

Hassan, K. and Lewis, M. (2014), *Handbook on Islam and Economic Life*, Edward Elgar, UK.

Iqbal, Z. and Mirakhor, A. (2007), *An Introduction to Islamic Finance: Theory and Practice*, John Wiley, Singapore.

Islahi, A.A. (2014), 'Muslim contributions to economic science', in Hassan, K. and Lewis, M. (eds), *Handbook on Islam and Economic Life*, Edward Elgar, Cheltenham, UK, pp. 21-44.

Kahf, M. (2014), *Notes on Islamic Economics: Theories and Institutions*, Monzer Kahf, USA.

Khan, M.F. (2012), *Theorising Islamic Economics: Search for Our Framework for Islamic Economic Analysis*, presented at Workshop on the Future of Islamic Economics: A call for discussion, Islamic Economics Institute, King Abdul Aziz University, Jeddah, Saudi Arabia, 12-13 November.

Mannan, M.A. (1970), *Islamic Economics: Theory and Practice – A Comparative Study*, Kazi Publications Inc. Dhaka.

Mirakhor, A. and Askari, H. (2017), 'The rules governing an Islamic economy', in *Ideal Islamic Economy*, Palgrave Macmillan, New York, pp. 139-178.

Nomani, F. and Rahnema, A. (1995), *Islamic Economic System*, S. Abdul Majeed, Kuala Lumpur.

Qureshi, A.I. (1991), *Islam and the Theory of Interest*, Sh. Muhammad Ashraf Publishers, Lahore, Pakistan.

Roy, O. (1994), *The Failure of Political Islam*, Harvard University Press, USA.

Siddiqui, S.A. (2014), 'Riba, time value of money and discounting', in Hassan, K. and Lewis, M. (eds), *Handbook on Islam and Economic Life*, Edward Elgar, Cheltenham, UK, pp. 113-131.

Zaman, A. (2012), 'An Islamic critique of neoclassical economics', *Pakistan Business Review*, April, pp. 9-58.

Zaman, S.M.H. (1984), 'Definition of Islamic Economics', *Journal of Research in Islamic Economics*, 1(2), pp. 49-50.

3 Introduction to the Islamic financial system

Learning Objectives

Upon completion of this chapter you should be able to:

- explain the meaning and styles of financial systems

- discuss the Islamic financial system

- identify and describe the five components of a financial system

- explain the concept, functions and evolution of money

- discuss the Islamic concept and functions of money

- critically evaluate the Islamic view on various types of money

- discuss the functions of central banks and their role in the Islamic financial system framework

- explain the roles performed by conventional and Islamic financial intermediaries

- discuss the roles of conventional and Islamic financial markets

- explain the nature of conventional and Islamic financial instruments

3.1 Introduction

Economic growth is important for the development of a country, as the more developed the country is, the higher will be the standard of living enjoyed by its citizens. To attain economic development, a country needs to engage in more investment and production activities to stimulate economic growth. This can only happen when savings and surplus funds in the country are mobilized to productive resources in the form of investment and lending to households, businesses and governments for the purpose of production and distribution. This calls for a mechanism or system to be in place in the country to facilitate the mobilization of funds for productive use.

Therefore, in this chapter we will look more closely at this mechanism, which is called the financial system. We will specifically provide answers to the following basic questions related to a financial system: *what is it and what it consists of, who uses it and for what purposes, and how its performance is relevant to the rest of the economy*. We will begin by introducing some of these important concepts for those with no prior knowledge of financial economics before addressing them from an Islamic perspective.

3.2   What is a financial system and who uses it?

Before answering the above two questions, it is first helpful to understand the meaning of the words *financial* and *system*. The word *financial* is a broad term used in describing various aspects of finance or the financial industry, while the word *system* refers to a set of rules, an arrangement of things or a group of related things that work towards a common goal. Hence, a *financial system* refers to the set of rules or arrangements related to various aspects of finance or the financial industry in helping participants to achieve a common goal which is typically related to the productive use of funds.

Howells and Bain (2008, p. 4) define a financial system as '*a set of markets for financial instruments, and the individuals and institutions who trade in those markets, together with the regulators and supervisors of the system*.' From the definition, it is clear that a financial system consists of *institutional units* such as a household, corporation or government agency that is capable in its own right of owning assets, incurring liabilities, engaging in economic activities and making transactions with other entities. These institutional units can interact either directly with each other or through organized *financial markets* and *financial intermediaries* for the purpose of mobilizing funds through the use of various *financial instruments*. These interactions are often monitored and supervised through a system of regulations and governance. Figure 3.1 presents the three possibilities for the flow of funds in the financial system.

Figure 3.1   Flow of funds in the financial system

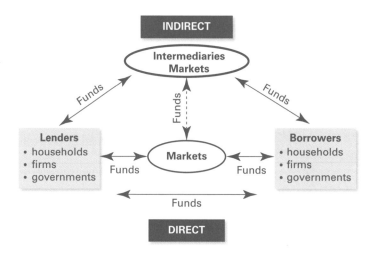

In short, a *financial system* allows the transfer of funds between lenders and borrowers to generate capital and also to meet the short term and long term capital needs of households, corporations and governments. The users of the facilities provided by a financial system are people, corporations and other organizations as well as government agencies, known collectively as *institutional units*. They interact with each other to channel funds to the end users of the financial system, i.e. the ultimate lenders and borrowers. *Lenders* are those willing to lend their financial surplus which arises when income exceeds consumption. Owners of financial surplus have a choice on how to use the surplus: they can invest in real assets such as machinery and properties; simply accumulate or build up money, which in this case is considered as hoarding; or to lend the money to others. Thus, not all owners of financial surplus are willing to be lenders, as their decision to lend may typically be induced by the amount of return they will gain, level of risk they are willing to take and the ease of liquidity, i.e. how easy they can convert the asset into cash when the need arises. *Borrowers*, on the other hand, are those with financial deficit which arises from having to incur financial liabilities (debts) or the result of accumulating financial assets in the past. In the case of firms, this could take the form of acquiring capital equipment, while for households this could be for acquiring consumer durables like cars or houses. The preferred choice of borrowing may be influenced by the *terms of borrowing*, i.e. cost of borrowing and period for repayment. Financial systems can operate at the micro, macro and global levels. At the *micro level*, i.e. households and firms, the financial system is related to a set of implemented procedures in tracking the financial activities of the individual or firm such as the level of and change in the revenues, expenses, assets, liabilities and capital. At the *macro level*, a financial system involves the exchange of funds between lenders and borrowers through organized financial markets and intermediaries within the country and across countries. At the global level, the financial system not only encompasses financial markets and intermediaries but also includes the central banks and finance ministries, the International Monetary Fund (IMF) and the Bank of International Settlement, the World Bank and other major institutions involve in international lending, such as private banks and hedge funds, and regional institutions such as in the Eurozone.

3.3   Styles of financial systems

Financial systems can be classified into market based (decentralized financial system) and bank based (centralized financial system), depending on the relative importance of banking and stock market institutions in the country. Table 3.1 presents the main characteristics of the two styles of financial systems.

Table 3.1 Styles of financial systems

Characteristics	Market based	Bank based
Financial markets	substantial, liquid	small, less liquid
% of listed companies	high	low
Risk dissemination	via market mechanisms, spatial	via market mechanisms, temporal
Ownership and control	dispersed	concentrated
Corporate control change	frequent hostile acquisitions	rare hostile acquisitions
Principal agent problem	shareholders vs. management	major vs. minor shareholders
Bank role in external financing	low	high
Debt to equity	low	high

In *market based systems* (e.g. Anglo–Saxon countries like the UK and the USA), the market institutions are often well developed and households' assets are sometimes held in the form of shares and bonds. Businesses raise capital through IPOs (initial public offerings) and corporate equities. The ownership structure of companies is often very diluted and dominated by institutional investors who play a major role in the efficiency of the capital market. Monitoring is conducted by the capital markets authorities, securities commissions, special government entities and rating agencies. Market based systems rely heavily on information quality and accounting transparency.

By contrast, in a *bank based system* (e.g. Germany and Japan), the capital markets are relatively underdeveloped and the main role of financing is played by banking institutions. Households' assets are held as claims on insurance companies and banks. The majority of companies are not listed, and for those that are listed there are limited numbers of major shareholders, and institutional investors play a minor role. In such system, the relationship between financial intermediaries and companies are of long term nature and are based on mutual information sharing. Such relationships decrease information asymmetry and borrowing costs. Financial monitoring is conducted by banks which monitor investment projects, and they will intervene, if necessary.

3.4   Islamic financial system

An *Islamic financial system* works on the flow of funds from the surplus spending unit to the deficit spending unit, which is governed by a set of Divine rules and regulations embodied in the *Qur'an* and *Sunnah*, such as avoiding *riba* (usury or interest), *gharar* (ambiguities and uncertainties), *maysir* (gambling), *haram* (dealing in unlawful activities), and avoiding unethical or immoral transactions such as market manipulation, insider trading, short-selling, etc. Figure 3.2 illustrates the underlying principles of an Islamic financial system.

Figure 3.2 Principles of an Islamic financial system

In some Muslim majority countries, the Islamic financial system often runs parallel with its mainstream counterpart. Given that they have to abide with the conventional legal system in their own jurisdiction, their claims on *shari'ah* legitimacy are by virtue of contracts (*aqd*) employed in their financial transactions. In other words, the institutions may be similar to the conventional counterparts but the operations and the nature of transactions are dissimilar. Figure 3.3 presents the typical institutions that can be found in an Islamic financial system.

Figure 3.3 Institutions in the Islamic financial system

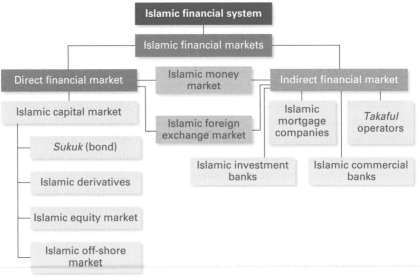

As illustrated in Figure 3.3, the surplus spending unit who wants to adhere to the Divine rules and regulations can purchase or invest in financial assets either directly or indirectly. In the direct financial market (without intermediation), they can choose to participate in the *Islamic capital market* by investing in the *Islamic equity market* or *Islamic bond market (sukuk)*. The securities traded in those markets are less liquid. If they are interested in investing in securities with higher liquidity, they can do so through the *Islamic money market* where Islamic treasury bills (i-TBs), Islamic negotiable certificates of deposit (i-NCDs) and overnight funds are traded. For those who do not have the time or skills to undertake investments or funding activities on their own, they can use financial intermediaries, such as Islamic commercial and merchant banks, Islamic financial services companies, *takaful* operators (Islamic insurance companies), unit trusts companies, Islamic cooperatives, Islamic micro financing institutions and other institutions such as *waqf* (endowment) and *zakat* (alms and charity) institutions.

Since the Islamic financial system is based on *shari'ah*, the services rendered by the system with regards to risk sharing, liquidity and information disclosure must also be *shari'ah* driven. Investors need greater product choices so that risks can be minimized, and this requires Islamic financial institutions to engage in product innovation so that investors can have more product choices. It is worth noting that Islam enjoins risk aversion and prohibits risk avoiding behaviour. *Risk aversion* from an Islamic perspective refers to willingness to take more calculated risks with the expectations of earning higher returns, which is based on the principle of *al-ghorm bil ghonm* (no reward without risk). This legal maxim stresses that reward can only be attained by the taking of risk. Such behaviour is directly opposite to *riba*, where risk taking is absent from the taking of surplus out of a debt, and it also allows capital to appreciate without any possibility to decline. *Risk avoiding* behaviour is prohibited because such investors expect fixed return as well as capital protection, which amount to *riba*.

Since the style of financial system, as discussed earlier, is either market based or bank based, the style of Islamic financial system can be said to be similar to a bank based system for the following reasons (Iqbal and Mirakhor, 2007):

- The prohibition of *riba* and debt-like securities limit the activities in the debt-based capital market, so the role of intermediaries will continue to be important.
- The equity market still faces a number of operational issues that need resolutions from *shari'ah* scholars, and this means that the role of intermediaries for capital formation will need to continue.
- Asset backed securities market development will increase the securitization activities performed by intermediaries.
- Limited application of derivative market instruments increases the burden of financial intermediaries to perform the function of risk sharing and mitigation.

Now that we understand what a financial system is and the different styles of financial systems, including the Islamic financial system, let us now turn our attention to the components of a financial system, in general, and how the Islamic financial system fits into the framework.

3.5 Components of financial systems

Every system is constrained by some rules. In the case of financial systems they are to some extent constrained by the regulations and governance practices of the country or by religious law such as *shari'ah*. Hence, financial systems are not the same in all countries mainly due to differences in their approaches to the regulation of financial activities and institutions, including religion. Nevertheless, they all share the same five main components in the system: *money*, *central banks*, *financial intermediaries*, *financial markets* and *financial instruments*, as illustrated in Figure 3.4.

Figure 3.4 Components of a financial
system

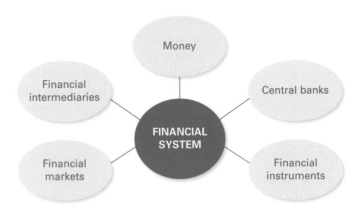

3.5.1 MONEY

a) Concept and evolution of money

Money refers to anything that is generally accepted as payment for goods and services or for repayment of loans. Central to the concept of money is general acceptability, i.e. as long as something is acceptable for exchange, then it can be considered as money. This is best understood by looking at how money has evolved over the years, as illustrated in Box 3.1.

In early human societies, there was no money and people engaged in *barter*, which involved the exchange of merchandise for merchandise without value equivalence. Later, some commodities assumed the role of currency as they were more sought after due to their utility. Salt, wheat, barley, cattle and even shells have been used as a medium of exchange and such money is referred to as *commodity money*. This form of money is problematic as it is not easily transferable. It is difficult to find coincidence of wants and to determine common measure of value, as well as to store the value. When precious metals were discovered, coins made from gold, silver and nickel were used as a basis for storing wealth and also as a medium of exchange, thus replacing commodity money. This *metallic money* was at first full bodied money, i.e. the metallic value was equal to the face value.

Later, the full metallic money was replaced by minted coins for small denominations and paper notes for larger denominations as *tender money*, i.e. they can be used to discharge debt and nobody can refuse to take it. At first the paper notes were convertible into pre-set, fixed quantities of gold and these gold standard notes were made legal tender. By the beginning of the 20th century almost all countries had adopted the gold standard, backing their legal tender notes with fixed amounts of gold.

However, after World War II, the Bretton Woods Agreement made the US dollar the default global reserve currency and only the USD was redeemable for gold. In 1971, the USD was removed from the gold standard, partly due to the inability of the USA to maintain enough gold reserves. As a result, the other countries also abandoned the gold standard. Hence, the *paper money* in circulation today is not derived from any intrinsic value or guarantee that it can be converted into a valuable commodity (such as gold). Instead, it has value only by government order (fiat) and is printed by the central bank of the respective country as legal tender.

Another form of money is *bank money*, which refers to *cheques*, *bills of exchange* and *bank drafts*, which play a vital function in the economy, as various transactions can be settled without the use of paper money. A *cheque* is an order to transfer funds from the payer's bank account to the payee's bank, where both banks may charge a fee for the service. It is a form of credit and involves fixed costs that are independent of the amount of the cheque. Now electronic payments are easier and cheque guarantee cards are hardly ever used. *Float* refers to cheques in the process of clearing. Until the cheque is processed through the clearing system, the payer continues to receive credit on his account. Thus, float represents an interest free short term loan to the payer. A *bill of exchange* is a written order that obliges one party to pay another party a fixed sum of money upon request or at a predetermined date. This is primarily used in international trade. It is generally transferable by endorsements and involves three parties: the *drawee*, who pays the sum specified by the bill of exchange; the *payee*, who is the

Box 3.1 EVOLUTION OF MONEY

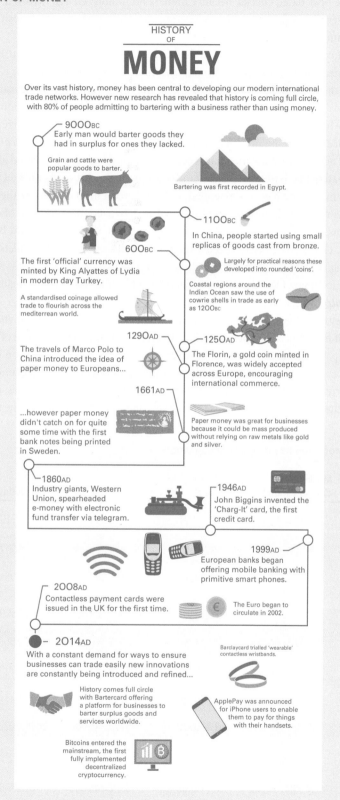

one who receives that sum; and the *drawer*, who is the party that requires the drawee to pay the payee. Bills of exchange are in essence post-dated checks, because there is no interest charge involved. A *bank draft* is a payment on behalf of a payer that is guaranteed by the issuing bank. When the payee deposits the draft in his bank, he receives credit the same day for that amount.

The development of computer technology and the birth of the World Wide Web in 1991 have allowed systems to develop for transactions to take place through *electronic money* (abbreviated as e-money). *E-money* can be either decentralized or centralized. The former is where the control over the money supply comes from various sources while in the case of the latter, the money supply is controlled by a central point.

Centralized e-money includes *debit cards, credit cards* and *charge cards* whereby currency and payments can be exchanged electronically at the point of sale instead of paper money. With a *debit card*, the payment comes right out of the current account into the merchants account when the card is presented at the point of sale. The debit cards issued by banks like Barclays and Santander are typical debit cards in the UK. With a *credit card*, charges are either paid in full or finance is extended up to the credit limit offered by the card issuer, as long as a minimum payment is made each month. The two most widely used networks are MasterCard and Visa. In contrast, a *charge card*, as offered by American Express, must be paid off in full monthly. Besides the *plastic cards* (debit card, credit card, charge card), centralized e-money includes *mobile digital wallets* (e-wallets), which are essentially systems using contactless payment transfer to facilitate easy payments by giving the payee more confidence without having to let go of the electronic wallet during the transaction. This includes *Google Wallet*, and *ApplePay* and *Apple Watch*, which were launched in 2011 and 2014, respectively.

Decentralized e-money takes the form of *cryptocurrency*, which is essentially a digital or virtual currency, designed to work as a medium of exchange. The appeal of virtual currency is due to its promise of lower transaction fees than traditional online payment mechanisms. Cryptocurrency prices are purely based on supply and demand. In 2009, Bitcoin, the first cryptocurrency, was invented under the pseudonym Satoshi Nakamoto. It became the 'gold standard' for virtual currencies. There are currently over 800 alternative cryptocurrencies, called Altcoins, such as Ethereum, Ripple and Litecoin. Table 3.2 presents the market capitalization for some of the top cryptocurrencies.

Table 3.2 Top ten cryptocurrencies market capitalization

	Name	Market capitalization $	Price $	Volume $ (24 hr)	Circulating supply	Change (24 hr)
1	Bitcoin	$157 745 044 309	$9 328.01	$6 849 900 000	16 910 900 BTC	6.46%
2	Ethereum	$71 117 672 054	$724.97	$1 854 210 000	98 097 806 ETH	7.75%
3	Ripple	$32 376 974 935	$0.828226	$737 943 000	39 091 956 706 XRP*	6.49%
4	Bitcoin Cash	$17 707 189 721	$1 041.01	$421 598 000	17 009 625 BCH	8.04%
5	Litecoin	$10 412 764 574	$187.40	$858 576 000	55 563 193 LTC	13.04%
6	NEO	$5 969 112 500	$91.83	$176 172 000	65 000 000 NEO*	10.35%
7	Stellar	$5 729 792 493	$0.309745	$32 067 700	18 498 418 032 XLM*	8.98%
8	Cardano	$5 621 740 778	$0.216829	$177 346 000	25 927 070 538 ADA*	8.50%
9	Monero	$4 516 541 225	$285.70	$111 715 000	15 808 463 XMR	11.98%
10	EOS	$4 358 166 501	$6.06	$328 244 000	718 588 353 EOS*	7.93%

* Not Mineable.

Source: coinmarketcap.com/

b) Functions of money

From the evolution of money described earlier, we can distinguish the functions of money into four: as medium of exchange, as unit of account, as store of value and as standard of deferred payment. These functions are further explained below.

(I) MEDIUM OF EXCHANGE Money as a *medium of exchange* means that it can be used to pay for goods and services, which in turn helps in promoting economic efficiency by reducing transaction costs, such as time and effort spent in exchange. Without money, trade must take place through barter which is not only costly but also problematic in finding a 'double coincidence of wants'.

Furthermore, money does not have to have any inherent value to function as a medium of exchange as long as everyone believes that other people will exchange it for their goods. Money provides the owner with *generalized purchasing power*, giving the owner flexibility over the type and quantities of goods to buy, the time and place of the purchase and parties to whom s(he) chooses to deal with.

(II) UNIT OF ACCOUNT Money as a *unit of account* means that it is used as a common denominator to measure the relative values of goods and services. As such, it reduces transaction costs by allowing all prices to be stated in common terms. With barter, there is a need to track the price of each good relative to all other goods, whereas with money the price of each good is tracked in terms of money. Without a measure of value in the form of money, there can be no pricing process, and without a pricing process organized marketing and specialized production may not be possible. Money as unit of measurement is also essential to all forms of economic planning. The values of alternative purchases are compared by consumers in terms of money. Likewise, producers also compare the values of alternative purchases and plan their production outputs and profits in monetary terms. Hence, it is vital to have a stable value of money over a long period of time.

(III) STORE OF VALUE Money is a financial asset that can be stored as wealth (income saved and not consumed). Although other assets such as real estate, shares and bonds may also serve as a *store of value*, money is unique in terms of its liquidity, i.e. the ease and speed with which it can act as medium of exchange. By definition, money is the most liquid store of value. However, money's usefulness as a store of value depends on how well it is able to maintain its value. During inflation, there is a general rise in the prices of all goods. If all prices double, then the value of money will be cut in half. In contrast, under conditions of hyperinflation, where the inflation rate exceeds 50 per cent per month, consumers have been known to have abandoned the use of money altogether and resort to barter. Money, being the most liquid of all resources, is generally accepted as commodity. The possession of money provides the owner with power to acquire almost any commodity in any place. It is this unique quality that distinguishes money from all other commodities. Hence, preference for liquidity means preference for money.

(IV) THE STANDARD OF DEFERRED PAYMENTS *Deferred payments* refer to payments which are made some time in the future for transactions in the present. Since money generally maintains a constant value through time, it immensely simplifies borrowing and lending operations as the *standard of deferred or delayed payments*. Thus, money assists in the formation of capital markets and the activities of financial intermediaries like the stock exchanges, investment trusts and banks. In short, money is the link connecting today's values with the future.

c) Islamic concept of money

As discussed in the last section, money is an instrument of wealth and the lubricant which enables the efficient transfer of resources. Islam encourages Muslims to invest their money and participate in partnership in order to share profits and risks in business instead of becoming creditors. Hence, the concept of money in Islam emphasizes three aspects: ownership, utilization and earning of money.

(I) OWNERSHIP OF MONEY In Islam, ownership of all things in existence belongs to Allah alone and that any wealth in people's possession is only a favour bestowed to whom He chooses to be shared with others. Since man is not the owner of wealth and only has the right to utilize it, it serves as a kind of trial and test. In the last chapter, we saw some of the verses related to ownership and wealth being a test on human. Further emphasis on these aspects can also be seen in other verses in the *Qur'an*:

> *To Him belongs what is in the heavens and on earth, and all between them, and all beneath the soil* (Ta-Ha, 20:6).[1]
>
> *Ye shall certainly be tried and tested in your possessions and in your personal selves; and ye shall certainly Hear much that will grieve you, from those who received the Book before you and from those who worship many gods. But if ye persevere patiently, and guard against evil,-then that will be a determining factor in all affairs* (Al-'Imran, 3:186).[2]

(II) UTILIZATION AND SPENDING OF MONEY Since wealth and money is a divine favour by Allah to humans, it needs to be managed and utilized in the best ways as prescribed in the *Qur'an* and *Hadith*. Firstly, is the need to spend to benefit the deserving, such as parents, next of kin, the needy, as well as for oneself, as mentioned in the *Qur'an*:

> *Believe in Allah and His apostle, and spend (in charity) out of the (substance) whereof He has made you heirs. For, those of you who believe and spend (in charity), – for them is a great Reward* (Al-Hadid, 57:7).[3]
>
> *It is prescribed, when death approaches any of you, if he leave any goods that he make a bequest to parents and next of kin, according to reasonable usage; this is due right on the pious* (Al-Baqarah, 2:180).[4]
>
> *To those weak of understanding Make not over your property, which Allah hath made a means of support for you, but feed and clothe them therewith, and speak to them words of kindness and justice* (An-Nisaa'; 4:5).[5]

Islam prohibits spending of money in unlawful ways and also wasting money which has been entrusted by Allah. These aspects are emphasized in the following verse in the *Qur'an* and also in the *Hadith*:

> *O children of Adam! Wear your beautiful apparel at every time and place of prayer, eat and drink, but waste not by excess, for Allah loves not those who are wasteful* (Surah Al-A'raf, 7:31).[6]
>
> *Abu Huraira reported that the Prophet said: 'Allah has prohibited three things: gossip, much questioning, and wasting money'* (Muslim).[7]

Islam prohibits stinginess and encourages moderation and it also prohibits squandering. The *Qur'an* states:

> *Those who, when they spend, are neither extravagant nor niggardly, but hold a just (balance) between those (extremes)* (Surah Al-Furqan, 25:67).[8]
>
> *And render to kindred their due right, as (also) to those in want, and to the wayfarer; but squander not (your wealth) in the manner of a spendthrift. Verily, spendthrifts are brothers of the Evil One (Satan); and the Evil One is to his Lord ever ungrateful* (Surah Al-Isra', 17:26-27).[9]

(III) EARNING MONEY Islam encourages man to seek lawful livelihood and it is an obligation upon every Muslim, besides their religious obligations such as prayer, fasting, pilgrimage, and *zakat* (alms giving). All the Prophets and Messengers of Allah work to earn their livelihood and as human beings having the same human

---

[1]www.wright-house.com/religions/islam/Quran/20-ta-ha.php, accessed 22 May 2018.

[2]www.wright-house.com/religions/islam/Quran/3-family-of-imran.php, accessed 22 May 2018.

[3]www.wright-house.com/religions/islam/Quran/57-iron.php, accessed 22 May 2018.

[4]www.wright-house.com/religions/islam/Quran/2-cow.php, accessed 22 May 2018.

[5]www.wright-house.com/religions/islam/Quran/4-women.php, accessed 22 May 2018.

[6]www.wright-house.com/religions/islam/Quran/7-heights.php, accessed 22 May 2018.

[7]Book 18, Hadith 4255 sunnah.com/muslim/30, accessed 22 May 2018.

[8]www.wright-house.com/religions/islam/Quran/25-criterion.php, accessed 6 June 2018.

[9]www.wright-house.com/religions/islam/Quran/17-isra.php, accessed 6 June 2018.

qualities, they were the perfect exemplars on the need of earning. The *Qur'an* and *Hadith* emphasized on the importance of work:

> And the Messengers whom We sent before you were all (men) who ate food and walked through the streets; We have made some of you as a trial for others, will you have patience? And Allah is One Who sees (all things) (Al-Furqan, 25:20).[10]
>
> Abu Huraira reported that the Prophet said: 'Prophet David used not to eat except from the earnings of his manual labour' (Bukhari).[11]

Besides obligation of earning money to spend on one's family, it is also important when one has debt to pay. Islam emphasizes the obligation to pay one's debt and to not procrastinate in doing so, as stated in the following *Hadith*:

> Abu Huraira reported that the Prophet said: 'Procrastination (delay) in repaying debts by a wealthy person is injustice' (Bukhari).[12]

Besides emphasizing the need to work and earn money, Islam also provides guidance on avoiding unlawful ways of gaining money. These include earnings from (i) usury or interest through money lending and other *riba* related activities; (ii) cheating through deception in weights, measures, numbers, length or size, etc., concealing defects and real profit, hiding the nature of production of a commodity, quality or its expiry date, overcharging, etc.; (iii) monopoly through hoarding and destroying competitors in the market; (iv) gambling; (v) stealing; and (vi) bribery and corruption. These aspects are emphasized in the *Ahadith*:

> Ibn Mas'ud reported that the Prophet said: 'Cursed the one who consumed riba, and the one who charged it, those who witnessed it, and the one who recorded it' (Tirmidhi).[13]
>
> Aby Huraira reported that the Prophet said: 'Do not practice Najsh (to cheat)' (Muslim).[14]
>
> Abdullah bin 'Amr reported that the Prophet said: "The curse of Allah is upon the one who offers a bribe and the one who takes it" (Ibn Majah).[15]

d) Functions of money in Islam

The Prophet approved the functions of money in Islam as a medium of exchange and store of value. Muslims are discouraged from engaging in barter trading as some of such practices could lead to injustice and exploitation. For instance, any transactions involving two similar commodities when exchanged in unequal quantities or the possession of a commodity that failed to be immediately transferred, constitute *riba al-fadl* (interest on excess in counter value). Muslims are also advised to buy and sell products using money, thus, confirming acceptance of money as medium of exchange. The role of money as a store of value is endorsed by the Prophet when *zakat* (alms) is levied on any wealth having the potential to grow. Since *zakat* is charged on monetary assets, this suggests that money is an important productive agent as it has the potential to grow and create more value.

However, the use of money as commodity and for lending is forbidden in Islam. The reason why Islam forbids the use of money as commodity is because money by itself has no intrinsic value, and thus it cannot be rented out nor sold to generate surplus value by itself. But commodities that have value in themselves such as gold (*dinar*) and silver (*dirham*) can still be used as commodity money and at the same time allow the owners to enjoy the usufruct in the commodities.

---

[10]www.wright-house.com/religions/islam/Quran/25-criterion.php, accessed 6 June 2018.

[11]Vol. 3, Book 34, Hadith 287 sunnah.com/bukhari/34, accessed 22 May 2018.

[12]Vol. 3, Book 41, Hadith 585 sunnah.com/bukhari/43, accessed 22 May 2018.

[13]Vol. 1, Book 12, Hadith 1206 sunnah.com/tirmidhi/14/3, accessed 22 May 2018.

[14]Book 18, Hadith 1580 sunnah.com/riyadussaliheen/18/70, accessed 22 May 2018.

[15]Vol. 3, Book 13, Hadith 2313 sunnah.com/ibnmajah/13/6, accessed 22 May 2018.

Islam also forbids the lending of money to make a profit, as such practice would be tantamount or identical to making money from money, which is *riba*. In Islam, money can only be generated through lawful investment and trade where all parties share the rewards and risks. In other words, money is only recognized as capital when it is combined with other factors of production because money, by itself, has no opportunity cost. Hence, creditors cannot lend money and expect compensation for parting with the money during the credit period without sharing any risks. Only investors who contribute capital and become partners in commerce and sharing the risks can earn rewards.

While both Islam and the capitalist system recognized money as a factor of production, the latter treats money as capital that deserves getting rewards (technically known as interest) irrespective of the results of the productive activity. Unfortunately, the concept of money has become intertwined with the institution of interest, which led to the present interest based banking system. Table 3.3 presents the differences in the concept of money between capitalist and Islamic perspective.

Table 3.3 Capitalist and Islamic concept on functions of money

Capitalist	Purpose	Islam
Yes	Medium of exchange	Yes
Yes	Commodity	No
Yes	Purchase of goods and services	Yes
Yes	Loan to make profit	No

e) Islamic view on various types of money

If you recall the evolution of money discussed earlier, it should become apparent that not all of the types of money meet the Islamic criteria. The *metallic money* in the form of gold and silver and the *tender money* backed by gold standard are acceptable in Islam, as they reflect the actual face value. However, the *paper money* that we currently use is problematic because it is not derived from any intrinsic value and there is no guarantee of the value being maintained. Hence, there have been calls in some Islamic countries for the return to Islamic *dinar* (gold coin) and *dirham* (silver coin) in place of the monetary system built around the US dollar. The *Qur'an* clearly states on the importance of using *dinar* and *dirham* as money in the following verses:

> Among the People of the Book are some who, if entrusted with a hoard of gold, will (readily) pay it back; others, who, if entrusted with a single silver coin, will not repay it unless thou constantly stoodest demanding, because, they say, 'there is no call on us (to keep faith) with these ignorant (Pagans).' but they tell a lie against Allah, and (well) they know it (Al-'Imran, 3:75).[16]
>
> The (Brethren) sold him for a miserable price, for a few dirhams counted out: in such low estimation did they hold him! (Yusuf, 12:20).[17]

Furthermore, the following *Hadith* clearly suggests the eventual collapse of the monetary system that is now functioning around the world, and the significance of the *dinar* and *dirham* in the near future:

> Abu Bakr ibn Abi Maryam reported that he heard the Messenger of Allah say: 'A time is certainly coming over mankind in which there will be nothing (left) that will be of use (or benefit) save a Dinar (i.e., a gold coin) and a Dirham (i.e., a silver coin)' (Musnad, Ahmad).[18]

What about *bank* and *electronic money*? When currency and payments are exchanged at the point of sale without any interest being involved, they are permissible. Hence, bank drafts, debit cards and charge cards are

---

[16]www.wright-house.com/religions/islam/Quran/3-family-of-imran.php#75, accessed 22 May 2018.

[17]www.wright-house.com/religions/islam/Quran/12-joseph.php#20, accessed 22 May 2018.

[18]garsoor.wordpress.com/2008/10/06/gold-dinar-silver-dirham-islam-and-the-future-of-money/ accessed 6 June 2018.

permissible. In the past, the issue of whether credit cards are permissible (*halal*) has received attention because they are essentially a short term loan facility that charges a high interest rate (more than most other consumer loan rates) due to high loan default risk, overheads and the cost of financing the loans. Furthermore, only about 40 per cent of credit card holders use them as payment devices and pay off their short term loans before the issuer charges interest. Today, Islamic credit cards are well accepted by all customers who prefer to utilize a credit card based on *shari'ah* principles. The Islamic credit card provides customers with all the benefits of a conventional credit card while ensuring that all payments and repayments are fully compliant with *shari'ah* principles. Using the principles of deferred payment sale, the bank issues an interest free and penalty free credit card. As goods are purchased using this credit card, the bank will render the transaction on behalf of the credit card holder and simultaneously sell it back to the customer. This credit is payable over a deferred period through instalments within a certain time frame.

The latest controversial issue in the Muslim world is related to the status and role of cryptocurrencies. There are differing opinions among *shari'ah* scholars on its permissibility. The use of digital currencies and blockchain technologies to create innovations in Islamic finance are well received in Muslim jurisdictions such as Malaysia, Indonesia, Saudi Arabia and the UAE. In fact, they are currently working on market regulations related to this type of money.

In Indonesia, Blossom, a micro finance provider, supports entrepreneurs and Islamic finance start-ups using cryptocurrency. In Qatar, a project aimed at establishing digital payment corridors across the Middle East and the Philippines has been launched. Recently, the Commercial Bank, in cooperation with banks in Oman and Turkey, has announced that it was in the process of testing a blockchain prototype designed specifically for the purpose of international remittances. In Dubai, an Islamic cryptocurrency called OneGramCoin, was introduced by a company called OneGram. Since Islamic finance requires an underlying asset to be *shari'ah* compliant, the OneGramCoin tokens introduced by the company were backed by actual gold. Hence, the coins have intrinsic value, as gold physically existed and the market price of gold will be the minimum exit price for these coins. Payments in cryptocurrencies have been accepted for their projects by two property developers in Dubai, Aston Plaza and Residences and MAG Lifestyle Development. In December 2017, a pilot initiative of a new cryptocurrency for the purpose of cross border payments between banks was launched by the central banks of the UAE and Saudi Arabia. The governor of the UAE's central bank stated that faster and more efficient transactions are now made possible through the deployment of blockchain technology.

However, more recently, Shawki Allam, the Grand Mufti in Egypt, released a *fatwa* (religious edict) against the use of all cryptocurrencies. His reason for stating cryptocurrencies as forbidden according to *shari'ah* is they carry risks of fraud through lack of information and knowledge which may be tantamount to gambling. Similarly, Bitcoin is considered to be contrary to Islamic rules by the Religious Affairs Directorate of Egypt. It justifies its decision because since it is not linked to any central authority, the cryptocurrency carries high risks of deception, fraud and forgery that would potentially have detrimental effects on individuals, groups and institutions.

In Turkey and Saudi Arabia, some of the clerics in both these countries have also voiced their objections, echoing the opinion by Egypt's Grand Mufti. In Indonesia, its central bank has cautioned against the risky and excessive speculative trading nature of cryptocurrency. In other Muslim countries, such as Algeria, Morocco and Bangladesh, Bitcoin and all other cryptocurrencies have been declared illegal.

3.5.2 CENTRAL BANKS

The second component in the financial system, *central banks*, are the national financial institutions that exercise control over key aspects of the financial system. They are responsible in supervising a nation's or group of nations' monetary system with the goals of managing monetary policy, stabilizing the nation's currency and fostering economic growth and monitoring inflation. *Monetary policy* refers to the macroeconomic policy and process by which the central bank, monetary authority or currency board of a country controls the supply of money, often targeting an inflation rate or interest rate to ensure price stability and general trust in the currency.

One of the oldest central banks in the world, which became the model on which most other central banks are based, is the Bank of England, formally known as the Governor and Company of the Bank of England, which was incorporated through an act of Parliament in 1694. The original Royal Charter of 1694, signed by King William III, explained that the bank was founded to 'promote the public Good and Benefit of our People' which still remains in the Bank's current mission statement: 'Promoting the good of the people of the United Kingdom by maintaining monetary and financial stability'. Almost every country in the world now has a central bank, which serves as one of the most important institutions in government.

a) Functions of central banks

Central banks play many important roles in the economy. Their main functions encompassed the following:

(I) ISSUER OF CURRENCY NOTES AND COINS The central bank, for the purpose of uniformity and simplicity, has been granted an exclusive monopoly on printing and issuing currency notes which are declared as unlimited legal tender throughout the country. This monopoly status allows it to restrict the amount of private issues of notes and coins as well as to regulate the country's currency and the total supply of money in the economy. To maintain people's confidence in the currency and to achieve the goal of financial stability, the central bank is required to keep gold, silver or other securities against the notes it issued.

Since the central bank is responsible for price stability, it needs to control the supply of money. It does this through what is known as monetary policy, which influences the availability as well as cost of money and credit by taking some measure(s) to control the supply of money and/or the level and structure of interest rates. When the central bank wants to increase the amount of money in circulation and decrease the cost for borrowing, i.e. interest rate, it can buy government bonds, bills or other government issued notes to stimulate economic growth. To reduce inflation and contract the economy, the central bank can sell government bonds on the open market in order to absorb money. Subsequently, the interest rate will rise, which in turn will discourage borrowing. Hence, through *open market operations*, i.e. buying and selling of government securities in the open market in order to expand or contract the amount of money in the banking system, the central bank is able to control inflation, the money supply and prices.

(II) BANKER, AGENT AND ADVISER TO THE GOVERNMENT As banker to the government, the central bank holds the government's bank account and performs the various banking operations on behalf of the government, such as receiving payments and making disbursements and remittances, floating public loans and managing public debts as well as advancing short term loans to the government during stressful economic situations. As an agent of the government, the central bank ensures that general exchange control is in force (where applicable). As for its role as adviser to the government, it counsels the government on all monetary and economic matters.

Although the central bank is frequently termed as the 'government's bank' due to its handling of all trading (creating, selling and buying) of government bonds and other instruments, it should ideally be independent and its operations should not be influenced by political decisions. However, in practice, the nature of the relationship between the central bank and the governing regime differs from one country to another.

(III) CUSTODIAN OF FOREIGN BALANCES Foreign currencies and gold are kept by the central bank as reserve note issue and also to cater for any deficits in the balance of payment with other countries. Hence, it becomes a custodian of the nation's reserves of international currency or foreign balances. In some countries, it is its responsibility to maintain the exchange rate fixed by the government as well as manage exchange control and other restrictions imposed by the state. It also intervenes in the foreign exchange markets at the behest of the government in order to influence the exchange value of the domestic currency in some countries.

(IV) CUSTODIAN OF CASH RESERVES All commercial banks in most countries are required to deposit a part of their cash balances with the central bank based on a specified ratio, for example, 1:10 reserve/deposit ratio. They can use these deposits to facilitate the banks' clearing process and also allow them to draw and pay back during busy and slack seasons, respectively. This enforcement policy by the central bank on commercial banks is another way to control the supply of money in the market.

The concentration of cash reserves in the central bank represents the strength of a country's banking system, as it provides a more elastic credit structure than if they were dispersed among individual banks. Moreover, the pooling of reserves in one institution such as the central bank will enable the reserves to be utilized in the most effective manner during periods of seasonal strain and in general emergencies or financial crises. In other words, centralization of cash reserves is conducive to the overall economy in terms of extent of usage and in increasing liquidity and elasticity of the banking system as well as the credit structure as a whole.

(V) CLEARING HOUSE Central banks facilitate commercial banks to offset the mutual claims of banks on one another and to make settlement on the outstanding payments. As the bankers' bank, the central banks hold the cash reserves of commercial banks to ease the member banks in adjusting or settling their claims against each other through the central bank.

(VI) CONTROLLER OF CREDIT The control or adjustment of credit of commercial banks is recognized as one of the main functions of the central bank. Since commercial banks create a lot of credit, the increase or decrease in the currency and credit may not only cause business fluctuations but also determines the levels of output, incomes, employment and inflation.

(VII) PROTECTION OF DEPOSITOR'S INTEREST In order to maintain a sound banking system and to safeguard against bank failures, legislation has been introduced to enable the central bank to monitor the functioning of commercial banks as well as protecting the depositors' interest. The central bank has the authority to inspect commercial banks to ensure that they have adequate financial resources and their management are operating in conformity with the banking laws and regulations as well as public and national interests.

(VIII) LENDER OF LAST RESORT (LOLR) Central banks need to oversee the financial sector in order to prevent crises or panics which may develop into a 'run' on banks or when there is a cyclical strain. Central banks may sometimes have to step in to prevent widespread withdrawals by depositors to avoid damage to the economy and the collapse of financial institutions. Thus, by acting as the lender of last resort, the central bank assumes the responsibility of meeting all reasonable demands by commercial banks in times of strains and difficulties. This normally involves giving cash to member banks to boost the position of their cash reserves through rediscounting of first class bills when there is a crisis. Member banks can also utilize advances on approved short term securities from the central bank to enable them to increase their cash resources in the shortest time possible. In other words, if a commercial bank lacks liquidity in meeting its clients' demands, i.e. not holding enough reserves to fulfil the needs of its own customers, it can rely on the central bank to lend them additional funds and will be charged at the prevailing discount rate set by the central bank.

b) Role of central banks in the Islamic financial system framework

As discussed earlier, central banks are responsible for the issuance of currency, the management of the banking system in order to ensure the value of the currency, the formulation of monetary policies to govern bank operations and also the regulation of the fluctuations (inflation and deflation) in the value of currency. Changes in the supply of money are closely related to changes in the aggregate economic activities and price level. The irregular periodic upward and downward trend of aggregate economic output is called *business cycles*. A sustained or persistent downward and upward trend in the business cycle is referred to as recession and inflation, respectively. *Recession* signals deep decline in the growth rate of money, while *inflation* signals rapid growth of money supply. Both conditions will not only have significant impact on the economy and economic players but also to every individual in the society in one way or another.

Central banks also play a major role in supervising activities of banks in different parts of the world and are also involved in regulating their operations in general. In addition, they help banks to establish a range of dealings with specific activities and clients. These activities mostly take place within the interest based system which is outlawed by *shari'ah*.

With the advent of Islamic finance, the cooperation between the central banks and Islamic banks is vital in fostering the growth and development of Islamic banks. The nature of their relationship differs from one country to another and this is largely dependent on the legal framework which regulates the status of Islamic banks within these countries. In a number of Muslim majority countries, the Islamic Financial Services Board (IFSB) has been established by the central banks to aid in the development and promotion of *shari'ah* compliant financial services industry, characterized by prudence and transparency via the adoption of international standards that are compatible with Islamic banking principles and methods.

In countries with a dual banking system, special legislation for Islamic banks has been enacted in addition to the legislation for conventional banking system. In other countries, initiatives have been undertaken to develop and enforce legislation that allows for the setting up of Islamic banks in line with specific laws and regulations. Regardless of the jurisdiction, central banks are deemed to be in a good position to provide the much needed assistance to compete with the conventional banks. Similarly, they are capable of buttressing the role that Islamic banks play in the socio-economic sector of a country by establishing special funds, as well as restrictions on equity, licensing and setting up of new branches.

Irrespective of the host country, particular attention should be paid to three features in the relationship between Islamic banks and central banks: as lender of last resort, as clearing house and as supervisor in regard to monetary policy. As a *lender of last resort*, the central bank can control the supply of money to the commercial banks, and in turn the public. They can lend directly to banks to provide them with the needed liquidity in order to protect depositors, prevent crises and widespread panic withdrawal, and the potential damage to the economy caused by the collapse of banks. However, these loans are given on the basis of interest accumulation, which is outlawed in Islamic finance. To accommodate the *shari'ah* requirement, central banks can provide liquidity for Islamic banks on the basis of profit and risk sharing in the form of *mudarabah* (partnership) or *musharakah* (joint venture) capital. Any profits generated from the Islamic bank's investment of the funds advanced by the central banks would be shared between them (we will discuss this in more detail in Chapter 12).

With regards to its role as a *clearing house*, the central bank can play an important role in providing Islamic banks with facilities for the settlement of cheques and other payments, and services related to letters of credit and guarantee in return for a commission. Islamic banks are required to open a current account with the central bank for its use of the clearing system and to meet limited temporary interest free overdraft facilities to cover any temporary shortfalls for settlement purposes. In addition, the central bank creates specific interest free scheme of funds that allows Islamic banks to utilize on the basis of profit sharing during the period of the shortfall.

Lastly, as *supervisor for monetary policy*, the central bank ensures stability in economic growth through stringent policies in controlling the money supply in the market by requiring Islamic banks to maintain a certain level of liquidity in their books. Since the structure of Islamic dealings are different, the central banks have created a blueprint based on standard data collected from Islamic banks to facilitate the central bank itself and the Islamic banks' agents in adhering to the principles of Islamic banking procedures. Through better understanding of the specific nature of dealings of Islamic banks, the central bank has now set a lower level of liquidity ratios for Islamic banks relative to their conventional counterparts.

Besides liquidity control, central banks need to also consider other types of control, including statutory cash reserve requirements, deposit insurance schemes, credit ceilings, distribution of Islamic banks' profits, inspection of banks, profit equalization funds and monetary assets. Given the unique characteristics of Islamic banks, it is important for the central bank to first approve the statute of the Islamic bank before granting permission for it to operate. This will facilitate the central bank in controlling the activities of the Islamic bank and examination of its processes. To safeguard the interests of investors in Islamic banks and evaluation of its investment programmes, the central banks must produce a distinctive set of guidelines and regulations for inspection purposes. Another aspect for central banks to consider is in terms of payment of interest on cash reserves. Since Islamic banks cannot deal with interest, the ratio of reserves required from Islamic banks could be reduced by the central banks. The central banks should give special consideration to Islamic banks in terms of credit ceilings and instead of applying the minimum interest rates as prescribed for commercial banks on savings and time deposits, a weightage system should be implemented for the purpose of profit distribution to such depositors in Islamic banks.

3.5.3 FINANCIAL INTERMEDIARIES

The next component in the financial system is *financial intermediaries*. They are institutions that channel funds from those having surplus to those desiring the funds but have shortage of it. In other words, through the intermediation process, financial intermediaries help to create assets for lenders and liabilities for borrowers by transforming a pool of short term funds into a few large loans for longer periods for the borrower. The intermediary makes a profit by charging a higher interest rate to the borrower and paying some interest to the lender.

Another important function of financial intermediaries is related to the administration of the accounting and payment systems (electronic funds transfer, settlement, clearing). The *Electronic Fund Transfer at Point of Sale (EFTPOS)* is a real-time gross settlement system in which all banking institutions initiate transfers of funds that are immediate, final and irrevocable when processed. Banking institutions that maintain a reserve or clearing account with the central bank may use EFTPOS to send large value, time critical payments such as payments for the settlement of interbank transactions; the purchase, sale and financing of securities transactions; the disbursement or repayment of financings; and the settlement of real estate transactions, or receive payments from other account holders directly. The Clearing House Interbank Payment System (CHIPS) is the only large value system in the world that has the capability of carrying extensive remittance information for commercial payments by cheques. Most payments over CHIPS are related to the foreign exchange and Eurodollar markets. *Automated Clearing House (ACH)* is a less expensive and slower method of electronic payment and usually payroll payments are handled this way. The data on payment instructions together with information from other banks are sent to an ACH for cross settlement and the net positions is made over EFTPOS.

In short, financial intermediaries benefit not only lenders and borrowers but also society in general. They help in improving economic efficiency by facilitating transactions and portfolio creation, reducing transaction costs associated with lending and borrowing, easing household liquidity constraints, spreading risks over time and reducing the problem of asymmetric information.

Financial intermediaries consist of *banking (deposit taking)* institutions and *non-banking (non-deposit taking)* institutions. *Deposit taking institutions* include commercial banks and savings institutions whose main source of funds consist of deposits from households, businesses and government agencies while for credit unions, the source is from deposits by credit union members. In terms of usage of funds, both commercial banks and savings institutions use the funds to purchase government and corporate securities, give out loans to businesses and households while credit unions use the funds to provide loans to credit union members. *Non-deposit taking institutions* can be further classified into *contractual savings institutions*, such as insurance and pension funds companies, and *investment intermediaries,* such as companies offering mutual funds, financial loans, investment services and brokerage houses. Figure 3.5 illustrates the various institutions that act as financial intermediaries.

Figure 3.5   Classification of financial intermediaries

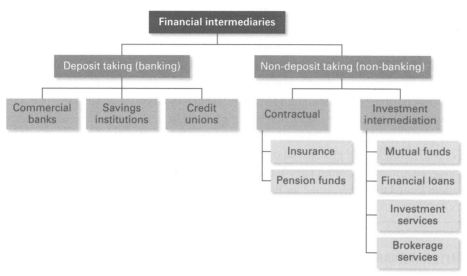

a) Islamic financial intermediaries

As mentioned earlier, the role of various Islamic financial intermediaries cannot be underestimated.[19] All the activities of intermediaries must follow the Islamic principles (see Figure 3.2). Islamic commercial banks (see Figure 3.3) play the role of intermediaries indirectly by buying funds through offering a variety of *shari'ah* compliant deposit products such as current accounts (*wadiah and qard-hassan*), savings accounts (*mudarabah* based) and investment accounts. They then sell the funds through a variety of Islamic equity based and debt based financing products. Equity based financing products facilities comprise trustee partnership (*mudarabah*), joint venture (*musharakah*) and declining partnership (*musharakah mutanaqissah*), while debt based facilities include cost plus sale (*murabahah*), leasing (*ijarah*), deferred delivery sale (*salam*), manufacturing sale (*istisna*), recurring sale (*istijrar*) and benevolent loan (*qard-hassan*). Some highly controversial financing products (due to differing opinions of *shari'ah* scholars) offered by some Islamic commercial banks include tripartite resale (*tawarruq*), bill discounting (*bay al-dayn*) and repurchasing (*bay al-innah*). A wide range of fee-based services, such as letter of credit (*wakalah*) and letter of guarantee (*kafalah*), is also offered by Islamic commercial banks. We will discuss more on these products or contracts in Chapter 4 and the intermediation activities of Islamic banks, *takaful* operators and micro finance institutions in Chapter 6, Chapter 7 and Chapter 8, respectively.

The range of intermediation services provided by Islamic commercial banks depends on whether they are fully fledged Islamic banks, Islamic subsidiaries of conventional banks or operating as Islamic windows. A *fully fledged Islamic bank* refers to a bank that fully operates based on Islamic principles and offers only *shari'ah* compliant products. Al Rayan Bank, Bank of London and The Middle East, and Gatehouse Bank are examples of such banks in the UK. The advantage of a fully fledged Islamic bank is the standalone management and banking infrastructure, while its disadvantage is high operating costs. An *Islamic subsidiary* is an Islamic bank leveraged on conventional bank (parent) but with separate operations and management. An example of Islamic subsidiary is the HSBC Amanah whose parent, HSBC, is a conventional bank. Advantages of Islamic subsidiary include medium operating cost, being still within the same banking infrastructure but with an 'Islamic brand name' to differentiate the services being offered, and having an independent management. The main disadvantage of Islamic subsidiary is that it may be costly to set up Islamic branches. An *Islamic window* refers to Islamic banking products and services provided by conventional banks as an option to customers. Barclays, Lloyd's Banking

---

[19]The different types of contracts for the products offered by financial intermediaries will be discussed in detail in Chapter 4.

Group and Bristol & West are some of the conventional banks that operate Islamic windows in the UK. Advantage of Islamic windows is that their operating costs are low, as they are still within the existing banking infrastructure, but their disadvantages include limited range of products or services being offered and dependence on conventional bank management.

The second type of intermediaries are Islamic insurance (*takaful*) operators. They are contractual savings institutions that mobilize funds through a variety of *takaful* policies and the mobilized funds are, in turn, invested in *shari'ah* compliant avenues. We will look in more detail on *takaful* in Chapter 7. The third type of financial intermediaries are mutual funds and unit trusts. They mobilize funds by selling fund units that are similar to *mudarabah* certificates and the funds are then invested in *shari'ah* compliant avenues.

In short, the primary function of financial intermediaries is asset transformation, which takes place in the form of matching the demand and supply of financial assets and liabilities (deposits, credit, loans and insurance) and transforming the maturity, scale and location of the financial assets and liabilities of the ultimate borrowers and lenders.

Islamic financial intermediaries also offer brokerage and matchmaking between borrowers and lenders and facilitate the demand and supply of non-tangible and contingent assets and liabilities such as collaterals, guarantees, financial services and custodial services. Figure 3.6 shows the range of services that Islamic intermediaries may provide.

Figure 3.6   Services provided by Islamic financial intermediaries

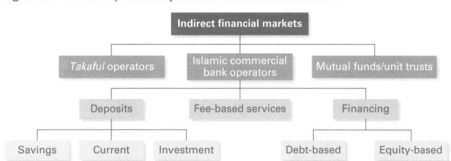

3.5.4 FINANCIAL MARKETS

Financial markets are mechanisms that facilitate the buying and selling of financial *securities* (equities and bonds), *commodities* (precious metals, oil and gas as well as agricultural products), *currencies* and other fungible items of value. These markets do not need specific physical locations to conduct transactions. With the advance in communication technology, exchange and trading can be conducted electronically in different parts of the world almost instantaneously.

Financial markets may be classified based on the nature of the assets and transactions, such as *type of transaction* (direct or indirect), *duration or the term to maturity* (e.g. money markets and capital markets), *selling and reselling* (e.g. primary and secondary markets), *size of transaction* (e.g. retail and wholesale markets), and also *style and complexity of transaction* (e.g. auction markets and over-the-counter markets). Figure 3.7 presents the components of the financial markets.

Money markets deal with monetary assets of short term nature, usually less than a year, to enable participants to meet temporary shortage of funds and temporary deployment of excess funds. They are more widely traded and also more liquid compared to securities. One specific money market is the *interbank market*, which allows banks with excess liquidity to lend their funds to other banks with a shortage of funds, often overnight and usually on an unsecured basis. An efficient interbank market improves the functioning of the financial system by enabling the central bank to add or drain liquidity from the system more effectively. It also allows banks to redistribute their individual excesses and shortages of liquidity among themselves without causing undue interest rate volatility.

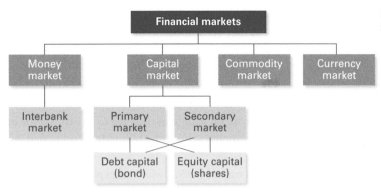

Figure 3.7   Components of financial markets

Capital markets, on the contrary, deal with longer term *equity capital* (shares) and *debt capital* (bonds). The participants in the capital markets include individual and institutional investors (pension funds, hedge funds and mutual funds), governments, companies, organizations, banks and other financial institutions. Suppliers of capital expect to get the maximum possible return at the lowest possible risk on their investment while the users of capital seek to raise capital at the lowest possible cost. Capital markets can be further categorized into primary and secondary markets. *Primary markets* (new issue markets) provide opportunities for issuers of financial securities to raise capital or debt for the first time through underwriting and initial public offering (IPO). *Secondary markets* provide the platform for the exchange of existing or previously issued securities (shares and debts).

Commodity markets deal with the trading of raw or primary products which can be split into two types: hard and soft. *Hard commodities* are natural resources that must be mined or extracted, such as gold, oil and tin. On the other hand, *soft commodities* consist of agricultural or livestock products such as coffee, wheat, corn, sheep and cattle. The most typical form of investments in commodities is by buying into a *futures contract* which obligates the holder to buy or sell at a predetermined price for delivery on a future date.

Foreign exchange or currency markets, also known as Forex or FX, deal with the trading of currencies. The main participants are commercial banks, securities dealers, hedge funds, large multinational companies, institutional investors as well as central banks. This network of participants buy and sell currencies of different countries for the purpose of financing international trade, investing or doing business abroad, or speculating on currency price changes. Table 3.4 shows the top ten currency traders in the world and their market share.

Table 3.4 Top ten currency traders

Rank			Market Share	
2017	**2016**	**Bank**	**2017**	**2016**
1	1	Citi	10.74%	12.93%
2	2	JPMorgan	10.34%	8.79%
3	3	UBS	7.56%	8.78%
4	5	Bank of America Merrill Lynch	6.73%	6.41%
5	4	Deutsche Bank	5.68%	7.88%
6	8	HSBC	4.99%	4.57%
7	6	Barclays	4.69%	5.68%
8	7	Goldman Sachs	4.43%	4.66%
9	15	Standard Chartered	4.26%	1.82%
10	11	BNP Paribas	3.73%	3.06%

Source: Euromoney FX Survey 2017 www.euromoney.com/article/b1348tjhnv7h99/euromoney-fx-survey-2017-results-released?

a) Islamic financial markets

Unlike the conventional financial markets, Islamic financial markets only began in the 1990s when the Islamic financial institutions (IFIs) managed to successfully mobilized funds from growing deposits and invested them mostly in commodities or trade financing financial instruments. Due to limited investment opportunities and lack of liquid assets, IFIs had to focus on short term financial instruments, but they realized that the development of capital markets was vital for their long term growth and survival. The wave of deregulation and liberalization of capital in the late 1990s allowed for close cooperation between conventional financial institutions and IFIs to find solutions for liquidity and portfolio management. This resulted in efforts being focused in two main areas: debt like security in the form of an *asset backed security* and *portfolio of Islamic securities*, mainly in the form of equity shares and commodities.

At the beginning, most of the financial transactions occurred in a located market such as an Islamic bank's office. However, this market has undergone transformation with the advancement in technology and IT investments by Islamic banks. Today, many financial transactions are handled by electronic networks, which help reduce the cost of processing financial transactions and enable small fund providers to participate in the market. Buyers and sellers obtain price information and initiate transactions, including making the offer and acceptance of financial transactions, from their desktop computers or from handheld devices. Hence, the Islamic financial markets today offer a broader array of financial instruments than those available 30 years ago.

In relation to the equity market, equity financing would be the preferred financing or investing technique from an Islamic perspective, as returns are tied to the earnings of the underlying business and there is no promise of fixed returns. Thus, equity financing is very much profit and loss sharing, and investment in a stock resembles the provision of partnership financing. The underlying *shari'ah* contract of shares issuance by companies is based on principles that relate to a contract that involves two or more parties in a project or business where each of the parties contribute to the capital and are actively involved in the management of the project or business. Thus, the investor who holds the shares of a company will share the company's fortune in the form of higher dividends and value of the share, and if the company suffers losses, the investor may receive lower dividends and accept possible declines in the share value.

However, not all stocks listed in an exchange may be acceptable from the *shari'ah* perspective, and this requires careful evaluation and identification of *shari'ah* compliant stocks. This has led to the development of *shari'ah* filters, *shari'ah* indices, *shari'ah* compliant REIT (Real Estate Investments Trust) and Islamic ETFs (Exchange Traded Funds). *Shari'ah* filters, or also known as *shari'ah* screening, is the methodology applied in ensuring that the activities of the companies are *shari'ah* compliant. The screening normally involves two stages: the first stage of screening is based on the line of business or core business of the underlying company, i.e. not involved in non-permissible activities such as gambling, alcohol, pornography, pork, etc. The second stage is based on the company's finances, i.e. whether it is involved with payment and receipt of interest. *Shari'ah index* shows companies that are found to be compliant with the stringent rules of *shari'ah*, and this list is monitored by a separate body. For example, the indices in the Standard & Poor's S&P/TSX 60 *Shari'ah* Index is evaluated and re-categorized every month by an outside agency, Rating Intelligence Partners, before it is passed on to a panel of Middle East based *shari'ah* scholars with financial backgrounds. The underlying principle behind the creation of a separate *shari'ah* index is to help the Islamic investor community to identify and invest in businesses that are compliant with *shari'ah*.

The OIC Fiqh Academy rules that it is permissible to purchase, hold or sell shares even if the company undertakes prohibited activities such as borrowing money and/or invest its money on the basis of interest provided they fulfil certain criteria. There is also no objection from *shari'ah* in relation to cash dividends, bonus shares, rights issue and other perks. With regard to preference shares, the OIC Fiqh Academy ruling is that it is not permissible. As for convertible preference shares, there is no formal ruling, but most *shari'ah* scholars are concerned about the possible element of *gharar* (uncertainty).

Commodities funds generate profits by buying and reselling *halal* commodities. However, due to the restrictions on the use of derivatives, commodities fund make use of two types of *shari'ah* approved contracts. The first is a contract where the buyer of an item pays upfront for the production of the item, agreeing on the specification and cost before production starts. The second is similar to a *forward contract* where the buyer pays in advance for the delivery of raw materials or fungible goods at a given date with the delivery price of the contract being calculated at spot price minus a discount to compensate the buyer of the credit risk for the upfront payment.

Islamic Real Estate Investment Trusts (i-REITs) are liquid assets that can be sold fairly quickly to raise cash and/or to take advantage of other investment opportunities. The advantages of investment in i-REITs are higher cash dividends relative to the market and tax benefits for certain foreign investors. However, there are two issues with i-REITs: the high distributions of annual profit and lower reinvestment may lead to a slower growth rate and despite being quite stable, it is still subjected to *shari'ah* risk, which restricts scope of investment.

Islamic Exchange Traded Funds (i-ETFs) are similar to conventional ETFs except that the Islamic Benchmark Index comprises of companies which are *shari'ah* compliant, as advised by the *shari'ah* adviser or *shari'ah* committee. Advantages of investing in i-ETFs include allowing diversification of risk, having lower expense ratio and transaction costs, higher transparency and are *shari'ah* compliant investments. Disadvantages include risk of speculation and tracking error.

Sukuk are Islamic bonds which have similar characteristics to conventional bonds. They are mostly asset backed and free from interest. The returns and cash flows of the financing are linked to the assets purchased or return from the assets purchased. We will discuss more on *sukuk* in Chapter 5.

Islamic Interbank Money Market (IIMM) was introduced as a short term intermediary to provide a ready source of short term investment outlet based on *shari'ah* principles through which the Islamic banks and banks participating in the Islamic Banking Scheme (IBS) would be able to match funding requirements effectively and efficiently. The IIMM covers the *Mudarabah Interbank Investment (MII),* which refers to a mechanism whereby a deficit Islamic banking institution (investee bank) can obtain investment from a surplus Islamic banking institution (investor bank) based on profit sharing. The period of investment ranges from overnight up to 12 months, while the rate of return is determined based on the gross profit before distribution for investments of one year of the investee bank. The parties involved can negotiate on the profit sharing ratio. Normally, the investor bank is uncertain of the return during the time of negotiation and it is only towards the end of the investment period that the bank will know the actual return. At the end of the investment period, the investee bank will repay the principal together with the share of the profit arising from the used of the fund. *Interbank trading* of Islamic financial instruments is the trading of Government Investment Issue (GII), which is non-tradable but the players may exchange the papers among themselves.

3.5.5   FINANCIAL INSTRUMENTS

Financial instruments, also known as financial claims, are monetary contracts that can be created, traded, modified and settled between two or more parties. Financial instruments can be in the form of cash (currency), evidence of an ownership interest in an entity (e.g. shares) or a contractual right to receive or deliver cash (bond) or other assets (e.g. commodities and currencies). The International Accounting Standards IAS 32 and 39 define a financial instrument as 'any contract that gives rise to a financial asset of one entity and a financial liability or equity instrument of another entity'.

Financial instruments can be classified into cash or derivative instruments. *Cash instruments* include securities, loans and deposits and their value is determined by the market. *Derivative instruments*, on the other hand, derive their values from the characteristics of one or more underlying entities such as an asset, index or interest rate.

Financial instruments can also be classified based on asset class, depending on whether they are equity based or debt based (short and long term). However, foreign exchange instruments are in a class of their own as they are neither equity nor debt based. A matrix on the classification of the conventional financial instruments is shown in Table 3.5.

Table 3.5 Classification of financial instruments

Asset class	Instrument type		
	Securities	**Other cash**	**Derivatives**
Debt (long term) >1 year)	Bonds	Loans	Bond futures Options on bond futures Interest rate swaps Interest rate options
Debt (short term) ≤1 year	T-bills Commercial papers	Deposits Certificate of deposits	Short term interest rate futures Forward rate agreements
Equity	Shares	N/A	Stock options Equity futures
Foreign exchange	N/A	Spot foreign exchange	Currency futures Foreign exchange options Foreign exchange swaps Currency swaps

a) Islamic financial instruments

IFIs and markets offer different instruments to satisfy providers and users of funds in a variety of ways: sales, trade financing and investment. The types of financial instruments offered depend on the nature of contracts dealing with commercial and business transactions based on Islamic principles. Iqbal and Mirakhor (2007) classify such contracts into four categories: transactional, financing, intermediation and social welfare.

Transactional contracts deal with the economic transactions that facilitate the exchange, sale and trade of goods and services in the real sector. *Financing contracts* deal with ways to create and extend credit, facilitate financing of transactional contracts and provide channels for capital formation and resource mobilization between entrepreneurs and investors. *Intermediation contracts* facilitate the economic agents to perform financial intermediation activities in an efficient and transparent way. The *social welfare contracts* are between individuals and society to promote wellbeing and welfare of the underprivileged and this can be institutionalized through an intermediary. Figure 3.8 illustrates the various contracts and financial instruments.

Figure 3.8 Islamic financial contracts/instruments

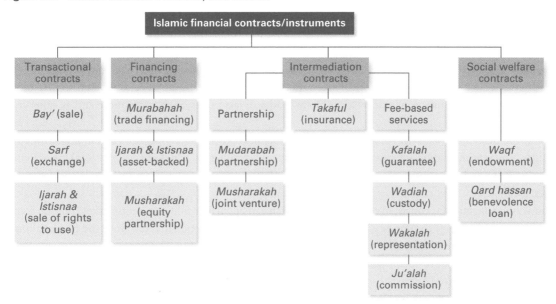

Source: Iqbal and Mirakhor (2007).

As can be seen, the basic instruments include trade or cost-plus financing (*murabahah*), profit sharing (*mudarabah*), leasing (*ijarah*), partnership (*musharakah*), and forward sale (*bay' salam*). These instruments serve as the basic building blocks for developing a wide array of more complex financial instruments, suggesting that there is great potential for financial innovation and expansion in Islamic financial markets. We will discuss these instruments in further detail in the next chapter.

Summary

A financial system facilitates the transfer of funds from the surplus units to the deficit units. It operates at three levels: micro (individuals and firms), macro (through organized financial markets and intermediaries within a country) and global (central banks, IMF, World Bank, etc.). A financial system can be either market based, whereby financing is raised in well-developed capital markets, or bank based with financing provided by banking institutions. The underlying principles of an Islamic financial system are risk sharing, observing the sanctity of the contracts, involved only in *shari'ah* compliant activities, avoiding prohibited transactions involving interest and speculation, and treating money as potential capital.

There are five components in a financial system: money, central bank, financial intermediaries, financial markets and financial instruments. Money has evolved from barter and commodity money to metallic money, paper money, bank money, electronic money and the latest is digital money in the form of cryptocurrency. Not all forms of money are acceptable from an Islamic perspective, and some Muslim scholars have encouraged for the return of *dirham* (gold coin) and *dinar* (silver coin). Three main functions of money are as medium of exchange, unit of account and as store of value. The concept of money in Islam emphasizes three aspects, i.e. ownership (recognize that money is just a favour bestowed by the Almighty to be shared with others), utilization (to manage and make good use of the money) and earning of money (through ethical ways).

Central banks play a crucial role in controlling the demand and supply of money through effective monetary policies. Changes in the supply of money are closely related to changes in the aggregate economic activities and price level. The irregular periodic upward and downward trend of aggregate economic output is called *business cycles*. A sustained or persistent downward and upward trend in the business cycle is referred to as recession and inflation, respectively. *Recession* signals deep decline in the growth rate of money, while *inflation* signals rapid growth of money supply. Both conditions will not only have significant impact on the economy and economic players but also on every individual in society in one way or another. Central banks perform eight main functions: issue currency, advise the government on monetary and economic matters, act as custodian of cash reserves and foreign balances, facilitate settlement of accounts between banks, control credit, protect depositors and act as lender of last resort to banks. Three aspects needing the attention of central banks to help in the development of Islamic finance include relationship as lender of last resort, as clearing house and as supervisor of monetary policy.

Islamic financial intermediaries comprise Islamic commercial banks, *takaful* operators and mutual funds and unit trusts. The intermediation activities performed by Islamic commercial banks cover deposit taking activities (savings, current and investment accounts), financing activities (debt based and equity based) and fee-based services.

Islamic financial markets consist of capital market, which can be further split into debt market (*sukuk*), equity market, derivative market, commodity market, money market and currency market. Both the financial markets and financial intermediaries offer various Islamic financial instruments. The financial instruments being offered depend on the nature of contracts, which falls under four categories: transactional, financing, intermediation and social welfare. The basic contracts form the building blocks in developing more complex financial innovation.

Key terms and concepts

al-ghorm bil ghonm	*Dirham*	Islamic window
bank based system	electronic fund transfer at point of sale	Lender of last resort (LOLR)
bank draft	electronic money	lenders
bank money	financial instruments	market based system
barter	financial intermediaries	medium of exchange
bill of exchange	financial markets	metallic money
borrowers	financial system	mobile digital wallets
business cycles	financing contracts	monetary policy
capital market	float	money
cash instrument	fully fledged Islamic bank	money market
centralized e-money	futures contract	non-deposit taking institutions
charge cards	generalized purchasing power	open market operations
cheque	hard commodity	paper money
clearing house	institutional units	plastic cards
Clearing House Interbank	interbank market	primary market
Payment System (CHIPS)	interbank trading	protection of depositor's interest
commodity money	intermediation contracts	risk aversion
controller of credit	Islamic bond market	risk avoiding
credit card	Islamic capital market	secondary market
cryptocurrency	Islamic equity market	*shari'ah* filter
currency market	Islamic Exchange Traded Funds (i-ETFs)	*shari'ah* index
custodian of cash reserves	Islamic financial system	social welfare contracts
custodian of foreign balances	Islamic Interbank Money	soft commodity
debit card	Market (IIMM)	standard of deferred payments
decentralized e-money	Islamic money market	store of value
deposit taking institutions	Islamic Real Estate Investment	tender money
derivative instrument	Trusts (i-REITs)	transactional contracts
Dinar	Islamic subsidiary	unit of account

Questions

1. Explain financial system and their participants.

2. Distinguish the styles of financial systems.

3. Discuss the underlying principles of an Islamic financial system.

4. Explain the concept of *al-ghorm bil ghonm*.

5. Discuss the components of a financial system.

6. Describe the evolution of money.

7. Critically evaluate the concept and functions of money from an Islamic perspective as opposed to mainstream perspective.

8. Discuss the Islamic view on the various types of money.

9. Since central banks' activities are based on interest, explain how they can support IFIs without jeopardizing the *shari'ah* aspect.

10. Describe the roles of the various types of conventional and Islamic financial intermediaries.

11. Distinguish between a fully fledged Islamic bank, an Islamic subsidiary and an Islamic window, including their advantages and disadvantages.

12. Describe the components of financial markets.

13. Distinguish between *shari'ah* filter, *shari'ah* index, Islamic Real Estate Investment Trusts (i-REITs), Islamic Exchange Traded Funds (i-ETFs) and Islamic Interbank Money Market (IIMM), including their advantages and disadvantages.

References and further readings

Allen, F. and Gale, D. (2001), *Comparing Financial Systems*, MIT Press, Cambridge, USA.

Askari, H., Iqbal, Z. and Mirakhor, A. (2017), *Introduction to Islamic Economics: Theory and Application*, John Wiley & Sons Singapore Pte. Ltd.

Askari, H., Krichene, N. and Mirakhor, A. (2014), 'On the stability of an Islamic financial system'. *PSL Quarterly Review*, 67(269), pp. 131-167. ssrn.com/abstract=2508177, accessed 22 May 2018.

Hassan, M.K. and Lewis, M.K. (2007), *Handbook of Islamic Banking*, Edward Elgar Publisher, Cheltenham, UK.

Howells, P. and Bain, K. (2008), *The Economics of Money, Banking and Finance: A European Text*, Pearson Education, Cambridge, UK.

Iqbal, Z. and Mirakhor, A. (2007), *An introduction to Islamic Finance: Theory and Practice*, John Wiley & Sons, Asia.

Rosly, S.A. (2005), *Critical Issues on Islamic Banking and Financial Markets*, Dinamas Publishing, Kuala Lumpur.

Zarrouk, H., El Ghak, T. and Elias Abu Al Haija, E.A. (2017), 'Financial development, Islamic finance and economic growth: Evidence of the UAE', *Journal of Islamic Accounting and Business Research*, 8(1), pp. 2-22, doi.org/10.1108/JIABR-05-2015-0020, accessed 22 May 2018.

Islamic financial institutions, markets and instruments

PART II

4 Introduction to Islamic contract law and financial contracts

Learning Objectives

Upon completion of this chapter you should be able to:

- define contracts according to Islamic commercial law

- describe the essential elements of a valid contract and other legal consequences

- explain the classification of contracts in Islamic banking

- discuss the features, basis and terms of each contract

- describe the application of the contracts in Islamic banking products

4.1 Introduction

Business transactions between two or more parties often involve a contract, either in oral or written form, without which the transactions may be void of legal significance. The basic purpose of any contract is to establish that the parties have made an agreement, and to reflect the intentions and consents as well as the rights and duties of each party, in accordance with that agreement. Issues of contract and legal effects arising from the contract are generally dealt under commercial law of the country, e.g. English commercial law (common law) or French commercial law (coded law). However, for Islamic contracts, they are specifically dealt under *fiqh al-mu'amalat* or Islamic commercial law, with the key underlying factors being justice, equity and mutual satisfaction. All contemporary Islamic financial transactions and products have their own underlying contracts designed to suit different needs and circumstances. Hence, it is not surprising that besides the classical types of contracts developed by early Muslim scholars, there have been many innovations in developing new contracts that comply with *shari'ah* to meet the demands of the fast developing Islamic finance industry.

In this chapter, we will look at the definitions and elements of a valid contract, as well as the classification and features of various contracts based on Islamic commercial law. These contracts are used in structuring various Islamic financial instruments.

4.2 Definitions of contracts in Islamic law

The word *aqd* (plural *uqud*), or contract, in the Arabic language means 'tying tightly'. It also carries the meaning of obligations as can be found in one chapter in the *Qur'an* known as 'Chapter on Contracts' (*Al-Maidah*) which mentions various kinds of contracts between man and Allah, and between man and man, and how these obligations should be fulfilled in this life (Haniffa, Hudaib and Mirza, 2008). The first verse of the chapter begins with:

> *O you who believe! Fulfil (your) obligations (contract)* (Al-Maidah, 5:1).[1]

Other affirmative evidence related to contracts can be found in these verses from the *Qu'ran*:

> *and fulfil (every) engagement, for (every) engagement will be enquired into (on the Day of Reckoning)* (Al-Isra, 17:34).[2]
> *Fulfil the Covenant of Allah when ye have entered into it, and break not your oaths after ye have confirmed them; indeed ye have made Allah your surety; for Allah knoweth all that ye do* (An-Nahl, 16:91).[3]

According to Bakar (2008), there are over 40 verses in the *Qur'an* related to commercial contracts alone besides another 30 verses related to other types of contract about marriage, divorce, bequest and endowment. These contracts were later developed by Islamic jurists into principles of contract. Although contracts are mentioned in the *Qur'an*, the definition of contract, or *aqd*, according to Islamic law cannot be found in any of the treatises before the 19th century, because a general theory of contract has never been developed by Muslim jurists (Bakar, 2008). A precise definition of contract only emerged in the 19th century in the Islamic Civil Law Codification of the Ottoman Empire, namely *Majallah al-ahkam al-adliyyah* (also known as *Mejelle*) under Articles 103-104:

> *'Aqd' is the two parties taking upon themselves an undertaking to do something. It is composed of the combination of an offer (ijab) and acceptance (qabul). The making of 'aqd' is connecting in a legal manner, one's offer (ijab) and acceptance (qabul) with the other, in a way which will be clear evidence of being mutually connected.*

Another definition of *aqd* is by Al-Sanhuri, who refers to that found in *Murshid al-Hayran* (the 1891 Egyptian version of the Ottoman's *Mejelle*):

> *…the conjunction of the offer emanating from one of the two contracting parties with the acceptance of the other in a manner that it may affect the subject matter of the contract. It is further explained that as a result of this conjunction both are under obligation to each other. It therefore follows from this that the origin of a contract in Islamic jurisprudence is an obligation"* (cited in Hassan, Kayed and Oseni, 2013).

From the two foregoing definitions, it is clear that for a contract to be valid under Islamic law certain conditions must be met and this is explained in the next section.

4.3 Elements of a valid contract

According to Islamic law, there are four elements for a contract to be valid: (i) a minimum of two parties with one being the *offeror* and the other *offeree*; (ii) there must be an offer (*ijab*) and acceptance (*qabul*); (iii) existence of a subject matter; and (iv) consideration. These elements are further elaborated in the following sections.

[1] www.wright-house.com/religions/islam/Quran/5-table.php, accessed 22 May 2018.
[2] www.wright-house.com/religions/islam/Quran/17-isra.php, accessed 22 May 2018.
[3] www.wright-house.com/religions/islam/Quran/16-bee.php, accessed 22 May 2018.

4.3.1 OFFEROR AND OFFEREE

For a contract to be valid, parties entering into the contract must be legally competent or have the capacity to enter into a contract. Competence to transact is based on two aspects, physical puberty and prudence in making sound judgement. Capacity refers to the quality that qualifies a person in acquiring rights and undertaking duties and responsibilities. The importance of this is revealed in the *Qur'an*:

> *Make trial of orphans until they reach the age of marriage; if then ye find sound judgment in them, release their property to them* (Al-Nisa', 4:6).[4]

4.3.2 OFFER (*IJAB*) AND ACCEPTANCE (*QABUL*)

Offer means a specific action that reflects consent or willingness by one of the contracting parties which can be done either in writing or verbally. *Acceptance* represents a statement uttered indicating assent to the offer. Offer and acceptance may also be concluded by means of representatives, or modern communication systems, such as the telephone, telex, fax, email and letter.

4.3.3 SUBJECT MATTER

In relation to the subject matter, there are four aspects that Islamic law stresses: existence, lawfulness, deliverability and precise determination.

At the time of the contract, *existence* means that the object of the contract must exist, except in the case of deferred delivery sale and manufacturing contracts. For both the latter contracts, the object of the promise to deliver need not be in existence at the time of the contract, but the object must be capable of certain delivery and its essence, quantity and value must be determined precisely.

Lawfulness indicates that the object of the contract must be lawful and permitted for trading purposes, so it must not be something that is prohibited by Islamic law or *shari'ah*, nor would it harm morality or cause disruption in public order.

Deliverability indicates that the object of the contract can be certainly delivered as promised. Therefore, sale of a fish in water or a bird in the air is prohibited by Muslim jurists due to high uncertainty (*gharar*) of the availability of the object for delivery at the promised time.

Precise determination of the object in terms of quantity, quality and value in the contract is important for the contract to be valid. Hence, delivery of the wrong quantity or value or inferior quality may nullify the contract.

4.3.4 CONSIDERATION

According to Islamic law, the consideration in the contract is not restricted to only monetary price, but may also be in the form of another commodity. For the contract to be valid, the consideration or price must be in existence and determined at the time of the contract. It cannot be fixed at a later date with reference to the market price or be left to the determination by a third party.

4.4 Legal consequences of contracts

While the four elements discussed above are conditions for a valid contract, there are five other legal classes of contracts: *deficient*, *void*, *binding*, *enforceable* and *withheld*.

A *deficient* contract is lawful in substance but unlawful in description. The *lawful substance* of a contract comprises the offer, acceptance and subject matter. If the description of the specification of price or the quality of the subject matter is missing in the contract, then the contract is declared deficient. However, such contract can still be validated by duly addressing the item that causes it to be deficient.

---

[4]www.wright-house.com/religions/islam/Quran/4-women.php, accessed 22 May 2018.

A *void* contract is one that has any of the four key elements and the descriptive elements missing. Therefore, it is unlawful in both its substance and description. For instance, an agreement to sell alcohol is considered void from the beginning because the subject matter, alcohol, is prohibited in Islam.

A *binding* contract is when the contract is sound both in its substance and description, making it binding on the parties as well as enforceable under the law. A binding contract can be further classified as either revocable or irrevocable. A *revocable* contract is a binding contract that allows either of the parties the option to revoke the contract at any stage; for example, in a partnership or agency type of contract, whereby a partner quits due to ill health. An *irrevocable* binding contract, on the other hand, is one that cannot be revoked by either party at any stage once they are concluded; for example, a sale contract where both its substance and description are lawful.

An *enforceable* contract is a valid and binding contract that can be enforced by the law on the parties concerned without affecting a third party. All binding contracts are enforceable contracts.

A *withheld* contract is a binding contract that has been concluded by someone, but is waiting for final approval by the real owner of the subject matter or final ratification of the negotiated price. This is quite common when buying or selling property.

4.5 Classification of contracts

Muslim jurists permit a wide range of contracts to be designed and implemented within the principles of *shari'ah*. Some of these contracts were developed during the period of the first Islamic state while others have emerged more recently to meet contemporary financing requirements based on Islamic teachings. From an Islamic legal perspective, contracts can be conceptually divided into two main categories: unilateral and bilateral. The former category of contracts include: (i) gift (*hadiah, hibah*); (ii) off-set of debt (*ibra'*); (iii) benevolence loan (*qard hassan*); (iv) endowment (*waqf*); and (v) will (*wasiyyat*). As for bilateral contracts, there are six types of contracts: (i) partnership (*shirkah*); (ii) exchange or trading (*al-mu'awadat*); (iii) utilization of usufruct (*al-manfa'ah*); (iv) security (*al-thawtiqat*); (v) safe custody (*wadi'ah*); and (vi) agency (*wakalah* and *ju'alah*). Figure 4.1 presents the classification of the various contracts under the two main categories which will be further elaborated in this section.

Figure 4.1 Classification of Islamic contracts

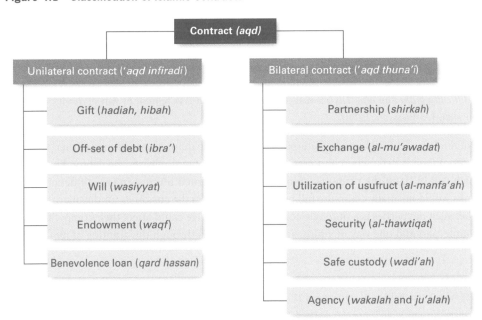

4.5.1 UNILATERAL CONTRACTS

This category of contracts is initiated and concluded by a single party, and involves some form of benefit being transferred to another party. It is gratuitous in nature and does not always require the consent of the recipient. The transactions are always in favour of the recipient(s).

a) Contract of gift (hibah, hadiah)

A gift contract involves the granting of items that have value or provide some form of benefits, such as property, cash, jewellery, share certificates, etc., which occurs during the lifetime of the *hibah* provider. In Islam, the habit of giving gifts and charity is highly encouraged, especially to the immediate family, as revealed in the following verse of the *Qur'an* and also in the *Hadith*:

> …and do good – to parents, kinsfolk, orphans, those in need, neighbours who are near, neighbours who are strangers, the companion by your side, the wayfarer (ye meet), and what your right hands possess: For Allah loveth not the arrogant, the vainglorious (An-Nisa', 4:36).[5]
>
> Narrated `Aisha: Allah's Messenger used to accept gifts and used to give something in return (Bukhari).[6]

For a *hibah* contract to be valid, certain conditions related to the *hibah* provider, *hibah* recipient(s) and the object of *hibah* must be fulfilled. With regards to the *hibah* provider, s(he) must have attained puberty and have the capacity to make sound judgement as well as being the genuine owner of the items intended for *hibah*. The act of giving is done voluntarily and not through coercion. As for the *hibah* recipient, s(he) can be anyone as long as s(he) has the capability to own the property. If the *hibah* recipient has not reached puberty or is disabled, then it is to be given to a guardian or a trustee on his/her behalf. S(he) must have received or accepted the *hibah* and have the authority to hold on to it without any interruptions. In terms of the object of *hibah*, it must be something lawful (*halal*) and have value, exists at the time the gift is made, must be eligible for sale and must be uncompensated.

The *hibah* contract is used by some Islamic banks to award discretionary *hibah* to their savings depositors from the profits the banks made for utilizing their funds. However, the amount is not fixed up front, otherwise it will be the same as the interest paid by conventional banks to their depositors. Some have criticized this practice because savings deposits should be held as safe custody and should not receive any additional returns, while others argued that awarding *hibah* to depositors is deemed necessary to allow Islamic banks to compete for customers, especially when there exist a dual-banking system in the country.

b) Contract of off-setting debt (ibra')

This refers to a contract through which a person waives or drops a right that is established as a liability to another. It is a recommended practice, as it helps the creditor to release some burden off the debtor. The permissibility of off-setting debt and imposing rebate on any early settlement is stated in the *Qur'an*:

> If the debtor is in a difficulty, grant him time Till it is easy for him to repay. But if ye remit it by way of charity, that is best for you if ye only knew (Al-Baqarah, 2:280).[7]

The subject matters of *ibra'* are debt, right and claim over a non-fungible item. As mentioned earlier, the most common subject matter of *ibra'* is debt, whereby a creditor drops the debt and releases the debtor. Unlike conventional banks, which would claim the principal amount plus the accrued interest in case of default by the customer, Islamic banks would normally claim the full purchase price from the customer for default of payment since the agreement between the parties is a pure sale contract. This practice could affect their competition with their conventional counterpart and one way of addressing this problem is through the granting of *ibra'* in cases

---

[5]www.wright-house.com/religions/islam/Quran/4-women.php, accessed 22 May 2018.

[6]Vol. 3, Book 47, Hadith 758 sunnah.com/bukhari/51/19, accessed 22 May 2018.

[7]www.wright-house.com/religions/islam/Quran/2-cow.php, accessed 22 May 2018.

of early settlement of debt as a 'matter of obligation'. This is achieved by incorporating an *ibra'* or a 'reduce and expedite' clause in the finance agreement.

c) Contract of benevolence loan (qard hassan)

Qard ul hasanah literally means 'beautiful loan', a terminology derived from various verses in the *Qur'an*. It is a unique contract in that the business transaction establishes a relationship between lender and borrower without any accrued tangible profits. In Islamic banking, this is known as interest free loans. Thus, *qard ul hasanah* may be utilized as an overdraft facility for clients. The act of lending to those in need is encouraged in Islam as mentioned in the following *Hadith*:

> It was narrated from Anas bin Malik that the Prophet said: 'On the night on which I was taken on the Night Journey (Isra), I saw written at the gate of Paradise: "Charity brings a tenfold reward and a loan brings an eighteen fold reward." I said: "O Jibril! Why is a loan better than charity?" He said: "Because the beggar asks when he has something, but the one who asks for loan does so only because he is in need" (Ibn Majjah).[8]

There are three conditions for a *Qard ul hasanah* contract to be valid: (i) loans must be concluded through the appropriate language of offer and acceptance; (ii) both lender and borrower must be of legal age and have the mental faculties that make them eligible to give charity; and (iii) the loan amount is known, in terms of volume, weight, number or size, so that repayment of its equal is possible.

d) Contract of endowment (waqf)

A contract of endowment is established by the founder for the asset(s) that s(he) owns to be used for an assigned objective or cause that will benefit others. The permanent nature of *waqf* results in the accumulation of *waqf* properties that are devoted to provide a capital asset that produces an ever increasing flow of revenues/*usufructs* to serve its objectives as documented in history. Information extracted from the registers of *awqaf* (plural form of *waqf*) in Istanbul, Jerusalem, Cairo and other cities indicates that lands of *awqaf* cover considerable proportion of total cultivated area. The grand mosque in Algeria and Al-Azhar University in Cairo also benefit from deeds of *awqaf*. Today, cash *waqf* has been used to help micro enterprises and the underprivileged to have access to funding to help them improve their circumstances.

Waqf can be categorized as *charitable, family* or *private* and *joint*. *Charitable* or *public waqf* includes any kind of benefit to the public such as hospitals, mosques, churches, schools, cemeteries, orphanage, etc. while *family or private waqf* is intended to benefit a specific person such as descendant(s) of the founder, neighbour, relative, etc. *Joint waqf* is where part of the benefit is assigned to private persons and the other part to the public, such as a piece of land with one section being used to build a mosque and the other section of the land for use by family members to build their house. There are many verses in the *Qur'an* encouraging voluntary charity or endowment. For example, as can be seen in the following verse:

> For, Believers are those who, when Allah is mentioned, feel a tremor in their hearts, and when they hear His signs rehearsed, find their faith strengthened, and put (all) their trust in their Lord; Who establish regular prayers and spend (freely) out of the gifts We have given them for sustenance: Such in truth are the believers: they have grades of dignity with their Lord, and forgiveness, and generous sustenance (Al-Anfal, 8:2-4).[9]

There are four aspects in a *waqf* contract: the founder (*waqif*), the asset held as *waqf*, the proclamation for establishing the *waqf*, and the objective of the *waqf*. The founder must be a person who is eligible to undertake the contract and is the owner of the asset. The asset to be held as *waqf* must be permissible under *shari'ah*; hence,

[8]Book 15, Hadith 2525 sunnah.com/urn/1267490, accessed 22 May 2018.

[9]www.wright-house.com/religions/islam/Quran/8-spoils-of-war.php, accessed 6 June 2018.

a casino or brewery and earnings from such activities cannot be given as *waqf*. The founder must make the proclamation of *waqf* clearly, such as 'Do not sell the orchard, but manage it and distribute the fruits to the poor and needy.' The objective of *waqf* must be an act of benevolence and righteousness for the reward to the founder promised in the hereafter, while others benefits from it in this world.

e) Contract of a will (wasiyyat)

A will is the act of conferring a right in the substance or the usufruct of an asset after one's death. *Wasiyyat* is emphasized in many verses in the *Qur'an,* for instance:

> *It is prescribed, when death approaches any of you, if he leave any goods that he make a bequest to parents and next of kin, according to reasonable usage…* (Al-Baqarah, 2:180).[10]

Central to a will contract is the *disposition by the testator* and the *object of the will*. With regards to the testator, certain conditions related to the testator are required to make the will valid: one must be of the age of maturity and be in full possession of their senses at the time of making the will; must not be acting under compulsion, or under influence, or in jest; and must not be indebted to an extent that the debt is equivalent in value to the whole asset. The will can be either in written form, verbal or even by signs. With regards to the object of the will, the *wasiyyat* may be of anything useful, and it is not necessary for the testator to say that it would come into effect after his death as this is legally implied. The bequest can only be to the extent of a third of the testator's assets. Any amount exceeding a third is not valid unless the heirs consent to it. A bequest to any one of the heirs is not valid without the consent of the others and where the will is in favour of non-heirs, or for a pious or charitable purpose, it is valid and operative only in respect of one-third of the testator's estate without the consent of the heirs and in respect of more than one-third with their consent.

4.5.2 BILATERAL CONTRACTS

This contract involves at least two parties, with one party making an offer and the other accepting the offer. In other words, there is mutual consent between the parties and certain rights and obligations are also established. Once the offer is accepted, a legal relationship is established and is binding on both parties. Muslim jurists further divide the bilateral contracts into six types based on the purpose and *raison d'etre* of the agreement, which are further explained below.

a) Contracts of profit sharing or partnership (shirkah)

There are two contracts under this category: contract of *mudarabah* and contract of *musharakah*. The former is related to a special type of business arrangement in which one party provides the capital and the other party provides the labour or effort, while the latter involves sharing in capital and effort in such a way that one of them cannot be distinguished from the other. The permissibility of *mudarabah* (profit sharing) is evidenced in the following *Hadith*:

> *Ibn Abbas used to pay money for mudarabah and to stipulate to the mudarib that he should not travel by sea, pass by valleys or trade in livestock, and that the mudarib would be liable for any losses if he did so. These conditions were brought before the Prophet (SAW) and he approved them* (Reported by al-Bayhaqi).[11]

The validity of *musharakah* is established in the *Qur'an,* as in the following verse:

> *And, verily, many partners (in business) oppress one another, except those who believe and do righteous good deeds, and they are few* (Sad, 38:24).[12]

Under these two categories, there are different types of contracts. Figure 4.2 illustrates the different types of partnership contracts.

---

[10]www.wright-house.com/religions/islam/Quran/2-cow.php, accessed 22 May 2018.

[11]Narrated by Al-Bayhaqi in Al Sunan al-Kubra, www.australianislamiclibrary.org/sunan-al-kubra---bayhiqi.html, accessed 6 June 2018.

[12]www.wright-house.com/religions/islam/Quran/38-S.php, accessed 22 May 2018.

Figure 4.2 Types of partnership contracts

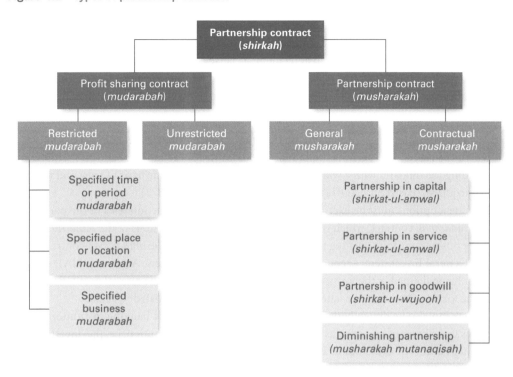

(I) MUDARABAH (PROFIT SHARING) As mentioned earlier, *mudarabah* is a partnership in profit whereby one party provides the capital and the other party provides skill and labour. The provider of capital is called *rabbul mal* while the provider of skill and labour is called *mudarib*. Hence, *mudarabah* can be defined as:

A partnership contract between rabbul mal and mudarib in which the rabbul mal provides capital to the mudarib to invest in a business enterprise by applying his skill, labour and endeavour with both parties sharing the profits at a pre-agreed ratio and the losses (if any) being entirely borne by the rabbul mal except if it is incurred due to breach of trust, for example, misconduct, negligence or violation of the conditions agreed upon by the mudarib. If any loss is incurred due to breach of trust, for example misconduct, negligence or violation of the conditions agreed upon by the mudarib, the mudarib will then become liable for it. (based on AAOIFI's Shari'ah Standard No. 13, pp. 370-378)

One of the advantages *of a mudarabah* transaction is that it helps in facilitating investment cooperation between the *rabbul mal* who has the capital but lacks business or investment expertise or time and the *mudarib* who lacks capital but has the skill and time. Since *mudarabah* involves joint efforts of money and entrepreneurship, any return earned by the *mudarib* is permissible under *shari'ah*.

There are several terms and conditions that need to be fulfilled between the contracting parties to make the *mudarabah* contract valid. Firstly, the contracting parties have the right to share the profit in an agreed ratio, while liability for losses is borne only by the capital provider or financier. Secondly, the capital in this partnership must be in absolute currency in the form of cash and not debt. Thirdly, the financier has no right to participate in the management of the project, which is carried out by the entrepreneur only.

Mudarabah contracts are of two types, restricted and unrestricted. *Restricted mudarabah (Al Mudarabah Al Muqayyadah)* may be defined as:

A contract in which rabbul mal restricts the actions of mudarib to a specified period or to a particular location or to a particular type of business that the rabbul mal considers appropriate, but not in a manner that would unduly constrain the mudarib in his operations. (based on AAOIFI's Shari'ah Standard No. 13, p. 372)

Thus, a *restricted mudarabah* contract may be restricted based on one of the following:

- *in respect of specified time or period* and in such an agreement, a clause on duration of the business will be included and the contract shall become void after the expiry of that period
- *in respect of specified place or location* and in such agreement, a clause covering the place or location of the business and the *mudarib* is bound to do the business within the specified area of such place or location
- *in respect of specific business,* which means that the *mudarib* is bound to do business as specified by the *rabbul mal*

Unrestricted mudarabah (Al Mudarabah Al Mutlaqah), on the other hand, may be defined as:

A contract in which the rabbul mal permits the mudarib to administer the mudarabah fund without any restriction, thus providing the mudarib with a wide range of business options on the basis of trust and the business expertise he has acquired. (based on AAOIFI's Shari'ah Standard No. 13, pp. 372)

Such unrestricted business options must be exercised only in accordance with the interests of the parties and the objectives of the *mudarabah* contract, which is to earn profit. Therefore, the actions of the *mudarib* must be in accordance with the business customs relating to the *mudarabah* operations. The *mudarabah* contract forms the basis of both the General Investment Accounts (GIA) and Specific Investment Accounts (SIA), with the investment project not being defined in the former but defined in the latter. Also, the ratio of profit distribution is normally fixed in the former whereas in the latter it is usually individually negotiated.

Mudarabah contracts can also be drawn between two banks so a deficit Islamic banking institution, i.e. the 'investee bank', receives investment from a surplus in another Islamic banking institution, i.e. the 'investor bank'. Such financial instrument is known as the *Mudarabah interbank investments* (MII).[13] The investment period for *mudarabah interbank investments* ranges from overnight to 12 months. The investee bank invests the surplus fund from the investor bank and promises to share the profit based on a negotiated pre-agreed ratio. The investee bank will deduct the principal amount of the invested fund from the gross profit and the remaining is recognized as the net profit to be shared resulting from its use of funds from the investor bank. It is important to note that at the time of profit sharing ratio negotiation between the two parties, the investor bank is aware that there is no guarantee of return or profit from the investee bank and even if there is, the exact amount is unknown. The investor bank will only know the exact return it will receive from the investee bank towards the end of the investment period in addition to the principal fund it provided to the investee bank.

In the context of Islamic banking, deposits may be accepted by Islamic banks on the basis of a *mudarabah* contract where profit and loss are shared. Under this agreement, depositors provide the capital and the bank provides administration and investment opportunities. Thus, the depositing customers are known as the *rabbul mal* who agree to provide the bank with capital for it to manage and to yield profits that will be shared between the two parties according to specific percentages or ratios agreed upon in advance. However, when there is a loss in the investment, only the depositors bear the loss and the bank only loses its time, effort and estimated profit.

The contract normally involves a two-tier *mudarabah* agreement, whereby the first-tier agreement will be between the bank and the depositor(s) and the second-tier agreement is between the bank and the entrepreneur. In the former agreement, depositors who agree to put their money into the bank's investment account (investment account holders, IAHs) are the providers of the capital and the bank functions only as the manager of the funds. Profits will be shared between them in an agreed proportion, but in the case of a loss, the IAHs will bear the loss. In the latter agreement, the bank acts as the financier to the entrepreneurs who seek finance from the bank on condition that profits accruing from their business will be shared between them in mutually agreed proportion. However, that loss shall be borne by the financier (bank) only. If there is more than one financier of

---

[13]We will look at this mechanism further in Chapter 12.

the same project, i.e. the project is financed by several banks, then profits are to be shared in a mutually agreed proportion previously determined, but any loss is to be shared in the proportion in which the different financiers have invested their capital. Figure 4.3 further illustrates an example of a two-tier *mudarabah*.

Figure 4.3 Example of a two-tier *mudarabah*

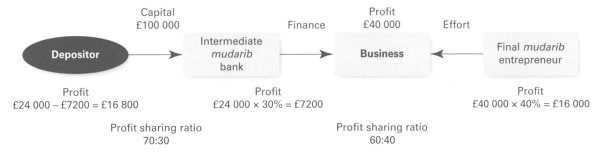

Example:
There are three parties involved in two-tier *mudarabah*: the capital provider (depositor), intermediate *mudarib* (bank) and final *mudarib* (entrepreneur). Assume that the depositor deposits £100 000 which is used by the bank to provide capital to Adam, the entrepreneur. The bank agrees to share profit with the depositor in the ratio of 30:70 and agrees to share profit with Adam in the ratio 60:40.

If the business makes a profit of £40 000:
Adam's share = 40% × £40 000 = £16 000
Bank's share = £40 000 − £16 000 = £24 000 × 30% = £7200
Depositor's share = £24 000 × 70% = £16 800 + £100 000

If the business makes a loss of £20 000:
Both Adam and the banker would lose their efforts and will not receive anything. Depositor will lose £20 000 and will only recover £80 000 of the capital.

(II) *MUSHARAKAH* (PARTNERSHIP) *Musharakah* is a contract of partnership between two or more parties in which all the partners contribute capital, participate in the management, share the profit in proportion to their capital contribution, or in the pre-agreed ratio, and bear the losses (if any) in proportion to their capital ratio. Based on Islamic jurisprudence, *musharakah* is the commingling of funds for the purpose of sharing in profit.

In the context of Islamic finance, *musharakah* financing is a partnership between the Islamic bank and its clients. Both parties contribute capital to establish a new project or share in an existing one. Either both of them or the client alone will take part in the management of the business as stated in the contract and will share the profits at a pre-agreed ratio, or bear the losses (if incurred) as per their capital ratio. The capital can be on permanent or declining capital basis and the fund providers will receive due share of profits. Partners share proportionate losses according to the capital contribution and not otherwise.

Several terms and conditions need to be fulfilled between the contracting parties for the *musharakah* contract to be valid. Firstly, the contracting parties involved in the partnership arrangement must all contribute capital to the project. Secondly, all parties will have the right to exercise executive powers in accordance with an agreed formula. Thirdly, it is better for the partners to belong to the same trade and can participate in actual work, with all the partners getting profit according to their work. In terms of risk, *musharakah* financing entails lower risks since it involves risk sharing through partnership. The number of individuals who are in a position to provide *musharakah* financing is limited, but *musharakah* funding through equity market participation may have much smaller risks because of the ease of divestment.

There are two types of *musharakah* contract*,* general and contractual. *General musharakah*, or partnership by joint ownership (*shirkat ul-milk*), implies co-ownership that comes into existence when two or more persons come together to get joint ownership of some asset without having entered into a formal partnership agreement, although Islam encourages for contracts to be written.

In contrast, *shirkat-ul-aqd* (partnership by contract) or *contractual musharakah*, is effectively a proper partnership, since the parties involved have freely entered into a contract for joint investment as well as sharing the profits and risks. Such contractual partnership takes a variety of forms: *shirkat-ul-amal* (partnership in services or labour), *shirkat-ul-wujooh* (goodwill partnership) and *shirkat-ul-amwal* (equity participation partnership). In the case of *shirkat-ul-amal*, all the partners jointly agree to render some services for their contracted customers, and the payment received from them is shared out among the partners in accordance to an agreed ratio. For example, two friends who are keen gardeners decided to provide garden landscaping services in the neighbourhood. They agreed for the revenues received from their customers to be accumulated into a revenue pool which will later be shared between them according to the agreed ratio irrespective of the amount of work each partner has actually provided. Goodwill partnership, which is also known as *shirkat-ul-wujooh*, is another form of *musharakah* partnership. This type of partnership is useful for those who do not have capital but have a good reputation and credibility. Hence, the partners will use their reputation or goodwill to purchase assets on a deferred payment basis and sell them at spot to customers in the market. Any profit earned is shared among the partners at the agreed ratio. Another common form of contractual *musharakah* is partnership by capital (*shirkat-ul-amwal*). Under this form of contract, partners jointly contribute capital and use it to generate profit. Any profit or loss will be shared among the partners usually based on each partner's capital contribution or some kind of agreed formula of distribution. The idea of *shirkat-ul-amwal* has been widely accepted in the form of limited companies and cooperative association and societies, whereby the capital is invested in these organizations in the form of equity or shares. Prospective partners or shareholders can buy as many share units as they wish.

In the case of Islamic banks, a *musharakah* financing arrangement would involve both the bank and the customer contributing their capital as well as expertise in a project, and the profit and loss will be shared based on the capital contribution. Figure 4.4 illustrates the mechanics of a *musharakah* joint venture.

Figure 4.4 Example of a *musharakah joint venture*

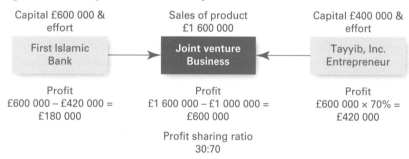

Profit sharing ratio
30:70

Example:
Tayyib, Inc., establishes a joint venture project with First Islamic Bank, with the former contributing £400 000 and the latter £600 000. Both parties agreed for the major part of the project to be managed by Tayyib, Inc. as it has more expertise on the project, with the bank involved in the financial management aspect. It was agreed that the share of the profit will be 70 per cent for Tayyib, Inc. and 30 per cent to the bank, with loss being shared based on capital contribution.

    If the joint venture was successful and the end product was sold for £1 600 000
        Profit generated = £1 600 000 – £1 000 000 = £600 000
        Tayyib, Inc.'s share of profit = 70% × £600 000 = £420 000
        Bank's share of profit = £600 000 – £420 000 = £180 000

    If the joint venture fails and the end product was sold for £800 000
        Loss incurred = £1 000 000 – £800 000 = £200 000
        Tayyib, Inc.'s share of loss = 40% × £200 000 = £80 000
        Bank's share of loss = £200 000 – £80 000 = £120 000

Many Islamic banks have also used *diminishing partnership* (*musharakah mutanaqisah*) as an effective financial instrument for house financing and fixed assets. This involves a chain of three contracts. The first contract is joint ownership between the client and the financier (enterprise), the second is a lease contract between the client and the financier for joint ownership whereby the financier provides units of shares to the client, and the third contract allows the client to conclude by gradually purchasing the remaining shares from the financier until the client owns the underlying property.

Example:

Alam wishes to purchase a property for £300 000 and he pays 20 per cent (£60 000) to the developer with the outstanding 80 per cent (£240 000) being paid for by the Islamic bank, who took the title to the property. Hence, the capital contribution ratio (CCR) is 20:80 between Alam and the Islamic bank. Assume that the bank allows Alam to defer payment for the 80 per cent over a period of say 20 years. Since no interest can be added to this, Alam will pay back the exact amount paid out by the fund provider.

At the same time of entering into the diminishing ownership agreement, Alam also enters into a lease agreement which runs concurrent with the diminishing ownership agreement, whereby the bank agrees to lease its share of the property to Alam for a variable amount of rent including payment of any outgoings related to the property as well as all administrative and legal costs, arrangements fees and stamp duty. Assume rental agreed upon is £1500 per month for the first five years, but would be revised to £1800 for the following five years and £2000 for the remaining ten years.

Both the amounts repaid under the diminishing ownership agreement and the amount paid under the lease agreement are amalgamated and used to calculate how much of the bank's share of the property has been purchased per month by Alam. As the bank's share in the property decreases, so does the amount paid under the lease agreement. At the end of 20 years upon fulfilment of all the conditions contained within the two contracts, the bank will pass the title to the property to Alam under the diminishing ownership agreement, normally for an additional payment. The mechanics are illustrated in Figure 4.5.

Figure 4.5 Diminishing *musharakah* contract

Rental payment cum buying share of bank on joint property.
Each year, bank's share decreases and client's share increases.

In summary, *mudarabah* and *musharakah* constitute, at least in principle if not in practice, the twin pillars of Islamic banking. As far as depositors are concerned, an Islamic bank acts as a *mudarib* which manages the funds of the depositors to generate profits subject to the rules of *mudarabah* as outlined earlier. The *musharakah* principle is invoked in the equity structure of Islamic financial institutions and is similar to the modern concepts of partnership and joint stock ownerships.

b) Contracts of exchange or sale (al-mu'awadad)

Contract of sale (*al-bay'*) is one of the most significant contracts as an alternative to interest-bearing loans. It is defined as:

an exchange of a useful and desirable thing for a similar thing by mutual consent in a specific manner.

Generally, a sale involves an exchange of something with something. They could fall under (i) sale of asset for a price; (ii) sale by immediate payment against future delivery; (iii) sale by barter which consists of exchange of a commodity for another commodity with no money payment; and (iv) sale by exchange of money for money (*sarf*) which consists of selling cash for cash, e.g. currency trading. Contracts of the third and fourth type are more susceptible to *riba* elements, especially *riba al-fadl* (unequal exchange of usurious commodities or exchange of money for money with different quantities) and *riba al-nasi'ah* (exchange without simultaneous transfer and immediate delivery), hence *shari'ah* has laid down stricter principles to ensure the legality of the contract. Figure 4.6 presents the different types of sales contracts which will be discussed in the following sections.

Figure 4.6   Different types of exchange or sale contracts

(I) COST-PLUS SALE CONTRACT (*BAY' AL-MURABAHAH*)   Cost-plus sale contract, or *bay' al-murabahah*, can be defined as:

> *a contract between a buyer and a seller under which the seller sells specific goods allowed under* shari'ah *principles and the law of the land to the buyer at a cost plus agreed profits payable in cash on any fixed future date in a lump sum or by instalments.*

Since the price and profit of a *bay' al-murabahah* contract is fixed based on the mutual consent of the buyer and seller, this is permissible according to the *Qur'an*:

> *… whereas Allah has permitted trading and forbidden riba* (Al-Baqarah, 2:275).[14]

The conditions of *bay' al-murabahah* are that the price at which the seller obtained the goods must be measured by weight, volume or number, regardless of whether the trade is concluded with the initial seller and/or the profit margin is specified in goods of the same genus. Secondly, profit should be fixed and added to the cost price and stated in the contract. Thirdly, knowledge of the profit margin is essential.

From the perspective of Islamic banking, *murabahah* financing provides customers with access to short term financing arrangements for covering their working capital financial needs and also as a letter of credit for trade financing. Under this arrangement, the customer may request the bank to fund some of its specific working capital needs such as purchasing raw materials or finished goods, completing its semi-finished products or replenishing its inventory. The bank will acquire the needed asset and subsequently sell it to the customer at an agreed price, which usually covers the purchase price and a profit mark-up. The total amount will be paid by the customer on a deferred term basis of one month, two months, three months or any other period agreed

[14]www.wright-house.com/religions/islam/Quran/2-cow.php, accessed 23 May 2018

by both parties. The cost (capital outlay) includes the purchase price and any other expenses related to it, such as delivery cost. Figure 4.7 illustrates the basic mechanics of *murabahah*.

Figure 4.7   Cost-plus *murabahah* contract

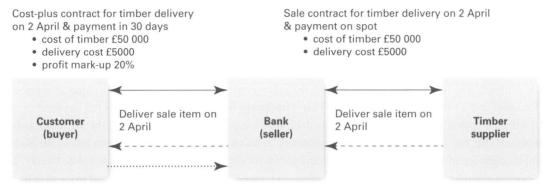

Example:
A manufacturer needs to buy £50 000 worth of timber to complete job order 201R but it hasn't got enough funds. The manufacturer approaches the bank and signs an agreement to purchase the timber from the bank at cost plus 20 per cent profit with payment to be made 30 days after receiving the timber. Delivery cost is £5000. The mark-up profit is a percentage of cost or purchase price of the goods for a lump sum payment. Hence, the manufacturer is liable to pay the bank £66 000 (£50 000 + £5000 = £55 000 × 120%) in 30 days time after the bank delivers the goods. Both parties know the profit and the cost of the product at the onset; there's no financial uncertainty in the transaction.

The majority of financing arrangements in Islamic financial markets today are based upon *murabahah with deferred payment*. One controversy that surrounds *murabahah* being a truly *shari'ah* compliant financing mechanism arises from the differentiation between the price for spot payments and the price for deferred payments. It has been argued that it is often unclear as to what extent the providers of such finance undertake risks that are substantially different compared with risks undertaken by interest based banks. In response to this, some scholars rationalize the difference between *murabahah* and conventional loans on three aspects.

Firstly, in *murabahah*, the price and profit margin are known and will not increase in future, while for conventional loan, the interest may fluctuate and all risks are transferred to the client. Secondly, after the *murabahah* contract is signed, the amount being financed cannot be increased in the case of late payment or default, nor can a penalty be imposed, unless the buyer has deliberately refused to make a payment. However, in a conventional loan contract, the amount can increase due to compound interest and a penalty may be imposed for default. Third, the aggregate value paid under *murabahah* equals the spot price and the loan advanced by the seller to the buyer becomes interest free. In conventional loans, the loan is an exchange of money now for money later, hence constitutes *riba*.

(II) FORWARD SALE CONTRACT (*BAY' AL-SALAM*)   *Bay' Al-Salam* is a contract in which advance payment is made for goods to be delivered later on, hence can be defined as:

> *the purchase of a commodity for deferred delivery in exchange for immediate payment according to specified conditions, or sale of a commodity for deferred delivery in exchange for immediate payment.*

The permissibility of a forward sale contract can be found in the *Qur'an*:

> *O you who believe! When you contract a debt for a fixed period, write it down. Let a scribe (writer) write it down in justice between you. Let not the scribe refuse to write as Allah has taught him, so let him write* (Al-Baqarah, 2: 282).[15]

[15]www.wright-house.com/religions/islam/Quran/2-cow.php, accessed 23 May 2018.

A valid contract of sale by deferred payments requires the fulfilment of the following conditions, which are over and above the conditions of an ordinary sale. The *salam* contract needs to satisfy six conditions in order to be valid: (i) the *object of sale* is of known genus and if there are multiple types of the specified genus of the commodity, then the type must be clearly specified; (ii) amount must be clearly stated by volume or by weight; (iii) the term of deferment of *payment* is known; (iv) the *price* is known and has to be specified in monetary form; (v) the place of *delivery* is specified; and (vi) characteristics are known.

With regards to the *object of sale*, besides knowing the genus and type, it cannot be stated in the contract that the price will be part of the conditions to be agreed upon because the products are not yet produced, as this will cause the contract to be invalid. As for the *payment*, the *salam* contract is only valid if the buyer pays the price in full to the seller at the time of effecting the sale. This is necessary because in the absence of full payment by the buyer, it will be identical to sale of a debt against a debt, which is prohibited. Therefore, all the Muslim scholars are unanimous that full payment of the price is necessary in *salam,* while those scholars who follow the Maliki school of thought are of the view that the seller may give a concession of two or three days to the buyers, but this concession should not form part of the agreement. In terms of *delivery*, the exact date and place of delivery must be specified in the contract. *Salam* cannot be effected for things which must be delivered on the spot. For example, if gold is purchased in exchange for silver or if wheat is bartered for barley, it is necessary, according to *shari'ah*, that the delivery of both takes place simultaneous. Without simultaneous delivery of both, the contract of *salam* becomes invalid. Finally, the *characteristic* of the commodity for a *salam* contract must be such that the quality and quantity can be specified exactly, otherwise it cannot be sold through a *salam* contract. For instance, precious stones cannot be sold on the basis of *salam* because the quality, size and weight are not exact, hence difficult to specify in the *salam* contract. Similarly, agricultural products such as wheat and fruits are subject to natural variations and hence the delivery remains uncertain. The same rule applies to any commodity in which the supply cannot be guaranteed.

There are two types of *salam* contracts, ordinary and parallel. In an *ordinary salam*, there are two parties to the contract, the buyer and the seller. However, in a *parallel salam*, the buyer after entering into the first sale contract with the seller by paying in advance for the goods to be delivered by a certain date, enters into another sale contract to sell the product awaiting delivery from the original seller to a buyer at a different price and delivering the goods on the same date as the buyer received delivery of the product.

Unlike their conventional counterparts that can make profit by advancing loan, Islamic financial institutions need to find alternative ways to earn permissible profit because *shari'ah* doesn't allow profit through advancing cash loans only. Hence they will have to deal in commodities in one way or the other by purchasing commodities through *salam* and to sell in spot markets. Figure 4.8 illustrates the mechanics of parallel *salam*.

Figure 4.8   Structure of parallel *salam*

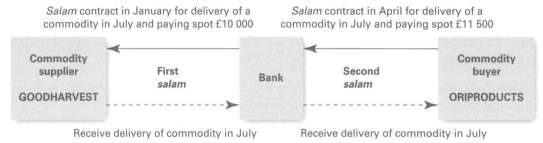

Example:
First Islamic Bank entered into a *salam* contract with GoodHarvest in January to supply a commodity in July and paying on the spot to the company £10 000. In April, the bank entered into a *salam* contract with Oriproducts to deliver commodity in July and was paid on the spot £11 500.

(III) DEFERRED INSTALMENT SALE CONTRACT (*BAY' BITHAMAN AJIL*) *Bay' bithaman ajil* (BBA) means 'deferred instalment sale'. Through this contract, banks may finance customers who acquire an asset but wish to defer the payment for a specific period (payment by instalments). Customers are allowed to settle the payment of the asset within a certain period of time.

Since BBA is basically a trading contract, four conditions must be observed to make it valid. Firstly, both parties (buyer and seller) are able to carry out their responsibilities and are not forced to enter into a contract. Secondly, the asset being traded must be in the form of a valuable asset which is lawful (*halal*), has trading value and is known by both parties. Thirdly, the price should be determined and the currency specified at the outset of the contract. Fourth, the offer and acceptance of the contract must be in clear language.

BBA is a financing facility that is widely used in Malaysia for financing the acquisition of assets and the payment is usually based on an instalment basis payable over longer periods compared to the *murabahah* repayment facility. The contract of BBA is utilized by the bank to provide its customers with medium and long term financing to acquire items which may include land, houses, motor vehicles, furniture, stocks and shares. The most popular financing granted under BBA is to purchase a house.

(IV) MANUFACTURING CONTRACT (*BAY' AL-ISTISNA'A*) *Bay' al-istisna'a* is an order of sale used mainly in financing assets that are under construction. Therefore, it is a contract for the acquisition of goods by specification or by order. For example, the purchase of house under construction where payments need to be made by the bank to the developer based on the stages of work completed.

For the contract of *istisna'a* to be valid, the buyer needs to express desire to buy a commodity and make an *istisna'a* request to the bank with a specific price and the agreed method of payment. The bank puts itself under obligation to manufacture and deliver the commodity within a specific period as stated in the agreement with the due date, being the same as or after the due date of receiving the commodity in a *parallel istisna'a* contract. The seller delivers the manufactured commodity to the bank directly or to any place decided by the bank in the contract, and the bank delivers the manufactured commodity directly to the purchaser or authorizes any party to deliver the commodity to the purchaser, who has the right to make sure that the commodity satisfies the specifications demanded in the contract.

Islamic financial institutions use *istisna'a* to finance the construction of houses or factories on a piece of land belonging to a client. The building is constructed either by the financier himself or by a construction company. But if the contract is concluded with the bank but the work will be carried out by the financier himself, then the sub-contract is not valid. It is necessary that the bank should have its own construction company and expert contractors to discharge the task. The price of construction may be paid by the client at the time of agreement or may be postponed till the time of delivery or any other time agreed upon between the parties. The payment may be in a lump sum or in instalments. In order to secure the payment of instalments, the title deeds of the house or land may be kept by the bank as security till the last instalment is paid by the client.

There are two types of *istisna'a* contracts: ordinary and parallel. In an *ordinary istisna'a,* there are two parties to the contract, the buyer and the seller. In a *parallel istisna'a* (see Figure 4.9), if the buyer does not stipulate in the contract that the seller should manufacture the product himself, then the seller may enter into a second *istisna'* contract in order to fulfil the contractual obligations in the first contract.

(V) CURRENCY SALE CONTRACT (*BAY' AS-SARF*) *Bay' as-sarf* is a contract of exchange of money for money or currency trading. The legitimacy of this contract is derived largely from the *Hadith*:

> *Abu Hurairah narrated that the Prophet said: '(Sell) silver for silver, gold for gold, barley for barley, wheat for wheat, like for like' (Ibn Majah).*[16]

[16]Vol. 3, Book 12, Hadith 2255 sunnah.com/urn/1265730, accessed 23 May 2018.

Figure 4.9   Flow of parallel *istisna'a* transaction

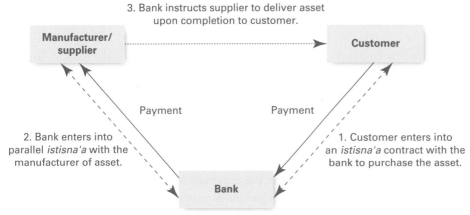

Those four items, i.e. gold, silver, wheat, barley, mentioned in the preceding *Hadith* are called *ribawi* items.[17] Based upon this *Hadith,* it is established that if gold is to be exchanged for gold, the exchange must be made on the spot with the amounts being of equal quality and quantity. A forward transaction in which one of the counter values is delivered at a future date or doing it on credit is not allowed. Given that exchanges must be equal, commissions on currency exchange have been questionable, as this contravenes the 'equal for equal' ruling, as any surplus is considered as usury. If gold is sold for silver or vice versa, *shari'ah* insists on equality and the delivery of the articles must be on the spot.

Hence, there are two main conditions of *sarf* contract. Firstly, a currency exchange contract must be on the spot and cannot be deferred. Secondly, if money is exchanged for other money of the same genus, for example, gold for gold, then the two compensations must be equal in weight, even if one of the two compensations is of a higher quality than the other.

Proponents of the view that any exchange of currencies of different countries is the same as *bay' as-sarf* argue that in the present age, paper currencies have effectively and completely replaced gold and silver as the medium of exchange. Hence, by analogy, exchange involving such currencies should be governed by the same *shari'ah* rules and injunctions as *bay' as-sarf*.

c) Utilisation of usufruct contracts (al-ijarah)

A *usufruct contract (al-ijarah)* is a form of exchange of value or consideration, return, wages or rent of service of an asset. Generally, it means 'to give something on rent'. It is also regarded as a contract by which the usufruct or the right to use and derive profit from a particular property is transferred to another person in exchange for a claim on rent. Thus, *ijarah* is defined as:

> a contract between two parties, the lessor and lessee, where the lessee enjoys or reaps a specific service or benefit against
> a specified consideration or rent from the asset owned by the lessor.

---

[17]Many scholars have used an analogy to argue that the *Hadith* on gold and silver represents all forms of monetary medium. Therefore all forms of currency should obey the rules established for gold and silver exchanges. This position is not however unanimous. There are those who argue that the rules do not apply to other items, such as copper, since copper is not one of the six *ribawi* items mentioned in the *Hadith*. Similarly, there are some scholars who argue that because money is to be regarded as gold and silver only, then paper money is not a proper form of money and a loan of £10 made today in return for £15 to be received tomorrow is not a form of *riba*, but this is only a minority held view.

The basis of *ijarah* being permissible is derived from the following verse in the *Qur'an*:

> *And said one of them (the two women): 'O my father! Hire him! Verily, the best of men for you to hire is the strong, the trustworthy'* (Al-Qasas, 28:26).[18]

The legitimacy of *ijarah* is also generated from consensus among the legal community. The *ijarah* is also acceptable by reasoning because it is a convenient means for people to acquire rights to use assets that they do not own, since not everyone is able to own tangible assets.

There are three conditions for the *ijarah* contract to be valid. Firstly, the object and purpose of the contract should be lawful. Secondly, the risk of the leased asset shall remain with the lessor throughout the lease period, in the sense that any harm or loss caused by factors beyond the control of the lessee shall be borne by the lessor. Thirdly, the lessee (customer) leases the goods from the owner or lessor (Islamic bank) at an agreed rental over a specific period.

Al-ijarah has two types of usufruct: *usufruct of property or capital assets* and *usufruct of labour, employment and service*. Thus, *al-ijarah* is not only related to the leasing of property alone but also includes services which we normally term as employment. In a conventional banking system, *ijarah* is a contract under which a bank buys and leases out for a rental fee equipment that is required by its client. The duration of the lease and rental fees are agreed in advance. The lessee will get the full benefit of using the leased asset within the specified period for as long as s(he) adheres to the lease terms and conditions. At the end of the lease period, the leased asset will be returned to the lessor. Figure 4.10 presents the different types of *ijarah* contracts.

Figure 4.10 Types of *ijarah* contracts

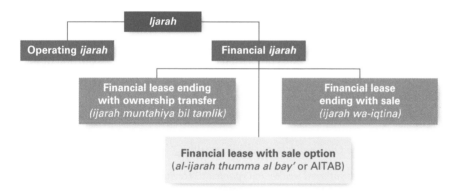

There are two main types of *ijarah*: operating and financial lease. *Operating lease (ijarah tashgheeliah)* is a lease contract where the lessee benefits from the asset for a specific time period but it does not result in the eventual transfer of ownership of the asset to the lessee. *Financial lease* is a lease contract which incorporates the option to transfer ownership of the leased asset from the lessor to the lessee at the end of the lease period. It has three variants: financial lease ending with sale, financial lease ending with ownership transfer and financial lease with sale option.

Financial lease ending with sale (ijarah wa-iqtina) is a lease agreement with the option for client to buy the leased asset at an agreed price from the bank at the end of the lease tenure, with rental fees previously paid constituting part of the price. In the case of *financial lease ending with ownership transfer (al ijarah muntahiya bil tamlik)*, the legal title is transferred to the lessee without any additional payments at the end of the lease period. As for *financial lease with sale option (al ijarah thumma al bay' or AITAB)*, the lessee will have the option to buy the asset at the end of maturity of the lease. AITAB consists of two different contracts, namely, the contract of *al-ijarah* and the contract of *al-bay'*. The objective of AITAB is to provide customers the opportunity to own an

[18]www.wright-house.com/religions/islam/Quran/28-story.php, accessed 23 May 2018.

asset they could not have bought on a cash basis, but can do so on a future date when payments are periodically made on a lease basis.

Transactions in AITAB involve the bank buying the asset from the dealer and then leasing the asset to the customer according to the terms and conditions, including specifying the market rental value and the leasing period. Hence, as owner of the asset, the bank will receive the lease payments and is responsible for ensuring that the customer is able to exercise the option to buy the house at a nominal value. Theoretically, the price of the asset should be equivalent to the total lease payments received by the bank during the leasing period. At the end of the lease period, transfer of ownership takes place from the bank to the customer when the latter exercises the option to buy the asset. If the customer does not want to continue with the *ijarah* contract, an offer will be made to buy the asset at a price equivalent to the difference between the total rental and the amount already paid as rent.

Example:
Assume that Zack is interested in a car with a price tag of £60 000. After paying a 20 per cent down payment, he approached the interest free bank for AITAB facility. The bank purchases the car for £48 000 and leases it to Zack. The monthly rental consists of the capital component and profit from the rent. Assuming that the bank wants a 5 per cent profit per annum and the rental contract is for seven years, then the expected profit for the duration is £16 800 (5% × 7 years × £48 000). The monthly rental shall be equal to £48 000 + £16 800 = £64 800/84, which is about £771.43.

d) Deposits or safe custody contract (al-wadi'ah)

Al-wadi'ah is a contract between the owner of goods and the custodian of goods whereby the latter undertakes the responsibility to protect the goods from being stolen or destroyed and to ensure safe custody. In Islamic banking operations, the bank has the authority to use a client's deposits in savings and current accounts, giving a guarantee to return it to the client when s(he) needs it. The client will periodically obtain a share of the profits earned by the bank when it utilizes the depositors' money to invest in its business ventures. The portion of profit to be shared with the client is at the absolute discretion of the bank. This reward is the replacement of the interest income that the client would otherwise receive from a conventional bank.

The action by the bank is permissible as it helps to mobilize deposits from the savings of capital owner and to make these deposits available for investment in ensuring production and distribution for the establishment of equity, justice and the welfare of society, as the *Qur'an* discourages idle wealth:

> Woe to every slanderer and backbiter. Who has gathered wealth and counted it. He thinks that his wealth will make him last for ever! Nay! Verily, he will be thrown into the crushing Fire (Al-Humazah, 104:1-4).[19]

The conditions for the contract to be valid include an offer and acceptance existing between depositor and the custodian (depository institution) and the deposited object must be in the form of an asset that is tangible and can be possessed physically.

There are two types of *wadi'ah*: safe custody trust and guaranteed custody. Safe custody trust *(wadi'ah yad amanah)* is a contract where the trustee or custodian has a duty to safeguard the property held in trust by not mixing or pooling the properties (money) under custody, not using the properties and not charging fees for safe custody. On the other hand, guaranteed custody *(wadi'ah yad dhamanah)* allows the custodian to pool the funds for utilization, with service charges being imposed and the custodians guaranteeing the safety of money, returning the funds as and when requested by the customer. The bank may give *hibah* (gift/reward) to the depositor and the *hibah* depends solely on the bank's discretion and cannot be promised by the bank, otherwise it becomes *riba*.

---

[19]www.wright-house.com/religions/islam/Quran/104-traducer.php, accessed 23 May 2018.

e) Security contract (al-tawthiqat)

The purpose of this type of contract is for documentation and safeguarding of contractual rights. Normally a fee is charged for the service. There are three types of contracts that fall under this category: *kafalah* (suretyship), *hawalah* (transfer of debt) and *rahn* (collateralization or pledging).

(I) SURETYSHIP CONTRACT (AL-KAFALAH) *Al-kafalah* is a contract between two parties whereby one party agrees to discharge the liability of a third party in the case of default by the third party. As a surety, the third party will give the party that agrees to discharge liability some form of collateral and pay a small fee for the service. Legally, it is the pledge given by the guarantor or the surety to a creditor on behalf of the principal debtor to ensure that the guaranteed, i.e. the debtor, will be present at a definite place, e.g. to pay his debt or fine or to undergo punishment. However, surety in Islamic law is the pledge to the claim and not the debt. The legitimacy of *al-kafalah* is recognized in the *Qur'an*:

> He [Ya'qub (Jacob)] said: 'I will not send him with you until you swear a solemn oath to me in Allah's Name, that you will bring him back to me unless you are yourselves surrounded (by enemies)' (Yusuf, 12:66).[20]

Al-kafalah may involve more than one guarantor or surety for a single obligation. If two parties who are jointly indebted provide surety for each other, then each of them is liable for the whole debt. However, the discharge of the surety does not necessarily discharge the liability of the principal debtor concerned. If the principal debtor is granted a delay for the payment of his debts, his guarantor should also be granted a delay.

Based on the way the offer and acceptance is expressed, *kafalah* can take the form of being immediate, conditional or contingent. *Immediate kafalah,* as the name suggests, takes immediate effect. For instance, when a person guarantees the payment of loan or becomes a guarantor for a particular loan, then the guarantee will follow the loan. If the loan has to be paid immediately, then the guarantor is liable to pay it immediately, and if the loan is deferred or payable by instalments in a certain period, then the guarantor is liable to settle the loan accordingly. Any variation has to be agreed upon by the creditor. *Conditional kafalah* is when the guarantor puts certain conditions in place before accepting to become a guarantor. For instance, a guarantor may specify that he will only become a guarantor if the creditor lends a specific amount to the principal. *Contingent kafalah* is a guarantee that is contingent on a specified event taking place or for a specified time. For instance, the guarantor specifying that the guarantee is only effective until next year or upon travelling abroad.

There are two types of *al-kafalah*: surety for the person and surety for the claim. In the case of *surety for the person (kafalah bi al-nafs)*, the person providing surety is assuming liability for the appearance of the debtor or of his agent in a lawsuit. Hence, any guarantor who had failed to perform his obligation could be detained. *Surety for the claim (kafalah bi al-mal),* on the other hand, can be independent or in addition to the surety for the person. For instance, *kafalah* for the property can be both for the settlement of a debt or a guarantee that a specific asset would be returned. Thus, the guarantor is liable if the debtor or the owner of the asset dies.

Islamic banks use *al-kafalah* to issue bank and shipping guarantees. Under the *kafalah* shipping guarantee, the bank gives surety to the owner of the shipping vessel to discharge goods to the importer pending receipt of the original bill of landing. Under the *kafalah* bank guarantee, the bank guarantees the company's standing to facilitate any business endeavours that may require such guarantees.

(II) TRANSFER OF DEBT (AL-HAWALAH) *Al-hawalah* means transferring a claim of a debt by shifting the responsibility from one person to another. This involves transfer of debt from a debtor (transferor) to another party who accepts the transfer (transferee) of debt, which releases the former from any obligation to pay the debt.

---

[20]www.wright-house.com/religions/islam/Quran/12-joseph.php, accessed 23 May 2018.

The creditor can only now claim the debt from the transferee. The permissibility of *al-hawalah* can be found in the *Hadith*:

> Abu Hurairah narrated that the Prophet said: 'Procrastination in paying debts by a wealthy man is injustice. So, if your debt is transferred from your debtor to a trustworthy rich debtor, you should agree' (Bukhari).[21]

There are two types of *al-hawalah*, either absolute or conditional. Absolute *hawalah (mutlaq)* refers to a contract where payment is not restricted to the property of the transferor in the hands of the transferee. Conditional *hawalah (muqayyad)* is a contract that contains a stipulation that the creditor's debt may be paid up from the debt of the debtor due from the transferee or anything belonging to the debtor, which the transferee keeps as security.

In Islamic banking operations, *hawalah* refers to a transfer of funds/debt from the depositor's/debtor's account to the receiver's/creditor's account, thus serving as a guarantee for the payment of debt to the creditor. It also serves as a medium of commercial transaction whereby a commission may be charged for such services. *Hawalah* resembles negotiable instruments in that its purpose is to guarantee the payment of debt to the creditor and also for the purpose of guaranteeing or securing the payment of loan due on a bill of exchange. This is a mechanism used for settling international accounts by book transfers.

(III) COLLATERALIZATION OR PLEDGING (AR-RAHN)   *Ar-rahn* is an arrangement whereby a valuable asset is placed as collateral for a debt. The collateral may be disposed in the event of a default. The legality of *al-rahn* is stated in the *Qur'an*:

> And if you are on a journey and cannot find a scribe, then let there be a pledge taken (mortgaging); then if one of you entrust the other, let the one who is entrusted discharge his trust (faithfully), and let him be afraid of Allah, his Lord (Al-Baqarah, 2:283).[22]

There are certain conditions attached to an *ar-rahn* contract. Firstly, the pledged asset must be owned by the pledger or debtor. Secondly, the reason for pledging is as security of a debt and not for investment and profitable use, otherwise this is considered as usury. However, in certain cases, the pledgee can utilized the usufruct of the pledged property as payment for their maintenance cost and as a right of security. Thirdly, it is not permissible for the pledgee to dissolve the contract until the debt is paid by the pledger. Fourth, the provision and supply or encumbrance of security which is not guaranteed, including the cost of its maintenance, its return and its substitution, are payable by its owner and its beneficial use is also returned to the pledger. Lastly, if the pledged security damages itself, the pledger loses right of security and no liability will be incurred on the pledge, and if either of the parties in the contract dies, the contract will be dissolved automatically.

f) Agency contract (wakalah and ju'alah)

(I) WAKALAH   *Al-wakalah* means agency or the delegation of duty to another party for specific purposes, under specific conditions. It is a contract between two parties where one party (the principal) appoints another party (agent) to act on his behalf. The agreement is to authorize power to the agent to represent him or to exercise the power on his behalf as instructed by the principal. The legitimacy of *al-wakalah* can be found in the *Qur'an*:

> … So send one of you with this silver coin of yours to the town, and let him find out which is the good lawful food, and bring some of that to you. And let him be careful and let no man know of you (Al-Kahf, 18:19).[23]

---

[21]Vol. 3, Book 37, Hadith 486 sunnah.com/bukhari/38/1, accessed 23 May 2018.

[22]www.wright-house.com/religions/islam/Quran/2-cow.php, accessed 23 May 2018.

[23]www.wright-house.com/religions/islam/Quran/18-cave.php, accessed 23 May 2018.

There are two main conditions for the validity of an agency contract. Firstly, the principal should have full authority of disposing the matter being entrusted to another person to perform on his behalf. Secondly, the agent appointed should have the capacity, i.e. knowledge and experience, to execute the trust given to him and to only act for what he is appointed for. The power to exercise is not vested on the agent to take an oath on behalf of the principal, to perform an illegal act, to sell the principal's property and any other matter which is not covered by the condition of the agreement.

There are two types of *al-wakalah: absolute agency (al-wakalah mutlaqah)*, where full freedom is given to the agent to exercise the power, and *limited agency (al-wakalah al-muqaiyadah)*, whereby the agent is bonded by certain conditions before power can be exercised.

Under this concept, the bank acts as the agent in completing a particular financial transaction, and as an agent the bank will be paid a certain fee for the services it provides. Under *al-wakalah*, the Islamic insurance (*takaful*) operator, being the agent of the participants can use part of the funds to cover the agent's management costs. Any surplus of the funds from underwriting will be redistributed to the participants as the funds belong to them.

(II) COMMISSION *(AL-JU'ALAH)* This contract involves one party undertaking to pay another party a specified amount of money as a fee for rendering a specific service in accordance to the terms of the contract stipulated between the two parties. Evidence for the legality of *al-ju'alah* can be found in the *Qur'an*:

> … *and for him who produces it is (the reward of) a camel-load; I will be bound by it* (Yusuf, 12: 72).[24]

In general, *al-ju'alah* is allowed as an exception, as the legality of *al-ju'alah* is based on its necessity (*darurah*). Hence, despite the existence of certain elements of uncertainty or *gharar,* it is permitted. The Malikis require that the *ju'alah* had no time component, while other scholars permit combining a task and a time period in the contract. For example, an uncertain work may be carried out by uncertain people but Islamic law does not recognize the unauthorized agency or persons who carry out the work. In this contract, two elements of certainty exist, namely, the amount of reward offered and a specified service to be accomplished.

Summary

Contracts are given special attention in Islam. Many verses from the *Qur'an* emphasize the importance of contracts, and in fact there is one whole chapter in the *Qur'an* that covers the various contracts in life related to the relationships between man and man, and man and God. Islamic commercial law provides guidance on business transactions that are lawful and just. The legal consequences of a contract may fall under one of the following: valid, void, deficient, enforceable, binding and withheld. Contracts can be classified into unilateral, which involves a single party, or bilateral, involving at least two parties. The remainder of the chapter discussed the various types of contracts and their application in Islamic banking and finance. It is important to note that many of these contracts are unique to Islamic banking and financing, because the product and services they offered need to be *shari'ah* compliant.

[24]www.wright-house.com/religions/islam/Quran/12-joseph.php, accessed 23 May 2018.

Key terms and concepts

al ijarah muntahiya bil tamlik	contract	musharakah mutanaqisah
al-wakalah	contractual musharakah	offeree
al-hawalah	deficient contract	offeror
al-kafalah	enforceable contract	qabul
al-wadi'ah	general musharakah	qard ul hasanah
ar-rahn	hibah	restricted mudarabah
bay' al-istisna'a	ibra'	revocable contract
bay' al-murabahah	ijab	subject matter
bay' Al-Salam	ijarah thumma al bay	two-tier mudarabah
bay' as-sarf	ijarah wa-iqtina	unilateral contract
bay' bithaman ajil	irrevocable binding contract	unrestricted mudarabah
bilateral contract	Islamic commercial law	void contract
binding contract	mudarabah interbank investments	waqf
consideration	musharakah	wasiyyat

Questions

1. Define contracts from the perspective of Islamic law.

2. Explain the elements for a contract to be considered valid.

3. Using appropriate examples, illustrate the difference between a deficient, void and binding contract.

4. Distinguish between unilateral and bilateral contracts and describe the various types of contracts under these two categories.

5. Explain the differences between *mudarabah* and *musharakah* and distinguish the various types of contract under each of these categories.

6. What is the difference between *murabahah* and a conventional loan?

7. Discuss the terms and conditions for a *bay Al-Salam* contract to be valid.

8. Explain the differences between the three types of *al-ijarah*.

9. Discuss the types of contract that can be used for documentation and safeguarding of contractual rights.

References and further readings

Bakar, M.D. (2008). 'Contracts in Islamic commercial law and their application in modern Islamic financial system'. In Bakar, M.D. and Engku Ali, E.R.A. (eds), *Essential Readings in Islamic Finance*, CERT, Kuala Lumpur, Malaysia, pp. 47-84.

Haniffa, R., Hudaib, M. and Mirza, A.M. (2008). 'Accounting policy choice within the *Shari'ah Islami'iah* framework'. In Bakar, M.D. and Engku Ali, E.R.A. (eds), *Essential Readings in Islamic Finance*, CERT, Kuala Lumpur, Malaysia, pp. 317-340.

Hassan, M.K., Kayed, R. and Oseni, U.A. (2013), *Introduction to Islamic Banking & Finance: Principles and Practice*, Pearson Education Limited, Cambridge, UK.

Iqbal, Z. and Mirakhor, A. (2007), *An Introduction to Islamic Finance: Theory and Practice*, John Wiley & Sons (Asia).

Ismail, A.G. (2010), *Money, Islamic Banks and the Real Economy*, Cengage Learning, Singapore.

Kamali, M.H. (2002), *Islamic Commercial Law: An Analysis of Futures and Options*, Ilmiah Publishers, Kuala Lumpur.

Ma'sum Billah, M. (2006), *Shariah Standard of Business Contract*, A.S. Noordeen, Kuala Lumpur.

Razali, S.S. (2010), *Islamic Law of Contract*, Cengage Learning Asia Pte. Ltd, Singapore.

Shari'ah Standards (2015), *The Accounting and Auditing Organization for Islamic Financial Institutions (AAOIFI)*, Manama, Bahrain.

5 Islamic bonds (*sukuk*) and derivatives

Learning Objectives

Upon completion of this chapter you should be able to:

- describe the nature, types, features and ratings of conventional bonds

- discuss the nature of *sukuk*

- identify the main differences between conventional bonds and *sukuk*

- explain the advantages and disadvantages of *sukuk*

- discuss the classifications and types of *sukuk* structures

- explain the various rating methodologies for *sukuk*

- discuss the development of and contemporary issues on *sukuk*

- explain the principles of derivatives and the concept of hedging

- discuss the various types of derivatives from an Islamic perspective

5.1 Introduction

The Islamic capital market is an important component of Islamic finance as it facilitates investment in Islamic financial instruments such as Islamic equity, *sukuk* and Islamic derivatives. *Sukuk* (Islamic bonds) is an innovative financing product that has changed the dynamics of the Islamic finance industry by offering an alternative product to investors seeking to invest and transact business in an Islamic capital market. They are structured in such a way that returns can be generated to investors without infringing *shari'ah*, which prohibits *riba*, or interest. The first *sukuk* was issued by Malaysia in 2000, followed by Bahrain in 2001. It has gradually become the most significant group of securities in Islamic finance because it enables the flow of funds between countries as well as domestically. In the past few years, *sukuk* has been used by the governments in different countries to raise funds through sovereign issues and also by corporate giants like Emirates, Goldman Sachs and GE through the offer of corporate *sukuk*. According to IIFM Sukuk Report 2017, $88 billion worth of *sukuk* were issued globally in 2016, an increase of 44 per cent over the 2015 issuance of around $61 billion. In short, *sukuk* has developed into one of the most significant mechanisms for raising finance in the international capital markets using Islamically acceptable structures.

In this chapter, we will briefly review the concept, types and features of bonds before focusing our attention on the nature of *sukuk*. We will consider the underlying principles of *sukuk* by focusing on their types, characteristics, structures and rating methodologies and also highlighting the key differences between bonds and *sukuk*. The development of *sukuk* and some of the controversial issues related to securitization of such products will also be discussed.

We then turn our attention to derivatives by explaining their relationship to the concept of hedging and discuss the various types of conventional derivative structures before considering the Islamic perspective on the concepts of hedging and derivatives.

5.2   Bonds: types, features and ratings

Bonds are securities representing debt owed by the issuer to the investor with a promise to pay the *par, face or maturity value* of the bond at the maturity date and also a periodic interest payment or the *coupon payment*. The rate of interest that the issuer must pay is known as the *coupon rate* and it is fixed for the duration of the bond, thus will not fluctuate with the market interest rate. If the issuer fails to meet the repayment terms of the bond, then the bondholder has a claim on the assets of the issuer.

The types of bonds traded in the capital markets include long term government or treasury bonds, municipal bonds and corporate bonds. Figure 5.1 illustrates the different types of bonds. We will consider each type including their main features.

Figure 5.1   Types of bonds

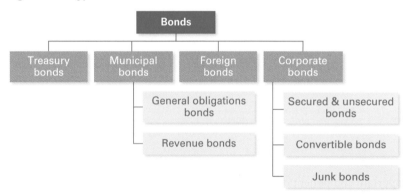

5.2.1 TYPES AND FEATURES OF BONDS

a) Treasury bonds/government bonds/municipal bonds/state bonds

Treasury or government bonds are issued by the government and considered as having the lowest *default risk* (not being able to make required payments on debt obligations), as the government is reasonably expected to make good on its promised payments. Municipal and state bonds are similar to government bonds as they are issued by the state or municipal government, but their default risk are higher than treasury bonds. However, there have been, over the years, governments who have defaulted on their debts. There are currently high levels of government debt even in the developed world, e.g. Japan's debt is 200 per cent of GDP, UK's is 90 per cent and Greece 175 per cent. Such high levels of debt in those countries may increase the default risk.

b) Foreign bonds

Foreign bonds are issued by foreign governments or corporations and are exposed not only to default risk but also *currency risk* (fluctuations in foreign exchange rate) if the bonds are denominated in a currency other than that of the investor's home currency. For instance, even if there is no default on the bond, a Japanese investor who purchased a bond denominated in pounds sterling will lose money when the pound falls relative to the Japanese yen.

c) Corporate bonds

Corporate bonds are issued by companies and the level of default risk is dependent on the characteristics of the issuer and the terms of the specific bonds. A *secured bond* is one where the issuer pledges a specific asset in the form of collateral on the loan. In the event of a default, the bond issuer passes the title of the asset onto the bondholders. An *unsecured bond* (debenture) is not backed by any specific assets or revenue and the issuer only promises payment in full. A *convertible bond* is one that gives investors the option to convert it into a fixed number of shares, thus giving them the chance to share in the upside when the company performs well in the market. Hence, its coupon rate is lower than an otherwise identical but non-convertible bond. *Junk bonds* are high yield fixed income bonds that carry a credit rating of BB or lower by Standard & Poor's rating and thus have higher default risk.

5.3 *Sukuk*

5.3.1   WHAT IS *SUKUK*?[1]

Sukuk is an Arabic term meaning financial certificates. It is an Islamic equivalent to conventional bonds whereby governments and corporations can issue such investment certificates to raise funds while adhering to *shari'ah*. Similar to bonds, *sukuk* have a maturity date and the *sukuk* holders may receive a regular stream of income (fixed or variable) over the life of the certificate and/or with a balloon payment at maturity, depending on the structure of the *sukuk*. However, unlike bonds, where the issuer owes the investor an amount of money consisting of the principal and interest payment (debt instrument), the *sukuk* investor has an ownership interest in a real underlying asset. In other words, the financing instrument represents undivided ownership of tangible asset based investment, usufruct or services of revenue generating issuers, with the underlying asset being *shari'ah* compliant in both nature and use. This is reflected in the definitions by the IFSB and AAOIFI which define *sukuk* as follows:

> ...*certificates that represent the holder's proportionate ownership in an undivided part on an underlying asset where the holder assumes all rights and obligations to such asset* (IFSB-2).
>   ...*certificates of equal value representing undivided shares in the ownership of tangible assets, usufruct (the legal right of using and enjoying a property leased), and services, or (in the ownership of) the assets of particular projects or special investment activity; however, this is true after the receipt of the value of the sukuk, the closing of the subscription and employment of funds received for the purpose for which the sukuk were issued* (AAOIFI, 2010).

In simple terms, *sukuk* are certificates that represent the value of an underlying asset which may be in the form of a tangible asset (airport, hospital, real estate), *usufruct* (right to the benefit derived in a property such as rent) and service (e.g. education programme), and the share of the *sukuk* holder in that underlying asset, usufruct or service.

The *sukuk* price may vary with the creditworthiness of the issuer and the market value of the underlying asset. As such, the return is not fixed or guaranteed but subject to performance of the underlying assets. The certificate value that is repaid at maturity reflects the current market price of the underlying asset rather than the original amount invested.

There are three important economic agents involved in *sukuk*: the *sukuk originator*, *sukuk investors* and *special purpose vehicle* (SPV). The *sukuk* originator (obligor or issuer) is the government or corporations needing the funds. The SPV is an entity set up to raise financial capital through *sukuk* issuance and acts as trustee in

---

[1]Note that the word *sukuk* is often used both as singular as well as plural outside of Arabic speaking countries. In the Arabic language, *sukuk* is plural and *sakk* is singular.

respect of the underlying asset or activities related to the usufruct or service for the benefit of the *sukuk* holders. The *sukuk* investors are subscribers of *sukuk* who become *sukuk* holders and jointly own the underlying assets with the SPV or enjoy the benefits derived from activities related to the usufruct or service. The service of an underwriter for *sukuk* is not always needed but may be brought in as insurance to the SPV in guaranteeing that any unsold *sukuk* will be purchased. Among the leading banks that act as underwriters for *sukuk* are CIMB Investment and Standard Chartered Bank.

5.3.2   COMPARISON BETWEEN *SUKUK* AND BONDS

There are many differences between *sukuk* and conventional bonds, and Table 5.1 presents a summary of eight major differences between them. Firstly, the relationship between the *sukuk issuer* and the *sukuk subscriber* is very different from the relationship between the bond issuer and the investor. In the case of the former, the relationship is a partnership, while the contractual relationship for a bond is that of debtor (issuer) and creditor (investor).

Table 5.1 Distinguishing *sukuk* from conventional bonds

	Features	Sukuk	Conventional bonds
1	Relationship	issuer and investor as partners	issuer as debtor and investor as creditor
2	Asset ownership	the investor has partial ownership of the underlying asset or usufruct on which the *sukuk* are based	debt obligation by the issuer to the bond holder, with no share in the ownership of the asset
3	Investment criteria	the underlying assets must be shari'ah compliant	can be used to finance any asset, project, business or joint venture that complies with local legislation
4	Type of asset	tangible asset, usufruct or service	receivables, financial assets
5	Investment rewards or returns	share of profits from the underlying asset, so can increase in value when the assets increase in value	fixed rate interest payments and principal at the bond's maturity date
6	Issue unit and issue price	each *sukuk* represents a share of the underlying asset, so the face value is based on the market value of that underlying asset	each bond represents a share of debt, with the bond price based on the issuer's credit worthiness
7	Sale	sale of ownership of the asset	sale of debt
8	Effects of costs	profit is affected by costs related to the underlying asset	return to bondholders is not affected by costs related to the asset, project, business or joint venture they support

Secondly, *sukuk holders* have proportional ownership of the underlying assets, usufruct or service on which the *sukuk* issuance is based. However, bonds do not give bondholders any share of ownership of the asset, project, business or joint venture they support, as they are creditors to the bond issuer.

Thirdly, the nature of investment is different. For *sukuk*, the investment must be in assets or usufruct that complies with *shari'ah*. The *sukuk* holder is assured that the value of the certificate corresponds to assets that are in the public good and not related to activities or products that are against Islam. In the case of bonds, the bond certificate may be backed by investment activities or assets that are not *shari'ah* compliant, and they may sometimes be bundled together with other types of assets without the investors' knowledge.

Another difference between *sukuk* and bonds is that *sukuk* are backed by tangible assets, usufruct or service that has value, while bonds simply indicate a debt obligation, so the assets will mainly be in the form of receivables and financial assets.

The next difference is in terms of returns or rewards. *Sukuk* holders receive a share of profits from the underlying asset and accept a share of any loss incurred. In contrast, bondholders receive regularly scheduled (and often fixed rate) interest payments for the life of the bond, and their principal is guaranteed to be returned.

The main advantage of *sukuk* over conventional bonds is that their value increases in relationship to the assets backing the *sukuk* certificate. If the asset rises in value, then the value of the ownership of the asset backed by the *sukuk* will also increase. Bonds do not have this characteristic. It is not possible to change the main debt in a bond. The income from a bond is the direct result of the fixed interest rate, while the value is linked to changes in the market interest rate and the creditworthiness of the issuer rather than from any kind of tangible increase in value or productivity.

The sixth difference between *sukuk* and bonds is in terms of *issue unit* and *issue price*. Each unit of *sukuk* represents a share of the underlying asset, and the *sukuk* is priced according to the real market value of the assets that are backing the *sukuk* certificate. However, each unit of bond represents a share of the underlying debt, and bond pricing is based on the credit rating of the issuer.

Another difference between *sukuk* and bonds is in terms of their sale in the secondary market. The sale of a *sukuk* is simply the sale of ownership of the asset but the sale of a bond in the secondary market is actually the sale of debt in the underlying loan relationship.

The last difference between *sukuk* and bonds is in terms of the effect of cost. *Sukuk* holders are affected by costs related to the underlying asset, so higher costs may translate to lower investor profits and vice versa. In contrast, bondholders generally are not affected by costs related to the asset, project, business or joint venture they support, and the performance of the underlying asset does not affect investor rewards.

Besides those differences, *sukuk* and bonds share some common features. Both can be liquidated or turned into cash by selling them on the secondary market. Based on the strength of their backing, both *sukuk* and bonds can be ranked by ranking institutions. There are also similar variations in *sukuk* and bond designs and issuers, allowing both Muslim and non-Muslim investors to have a variety of options when looking into these financial instruments.

Some sceptics argued that the differences between bonds and *sukuk* instrument are only in terms of mechanics. However, others argued that the discrepancies are beyond technicalities because the underlying principle is different and it is this fact that matters to Muslims. The economic difficulties that have plagued the world economy in the last decade are largely driven by the obsession on making profit from money alone rather than investment in the real economy. The artificial increase of prices based on debt and the volatility of interest rates have caused economic bubbles to form and burst, which subsequently lead to depressions and recessions in the economy.

5.3.3 ADVANTAGES AND DISADVANTAGES OF *SUKUK*

There is no doubt that there are many benefits or advantages of *sukuk* to the investors, issuers and the economy as a whole. For corporate bodies and states, *sukuk* is one of the alternative ways to raise funds to finance large business and capital projects that are beyond the ability of a single party, such as financing airports, bridges, tunnels, etc. For instance, in 2015, Emirates Airlines issued *sukuk* worth $107.5 billion, with maturity in 2025, to fund the orders for A380-800 aircrafts from Boeing and Airbus. *Sukuk* issuers may also gain reputational benefit by entering the broader ethical investment market. This can be seen in the case of the UK supermarket chain, Tesco, which issued *sukuk* worth $221 million in 2008 to fund its domestic operations in Malaysia. This indirectly signals corporate interest in attracting ethical investors. Furthermore, by issuing *sukuk*, the issuer can enhance their profile in the international markets, as they are assessed and rated by international rating agencies. If the *sukuk* is well managed and has a good rating, it will attract investors looking to invest in reputable companies. For example, Goldman Sachs issued *sukuk* with the proceeds used in the commodities business of J. Aron & Co, a Goldman unit. The *sukuk* was rated A minus by Standard & Poor's and A by Fitch Ratings, identical to the ratings of the investment bank.[2] There is a large base of untapped Islamic-compliant investors

---

[2]www.reuters.com/article/goldman-sukuk-launch/update-1-goldman-sachs-gets-strong-demand-for-landmark-sukuk-issue-idUSL6N-0RH2RH20140916, accessed 23 May 2018.

looking for products such as *sukuk*, and corporate bodies and states could issue *sukuk* as alternative way to raise funds and tap this significant source. *Sukuk* issuers who are active in Islamic markets will have marketing advantage, should they be seeking investments in those markets. For instance, Chinese entities such as Country Garden and Beijing Enterprises Water Group have issued *sukuk* through their Malaysian subsidiaries in 2015 and 2017, respectively, to finance their projects in the Southeast Asia region. *Sukuk* can be used as an instrument for socio-economic and infrastructural development of dams, highways, hospitals, schools, etc., within and outside the Muslim world.

Now, let's turn our attention to advantages of *sukuk* for investors. Firstly, *sukuk* provide investors the opportunity to deploy their capital and the ability to liquidate with ease whenever the need arises. Secondly, since *sukuk* have a maturity horizon and are in small denominations, investors can be confident with the security and profitability of the project as well as ease for clearing and settlement at the maturity date. Thirdly, *sukuk* investors can gain liquidity by freely trading their securities in the secondary market. Similarly, *sukuk* represent an excellent way for banks and Islamic financial institutions to manage their liquidity effectively. In addition, *sukuk* serve as a means for the equitable distribution of wealth, as they allow all investors to benefit from the true profits resulting from the enterprise in equal shares. Hence, it allows for the circulation of wealth on a broader scale instead of only among a handful of wealthy individuals.

However, *sukuk* also have some limitations or disadvantages. Firstly, since the key element for attracting investors is good rating of the issuer or obligor, it may be difficult for corporations or states to tap into this market without a good rating from the international rating agencies. Secondly, the standardization of documents for *sukuk* issuance has been slow to develop, which in turn has adverse cost implications. Furthermore, there is no absolute unified and settled body of opinion on the extent of *shari'ah* compliance of the structures, as *shari'ah* scholars have differing views. This may create confusions among investors. Another limitation of *sukuk* is the need to involve *shari'ah* scholars for all transactions, including the extent to which the structure used for the *sukuk* departs from the typical structures already well recognized in the market. This can add some additional cost and an element of unpredictability to the transaction structuring process. Next, the tax treatment for *sukuk* may be dissimilar to conventional bonds in certain jurisdictions. Lastly, *sukuk* based on the *ijarah* (lease) structure requires the obligor to have at its disposal permissible (*halal*) income producing assets on which to base the transaction. If the correct mechanics are not included within the documentation, the substitution of similar assets into and out of the structure would be impossible and this could limit the obligor's ability to sell or deal with the asset during the life of the transaction.

5.4   Structuring *sukuk*: types and features

5.4.1   CLASSIFICATION OF *SUKUK*

Various structures of *sukuk* have been implemented in practice. Depending on their characteristics, they may be classified based on the tradability of the certificates, the nature of the underlying assets and nature of the contract. The various classifications of *sukuk* and their characteristics are summarized in Table 5.2.

Sukuk may be classified as tradable or non-tradable. *Tradable sukuk* are investment certificates that represent tangible assets or proportionate ownership of a business or investment portfolio that can be traded in the capital market. They include, among others, *sukuk al-ijarah*, *sukuk Al-Musharakah* and *sukuk Al-Mudarabah*. On the contrary, *non-tradable sukuk* are investment certificates that represent receivables of cash or goods such as *sukuk al-murabahah* and *sukuk Al-Salam*. They cannot be traded, as they are essentially financial assets and selling them may amount to a sale of debt which is not allowed by *shari'ah*.

Sukuk can be classified as asset based or asset backed, depending on the nature of the underlying assets. Under *asset based sukuk*, the *sukuk* holders have beneficial ownership of the underlying asset and they have recourse to the originator if there is a shortfall in payments. Under *asset backed sukuk*, the *sukuk* holders own the asset and as a result do not have recourse to the asset, but to the originator, if there is a shortfall in payment.

Table 5.2 Summary on the classifications of *sukuk* and their distinguishing features

Classifications	Categories	Characteristics	Type of *sukuk*
Tradable *sukuk*	type of assets	tangible assets or proportionate ownership of a business or investment portfolio that can be traded in the capital market	*sukuk al-ijarah* *sukuk Al-Musharakah* *sukuk Al-Mudarabah* *sukuk Al-Wakalah* *sukuk Al-Istisna'a*
Non-tradable *sukuk*		receivables of cash or goods	*sukuk al-murabahah* *sukuk Al-Salam*
Asset based *sukuk*	issuer	company or government	*sukuk al-ijarah*
	sukuk holders' ownership	beneficial ownership with no right to dispose of the asset	
	recourse	purchase undertaking at par from obligor is the ultimate recourse. The recourse is only to obligor and not the asset	
	source of payment	originator/obligor's cash flows	
	presentation/disclosure of the asset	asset stays on the balance sheet of originator/obligor	
	characterization	debt like	
	rating	corporate credit rating	
Asset backed *sukuk*	issuer	SPV	*sukuk Al-Musharakah* *sukuk Al-Istisna'a*
	sukuk holders' ownership	legal ownership with right to dispose of asset	
	recourse	*sukuk* holders only have recourse to the asset, thus the asset plays a genuine role in defaults	
	source of payment	revenue generated by the underlying asset	
	presentation/disclosure of the asset	the asset is separated from the originator's books	
	characterization	equity like	
	rating	strength of cash flows	
Debt based	fixed return	pay a predetermined rate of return to investors	*sukuk al-murabahah* *sukuk Al-Salam* *sukuk Al-Istisna'a*
Equity based	variable return	profit and loss sharing based on pre-agreed ratio	*sukuk al-ijarah* *sukuk Al-Mudarabah* *sukuk Al-Musharakah* *sukuk Al-Wakalah*

In terms of disclosure, asset based *sukuk* will be disclosed in the balance sheet of the originator, while asset backed *sukuk* will be disclosed separately from the originator. Hence, asset based *sukuk* is closer to debt while asset backed *sukuk* is closer to equity. The issuer of asset backed *sukuk* is the SPV and its rating is based on strength of the cash flows. On the contrary, the issuer of asset based *sukuk* is the company or government and its rating is based on credit rating.

Another classification for *sukuk* is based on the nature of the contract. *Sukuk* structures can follow debt based or equity based principles. *Debt based instruments* such as *ijarah* (rental/lease agreement) and *murabahah* (cost plus sale) pay a predetermined rate of return to investors and are thus less recognized under *shari'ah* as they mimic conventional bonds compared to equity based investments. In contrast, *equity based instruments* follow profit and loss sharing principles of *musharakah* and *mudarabah*, which are partnership contracts in which the financier and entrepreneur share profits based on pre-agreed ratios, while losses will be shared according to their contribution (financial or physical) to the partnership.

5.4.2 TYPES OF *SUKUK*

There are many different structures of *sukuk*, but there are currently eight most commonly used in the market, as presented in Figure 5.2. In this section, we will look more closely at each of them.

Figure 5.2 Types of *sukuk*

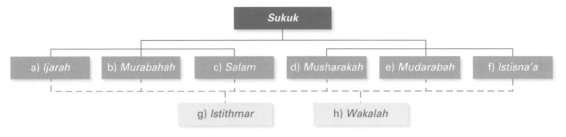

a) Sukuk al-ijarah *(lease-based* sukuk)

This is the most popular type of *sukuk*, probably because of its simplicity and also because it is highly favoured by *shari'ah* scholars. It is structured based on the *ijarah*, or lease contract, which allows for the mobilization of funds for long term infrastructure projects and also as means for securitization of tangible assets and usufruct in exchange for a rent. An example of the use of *sukuk al-ijarah* is that issued in Dubai by Nakheel Development Limited in 2006. Figure 5.3 illustrates the structuring process for *sukuk al-ijarah* based upon a sale and leaseback approach.

Figure 5.3 *Sukuk al-ijarah* based on sale and leaseback structure

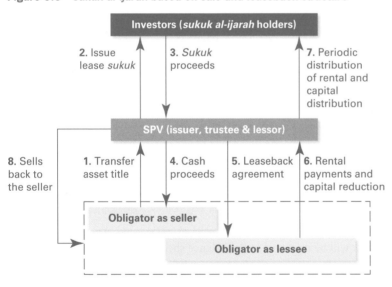

Steps involved in the structure

1. The obligator or originator needs financing and decides to liquidate some of its assets. It either establishes an SPV (issuer of *sukuk*) or enters into a sale and purchase arrangement with the SPV to sell certain assets at an agreed predetermined purchase price and transfers the title of the asset to the SPV.
2. The SPV raises financing required by issuing *sukuk al-ijarah* certificates in an amount equal to the purchase price to be subscribed by investors.
3. The SPV receives payments from *sukuk* holders for the sale of *sukuk al-ijarah* certificates.
4. The cash proceeds are passed on to the obligator (as seller) by the SPV.

5. A lease agreement is signed between the SPV and the obligator for a fixed period of time, where the SPV (lessor) leases back the assets to the obligator (as lessee).
6. SPV receives periodic rentals from the obligator and also amount for capital reduction. The amount of each rental is equal to the periodic distribution amount (PDA) payable under the *sukuk* at that time. This amount may be calculated by reference to a fixed rate or variable rate (e.g. LIBOR, i.e. London interbank offering rate) depending on the denomination of *sukuk* issued and subject to mutual agreement of the parties in advance.
7. The proceeds received by the SPV from the lessee will be distributed among the *sukuk* holders.
8. At maturity, or on a dissolution event, the SPV sells the assets back to the seller at a predetermined value which should be equal to any amounts still owed under the terms of *sukuk al-ijarah*. At this stage, the SPV may cease to exist if it has been established merely for a specific task.

b) Sukuk al-murabahah *(deferred payment or cost-plus* sukuk*)*

This type of *sukuk* structure is not frequently utilized compared to some of the other types of *sukuk* structures. However, it could be considered as a possible option when it is impossible to identify a tangible or real asset for the purpose of the underlying investment. Since *sukuk al-murabahah* certificates signify rights of the *sukuk* holder to share in receivables from the purchaser of the underlying *murabahah*, they cannot be traded on the secondary market as non-negotiable instruments. The reason for not permitting trading of this type of *sukuk* on the secondary market is due to *shari'ah's* prohibition of trading in debt except at par value. Hence, it comes as no surprise that *sukuk al-murabahah* is less attractive for prospective investors. Nevertheless, it is a popular instrument in Malaysia and is mainly used for short term financing, when liquidity is less important. Examples of the use of such *sukuk* include the one issued by Arcapita Bank based in Bahrain in 2005 and MBSB based in Malaysia in 2013. Figure 5.4 illustrates the structuring process for *sukuk al-murabahah*.

Figure 5.4 *Sukuk al-murabahah* **structure**

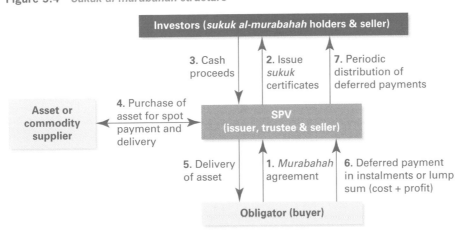

Steps involved in the structure

1. The obligator (as purchaser) enters into a *murabahah* agreement with the SPV (as seller) who agrees to sell to the obligator certain commodities on spot delivery and deferred payment terms. The period for the payment of the deferred price will reflect the maturity of the *sukuk*.
2. The SPV then issues *sukuk al-murabahah* certificates, which represent an undivided ownership interest in an underlying asset or transaction. They also represent a right against the SPV for payment of the deferred price.
3. Investors subscribe to the *sukuk al-murabahah* and pay the proceeds to the SPV who acts as trustee on behalf of the investors over the proceeds and also any commodities acquired using the proceeds.

4. The SPV purchases the required commodities from a third party or commodity supplier for a cost price representing the principal amount for spot payment. The commodity supplier makes spot delivery of the commodities to the SPV in consideration for the cost price.

5. Upon delivery from the commodity supplier, the SPV passes on the commodities to the obligator in accordance with the terms of the *murabahah* agreement.

6. The obligator makes payments of deferred price at regular intervals to the SPV. The amount of each deferred price instalment is equal to the returns payable under the *sukuk* at that time.

7. The SPV pays each deferred price instalment to the investors using the proceeds it has received from the obligator.

c) Sukuk Al-Salam *(deferred delivery purchase* sukuk*)*

In a *salam* contract, an asset is delivered to a buyer on a future date in exchange for full advance spot payment to the seller. This is allowed by *shari'ah* if the object forming the subject matter of the sale is in existence and it is in the physical or constructive possession of the seller. The use of *sukuk Al-Salam* is uncommon compared to other types of *sukuk* due to its non-tradability feature and the requirement for the originator to deliver certain 'standardized' assets to the SPV at certain future dates, which may be difficult when the originator's business model does not provide for this. An example of the use of this *sukuk* is by the Bahrain government whereby it promises to sell aluminium to the buyer at a specified future date in return of a full price payment in advance, with Bahrain Islamic Bank (BIB) being nominated to handle the transaction. *Sukuk Al-Salam* are usually used to support a company's short term liquidity requirements. Figure 5.5 illustrates the structuring process for *sukuk Al-Salam*.

Figure 5.5 *Sukuk Al-Salam* structure

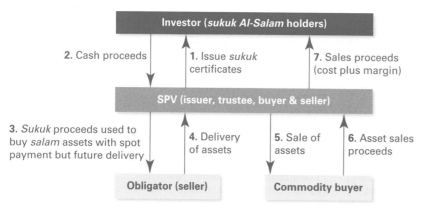

Steps involved in the structure

1. SPV issues *sukuk Al-Salam* certificates for subscriptions by investors.
2. The *salam* proceeds from *sukuk* holders are passed onto the SPV.
3. SPV signs an undertaking with the obligator to source both commodities and buyers and paying on spot to the obligator for future delivery.
4. The obligator will deliver the specified *salam* assets to the SPV.
5. The SPV will sell the *salam* assets to the commodity buyer at cost plus profit.
6. Asset sales proceeds will be paid to SPV.
7. SPV will pass on the capital and profit from sale of assets to the *sukuk* holders.

d) Sukuk Al-Musharakah *(joint venture sukuk)*

Sukuk Al-Musharakah is useful when huge sums are required for mega projects. The *sukuk* holders (investors) are the owners of the joint venture, asset or business activity and therefore have the right to share its profits on agreed upon ratios and loss according to the individual contributions. A committee of investor representatives participates in the decision making process. They are negotiable instruments that can be traded in the secondary market. An example of the use of this type of *sukuk* was by Emirates, Dubai's national airline, involving a US$ 550 million *sukuk* transaction in 2005 for a seven-year deal. The *musharakah* or joint venture was set up to develop a new engineering centre and a new headquarters building on land situated near Dubai's airport which was ultimately leased to Emirates. Profit, in the form of lease returns, generated from the *musharakah* or joint venture was used to pay the periodic distribution on the trust certificates. Figure 5.6 illustrates the structuring process for *sukuk Al-Musharakah*.

Figure 5.6 *Sukuk Al-Musharakah* **structure**

Steps involved in the structure

1. SPV issues *sukuk Al-Musharakah* certificates to raise funds from subscribers.
2. Investors subscribe to the *sukuk* and pay the proceeds to the SPV who acts as trustee over the proceeds and any assets acquired using the proceeds on behalf of the investors.
3. The SPV and the obligator enter into a *musharakah* arrangement by contributing capital and expertise to the *musharakah* entity. They will be allocated a number of units in the *musharakah* in proportion to their capital contributions.
4. On each periodic distribution date, the SPV and the obligator shall receive a pre-agreed percentage share of the expected profits generated by the *musharakah* entity. If the *musharakah* entity generated a loss, the SPV and the obligator share that loss in proportion with their capital contribution to the *musharakah* entity.
5. The SPV then pays each PDA to the *sukuk* holders using the profit it has received from the *musharakah* entity.

e) Sukuk Al-Mudarabah *(equity partnership sukuk)*

In *sukuk Al-Mudarabah*, the *sukuk* holders are the silent partners who do not participate in the management of the underlying asset, business or project. The working partner is the *sukuk* obligator, and as such is entitled to a fee and/or share of the profit as spelt out in the initial contract with investors. Examples of *sukuk Al-Mudarabah* issuances include Shamil Bank of Bahrain which raised capital worth 360 million Saudi riyal through the Al Ehsa Special Realty *Mudarabah* for investment participation in a land development transaction with a real estate development company in the Kingdom of Saudi Arabia, and the other is IIG Funding Limited, which was issued in July 2007 and listed on NASDAQ Dubai. Figure 5.7 presents the structuring process for *sukuk Al-Mudarabah*.

Figure 5.7   *Sukuk Al-Mudarabah* structure

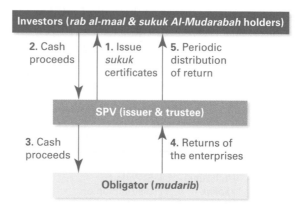

Steps involved in the structure

1. SPV issues *sukuk Al-Mudarabah* certificates which represent an undivided ownership interest in an underlying asset or transaction and a right to periodic distribution amount and the dissolution amount.
2. Investors subscribe to the *sukuk* and pay the proceeds to the SPV who acts as trustee over the proceeds and any assets acquired using the proceeds on behalf of the *sukuk* holders who are the *rab al-maal* (capital provider).
3. SPV enters into a *mudarabah* agreement with the obligator as *mudarib* and passes the proceeds to the latter who agrees to contribute its expertise and management skills to the *shari'ah* compliant *mudarabah* enterprise, with responsibility for managing the *rab al-maal's* cash contribution in accordance with specified investment parameters.
4. Profits generated from the *mudarabah* enterprise are divided between the SPV and the obligator in accordance with the profit sharing ratios set out in the *mudarabah* agreement. In addition to its profit share, the obligator as *mudarib* may be entitled to a *performance fee* for providing its expertise and management skills if the profit generated by the *mudarabah* enterprise exceeds the benchmark return. This performance fee (if any) would be calculated at the end of the *mudarabah* term and upon liquidation of the *mudarabah*.
5. SPV then pays the *mudarabah* profits it has received under the *mudarabah* agreement to the *sukuk* holders.

f) Sukuk Al-Istisna'a *(Islamic project sukuk)*

Istisna'a is an agreement made between the buyer and manufacturer or contractor for the delivery of a product or completion of a construction project at an agreed upon price and product specifications by some future date. In the case of *sukuk Al-Istisna'a*, the *sukuk* holder becomes the buyer of the project and the manufacturer or contractor is the obligator who agrees to deliver or complete the project by the agreed future date. The SPV then leases the manufactured asset for regular rental instalments. Examples of the use of *sukuk Al-Istisna'a* structure include the *sukuk* offering in 2006 by the Qatar Real Estate Investment Company (QREIC) which is listed on the Euro MTF market of the Luxembourg Stock Exchange, and the 2008 issue of *sukuk* by National Central Cooling Company (Tabreed) which is listed on the London Stock Exchange. Figure 5.8 illustrates the structuring process for *sukuk Al-Istisna'a*.

Figure 5.8 *Sukuk Al-Istisna'a* structure

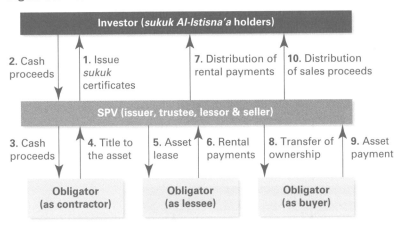

Steps involved in the structure

1. SPV issues *sukuk Al-Istisna'a* certificates, which represent an undivided ownership interest in an underlying asset or transaction and a right to periodic distribution amount and the dissolution amount.
2. Investors subscribe to the *sukuk* and pay the proceeds to the SPV who acts as trustee on behalf of the investors.
3. The SPV and the obligator enter into an *istisna'a* arrangement for the latter to manufacture or construct certain project and to deliver those assets at a future date. The SPV pays a price, typically by way of staged payments against certain milestones, to the obligator as consideration for the assets in an aggregate amount equal to the principal amount.
4. The originator will pass the title of the asset to the SPV.
5. SPV undertakes to lease the assets to the obligator under a forward lease arrangement known as *ijarah mawsufah al-dimmah*, i.e. leasing something (such as a home, office, or factory) that is not yet constructed, for an overall term that reflects the maturity of the *sukuk*.
6. The obligator, as lessee, makes advance rental payments prior to the delivery of the assets, and actual rental following the delivery of the assets at regular intervals to the SPV (as lessor). These amounts of periodic distribution may be calculated by reference to a fixed rate or variable rate (e.g. LIBOR) depending on the denomination of the *sukuk* issued and subject to mutual agreement of the parties in advance.
7. SPV pays each periodic distribution amount to the *sukuk* holders, either based on the advance rental or actual rental payments it has received from the obligator.
8. The SPV may sell the assets to the obligator in the event of maturity and transfer ownership of the assets to the originator.
9. The originator will pay the SPV for the assets which will be equal to the principal amount plus any accrued but unpaid PDAs owing to the investors or an amount sufficient to cover the dissolution amount.
10. SPV pays the dissolution amount to the *sukuk Al-Istisna'a* holders.

g) Sukuk al-istithmar *(investment sukuk)*

The term *istithmar* is broadly understood to mean an investment. When it is not possible to identify a tangible asset and if the business of the obligator is largely intangible, it is still possible to structure *sukuk* (although not universally accepted) by packaging the rights under the Islamic contracts and selling it as an investment known as *sukuk al-istithmar*. Under a *sukuk al-istithmar* structure, it is possible for *ijarah* contracts (and the relevant underlying assets), *murabahah* receivables, and/or *istisna'a* receivables (each generated by the originator), as well as shares and/or *sukuk* certificates to be packaged together and sold as an investment. The income generated by such investment can then be used to make payments to the investors. Examples of the use of such *sukuk* include the 2016 Dubai Islamic Bank's (DIB) *sukuk al-istithmar* with a value of US$ 500 million listed on Nasdaq Dubai and the Islamic Development Bank's 2009 issuance listed on the London Stock Exchange. Figure 5.9 illustrates the mechanics of the *sukuk al-istithmar* structure.

Figure 5.9   *Sukuk al-istithmar* structure

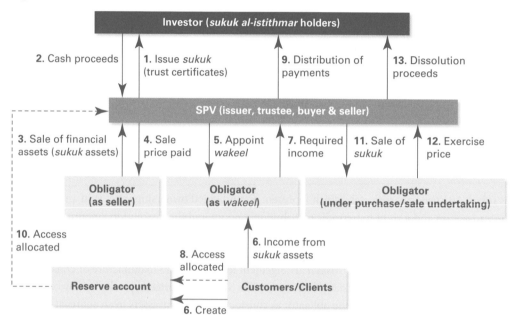

Steps involved in the structure

1. SPV issues *sukuk al-istithmar* certificates which represent an undivided ownership interest in an underlying transaction and a right to payment of the periodic distribution amount and the dissolution amount.
2. Investors subscribe to the *sukuk al-istithmar* and pay the proceeds to the SPV who acts as trustee on behalf of the investors.
3. The obligator enters into a sale and purchase arrangement with the SPV by selling a certain portfolio of financial assets.
4. The SPV pays the obligator for its purchase of the *sukuk al-istithmar* in an amount equal to the principal amount.
5. The SPV appoints another obligator as its *wakeel* (or agent) to be responsible in collecting the income comprising principal and profit for the *sukuk* assets from the relevant customers/clients for a term that reflects the maturity of the *sukuk*.
6. The obligator collects income in respect of the *sukuk* assets from the relevant customers/clients and will deposit these amounts into a collection account.
7. At regular intervals, the obligator will make income payments to the SPV in respect of the *sukuk* assets based on a target amount which is agreed for each collection period. The amount is equal to the periodic distribution amount payable under the *sukuk* at that time and may be calculated by reference to a fixed rate or variable rate (e.g. LIBOR) depending on the denomination of the *sukuk* issued and subject to mutual agreement of the parties in advance.
8. During a particular collection period, if the income amount collected in respect of the *sukuk* assets as reflected in the collection account is in excess of the required income, such excess will be credited to a reserve account of the obligator.
9. SPV pays each PDA to the investors using the required income it has received from the obligator.

10. Upon redemption of the *sukuk*, the balance of the reserve account (if any) will be paid to the SPV in order to enable the payment of the dissolution amount to the *sukuk* holders. The excess (if any) will be retained by the obligator as incentive fees.

11. In the event of default or at maturity, the SPV will sell to the obligator the *sukuk* assets at the applicable exercise price which will be equal to the principal amount plus any accrued but unpaid PDAs owing to the investors less the distributed reserve amount (if any).

12. Payment of exercise price by the obligator to the SPV.

13. SPV pays the dissolution amount to the investors using the exercise price and the distributed reserve amount (if any) it has received from the obligator.

BASIC REQUIREMENTS WHEN USING *SUKUK AL-ISTITHMAR*   Based on the principles set out in AAOIFI *Shari'ah* Standards No. 17 (Investment *Sukuk*), No. 21 Financial Paper (Shares and Bonds) and No. 23 (Agency) and other established principles relating to the concept of *istithmar*, there are a number of basic requirements to be wary of when using *sukuk al-istithmar*. They include the following:

(a) The customers/clients whose financial assets are included in the *sukuk* assets sold to the SPV must be informed of (and, in some instances, requested to consent to) the sale of those financial assets and also the role of the obligator in collecting income on behalf of the SPV.

(b) To ensure the continuing acceptance and tradability of the *sukuk*, safeguards must be included in the documentation such that the net asset value of *ijarah* contracts (together with underlying assets), shares and asset based *sukuk* certificates (i.e. non-*sukuk al-murabahah*) comprised in the *sukuk* assets at any given date is not less than 30 per cent of the net asset value of the *sukuk* assets (taken as a whole) as at the closing date. Note that 30 per cent is the minimum percentage of tangible assets as prescribed by AAOIFI, but some *shari'ah* scholars suggest a higher threshold, up to 51 per cent in some cases.

(c) To ensure that the *sukuk* assets are sufficiently segregated from the other financial assets of the obligator, appointment of a custodian may be required.

(d) The principal amounts from the underlying financial assets should never be used to service coupon payments under the *sukuk*.

(e) Although the *wakala* arrangement will require an upfront fee to be paid to the obligator as *wakeel*, it can be combined with incentive fees payable at maturity based on the overall performance of the *sukuk* assets (but care should be taken to ensure that this does not amount to profit sharing).

Besides the AAOIFI's requirements set out above, *shari'ah* scholars also hold different views on some aspects of *sukuk al-istithmar*:

(a) Dealing with a shortfall during a collection period: some *shari'ah* scholars prefer to avoid using the purchase undertaking and instead suggest that the obligator should make up any shortfall through either payments on account or provision of *shari'ah* compliant liquidity funding.

(b) There exist minimum thresholds and asset types in order to maintain the tradability of the *sukuk*.

(c) Certain roles of the obligator need to be performed by another entity altogether and/or a sub-agency or delegation arrangement needs to be put in place in order to overcome any residual concerns over the entity that will ultimately provide the purchase undertaking.

h) Sukuk Al-Wakalah *(agency sukuk)*

A more recent innovation in *sukuk* structures is *sukuk Al-Wakalah*. A *wakalah* simply refers to an arrangement whereby one party (principal) entrusts another party (agent or steward) to make decisions and/or act on behalf of the other party. The *wakalah* agreement will cover issues such as the appointment, scope of services and remuneration payable to the *wakeel*. The *sukuk Al-Wakalah* innovation structure is particularly useful in situations where there is no specific tangible asset or assets. In this case, the obligator will make a pool of assets or portfolio of investments as underlying assets to secure the issuance of the *sukuk*, which will be passed to a *wakeel* who will use his or her expertise to manage the resources made available to him or her for the best interests of the investors. Good stewardship ensures that the portfolio generates the profit expected by the principal owners. While the *wakalah* structure has some similarities with the *mudarabah* structure, what distinguishes them is in terms of profit distribution. In a *mudarabah* structure, the profit is distributed among the parties according to certain ratios, but in the *wakalah* structure the investor will only receive dividends from profits as agreed at the outset of the deal and the *wakeel* will keep any profit in excess of the agreed upon profit return as a performance or an incentive fee.

There are a number of structural issues relating to the *wakalah* which made it a less popular structure for *sukuk* issuances. An example of the use of this structure is by Dar Al Arkan Sukuk Company, which is incorporated in Cayman Island, in relation to its US$ 1.8 billion *sukuk* issuance in 2013. Figure 5.10 illustrates the structuring process of *sukuk Al-Wakalah*.

Figure 5.10   *Sukuk Al-Wakalah* **structure**

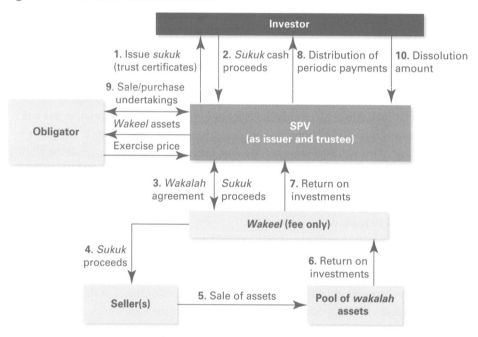

Steps involved in the structure

1. *Sukuk Al-Wakalah* certificates are issued by the SPV. The certificates represent an undivided ownership interest in the *wakalah* assets. These assets also represent a guaranteeing right for the investors against the issuer SPV to periodic distribution and dissolution amounts.
2. Investors purchase the *sukuk Al-Wakalah* certificates for a specific fixed principal amount (the *sukuk* proceeds) payable to the issuer SPV.
3. The issuer SPV, in its capacity as principal, engages a *wakeel* under a *wakalah* agreement to invest the *sukuk* proceeds in a pool of assets or portfolio of investments (the *wakalah* assets), selected by the *wakeel* and in accordance with specified criteria.
4. The *wakeel* purchases the selected *wakalah* assets from one or more sellers using the proceeds received from the *sukuk* issues.
5. The *wakeel* will manage the *wakalah* assets on behalf of the issuer SPV with the main objective of generating the expected return agreed upon with the principal. The duration of such stewardship is expected to last for the duration of the *sukuk*. Under this *wakalah* agreement, the *wakalah* assets will remain as trust assets held by the issuer SPV on behalf of the investors.

6. The profit generated from the *wakalah* assets will be passed on to the *wakeel*.

7. The *wakeel* then transfers the exact profits to fund the periodic distribution amount committed by the issuer SPV to the investors, and any profits in excess of the periodic distribution amount will be kept by the *wakeel* as incentive remuneration.

8. The periodic distribution amount will be paid to the investors on the relevant periodic distribution dates by the issuer SPV. The periodic distribution amount will be calculated based on either fixed or variable rate (e.g. based upon LIBOR).

9. Upon the maturity or in the event of default, the issuer SPV can exercise its option to require the obligator to repurchase the *wakalah* assets at an exercise price under the purchase undertaking. The exercise price is equal to the dissolution amount payable to investors together with any accrued but unpaid periodic distribution amount.

10. The issuer SPV, in its capacity as trustee, will pay the dissolution amount to *sukuk* investors using the exercise price received from obligator. By paying the dissolution amount, the *sukuk* will be redeemed and the SPV's role as trustee will end.

(I) BASIC REQUIREMENTS WHEN USING *SUKUK AL-WAKALAH* Set out below is a summary of the basic requirements that should be considered when using *sukuk Al-Wakalah* as the underlying structure:

(a) The scope of the *wakalah* arrangement must be within the boundaries of *shari'ah* compliant financial products, which implies that the principal (e.g. the SPV or the investor) cannot request the *wakeel* to perform tasks that would not otherwise be *shari'ah* compliant.

(b) The *wakalah* agreement must clearly state key issues such as the type or criteria of assets that the *wakeel* can select, the duration of the *wakalah* and the conditions for termination of the *wakalah* agreement. Additionally, the fees payable to the *wakeel* for his or her services must be specified, even if nominal, in order for the *wakalah* agreement to be valid.

(c) The principal (e.g. the SPV) can only receive the expected return, i.e. the amount to be used to fund the periodic distribution amount to investors. The excess return will be held by the *wakeel* for his or her own gain.

(d) The obligator must hold at least 30 per cent of the whole *wakalah* assets portfolio which comprise of tangible assets (such as equities or asset based *sukuk* or *ijarah* assets). In addition, the *shari'ah* supervisory board would usually impose other supplementary criteria, that may include (but not be limited to) the following:

- If the assets pool comprises equities, the *wakeel* should only buy equities where the primary business activities of the companies are *shari'ah* compliant, i.e. not connected with interest, pork related products, alcohol, gambling or other *haram* activities. Given the difficulties in finding companies that are 100 per cent *shari'ah* compliant, some *shari'ah* supervisory boards permit the buying of equities in businesses involving prohibited activities as long as the revenue generated from such activities only forms no more than five per cent of the aggregate revenue of the business.

- The *shari'ah* supervisory board may restrict the *wakeel* in engaging in highly leveraged companies as evidenced in certain financial ratios, such as debt to equity, due to *gharar*. The *wakeel*, as an alternative, may purchase equities of businesses listed on an index that has been endorsed as *shari'ah* compliant, such as the Dow Jones Islamic Index.

- If the pool of *wakalah* assets comprises *sukuk*, they must be approved by the relevant *shari'ah* supervisory board and must also be fully backed by tangible assets.

(e) A mechanism must be in place for substituting assets that are no longer *shari'ah* compliant from the pool of assets at any time during the duration of the *wakalah* and or the *sukuk*. This may be achieved through the SPV purchase undertaking or a separate replacement undertaking whereby the obligator may be required to buy back the non-compliant asset from the pool in consideration for a new *shari'ah* compliant asset.

(f) AAOIFI has restricted the obligator, under the purchase undertaking, from buying certain proportions of the *wakalah* assets for a fixed price to fund payments of periodic distribution amount provided that the obligator and seller are different entities and are independent of one another. Even when the relevant investments are held by the obligator, they should first be sold to the seller, who will in turn sell the assets on to the *wakeel*.

(II) ADVANTAGES OF ADOPTING THE *WAKALAH* STRUCTURE Despite the limitations of the *wakalah* structure, there are a number of advantages in adopting this structure, as listed below:

(a) The portfolio of assets selected by the *wakeel* may comprise a broad range of *shari'ah* compliant assets approved by the relevant *shari'ah* supervisory board for a period of time that matches the duration of the *sukuk*.

(b) The obligator, and to some extent also the *wakeel*, is able to build its statement of financial position by acquiring the investments comprised in the portfolio and to utilize them as underlying assets for the issuance of *sukuk*.

(c) The obligator is able to utilize assets that would otherwise be difficult to use as underlying assets. For instance, due to *murabahah* and *istisna'a* contracts assets being debt arrangements which are considered as financial assets, they cannot be traded on the secondary market and are also unsuitable to be used as underlying assets for the issuance of *sukuk*. However, given the nature of their contractual debt, they could be part of a portfolio of assets, provided that at least 30 per cent of the portfolio pooling comprises various tangible assets (such as equities or *ijarah* or other asset based *sukuk*). Therefore, *wakalah* structure enables the obligator to construct tradable assets of different types including those assets which, by themselves, may defy the tangibility criteria. Hence, this structure may be particularly useful for Islamic financial institutions that tend to have a large number of commodity *murabahah* and *istisna'a* contracts on their statements of financial position.

5.5   Rating of bonds and *sukuk*

Investors who want to subscribe to securities issued by companies and governments often rely on *credit rating agencies,* as they provide them with independent assessment regarding the creditworthiness and probability of default by those borrowers. There are more than 50 rating agencies globally, some being set up by the government while others by multilateral financial agencies such as the International Finance Corporation (IFC) and Islamic Development Bank (IDB). In the case of the IDB, it took the initiative to establish a transnational rating agency known as the Islamic International Rating Agency (IIRA) that focuses specifically on Islamic finance products. However, three major international rating agencies, both in the United States and globally, are Standard & Poor's Ratings Services (S&P), Moody's Investors Service (Moody's) and Fitch Ratings, with a combined market share above 90 per cent (Tichy, 2011). Besides those three, different countries have also set up their own rating agencies, such as Credit Rating Agency of Bangladesh (CRAB), Indian Credit Rating Agency (ICRA), Malaysian Rating Corporation Berhad (MARC) and Agence d'Evaluation Financiere (ADEF).

Bond ratings are based on both quantitative and qualitative factors. The former include financial ratios (especially ROE and debt ratio) and bond contract term (whether secured or not). The latter include sensitivity of earnings to the strength of the economy, impact of inflation, stability in country of operations, etc. Triple A and double A bonds are extremely safe and rarely default, single A and triple B are strong enough to be considered *investment grade bonds* (the lowest allowed for financial institutional investors by regulation) and double B and below are considered junk bonds.

5.5.1   *SUKUK* RATING AGENCIES AND METHODOLOGIES

Similar to their conventional counterpart, *sukuk* can be rated on two bases, sovereign and corporate. *Sovereign credit rating* refers to credit rating of the sovereign entity or national government by taking into consideration the risk level of its regulatory, political, economic and legal environment. The IIRA provides credit rating for a country so that a credit benchmark and sovereign ceiling for transactions involving foreign currency can be established for the purpose of *sovereign sukuk*. It analyses six basic criteria in determining the likelihood of default on *sukuk* obligations at maturity: (i) politics and policy continuity, (ii) the structure and growth of the economy, (iii) budgetary and fiscal policy, (iv) monetary policy and flexibility, (v) external accounts and (vi) internal and external debt.

Corporate credit rating is not only related to creditworthiness of the issuer but also risk level related to other aspects such as corporate governance rating, real estate rating and *shari'ah* quality rating, etc. Besides the Big Three (S&P, Moody's, Fitch) the other two principal agencies that have experience in rating *sukuk* are MARC and IIRA. The methodology adopted by these rating agencies differs, hence it is important to understand the underlying criteria or factors being considered in coming up with the rating.

The ratings of S&P are an opinion about the ability and willingness of an issuer to meet financial obligations in a timely manner, without actually commenting on *shari'ah* compliance. Although it distinguishes between three types of *sukuk* (i.e. *sukuk* with full credit enhancement mechanisms, *sukuk* with partial credit enhancement mechanisms and *sukuk* with no credit enhancement mechanism), it applies the same definition of default to *sukuk* as it does to conventional bonds (Hassoune, 2007).

Moody's ratings address credit risk and not legal compliance of an instrument with *shari'ah* criteria and uses English law as a reference for contractual obligations (Howladar, 2006). According to Hassoune (2007), Moody, in April 2007, established rating methodologies applicable to *sukuk* which hinged on whether they were asset based or asset backed *sukuk*. The rating methodology used for assessing the risk of unsecured asset based *sukuk* focuses on the creditworthiness of the sponsor, an approach which is similar as for conventional bonds. As for the secured asset backed *sukuk*, the ratings approach is similar to that for tradable securitization transactions, while also acknowledging the Islamic features.

Fitch Ratings agency is known to provide constructive and objective credit ratings on the Islamic finance market (i.e. rating instruments such as *sukuk* and institutions) for more than a decade. Given its strong track record in Islamic finance, Fitch Ratings was able to rate 95 outstanding Islamic finance instruments worldwide and 31 Islamic finance based issuers (See Figure 5.11). Fitch Ratings agency has a special group called Islamic Finance Group/Team which coordinates all the activities related to Islamic finance across the sovereign, financial institutions, corporates, structured finance, infrastructure and insurance teams. Besides involvement in the rating process of Islamic finance instruments, the group also monitors and reports on the sector's growth development through specialized commentary and research. Since the group spans various time zones and continents, they are able to combine local knowledge with strategic global perspective to provide the latest update on major developments across regions and sectors, industry outlooks, market trends, including Rating Action Commentaries (RACs) on different debt issuance, and Fitch Wires, special reports on specific commodities, services and sectors worldwide, etc.

MARC analyses five components in the rating of a *sukuk* transaction: (i) the basic structure of the *sukuk* by distinguishing between the application for conventional corporate and project finance and asset backed methodology; (ii) assessment of credit quality and the roles and performance ability of key transaction parties – originator/borrower, lessee(s) or obligor(s), guarantor(s), contractor, and servicer/back-up servicer; (iii) asset and cash flow analysis of asset backed and non-recourse or limited recourse project finance *sukuk*; (iv) assessment of credit enhancement and structural protections, such as reserve accounts, payment waterfalls and collateral value in addition to external credit support; and (v) legal analysis not only in the context of any securitization but also from the perspective of any secured financing (Leong, 2006; 2008).

The IIRA has a total of eight different ratings for Islamic products: sovereign rating, issuer rating, *sukuk* rating, insurer financial strength rating, *shari'ah* quality rating, corporate governance quality rating, bank financial strength rating and real estate rating. We have mentioned earlier the criteria used in assessing sovereign rating for *sukuk* and will instead focus on the other types of rating.

Figure 5.11   Fitch Ratings of Islamic Finance Coverage by Regions, Sectors and Volumes for 2016

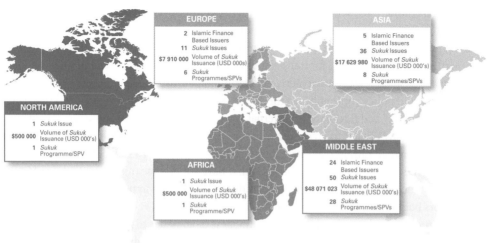

Source: www.internationalfinance.com/magazine/sukuk-issuance-promises-a-good-year

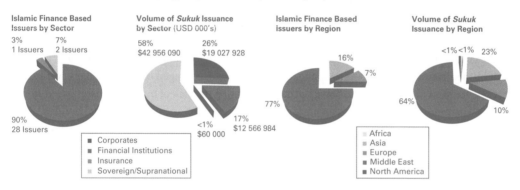

Issuer rating relates to the *sukuk* issuer's overall financial and institutional creditworthiness, which would determine the level of confidence potential investors would have in it. *Sukuk rating* is related to the viability of the *sukuk* in the secondary market. This is assessed based on the documented terms and covenants along with the risk/return measures which would determine the number of potential *sukuk* subscribers. *Insurer financial strength rating* is related to the financial strength of the *sukuk*'s insurer in meeting contractual obligations and this is assessed based on both qualitative (country risk of the domicile of the company and its business profile) and quantitative (strength of company's balance sheet and operating performance) factors. The strength of this rating is important to potential investors in their consideration for avoiding or mitigating risks.

Shari'ah quality rating, which does not form part of the assessment of the Big Three (S&P, Moody's, Fitch), is one of the most fundamental aspects of IIRA's assessment that is vital to the investing public looking to invest in *shari'ah* compliant corporate entities and products. The methodology adopted by IIRA in assessing level of *shari'ah* compliance involves looking at the following major elements:

- procedure of authentication of products and services
- safeguards against comingling of funds in the case of an Islamic window or branch of a conventional financial institution
- code of ethics adopted by the institution
- policy on the calculation of profit or loss
- whether type of business undertaken are *shari'ah* compliant
- whether assets and liabilities are *shari'ah* compliant

Corporate governance quality rating is related to the standard or quality of governance of the corporate entity responsible for managing the issuance of *sukuk*. This is assessed based on key elements of the corporate governance structures recognized at the global level as well as best practices in the field as benchmarks for transparency, fairness, responsibility and accountability.

Bank financial strength rating is related to asset quality, covering aspects such as the banking environment, investment policies and loan administration procedures, portfolio composition and characteristics as well as quality of forecasting, risk management practices, lending history and performance and economic values. Those aspects are assessed via the following set of fundamentals: liquidity and funds management, market assessment, information systems, earnings performance, asset/liability management, capital adequacy, etc. Higher rating denotes ability of the entity to make profits and pay dividends.

Lastly, *real estate rating* deals with the overall rating of the developer and this is assessed based on the developer's activities such as the performance of its architects, engineers, contractors and other important personnel.

5.6 Development and contemporary issues related to *sukuk*

As a recent innovation, *sukuk* has changed the dynamics of the Islamic finance industry. Today it is recognized as the main contributor to the exponential growth of Islamic financial assets in recent years (Godlewski, Turk-Ariss and Weill, 2011). The early issuance of *sukuk* in Malaysia in 2000 and Bahrain in 2001 was based on the simple *ijarah* structure. However, in the last decade, new approaches in *sukuk* structuring (as discussed in the preceding section) have made it popular both as a means for government to raise finance through *sovereign sukuk* as well as companies to raise funding through the offer of *corporate sukuk*.

Sovereign and quasi sovereign issuers dominate the *sukuk* market, representing more than half of aggregate issuances, while supra-national bodies, such as the IDB and the Islamic Liquidity Management Corporation (IILM), additionally drove the business with substantial issuances. Corporate guarantors were chiefly from the financial segments of Turkey and Malaysia. While most *sukuk* before 2010 were based on debt structures, especially *murabahah*, there is now an increasing trend in issuing investment based structures based on *ijarah* and *wakalah*.

Multinational corporations, state corporations and financial institutions have all used international *sukuk* issuance as an alternative to syndicated financing. For instance, *sukuk* have provided the government with financing during economic downturn to finance public development projects such as hospitals, motorways, ports and airports. *Sukuk* have also been used as an instrument for project financing in numerous cases, including Kuala Lumpur International Airport and the Dubai Palm Islands. Real estate developers, construction companies, energy producers, transport companies, civil aviation and other sectors have issued *sukuk* to finance their projects. Rated issuers and the various issuances have helped Islamic financial institutions manage short term liquidity. *Sukuk* were also issued for social responsibility causes such as financing for tsunami victims and rehabilitation in Acheh in 2005, and in the Middle East to increase food production capacity (Abdelhady, 2012). The most recent phenomenon is the Green *Sukuk* or 'Socially Responsible Initiatives (SRI) *Sukuk*' which will be utilized to fund activities related to the protection of natural resources, advancement of renewable energy and economic development.

Sukuk are a truly global security. Asia has the most number of *sukuk* issues and the developed primary and secondary market for *sukuk* are worth $20.8 billion. Malaysia is the largest issuer with 70.5 per cent of the Asian market share[3] and 1897 issues compared to 386 from the MENA region. Other issuers include Pakistan, Singapore and Brunei. Indonesia and Bangladesh have also been involved in issuing *sukuk* to meet capital development and working capital needs and liquidity management, respectively. In the MENA region, GCC countries dominate the *sukuk* market with issuance of $94.4 billion, of which Saudi Arabia has the highest issuance worth $10.5 billion. Tunisia and Libya have amended their legislation to allow for sovereign *sukuk* issues. In the African continent, Gambia, Sudan, Egypt and Kenya have issued *sukuk* while South Africa planned to issue a sovereign *sukuk*.

---

[3]GIFF 2012 www.assaif.org/content/download/31707/162231/file/2.1%20An%20Overview%20of%20the%20Islamic%20Finance%20Industry.pdf, accessed 18 June 2018.

In the non-Muslim world, IFC has issued $200 million worth of *sukuk*, East Cameron Gas Company $165.7 million and GE Capital $500 million (GIFF, 2012). According to Zawya.com, 22 countries have outstanding *sukuk* in 13 currencies. *Sukuk* are listed globally on many European Stock Exchanges, especially the London Stock Exchange which has listed 65 *Sukuk* worth $48 billion, making it a major listing centre. Within the EU, Luxembourg became the first AAA rated government to issue a euro denominated Islamic sovereign sukuk in 2014. This was followed by the Irish Stock Exchange, with France recently amending its rules to allow *sukuk* listing (GIFF, 2012).

Despite *sukuk* being issued under various structures and accepted as a global financial instrument, this mode of finance is said to be far from fully developed. The *sukuk* market experienced over 50 per cent decline in the number of *sukuk* issues in 2008 and market experts have partly blamed it on the criticism made by Sheik Muhammad Taqi Usmani, a leading *shari'ah* scholar and *shari'ah* board chairman at AAOIFI. He stated that as much as 85 per cent of the outstanding *sukuk* had failed the test of *shari'ah* compliance and declared the reasons being as follows:

- Existence of cases where the assets in the *sukuk* were the shares of companies that do not confer true ownership, but merely offer *sukuk* holders a right to returns.
- Most *sukuk* issued are identical to conventional bonds in terms of the distribution of profits from their enterprises at fixed percentage, bench marked on interest rates, while the legal presumption regarding *sukuk* is that no fixed rate of profit or the refund of capital can be guaranteed.
- Almost all *sukuk* issues guarantee the return of the principal to the holder at maturity (just as in conventional bonds) through a binding promise from either the issuer or the manager to repurchase the assets at the stated price regardless of their true or market value at maturity.

To enhance transparency and bring the substance of *sukuk* products closer to the basic principles of *shari'ah*, AAOIFI made an amendment to FAS 17 in February 2008 and issued a guidance statement on accounting for investments which included:

- *Sukuk* issuances have to be backed by real assets, the ownership of which has to be legally transferred to the *sukuk* holders to be tradable.
- *Sukuk* must not represent receivables or debts, except in the case of a trading or financial entity selling all its assets or a portfolio with a standing financial obligation in which some debts, owed by a third party and incidental to physical assets or usufruct, are unintentionally included.
- The manager of the *sukuk* is prohibited from extending loans to make up for the shortfall in the return on the assets, whether acting as a *mudarib* (investment manager), *sharik* (partner), or *wakeel* (agent).
- Guarantees to repurchase the assets at nominal value upon maturity are prohibited, except for *sukuk ijarah* structures.

Recently, three issues on the development of equity based *sukuk* have been debated. They are in relation to:

(i) *sukuk* structure risk
(ii) pricing mechanism for *musharakah sukuk*
(iii) identifying a common structure for *ijarah sukuk* that is compatible with all *madhahib* (Islamic doctrines)

The focus on this type of *sukuk* is understandable given that the ownership of the assets associated with equity based *sukuk* are not owned by the *sukuk* holders but merely a partner in loss but not in profit. We will briefly look at each of these issues more closely.

5.6.1 SUKUK STRUCTURE RISK MATRIX

In Islam, risk sharing in profit and loss is considered as the best method for establishing justice among parties involved in terms of efforts and rewards, and between labour and capital. The commingling of capital and labour to establish a partnership is an essential feature of the risk management framework, and the behavioural norms of individuals are crucial in establishing the system of justice. Equity based *sukuk* is seen as attractive from the investor's perspective, since they are either asset backed or at least asset based when the offering reduces investment risks, the value of the issue is largely stable, and the investment time horizon is fixed. However, this type of *sukuk* encounters several unique risks. IFSB Standard 7 (2005) recognizes that *sukuk* risks are quite complex due to the innovation of *sukuk* structures. The standard identifies five *sukuk* risks components: originator, servicer, issuer, SPV and holder (investor). Tariq and Dar (2007) present risk characteristics of each type of *sukuk* structure by linking them to the underlying *shariʾah* structures. They identified eight risk factors associated with the types of *sukuk*: credit risk, rate of return risk, foreign exchange risk, price risk, liquidity risk, business risk, *shariʾah* compliance risk and infrastructure rigidities. Alswaidan *et al.* (2017), drawing upon the work of Tariq and Dar (2007) and information contained in IFSB Standard 7 (2005), illustrate the risks associated with *sukuk* securitization in a horizontal structure. They expanded the classification of *sukuk* risk into a matrix with four categories: debt based, equity based, assets based and agency based. Having such a *sukuk* structure risk matrix classification provides a better understanding of the risks underlying *sukuk* structures and in identifying risks and estimating the reward measurement of each structure.

5.6.2 PRICING MECHANISM FOR SUKUK MUSHARAKAH

Another recent issue discussed in the literature is the pricing mechanism for *sukuk musharakah* (joint venture). The current practice of pricing *musharakah sukuk* is based on the profit and loss sharing ratio between the financiers and entrepreneurs. However, companies tend to keep a portion of the profits made for reinvestment. This means that investors do not get their full share of the profit and they may be substantially underpaid especially if the company aims to retain more profit to strengthen its capital and expand its activities. Furthermore, Ahroum and Achchab (2017) argue that the pricing of *sukuk musharakah* is affected by the high costs of issuance including high legal and accounting fees, lack of established norms in the structuring process of *sukuk*, and *sukuk* secondary markets that are relatively non-liquid. Similarly, due to limited issuance of sovereign *sukuk*, it makes it difficult to construct benchmark yield curves to price *sukuk*. According to Jobst *et al.* (2008), the price discovery in *sukuk* secondary market is inefficient and they are traded at a premium over conventional bonds due to the inadequacy of the evaluation model in capturing the underlying nature of *sukuk*.

5.6.3 IDENTIFYING STRUCTURE FOR SUKUK IJARAH COMPATIBLE WITH ALL MADHAHIB

One of the major problems with structuring of Islamic financial instruments is the differences in the Islamic *madhahib* (school of thoughts of Islamic jurisprudence). There are four prominent *madhahib* that have survived, namely, the *Hanafi, Hanbali, Maliki* and *Shafi*. The *Hanafi madhab* method of interpretation is based on *qiyas* (analogy), *Hadith* or *Sunnah* for the *Maliki* and *Hanbali madhahib*, and for the *Shafi madhab*, a combination of *Hadith* and *qiyas* (they used *hadith* more than the *Hanafi* and *qiyas* more than the other two).

Over time, each school has found some semblance with a particular region and this has led to geographical concentration of followers of a *madhab* in certain locations. The *Hanbali madhab* is primarily located in Saudi Arabia; *Maliki madhab* is dominated in Arabian Gulf States (Kuwait, Qatar, Bahrain, Dubai and Abu Dhabi), Spain, East and West African countries (upper Egypt, the Sudan, Tunisia, Algeria, Libya, Morocco, Mali, Nigeria, Chad, Niger, Senegal, Mauritania), Basra, Syria and Yemen; *Shafi madhab* is dominant in Indonesia, Malaysia, Brunei, East Africa and parts of Yemen and Egypt, while the most dominant and far spread followers of the *Hanafi madhab* live in Turkey, Egypt, Syria, Lebanon, Jordon, Iraq and the Indian subcontinent.

Since the *madhahib* are regionally located, the financial policies and types of products offered in a particular region follow a particular *madhab*. Thus, financial instruments or products acceptable under a particular regional *madhab* may not be acceptable under another *madhab*. This has created confusion for both Muslim and non-Muslim potential investors. Therefore, there have been calls to search for commonalities that are acceptable to all *madhahib* and that can satisfy the followers of any *madhab of Islamic Fiqh* when developing products. Rafay *et al.* (2017) studied 21 *sukuk ijarah* issuances in their attempt at developing a unified framework acceptable by all *madhahib* for *ijarah sukuk*. They conclude that the following steps must be taken by *shariʾah* scholars, regulatory bodies and Islamic financial institutions to ensure a globally uniform protocol for *ijarah sukuk*:

- The issuer of *sukuk al-ijarah* should not involve itself with *haram* activities and the underlying assets should have *halal* usage.
- After the issuance of *sukuk al-ijarah*, the lessee should aim for the underlying asset to be used in *halal* operations.

- *Sukuk al-ijarah* should be structured along the lines of sale and leaseback structure or a joint *istisna'a*. It should be followed by *ijarah* contract with the *ijarah* rentals beginning when the *istisna'a* terms are fulfilled, the underlying asset is ready for use and is in the possession of the lessee.
- *Sukuk al-ijarah* can be issued for any tenure and any currency.
- *Sukuk al-ijarah* should be asset backed and it is preferable that the issuer transfer not only the usufruct but also the title.
- The SPV should be independent of the originator.
- Only credit guarantee can be attached to the *sukuk al-ijarah* and performance guarantee should be avoided.
- Mandatory liquidity facility should not be required for *sukuk al-ijarah*.
- The underlying asset should not be subordinated.
- The rentals can be fixed or floating, preferably with unconventional benchmarks and the amount due to investors in either case should be known before the start of period to avoid *gharar*.
- *Sukuk al-ijarah* should preferably be listed and tradable on a recognized stock exchange and rated by any international credit rating agency.
- The buyback of assets should be agreed with a unilateral promise acceptable with a post *ijarah* sales price.
- *Sukuk al-ijarah* should not be convertible in kind for principal repayment.

5.7 Derivatives

5.7.1 CONCEPT OF HEDGING

Hedging refers to the act of engaging in financial transactions as a proactive measure purposefully directed at reducing or eliminating exposure to various risks within the market environment. It may be likened to insurance where a person buys an insurance policy to reduce the impact of loss from unexpected death or destruction to the property. Similarly, portfolio managers, investors, and corporations use hedging to reduce the potential effects of future business risks arising from adverse price movements in the value of an asset.

There are three approaches to hedging: economic hedging, cooperative hedging and contractual hedging. *Economic hedging* involves a strategic arrangement by the corporate management to diversify investment without dealing with third parties or agents to achieve their purpose of hedging. It can be independent of or complementary to other hedging strategies. *Cooperative hedging*, on the other hand, involves a strategic partnership among market players to overcome economic problems. Hence, it requires social interaction among the market players through cooperation and partnership in investment activities. It is similar to cooperative insurance which involves risk sharing and proper management of the risk. *Contractual hedging* involves contractual financial instruments, which are, in most cases, for profit instruments. The same financial instruments can be modified to accommodate finance, risk management and ownership together. Hedging can be undertaken by investors as a risk mitigation technique through the use of complex financial instruments known as derivatives.

5.7.2 DEFINITION AND TYPES OF DERIVATIVES

Derivatives are financial instruments or securities whose value or price depends upon or is derived from the value of one or more underlying assets, or from the value of a rate or index of asset value. Derivatives are generally used as an instrument to hedge risks. This is why they are considered to be financial instruments for trading risks. They are also used for speculative purposes within the *secondary market* (a financial market where previously issued securities such as bonds and shares are bought and sold).

The most common types of derivatives are *forward contracts, futures contracts, options* and *swaps*. These derivatives are contracts that can be structured in a way to serve as underlying assets. We will first look at the mechanics of each instrument to gain a good understanding, which will later help us comprehend the Islamic paradigm for risk mitigation using such derivatives that are *shari'ah* compliant.

a) Forward contracts

Forward contracts are *non-standardized agreements* (flexible in terms of quantity and date of delivery) by two parties to involve in the future sale or purchase of an asset at a price agreed on the spot (*forward price*), but the underlying asset is delivered at a future date. Hence, a forward contract is generally regarded as a contract where the parties *lock in* the price when entering into the contract to avoid future fluctuations in the market. In other words, the agreed price for the asset is paid before delivery. Such contracts are typically used for commodities and exchange rates. For example, a farmer can enter into a forward contract with a bank to lock in a price for wheat from the upcoming harvest to hedge against price fluctuation. Forward contracts can also be used by investors and portfolio managers as a means of speculation on future fluctuations in the market value to hedge for currency or exchange rate risks.

The advantage of forward contracts is that both parties can be as flexible as they would like to be. The disadvantage of forward contracts is lack of liquidity, as the seller must find a counterparty willing to buy the contract, giving rise to liquidity risk as there is limited market for trading them. Another disadvantage is that parties to the contract are still subject to default risk, hence it is important for the parties involved to check on the credibility of their counterparty.

b) Futures contracts

Futures contracts are standardized agreements between two parties to exchange a specified asset with a known standardized quantity and quality at a price agreed upon by the parties on the spot (known as *futures price or strike price*), while delivery is made at a specified future date. The difference between forward and futures contracts is that the former is not exchange-traded while futures are exchange-traded derivatives. For instance, a wheat supplier or trader would like to secure the selling price of wheat for the next crop season, and at the same time there is a manufacturer or trader who seeks to secure its buying price of wheat. Since both have similar objectives, i.e. to secure the asset at a certain price, they will enter into a futures contract providing that in the next six months, 1000 tonnes of wheat will be delivered to the manufacturer at a price of US$ 3000 per tonne regardless of price fluctuations in the market. In other words, by entering into the futures contract, the parties have hedged or prevented future market risks.

Futures contracts are traded on the floor of a *futures exchange*, which is a centralized financial market where contracting parties can trade standardized futures contracts. Note that it is the contract instrument that can be sold or bought in the futures market and not the wheat itself. Financial futures are traded either to speculate on prices or to hedge exposure to price movements. *Speculators* commonly serve as the counterparty to hedgers for futures transactions and provide liquidity to the futures market.

The advantage of a futures contract is that it is easier to match parties due to the standardized nature of the quantity and delivery date. Furthermore, once the contract has been bought, it can be traded again at any time until the delivery data, hence help overcome liquidity risk. Another advantage is that the default risk is lower in the case of futures contract, because it is the clearing house that oversees the activities rather than on individual basis.

c) Options

An *option* is a financial derivative that gives the holder the option (*right*) to buy or sell the underlying asset at a specified price (exercise or strike price) within a specific period of time (*term to expiration*). The holder is only given the right and it does not constitute an obligation. The seller of the option is called the *writer* and the buyer of the option is called the *owner*. Since the option to buy or sell at a specified price has value, the buyer is willing to pay an amount called a *premium* at the start of the contract. The options contract can be an American or European option. An *American option* can be exercised at any time up to the expiration date while a *European option* can be exercised only on the expiration date.

A *call option* grants the holder the right *to buy* an underlying asset at the exercise price within a specific period of time while a *put option* grants the holder the right *to sell* an underlying asset at the exercise price within a specific period of time. The *call contract* guarantees the buyer a *maximum price* or the *strike price*: if the price of the underlying asset is above the strike price, a claim (difference between strike price and market price) can be made, and if the price is below the strike price, the option is not exercised. A *put contract* guarantees the seller a *minimum price* or the strike price: if the price of the underlying asset is *below* the strike price, a claim can be made, and if the price is above the strike price, the option is not exercised. For example, assume an investor holds a *call option* that gives him the right to purchase the shares of a company at a striking price of £110 and paying a premium of £9 for the right. This means that he will only exercise his option or right when the price on the maturity date exceeds £110, as there is a gain to be made. The net gain will be after deducting the premium. In contrast, if the investor holds a *put option* with the same striking price and premium, he will only exercise his option or right when the price on the maturity date falls below £110 to make a gain. Table 5.3 illustrates the gain or loss from a call and put option at different maturity prices.

Table 5.3 Contingency table showing gains or losses for various maturity prices

Item	Call contract strike price of £110, premium £9				
	£	£	£	£	£
Possible market price at maturity	105.00	110.00	115.00	120.00	125.00
Maturity price above the strike price?	N	N	Y	Y	Y
How much to claim?	0.00	0.00	5.00	10.00	15.00
Less contract premium	(9.00)	(9.00)	(9.00)	(9.00)	(9.00)
Net gain (loss)	(9.00)	(9.00)	(4.00)	1.00	6.00
Item	Put contract strike price of £110, premium £9				
Possible market price at maturity	105.00	110.00	115.00	120.00	125.00
Maturity price above the strike price?	Y	N	N	N	N
How much to claim?	5.00	0.00	0.00	0.00	0.00
Less contract premium	(10.00)	(10.00)	(10.00)	(10.00)	(10.00)
Net gain (loss)	(5.00)	(10.00)	(10.00)	(10.00)	(10.00)

The advantages of options are that they can be used to limit losses from fluctuations in market prices and thus enhance their asset returns. They also enable investors to obtain additional gain on the contract through a small premium payment. Moreover, options are an inexpensive way to gain access to the underlying investment without having to buy the assets. Since the terms of listed options are regulated and traded on an exchange, they are standardized. The disadvantages of options include the option contract expiring worthless and the default risk increases the shorter the time to its expiration. Similarly, regulatory intervention such as tax may prevent investors from exercising their options, as they are perceived as not desirable for their purpose. Options, as a diversification strategy, cannot eliminate risk, thus rendering the investors' attempt at enhancing their portfolio returns worthless.

d) Swaps

A *swap* can be defined as an agreement between two parties to exchange a series of cash flows for a set period of time. The exchange normally involves one financial instrument for another for the mutual benefit of the parties. Similar to other derivative instruments, they are both used either to hedge for risks or to speculate. Firms may engage in swaps to change the quality of issues, either as bonds or stocks, or due to a sudden change in their investment objectives. This provides them with benefit in the form of cash flow where each of the parties exchanges their individual cash flow streams (legs of swap) for the other in order to mutually benefit from the exchange.

Unlike the futures and options contracts which are standardized financial instruments that can be exchanged in the market, swaps are customized contracts traded over-the-counter (OTC) market between private parties. The swaps market is dominated by firms and financial institutions. When counterparties enter into a swap agreement, the agreement must clearly stipulate the way the cash flows are calculated and the dates they will be paid. At the initiation of the contract, the series of cash flows may be determined by some variable such as *interest rate, foreign exchange rate, equity price* or *commodity price*. There are various types of swaps: *interest rate swaps, currency swaps, credit default swaps* and other more complicated versions of interest rate swaps such as *commodity swaps, equity swaps, forward swaps* and *options swaps*. We will briefly consider three types of swaps, namely, *interest rate swaps, currency swaps, credit default swaps*.

Interest rate swaps, as the name implies, involve the exchange of one set of interest payments for another set of interest payments, all denominated in the same currency. The most common and simplest interest rate swap is the *plain vanilla swap* or *fixed-for floating swap*. In this swap, the parties specify: the interest rate on the payments that are being exchanged; the type of interest payments (*fixed or variable/floating*); the amount on which the interest is paid (*notional principal*); and the time period over which the exchanges continue to be made. The specified payment dates are called *settlement dates*, and the time between are called *settlement periods*. Because swaps are customized contracts, interest payments may be made annually, quarterly, monthly or at any other interval determined by the parties.

For example, Bank A has negotiated a plain vanilla swap in which it agrees to pay Bank B a fixed interest rate of 9 per cent for a floating interest rate equal to LIBOR (London Interbank Offer rate) plus 1 per cent on a notional principal of US$ 100 million. Assume that at the settlement date, the LIBOR rate is 7 per cent. Hence, the floating rate will be 8 per cent (LIBOR +1%). Therefore, Bank A will pay Bank B interest payments of US$ 9 million (9% × $100m) and Bank B will pay Bank A US$ 8 million (8% × $100m). Since swap contracts allow for payments to be netted against each other to avoid unnecessary payments, Bank A will pay Bank B US$ 1 million and Bank B pays nothing to Bank A. Assume now that the LIBOR is 9 per cent, which means the floating rate will now be 10 per cent. Therefore, Bank A will pay Bank B interest payments of US$ 9 million (9% × $100m) and Bank B will pay Bank A US$ 10 million (10% × $100m). Since swap contracts allow for payments to be netted against each other to avoid unnecessary payments, Bank B will pay Bank A US$ 1 million and Bank A pays nothing to Bank B.

An advantage of interest rate swap is that it helps financial institutions to reduce transaction costs which banks need to incur when rearranging their balance sheet without the swap. Disadvantages of interest rate swap are similar to that of forward contract. It lacks liquidity as it cannot be exchanged and also suffers from default risk, but not on the full amount of notional principal.

Currency swaps involve the exchange of a set of payments in one currency for a set of payments in another currency at a specified exchange rate and at specified intervals. Assume there are two parties: Company A is based in the USA and it trades with Company B which is based in Brazil. Company A borrow the funds that Company B needs from an American bank while Company B borrows the funds that Company A will need through a Brazilian bank. In other words, they have effectively taken out a loan for each other. If the exchange rate between Brazil (BRL) and the US ($) is 1.60BRL/1.00$ and both companies require the same equivalent amount of funding, then Company B will receive $100 million from Company A in exchange for 160BRL real notional amount when the loans are swapped. Nevertheless, both companies must still incur interest payments equivalent to the other party's cost of borrowing. This last point forms the basis of the advantage that a currency swap provides.

Credit default swaps (CDS) are privately negotiated contracts to protect investors against default risk on a particular debt instrument such as bonds. They involve two parties, a buyer who is willing to make periodic payments to the seller, who receives payments but is obligated to reimburse the buyer if the debt instrument specified in the swap agreement default. For example, firm A purchased bonds issued by firm B with par value £100 million and a bank is willing to sell the contract over five years for a premium of 2 per cent. This means that the payments to be made by the firm to the bank will be £2 million annually (2% × £100m). If firm B files for bankruptcy, then the bank is obligated to pay £100 million to firm A. If the bonds do not default, then firm A is not obligated to pay the bank.

5.8   Islamic derivatives

5.8.1   THE ISLAMIC PERSPECTIVE ON HEDGING

In conventional hedging, speculation in derivatives is often carried out to maximize profit rather than to facilitate business activity. That is why it is uncommon to see the actual delivery of the underlying asset in the contract and this is where the speculative elements of *gharar* (uncertainty) and *maysir* (gambling) are prohibited by the *shari'ah*. Hence, when the speculative and gambling elements are removed from the process of hedging in conventional practice, it may be adopted within the *shari'ah* framework of investments.

The majority of Islamic finance experts have agreed that hedging can be modified to suit the requirements of *shari'ah* and this is allowed in order to reduce risk and protect investments as long as the fundamental prohibitions in Islamic commercial transactions are excluded. This is also applicable if the sole purpose of hedging is to protect against loss of value as a result of various factors such as currency fluctuation, change in benchmark rates, etc., in the transaction involving an underlying real asset. Market speculators are not allowed to deliberately expose themselves to risk in order to gain profit from currency fluctuations as this is tantamount to gambling. Any type of derivatives, i.e. futures, forwards, swaps or options contracts, involving market speculation is not *shari'ah* compliant.

5.8.2   DEFINITION AND TYPES OF ISLAMIC DERIVATIVES

As the concept of hedging involves the use of the different types of derivatives to reduce potential risks, this section examines the Islamic perspectives on the main derivatives we discussed earlier but are modified to make them *shari'ah* compliant. The *Shari'ah* Compliant Derivative Instrument Islamic Financial Service Act 2013 defines Islamic derivatives as:

> *Any agreement, including an option, a swap, futures or forward contract, that is made in accordance with* shari'ah, *whose market price, value, delivery or payment obligations is derived from, referenced to or based on, but not limited to, Islamic securities, commodities, assets, rates (including profit rates or exchange rates) or indices.*

The type of Islamic derivatives that are currently in use include *Islamic Forward Contract (IFC)*, *Islamic Foreign Exchange Swaps (IFXS)*, *Islamic Cross Currency Swaps (ICCS)*, *Islamic Profit Rate Swaps (IPRS)* and *Islamic Options Futures (IOF)*. Figure 5.12 presents the various types of Islamic derivatives.

Figure 5.12   Islamic derivatives instruments

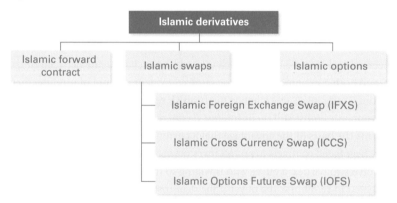

a) Islamic forward and futures contracts

The main feature of forward and futures is deferment in price and asset transfer to a future date. However, to defer both price and asset to future date is controversial, due to the issue of *gharar*. The OIC *Fiqh* Academy ruled that deferring both the counter values in the trading of commodities (forward contract) is not permissible. However, if the *salam* rules are followed, then this becomes permissible. Other instruments/contracts that exist in Islamic finance such as *istisna'a* and *ju'alah* (refer to Chapter 4 for explanation of these contracts) could also be considered as a basis for structuring forward/futures contracts within an Islamic framework. Each of those contracts is concerned with deferred transactions and applies to different situations.

In futures trading, buyer and seller are required to take or make physical or cash settlement delivery upon expiry of the time specified, unless they close their position, i.e. re-sell the futures before its expiry. This normally happens when the parties feel that the contract has risen or fallen in their favour. For example, a trader who bought a futures contract will sell it to close out when the price goes up. On the other hand, if a trader has sold a futures contract, he will buy back to close out when the price goes down. The OIC *Fiqh* Academy ruled that the practice of closing out is not permissible, because by paying a percentage of the contract value a futures trader may stand to gain (or lose) an amount of profit (or loss) that is calculated based on the whole contract value when the price swings in (or against) his favour.

(I) *SALAM* FUTURE CONTRACT *Salam* is essentially a transaction where two parties agree to carry out a sale/purchase of an underlying asset at a predetermined future date, but at a price determined and fully paid today. Since there is full pre-payment, a *salam* sale is clearly beneficial to the seller, so the predetermined price is normally lower than the prevailing spot price. The difference between the *salam* price and the spot price is the 'compensation' from the seller to the buyer for the privilege received. To be *shari'ah* compliant, the *salam* futures contract is subject to several conditions:

● Full payment by buyer at the time of effecting sale.
● The underlying asset must be easily quantifiable and its quality determinable.
● Cannot be based on a uniquely identified underlying asset.
● Quantity, quality, maturity date and place of delivery must be clearly enumerated.

(II) ISLAMIC PROMISSORY FORWARD CONTRACT (IPFC) This instrument is structured in a manner that reflects the concept of *wa'ad* (promise) in forward contracts. When the Islamic forward contracts such as *salam* or *murabahah* are backed with a promise, an IPFC is established. This is used for hedging risks associated with contracts such as commodity *murabahah*. It is important to emphasize that conventional futures in which payment and delivery of goods are postponed are not allowed under *shari'ah* due to the presence of *gharar* and *riba* elements.

b) Islamic swaps

An *Islamic swap* is a derivative contract where two parties exchange one financial instrument for another backed with an underlying asset for the mutual benefit of the parties and excluding all prohibitive elements under the *shari'ah* such as *riba, gharar* and *jahl* (ignorance). The three main instruments of Islamic swaps that have been structured in a manner that complies with the precepts of the *shari'ah* are *Islamic foreign exchange swap, Islamic cross currency swap* and *Islamic profit rate swap*.

(I) ISLAMIC FOREIGN EXCHANGE SWAP (ISLAMIC FX SWAP) The *Islamic foreign exchange swap* is a contract designed as an Islamic hedging mechanism to minimize the exposure of market participants to the volatile and fluctuating currency exchange rate in the market. To maintain absolute *shari'ah* compliance in the contract, the Fx swap generally involves the exchange and re-exchange of foreign currency. Islamic Fx swaps involve two stages. The first foreign exchange of monetary currencies occurs at the beginning and another exchange occurs at the expiry date.

For example, assume that two people, one British and one Emirati, agree to enter into a Fx swap contract. They agree to exchange £50 million which will result in an initial conversion of AED 252.3 million based on the current spot price. They also agree on the exchange rate fixed for the second stage of the contract, regardless of market volatility or fluctuations in the value of the currency. At the maturity date, the parties would convert the AED back to GBP based on the mutually agreed future exchange rate at the initial stage of the contract and not at the prevailing market rate. This swap is meant to avoid the effects of market volatility with regard to currency fluctuations in the future. This is different from a Fx forward contract, which is only a *one stage contract*, i.e. it involves only one initial exchange to conclude the contract.

(II) ISLAMIC CROSS CURRENCY SWAP (ICCS) An *Islamic cross currency swap* is a bilateral contractual arrangement between two parties to exchange a series of profit and/or principal payments denominated in one currency for another series of profit and/or payments denominated in another currency, based on a notional principal amount, over an agreed period of time. The mutually agreed underlying asset used to legitimize the transactions is based on commodity *murabahah*. Through this arrangement, Islamic banks are able to hedge the interest and currency exchange risks of their investments in foreign denominated assets. Besides serving as a tool for risk management, the ICCS also helps reduce the cost of raising resources and enhances asset–liability management.

(III) ISLAMIC PROFIT RATE SWAP (IPRS)   An *Islamic profit rate swap* is a bilateral contract to exchange profit rates between a fixed rate party and a floating rate party or vice versa. A *fixed rate party* is the one who intends to swap its fixed rate profits with a floating rate while a *floating rate party* is the one who intends to swap its floating rate profits with a fixed rate in the profit swap arrangement. Funding rates are matched with the return rates of investment to have a healthy profit rate swap. This is implemented through the execution of a series of underlying contracts to trade certain assets based on the *shari'ah* principles of *bay'* and *bay' bithaman ajil*. Since Islamic financial institutions cannot deal in transactions involving interest, IPRS serves as an appropriate *shari'ah* compliant mechanism to reduce risk exposures from the fluctuating borrowing rates.

c) Islamic options

An *Islamic* option is a contract to buy or sell an asset at a predetermined price within a stipulated period of time. This is a kind of risk management technique where the buyer tries to avoid or eliminate future market volatility. There are mixed opinions on the permissibility of this instrument. In Islamic jurisprudence, there is a reference to options in commercial transactions under the doctrine of contractual stipulations (*al-khiyarat*) and also in *bay al-arbun*, which is a transaction in which a buyer pays a deposit to secure the underlying asset as well as the price at the time of concluding the contract. However, this is only permitted by the Hanbali jurists while the other three schools of thought disallow it as they consider it a void contract. The OIC *Fiqh* Academy argued that while options are acceptable when viewed in the light of *bay-al-arbun*, they become unacceptable as they are detached and independent of the underlying asset. Similarly, promises as part of a contract are acceptable in *shari'ah* but the trading and charging of a premium for the promise is not acceptable. Furthermore, it stated that option contracts, as currently applied in the world financial markets, are a new type of contract which do not come under any of *shari'ah* denominated contracts. Since the subject of the contract is neither a sum of money nor a utility nor a financial right, which may be waived, the contract is not permissible in *shari'ah*. Other scholars argued against options as they are similar to *maysir*, since the profits from options are unearned gains. In short, Muslim scholars are not unanimous with regards to the validity of options as a derivative for the purpose of hedging within the Islamic financial market. As trading in options is prohibited by the resolution of the OIC *Fiqh* Academy, it therefore has a limited scope of utility in Islamic banks as a risk management technique.

Summary

Bonds and *sukuk* are important financial instruments in the capital markets. *Sukuk*, as an innovative Islamic financial product, has developed into a truly global product appealing to both Muslim and non-Muslim investors. Three important economic agents involved in *sukuk* are the *sukuk originator*, *sukuk investors* and *special purpose vehicle* (SPV). There are many differences between conventional bonds and *sukuk*, but the fundamental difference is that bonds are purely debt instruments while *sukuk* are attached to an underlying asset. *Sukuk* provide many advantages, not only to investors but also to the issuers and the economy. *Sukuk* structures may be classified based on their tradability, their underlying assets and nature of contract. Although AAOIFI recognized 14 different *sukuk* structures, there are eight commonly used in the market: *sukuk al-ijarah*, *sukuk al-murabahah*, *sukuk Al-Salam*, *sukuk Al-Musharakah*, *sukuk Al-Mudarabah*, *sukuk Al-Istisna'a*, *sukuk al-istithmar* and *sukuk Al-Wakalah*. The structuring process for each type of *sukuk* is different, with some involving very complex arrangements, such as *sukuk al-istithmar* and *sukuk Al-Wakalah*, which involve a number of different contracts to make them *shari'ah* compliant. Rating agencies provide independent assessments on creditworthiness and other aspects of corporations and states to help investors make informed decisions. Different methodologies are used by rating agencies in producing the output of their assessments. Islamic International Rating Agency (IIRA), set up by IDB, provides eight different types of rating related to Islamic financial products: sovereign rating, issuer rating, *sukuk* rating, insurer financial strength rating, *shari'ah* quality rating, corporate governance quality rating, bank financial strength rating and real estate rating. *Shari'ah* scholars have reservations on some types of *sukuk* structures in the market and they have set some safeguards to mitigate specific issues in order to ensure that the *sukuk* are *shari'ah* compliant.

Derivatives, as Islamic financial instruments, are more controversial as they often contain the elements of *gharar*, *riba* and *maysir*. A number of criteria have to be considered when structuring Islamic derivatives. This may involve a number of contracts being drawn to make them *shari'ah* compliant.

Key terms and concepts

American option
asset backed *sukuk*
asset based *sukuk*
bank financial strength rating
call option
contractual hedging
convertible bond
cooperative hedging
corporate credit rating
corporate governance
   quality rating
coupon payment
coupon rate
credit default swaps
credit rating agencies
currency risk
currency swaps
debt based instruments
default risk
derivatives
economic hedging
equity based instruments
European option
exercise price
fixed rate party
floating rate party
forward contracts
forward price
futures contract
futures exchange
futures price
ijarah mawsufah al-dimmah

insurer financial strength rating
Islamic cross currency swap
Islamic cross currency swaps
Islamic foreign exchange swap
Islamic FX swaps
Islamic option
Islamic options futures
Islamic profit rate swap
Islamic profit rate swaps
Islamic promissory forward
   contract
issue price
issue unit
issuer rating
junk bonds
LIBOR
madhahib
maturity value
municipal bonds
non-standardized agreements
non-Tradable *sukuk*
one-stage contract
option
options
performance fee
periodic distribution amounts
plain vanilla swap
put contract
put option
real estate rating
salam future contract
secured bond

settlement dates
settlement periods
shari'ah quality rating
sovereign credit rating
special purpose vehicle (SPV)
speculators
strike price
sukuk
sukuk al-ijarah
sukuk Al-Istisna'a
sukuk al-istithmar
sukuk Al-Mudarabah
sukuk al-murabahah
sukuk Al-Musharakah
sukuk Al-Salam
sukuk Al-Wakalah
sukuk holders
sukuk investors
sukuk issuer
sukuk obligator
sukuk originator
sukuk rating
sukuk subscriber
swap
swaps
tradable *sukuk*
treasury bonds
underwriter
unsecured bond
usufruct
writer

Questions

1. Describe the types and features of conventional bonds.

2. Define *sukuk* and identify the economic agents involved in the *sukuk*.

3. Distinguish between *sukuk* and bonds.

4. Explain the advantages and disadvantages of *sukuk* for the issuer and the investor.

5. Discuss the classifications of *sukuk* and their distinguishing features.

6. List eight types of *sukuk* and explain any two of them by illustrating your answer using relevant examples.

7. Discuss the requirements stated in AAOIFI Shari'ah Standards when structuring *sukuk al-istithmar*.

8. Discuss the requirements when structuring *sukuk Al-Wakalah*. What are the advantages of using this structure?

9. Distinguish between *sovereign credit rating* and *corporate credit rating*.

10. Identify any four rating agencies that have experience in rating *sukuk* and discuss their rating methodologies.

11. Critically evaluate the debates surrounding the issue of *sukuk* as highlighted by Sheik Taqi Usmani and AAOIFI.

12. Describe the different types of derivatives and highlight their advantages and disadvantages.

13. Define Islamic derivatives and critically evaluate the problems of each type of derivative from an Islamic perspective.

Case Study

You are the *sukuk* specialist at Regal Consultancy. The CEO of the company was approached last week by two clients, Abdul & Sons and Horizon Premia, who are both looking to raise funds in a *shari'ah* compliant way for their business. The following information was passed on to you by the CEO and he has asked you to prepare a separate report for each client to advise them on which *sukuk* structure would be best to serve their needs. Also he has asked you to illustrate the mechanics of the proposed *sukuk* structure using diagrams to help the clients understand the recommended *sukuk* structures better.

Abdul & Sons needs more liquidity to finance its activities following successful bids on two big contracts in Kazakhstan. It needs to raise £8 million and would like to raise the funds in a *shari'ah* compliant way without involving any interest. It has a collection of assets in its books that can potentially be used to help raise the funds.

Horizon Premia also needs to raise funds as it is facing a shortage of liquidity to expand its business. Among its portfolio of assets is a piece of land which it has owned since 2005. Max, the finance manager at Horizon Premia, wanted the land to be used to generate income to support the company's other business activities. The land is located next to the Castle Hill Hospital, which currently has limited parking for patients and visitors.

References and further readings

AAOIFI (2010). Shari'ah Standards for Islamic Financial Institutions, Bahrain, AAOIFI.

Abdelhady, H. (2012), 'Islamic finance as a mechanism for bolstering food security in the Middle East: Food security waqf', *Sustainable Development Law and Policy*, 13(1), pp. 29-35.

Ahroum, R. and Achchab, B. (2017), 'Pricing of sukuk musharakah with joint venture as underlying, beyond the use of PLS ratio', *Journal of Islamic Accounting and Business Research*, 8(4), pp. 406-419.

Alswaidan, M.W., Daynes, A. and Pasgas, P. (2017), 'Understanding and evaluation of risk in Sukuk structures', *Journal of Islamic Accounting and Business Research*, 8(4), pp. 389-405.

Godlewski, C.J., Turk-Ariss, R. and Weill L. (2011), Do markets perceive Sukuk and conventional bonds as different financing instruments? *BOFIT Discussion Paper* No. 6/2011.

Hassoune, A. (2007). 'Standard & Poor's approach to rating sukuk', *S&P Ratings Direct*. September.

Howladar, K. (2006). Shari'ah and sukuk: A Moody's primer. *Moody's Investors Service*.

IFSB (2005). *Guiding principles of risk management for institutions (other than insurance institutions) offering only Islamic financial services*, Islamic Financial Services Board: Malaysia.

Jobst, A., Kunzel, P., Mills, P. and Sy, A. (2018). Islamic Bond Issuance – What Sovereign Debt Managers Need to Know, *IMF Policy Discussion Paper* PDP/08/3.

Leong, M. (2006). *Islamic financial institutions enhancing current methodologies*, Malaysian Rating Corporation Berhad.

Leong, M. (2008). *Rating approach to sukuk, a MARC perspective*, Malaysian Rating Corporation Berhad.

Rafay, A., Sadiq, R. and Ajmal, M. (2017). 'Uniform framework for Sukuk al-Ijarah – a proposed model for all madhahib', *Journal of Islamic Accounting and Business Research*, 8(4), pp. 420-454.

Tariq, A.A. and Dar, H. (2007). 'Risks of sukuk structures: Implications for resource mobilization', *Thunderbird International Business Review*, 49(2), pp. 203-223.

Tichy, G. (2011). 'Credit rating agencies: Part of the solution or part of the problem?' *Intereconomics – Review of European Economic Policy*, 46, pp. 232-262.

6 Islamic banking and financial institutions

Learning Objectives

Upon completion of this chapter you should be able to:

- describe the origin of modern banking

- discuss the role of banking

- identify the benefits of intermediation

- describe the different types of banking

- explain the evolution of Islamic banking

- discuss the emergence and growth of Islamic banking in different regions

- explain the principles underlying Islamic banking

- distinguish between conventional and Islamic banking

- explain the management structure of Islamic banking

- discuss the product launch structure

6.1 Introduction

This chapter looks at the role of Islamic banks as one of the important organs in the Islamic financial system and economy. As discussed in Chapter 3, banks are one of the financial intermediaries that provide a mechanism by which funds are transferred and allocated to the most productive opportunities. The first part of this chapter introduces the concept and types of banking as well as their typical activities, while the latter part focuses on Islamic banking, its operating structure and contribution to the economy, as well as its growth in difference regions.

6.2 The origin of modern banking

The word *bank* is derived from the Italian word *banco* meaning table or bench where Italian money changers used to display the monies and records when conducting their transactions (de Roover, 1954). Hence, the origin of modern banking can be traced to the practices in the medieval Italian cities of Florence, Venice, and Genoa where trading families made loans to princes to finance wars and their lavish lifestyles, and also to merchants engaged in international trade. According to Hoggson (1926), two prominent families in Florence in the 14th century were the Bardi and Peruzzi families, who extended substantial loans to King Edward III of England to finance the Hundred Years' War against France. The two banks failed when King Edward defaulted (Hoggson, 1926). Another important figure is the money changer, Giovanni Medici, who set up the Medici bank in 1397 with branches all over the Italian cities and across Europe (Goldthwaite, 1995). Most business of the medieval banks was carried out through the use of bills of exchange, and since the church prohibited direct interest charges, bankers would take deposits in one city, make a loan to someone transporting goods to another city, and then take repayment at the other city.

The origins of the English banking system can be attributed to the activities of the goldsmiths in London during the 16th century, who used their premises to store gold for merchants who needed somewhere to safely deposit their wealth (de Roover, 1954). Receipts were then issued and the gold would be subsequently returned when the receipts were presented to the goldsmiths. With the passage of time, people began to trade using the paper receipts in place of the real gold pieces and coins. The effectiveness of this paper based system strongly depends on the capability of the goldsmiths to return the gold on instant demand. This is the starting point for the obligatory promise on each and every banknote stating: I promise to pay the bearer on demand the sum of specific pounds or dollars (Turk and Rubino, 2013). These receipts became a widely accepted form for settling payments among traders and accumulation of wealth.

At this significant point in time, it came to the attention of the goldsmiths turned bankers that the general public were relying entirely on the paper receipts which had become *legal tender* and were no longer approaching them regularly for their gold deposits. This provided them with one of the greatest, legal but unethical, money making ideas of all time. They reasoned that if the general public has confidence in these paper receipts, then it makes sense to print and issue more of them without needing any equivalent increase in the amount of gold being deposited. Hence, the goldsmiths started issuing receipts in excess of the gold and silver which they held and lending them to others through the creation of what became known as the *business or consumer loans* (Turk and Rubino, 2013).

This caused the market to be flooded with 'artificial' receipts that could be used as legal tender and would also allow huge loans to be made to the general public, thereby earning interest for the goldsmiths cum bankers. They also realized that the more deposits they had, the more profits they could make. They began paying for deposits of gold and silver instead of charging for storage which led to the innovation of the interest bearing account (Turk and Rubino, 2013). Subsequently, the goldsmiths started lending the paper money to those who needed them by charging a high interest rate and paying some interest to those who deposited money with them to attract more savings.

Besides individuals, the government also borrowed money from these goldsmiths, especially to finance wars, which the government paid back with interest raised from taxation. The colossal amount of funds needed by the government to finance the war in France at the end of the 17th century resulted in a group of financiers coming together to set up the Bank of England in 1694 to provide the loan required by the government. In return, the bank received interest on the loan, and the right to issue notes and lend money, as well as to buy and sell gold. Since the activities of the Bank of England were confined to London, many small banks began to emerge in the provincial towns of England by the late 18th century. In 1833, banknotes issued by the Bank of England were made legal tender, so were accepted as payment for a debt.

With the passage of time, these goldsmiths cum bankers further realized that they needed to hold less gold in relation to the receipts issued, leading to the birth of the *fractional reserve system*. This reserve system is deceptive, as it allows an expansion in the supply of paper money without a corresponding rise in the assets held by the bank. For example, consider that a bank has £1000 as capital and through experience realized that only 20 per cent or £200 is needed to be held as reserve to fulfil the daily withdrawal request. This means the bank can lend out £800. When the loan recipient makes a deposit in another bank, the bank can lend out £640 (80% of £800) and the process continues until a huge multiple of the original deposit base is being turned into circulating currency, creating an elastic money supply. This new money is only available to society through taking an interest bearing loan from the bank, and this has been the cornerstone of the western economic system to the present day.

Consequently, the money that we own today is not backed by real assets. It is purely worth only the paper it is written on and is only deemed to have additional value because society has confidence in the economic system. Modern banking replaces the traditional asset based medium with paper based banknotes, with interest being a dominant feature in all the transactions. Having understood the origins of conventional banking, we will now turn our attention to the nature of banking and banks' activities, before turning our attention to Islamic banking and finance in the later sections.

6.3   Nature and types of banking

The term bank refers to any establishment licensed to accept deposits, pay interest or profit, clear cheques, make loans and offer a range of other financial services to their customers. Individuals and organizations generally use banks as places to store their surplus funds for safekeeping. Since banks have access to these funds, they are in a position to lend money to individuals and organizations that for one reason or another need to spend or have access to some funds. Thus, banks can use the funds they hold for safekeeping to generate returns for the individuals and organizations that have deposited with them and make them grow in value. In this way, the banking system acts to channel society's surplus wealth to individuals and organizations that can use it productively for building factories, airports, railways, roads and other economic assets, which help society as a whole to grow richer. At the same time, it makes those who deposit their money with the banks become wealthier through payment of profits the banks made from lending or investment, thus encouraging them to continue to save and deposit their surplus funds. Banks also help companies trading internationally to bring their wealth into the country. They also help governments and large corporations to raise funds by issuing bonds and shares in the capital markets, offer advice and underwrite the issues, by taking much of the risk out of them. In short, banks are therefore essential for economic growth.

As we have seen in Chapter 3, mobilization of funds may take place directly in the financial markets or indirectly through intermediaries. The core activity of banks as financial intermediaries is to facilitate the exchange of funds between savers/depositors and borrowers. In general, the majority of savers/depositors want to lend their assets for short period of time for the highest possible return, while the majority of borrowers demand liabilities for long period at a low cost. The role of the financial intermediary is therefore to bridge the gap between the two parties and reconcile their incompatible needs and objectives. In order to fully appreciate the significance of the intermediation process, we need to understand the role of the banks and the benefits of intermediation.

6.3.1 ROLE OF BANKS AND BENEFITS OF INTERMEDIATION

As mentioned earlier, banks typically accept funds from various savers/depositors for safekeeping and investment, which are recorded in the banks' books as their *liabilities*. Most of the deposits have the following characteristics: *small size, low risk* and *high quality*. The large source of funds from deposits held by banks provides them with opportunities to lend the funds as loans and investments. These loans and investments are recorded in the banks' books as *assets* and they have the following characteristics: *larger in size, higher risk and illiquid*. Banks can therefore bridge the gap between the needs of the surplus units and deficit units by performing three transformation functions: *size, maturity* and *risk* as shown in Figure 6.1.

Size transformation involves banks collecting small deposits and repackaging them into large loans such as mortgages. *Maturity transformation* involves banks transforming their liabilities (funds from savers/depositors) which are repayable on demand or at relatively short notice into banks' assets (funds lent to borrowers) that are

Figure 6.1 Role of banks

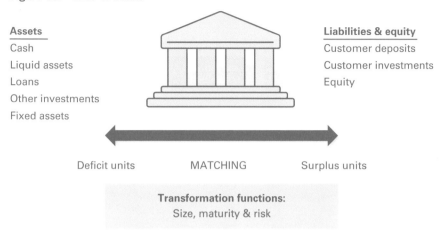

Assets		**Liabilities & equity**
Cash		Customer deposits
Liquid assets		Customer investments
Loans		Equity
Other investments		
Fixed assets		

Deficit units   MATCHING   Surplus units

Transformation functions:
Size, maturity & risk

repayable in the medium to long term. *Risk transformation* involves banks minimizing the risk of individual loans by diversifying their investments, pooling of risks, screening and monitoring borrowers besides holding capital and reserves as a buffer for unexpected losses. Hence, the role of banks as intermediary is of great significance. Table 6.1 presents a summary of the benefits to three important groups of stakeholders in conventional banking.

Table 6.1 Benefits of conventional financial intermediation

Ultimate lenders (surplus units)	Society	Ultimate borrowers (deficit units)
Greater liquidity	efficient utilization of funds within the economy	loans available for longer periods and larger amounts
Lower transaction cost	more borrowing and lending activities	lower transaction cost
Less risk	funds available for higher risk ventures	lower interest rate
Lending decision simplified		loans available when required

6.3.2 TYPES OF BANKING

The banking business has substantially evolved from offering the relatively restricted products and services of *traditional banking* (loans and deposits) to *modern banking* that offers *universal* or *full service banking* (loans, deposits, insurance, securities/investment, pensions and other financial services).

A number of factors have contributed to the change of the banking business. These include: (i) deregulation in the 1990s, which saw many banks merging with investment companies enabling more services to be provided as well as increasing competition; (ii) redefinition of the constituents of banking business to include other services such as insurance, pensions, leasing, etc.; (iii) free flow of funds across national boundaries that facilitated the growth of international banking; and (iv) advances in technology that allowed other financial services firms to offer accounts and services similar to banks. Another development is the rise of ethical financial services and among them Islamic banking.

Banks refer to several different types of financial institutions that conduct different kinds of activities. Some are very large carrying out many different functions while others are more specialized. Figure 6.2 presents the different types of banking that exist today.

Banks can generally be classified into five types: *retail or personal banks, private banks, corporate banks, investment banks* and *Islamic banks*. There are various types of banks that offer personal banking services. Firstly,

Figure 6.2   Types of banking

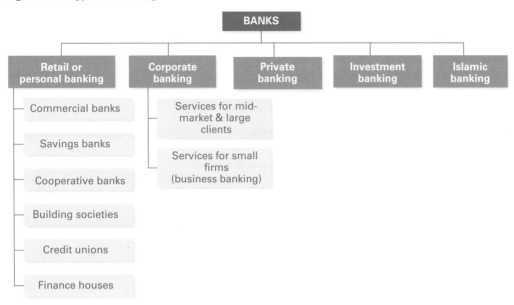

there are *commercial banks* that cover the majority of business of households and the corporate sector. They deal with both retail and corporate customers, have well diversified deposit and lending portfolios, and offer full range financial services. They are typically limited companies which may be publicly listed or privately owned. *Savings banks* and *cooperative* banks share similar features. Firstly, both have mutual ownership i.e. being owned by members or shareholders who are usually depositors or borrowers. Secondly, unlike commercial banks, their strategic objective may be other than profit maximization and thirdly, they tend to focus on retail and business customers. *Building societies* are also similar to savings banks and cooperative banks but they focus on retail deposit taking and mortgage lending. *Credit Unions,* on the other hand, are non-profit cooperatives owned by members who pooled their savings and lend to each other, while *finance houses* provide finance for leasing and factoring services.

Corporate banking is generally related to banking services provided to companies regardless of size. However, some have used the term corporate banking to refer to services offered to only very large firms and the term *business banking* for small firms. The typical services for large firms focus on cash management and transaction services, credit and other debt finance facilities, foreign exchange and securities underwriting and fund management services. Services for smaller firms cover payment services, debt finance, equity finance and other special financing schemes. Examples of those offering corporate banking services include Barclays, Deutsche Bank and HSBC.

Private banking, which has substantially grown in recent years, refers to high-quality provision of financial services to wealthy clients, both individuals and families. Examples of such banks include UBS, Wells Fargo, Credit Suisse and Morgan Stanley. Those with $1 million or more investable assets are known as *high net worth individuals.*

Investment banking helps companies and governments raise funds in the capital market either through equity or debt, provide corporate advisory services on mergers and acquisitions, and asset management as well as other securities services, e.g. brokerage, financing services and securities lending. Examples of such banks are JP Morgan, Goldman Sachs and Citi.

Islamic banking, unlike the conventional interest based or western based banks, offers a wide variety of products and services that do not charge or pay interest as this is prohibited by *shari'ah*. Instead, the products and services are based on profit and risk sharing which symbolizes entrepreneurship and wealth creation. The remaining sections of this chapter will now focus on Islamic banking.

6.4   Evolution of Islamic banking

6.4.1 EARLY MODES OF TRANSACTIONS IN THE ISLAMIC EMPIRE

The people of Makkah were known as experienced traders and the city of Makkah had been a great centre of inter-regional trade. The Prophet Muhammad himself was involved in trading, travelling between Makkah and Syria. His truthfulness and trustworthiness in commercial dealings earned him the titles of *al-sadiq* (the truthful one) and *al-amin* (the trustworthy).

The caravan trades in the Arabian Peninsula involved agents employed to represent their principals to carry out specific transactions and they were compensated either through financial payments or proprietary benefits as agreed by the parties in the form of *wakalah* (agency contract). In addition, the Prophet was reported to sometimes borrow money from the Jews and facilitated interest free loans in the form of *qard* (benevolent loan) for his needy companions. The Prophet and his companions were also engaged in *salam* (forward) contracts against cash payment until the season when the commodity is available for delivery. Another important mode during this period includes *sarf* (exchange of money in the form of gold for gold and silver for silver at the same time).

It was during this period that *shari'ah* began to regulate economic policies and transactions, such as prohibiting those tainted with *riba*, having excessive risk or speculation (*gharar*), dealing in prohibited commodities and goods, dealing in stolen goods, exploitation and unjust practices in the market place, giving short measures, hoarding of foodstuff or other essential commodities, and cheating and fraud in business, as discussed in previous chapters.

During the 30-year period (632-661 CE) of the Orthodox caliphates, various far reaching economic transformations were also introduced. During the time of Caliph Abu Bakar, the attention was focused on *zakat* (alms) as this is not only one of the pillars of Islam but also an important distributive tool. The expansion of the Islamic state under the Caliphate of Umar Al-Khattab resulted in increased state revenues, requiring a central monetary agency to manage the funds in Medina. Hence, the Caliph Umar set up a centralized, state administered *baitul mal* (house of treasury) for distribution of revenues from *zakat* and other sources. The official mediums of exchange were the *dinar* and *dirham* (gold and silver weights, respectively, made by Persians). During the Caliphate of Uthman Affan, the Islamic Empire experienced unprecedented increase in wealth, so much so that citizens could apply for benevolent loans. It was also during this time that the first Muslim coins were used based on the coin standard set during Caliph Umar, which was ten dirhams equivalent to seven dinars. According to Islamic law, one dinar is a specific weight of 22k gold, equivalent to 4.25 grams and one dirham is a specific weight of pure silver equivalent to 2.975 grams.

During the Umayyad period, Muslims who had been trading using Byzantine gold dinars and Persian silver dirhams before this, began to mint their own silver coins showing a crescent, the star and '*bismillah*' (in the name of God) around the rim instead of human and animal figures present on the Persian coins. The state had a monopoly on coinage based on the coin standard of Caliph Umar and any tampering with their weight or purity was severely punished.

According to Chachi (2005), the term *sarraffeen* was used to refer to financial clerks, money changers, treasury receivers, government cashiers, experts in examining and collecting coins, and licensed merchant bankers that exist during the Abassid period (after 750 CE). A single currency became the standard throughout the Islamic Empire. As trade and commerce expanded to North Africa, Spain and a large part of Asia, some basic financial instruments, such as the *suftaja* (bill of exchange) and the *shekk* (cheque), were used. Nasser (1996) highlighted that there were different types of commercial papers and banknotes that were widely accepted such as, bills of exchange (*suftaja*), promissory notes (*reqaah al-sayarifah*), and goods *sukuk*. During this time, licensed bankers with offices or agencies in different parts of the Islamic Empire performed various functions such as exchanging money, accepting deposits, assigning debts (*hawalah*) and issuing banknotes. In the Medieval Near East, the first and most important forms of commercial credit papers known as *hawalah* and *suftaja* were traded in the form of written obligations. Muslim societies managed their economies and carried on extensive domestic and international trade without the use of interest, as profit sharing and various kinds of participation arrangements were adequate to serve the demand for savings and investment (Siddiqi, 1983). Contracts that are customary for the people in the Arabian Peninsula and other parts of the Islamic regions were widely used. Any financial or contractual practices that were found to violate one or more of the prohibitions in *shari'ah* were rejected outright, but might be considered if they could be modified to meet the standards of Islamic justice and fairness.

In short, Muslims were able to contribute greatly to the development of financial and banking practices during the Islamic Empire, due not only to the existence of a legislative system that incorporated firm conventions and regulations in governing all transactions and contracts, but also a strong judicial system capable of enforcing all legitimate contracts and resolving any commercial disputes.

6.4.2 THE RISE OF MODERN ISLAMIC BANKING AND FINANCE

The decline of the Islamic Empire from about the 12th century led to the weakening role of the *sarraffeen* in Muslim countries and the rise of modern banking in different parts of Europe. From the 18th century onwards, the rise of European colonial powers with their aggressive colonial mercantile system challenged the traditional Islamic business model (Chapra, 2000). Through colonization, the western influence penetrated many aspects of life including adoption of the western banking model. The 19th century witnessed the establishment of western banks in the Islamic world (Wilson, 1995) which started with the opening of branches by foreign banks or by establishing banks within the countries. For instance, in Egypt, the first conventional bank opened its doors in 1856 under the name Bank of Egypt (as a branch of an English bank) but was closed in 1911, while the National Bank of Egypt which was established in 1898 by Ralph Suarez and Constantine Salvagos (both were Jewish Egyptian businessmen) with an English partner is still in operation today (Nasser, 1996).

By the mid-20th century, the feelings of economic injustice and nationalist sentiments grew in the Muslim world. There was widespread interest to revive Islamic economics and there were three opinions at that time regarding western banking system (Nasser, 1996). The first group believed that all bank activities are *shari'ah* compliant, an opinion that is also shared by the founder of the Bank of Egypt. The second group deemed all bank activities to be not *shari'ah* compliant (*haram* or contradictory to *shari'ah* principles) but they were essential at that time due to the significant role they played in the economy. Hence, they endorsed the establishment of a western model of banking based on the basic Islamic juristic rules of *al-darurat tubeah al-mahdurat* (necessity supersedes prohibition), which allows engagement in activities that contradict *shari'ah* because of necessity and in the absence of other alternatives that are *shari'ah* compliant. The third group acknowledged the importance of banking activities for the economy, but *riba* is not indispensable for banks' commercial dealings, as Islamic jurisprudence offers many forms of financial contracts which can be implemented by the banks to assist their customers in avoiding *riba*.

The first and second opinions were strong in the mid-1900s, influenced by the political and socio-economic conditions at that time. The political and western educated elites supported western banking model as they were considered well established and that Muslims did not have enough knowledge on an appropriate business model for Islamic banking practices after the golden age of Islam (Nasser, 1996).

From the 1940s onwards, the Islamization agenda saw the mushrooming of Islamic financial institutions. Modern Islamic banking and finance underwent several phases before it came to be what it is today. The various phases are further explained in the following sections.

a) Phase 1: Origins of ideas in developing interest-free banking (1930s-1960)

The efforts to establish modern Islamic finance began in the mid-1930s by a number of Muslim economists and political Islamists. Their discontent with the western style economic and banking system, which was largely based on interest, prompted them to focus their attention on developing economic activities that are more compatible to *shari'ah*. The initial idea may be attributed to an Indian Muslim, Abul Al-ala Mawdudi (1937). He was the founder of *Jamaat-i-Islami* and author of the book *Al-riba,* which proposed changes in behavioural norms based on the Islamic traditions. Other important figures from the sub-continent contributing to Islamic economic activities include Hifz Al-Rahman Seoharvi (1942) who published his book *Islam as an Economic System*, Muhammad Hamidullah (1944) who was considered the first to coin the term 'Islamic Economics' and wrote a paper titled *Islam's Solution of the Basic Economic Problems – the Position of Labour*, Anwar Qureshi (1946) who wrote *Islam and the Theory of Interest*, and Naiem Siddiqi (1948) who wrote *Banking According to Islamic Principles*.

There was also development of similar ideas in Egypt. One of the most prolific writers was Hasan Al-Banna who founded one of the largest and most influential Islamic revivalist organizations that exists today, the Muslim Brotherhood. He called for Islamization of not only the state and society but also the economy, and elaborated on an Islamic fiscal theory where *zakat* are reserved for social expenditure to reduce inequality in society. Another important figure is Sayyid Qutb (1952) who published a major theoretical piece of work on social criticism, *Al-'adala al-Ijtima'iyya fi-l-Islam* (*Social Justice in Islam*), when he was studying in the USA. The pioneer of Islamic banking was Muhammad Uzair (1955) who published *An Outline of Interestless Banking*, which is considered a major piece of work by a professional economist specifically on banking.

b) Phase 2: The emergence and establishment of Islamic banks (1963-1989)

Unlike the first phase where efforts were channelled at developing ideas on how to Islamize the banking system, the second phase involved the implementation of those ideas into practice. Hence, a number of Islamic banks were established during this period offering a relatively limited range of products and services compared to their conventional counterparts, especially during the 1960s. This was partly due to lack of awareness and knowledge. In the 1970s, a number of academic institutions and research centres were set up. Many conferences were held and books were written on the subject to increase the level of knowledge and awareness on Islamic banking. The 1980s saw a growth in the sector, with some government interventions in countries like Sudan and Iran where the system became fully 'Islamized'. This decade also saw a variety of Islamic banking products other than *mudarabah* (profit and loss sharing) and *musharakah* (equity sharing) being introduced. Also, a number of conventional banks started offering Islamic banking products through their Islamic windows.

Table 6.2 illustrates the development of Islamic banks during this phase. The experiment with Islamic banking systems as an organization was first tried with the establishment of a small private Islamic bank in Pakistan in the 1950s, which was subsequently closed down.

Another attempt was made in 1963 with the establishment of Mit Ghamr in Egypt and Tabung Haji in Malaysia. While the former no longer exists, the latter is still in business today, profitably investing money from savers to help them meet the cost of their pilgrimage to Makkah, and with a very strong portfolio of investments and business diversification. In 1973, Philippine Amanah Bank was established by President Ferdinand Marcos to enable Muslims in the country to meet some of their financial needs without involving interest.

Islamic banks were established in a wider scale from 1974 as a result of increased oil prices during this decade which benefited countries like Saudi Arabia, Kuwait, United Arab Emirates, Qatar and Bahrain. The first international Islamic bank, Islamic Development Bank (IDB) was set up in 1974 and since then it has played a pivotal role in the development of the Islamic banking and finance industry, while fostering economic development and social progress in Muslim communities in accordance with *shari'ah* principles. Dubai Islamic Bank (DIB) was set up in 1975 under a special law allowing it to engage in business enterprises while accepting deposits into current accounts that were guaranteed, and investment accounts that were to receive a share in the profits accruing from their use in business by the bank. It was established by a reputable entrepreneurial family, the Lootah brothers and Abdallah Saeed, who have social and political connections with the governor of Dubai, Sheikh Rashid Al-Maktoum.

In 1977, the Faisal Islamic Bank, owned by Prince Al-Faisal of Saudi Arabia was set up in Egypt and Sudan. This was later followed through private initiatives by people such as Ahmed Al-Yasin for Kuwait Financial House in 1977 and Sami Hamoud for Jordan Islamic Bank in 1978. The first Islamic financial institution set up in the west was in Luxembourg in 1978. In 1979, another two banks were set up, Bahrain Islamic Bank and

Table 6.2 Development of Islamic financial institutions (1963-1989)

The institution name	Country	Date of establishment
Local Saving Bank (Mit Ghamr)	Egypt	1963
Tabung Haji	Malaysia	1963
Nasser Social Bank	Egypt	1971
Philippine Amanah Bank	Philippines	1973
Islamic Development Bank	Saudi Arabia	1974
Dubai Islamic Bank	UAE	1975
Faisal Islamic Bank	Egypt, Sudan	1977
Kuwait Financial Home	Kuwait	1977
Jordan Islamic Bank for Financing and Investment	Jordan	1978
Islamic Finance House	Luxembourg	1978
Bahrain Islamic Bank	Bahrain	1979
Trust National for Investment	Pakistan	1979
Islamic Financing Home (Dar Al-mal Al-Islami Group)	Switzerland	1981
Tadamon Islamic Bank	Sudan	1981
Qatar Islamic Bank	Qatar	1982
Islami Bank	Bangladesh	1983
Faisal Islamic Bank	Bahrain	1983
International Islamic Financial Institution	Denmark	1983
Islamic Banks	Iran	1983
LUBS Islamic Investment Pool	Switzerland	1985
Al Ameen Islamic Financial and Investment Corp. Ltd.	India	1985
La Ningxia Islamic Trust and Investment Corporation	China	1985
Al-Baraka Banking Group	Worldwide	1985
Bank Islam Malaysia	Malaysia	1987
Al Rajhi Financial Company	Saudi Arabia	1988
Al Jazeera Finance	Qatar	1989

National Investment Trust in Pakistan, making the total number of Islamic banks in operation to 12 by the beginning of 1980.

Another 24 Islamic financial institutions were established between 1981 and 1985. They included Dar Al-mal Al-Islami Group and the Al Baraka Banking Group owned by Prince Al-Faisal and Shaykh Saleh Kamil, respectively. By 1985, more than 50 conventional banks were offering Islamic financial products including in major financial hubs such as London. By the beginning of the 1990s, banks, such as Grindlays in Karachi, Citi-Islamic in Bahrain and the National Commercial Bank in Saudi Arabia, had established more than 50 Islamic branches dealing exclusively in Islamic products.

c) Phase 3: Metamorphosis of Islamic banking and finance industry (1990-present)

The oil boom in the 1990s led to rapid growth and expansion of the industry as there was surplus foreign currency from oil revenues which needed to be invested in other sectors. More innovative products were introduced and the financial infrastructures were developed to support the booming sector. In the 1990s there was significant growth in Islamic windows and asset based financial instruments were enhanced. Regulations and supervision of the sector were also given more attention. From the 2000s onwards, the sector continue to expand and more attention given to risk management and control. Asset based securities markets began to develop and more complex financial instruments are being introduced.

A number of Islamic mutual funds appeared in the 1990s, many of which are managed by reputable western firms. It was during this period that the Islamic equity and bond markets were introduced. Dow Jones Islamic Index provides investors with the opportunity to participate in ethical investment. This period also saw the introduction of *takaful* (Islamic insurance). Islamic banks also started to increase in scale by introducing more complex financing schemes such as *sukuk* (Islamic bonds). In 2004, the global issuance of *sukuk* reached $6.7 billion, almost five times that of 2003.

The new millennium further witnessed rapid growth leading to internationalization of the industry. By the early 2000s, western financial institutions such as Citibank, ABN AMRO, HSBC and others established their own Islamic windows or subsidiaries to attract petrodollars deposits from the Middle East and other Muslims clientele into local markets (Khan and Bhatti, 2008, p. 709). Bosnia Bank International Sarajevo was established on 19 October 2000. In February 2001, ABCIB Islamic Asset Management was established as a wholly owned subsidiary of ABC International Bank, located in the UK.

The number of Islamic banks and financial institutions grew to 200 by the year 2002. Their capital and deposits were over $8 billion and $100 billion, respectively. Their assets were worth more than $160 billion, which contributed significantly to the world's economic stability and growth. About 40 per cent of these institutions are located in south and southeast Asia, and another 40 per cent in the Middle East. The remaining 20 per cent is equally divided between the Americas, Europe and Africa. About 67 per cent of these institutions are very small, with assets of less than $100 million.

In August 2004, the Islamic Bank of Britain (now renamed Al-Rayan) was established in the UK, making it the first fully fledged Islamic bank to operate in the country, being regulated by the British government's Financial Services Authority (FSA). Also, the European Islamic Investment Bank was incorporated in January 2005 and received authorization from the FSA in March 2006. Later in July that year, Bank of London and the Middle East were incorporated and received authorization from the FSA.

The Islamic financial market in the United States stands at about $1.5 billion with Guidance Financial, a licensed mortgage lender, being the market leader in the Islamic residential finance sector. It uses a *musharakah* contract to abide with *shari'ah* and since such a type of contract is not considered a legal asset for the bank, it has to operate as a one product company. It cannot offer any other financial services to avoid acting like a bank. Guidance Financial operates in 32 states and has to date achieved over $900 million in sales from *musharakah* transactions. In the area of Islamic commercial real estate financing, Devon Bank, which was established by a Jewish family in Chicago, is the major player in the USA. The bank operates in several US states with a $20 million portfolio (Ranzini, 2007). HSBC is another player in the US Islamic financial market, offering several Islamic solutions to its customers.

Many conventional banks and financial institutions are becoming increasingly interested in Islamic banking, as they believe that competition is always in favour of the most suitable, efficient, and fittest Islamic banks. Such competition from their conventional counterparts has prompted Islamic banks to exercise more diligence and care in introducing better quality products and conducting their activities more efficiently. Its resilience in performance during the financial crisis further strengthened the confidence in the market. In countries with dual banking systems, competition drove a number of conventional banks to convert into fully fledged Islamic banks, as they have acquired adequate practical experience and *shari'ah* practices in this field. Other conventional banks have started to operate Islamic windows to serve their Muslim customers, for instance, Lloyd's Bank in the UK.

The Organization of Islamic Conference (OIC) also helped to establish Islamic banks in several Islamic countries via the IDB. These steps included capital injection for newly established Islamic banks. The IDB also fosters the economic development and social progress of member countries and Muslim communities individually and jointly in accordance with the principles of *shari'ah*. It provides funds for development projects without dealing in interest. Instead, it charges service fees according to the actual administrative expenditures for managing investment portfolios in which individual Islamic banks place their surplus liquidity, and also being involved in profit sharing financial assistance to member countries.

6.5   Emergence and growth of Islamic banking in different regions

In the last section, we looked at how Islamic banking and finance have evolved from being an idea as part of the 'Islamization' agenda to become an important industry recognized globally. The industry has transformed into a more cohesive and competitive system in the post crisis period and is gradually emerging as an important component supporting international economic and financial linkages. Islamic financing facilities are now increasingly used to fund various transactions including cross border trade financing, national infrastructural and developmental projects, supporting the international *halal* trade industry and also facilitating foreign direct and portfolio investments.

Apart from the industry's strongholds in Malaysia and the Gulf Cooperation Council (GCC), the industry's growth has now gained stronger footing in other parts of Asia such as Turkey, Pakistan and Bangladesh as well as in African countries like Kenya, South Africa and Nigeria. Similarly, there have been increased Islamic finance activities in advanced economies such as the UK, Hong Kong, Singapore and Germany in recent years. In the following sections we will consider the development of the industry in different regions to provide insights on the status quo of Islamic banking.

6.5.1 UK, EUROPE AND USA

Islamic finance in the west is still at an embryonic stage. However, it is expected to grow and develop further following government incentives and the measures introduced to create an environment that is more conducive to support the industry as shown in Figure 6.3. Furthermore, the increased emphasis on alternative financial solutions in the wake of the financial crisis and realization of the value of Islamic financing techniques have caused conventional banks to start incorporating them into their existing financing practices or opening up separate Islamic windows. Another important factor that will drive the industry is the growing Muslim population within European jurisdictions. The Muslim population in Europe is expected to grow by 62 per cent by 2030, from 16.77 million to just over 27 million. Thus, demand for Islamic financial products and innovation is expected to increase.

a) United Kingdom

Islamic financing activities started in the UK in the 1980s when the London Metal Exchange provided *shari'ah* compliant overnight deposit facilities based on the *murabahah* principle. Today, London has become an important financial hub with major international firms and the Middle East's biggest traditional banks offering Islamic products in this city. The country is home to the west's first fully fledged *shari'ah* compliant retail bank and currently there are five of such banks. The growth of the Islamic industry is made possible with strong support offered by the UK government through the Islamic Finance Task Force, abolition of double taxation in 2004 and bringing the whole Islamic financial sector to operate under a single piece of legislation (Financial Services and Market Act, 2000). There is continued effort to ensure consistent regulatory treatment of Islamic finance with its statutory objectives and principles.

b) France

In 2007, amidst the increasing crude oil price, the French Minister of Economy at that time, Christine Lagarde, requested a viability assessment be conducted on France's capability to attract Islamic finance to boost its economy. The idea was mainly to attract a pool of liquidity from overseas Islamic investors via the creation of capital market instruments and wholesale banking that permit local authorities and corporations to benefit from such potential new sources of funding. The increasing support by the French authorities towards having an innovative financing environment led to the launch of an Islamic friendly approach of *shari'ah* compliant deposit schemes and tax regulation for *musharakah* and *mudarabah*. The changes are expected to result in growth in assets under management beyond the current level of $147.2 million with increases in trade flow from Islamic countries and Muslim population with French ties.

Figure 6.3 Factors contributing to growth of Islamic finance in Europe

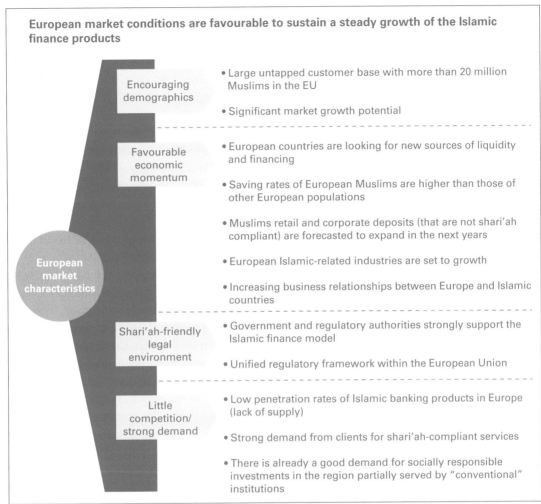

European market conditions are favourable to sustain a steady growth of the Islamic finance products

European market characteristics

Encouraging demographics
- Large untapped customer base with more than 20 million Muslims in the EU
- Significant market growth potential

Favourable economic momentum
- European countries are looking for new sources of liquidity and financing
- Saving rates of European Muslims are higher than those of other European populations
- Muslims retail and corporate deposits (that are not shari'ah compliant) are forecasted to expand in the next years
- European Islamic-related industries are set to growth
- Increasing business relationships between Europe and Islamic countries

Shari'ah-friendly legal environment
- Government and regulatory authorities strongly support the Islamic finance model
- Unified regulatory framework within the European Union

Little competition/ strong demand
- Low penetration rates of Islamic banking products in Europe (lack of supply)
- Strong demand from clients for shari'ah-compliant services
- There is already a good demand for socially responsible investments in the region partially served by "conventional" institutions

Source: www2.deloitte.com/content/dam/Deloitte/lu/Documents/financial-services/lu-en-islamicfinance-ineurope-11042014.pdf

c) Switzerland

Swiss banks, particularly Faisal Private Bank SA, UBS and Credit Suisse, were among the first few institutions to provide Islamic financial products in the country. This is made possible thanks to their worldwide networking pioneer vision. It is also well known that high net worth individuals often keep their funds in Swiss Banks which guarantee higher privacy.

In 1982, Faisal Private Bank (Switzerland), an investment bank located in Geneva was established, and in October 2006 it was registered with the SFBC (Swiss Federal Banking Commission) and became a bank under Swiss law. Faisal Bank SA is the first Swiss bank to operate completely in compliance with *shari'ah*. Its main shareholder (79 per cent) is the Ithmaar Bank BSC, a major provider of Islamic investment products in the Middle East with headquarters in Bahrain. The bank provides products in the wealth management and private investment sectors for its clients and offers nearly the full range of Islamic financial structures: *mudarabah, musharakah, ijarah, sukuk*, etc. The bank invests about 55 per cent of its assets in short term projects (parallel purchase and sale of currencies and commodities) and about 36 per cent are invested in real estate. These products are designed and offered mainly for the needs of the bank's customers, wealthy private clients as well as institutional investors.

UBS AG is a Swiss bank with subsidiaries all over the world. It operates in the wealth management, investment banking and asset management sectors, and has a long history of active involvement in Islamic banking.

Due to the increasing demand for Islamic products, Noriba Bank, a 100 per cent subsidiary established in Bahrain in 2002, was integrated into UBS in 2006 as a part of the restructuring of the UBS business units. Today UBS provides a wide range of Islamic products. In the asset management sector, UBS has offered a fund through Noriba in Luxemburg since 2000, called UBS Islamic Global Equities (formerly the Noriba Global Equity Fund), which is an open ended fund that invests in diversified *shari'ah* compliant companies around the globe and is part of the Dow Jones Islamic Market 100 Titan Index^{SM}. In the equity sector, UBS offers its customers the UBS *sharia* compliant GOAL (*Geld oder Aktien Lieferung*: cash or share delivery), structured products based either on a *shari'ah* index or a product that is approved by the *shari'ah* board. UBS also provides long term *shari'ah* compliant products; for example, the UBS Sharia Compliant Deposit, based on a commodity *murabahah*, which cannot be cashed in before maturity. Another long term product is the UBS *sharia* compliant FX BLOC, which operates exactly like the UBS Sharia-Compliant Deposit, except that at maturity the bank also has the right to convert the invested capital into another currency. UBS also offers the UBS Range *Murabahah* investment, also based on a commodity *murabahah*. This product offers full capital protection, but the profit is limited by a cap (profit rate payment). Further products offered by UBS are different forms of *sukuk* – for example, *Musharakah Sukuk, Ijarah Sukuk* and *Murabahah Sukuk*. All these products are designed for both private and institutional investors. The Islamic banking sector is becoming more and more important to UBS.

Credit Suisse is a globally active financial services company offering a wide range of financial products for the private banking, wealth management and investment banking sectors, with its headquarters in Zurich. Since 2006, Credit Suisse has provided Islamic financial products. A team has been built up with Islamic financial experts in both Zurich and London. At present, the products are aimed mainly at institutional investors, but demand by private customers are expected to be addressed soon. The current fund that Credit Suisse is offering is the CS SICAV One (Lux) Equity Al-Buraq, issued in May 2007 and operated in compliance with *shari'ah*. At least two-thirds of the total capital is invested in shares or equities. Any profit earned that is not compliant with *shari'ah* is donated to charity organizations.

Pictet & Cie, established in 1905 in Geneva, founded Al Dar Islamic Fund in Luxembourg in 1988 to invest in *shari'ah* compliant open ended equity mutual fund worldwide equities.

d) Luxembourg

While the UK hosts several Islamic banks, Luxembourg is recognized as a leading hub for Islamic funds and is one of the major financial markets in Europe offering competitive pricing, incentives and access to European clients. Since 2002, when Luxembourg became the first European country to list *sukuk*, it now has a total of 16 *sukuks* listed on the exchange and 111 Islamic funds worth $3.4 billion. The government strongly supports foreign investments from oil rich countries and emerging wealthy nations. Luxembourg became the first EU jurisdiction to adopt UCITS IV at the end of December 2010, and as a major domicile for both conventional and Islamic investment funds it had a first-mover advantage.

e) Germany

In comparison to Luxemburg, Switzerland, France and UK markets, the German Islamic market is more moderate. There are currently about 4 million Muslims in Germany with a total accumulated wealth of €25 billion. Only 8 per cent of Muslims in Germany own their own homes, compared to a country-wide average of 42 per cent. Hence, it is not surprising to find the Islamic mortgage is high on the list.

The first retail Islamic banking institution was set up in 2015. It is a subsidiary of Kuveyt Turk Katimim Bankasi (KT Bank), the largest Islamic bank in Turkey, owned 62 per cent by Kuwait Finance House. KT Bank offers both deposit and financing facilities to local customers, and focuses on Germany's large Turkish community. The licensing of KT bank led to further expansion of *shari'ah* compliant banking activity in Germany.

Deutsche Bank AG, founded in 1870, has been actively operating for the last three decades within Arab markets, with a major focus on Islamic banking and *shari'ah* compliant products. It was awarded the 'Most Innovative Custodian Bank – First Islamic Custodian Bank' in 2007, and 'The Biggest and Most Active Custodian Bank for Islamic

Funds' in 2008. Deutsche Bank always engaged in cooperation with local banks, like the joint venture with Abraaj Capital of Dubai and Ithmaar Bank of Bahrain for the launch of financial funds that are run according to the rules of *shari'ah*. Part of Deutsche Bank's asset management division is DWS, a global mutual fund company, with €269 billion assets under management. A range of *shari'ah* compliant funds is offered by DWS in Africa and the Middle East to invest in precious metals securities and equities. All these funds require a minimum investment amount of $10 000 and $25 000 for private and institutional clients, respectively, and deals only with *shari'ah* compliant securities.

Commerzbank is one of the largest German banks, with its headquarters in Frankfurt. Its subsidiary company, Commerz International Capital Management (CICM), launched the Al-Sukoor European Equity Fund in 1999. This fund was initially designed only for institutional investors from the Middle East, but CICM later partnered with Al-Tawfeek group, a subsidiary company of Dallah Albaraka which is one of the world's biggest banking groups, to help with the design and sale of the fund. However, the fund had to be closed in 2005. According to Commerzbank, Islamic banking is not one of its core divisions and the Al-Sukoor European Equity Fund was the only Islamic product that was offered to its German clients.

Allianz, also offers *shari'ah* compliant products to customers outside Germany, especially in Indonesia, the Gulf States and Malaysia. As one of the biggest global providers of insurance, banking and asset management services, it opened a branch in Indonesia in 2006, which specialized in *shari'ah* compliant products. Hannover Re Group is one of the major reinsurance groups worldwide offering *takaful* (insurance) to companies that operate according to *shari'ah* in Indonesia, the Gulf States and Malaysia. In 2006, the €660 million Gulf German Residence Fund was issued by Abu Dhabi Investment House, which invests in real estate properties all over Germany. Another real estate fund investing in Germany is the German AIL Fund 1, which was launched in 2007 by Arab Investment Ltd.

Saxony-Anhalt was the first western organization to tap into the Islamic capital market (*sukuk*). In 2004, the federal state of Saxony-Anhalt was the first European issuer of a €100 million asset backed *sukuk*, structured as a *sukuk al-ijarah*, which was listed on the Luxembourg Stock Exchange. The German State, represented by the Ministry of Finance, sold a number of buildings to a special purpose vehicle (SPV) and then leased them back for five years. The subscribers of the SPV receive a variable rent over the whole period. This rent is aligned to the EURIBOR, which was chosen as the benchmark. The debts of Saxony-Anhalt are guaranteed by the German state.

f) Italy

As of 2014, a number of initiatives have been taken by the Italian authorities to study issues related to an expanded presence of Islamic finance. The Banca d'Italia, for example, has hosted a number of conferences on the subject. ABI, the Italian Banking Association, is currently coordinating a working group related to the issuance of a corporate or sovereign *sukuk*. There is also a plan to launch a 'Mediterranean Partnership Fund' dedicated to promoting small and medium-sized enterprises in the MENA region. Part of the fund, in collaboration with Arab governments and IDB, would be *shari'ah* compliant. Islamic retail banking deposits are planned to rapidly increase from $5.8 billion by 2015 to $33.4 billion by 2050 with significant increase in revenue from $218 million by 2015 to $1.2 billion by 2050. The Italian market has good future prospects, especially for some of its wholesale banking institutions that are active in using *murabahah*, trade financing and participation in syndication facilities (i.e. Islamic capital market). More recently, Italian banks have also been active in private–public partnerships initiatives in the GCC region, and a number of bilateral trade ties between Italian based institutions and GCC based financial institutions are known to have succeeded in introducing and managing Islamic insurance products for group employee benefit purposes.

g) Ireland

The Irish market has a strong foundation for the Islamic finance industry with a comprehensive tax treaty network and a specific tax code for Islamic instruments. The Irish government is highly supportive of Islamic finance development which is part of its International Financial Services Strategy launched in 2015. A dedicated team was set up to deal with the establishment of *shari'ah* compliant investments funds. The Irish market has growth potential due to its easy access to the European market. It is home to more than 50 world class fund service providers who will take the opportunity to participate in Islamic finance given the facilities provided by the government.

h) USA

Today, the USA is home to at least 19 providers of Islamic banking products and services, including retail banks, investment banks, mortgage companies, investment advisers and community based finance providers (such as University Bank, Devon Bank, Broadway Bank of Chicago, Zayan Finance, Guidance Residential, City of Minneapolis – Alternative financing programme, African Development Centre, Ameen Housing Cooperative, Saturna Capital, Azzad Asset Management, Arcapita and Innovest Capital). With the estimated number of American Muslims living in the country increasing and a reduction in the complexity of the USA's regulatory regime, it is expected that the growth of the Islamic financial market will be prompted by the existing providers as well as newcomers.

6.5.2 MIDDLE EAST AND TURKEY

a) Middle East

Since the establishment of DIB in 1975, the region has witnessed strong growth in Islamic banking. The GCC[1] became the incubating ground for Islamic banking and finance, which saw further development in Islamic insurance (*takaful*) and *shari'ah* compliant asset management, as well as retail and investment banking. The region's Islamic financial institutions became the major provider of capital for the development of Islamic finance worldwide, especially in Asia. The GCC's unique position in the heart of the Islamic world further enable it to function as an Islamic financing centre linking Europe, Asia and Africa, as can be seen in the spread of GCC's Islamic banking subsidiaries in other parts of the world. For instance, Al Rajhi Bank in Saudi Arabia has successfully developed a range of deposit and financing products that attracted millions of customers, making it the largest listed Islamic bank in the world with subsidiaries in other countries. Among the authorities in the GCC that have been very supportive of Islamic banking and finance is Bahrain, which has become the main centre for Islamic banking and *takaful*. Kuwait, Oman and Saudi Arabia also offer useful legislative support to allow the Islamic financial sector to play an important role in the development of their local economies. While major international banks were severely weakened during the financial crisis of 2008-2009, Islamic banks in the GCC were not affected, and in fact the crisis presented them with opportunity for growth and market share expansion which saw further internationalization of Islamic banking and finance which supplies fresh liquidities to the global economy. For example, Kuwait Finance House and Al Rajhi Bank's Islamic retail banking investments in the Asian market have remained resilient.

The most popular Islamic financial products, *murabahah* and *ijarah*, were initiated and refined in the Gulf region. Another popular product in Bahrain, Kuwait, Qatar and the UAE is the *mudarabah-investment* deposits. *Shari'ah* compliant mutual funds are offered for those looking for returns on investment. However, the GCC's Islamic financial institutions have been criticized for simply mimicking conventional banks and focusing on wealthy clients rather than playing a social role and helping the poor entrepreneurial.

b) Turkey

Turkey is home to a number of dedicated Islamic banks as well as Islamic window operations offered through conventional banks. Some of the listed banks provide only investment or wholesale banking, while others are more retail focused. The Islamic banking industry in Turkey is known as 'participation banking' (katılım bankacılığı), offering *shari'ah* compliant services and products to customers. Turkish Islamic banks collect deposits

---

[1]The GCC is a regional political organization comprising the energy rich Gulf monarchies – Bahrain, Kuwait, Oman, Qatar, Saudi Arabia and the United Arab Emirates.

on the bases of *mudarabah* structure and use *murabahah* structure to cater for the financing needs of their customers. Other financial structures such as *musharakah* is used to finance construction contracts, *istisna'a* for financing housing projects, and *ijarah* is used to finance equipment, machinery and other investment tools by companies while *qard hasan* is used for credit card cash withdrawals. In 2010, the first *sukuk al-ijarah,* an asset based instrument, was issued. With the upswing in Turkish economy, the banks were able to obtain their own funding from international markets in the form of *murabahah* syndications.

The practice of Islamic finance in the Turkish banking sector first gained legitimacy in 1983 when 'special finance houses' were introduced. Between 1985 and 1991, six interest free finance companies, Al Baraka, Kuveyt Turk, Faisal Finans, Anadolu Finans, İhlas Finans and Asya Finans, were established. In 2001, Turkey experienced a devastating economic crisis, during which İhlas Finans, the key player, went into bankruptcy because of a liquidity problem. Kuveyt Turk (Kuveyt Turk Participation Bank Inc.) whose largest shareholder is Kuwait Finance House, offers participation services in Turkey and Germany. Türkiye Finans is a participation bank and a joint venture with Saudi Arabia's National Commercial Bank, Boydak Group and Ülker Group. Bank Asya (Asya Participation Bank Inc.) provides interest free banking services in Turkey. Participation banks have encouraged their customers to invest in gold funds as either current accounts and/or participation accounts. There has consequently been a 500 per cent increase in investment since 2010.

Since the last decade, the Turkish government has reasserted its commitment to accelerate the growth of Islamic banking and finance in the country and also globally. Recent developments indicate the initial success of its strategy. For instance, the World Bank Global Islamic Finance Development Centre was inaugurated in Istanbul in 2013 to assist international banks to benefit from the rapid growth and potential Islamic investments for economic development. In 2014, the largest bank owned by the government, T.C. Ziraat Bankası A.Ş., received approval to go ahead in establishing a fully fledged Turkish Islamic Bank.[2] In 2015, another large state owned bank, Türkiye Halk Bankası A.Ş. (also known as Halkbank), was given the approval from the Turkish Banking Regulatory and Supervisory Authority to establish an Islamic bank division in Turkey with a share capital of TRY1 billion (about £180 million). Similarly, in 2015, Kuveyt Turk, a Turkish lender, announced the establishment of Germany's first fully fledged Islamic bank outside Turkey.

6.5.3 SOUTH-EAST ASIA AND SOUTH ASIA

a) Malaysia

Malaysia is a pioneering country in the development of global Islamic finance industry beyond the 1970s nascent. The industry has experienced transformative changes, which support the overarching goal of Islamic finance as a more inclusive and equitable financial system. The evolution of Malaysian regulations related to Islamic finance and the ensuing product innovation have boosted Islamic financial institutions' (IFIs) ability to serve the economy through *shari'ah* compliant instruments.

Its Islamic finance ecosystem has grown in strength since the launch of its Financial Sector Masterplan in 2001. The plan outlines a comprehensive set of strategies to be implemented to strengthen the foundation of the Islamic financial sector and it has since shown positive outcome. Total assets of the Islamic banking subsector grew by more than 8 per cent in 2016 (2015: 11.5 per cent), accounting for about 28 per cent of the overall banking industry (2015: 26.8 per cent). Intermediation financial related activities expanded following the growth in investment intermediation. The *takaful* industry also witnessed higher growth as reflected in the reported net *takaful* contributions of RM7.5 billion in 2016 compared with RM6.8 billion in 2015, an increase which accounts for about 15 per cent of total industry premiums and contributions. In short, IFIs in Malaysia are expected to play a bigger intermediation role to sustain its growth trajectory and deliver better value to

---

[2]Vizcaino, Bernardo, and Shri Navaratnam. 'UPDATE 1-Turkey's Ziraat Bank Gets Fast-track Approval for Islamic Unit.' *Reuters.* Thomson Reuters, 15 Oct. 2014. Web. 4 Sept. 2015.

consumers through business diversification and use of technology as well as contribute effectively towards the broader economic and social development.

b) Indonesia

Indonesia is among the latecomers to the Islamic finance and banking industry and it is almost a decade behind Malaysia. Bank Muamalat, Indonesian first Islamic bank, was established in 1992 but it was only in 1999 that the Indonesian central bank endorsed the use of Islamic financial instruments and structure. However, the Indonesian central bank has since then accelerated reforms in its monetary policies to further support liquidity instruments and capital markets activities which saw the Islamic financial sector growing at twice the rate of conventional finance. Among the plans of the central bank is to have at least one in five banks in the country to be *shari'ah* compliant by 2020 and to have all financial institutions, including Islamic banks and cooperatives, under the supervision of the Indonesian FSA.

Islamic microfinance plays a crucial role in supporting sustainability of the rural socio-economic sector. Hence, the government plans to provide financing available to micro, small, and medium enterprises (MSMEs) in so-called productive sectors, which include agriculture and infrastructure. The most commonly used financial structure by Islamic rural banks (BPRS) and microfinance cooperatives (*Baitul Maal wat Tamwil*) in Indonesia's microfinance sector is *murabahah* contracts. Another important player in this sector is Bank Rakyat Indonesia Syariah (BRI Syariah), which is a subsidiary of Indonesia's largest microfinance institution, Bank Rakyat Indonesia (BRI).

c) Pakistan

Efforts to provide a blueprint for an Islamic economy were initiated in 1977 by the then president of Pakistan, General Mohammed Ziaul Haq, who passed the task to the Council of Islamic Ideology (CII). In 1980, the CII developed a theoretical model of the Islamic economy through the help of top economists and bankers in Pakistan. The State Bank of Pakistan (SBP) concluded the task of implementing the Islamic banking and finance sector in 1984 by issuing a circular that prescribed 12 financing modes for practising fully fledged Islamic banking: service charges and *Qard-Hasanah* systems for financing by lending, six trade based modes, such as mark-up or mark-down financing under buy-back agreement (*Bai muajjal/murabahah*), leasing, hire-purchase and financing for property development on the basis of development charges, investment type modes of financing that include *musharakah*, equity participation, *mudarabah* and rent sharing.

In 2001, the Islamic banking industry was relaunched under the supervision of the SBP and in 2002, the government abandoned its Islamization policy. The strategy developed by the SBP in 2001 has permitted the introduction of Islamic banking services by fully fledged Islamic banks as well as Islamic banking subsidiaries and branches of conventional banks. In light of the government's reliance on the banking sector as an essential source of finance to cover its budget deficits, this market driven approach is intended to achieve the transformation of the financial industry towards *shari'ah* compliance in a gradual and non-disruptive manner.

Meezan Bank was the first fully fledged Islamic bank to be granted a license in 2002, and there are six such banks operating in Pakistan. The most recent entrant, MCB Islamic Bank, is a subsidiary of the fourth largest commercial bank in Pakistan. In addition, 17 out of the remaining 21 local commercial banks in the private and public sectors operate dedicated branches for Islamic banking.

Figure 6.4 illustrates the growth and global assets in major regions: the GCC, Turkey, ASEAN and South Asia.

6.5.4 AFRICA

Africa, with a Muslim population of about 491 million, holds a promising growth opportunity for Islamic finance. One of the challenges for the growth of the Islamic financial revolution in Africa is the high rate of its people still not having access to banking services while the banking system in other countries is growing increasingly sophisticated. Furthermore, the low literacy rate causes people not to have a bank account. Nevertheless,

Figure 6.4 Growth and global assets in major Islamic finance hubs

International participation banking assets* (US$b)

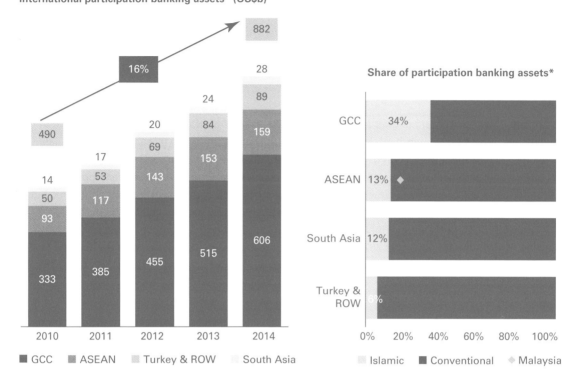

Share of participation banking assets*

Global share of Islamic finance banking assets, 2015

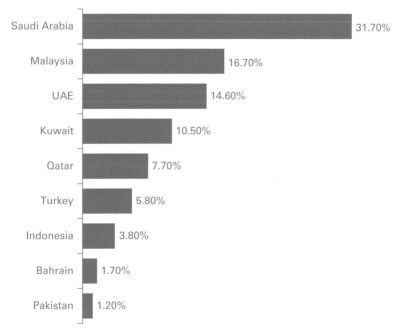

Source: www.consultancy.uk/news/3102/ey-islamic-banking-growth-on-the-increase-across-globe

Muslim population which makes about 43.3 per cent of the whole population of the continent perceives Islamic banking as a motivating cause to start utilizing banking services. Egypt, Algeria, Tunisia, Senegal, Gambia and Djibouti all have at least one Islamic financial institution. They all face similar challenges of operating in an environment that is not yet aligned to the requirements of *shari'ah* compliant financial products. Among the major challenges is the fact that Islamic scholars are very few in number, and only a few countries have legislation that is conducive to Islamic banking.

a) Egypt

Egypt is known as the first country to offer Islamic finance. The pioneering efforts by Ahmad El Najjar in introducing a business model for savings bank in the form of profit sharing in the Egyptian town of Mit Ghamr in 1963 paved the way for the introduction of Islamic banking to the world. The business model neither charges nor pays interest, but instead invests most of the deposits in business projects through partnerships and shares the profits and losses with depositors. However, the government banned such a business model in 1967, but it later supported the establishments of Nasser Social Bank (NSB) and Faisal Islamic Bank of Egypt (FIB) in 1971 and 1977, respectively. Since then the number of financial institutions offering Islamic banking services to their customers has grown substantially. As of 2015, there are about 39 banks, including the 14 banks licensed by the Central Bank of Egypt (CBE), offering Islamic financial products.

b) Kenya

Kenya made history when it became the first country in Eastern and Central Africa to permit the operations of a fully fledged *shari'ah* compliant commercial bank called First Community Bank (FCB). In 2008, Gulf African Bank became the second fully fledged *shari'ah* compliant bank operating in the country.

c) South Africa

South Africa became the first sub-Saharan African country to have an Islamic bank when Albaraka was established in 1989 to serve a niche market. In 2002, the First National Bank, which is one of the four largest national banks in the country, began offering Islamic products through their branches in South Africa and Botswana. In 2006, the largest retail banking group in the country, Absa, became the first bank offering comprehensive Islamic banking products which include vehicle financing, transactional and contractual savings accounts and other *shari'ah* compliant products such as Islamic will, short term *takaful* cover for businesses, vehicles and home, international cash debit cards and Western Union money transfers. There is also increasing popularity in *shari'ah* compliant ETFs listed on the JSE (Johannesburg Stock Exchange). The Shari'a New Gold and Top 40 ETFs are seen as ground breaking products offered in sub-Saharan Africa. Despite the wide range of *shari'ah* compliant products on offer in the South African banking system, critics highlighted that the pace for further development of the existing products and infrastructure is slow and does not match up with the growth in demand for more product offerings expected by both local and Muslim foreign nationals.

d) Nigeria

Nigeria is not only the most populous country in west Africa but also has the largest economy. There was a strong demand by Nigerian Muslims, who made up about 65 per cent of the population, for the establishment of a banking system that meets their religious and moral aspirations. To achieve this goal, a number of Islamic organizations, corporate bodies and individuals put on a concerted effort to make it a reality. In 2009, the regulatory framework for Islamic banking was assented by the Central Bank of Nigeria (CBN). As a result, in 2011, JAIZ Islamic Bank became the first fully fledged Islamic bank in the country. The bank was given a national license in 2016 to operate in all the different states of the federation.

e) Tunisia

In January 2009, the Central Bank of Tunisia granted a banking licence to Banque Zitouna to operate as a fully fledged Islamic bank which opened in 2010 with head office situated in Les Berges du Lac, near the country's capital, Tunis. Zitouna's authorized capital is $22.8 million, with Princesse El Materi Holding having a 51 per cent stake in the venture. Other shareholders include Groupe La Carte (insurance provider), Groupe Poulina Holding (a group of companies that covers the agricultural, food, industrial and service sectors), Groupe TTS (tourism services group), Groupe Délice-Danone (an agro–food company), Groupe UTIC (distribution) and Groupe Bouchamaoui. All banking products and services offered by Zitouna are fully *shari'ah* compliant and focus on lending and deposits. They are based on various profit and loss sharing mechanisms, including *murabahah, ijarah, mudarabah* and *musharakah*.

6.5.5 OTHER NEW HUBS

a) Hong Kong and China

The Hong Kong government has been encouraging more finance activity of Islamic instruments in the city. In 2007, Hang Seng Bank launched Hong Kong's first *shari'ah* compliant retail fund. Malaysian Hong Leong Bank became the first bank allowed to offer comprehensive Islamic financial services in Hong Kong in 2008. It aims to tap the markets of mainland China and west and north Asia by leveraging on Hong Kong's status as an international financial centre. The bank offers a *murabahah* security, a product which is based on a price mark-up structure and helps in liquidity management and plans to offer other products with *shari'ah* structures like *ijarah, mudarabah* and *musharakah*. Also in 2008, Hong Kong's first *shari'ah* compliant syndicated loan was launched for Noble Group raising $80 million.

In 2011, Khazanah, the investment holding arm of the Malaysian government, marketed Hong Kong's first yuan-denominated *sukuk* of 500 million yuan, attracting investors from Malaysia, Singapore, Hong Kong, the Middle East and Europe. In 2012, Malaysian telecommunications firm Axiata launched the first corporate yuan *sukuk* in Hong Kong, raising 1 billion yuan. Also in 2012, Hong Kong Monetary Agency (HKMA) and Bank Negara Malaysia introduced a pilot scheme that allowed bonds to be traded and settled across the Malaysian and Hong Kong borders. While the government is interested in *sukuk* (Islamic bond) market, the development of other Islamic services and products and hosting IFIs needs relentless promoting efforts especially at the political and local legislation fronts with China's government.

The People's Republic of China has been taking the steps necessary to facilitate Islamic finance transactions in China and Hong Kong, to prepare the country for competition in the *sukuk*, Islamic funds and Islamic finance industries. In 2006, the Chinese banking sector was opened to foreign banks. In the same year, Bahrain based Shamil Bank launched its $100 million Shamil China Realty *Mudarabah*. The four year *mudarabah* was invested in the Xuan Huang China Realty Investment Fund, a joint venture between Shamil Bank and the state-owned Chinese Conglomerate CITIC Group. In addition, Deutsche Bank, through its global mutual fund arm DWS Investments, launched its first *shari'ah* compliant mutual fund capability in December of 2006, which was marketed as DWS Noor Islamic Funds and included the DWS Noor China Equity Fund.

In 2009, Bank of Ningxia established an Islamic Banking Unit. In 2012, Bank Muamalat Malaysia and Bank of Shizuishan of China announced plans to establish an Islamic bank in Ningxia province. In addition, the two banks agreed to offer Islamic banking products through Bank of Shizuishan's network of 23 branches. In 2013, China approved Ningxia as an economic experimental zone for inland development, creating room for the introduction of Islamic finance in the country. Also in 2014, RHB Asset Management launched an Islamic fund for public investors and Affin Bank and Bank of East Asia announced plans to establish an Islamic bank in the People's Republic of China. In 2015, Industrial and Commercial Bank of China, China's largest bank by assets, signed a deal with IDB to develop *shari'ah* compliant banking products in China and the 52 IDB member countries. Gulf Finance House plans to invest at least $1 billion in Chinese infrastructure projects. Al Rajhi Investments (ARII) introduced *shari'ah* compliant investments in the Chinese market through its Shari'ah Investment Fund (SAIF) in partnership with China Resources (CRC). There are also plans to develop a Ninxia Islamic Finance Center in the province's capital Yinchuan, establish Islamic banks and banking products in China, and develop a wholesale Islamic capital market, including Islamic bonds, equities and funds.

b) Japan

Islamic finance became popular in Japan after the first issuance of *sukuk* in 2006 by Japan Bank for International Cooperation (JBIC), the state's finance arm for enhancing international trade and investment. As part of the Japanese government's plan for enhancing international trade and investment and strengthening Japanese local business, the Malaysian subsidiary of Bank of Tokyo-Mitsubishi UFJ (BTMU) in 2006 made a strategic alliance with Malaysian Commerce International Merchant Bankers (CIMB) to contribute to the sound development of Islamic finance. In 2007, Sumitomo Mitsui Banking Corporation (SMBC) established a branch in Dubai to encourage regional transactions, especially for Islamic financial transactions. Japanese asset management houses such as Nomura Investment Company and Toyota Motor Corp began providing *shari'ah* compliant investment funds in 2010 and 2012, respectively. In 2014, BTMU issued the world's first *sukuk* denominated in yen (Emas Sukuk).

With regards to *takaful*, Tokio Marine and Nichido Fire Insurance Co (Tokio Marine) launched their *takaful* business in 2001, targeting customers in Saudi Arabia. Seeing the tremendous opportunities in *takaful* products, the company in 2004 opened a branch for *takaful* and re-*takaful* in Singapore. In 2006, Tokio Marine and Malaysia's Hong Leong Group established a joint *takaful* operation in Kuala Lumpur. In 2007, Tokio Marine established its *takaful* business in Egypt.

JBIC's and Tokio Marine's successful venture with Islamic financial products prompted positive developments in regulatory reforms in the Japanese Banking and Insurance Business Acts. This is expected to promote more active *shari'ah* compliant transactions in Japanese public and private sectors in the years to come.

c) India

Islamic finance has a long history in India and some of the leading figures involved in the Islamization of the economic system were from India. The Muslim Fund Deoband (MFD) was established in 1961 and it is still operating today. Muslim Fund Najibabad (MFN) was established on the model of MFD in 1971 and in 1990, MFN floated a subsidiary, Al-Najib Milli Mutual Benefits Ltd. The Modern Education Social and Cultural Organization (MESCO) set up by a group of college students from Bombay (now Mumbai) in 1968 led to the establishment of Baitun-Nasr Urban cooperative credit society (BUN) which commenced functioning in 1973. Restriction on the operation beyond the geographical boundary of Bombay and other restrictions led to the formation of Barkat Investment Group (BIG) in 1983. BIG and Tata Mutual Fund came together in 1996 to launch a mutual fund scheme especially designed for Muslims, though it was never regarded as a truly *shari'ah* compliant fund since no *shari'ah* advisor was involved in the screening of the fund.

Over the last decade, a number of significant changes occurred in the Indian banking sector. Instead of being averse to anything Islamic as before, the Indian regulators have started to look at the positive side of *shari'ah* compliant activities and have allowed schemes that lay claim to such an undertaking. In 2005, the Indian government took important actions with important ramifications for the Islamic finance business in the country such as the establishment of Anand Sinha Committee under the Reserve Bank of India to study Islamic financial products. In 2008, the Raghuram Ramrajan Committee recommended Islamic banking for financial inclusion of the Muslim community in India, which prompted the government to call for reforms in the National Minority Development Finance Corporation (NMDFC) based on *shari'ah* principles. In 2009, the Securities and Exchange Board of India (SEBI) permitted the first *shari'ah* compliant mutual fund and venture capital fund, and the government of the state of Kerala announced the launch of an Islamic Investment company. In the same year, the General Insurance Corporation of India (GIC), one of the largest government owned company, appointed Taqwaa advisory & Shariah Investment Solutions (P) Ltd. (TASIS) to provide *shari'ah* advice to ensure financial activities are *shari'ah* compliant.

These actions indicate a cautious but systematic approach by Indian policymakers in allowing Islamic financial products and services in the country, which prompted many players from the private sector like HSBC, Benchmark, TATAS, Taurus, UTI, Kotak, Reliance and Bajaj Allianz to come up with *shari'ah* compliant products for the Indian market.

6.6 Operating structures of Islamic banking and finance industry

Let us now look at the operating structure of the Islamic banking system to help us better understand the nature of Islamic banking. *Operating structure* refers to the functions, departmental structure, main layout and mobilization of funds. Although the operating structures of Islamic banks on the surface may seem similar to conventional banks, there are significant differences as they are built on a totally different foundation arising from a single requirement: *shari'ah* compliance. In the following sections we will consider what these principles are and how they differ from conventional banking as well as their implications on the operating structure.

6.6.1 PRINCIPLES AND FUNCTIONS OF ISLAMIC BANKING

As we have seen in the earlier chapter 5, *shari'ah* lays the foundations for economic activities to ensure that the goal of social justice is achieved in society. In this section, we will look at seven principles pertinent to the business of banking from an Islamic perspective, as illustrated in Figure 6.5.

Figure 6.5 Principles underlying Islamic banking

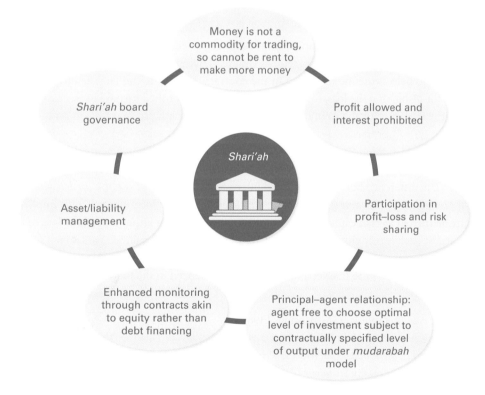

a) Money is not a commodity for trading

Central to the business of banking is of course money, as it is received from depositors/savers and disbursed to those who needed it for some reasons. The *modus operandi* for conventional banks is to lend the money deposited by depositors/savers to others who needed it in return for some fixed payments in the form of original capital and an excess return (interest).

For example, you take a loan of £20 000 from a conventional bank to be paid in a series of monthly payments of £400 over five years. If you add up the monthly payments, you will discover that the total payments you made exceeded the amount of your loan (£400 × 60 = £24 000). Thus, the extra £4000 is due to the interest that you paid on the loan to compensate the lender for the time during which you used the funds. In other words, you are paying rent for the use of resources from the bank. Hence, in conventional banking, money is treated as a commodity to make money and the concept of time value of money is recognized by incorporating a fixed compensation (interest rate, in this case about 7.5 per cent) in the monthly payment. In other words, conventional banks trade in money, buying money from depositors and selling money in the form of loans.

However, as discussed in Chapter 3, money from an Islamic perspective is only considered as a medium of exchange and store of value, and not a commodity that can be sold or rented out to generate surplus value by itself. Thus, money can only be exchanged for real assets or services and cannot be exchanged directly for money unless the exchange is spontaneous. This implies that lending of money and waiting passively to get back the capital and an excess return is *haram* (not permissible) under *shari'ah* as this constitute making money from money and the excess return is considered as *riba* (interest).

Since the paying or receiving of interest is prohibited, this implies that money should not be allowed to give rise to more money through predetermined fixed interest payments, but instead requires consideration of human efforts, initiatives and risks involved in the productive venture. Therefore, money is considered as *potential capital* rather than *actual capital*, meaning that money becomes capital only when it is invested in business.

b) Profit allowed and interest prohibited

The *sine qua non* of conventional banking is interest, which is perceived as a form of justifiable reward to the moneylender for saving and for undertaking the inevitable consequence of the difference in value today and the value after some time (time value of money) as well as a charge for the use of money as capital.

However, from an Islamic perspective, money advanced as a loan is regarded as a debt and not capital, and therefore the lender is not entitled to receive any excess returns (interest) because Islam encourages the act of lending to be a benevolent act to help someone in need. On the contrary, the profit and fees, as opposed to interest, charged by the bank for disbursing the loan to the borrower to be used for the purchase of real assets or services will be shared with the depositor or the capital owner, since the banker has put in efforts in arranging for the mobilization of funds.

In other words, interest received from lending is condemned as it is not a justifiable payment to the lender, while normal profit is recognized as the correct form of compensation to the lender. So what is the difference between profit and interest? The difference between profit and interest is that: *(i) profit is not a predetermined rate of return, (ii) it has a probability of loss and (iii) it is earned by exerting some efforts or work*. This implies that borrowed funds must be treated as risk capital which entails the possibility of either a profit or loss of a non-predetermined value and as such is recognized as a valid factor of production. Islamic scholars do not foresee problems for Islamic banks to make some profit on the amount they spend for procuring the assets as long as the prices and profits are determined by the market and not fixed, as evidenced in the following verses in the *Qur'an* and the Hadith, respectively:

> It is no crime for you to seek the bounty of your lord (Al-Baqarah, 2:198).[3]
>
> As narrated by Anas: During the life time of the Prophet (pbuh) price levels went up. They (people) said 'Prophet (pbuh)! Fix the prices for us.' On this, the Prophet (pbuh) said: 'Prices are fixed by Allah. He contracts and expands the sources of livelihood and I hope to meet my Sustainer (Allah) in a state that no one may raise a claim of injustice against me in respect of blood or money' (Abu Dawud).[4]

---

[3] www.wright-house.com/religions/islam/Quran/2-cow.php, accessed 25 May 2018.

[4] Book 23, Hadith 3444 sunnah.com/abudawud/24/36, accessed 25 May 2018.

c) Participation and risk sharing

While the first and second principles prohibited the use of money as commodity to make more money in the form of interest payment as practiced by conventional banks, the third principle emphasizes participation and risk sharing for all financial transactions. The principle of 'no reward without risk bearing' is applicable to both capital and labour. In the case of the former, no reward is due for the capital unless it is exposed to business risks while for the latter, no payment is allowed for labour unless it involves some work or effort. Thus, both the principal and agent should equally share the risk and rewards from the business ventures. Islamic banking offers depositors/investors returns through participation in risk sharing type packages rather than fixed interest on deposits and participates in the business venture by utilizing the funds at risk on a profit–loss sharing basis with the borrower/entrepreneur. Profits should be for both the principal and agent. The mechanism for distribution of profit should be on the basis of a pre-agreed ratio of the capital and must be clearly expressed to eliminate uncertainty and any possibility of dispute.

This is unlike the interest based conventional banking system where all the risks are transferred to the borrower who must pay back the loan with the addition of an agreed predetermined interest regardless of the success or failure of the venture. Therefore, the risk sharing principle should encourage investments that will benefit the community by deterring those who are risk averse from hoarding money and also stopping depositors from expecting increase on their funds with no risk other than the bank becoming insolvent. In other words, Islam leaves no other avenues available to those with surplus funds; either invest with risk or suffer losses through devaluation resulting from inflation by keeping the money idle. Islam also supports the notion of higher risks and higher returns, as high risk investments provide a stimulus to the economy and encourage entrepreneurs to maximize their efforts.

d) Rabbul mal *(principal)* and mudarib *(agent)* relationships

Closely related to the third principle is the nature of relationship between the bank and depositors and bank and borrowers/entrepreneurs. In Islamic banking operations, there is a two tier relationship in profit–loss sharing. The first tier involves the relationship between the depositor as the *rabbul mal* (principal) who provides the capital, and the bank as the *mudarib* (agent) who either acts as partner or manager of the fund. Therefore, the principal will hand over the agreed capital to the agent with no interference in the management but has the authority to oversee the agent's activities and will only work with the agent if the latter consents. The agent's responsibility is to assure the owner of capital or principal that the capital is in good hands and will act to find the best ways of investing it in a permissible manner. Hence, the agent may act in one of these capacities: (i) as a trustee to look after the investment responsibly except in the case of natural calamities, (ii) as an agent (*wakeel*) to purchase from the funds provided by the principal and (iii) as a partner (*shareek*) in sharing any profit.

The second tier relationship involves the borrower or entrepreneur as manager of fund and the bank functioning as provider of capital. In other words, the contractual relationships could be in the form of buyer–seller relationship (*murabahah*), lessor–lessee relationship (*ijarah*), partnership (*musharakah*), principal–agent relationship (*mudarabah*) or creditor–debtor relationship (*qard hassan*). These contractual relationships have implications on the structure of balance sheet (statement of financial position) of Islamic banks compared to their conventional counterparts, as we will see in the later section.

Hence, the principal–agent problem (agency conflict), often referred to as *the agency cost of equity*, i.e. tendency of agents to engage in excessive consumption and other opportunistic behaviour that benefits them without having to bear the full share of the cost to the firm, can be mitigated by contracts that force agents to bear more of the wealth consequences of their actions. Unlike conventional banking whereby the standard relationship is that of lender–borrower or creditor–debtor, contractual relationship based on profit–loss sharing contract allows Islamic banks as agents to freely choose the optimal level of effort in each state contingent on the specified level of investment.

e) Enhanced monitoring

Since Islamic financial contracting encourages profit–loss sharing, this means that banks have the obligations to monitor the performance of the entrepreneur, since they are partners in the endeavour. The advantage of such enhanced monitoring is that it will help ensure that the venture is profitable. However, this may be at a higher cost as Islamic banks need to invest relatively more in managerial skills and expertise in overseeing the different investment projects.

In contrast, the contractual relationship in conventional banking is that of lender–borrower or creditor–debtor and as such there is no obligation to closely monitor how the funds have been utilized. The only consideration is that payments are made on time by the debtor and failure to do may result in penalty and/or loss of assets.

f) Asset/liability management

Stability of the financial system is important to ensure that there is no financial panic or contagion in the form of bank runs that may cause collapse in the whole financial system. This requires mobilizing capital to their most productive uses, prudent management of risks and good management of assets and liabilities on the balance sheet. An important issue related to the balance sheet structure is the matching of assets and liabilities.

In Islamic banking, there is no predetermined rate on the deposits and investments as well as the depositors'/investors' share in the profits and losses on the asset side of the balance sheet. Therefore, the problem of asset–liability mismatch does not arise as the assets and liabilities are closely matched. This in turn contributes to the stability of the financial system. Furthermore, since the largest portion of income generated by an Islamic bank and a major percentage of assets is subjected to risk as a result of profit sharing, it is obvious that prudent management of risks is essential for ensuring the stability of Islamic banks. Risks can be managed prudently through effective regulatory and supervisory framework and having a sound internal Islamic banking policy.[5]

In the case of conventional banking, deposits which are on the liability side are accepted at a predetermined rate irrespective of the rate of return from loans on the asset side. This creates a fixed liability or commitment for the bank without certainty that it would earn more from the loans and investments on the asset side. When the rate on the asset side is not known, this can lead to mismatch between assets and liabilities which may result in financial instability.

g) Shari'ah governance

The most distinctive feature of Islamic banking is the existence of a *shari'ah* board that comprises religious scholars who will have significant influence on the board's decision making, as well as operations of Islamic banks. Any new products cannot be launched by the bank without prior approval by the *shari'ah* board who will oversee whether the product is permissible and meets the *shari'ah* gold standard, such as not investing in and providing financing to activities involved with *riba* and *gharar*, manufacturing and sale of non-permissible products, stockbroking or share trading in non-*shari'ah* based activities, etc. In making their decisions, the *shari'ah* board must ensure that they have taken into account all requirements of justice, customer protection, compliance with *shari'ah*, interpretation of customary civil practices as well as practicality of implementation. In short, decisions must be clear, defensible and without any doubt to their validity. This enhances the legitimacy of the products offered by the banks and also provides confidence and satisfaction to depositors that the board is monitoring the adherence and compliance by the institution with *shari'ah* principles.

6.6.2 COMPARISON BETWEEN CONVENTIONAL AND ISLAMIC BANKING

Now that we have understood the underlying principles of Islamic banking, let us now look at how these principles affect the practice of Islamic banking making it distinctive from conventional banking. Table 6.3 provides a comparative summary of the two banking systems. There are ten aspects that differentiate between the two banking systems.

---

[5]We will look in more detail on risks in Chapter 11.

Table 6.3 Summary of differences between conventional and Islamic banking

Aspect	Conventional banking	Islamic banking
1. Function of money other than medium of exchange and store of value	Money is treated as a commodity, hence it can be sold at a price higher than its face value and it can also be rented out.	Money is not a commodity, hence it cannot be sold at a price higher than its face value or rented out.
2. Impact of use of money on the economy	Conventional banking uses money as a commodity, which may lead to inflation.	Islamic banking links money to trade related activities, therefore contributing directly to the real economy.
3. Determinant of return	Compensation in the form of interest is for the use of money as capital and for giving up use of funds today which would have increase in value in the future (based on time value of money).	Charging fees and earning profit for the provision of service in mobilizing funds, not as debt but based on trading, sharing or leasing.
4. Late payment of loans	Interest will be compounded.	No compound charges are allowed and any penalty charged is not considered part of bank's income and must be given to charity.
5. Banking relationship	Loan arrangement and services.	Financing arrangements based on partnership, profit sharing, trading, agency, commodity sales.
6. Contractual terms	Debtor–creditor or lender–borrower.	Partners, fund provider and entrepreneur, buyer and seller, principal and agent, service provider.
7. Risk	All risks are transferred to the debtor.	Risk is based on the nature of contract and banks share some risk.
8. Rulings	Banking regulations and business laws of the country.	Islamic business law (*fiqh muamalat*) in addition to banking regulations and business laws of the country.
9. Product approval	Products are approved by the bank management.	Products are approved by the bank management *and Shari'ah Board*.
10. Governance	The organization is run by the board of directors.	The organization is run by the board of directors and *shari'ah* supervisory board.

The first two aspects are related to the first principle regarding money. While both banking systems recognize money as medium of exchange and store of value, conventional banking treats money as commodity that can be used for trading. The creation of money in this way may subsequently lead to inflation due to an oversupply of money in the market. However, Islamic banks do not treat money as commodity but instead use money for trading in real assets, which will help the economy to grow.

The next two aspects are related to the second principle on interest and profit. In conventional banking, the returns to the bank take the form of a fixed return in excess of the original money as compensation for use of money/funds as capital and for the lender giving up current value which will increase in the future. This excess return (interest) being charged is considered as *riba* which is prohibited because the bank has treated the money as capital. Furthermore, the fixed rate based on the time value of money assumes that the future is certain, that there is no risk of the possibility of loss on the part of the lender. Since conventional banking is interest based, they charged compound interest for late payment, which is unjust for the borrower as this will accumulate the debt further.

In contrast, money given out as a loan is considered a debt and Islam prohibits charging extra for lending money. The debt must be returned in the same amount, otherwise it is considered as *riba*. To be recognized as capital, some form of effort or work is needed which may take the form of trading, partnership, agency, etc. The difference between the amount of input and output will be the profit, not interest. Since interest is prohibited, Islamic banks cannot charge for late payment, as Islamic teaching encourages lenders to be kind to their debtors by considering their circumstances. If charges are made, the bank must not consider this as part of their income and must give them away to charity as recommended by the majority of *shari'ah* scholars.

Aspects number five to seven are interrelated to principles number three to six. Principles number three and four state that Islamic banking must be based on participation or profit–loss and risk sharing and the relationship takes the form of principal–agent, respectively. The banking relationship, contractual terms and risk are different between conventional and Islamic banking. Hence, banking relationship takes one form, loan arrangement and services in conventional banking, but in Islamic banking, the relationship takes various forms: financing based on partnership (*musharakah*), profit sharing (*mudarabah*), trading (*murabahah*), agency (*wakalah*) and commodity sales (*salam*). As a result of the different arrangements, the contractual relationships are also different; a single form as debtor–creditor in the case of conventional banking but as partners, buyer–seller, principal–agent, etc. for Islamic banking. The different forms of relationships that exist in Islamic banking affects the asset/liability structure (principle number six) whereby there is less mismatching of the two sides of the balance sheet compared to conventional banking. Also, given the profit–loss sharing nature of the relationship in Islamic banking, there is enhanced monitoring (principle number five) in ensuring the project or venture is successful or profitable. In contrast, monitoring is given relatively less attention as the lender is assured of returns from interest payments that are compounded. Similarly, risk sharing propagated under principle three means that Islamic banks share risk based on the nature of contracts while risk are transferred to borrowers in conventional banks.

The last three aspects are related to the last principle, *shari'ah* governance. Conventional banks must adhere to business and banking laws. Governance responsibility lies with the board of directors. In contrast, Islamic banks must follow Islamic business law, which prohibits interest related activities, high uncertainty and speculative activities, and unlawful activities such as investment in entertainment, weapons, etc., while the governance of its activities falls under the remit of both the *shari'ah* supervisory board and the board of directors.

6.6.3 MANAGEMENT STRUCTURE

The management structure of banks is not homogenous as it depends on each bank's specific requirements. However, both conventional and Islamic banks share common features, except for the existence of the *shari'ah* supervisory board (SSB) and *shari'ah* committee, in the case of the latter. Figure 6.6 illustrates a typical management structure for Islamic and conventional banks. All banks have shareholders who provide the primary resources supporting the bank's existence. They are investors who own the banks. All banks have boards of directors who oversee the operations and are responsible for exercising effective corporate governance. They consist of executive and non-executive directors. The latter are responsible in monitoring banks' decision making and performance, appointment of the chief executive officer (CEO) as well as contributing to the strategic directions. All banks must have audit committees that report directly to the board on whether the bank's operations are in compliance with industry regulations, there are effective internal control policies, and that the bank's operations are performed according to specific internal control procedures, as well as comply with the rules and regulations set by the governing bodies through the conduct of internal audit.

In the case of Islamic banks, there is the SSB whose membership comprises of *shari'ah* scholars who have expertise in *fiqh muamalat* (Islamic rulings governing commercial transactions) to endorse that the activities of the Islamic banks are *shari'ah* compliant. The SSB reports directly to the board of directors and like the audit committee will need to prepare a *Shari'ah* Supervisory Board Report to be included in the annual report to attest on the *shari'ah* compliance, and how aspects of non-*shari'ah* compliance has been dealt with. Before endorsing on *shari'ah* compliance, a *shari'ah* audit needs to be conducted by the *shari'ah* audit committee who reports to the SSB.

The bank's leadership is headed by the CEO, who reports directly to the board of directors and is responsible for ensuring the strategic direction and performance of the bank through effective mobilization of funds and risk management. Directly below the CEO is the operational level management team, comprising the operational managers for banking activities (the chief operating officers) and the departments of finance, marketing, human resources, legal affairs and compliance, information technology and risk management. The operations

Figure 6.6 Typical management structure of an Islamic and a conventional bank

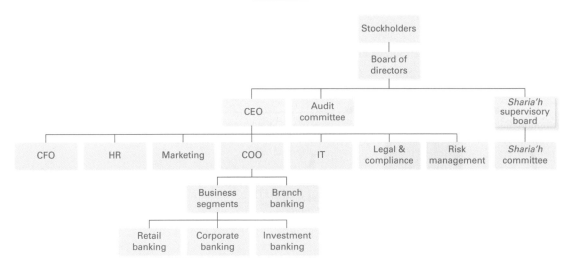

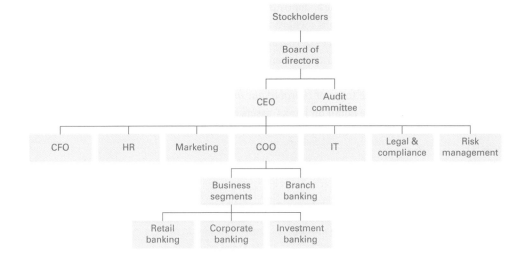

of the bank may be divided into business segments and branch banking. The business segments may consist of retail, corporate and investment banking, as explained earlier. Branch banking usually covers retail banking activities.

6.6.4 MANAGING THE OPERATIONS OF ISLAMIC BANKS

The underlying Islamic principles for bank operations are to channel funds from depositors to investors efficiently and effectively. This entails focusing on the sources and application of funds available to the Islamic bank. The operation is said to be effective when the customers' deposits and investments will enable the bank to generate a pool of funds that it can efficiently use to fund its financing portfolios or to deploy it towards attractive emerging investment instruments. Another important aspect in the management of the operations of an Islamic bank is to ensure instant determination and recognition of profits that can be derived from each investment opportunity, as well as allow for the sharing of profits between the bank and the customers (deposit/investment). Hence, it is the profit–loss sharing (PLS) structure that shapes the operation of the bank management and the way the whole bank is managed. Figure 6.7 illustrates the cycle of the Islamic banking model.

Figure 6.7 Islamic bank cycle of sources and uses of funds

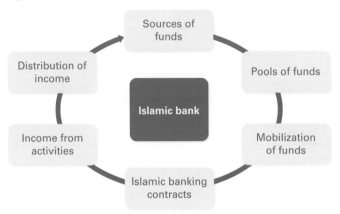

The main sources of funds for Islamic banks are deposits (current and savings) and investments. They are recorded as liabilities in the banks' books. These deposits and investment funds are pooled so that they can be mobilized effectively. Unlike conventional banks where the funds are used for lending as loans, Islamic banks offer a variety of products with different degrees of risk and return. They can be in the form of short term asset backed trade financing, PLS investments, equity partnership investments and other fee charging banking services. They are all recorded as assets in the banks' books. In order to avoid interest, Islamic banks have more complex contracts which may take the form of *murabahah, mudarabah, musharakah, ijarah, salam, istisna, ju'alah, kafalah*. We will look into more detail on banks' assets and liabilities in Chapter 9. Table 6.4 illustrates the various assets and liabilities of Islamic banks by functionality and maturity, and the various types of contracts (in brackets).

Table 6.4 Assets and liabilities of Islamic banks

Based on functionality		Based on maturity profile	
Assets	**Liabilities**	**Assets**	**Liabilities**
Cash	Demand deposits (*amanah*)	Cash	Demand deposits (*amanah*)
Financing assets (*murabahah, salam, ijarah, istisna'a*)	Investment accounts (*mudarabah*)	Short-term trade finance (*murabahah, salam*)	Investment accounts (*mudarabah*)
Investment assets (*mudarabah, musharakah*)	Special investment accounts (*mudarabah, musharakah*)	Medium term investments (*ijarah, istisna'a*)	Special investment accounts (*mudarabah, musharakah*)
Fee based services (*ju'alah, kafalah*)	Reserves	Long term partnerships (*mudarabah, musharakah*)	Reserves
Non-banking assets	Equity capital	Fee based services (*ju'alah, kafalah*)	Equity capital
		Non-banking assets	

Based on the type of contractual relationship, banks will receive income from their financing and investment activities, banking services, agency fees and share in profits from joint ventures. They also incur expenses for their operating and non-operating activities such as administrative and general expenses and depreciation. A bank's total revenue minus expenses including provisions for *zakat* will give the net income for the bank. We will also look into more detail on banks' income and expenses in Chapter 9.

Like their conventional counterpart, Islamic banks are equally concern about their income and pricing. However, they must also be concerned with the product they launch and the impact on customers, especially if the *shari'ah* compliance aspect of the product is doubtful, as this will significantly affect their revenue. Furthermore, they cannot charge fees for certain aspects of the operations, such as a penalty for late payment, which in contrast is an important source of income for conventional banks. Hence, the treasury functions in Islamic banks go beyond managing liquidity, risk and cost of funds to include ensuring *shari'ah* compliance in their investment activities.

The operations to support treasury management involve having a detailed work stream, commodity desk and *aqd* (contract) completion. The legal department will deal with all contractual relationships, *aqd* and transactional documents as well as Islamic terms and conditions. The execution of documents, completion of the *aqd* process, including non-*shari'ah* compliant events, are all handled by the *shari'ah* review and audit.

Since not all features of conventional banking operations and products can be used in Islamic banking, the contractual relationships between Islamic banks and their customers are more complex in order to avoid interest. The *shari'ah* committee handles the consideration and approval of new products, processes and structures, as well as decisions on how to deal with *shari'ah* non-compliance. Table 6.5 illustrates the steps involved before banks launch new products.

Table 6.5 Steps in launching new banking product

Conventional bank	Islamic bank
Is there is market demand and product competitor?	Is there is market demand and product competitor?
The same structure is copied.	The structure is researched by the *shari'ah* team for *shari'ah* suitability and any issues.
	The structure is deliberated by the *shari'ah* committee for decision and resolution of any issues.
Main documents are prepared: loan agreement or deposit application.	Main documents are prepared: this will depend on the approved structure (e.g. *murabahah, ijarah, wakalah,* etc.).
	The structure is assessed internally to ensure product meets *shari'ah* requirements and operations.
Submission to senior management.	Submission to senior management.
Submission to regulatory body.	Submission to regulatory body.
Review product and amend if necessary.	Review product and amend if necessary.
Launch product.	Launch product.
Review product and amend if necessary.	Review product, including *shari'ah* review, and amend if necessary with *shari'ah* committee approach.

Summary

Banks and financial institutions occupy an important intermediary position in a country's economic development. Their origin can be traced back to the medieval era in Europe when interest dealings were prohibited by the church, to later evolve into the modern banking system that we have today, fixated on interest. Conventional banking was established to offer a range of activities and financial services to their customers who deposit surplus funds to redirect them to those seeking loans to finance various social and economic projects. The mobilization of funds is one of the core activities that banks fulfil as financial intermediaries in bridging the gap between savers and borrowers and reconciling their incompatible needs and objectives.

Unlike the interest based conventional banks, Islamic banking offers a wide variety of services that do not charge or pay interest, as this is prohibited by *shari'ah*, and the products that are asset based. It is a system based upon profit and risk sharing, symbolizing entrepreneurship and eradication of exploitation. The origin of this system is attributed to the teachings of the Prophet Muhammad. Banking activities such as *wakalah* (agency contract), interest free loans in the form of *qard* (benevolent loan), *salam* (forward) contracts and *sarf* (exchange of money in the form of gold for gold and silver for silver at the same time) were reported to have been used and/or permitted by the Prophet. In addition, the Prophet established the foundation of the political economy by disallowing business transactions tainted with interest (*riba*), having excessive risk or speculation (*gharar*), dealing in prohibited commodities and goods, dealing in stolen goods, exploitation and unjust practices in the market place, giving short measures, hoarding of foodstuff or other essential commodities, and cheating and fraud in business. On the backdrop of such principles, the economy was developed throughout the Islamic Empire.

Muslims have further contributed to the development of Islamic finance through purifying the western banking system brought by European colonial powers to be closer to the traditional Islamic business model. They call for all bank activities to be *halal* (adhere to *shari'ah*) and avoid *haram* (contradictory to *shari'ah* principles) activities as much as possible without causing hardship on others as part of the basic Islamic juristic rules of *al-darurat tubeah al-mahdurat* (necessity knows no law).

Islamic finance has developed from offering just *mudarabah* (profit and loss sharing) and *musharakah* (equity sharing) products to a wider range of products including *takaful* (Islamic insurance), Islamic micro financing and more complex financing schemes such as *sukuk* (Islamic bonds). The resilience and competitiveness of the Islamic financial products and services attracted more and more organizations into considering Islamic financing as part of their strategic financial plans and this led to the industry's further growth outside its strongholds in Muslim majority countries such as Malaysia and the GCC, Turkey, Pakistan and Bangladesh, to African countries, Europe and East Asia.

There are seven underlying principles that distinguish Islamic banking from conventional banking. Firstly, money is not a commodity that can be traded. Secondly, Islam allows profit but forbids interest. Thirdly, the mode of financing is based on profit–loss and risk sharing. Fourth, the principal–agent relationship in Islamic banking involves a two-tier relationship: one between the depositor (principal) and the bank (agent) and the other between the bank and the entrepreneur, where the relationship can take many forms instead of simply creditor–debtor which is common in conventional banking. Fifth, depending on the contractual relationship, banks have the obligation to monitor activities of the entrepreneurs who are involved in the partnership. Sixth, assets and liabilities in Islamic banks are closely matched, and hence is more stable compared to conventional banks. Finally, the *shari'ah* supervisory board governs the *shari'ah* compliance aspects of the business.

Key terms and concepts

agency cost of equity	investment banking	*shari'ah* compliant
al-darurat tubeah al-mahdurat (necessity knows no law)	legal tender	*shari'ah* governance
asset/liability management	maturity transformation	*shari'ah* supervisory board
baitul mal	modern banking	size transformation
fractional reserve system	operating structure	traditional banking
high net worth individuals	private banking	
	risk transformation	

Questions

1. Discuss the origin of modern banking.

2. Describe the nature and types of banking and explain the benefits of intermediation.

3. Report on the evolution of Islamic banking.

4. Discuss the emergence and growth of Islamic banking in a region of your choice to provide insights on the status quo of the Islamic financial industry.

5. Assess the operating structures on the Islamic banking and finance industry.

6. Discuss the principles underlying Islamic banking.

7. What is the difference between profit and interest?

8. Distinguish between conventional and Islamic banking system.

9. Explain the difference between governance structure of an Islamic and a conventional bank.

10. Identify the various assets and liabilities of an Islamic bank.

11. Report on the steps involved before an Islamic and a conventional bank launch a new financial product.

References and further readings

Chachi, A. (2005), 'Origin and development of commercial and Islamic banking operations', *Islamic Economics*, 18, pp. 3-25.

Chapra, M.U. (2000), *The Future of Economics: An Islamic Perspective*, The Islamic Foundation, Leicester, UK.

De Roover, R. (1954), 'New interpretation of the history of banking', *Journal of World History*, 2.

Financial Services and Market Act 2000, www.legislation.gov.uk/ukpga/2000/8/contents

Goldthwaite, R.A. (1995), *Banks, Places and Entrepreneurs in Renaissance Florence*, Variorum, Aldershot, Hampshire, UK.

Hamidullah, Muhammad (1936), *Islam's Solution of the Basic Economic Problems – the Position of Labour*, Islamic Culture, Hyderabad (Deccan), April 10(2), pp. 213-233.

Haniffa, R and Hudaib, M. (2010), 'Islamic finance: From sacred intentions to secular goals?', *Journal of Islamic Accounting and Business Research*, 1(2), pp. 85-91.

Hoggson, N.F. (1926), *Banking Through the Ages*, Dodd, Mead & Company, New York.

Khan, M.M. and Bhatti, M.I. (2008), *Developments in Islamic Banking: The Case of Pakistan*, Palgrave Macmillan, Basingstoke and London.

Mawdudi, Abul Al-ala (nd), *Al-Riba*, trans. Muhammad Assim Al-Hadad, Beirut: Dar al-Fikr.

Nasser, A. (1996), *Essentials of Islamic Banks Assets and Operational Aspects* (in Arabic), Apollo, Cairo.

Qureshi, Anwar Iqbal (1946), *Islam and the Theory of Interest*, Sh. Muhammad Ashraf, Lahore, Pakistan: reprinted 1991.

Qutb, Sayyid (1952), *Al-'Adala Al-Ijtima'iyya Fil-Islam (Social Justice in Islam)*, translated by John B. and Algar Hardie, Hamid. Revised edition. Baltimore, MD: Islamic Publications International, 2000.

Ranzini, S.L. (2007), *Islamic Finance (Finally) Taking Root in North America*, www.eurekahedge.com/Research/News/833/Islamic_Finance_Finally_Taking_Root_in_North_America

Seoharvi, Al-Rahman (1942), *Islam ka iqtisadi Nizami (Islam as an economic system)*, archive.org/details/IslamKaIqtisadiNizamByShaykhHifzurRahmanSeoharvir.a_201406, accessed 18 June 2018.

Siddiqi, Naiem (1948), *Islami Usul par Banking* (Banking According to Islamic Principles), Paper in the Urdu monthly *Chiragh-e-Rah* (Karachi), 1(11&12) (Nov. & Dec.) pp. 24-28 and 60-64.

Siddiqi, M.N. (1983), *Banking Without Interest*, The Islamic Foundation, Leicester.

Turk, J. and Rubino, J. (2013), *The Money Bubble: What to Do before It Pops*, DollarCollapsePress, www.dollarcollapse.com, accessed 14 June 2018.

Uzair, Muhammad (1955), *An Outline of Interestless Banking*, Raihan Publications, Karachi, Dacca.

Wilson, R. (1995), *Economic Development in the Middle East*, Routledge, London; New York.

7 *Takaful* (Islamic insurance)

Learning Objectives

Upon completion of this chapter you should be able to:

- describe the history of insurance

- explain the concept of insurance and discuss the different types of insurance

- describe the history and evolution of *takaful*

- explain the principles of *takaful*

- distinguish between insurance and *takaful*

- describe the types of *takaful* products

- discuss the various models of *takaful* governance

- explain the treatment of surplus and deficit in *takaful* underwriting

- distinguish the concept of reinsurance and *retakaful*

- discuss the future prospects and challenges of *takaful*

7.1 Introduction

We are exposed to many uncertainties and calamities in our everyday life. We do not have any command on them, but we can try to minimize the risk and the potential financial and non-financial losses and distress associated with them. This can be done through what is known as insurance, which is a cooperative mechanism to spread the loss and also a social tool for accumulating funds to meet any further uncertain losses. Hence, the main function of insurance is to provide the policyholders or its members with some degree of protection and security by eliminating the worries and miseries of losses due to destruction of property and death. It also provides capital to society as the accumulated funds are invested in productive activities.

Since some aspects of the business of conventional insurance are not *shari'ah* compliant, Islamic insurance (*takaful*) serves the need of Muslims to manage risk. *Takaful* literally means mutual guarantee, because participants or policyholders jointly agree to guarantee among themselves against any hazard or loss incurred during the insurance period. It is the third component of the Islamic finance industry, the other two being Islamic capital markets and Islamic banking.

In this chapter, we will briefly look at the history of insurance and its main features to enable us to differentiate it from *takaful*. We then turn our attention to the concept of *takaful* and its development over the years, followed by the different models of operations of *takaful* and *retakaful*. The chapter ends with discussion of some of the contemporary challenges faced by the *takaful* industry.

7.2   Brief history of insurance

Insurance, as an economic related activity, can be said to exist simultaneously with the existence of human society. In natural or non-monetary economies (i.e. without money, markets, financial instruments, etc.), insurance entails agreements of mutual aid by families, neighbours, villagers, communities, etc., to help each other in overcoming any adversities that befall them. For instance, when a person's house is destroyed in the neighbourhood, the neighbours are committed to help rebuild the house. Similarly, when there is a death in the family, the others in the family and neighbours will help in paying for the burial expense. In other words, such forms of insurance are often informal or formally intrinsic to local religious customs, with some surviving to the present day in some countries where a modern money economy with its financial instruments is not widespread.

Individuals are exposed to losses, either as a result of the assets they hold or simply by the fact of their existence in this world. They would naturally form themselves into groups to aggregate those risks, price the risk and eventually sell it to investors. Thus the idea of risk transfer has been developed against the background of social philosophy towards the sanctity of individuals and the institutional arrangement that emancipated as a result of it. The arrangement includes separating *peril risk* (the cause of the loss) from of the risk of losing the value of the asset or equity. The peril risk is transferred to an external party who is able to bear it at a lower cost. This form of insuring idea is known as socialized or public good, that protects individuals and firms against infrequent (uncertain) but extreme losses at a cost which is small compared to the feared loss.

Insurance, in a modern sense of money economy, which involves transferring or distributing of risk, may be traced as far back as the 2nd and 3rd millennia BCE, as practiced by the Babylonian and Chinese traders, respectively (Sfetcu, 2014). The former developed a system which was recorded in the famous Code of Hammurabi (1750 BCE) whereby Mediterranean sailing merchants who received loans to fund their shipments would pay the lenders an additional sum in exchange for the lenders' guarantee to cancel the loan should the shipments be stolen or lost at sea. Similarly, Chinese merchants travelling treacherous river rapids would redistribute their wares across many vessels in their group to limit the loss due to any single vessel capsizing.

In the 4th century BCE, the people of Rhodes introduced the concept of *general average* whereby merchants whose goods were being shipped together would pay a proportionally divided premium which would be used to reimburse any merchant whose goods had to be jettisoned in order to lighten the ship and save it from total loss. The ancient Athenians introduced different rates for maritime loans based on whether the journey was during the safe or dangerous time of the year, thus implying an intuitive pricing of risk with an effect similar to insurance.

In the 6th century BCE, the Greeks and Romans introduced health and life insurance. They created guilds called benevolent societies which cared for the families of deceased members, as well as paying funeral expenses of members. Similar establishments, known as friendly societies, whereby people donated amounts of money to a general sum that could be used for emergencies, existed in England before the introduction of modern insurance in the late 17th century. The practice of underwriting primarily took place in a coffee house owned by Edward Lloyd, later known as Lloyd's of London. Insurance companies thrived in Europe, especially after the Industrial Revolution. The development of insurance institutions in the 18th century was spurred by advances in mathematical theories upon which the practical models of insurance are based. By the 19th century, leading insurance companies of the west began to offer their services in Muslim lands and Muslims utilized them in their trade relationships with Europe (Khan, 2005).

7.3 Features and types of insurance

Insurance is a form of risk management contract primarily used to hedge against the risk of a contingent or uncertain loss. Figure 7.1 illustrates the mechanics of conventional insurance. The entity which provides insurance is known as an *insurer, insurance limited company* or *insurance carrier*. A person or entity that buys insurance is known as an *insured* or *policyholder*. The fee paid by the policyholder to the insurer for agreeing to pay the policyholder a sum of money (or its equivalent) on the occurrence of a specified event is called the *premium*. The specified event must have some element of uncertainty about it: either the event is bound to happen in the ordinary course of nature but the timing of its occurrence is uncertain, or the occurrence of the event depends upon accidental causes which may never happen at all.

Figure 7.1   **Mechanics of conventional insurance**

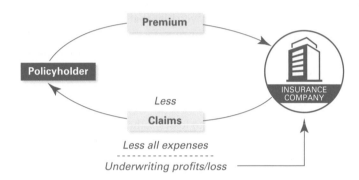

Insurance companies make money through pooling the money from premiums paid by policyholders to pay for claims and any expenses involved in selling and providing insurance protection to policyholders. This is known as the *underwriting profit* or income. Insurance companies will invest (often in stocks and bonds) funds reserved for meeting potential claims and the returned earnings from the investments help the insurer to keep down the premium cost of insurance to policyholders.

There are two main types of insurance, namely, life insurance and general insurance. *Life insurance* is an insurance coverage that pays out a certain amount of money to the insured or their specified beneficiaries upon a certain event affecting the individual who is insured. The coverage period for life insurance is usually more than a year and it requires periodic premium payments, either monthly, quarterly or annually. *General insurance* is basically an insurance policy that protects policyholder against losses and damages other than those covered by life insurance. The coverage period for most general insurance policies and plans is usually one year, whereby premiums are normally paid on a one time basis. Table 7.1 outlines the main products and risks covered by each type of insurance.

Table 7.1 Main products and risks covered by life and general insurance

Type of insurance	Main products	Risks covered
Life insurance	• whole life • endowment • term • investment-linked • life annuity plan • medical and health	• premature death • income during retirement • illness
General insurance	• motor insurance • fire/house owners/householders insurance • personal accident insurance • medical and health insurance • travel insurance	• property loss, for example, stolen car or fire damage to a house • liability arising from damage caused by yourself to a third party • accidental death or injury

7.4   Historical development of *takaful*

The idea of mutual assistance, which became the foundation of modern history of *takaful*, can be traced to the practice by ancient Arab traders in protecting themselves against the risks associated with long distance trade by caravan or sea. Such practices included *hilf* (confederation), *aqila* (pooling of resources) and *daman altarik* (surety), which gradually evolved into a system of community self-help and financial assistance (Fisher and Taylor, 2000). During the early development of Muslim community in Medina (1-20 AH), the Prophet Muhammad validated social insurance mechanism such as *diyah* (blood money or compensation for accidental killings, murder or injury paid by the perpetrator or his (her) relatives to the victim or his (her) relatives), *fidyah* (ransom paid to prisoners of war) and *zakah* (obligatory charity) as cooperative schemes to aid the needy, ill and poor.

In the second century of the Islamic era, the system of *aqilah* or a joint guarantee by a group of individuals to help each other in times of disaster or misfortune became popular when Muslim Arabs started to expand their trade to India, the Far East, and other countries in Asia (Sadeghi, 2010). In later centuries, Muslims from the Ottoman Empire used similar mutual help or indemnification practices in their trade relationships with Spanish merchants (Schoon, 2008) and *waqf* funds were used to provide rudimentary insurance for members of guilds in the Empire (Cizakca, 2004). There was not much development until the onset of Ottoman reform movements and the acceleration of trade with Europe in the 19th century which saw the Ottomans adopting a variety of modern financial institutions (Pamuk, 2004) based largely on western models (Kuran, 2005).

The development of insurance in its modern form in the Muslim world may be attributed to Ibn 'Abidin (1784-1836), a Hanafi scholar who developed the meaning, concept and legal basis of an Islamic insurance contract. Non-life insurance contracts, rooted on conventional modes, were endorsed by the Ottomans around 1839 and the Egyptians in 1845. In 1906, the Mufti of Egypt, Muhammad Baqit, approved the idea of insurance as described by Ibn Abidin (Mankabady, 1989). While some Muslim scholars had serious reservations regarding the morality of the practice of insurance (Ahmad, 1995), others view it as inevitable in the modern world (Bekkin, 2007), and Muslim businessmen had no options but to use western conventional contracts to manage their risks (Abdel Karim and Archer, 2002).

Following the rise of Islamic banking in the 1970s, concerned Muslim intellectuals and scholars started to find an alternative which is more compatible with Islamic financial principles. The *takaful* contract was born later out of this necessity and the recognition of mutual protection as an acceptable form of insurance was reinforced in 1976 during the first international conference on Islamic Economics in Makkah, Saudi Arabia. A resolution (fatwa) on *takaful* as a cooperative insurance, was passed by the Higher Council of Saudi Scholars in 1977 and a similar resolution was passed by the *Fiqh* Council of the Muslim World League. Sudan took the lead in establishing the first Islamic Insurance Company in 1979 based on the cooperative insurance model, followed by Saudi Arabia and the United Arab Emirates which established the Islamic-Arab Insurance Company in 1980. The prevailing social and economic environment during this period also gave an encouraging start to *takaful* operation in Western Europe which saw the establishment of Dar Al Mal Al Islamic in both Switzerland (1981) and the UK (1982), and the Islamic Takaful Company in Luxembourg (1983).

In 1984, the Takaful Act was enacted in Malaysia allowing for *takaful* business to be conducted. Syarikat Takaful Malaysia Berhad became the first *takaful* company which was incorporated in Malaysia in November 1984. It was only in 1985 that the OIC *Fiqh* Academy approved the *takaful* system followed by the Grand Council of Islamic Scholars in Makkah, *Majmak Al-Fiqh*, in 1986. This was a major boost to the creation of institutions to translate Islamic insurance ideals into practical solutions. Since then, the *takaful* industry has grown from strength to strength, offering various *takaful* products to meet the increasing demands for *shari'ah* compliant financial products.

7.5   Principles of *takaful*

The word *takaful* is an Arabic word meaning *solidarity* and *mutual guarantee*. It is derived from the root verb *kafala* which means to guarantee, to secure or to be responsible for others. It is an alternative to conventional insurance and is based upon an aspect of *shari'ah* that regulates and refines the affairs between people known as *muamalat* (dealings). Hence, the Islamic value of the responsibility of individuals to cooperate to protect each other against loss or damage is based on absolute rather than normative values as revealed by God, that are not subject to periodic reinterpretations. Islam encourages its followers to take appropriate measures of risk management in commercial as well as civil activities instead of leaving everything in God's hands as demonstrated in the following prophetic precedent:

> *One day Prophet noticed a Bedouin leaving his camel without tying it and he asked the Bedouin, 'Why don't you tie down your camel?' The Bedouin answered, 'I put my trust in Allah.' The Prophet then said, 'Tie your camel first, then put your trust in Allah' (Tirmidhi).*[1]

According to Fisher and Taylor (2000), there are four elements that must exist to establish a proper framework for a *takaful* system. The first is related to the *utmost sincerity of intention (niyyah)* by participants in the scheme to follow the guidance and adhering to the rule and purposes of *takaful*. The second is to integrate the framework of mutual assistance, solidarity and share of risk, whereby participants contribute money into a pooling scheme based primarily on the principles of *ta'awun* (mutual assistance) and tabarru' (donation). These principles are reflected in the Islamic Financial Services Board (IFSB, 2009) definition of *takaful*:

> *…joint guarantee, whereby a group of participants agree among themselves to support one another jointly for the losses arising from specified risks. In a Takaful arrangement the participants contribute a sum of money as a Tabarru' (donation) commitment into a common fund that will be used mutually to assist the members against a specified type of loss or damage.*

The concept of *joint guarantee (ta`awun)* indicates that participants of *takaful* jointly agree to guarantee and support each other when faced with hardship. This is premised on the Qur'anic verse encouraging Muslims to help each other in enjoining good:

> *Help ye one another in righteousness and piety* (Al-Maidah, 5:2).[2]

This is an important principle as it provides a platform for the participants to mitigate risks among themselves as an act of mutual assistance by creating a social network, and strengthening brotherhood and sense of community among them. Such a system also helps the majority of the fortunate ones in the community of participants to join the *takaful* scheme in order to ease the financial burden shouldered by the minority of the unfortunate ones by agreeing to share the financial burden mutually.

Another important concept of *takaful* is *donation (tabarru'),* which represents the amount of financial commitments made by all participants to the donation pool to help members facing perils without expecting any returns (Al-Zuhayli *et al.*, 2003). This should ideally eliminate the instances of moral hazard and adverse selection which are common in conventional insurance contract, where the insured feel that it is their right to benefit from the insurance and to profit from the loss resulting from the occurrence of risk events.

The third element is to incorporate moral values and ethics, conducting the business openly in good faith, with honesty, full disclosure, truthfulness and fairness in all dealings. Hence, the concepts of piety (individual purification), brotherhood (via *ta'awun* or mutual assistance), charity giving (based on *tabarru'* or donation), mutual guarantee of protection and sustainable operations as opposed to profit maximization, need to be upheld by participants in the scheme. In short, the key motivation for Muslims to utilize the *takaful* system is to perform acts of piety using *tabarru'* and *ta'awun* to promote community wellbeing, while achieving individual purification.

---

[1] Jami' at-Tirmidhi, 37 Chapters on the description of the Day of Judgement, Ar-Riqaq, and Al-Wara', sunnah.com/urn/727020, accessed 18 June 2018.

[2] www.wright-house.com/religions/islam/Quran/5-table.php, accessed 25 May 2018.

Box 7.1 *Takaful* industry reports double-digit growth in the GCC

Saudi Arabia and the UAE grows close to 20% in general takaful business

Published: 17:30 April 11, 2017
By Babu Das Augustine, Banking Editor

DUBAI

Takaful (Islamic Insurance) industry has grown in high double digits across the Gulf Cooperation Council (GCC) in recent years according to the Global Takaful Report 2017, released at the World Takaful Conference on Tuesday.

In terms of gross written contribution (GWC) equivalent of gross written premium in the conventional industry, the GCC markets grew by a compounded annual growth rate (CAGR) of 18 per cent during 2012 to 2015 period. While South East Asia reported a negative growth of 4 per cent due to currency depreciation, Africa reported a CAGR of 19 per cent during the same period.

"Regulatory reforms across several African markets along with large uninsured population are helping high growth rates across several countries in the continent. In terms of GWC, Saudi Arabia is the largest Takaful market with a GWC of $9.7 billion (Dh35.62 billion) in 2015. Saudi market is dominated by general insurance with limited life insurance business," said Safder Jaffer, Managing Director & Consulting Actuary — Middle East & Africa, Milliman, an actuarial and consulting firm that prepared the report.

Takaful: Gross written contribution ($)

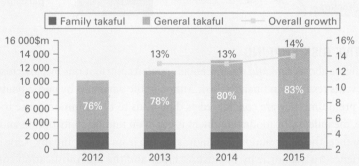

GCC markets continue to dominate general takaful whereas South East Asia continues to dominate life takaful. GCC had an overall market share of 88 per cent of general takaful market in 2015. Saudi Arabia and UAE reported the strongest growth in general takaful in 2015 with 20 per cent and 19 per cent growth in total contributions, respectively.

In the GCC, family takaful achieved a record growth of 34 per cent in 2015 in total contributions mainly as a result of high growth in the UAE driven by the introduction of compulsory health insurance in Dubai. "There are significant growth opportunities for family takaful in GCC given current low penetration rates," Jaffer said.

Global takaful GWC is estimated at $14.9 billion as at the close of 2015. There is strong growth in overall global takaful market in the range of 13 to 14 per cent per annum. The split of the family and general takaful market in 2015 is approximately 17 per cent and 83 per cent respectively.

"The growth in the Takaful industry is double-digit and is here to stay. However, to continue to meet profitability, the industry would need to meet customer needs and embrace modern technology and global best risk management practices," Jaffer said.

GCC continues to dominate the global takaful market with a 77 per cent market share (predominantly general takaful business), followed by South East Asia at 15 per cent (largely family takaful).

Africa and other remaining countries are relatively new to takaful and their GWC is small at $0.7 billion and $0.5 billion respectively and represent just about 3 per cent of the global market share. Despite the current low market share, these regions have some of the fastest growing markets.

According to the report, in addition to Africa, there is significant opportunity to grow the general takaful market in South East Asia. "There are large segments of Muslim populations who currently purchase conventional general insurance policies, but will over time gravitate towards general takaful, if general takaful companies can compete effectively with conventional insurance providers," Jaffer said.

Source: gulfnews.com/business/sectors/insurance/takaful-industry-reports-double-digit-growth-in-the-gcc-1.2009719

The fourth element is ensuring no unlawful element that contravenes *shari'ah* is present. This includes the following: parties participating in the scheme have the legal capacity and are mentally fit, agreement to provide mutual consent which includes voluntary purification, payment of the premium or donation is based on offer and acceptance, the insurable interest and the time period of policy and underlying agreement are clearly specified, and the principle of indemnity prevails.

7.6 Major differences between *takaful* and insurance

Based on the principles of *takaful* discussed earlier, there are a number of features that make it distinct from conventional insurance. Figure 7.2 illustrates the various components in a *takaful* system.

Figure 7.2 Core components of *takaful*

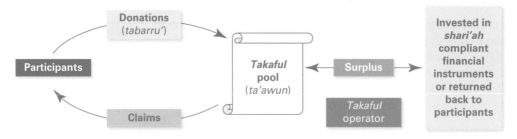

7.6.1 COOPERATIVE RISK SHARING

As can be seen in the figure above, a *takaful* scheme entails pooled contributions by participants to assist members in the occurrence of events resulting in financial loss. Although the payments by participants or policyholders are essentially similar to premium, they are considered as donations to the common cause to assist members who suffer any loss. Hence, the indemnification component is based on mutual contribution and reciprocal donation.

In the case of insurance, the contribution (premiums) to the insurance company is for individual protection from financial loss. Hence, risk is borne by the insurer alone and the indemnification component is based on commercial relationship between the insurer and the insured.

7.6.2 CONTRACTING PARTIES

There is more than one contractual relationship in a *takaful* scheme, although the basis of it is mutual assistance. The participants insure themselves against any loss based on mutual agreement and mutual sense of responsibility. The *takaful* operator is not an insurer and there is no sale and purchase agreement between the operator and the participants.

On the other hand, there are two parties in conventional insurance, the insurer or the insurance company and the insured party. The insurer and the insured party enter into a commercial contract with each other. The insured party is only concerned about itself and has nothing to do with the other insured parties in terms of guaranteeing one another against loss.

7.6.3 CLEAR FINANCIAL SEGREGATION

There is clear segregation between the participants and the operator (or *wakil*) of the *takaful* scheme. The company handling the *takaful* funds is not an insurer but merely an operator appointed to manage the portfolio and invest the contributions for and on behalf of the participants. *Shari'ah* restricts the role of the operator to that of an ordinary trustee who is responsible to the participants. Depending on the type of *takaful* model (which will be explained later in the chapter), the exact roles of the participants and the operator are clearly defined.

For the insurance business, the insurance company is a profit making entity that agrees to bear the financial burden and losses of all its policyholders. The shareholders own the insurance company and they are entitled to receive any surplus and to bear any deficit recorded at the financial year end from the investments.

7.6.4 PAYMENT OF PREMIUMS

In a *takaful* scheme, premiums are not paid as regular instalments to guarantee the receipt of compensation in the event that the insured for purpose actually occurred. Instead, they are donations from the participants into a common fund in order to indemnify other participants, and are held as a trust by the *takaful* operator. The participants remain as owners of the premiums and the *takaful* operator cannot make the participants to forfeit their premiums.

On the other hand, the regular premium instalments paid by the policyholders in conventional insurance is in exchange for insurance cover. Policyholders are guaranteed compensation by the insurance company if the contingent event stated in the insurance contract occurs. In other words, the contractual agreement for compensation is based on the probability of the event occurring or not occurring during the period of the insurance cover. The premiums paid may be forfeited in certain circumstances depending on the contract. The nature of the contract in insurance may give rise to issues related to *gharar* (excessive uncertainty), *maysir* (gambling) and exploitation.

a) *Issue of* gharar

This issue arises because the sale contract involves uncertainty, doubt and probability, which is against *shari'ah* rules. In conventional insurance, neither the insured nor the insurer knows when the loss will occur or what will be the amount, or whether it will occur in the first place.

However, in *takaful*, the policyholders fund is structured so that policyholders aid each other if a loss occurs and there is no guarantee from the *takaful* operator to the policyholder. The policyholders are grouped in a mutual assistance contract; there is no probability or uncertainty factor involved as they donate their contributions to the fund and they could receive a surplus from the principle of sharing the losses and profits. In fact there is no risk transfer (as the policyholder retain the risk), but there is risk sharing among the policyholders.

b) *Issue of* maysir

Similar to the case of *gharar*, the existence of *maysir* in the conventional insurance contracts bring in the consumption of wealth wrongfully. It transfers the wealth from the insured to the insurance company by gambling on the occurrence of the risk event of which its probability of occurring had been expected to be minimal. If the insured event happens, the insurer will have to pay the whole financial compensation covered by the premium to the insured. On the other hand, should the insured event do not materialize, the insured will have lost his premium.

Review of moral hazards and adverse selection suggest that the insured party aims to gain from the insurance contract (Donnelly *et al.*, 2013), which is basically to get a higher financial output as compared to input. The insurance services will be offered base on the rule of large numbers of people anticipating the loss, prompting them to insure themselves from the probable event leading to financial loss. To ensure the survival of the insurance company, the accumulated premium price must be set higher than the collective probable financial payments for instances of risk occurring, thus providing the expected profit to the insurer.

7.6.5 *Underwriting policies and strategies*

Takaful funds must be invested in *shari'ah* compliant products and companies by the *takaful* operators. This includes only investment in those activities that are *halal* or permissible, that do not cause harm to others and the environment, and that do not involve the elements of *riba*. The main return on investment in Islam is the returns from economic venture such as through partnership or contracts of sale where risk is undertaken. Should the investment be made in the shares of holding companies whose subsidiaries engaged in the supply or production of non-permissible goods and services, any profit or return relating to these activities is deemed to be unacceptable and must be discharged accordingly such as through charitable cause. Similarly, investment linked insurance such as savings based or life insurance with attached interest return to these investments are also prohibited due to the *riba* element. Life insurance is prohibited, as death is certain, though the time of death and the place of death is unpredictable. Insuring life would indicate that the person put his fate and trust of life to the insurer rather than Allah. Closely related to this is the issue of beneficiary getting access to all the financial compensation not according to the Islamic law of inheritance.

There are no strict restrictions on how and where insurance companies invest the funds. Normally, their investments are done through placement in interest bearing deposits or interest bearing financial instruments such as bonds, where the return in excess of the initial invested amount is stipulated. There are also no restrictions on the type and nature of business or products.

Table 7.2 presents a summary of specific differences between *takaful* and conventional insurance. It incorporates the issues discussed in the preceding paragraphs as well as some other differences.

Table 7.2 Differences between *takaful* and conventional insurance

	Takaful	**Conventional insurance**
Operations and regulations	Operational mechanisms and products must be in line with *shari'ah* rules and in accordance with required national laws and insurance regulations.	Operational mechanisms and products must be in line with the national insurance regulations and laws.
Contract	A combination of *tabarru'* contract and agency and/or profit sharing contract.	Contract of exchange (sale and purchase) between insurer and insured.
Company	Company is better known as an operator and acting as a trustee, manager and also entrepreneur to the policyholders jointly.	Company is known as insurer and the relationship between the company and the policyholders is on one to one basis.
Return to company	*Takaful* operator earns a fee for rendering service of managing the *takaful* fund and from the *mudarabah* profit sharing scheme as *mudarib*.	Insurance company makes a profit when there is underwriting surplus.
Indemnification	Indemnification component is based on mutual contribution, reciprocal donation.	Indemnification component is a commercial relationship between insurance company and the insured.
Premiums	Paid premium is treated as both donation (*tabarru'*) and saving (*mudarabah*).	Paid premium creates an obligation against the insurer on a sale and purchase relationship.
Policyholder fund	The policyholders fund belongs to the policyholders on collective basis and is managed by the shareholders.	All (i.e. both policyholders and shareholders) funds belong to the insurance company, though separation of assets may be maintained between shareholders and policyholders for specific insurances (e.g. with profits).
Policyholder duty	To make contributions to the scheme and expect to share the surplus mutually.	To pay premium in regular instalment to the insurer.
Investments	The funds must only be invested in interest free *shari'ah* approved assets and also meet any required national insurance regulations and laws.	The funds may be invested in any assets as long as they meet required national insurance regulations and laws.
Benefits	Paid from the related participants' funds under mutual assistance.	Paid from the company reserves.
Profit	Underwriting profit is distributed to the policyholders. Shareholders' profit is generated from the return on the investments of the shareholder capital and expenses paid to the shareholders by the policyholders for (i) managing the company on behalf of the policyholders; and (ii) managing the policyholders' investment funds on behalf of the policyholders.	Policyholders do not get any share of the underwriting profit (except in mutual companies); shareholders' profit is generated from the company's underwriting profit plus any investment returns.
Shari'ah rules	*Takaful* practices are free from the elements of *riba* and other prohibited elements, and evolved around the elements of *mudarabah*, *tabarru'* and other *shari'ah* justified elements.	Conventional insurance (including mutual insurers) may involve *riba*, *gharar*, *maysir* and some other elements, which may not be justified by *shari'ah* principles.

7.7   Types of *takaful* products

Takaful operators offer *shari'ah* compliant products for protection on property and family. The former category is known as general *takaful* or non-life contracts, while the latter falls under the category of life-related events. Table 7.3 presents some of the typical products offered under each scheme.

Table 7.3 General and family *takaful* products

Family *takaful*	General *takaful*
• **Individual family *takaful*** scheme that provides financial benefits for participant and beneficiaries arising from death or permanent disability	• **Home *takaful*** covers home against loss or damage caused by floods, fires and other such perils
• **Group family *takaful*** scheme for employers, clubs, associations and societies covering protection in the form of financial benefits arising from death or permanent disability	• **Motor *takaful*** covers against loss or damage to vehicle due to accidental fire, theft or accident, bodily injury or death of a third party as well as loss or damage of a third party's property
• **Retirement annuity** scheme that provides regular income upon retirement	• **Personal accident *takaful*** provides participant or beneficiaries with compensation in the event of death, disability or injuries arising from an accident
• **Child education *takaful*** provides protection and long term savings to finance the higher education expenses of the participants' children	
• **Medical and health *takaful*** scheme covers the cost of private medical treatment, hospitalization, surgery and treatment when the participant is diagnosed with certain illnesses or are involved in an accident	
• **Investment-linked *takaful*** scheme combines investment and *takaful* cover. The contribution provides the participant a *takaful* cover for death and disability benefits, and also an investment in a variety of *shari'ah* approved investment funds	

7.7.1   GENERAL *TAKAFUL*

These schemes are basically non-life contracts of joint guarantee on a short term basis (normally one year), designed to meet the needs for protection of individuals and corporate bodies in relation to material loss or damage resulting from a catastrophe or disaster inflicted upon real estate, assets or belongings of participants. The *takaful* contribution paid is pooled into the Participants' Risk Fund (PRF) under the principle of *tabarru'* (donation) to match the risk elements of the business that are inherent in its underwriting activities.

7.7.2   FAMILY *TAKAFUL*

The schemes deal with the provision of financial relief to the participants and/or their families in the event of misfortunes relating to the death or disability of the participants. Such products are aimed for life related covers including for systematic savings and investment purposes. In instances where the risks occurred before the targeted financial amount is being achieved, the participants agree to assist the unfortunate member to realize the target by donating an amount which represents the difference between the targeted amount and the accumulated savings together with any profit therein on the event date.

This category of *takaful* normally requires the *takaful* operator to engage in a longer term relationship over a defined number of years with the participants, throughout which the participant is required to make regular instalment payments in consideration for his or her participation in the *takaful* scheme. The contributions made are segregated based on certain percentages and the amounts are credited to the Participants' Risk Fund (PRF) and Participants' Investment Fund (PIF). Figure 7.3 illustrates the typical structures of family and general *takaful*.

Figure 7.3   Family and general *takaful* structures

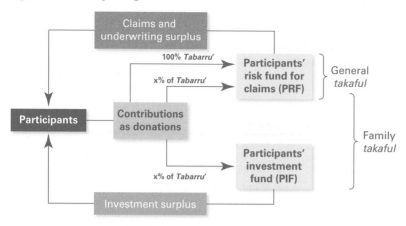

With the different products and services offered under the general and family *takaful* schemes, some regulators require segregation of reporting for the two funds handled by one *takaful* operator. However, in some regulatory jurisdictions, the two different *takaful* schemes need to be operated by two different *takaful* operators under different license requirements so as not to mix the operations of the two schemes, especially between the short term general *takaful* fund and the long term fund in family *takaful*. The segregation also allows for better governance of the funds by avoiding the comingling of both in instances of insufficiency.

7.8   Models of *takaful* governance

Like conventional insurance, the components of general and family *takaful* (participants, operator and fund) have been arranged under four different governing models offering different coverage schemes for the participants. The four governance models are *wakalah*, *mudarabah*, hybrid *wakalah-mudarabah* and the latest is the super-hybrid *waqf-wakalah-mudarabah*.

7.8.1   *WAKALAH TAKAFUL* MODEL

Wakalah in Arabic means *agency* whereby the agent (*wakil*) is entrusted to govern the *takaful* business by the participants. Under this model, the *takaful* operator and the *takaful* participants form a principal–agent relationship whereby the former acts strictly as an agent on behalf of the latter to conduct either underwriting activities only (for general *takaful*) or both the investment and underwriting activities (for family *takaful*). The *takaful* operator will in return receives a management fee, called a *wakalah fee*, which is usually a pre-agreed percentage of the premium contributions paid by the *takaful* participants for the service rendered as an agent. The *wakalah fee* to the *takaful* operator must be clearly stated in the *takaful* contract and this fee is expected to cover the total sum of:

- management expenses
- distribution costs, including intermediaries' remuneration
- a margin of operational profit to the *takaful* operator.

The agency fees can be collected upfront during the collection of the contribution as determined by the *takaful* operator. The agent's responsibility is to control expenses and costs distribution, paying claims and *retakaful* and invest the surplus. Hence, a profit is made if the *wakalah fee* received by the *takaful* operator is more than the management expenses incurred. Since the *takaful* operator is only an agent, it does not directly share in the risk borne by the *takaful* fund or any of its investment profit or surplus/deficit. The participants, as the principals, should observe the operators' role in managing the fund in accordance with their objectives via interval reporting. Figure 7.4 illustrates the mechanics of *wakalah takaful* model which involves the following five steps:

1. Participants pay contributions into a common fund.
2. A *takaful* operator is appointed as agent to manage the pooled funds in return for a fixed *wakalah* fee mutually agreed at the time of contract.
3. The donated portion of the pooled funds i.e. the PRF is used for underwriting activities. Any claims and underwriting surpluses will be returned to the participants in the form of a *hibah* (gift).
4. The investment portion of the pooled funds, i.e. the PIF, is invested in *shari'ah* compliant investment activities by the *takaful* operator. Any year end investment surplus will be paid to the participants.
5. A performance fee may be paid to the *takaful* operator as incentive for prudent management of the fund.

Figure 7.4 Mechanics of *wakalah takaful* model

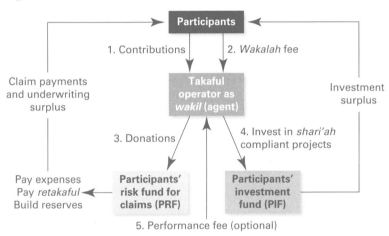

Figure 7.3 applies to family *takaful* schemes. However, in the case of general *takaful* under this model, there is no segregation of funds for the agent to manage. The agent may invest the donated contribution on behalf of the participants and all surplus after deducting the expenses will go to the participants as a *hibah* (gift).

The *wakalah takaful* governance tends to create high moral hazard as the agent may be passive since the *wakalah fee* or return is fixed. Similarly, if the agent is given a pre-fixed percentage from each policyholder's donation, this may make the agent to focus more on increasing the number of participants and neglecting managing the investment. Hence, as an additional incentive, the *takaful* operator in some *wakalah* models may also receive part of its remuneration as an agent in the form of a performance related fee which is typically related to the underwriting outcome. Advocators for the surplus sharing arrangement argues that the operator deserves to be rewarded for their efficiency in managing the fund which had generated profit from investment or lower the amount claimed resulting in the surplus of fund (Siddiqui and Athemy, 2008).

7.8.2 *MUDARABAH TAKAFUL* MODEL

Unlike the *wakalah* model where the relationship between the participants and the *takaful* operator is that of principal–agent, the *mudarabah takaful* model involves the participants acting as *rabb-ul-mal* (capital provider) and the *takaful* operator as the *mudarib* (entrepreneur). Figure 7.5 illustrates the mechanics of the *mudarabah takaful* model, which involves the following steps:

1. Participants pay contributions into a common fund and this is given as capital to the *takaful* operator for investment and underwriting purposes.
2. The *takaful* operator, acting as a *mudarib*, utilizes the capital provided by the participants in investment and underwriting of risk activities and both parties agree on the profit sharing ratio at the time the contract is signed. Neither the *takaful* operator nor the participants can unilaterally alter the pre-agreed sharing ratio on the investment profit and/or underwriting surplus.
3. The *mudarabah* profit from the investment activities will be shared based on the pre-agreed ratio.
4. The *mudarabah* profit from underwriting activities will also be shared on the pre-agreed ratio but the surplus, which represents the excess of the donated contribution accumulated with the returns from investment of fund less the claim amount disbursed, will be returned to the respective participants apportioned in accordance to their contribution earlier. Note that since the contribution paid is actually 'the capital' of the *rabb-ul-mal,* the surplus distribution may actually mean the payment of capital back to the participants rather than profit as it forms part of the surplus.

Figure 7.5 Mechanics of *mudarabah takaful model*

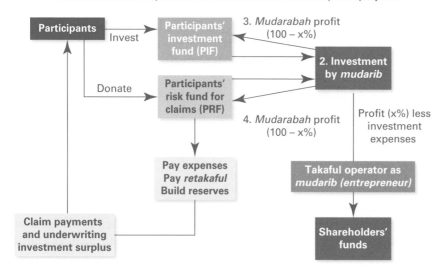

The model shown is for family *takaful*, which involves segregation of funds. In the case of general *takaful*, there is no segregation of funds and all the contributions will be treated as capital for underwriting and investment activities and the *mudarabah* profit from investment will be shared in the pre-agreed ratio with the surplus being returned to participants as gift.

In this type of *takaful* model, any financial losses suffered from the investment and underwriting activities are to be borne solely by the *takaful* participants as the *rabb-ul-mal*, provided that the losses are not attributable to the *takaful* operator's misconduct or negligence. Hence, the *takaful* operator can generally expect to make a profit only by ensuring that the expenses of managing the *takaful* operation are less than the total share of investment profit and/or underwriting surplus it may receive.

In the event that the fund is insufficient to honour all the claims made by the effected participants, the *takaful* operator is expected to extend the fund through *qard al hassan* (benevolent loan). In a *mudarabah* structure, this clearly violates the condition of the capital which is not supposed to be guaranteed by the entrepreneur who in this case is the *takaful* operator. Any expectation levied on the *takaful* operator in guaranteeing the sufficiency of the pool of fund is akin to guaranteeing the capital since the pool of fund is acknowledged as the capital in the *mudarabah* structure.

Issues that arise, especially in the application of general *takaful,* require both scholars and practitioners to review and improve them. The relationship between the participants, *takaful* fund and *takaful* operator must be appropriately defined as it will affect the validity of the *mudarabah* contract. This is the apparent reason why most *takaful* operators had abandoned the *mudarabah* structure in search for other acceptable alternative.

7.8.3 HYBRID *WAKALAH-MUDARABAH TAKAFUL* MODEL

The pure *mudarabah* and *wakalah* structures have been of concern to both scholars and practitioners, as the implementation of the *takaful* schemes closely resembles conventional insurance services and also due to moral hazard problems. Under the *wakalah* model, the *takaful* operator tends to focus more on the PRF since the fees are a fixed percentage of each donation. Similarly, under the *mudarabah* model, the *takaful* operator tends to focus more on the PIF, since the return is a fixed percentage of the profits generated from the investment. These moral hazard limitations can be eliminated when the *takaful* operator is incentivized towards both PIF and PRF activities. Hence, a hybrid model is introduced to bridge the limitations associated with the stand alone structures of *mudarabah* and *wakalah* and to make the scheme fair and suitable to all parties concerned.

The hybrid *wakalah-mudarabah takaful* involves the principles of *tabarru'* and *qard al hassan* (benevolent loan) in order to deliver profitable equity and pay agency ventures. This model segregates between the investors' fund and the participants' funds. The *takaful* fund donated by the participants for underwriting activities (PRF) will be entrusted through the *wakalah* structure. Hence, the *takaful* operator is entitled to an agency mutually predetermined *wakalah* fee to compensate for his/her role as a *wakil* (agent) who manages the *takaful* fund. The participants' portion of the contribution meant for investment activities (PIF) is given to the operator in the form of *mudarabah* capital. Thus, the operator will not earn any fees upfront from this participant fund, but will have the share of profit from investment of the fund in accordance to the pre-agreed profit sharing ratio. The modified structure provides the operator with the agency from the management of the PRF and a share of profit from the investment of the PIF. Figure 7.6 illustrates the mechanics of the hybrid *wakalah-mudarabah takaful* model, which involves the following steps:

1. The participants make contributions which are segregated into the PIF and PRF.
2. Participants appoint the *takaful* operator to act as an agent for a mutually agreed fee for handling the PRF.
3. A portion of the PRF will be utilized as capital by the *takaful* operator as a *mudarib* for investment at a pre-agreed profit sharing ratio. The *mudarabah* investment profit from PRF is added to the PRF account, which is used for underwriting activities. Any profits and underwriting surplus may be distributed to the participants as a gift.
4. The PIF is utilized by the *takaful* operator as a *mudarib* for investment at a pre-agreed profit sharing ratio.
5. The *takaful* operator sources of income are the agency fee, incentive fee and the profit share from the investment of the funds.

Figure 7.6   Mechanics of hybrid *wakalah-mudarabah takaful model*

1. Contributions segregated for underwriting and investment in *shari'ah* compliant projects

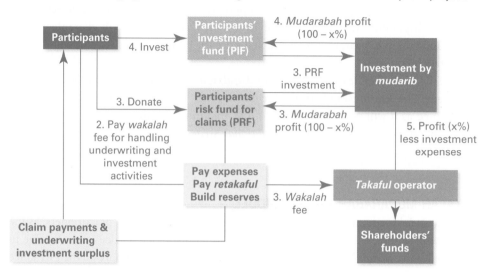

The twofold role of the *takaful* operator makes the hybrid model unique and is the reason why it is becoming more popular, and in fact, many scholars including AAOIFI and the Central Bank of Bahrain have endorsed it to be the most suitable and mutually beneficial model for all the parties concerned.

However, the model still has its limitations, especially in dealing with the rights of the participants on the return of surplus from the PRF. Since the fund is contributed as a donation, they lose their ownership to the fund. Furthermore, the *takaful* operator has to be mindful on the financial treatment required by utilizing these contracts as income is derived differently, which in turn affects how expenses are charged in relation to the fund management activities. For the model to be successful, relationships of all parties to the contacts must be properly observed and understood by all parties.

7.8.4   SUPER-HYBRID *WAQF-WAKALAH-MUDARABAH TAKAFUL* MODEL

Although the *wakalah-mudarabah* hybrid model addresses some of the moral hazard associated with the role of the *takaful* operator, issues still remain on how to deal with the surplus and the ownership of the fund (especially when participants leave the scheme and without receiving their remaining donation). To overcome such issues, a new super-hybrid *waqf-wakalah-mudarabah takaful* model was introduced by the renowned Islamic jurisprudence scholar, Muhammad Taqi Usmani. In this new model, *waqf* (endowment) was included in the *wakalah-mudarabah* model and besides *tabarru'* (donation), this model also introduces the concept of *qard hassan* (benevolent loan) to donate the funds to *waqf* (endowment).

In the *waqf* structure, the contributions of the participants are no longer taken on the basis of *tabarru'* (donation) but are transferred into the pool of fund under *waqf*. Hence, the contribution carries the notion of *waqf* rather than *tabarru'*. As such, the *waqf* structure is able to formalize the relationship between the *takaful* operator and the *waqf* fund participants. It also helps to eliminate issues such as the sharing of surplus and also moral hazard. The *wakalah* and *mudarabah* elements come into play with the role of the *takaful* operator. The shareholders of the *takaful* company make donations in order to establish a *waqf* fund and the *takaful* company then becomes the shareholders' agent (*wakil*), delegated to manage the *waqf* funds efficiently and make payments for any valid claims. This delegation of authority is in the form of a *wakalah* (agency) contract for which the *takaful* company receives an agreed *wakalah* fee. The *takaful* company also manages the investment of the *waqf* funds as a *mudarib* (entrepreneur) under a *mudarabah* contract, the implication being that the *takaful* company is also entitled to its share in the profit realized from the investment.

Figure 7.7 illustrates the mechanics of this super-hybrid *takaful* model. In this model, the participants of the *takaful* scheme will donate the contributions for PRF to a *waqf* fund and pay the *takaful* operator a *wakalah* fee for managing the fund. The shareholders of the *takaful* company will also make donations to the *waqf* fund to cover the underwriting activities. The *waqf* funds are invested in *shari'ah* compliant business activities and any surplus generated will be kept in the *waqf* fund. The PIF is given as capital to the *takaful* operator under a *mudarabah* contract for investment based on a pre-agreed profit sharing ratio. The returns from such investments are distributed for the benefit of the participants. The steps involved can be summarized as follows:

1. Participants donate PRF contributions as *waqf* into a common pool of funds for mutual indemnification.
2. Participants enter into a *wakalah* (agency) contract with the *takaful* operator who is paid a fixed *wakalah* or agency fee for undertaking underwriting activities.
3. The shareholders of the *takaful* company also donate to the *waqf* fund and delegate the operator to act as agent.
4. The *waqf* fund will be invested and any surplus generated will be accumulated in the *waqf* fund to underwrite the risks of the participants.
5. The *takaful* operator, acting as a *mudarib*, will invest the PIF portion of the contributions from the *takaful* scheme and the *mudarabah* profits are shared based on a pre-agreed profit sharing ratio and returned to participants.

Figure 7.7 Mechanics of super-hybrid *wakalah-mudarabah takaful model*

Contributions segregated for underwriting and investment in *shari'ah* compliant projects

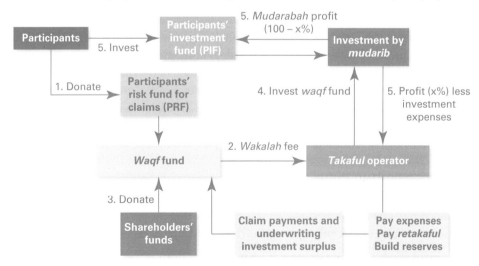

Table 7.4 presents a comparison of the main features of each *takaful* governance model being used in the industry.

Table 7.4 Comparison of the four *takaful* governance models

	Wakalah model	*Mudarabah* model	*Wakalah-mudarabah* hybrid model	*Waqf-wakalah-muarabah* super-hybrid model
Contract used	• *wakalah* only	• *mudarabah* only	• *wakalah* and *mudarabah*	• *waqf, wakalah* & *mudarabah*
Investment strategy	• savings and investment in *shari'ah* compliant assets	• investment in *shari'ah* compliant asset	• investment in *shari'ah* compliant assets	• investment in *shari'ah* compliant assets
Operator's responsibility	• administers the *takaful* undertaking and oversees the investment of the fund as a *wakil* (agent)	• invests the funds and manages the whole *takaful* undertaking as a *mudarib* (entrepreneur)	• administers the *takaful* undertaking as an agent and oversees the investment of the funds as an entrepreneur	• administers the *takaful* undertaking, oversees the investment of the funds, and manages the *waqf* fund
Initial capital used	• participants' premiums	• participants' premiums	• participants' premiums	• participants' premiums and charitable donations (*waqf*)
Benefits	• mutual guarantee against any risk for the participants and end of year surplus • agency fee for the operator	• mutual guarantee for the participants • *mudarabah* profit to be shared between operator and participants • surplus to be distributed to participants	• mutual guarantee for the participants • *mudarabah* profit to be shared between operator and participants • surplus to be distributed to participants • agency fee for the operator	• mutual guarantee for the participants • operator and participants share profit from the investment of cash *waqf* funds • returns from *waqf* investment of the participants to be added to PRF

7.9   Dealing with underwriting surplus and other technical provisions

As mentioned earlier, one of the main challenges faced by the *takaful* industry is to seek solution on the most appropriate manner to determine and allocate surplus in a way that does not contravene the *shari'ah*. This matter arises due to the nature of contributions from the participants and the origin of the surplus. As *takaful* institutions become more profit oriented in order to compete strongly with their conventional counterparts, there have been some misgivings on the appropriate method for the distribution of surplus in *takaful* undertakings. To address this issue, AAOIFI has issued a relevant standard, Financial Accounting Standard No. 13, to regulate the necessary disclosure of the bases for determining and allocating surplus or deficit in *takaful* companies.

7.9.1   RECOGNIZING UNDERWRITING SURPLUS

Underwriting surplus is the excess of the total premium continuations paid by policyholders during the financial period over the total indemnities paid in respect of claims incurred during the period, net of reinsurance and after deducting expenses and changes in technical provision. This can be simply expressed as follows:

Underwriting surplus = Total premium − All expenses and provisions

In most *takaful* undertakings, participants make donations to the common pool of funds for mutual indemnification and it is common to have an underwriting surplus from the process. In order to recognize this in the financial statements, the underwriting surplus is calculated for a specific financial year. Accordingly, all indemnities paid in respect of claims during the financial period are the underwriting activities carried out by the *takaful* operator to indemnify the participants. This must be taken into account when calculating the underwriting surplus and also should be reflected in the financial statements of the *takaful* operator. Similarly, the premiums paid by the *takaful* operator for the *retakaful* policy (see below) is an expense that should be deducted from the total premium contributions of the participants. Changes in technical provisions that must be deducted from the total premium contributions of the participants may be related to changes in estimation of provisions due to unpaid claims and unearned premiums, and any adjustment made in the method of accounting to reflect the actual financial position of the *takaful* fund as well as changes in the provisions related to the method of accounting and balancing the financial statement.

7.9.2   RIGHT OF POLICYHOLDERS TO SURPLUS AND METHOD OF ALLOCATION

AAOIFI's standard (FAS 13, 2010) addressed the *shari'ah* ruling on *takaful* surplus. The standard recognized the right of the policyholders or *takaful* participants to the surplus. It is the view of many *shari'ah* scholars that since the surplus originated from the financial contributions of *takaful* policyholders, it therefore collectively belongs to them. This must be clearly stipulated in the *takaful* agreement policy. Since a *takaful* undertaking must agree on the distribution method in the policy, transparency is vital. Hence, the *takaful* company must have a system in place to clearly segregate between the assets, obligations and results of operations of the policyholders and that of the *takaful* company's shareholders. The latter is not entitled to the surplus, but will receive dividends from any realized profits for their investments in the activities of the *takaful* undertaking. However, some *shari'ah* boards approve the sharing of surplus between the shareholders and the policyholders.

There are many ways for allocating *takaful* surplus. AAOIFI offers five options that the *takaful* undertaking may select. The first option is to allocate *takaful* surplus to all policyholders, regardless of whether or not they have submitted claims on the policy during the financial period. The second option is to allocate *takaful* surplus only among policyholders who have not submitted any claims during the financial period. The third option is to allocate *takaful* surplus to all but for those who have submitted claims during the financial period, they are only entitled to the difference between their financial contributions and their claims during the financial period. The fourth option is to allocate *takaful* surplus among current policyholders and shareholders, if this is permitted by the *shari'ah* board. The last option is to allocate *takaful* surplus based on other methods deemed appropriate. In the absence of rules or regulations in any jurisdiction on how to allocate *takaful* surplus, AAOIFI suggests the use of the first method, i.e., allocating the surplus equally among the policyholders.

7.9.3   COVERING *TAKAFUL* DEFICIT

Takaful undertakings may not always have surplus, but instead realize a deficit. This arises when there is a shortfall in the *takaful* pool to compensate for the amount of claims submitted by policyholders for their mishaps and/or to cover other operating costs. When a *takaful* undertaking experiences such shortfall, it needs to address this carefully as it may have implications on future underwriting activities and survival in the long run. In practice, *takaful* undertakings turn to *retakaful* companies to rescue and bail them. However, they first need to rectify the deficits and losses. Given that a *takaful* undertaking has two main funds, i.e. PRF and PIF, it needs to follow different frameworks in dealing with the deficit.

In the case of deficit in PRF, which occurs when the assets of the PRF are insufficient to meet the liabilities, it is the duty of the *takaful* operator to rectify the deficiency and loss in the PRF. The *takaful* operator may thus provide a *qard hasan* (benevolent loan) to the *takaful* fund to undertake the underwriting activities and there must be a sound repayment mechanism so that such a loan can be repaid through future surpluses. If the deficit arises due to mismanagement of the *takaful* operator, it may be rectified through the transfer of assets from the shareholders' fund.

When the deficit is related to the PIF, the shortfall will have to be absorbed by the shareholders via its general reserves or own capital, especially when the *takaful* fund is structured based on a *mudarabah* model. Thus, the participants will first bear the loss from the investment. A benevolent loan from the *takaful* operator cannot be used to rectify the deficit as the operator is an entrepreneur and the *shari'ah* does not allow guaranteeing a deficit for *mudarabah* capital. Therefore, the deficit must be made good through other means. However, if the deficit is due to the *takaful* operator's professional negligence or mismanagement, the loss in deficit would be absorbed by the shareholders' funds (reserves or capital).

AAOIFI, in its standard, provides a number of methods that can be used for covering the *takaful* deficit. One way is to settle the deficit using the general reserves of the policyholders, provided that such reserve exists. Another method is to borrow from the shareholders' fund based on qard hassan to cover the amount of deficit, repaying through future surpluses. The *takaful* undertaking can also consider requesting the policyholders to absorb the deficit pro-rata. The last method is to increase the future premium contribution payments of policyholders on a pro-rata basis.

7.10 Reinsurance and *retakaful*

It is well known in the conventional insurance industry that it is challenging for one insurance underwriter to bear all risks for the insured policies. Therefore, managing risk losses collectively is a key strategy for the whole insurance industry. This is done through what is known as reinsurance, a mechanism designed to transfer the pool of risks to a larger insurer.

The proliferation of *takaful* companies in many Muslim countries has invariably created the need for the establishment of reinsurance companies structured on Islamic principles. The Islamic alternative to reinsurance is *retakaful*, which has been structured to be *shari'ah* compliant. *Retakaful* operators carry out their operations in accordance with the structures and models of the *takaful* operators. Essentially, *retakaful* is a *takaful* undertaking for *takaful* operators. *Retakaful* involves *takaful* operators contributing an agreed amount of premium periodically to the *retakaful* company. Hence, all the underwriting risks of the *takaful* operators are insured by the *retakaful* company, who plays a significant role when *takaful* operators record deficits or losses. Figure 7.8 illustrates the relationship and flow of funds in a *retakaful* process.

Figure 7.8   Relationship and flow of capital in the *retakaful* process

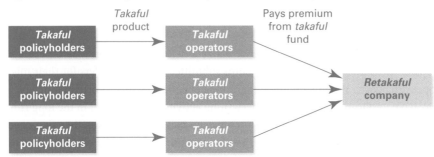

The initial capital required for *retakaful* undertakings is large due to the large pool of risks involved in reinsurance. However, the capital of many *retakaful* companies is not large enough to attain an A rating as required for reinsurance purposes, causing many *takaful* operators opting for reinsurance policies of conventional reinsurance companies. Given the circumstances, *shari'ah* scholars have allowed *takaful* operators to use reinsurance companies subject to certain conditions and particularly those that can cater for the large pool of risk of many *takaful* companies at an international level. Some of the conditions include the following:

● The business relationship should not cause financial harm to Muslims or result in destabilizing the financial system of any Muslim country.
● *Takaful* operator should reinsure on a net premium basis and not receive any reinsurance remunerations, profit commissions or interest on premiums it has retained from premiums payable to its reinsurer.

- *Takaful* operator must refrain from receiving interest from a conventional reinsurance company and if it is not possible, it may accept the interest and spend it on humanitarian activities and public infrastructure projects.
- The premium paid for securing reinsurance protection should be as low as possible.
- Preference should be given to Islamic reinsurance operators in the matter of securing reinsurance protection whenever possible.
- *Takaful* operators should appoint a *shari'ah* supervisory board to monitor their operations according to *shari'ah* principles.

The continuous growth experienced in the Islamic banking industry has increased demand for protection. In recent years, some conventional reinsurance companies have established *takaful* pools, arms or divisions based on the active demand for capacity from the *takaful* industry. Those companies include Swiss Re, Mitsui Sumitomo, Hannover Re, Kuwait Re, Trust Re and Labuan Re.

Box 7.2 London – a global takaful centre?

By Martin Mankabady 30 July 2015

Takaful is a market that for some time has been recognised as a sleeping giant. In London it is in the process of waking up, writes Martin Mankabady, corporate insurance partner at Clyde & Co.

Around a quarter of the world's population is Muslim, a vast potential market for takaful insurance products. Yet a number of barriers have been in place, which have so far prevented the market from taking off in a meaningful way. Insurance markets in Islamic centres such as the Middle East, Malaysia and Indonesia are relatively nascent, and the takaful market is characterised by a high proportion of smaller players held back by high start-up costs and an on-going struggle for profitability.

But signs show that this is about to change. Takaful insurance has been declared one of the eight pillars of the UAE's push to become the centre of the Islamic finance world. Regulators across the Middle East and beyond are introducing new rules designed to create fewer, stronger players in the insurance industry. It is expected that this will result in a number of takaful businesses emerging with sufficient scale to get themselves on the map. They should be well placed to grab a share of the growing global takaful market, which is expected to reach $20 billion by 2017, according to AM Best.

An appealing prospect

It is unsurprising then, that as one of the world's leading insurance centres, London is looking closely at this market. In 2013, at the World Islamic Economic Forum in London, Prime Minister David Cameron said that the UK was in a global race for its economic future and that it would be a "mistake" to miss the opportunity to encourage more Islamic investment. He outlined the government's ambition to establish London as a global Islamic finance centre along with Kuala Lumpur and Dubai, stating: "When Islamic finance is growing 50% faster than traditional banking and when global Islamic investments are set to grow to £1.3 trillion by 2014, we want to make sure a big proportion of that new investment is made here in Britain."

A further example of this resolve was the June 2014 issue by the UK government of a sovereign Sukuk – the Islamic equivalent of a bond – which attracted orders of more than £2 billion from global investors. The fact that the UK was the first country to issue such a bond outside the Islamic world is evidence of the country's desire to cement its position as the western hub for Islamic finance.

This appetite within the UK to embrace Islamic finance will only help to kick-start the takaful insurance market in London, predominantly on the commercial side. There is already evidence that this is starting to happen. Cobalt Underwriting, London's first Islamic insurance underwriting agency, was launched in 2012 and has recently been making the headlines. In October 2014 Cobalt entered into a partnership with AIG, a move that provided increased capacity and the opportunity to increase the lines of business it offers. In April this year, together with XL, Cobalt launched the first Shariah-compliant product to be made available through the Lloyd's platform, and then in July it announced that it had secured a major property portfolio placed by Lockton's Real Estate and Construction practice.

(Continued)

Barriers to success

London has a number of advantages that will play a key role in helping the takaful market to grow. It has a reputation for being a centre of innovation for global risk transfer, and has been a pioneer for new product development. It is well-placed geographically, English is the main business language, it is a cultural melting pot that is open to new ideas and products, and it has a talent pool which is hard to match.

However, despite these advantages – and the advances that have already been made – takaful will not take off overnight in London. This will be a slow-burn process and a number of challenges will need to be overcome. These challenges include ensuring that takaful products meet not only Sharia principles but are also compliant with UK rules and regulations. This will require the creation of a Sharia supervisory board or committee, made up of the right people, by those wishing to write takaful products. It will be important for London's credibility and efficiency as a takaful market to attract Islamic Scholars with the relevant knowledge and experience, to provide advice swiftly and consistently.

Equally important is the need for the retakaful and Islamic investment market to be large enough to support the primary takaful market and to help it to grow. This has been a challenge worldwide, but there are signs that the retakaful market is picking up. Sharia boards of takaful firms are increasingly pressing for retakaful options and the pricing gap with conventional insurance is narrowing, as more capital moves into the market.

Swiss Re, the world's second largest reinsurer, is in talks to set up a market retakaful pool, and Lloyd's has opened an office in Dubai and is in talks with regulators to access the Malaysian market. Others in the sector are also building capacity in the sector, including Dubai-based EmiratesRe, while PineBridge Investments, a New York-based asset manager, is exploring the launch of a retakaful firm in Dubai, according to a Reuters' report.

Accelerating development

To overcome these challenges, all participants in the insurance industry in London with an interest in the takaful market need to work together. To this end, the launch of the Islamic Insurance Association of London (IIAL) earlier this year, to act as a forum to bring together key stakeholders including underwriters, actuaries, lawyers and scholars, was an important development.

Speaking at the launch event, Chairman Max Taylor noted that (re)insurance was the last of the financial services sectors in London to establish Shariah compliant operations and products and the IIAL would provide it with "a strong and authoritative voice with both UK and international governments and regulators". This role will be vital in helping to ensure that the political will to seize the takaful opportunity does not waver. The IIAL will raise the profile of London as a genuine global centre for takaful and signal to the world that this is a city that is very much open for Islamic business.

Source: www.insurancetimes.co.uk/london–a-global-takaful-centre/1414931.article

7.11 Future prospects and challenges of *takaful*

Ernst & Young (2014) reported that the gross *takaful* contribution for 2014 was estimated to reach $14 billion, a figure higher than the previous year's $12.3 billion. Between 2007 and 2011, a high year on year growth rate was registered, moderated by an impressive Compound Annual Growth Rate (CAGR) of 22 per cent, but this slowed down to 14 per cent for the period 2012 through 2014.

Performance of the industry varies across countries depending on the prevailing regulation, business structure, investment avenues and products offered. The Ernst and Young Report (2014) noted that Malaysia has been the major contributor in the offering of family *takaful* products with gross contribution at $1.4 billion. However, Saudi Arabia, which contributes almost half of the global *takaful* gross contribution is expected to lead the industry in the future years.

At the current growth rate, the report observes that the penetration level is still low at 2 per cent of the population in the respective markets. This serve as the main driver for growth as the Muslim market still remain untapped in the provision of *takaful* services. The industry is predicted to grow at a moderate growth of

14 per cent over 2013 to 2016 (Ernst and Young, 2014). The report had also projected that the gross *Takaful* contribution will reach $20 billion in 2017 (Ernst and Young, 2014).

Although the *takaful* industry is still growing at a commendable pace for a young industry, it still faces several challenges. The main concern was how the scheme can be profitably run while at the same time providing products and services which are in accordance with the *Shari'ah* requirement. Hence they are mainly in terms of the different business models adopted, determination of contribution, penetration of products especially family *takaful,* and regulatory reforms. Furthermore, the availability of re*takaful* is limited, thus firms have to subscribe to reinsurance companies that are able to absorb the underwritten risks. Such instances provide additional challenge to the industry especially as it strives to adhere to *shari'ah* requirements.

Summary

The concept of insurance has always existed in human society as a mechanism to mitigate risk and to protect from economic and natural disasters. *Takaful* is an Islamic alternative to insurance aimed at helping individuals, societies and businesses to mitigate risks in a *shari'ah* compliant way. It is an important component in the Islamic financial system and with the growth of Islamic banking, the demand for *takaful* is expected to increase in the future.

The underlying principles of *takaful* are *ta'awun* (mutual assistance) and *tabarru'* (donation) and different *takaful* governance models have been developed based on these two principles. The policyholders in *takaful* schemes are known as participants and the payments to the pooled funds are known as contributions. The entity that handles the management of the pooled funds is known as the *takaful* operator. There are two main classifications of *takaful* products: family *takaful* and general *takaful*.

The contributions to the pooled funds for family *takaful* can be segregated into participants' risk fund (PRF) and participants' investment fund (PIF). The former is a donation to cover risks and is managed by the *takaful* operator as an underwriting activity while the latter is utilized for investment purposes to generate returns. The investment activities in *takaful* may either generate surplus or deficit and the challenge faced by those involved in the *takaful* industry is to find appropriate solutions to handling them without contravening *shari'ah*. *Takaful* operators contribute an agreed premium to a *retakaful* company to protect from losses.

Key terms and concepts

aqilah	life insurance	takaful
cooperative risk sharing	muamalat	takaful operator
family takaful	mudarabah takaful	technical provision
general average	Participants' Investment Fund (PIF)	underwriting
general insurance	Participants' Risk Fund (PRF)	underwriting surplus
general takaful	peril risk	wakalah-mudarabah takaful
indemnification	reinsurance	wakalah fee
indemnities	reinsured	wakalah takaful
insurance	reinsurer	wakil
insurance premium	retakaful	waqf
insured	ta'awun	waqf-wakalah-mudarabah
insurer	tabarru'	takaful

Questions

1. Briefly describe the development of insurance and the idea of risk transfer.

2. Discuss the main types of insurance and their features.

3. Describe the historical development of *takaful*.

4. Explain the key principles of *takaful*.

5. Distinguish between *takaful* and conventional insurance.

6. Advise on the types of *takaful* products.

7. Discuss the different models of *takaful* governance.

8. Explain how AAOIFI addresses the underwriting surplus and other technical provisions related to *takaful*.

9. Distinguish between reinsurance and *retakaful*.

10. Comment on the future prospects and challenges facing the *takaful* industry.

References and further readings

Abdel Karim, R.A., and Archer, S (2002), 'Introduction to Islamic finance'. In Abdel Karim & Archer (eds), *Islamic Finance: Innovation and Growth*, Euro money Books, London.

Ahmad, A. (1995), *The Evolution of Islamic Banking, Encyclopaedia of Islamic Banking and Insurance*, Institute of Islamic Banking and Insurance, London, pp. 15-30.

Al-Zuhayli, W. (2003), 'Al-Fiqh al-Islami wa adillatuhu' (Islamic jurisprudence and its proofs). In El-Gamal, M. (ed.) *Financial Transactions in Islamic Jurisprudence*. 1st ed. Dar al-Fikr, Damascus, Syria.

Archer, S., Abdel Karim, R.A. and Nienhaus, V. (eds) (2009), *Takaful Islamic Insurance: Concepts and Regulatory Issues*, John Wiley & Sons (Asia) Ltd.

Bekkin, R. (2007), 'Islamic Insurance: National Features and Legal Regulation', *Arab Law Quarterly*, 21, pp. 3-34.

Cizakca, M. (2004), *Cash Waqf as Alternative to NBFIs Bank*, International Seminar on Nonbank Financial Institutions: Islamic Alternatives, Islamic Banking and Finance Institute, Malaysia.

Donnelly, C., Guillén, M., and Nielsen, J.P. (2013), 'Exchanging uncertain mortality for a cost', *Insurance: Mathematics and Economics*, 52, pp. 65-76.

Ernst & Young (2014), Global Takaful Insights 2014. www.islamicfinance.com/wp-content/uploads/2015/01/EY-global-takaful-insights-2014.pdf, accessed 18 June 2018.

Fisher, O.C. and Taylor, D. (2000), *Prospects for the Evolution of Takaful in the 21st Century*, Proceedings of the Fifth Harvard University Forum on Islamic Finance: Islamic Finance: Dynamics and Development Cambridge, Massachusetts. Center for Middle Eastern Studies, Harvard University. 2000. pp. 237-254.

IFSB *Guiding principles on governance for takaful undertakings*, Kuala Lumpur, Dec. 2009.

Khan, A. (2005), *Insurance and the Opinions of Collective Institutions of Fiqh*, Seminar on Collective Ijtihad, Evolutionary Change and Practical Methods, Islamic Research Institute, Islamabad, Pakistan.

Kuran, T. (2005), 'The logic of financial westernization in the Middle East', *Journal of Economic Behaviour & Organization*, 56, pp. 4593-4615.

Mankabady, S. (1989), 'Insurance and Islamic law: The Islamic insurance company', *Arab Law Quarterly*, 4, pp. 199-205.

Pamuk, S. (2004), 'The evolution of financial institutions in the Ottoman Empire', *Financial History Review*, 11, pp. 7-13.

Sadeghi, M. (2010), 'The evolution of Islamic insurance – Takaful: A literature survey', *Insurance Markets and Companies: Analyses and Actuarial Computations*, 1(2), pp. 100-107.

Schoon, N. (2008), 'Islamic finance, a history', *Financial Services Review*, pp. 10-12.

Sfetcu, N. (2014), *Insurance Glossary*, Google books.

Siddiqui, S.A. and Athemy, A.A.R.A. (2008), 'Resolving controversial issues and setting goals for Islamic insurance: An evaluation of takaful companies of Brunei', *Journal of Islamic Economics, Banking and Finance*, 3(2), pp. 129-158.

8 Islamic microfinance

Learning Objectives

Upon completion of this chapter you should be able to:

- discuss the role and objectives of microfinance
- explain the emergence and development of microfinance
- discuss the role and objectives of Islamic microfinance
- explain the emergence and development of Islamic microfinance
- explain the different types of Islamic microfinance products and services
- distinguish the features of conventional and Islamic microfinance
- discuss the practice of Islamic microfinancing in different regions

8.1 Introduction

Microfinance or 'microcredit' refers to a financial intermediation between microsavers, micro borrowers and micro investors (Seibel, 2005). It is a new kind of banking system that works for the poor, who have no tangible collateral to access the conventional banks (Blanco-Oliver, Irimia-Dieguez and Reguera-Alvarado, 2016). Microfinance institutions (MFIs) provide a wide range of products and services, from savings to loans, insurance, remittances and payments, all on a small scale to help low income groups in society who are excluded from using commercial banks to access such products and services (Armendáriz and Murdoch, 2010). Proponents of microfinancing have argued that microfinance can be an effective tool to alleviate poverty in poor nations, as microcredits can help support entrepreneurial initiatives.

According to Obaidullah (2008), over half a billion individuals live on under $2 per day in Indonesia, India, Pakistan, Bangladesh, Egypt and Nigeria. It is estimated that nearly half of global poverty is concentrated in Muslim communities and that 75 per cent of the world's refugees come from Muslim nations. Many of them struggle to access sufficient liquidity, manage savings and transfer and receive money. Given the disproportionately high rate of poor and needy Muslims, Islamic microfinance is deemed as a valuable and novel tool for development and poverty alleviation.

Market surveys by financial institutions and other reports on Islamic microfinance consistently argue that poor Muslims, in particular, show significant rates of rejection of traditional micro loans (El-Gamal, El-Komi, Karlan, and Osman, 2014). Similarly, the 2008 Consultative Group to Assist the Poor (CGAP) report indicates that up to 40 per cent of potential microfinance clients reject non-*shari'ah* compliant micro loans

(Karim, Tarazai and Reille, 2008). Hence, efforts in developing *shari'ah* compliant microfinancing are warmly welcomed by stakeholders as it can promote the financial inclusion of populations who are excluding themselves from conventional microfinancing options (Kroessin, 2012; Khan and Phillips, 2010). Therefore, in the last few years, Islamic microfinance has been the subject of several international conferences, studies, and workshops sponsored by the Islamic Development Bank (IDB), the Accounting and Auditing Organisation for Islamic Financial Institutions (AAOIFI) and the Harvard Islamic Finance Project, among others.

In this chapter, we will consider the role and objectives of conventional and Islamic microfinance and their emergence and development, followed by discussion of their distinguishing features. We will then focus on the various types of Islamic microfinance products and services available and examine the practice of microfinancing in various regions.

8.2   Role and objectives of microfinance

Microfinance is a relatively new branch of financial services aimed at promoting self-sufficiency and economic development among people who do not have access to the traditional financial sector. This involves the provision of small loans without the strict requirements of traditional lenders. The recipients are not only the poor and unbanked, but also include those who are not poor but who lack the credit standing to borrow money to start or grow a business. Hence, MFIs provide underprivileged groups access to capital to get their business idea off the ground and turn micro loans into profitable business that will help them pay off their micro loan and continue to gain income from their venture indefinitely.

In addition, microcredits help the impoverished people to have enough financial stability and protection from sudden financial problems and in the long run to move from simply surviving to accruing savings. Their savings may allow for educational investment, improved nutrition, better living conditions and reduced illness. Another segment of the microfinance sector is micro insurance, which enables people to pay for health care when needed and also to receive treatment for health conditions before they become grave and more costly to treat.

Microfinance also provides women with the financial backing to enable them to readily participate in economic activity. The aim is to improve their status and make them more active in decision making, thus encouraging gender equality. According to the international CGAP, there has been evidence of a decline in violence against women in areas targeted by microfinance programmes.

Microfinance is further expected to have trickle down effects not only on the lives of direct recipients but also on their communities. For instance, the micro loans enable the recipients to get better health care and their new business ventures can provide jobs and employment opportunities, thereby increasing income among community members and improving their overall wellbeing.

In short, microfinance is deemed an important mechanism in alleviating poverty and enhancing the households' wellbeing at different levels, such as asset acquisition, household nutrition, health, food security, children's education, women's empowerment and social cohesion. However, more recently, the positive impact of microfinance has been questioned (Angelucci, Karlan and Zinman, 2013; Ganlea, Afriyie and Segbefia, 2015). The literature claims that the impact of microfinance works differently from one context to another and that the impact is dependent on the population density, attitudes to debt, group cohesion, enterprise development, financial literacy, financial service providers and others (Armendáriz and Morduch, 2010).

8.3   Development of microfinancing

Microfinance has a long history. Informal savings and credit groups have operated for centuries across the developing world. The simplest form and most widely used methods of informal savings are the Rotating Savings and Credit Association (ROSCA) whereby participants make regular contributions to a common fund which is given in whole or in part to each contributor in turn. Various types of ROSCAs exist in almost every developing country and they are known by different names: *tandas* (Mexico), *pasanaku* (Bolivia), *chit* (India), *cheetu* (Sri Lanka), *arisan* (Indonesia), *njangi* (Cameroon), *susu* (Ghana), *ekub* (Ethiopia), *upatu* (Tanzania), *tontines* (West Africa), etc.

Formalization of the microfinance institution (MFI) first occurred in Ireland at the beginning of 1700s (CGAP, 2009). The Irish Loan Fund system provided small loans to the rural poor with no collateral. By the 1840s, it became a widespread institution providing small loans with interest for short periods to 20 per cent of all Irish households annually. A decade later, larger and more formal savings and credit institutions that focused primarily on the rural and urban poor emerged in Germany. The concept of credit union was introduced to assist the rural population to break out of their dependence on moneylenders and to improve their welfare. From 1870, the unions expanded rapidly over a large sector of the Rhine Province and other regions of the German States. The cooperative movement also expanded rapidly to other parts of Europe, North America and eventually to developing countries. These institutions were known as People's Banks, Credit Unions, and Savings and Credit Cooperatives. In Indonesia, the Indonesian People's Credit Banks or Bank Perkreditan Rakyat (BPR) opened in 1895 and became the largest microfinance system in Indonesia with close to 9000 units.

In the early 1900s, various adaptations of those models began to appear in parts of rural Latin America with the goal of modernizing the agricultural sector through increased commercialization of the rural sector, by mobilizing idle savings and increasing investments through credit, as well as reducing oppressive feudal relations that were enforced through indebtedness. These new banks for the poor were owned by government agencies or private banks. The microfinance industry started to grow rapidly in the 1950s, driven primarily by the spread of the 'green revolution'[1] in rural Asia and Latin America (Harriss-White and Harriss, 2007) to overcome hunger and poverty in these countries. During this period, a large scale rural credit programme, subsidized by an international donors, was launched (Robinson, 2005), whereby credit was distributed as loans to farmers in order to encourage the adoption of new green technologies such as machinery, chemical fertilizer and rice seed.

In the 1970s, the strategy for tackling issues related to the poor shifted from a focus on agriculture to small enterprise development. People were encouraged to start small businesses to improve their livelihoods as well as reduce unemployment (Schreiner and Woller, 2003). Experimental programmes of microenterprise credit based on solidarity group lending in which every member of a group guaranteed the repayment of all members were launched in Bangladesh, Brazil and a few other countries. Such microenterprise lending programmes had an almost exclusive focus on credit for income generating activities (in some cases accompanied by forced savings schemes) targeting very poor (often women) borrowers. ACCION was launched in 1972 to address poverty in Latin America's cities and in 1973, members of the Self Employed Women's Association (SEWA) in India (Gujarat) founded their own bank called the Mahila SEWA Co-operative Bank to provide banking services to poor, illiterate, self employed women. In Bangladesh, Professor Muhammad Yunus of Chittagong University, who won the Nobel Prize in 2006, designed an experimental credit programme based on a special relationship with rural banks. Despite the credit programme being successful in disbursing and recovering thousands of loans, the bankers opted out and in 1983, Grameen Bank was formed through support from donors.

During the 1980s, microcredit programmes continue to improve and the cost recovery interest rates and high payments rate enabled the MFIs to achieve long term sustainability and reaching larger number of clients. In the 1990s, microcredit programmes began to be replaced by microfinance and the landscape of MFIs was characterized by high level of supervision, regulation and transparent systems (Cornford, 2001). Numerous MFIs were established with a lot of support from international donor agencies, such as the CGAP, the World Bank and the Asian Development Bank (ASB). Moreover, during this period, non-governmental organizations (NGOs) began to get involved in microfinancing activities. They combined credit schemes with development programmes to tackle issues regarding education, health and environmental awareness (Edwards and Hulme, 1995). From the 1990s onwards, MFIs spread rapidly across the globe in an unprecedented way by pursuing

---

[1]The term 'green revolution' refers to the harvest success in Mexico as a result of modern agricultural practices (Briney and Winter, 2010).

strategy of commercialization and transformation into profit-making organizations. In the 2000s, private investors and new players entered the market. The advancement of technology lead to innovation in microfinance products and services. Table 8.1 summarizes the change in the approach towards microfinancing.

Table 8.1 Shift in the approach of microfinancing

Role of financial markets	Stimulate production and transfer resources	⟹	Efficient intermediation
View of users	Beneficiaries (supply driven)	⟹	Clients (demand driven)
Sources of funds	Subsidized funds from donors or governments	⟹	Diverse pricing and sources
Financial performance	Loss making: depleting capital	⟹	Sustainability: capitalization
Accountability and evaluations	Activity based (focused on donor objectives)	⟹	Performance of institutions and systems

8.4   Role and objectives of Islamic microfinance

Islam views poverty to be a calamity that Allah has decreed upon an individual, society or nation as a test to teach people that every calamity that Allah decrees is for a reason. The poor should be patient with the decree of Allah and to turn to Him alone in seeking provision as mentioned in the *Qur'an*:

> *There is no moving creature on earth but its sustenance dependeth on Allah. He knoweth the time and place of its definite abode and its temporary deposit: All is in a clear Record* (Hud, 11:6).[2]

Islam also prescribed ways to solve the problem of poverty. Firstly, Islam encourages people to work and earn a living, and to travel in the land to seek provision as mentioned in the following verse in the *Qur'an* and also in the *Hadith*, respectively:

> *And when the Prayer is finished, then may ye disperse through the land, and seek of the Bounty of Allah and celebrate the Praises of Allah often (and without stint): that ye may prosper* (Al-Jumaah, 62:10).[3]
>
> *Abu Hurairah narrated that the Prophet said: 'If one of you were to take a rope and bring firewood on his back and sell it, thus preserving his dignity, that is better for him than asking of people who may give to him or withhold from him'* (Al-Bukhari).[4]

Secondly, it is the collective obligation (*fard kifayah*) of a Muslim society to take care of the basic needs of the poor. In fact, according to al-Shatibi, the noted Islamic scholar, this is the *raison d'etre* of society itself (Chapra, 2008). Islam has made *zakah* obligatory on the wealth of the rich and encourages charity giving and helping the weak and needy, as mentioned in the *Qur'an*:

> *So fear Allah as much as ye can; listen and obey and spend in charity for the benefit of your own soul and those saved from the covetousness of their own souls,- they are the ones that achieve prosperity* (At-Taghabun, 64:16).[5]

Several recent reports have focused on the unique considerations of the developmental need of the global Muslim population. According to these reports, there is a rich and underutilized resource for poverty alleviation based on the inherent Islamic social justice system. While conventional microfinancing shares the same objective as Islamic microfinancing, Muslims usually avoid conventional microfinance system due to its association with the prohibited exploitation of *riba*. As an alternative, Islamic microfinance has recently been institutionalized with the view of providing interest free financial services to those who reject the practice of *riba*.

[2]www.wright-house.com/religions/islam/Quran/11-hud.php, accessed 29 May 2018.

[3]www.wright-house.com/religions/islam/Quran/62-congregation.php, accessed 29 May 2018.

[4]Vol. 3, Book 23, Hadith 2585 sunnah.com/urn/1077610, accessed 29 May 2018.

[5]www.wright-house.com/religions/islam/Quran/64-mutual-disillusion.php, accessed 29 May 2018.

The Islamic scheme of poverty alleviation includes charity (*sadaqa, waqf* and *zakah*), economic empowerment, debt avoidance, mutual cooperation and solidarity, family cohesiveness, and *shari'ah* compliant financial contracts (Obaidullah, 2008). Therefore, there has been increasing recognition on the potential to tap into the scattered Islamic donor streams, namely, *zakat, sadaqa* and *waqf* and channel them towards the strategic, impact oriented goals of Islamic microfinance. Consequently, out of the background of the growing field of Islamic finance, a slow but steady growth of Islamic microfinance has recently become more dynamic, fuelled by increased attention from governments, central banks, NGOs, donors, and Islamic and financial institutions (IFIs) themselves. The key expected outcomes of Islamic microfinance is to provide access to liquid funds for poor clients who may be reluctant to engage with non-Islamic finance and other poverty alleviation related benefits, as well as expand its reach through partnerships and funding strategies and product innovation.

8.5 Development and evolution of Islamic microfinancing

The history of Islamic microfinance institutions (IMFIs) has not been extensively researched, thus there is a dearth of literature in this area. Nevertheless, the emergence and development of IMFIs are often associated with the philanthropic institutions of *waqf* (endowment) and *zakah* (almsgiving) that were dominant throughout Islamic history. *Waqf* is simply an Islamic charitable foundation (Çizakça, 1998) but more precisely, refers to 'the locking up of the title of an owned asset from disposition and allotment of its benefit for a specific purpose or purposes' (Sadeq, 2002, p. 139). The special characteristic of *waqf* is its perpetuity, as its assets and ownership cannot be transferred and can only be used for specific purposes such as financing education institutions, orphanages, roads, hospitals, establishing mosques, graveyards and so on. For more than a century, magnificent works of architecture, health, education and welfare activities were entirely financed and maintained by the *waqf* system (Çizakça, 2000). In short, the history of *waqf* is closely linked with the significant achievement in promoting the welfare of society in general and, serving the poor, in particular (Ahmed, 2007).

The other institution that is closely linked to IMFIs is the *zakah*, a compulsory percentage based almsgiving based on specific items of assets/properties that satisfactorily meet a set of conditions (Ahmed, 2004). While *waqf* is more flexible, the precise conditions of *zakah*, including the eight categories of beneficiaries of *zakah* funds, have been established in the *Qur'an*. The *zakah* mechanism enables the sharing of resources in a society, redistributing income and wealth, thus reducing the socio-economic gap between the rich and the poor (Kaleem and Ahmed, 2010). Therefore, similar to the institution of *waqf, zakah* is also considered to be an effective Islamic tool for the alleviation of poverty.

Both *zakah* and *waqf* played imperative roles in the Muslim world with the former being the backbone of philanthropy while the latter supported the infrastructure (Ahmed, 2004). Since both were administered by the government, the history of these institutions was impacted by the fates of the state (Çizakça, 1998). During the 19th century, most Muslim countries were under colonial rule, and as a result, to some degree lost their traditions, values and cultural heritage (Iqbal and Mirakhor, 2011), including the Islamic philanthropy institutions of *waqf* and *zakah*, (Çizakça, 1998). Upon these countries' independence from colonial power, Muslims started to rediscover their Islamic identity, and became determined to transform their way of life and bring it into closer alignment with the principles of Islam (Henry and Wilson, 2004). This reawakening also impacted the financial services sector including microfinance.

Although not fully adhering to *shari'ah* principles, since India has a secular government and an interest based banking system, the Muslim Fund Deoband which was established and registered as a charitable trust in India in 1961 could be considered as the first model of the IMFI (Islahi, 1997). It aims to release poorer Muslims from the strangle of moneylenders by disbursing interest free loans without collateral and mobilizing the savings from them (Khan and Nisar, 2004).

The idea to establish a financial institution in compliance with *shari'ah* principles was initiated in the remote village of Mit Ghamr in Egypt in 1963. Although it is widely recognized as the first modern Islamic bank (Iqbal and Mirakhor, 2011), it was actually a microfinance scheme to encourage microsavings and micro entrepreneurship. However, due to the perceived threat of Islamic fundamentalism by the administration, this savings institution and its branches were forced to close in 1967 (Memon, 2007).

The Pilgrim Savings Corporation, which was established in 1963 in Malaysia, was another interest free savings initiative to help Muslims save money towards their pilgrimage expenses (Dar and Presley, 2003). Although not much discussed in the literature, another IMFI is the Islamic Cooperative Bank which was established in 1965 in Karachi by S.A. Irshad (Dar and Presley, 2003). In Egypt, the first interest free institution, which contains bank in its name, the Nasser Social Bank, was established in 1971 by the Egyptian government after the closure of Mit Ghamr to provide loans to those with low incomes (Iqbal and Molyneux, 2005).

There were no other IMFI initiatives until 1986, when Malaysia established a microfinance project called Project Ikhtiar. This project replicated the Grameen Bank model, disbursing loans to 373 poor households in the Northwest of Selangor (Amanah Ikhtiar Malaysia, 2010). The project was successful, with the rate of payment reaching about 90 per cent, and was formalized into a private trust called Amanah Ikhtiar Malaysia, continuing its aim to provide interest free loans without collateral to borrowers, for the charge of only a service fee (Ismail, 2001).

Towards the end of the 1990s, another IMFI emerged in Hodeidah, Yemen (Al-Zamzami and Grace, 2001), aimed at helping the refugees of the Gulf War. This project was realized in 1997 with the assistance of the United Nation of Development Program (UNDP) under the Hodeidah Microfinance Program (HMFP). In the same vein, the UNDP provided support for the establishment of the Sanduq, a local IMFI which was owned and managed by the local people in Jabal a Hoss in Syria in 2000 (Imady and Seibel, 2003). This programme was different compared to other IMFIs, as the mobilization of funds was undertaken through member shared capital, which meant that it had multi shareholders. Another IMFI also emerged in Pakistan in 2001 called the Akhuwat (Akhter, Akhtar and Jafri, 2011), where the organizational structure and activities were based on the mosque. The Akhuwat operated without funding from either the government or donors, channelling only interest free charitable loans (*qard al-hassan*) with the obligation for borrowers to pay just 5 per cent of their loan as an administration fee. From the beginning of 2000 onwards, a number of IMFIs were established in various countries in different regions such as the Middle East, South East Asia and South Asia (Allen and Overy, 2009).

8.6   Components of Islamic microfinance

Beneficiaries of Islamic microfinance need a range of financial services which can be categorized into microlending (or microcredit), microsavings, micro-*takaful* (micro insurance) and microenterprise (micro equity). The main aspects of those financial services are summarized in Table 8.2.

Table 8.2 Four components of Islamic microfinance

Microlending	Microenterprise	Microsavings	Micro-*takaful*
extending small scale financial support to the poor or low income people	based on the concept of profit and loss sharing (PLS)	based on the concept of small saving deposits	benefiting from mutual cooperation, solidarity and protection
interest free loans or profit based loans such as murabahah, bay-bithaman-ajil, ijarah and bay-salam	provide capital based on *mudarabah, musharakah/mutanaqisah* and *muzaraah*	designed to secure the capital or profits realized in a savings account	mutual risks transfer arrangement within a group
flexible in terms of repayment of the loan	risk transfer through risk mitigation on behalf of the vulnerable party (*mudarib*)	encourages self-reliance in the management of funds	relevant for risks that are beyond financial capacity of members
based on the principle of *qard hasan* (benevolent loan)	based on various partnership based modes of equity financing	based on the concept of *wadiah* (safekeeping)	based on the principles of *takaful* (inclusive finance)

8.6.1   MICROLENDING (MICROCREDIT) SCHEMES

Microlending schemes involve the provision of credit facilities for low income people. To avoid the *riba* based microcredit offered by conventional MFIs, various microlending schemes that do not violate *shari'ah* is offered by the IMFIs worldwide. Such *shari'ah* compliant mechanisms that can benefit the entrepreneurial poor to grow their business and income include *murabahah, bay-bithaman-ajil, ijarah* and *bay-salam*. Based on the principle of *qard hasan* (interest free loans with flexible repayment period and with no penalty and extra compensation to lender), housing loans can be provided to the poor which will allow them to have a strong income generating, physical asset base, especially when such houses are leased to third parties.

8.6.2   MICROENTERPRISE (MICRO EQUITY)

A micro entrepreneur may achieve their financing requirements through either debt (microcredit or micro-lending schemes) or equity (microenterprise or micro equity). Microlending schemes may take any of the forms mentioned earlier, i.e. *murabahah, bay-bithaman-ajil, ijarah and bay-salam*. In an Islamic economic system, micro equity based products basically deal with the profit-loss sharing approaches. The major micro equity products include *mudarabah* (trustee financing), *musharakah* (joint venture) and *muzaraah* (share cropping) (Obaidullah, 2008). Micro equity provided to a first generation micro entrepreneur is called micro venture capital (MVC) and they are usually far smaller in number and outreach.

8.6.3   MICROSAVINGS

This scheme provides a platform enabling the poor people to plan and manage their finances sensibly. The capital from the credit facilities and the accumulated profits generated from their activities can help them to become more self-reliant. The money is deposited in *wadiah* (safekeeping) account, which is the underlying concept behind the introduction of the savings account in the formal banking system. Once the depositors accumulated reasonable capital, they can invest it in one of the permissible (*halal*) investments and plan for the repayment of any micro loan they may have benefited from.

8.6.4   MICRO-*TAKAFUL*

Micro-*takaful* is generally offered to the low income and underprivileged segment of the population. These people are usually excluded from the general *takaful* terms and conditions by various entities, which are subject to the regulatory and supervisory authorities of *takaful*/insurance or any other competent authority under the national laws of any jurisdiction.

   This group's ineligibility for normal *takaful* may be attributed to their inability to meet the basic financial and underwriting requirements set forth by *takaful* regulation, for reasons relating to their medical history, hazardous occupation, irregular income, insurable interest and various other considerations that fall within the purview of prudential regulation of exclusive finance. Another important cause is due to the unavailability of suitable insurance products that really fit the needs of this specific group of customers. They may also lack awareness and understanding of the usefulness of insurance to manage the risks in their private and working lives. Another contributing factor is the lack of expertise and will of *takaful* operators to make the investment needed to reach to these markets.

   Micro-*takaful* is therefore an important tool to protect this group from financial losses and help them break the cycle of poverty. Such schemes are designed to benefit low income earners and micro entrepreneurs through mutual cooperation, solidarity and protection from many forms of financial or material risk at an affordable cost. The mutual risk transfer arrangement within the group ultimately benefits all the members as well as their dependants. This form of arrangement is relevant for certain risks that are beyond the financial capacity of individual members.

It should be noted that micro-*takaful* does not directly solve the poverty problem but is instead one of the components in poverty alleviation strategies. The low income earners would usually use their own pocket money, borrowings or selling of assets in dealing with the risk management strategy that they have chosen. Without having a proper financial protection like micro-*takaful*, low income earners and micro entrepreneurs would easily fall into the poverty trap.

8.7 Islamic microfinance models

The Islamic microfinance model can be classified into *market based for profit* and *not for profit* modes of microfinance. The different types under each category will be discussed in turn.

8.7.1 MARKET BASED FOR PROFIT MODES OF ISLAMIC MICROFINANCE

Islam permits trading for profit and creation of wealth schemes. These schemes are to cater to the needs of the poor who fall into the economically active category but need financial stability for the business to grow and survive. There is a range of for profit microfinance modes in the form of debt (e.g. *qard hasan, murabahah, ijarah, salam* and *bay-bithaman ajil*) or equity (e.g. *mudarabah, musharakah* and *muzaraah*) available to those who need them. Most of these modes of finance have already been discussed in Chapter 4 and only those that have not been covered earlier will be discussed in the following section.

a) Bay muajjal–murabahah *model*

Bay muajjal–murabahah is a microcredit product that provides working capital to micro entrepreneurs. Under this model, the IMFI agrees to sell a commodity to the entrepreneur on a deferred payment of the price to a future date. When the commodity is supplied, the IMFI agrees to act as an agent for the entrepreneur in order to find a third party buyer for the commodity product. Figure 8.1 illustrates this model in six steps.

Figure 8.1 *Bay muajjal–murabahah* model

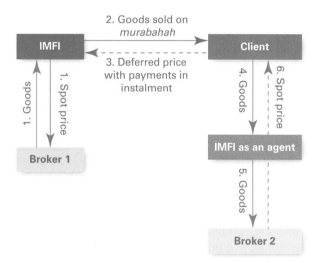

First, the IMFI buys goods requested by the client from Broker 1 for a price paid on the spot and the goods are supplied immediately to the IMFI. The IMFI then sells the goods to the buyer at a deferred mark-up price. This is a *murabahah* sale. In the third step, the client settles the deferred price in instalments over an agreed period. When the *murabahah* in the second step is combined with the deferred payments in the third step, it becomes a *bay-muajjal* microfinance product. In the fourth step, in a separate contract, the client supplies the goods to the IMFI and appoints them as an agent to sell the goods on a spot basis. In the fifth step, the goods are sold on the spot basis to Broker 2 and the price is paid immediately. Lastly, the IMFI remits the proceeds of spot sale to the client.

b) Mudarabah *and* musharakah mutanaqisah *(diminishing partnership)*

The diminishing partnership, known as *musharakah mutanaqisah*, is an Islamic financial product structured to strategically provide the poor access to fixed assets that they need. The IMFI and the client enter into a partnership contract whereby the former purchase the needed asset and lease it to the client for a specified term. The poor client's share is minimal and the IMFI provides the bulk of the capital share for the transaction. When the asset is leased, both parties share the profit based on a predetermined contractual ratio. The client then buys a specified unit every month out of the IMFI's shares, which would automatically gradually decreases the IMFI's capital ownership until the client has bought the total capital share in the property out of the profits over a period of time. The title then passes to the client, who will then fully own the property.

Musharakah mutanaqisah can also be combined with *mudarabah* and *musharakah* to become a microfinance product involving entrepreneurship and capital aimed at allowing the entrepreneur to undertake any type of business venture, and agrees to manage the same according to the terms of the agreement with IMFI. Profits are shared between the IMFI and the micro entrepreneur in the pre-agreed ratio. Losses are shared strictly in proportion to their respective capital contributions. The sharing of profit acts as a residual which should inspire the entrepreneur (*mudarib*) to undertake more risky ventures as well as exerting optimum efforts. Therefore better output may be expected from such type of agreement.

In a nutshell, *musharakah mutanaqisah* partnership consists of three contracts: (i) *musharakah* (partnership), (ii) *ijarah* (lease) and (iii) *bay* (sell). The customer enters into a partnership under the contract of *shirkat-al-milk* (joint ownership) with the IMFI and thus, they co-own the asset. In the next stage, the IMFI leases its share in the asset to the customer under the contract of *ijarah (leasing)*. The customer will buy the share in the asset under the contract of *bay* and gradually owns the total asset (Ahamed-Meera and Dzuljastri-Razak, 2009). The IMFI holds ownership of the property during the lease period and it bears all the liabilities, such as defects of or damage to the property following the principal of '*al Ghorm bil Ghonm*' (no reward without risk) and '*al Kharaj bil Daman*' (any benefit must be accompanied with liability) (Ahamed-Meera and Dzuljastri-Razak, 2005). Figure 8.2 illustrates a *mudarabah with diminishing partnership*.

Figure 8.2 *Mudarabah* and *musharakah mutanaqisah* model

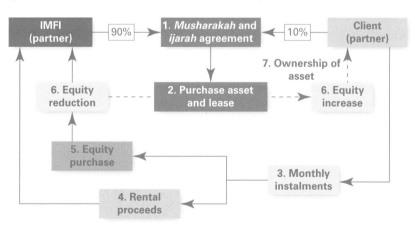

Alternatively, IMFI can create a specific fund for financing projects under *musharakah mutanaqisah* where a portion of the fund is used to purchase assets such as business outlets and another portion is used as capital for investment and business start-ups. These could be based on *mudarabah mutlaqah* (unrestricted trust financing) whereby the capital provider does not specify or restrict the business for investment, or based on *mudarabah muqayyadah* (restricted trust financing) whereby the capital provider specifies or restricts the business for investment while offering its purchased properties on rental basis. However, such schemes must also allow a provision that the *mudarib* can own the property (e.g. a shop) through *musharakah mutanaqisah* partnership at a certain stage of the business.

This partnership contract is possible only when the client (*mudarib*) would be able to add to their savings from the income. It is expected that the capital contribution, along with the managerial activities, will increase the income level of the *mudarib*. Furthermore, this practice must enhance the relationship and trust between the client and the IMFI. However, at this stage, the IMFI can extend the *musharakah mutanaqisah* partnership so that the *mudarib* can own the asset after a certain period of time. Upon ending the *musharakah* contract, the *mudarib* can either own the entire business or enter into another *musharakah* contract with the IMFI.

c) Salam *and* parallel salam *for agriculture*

Salam and *parallel salam* (see figure 8.3) are the most effective tools available to Islamic banks and financial institutions that support microcredit schemes for agriculture. A *salam* contract is important in the financing of micro farming, small scale farming that involves the cultivation of the family's plot of land, where the farmers require some money to grow their crops and feed their family up to harvest time. Islamic banks and financial institutions provide microcredit for this purpose after entering into a *salam* contract where the bank is the buyer and the farmer is the seller who undertakes future delivery. By providing microcredit facilities in advance and allowing the farmers to sell their cash crops for a price lower than the real market price, the transaction should result in a profit for the IMFI and at the same time allows small farmers to engage in sustainable agriculture through guaranteed sale of their produce in exchange for spot payment of price of the produce.

Under a *salam* agreement, a farmer or a trader in need of short term funds agrees to sell the produce or commodity to the IMFI on a deferred delivery basis but receives the full price of the commodity on the spot to serve its current financing need. For the validity of the *salam* contract, the price and the date of delivery are fixed on the date of signing the *salam* contract. The quantity and quality, with an exact description or specification, must also be stated in the underlying contract. It is also not permissible for the parties to stipulate that the *salam* contract will be effected on the produce of a particular field of the farm or fruits from a particular tree. This is because of the element of uncertainty (*gharar*) in such a stipulation. There is the possibility of the destruction of the farm or the tree before harvest. Therefore, the contractual terms must be clear, certain and specific in all ramifications. No room should be left for ambiguity that may result in a dispute between the parties.

After the delivery of the cash crops, the Islamic bank sells them on the open market on the basis of *parallel salam* at a price higher than the price at which it bought them from the farmer. The difference between the cost price of the crops as concluded with the farmer and the selling price on the open market is the profit realized by the IMFI. In practice, the IMFI could be an association of farmers or artisans or traders or an agency to undertake collective marketing of the members' produce. The profits from this kind of micro farming scheme are a major source of income for the Islamic microfinance portfolio of a financial institution.

Figure 8.3 *Salam and parallel salam*

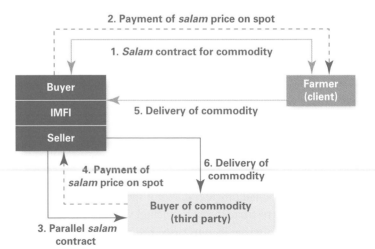

In short, this model involves a *salam* contract between the farmer and the IMFI which is essentially a forward agreement, where delivery occurs at a future date in exchange for spot payment of price and is used in conjunction with *parallel salam*, which is a forward contract concluded with a third party that is distinct and not in any way contingent upon the first *salam* contract, nor must its performance be contingent on the first contract.

8.7.2   NOT FOR PROFIT MODES OF ISLAMIC MICROFINANCE

There are four major *not for profit* modes of Islamic microfinance: *sadaqat (charity), zakat (alms), awqaf (endowment)* and *qard hasan (benevolence loans)* that can be utilized in poverty alleviation and social development schemes. They also allow for wealth circulation among the whole community and not only among the rich. The term *sadaqah* refers to various forms of charity, such as, *tabarru'* (donations), *hiba* (gifts), *infaq* (charitable spending) and may indeed connote any act of kindness and charity. Hence, *sadaqah* has broader meaning than just charity.

When benefits from *sadaqah* are expected to flow perpetually, it is called *sadaqah jaria* (perpetual *sadaqah*) and normally involves *waqf* or endowment of tangible assets e.g. land, property and farm, etc., for charitable purposes. The *sadaqah* that is prescribed and obligatory on Muslims refers to *zakah*. *Sadaqah* in the form of loans that is free from any benefit or return to the lender or more commonly referred to as interest free loan is called *qard hasan*. A combination of these three forms of *sadaqah* into an overarching framework is expected to drastically alleviate poverty in society. Despite the not for profit nature of an overarching model, it can be easily modified to accommodate the profit oriented modes explained earlier.

For instance, as suggested by Obaidullah (2008), the IMFI first creates a *zakah* fund to receive *zakah* and *sadaqah* contributions. Secondly, it collects charity which can be in the form of monetary assets (e.g. cash *waqf* funds) and physical assets (e.g. buildings and equipment for education and skills training). In the third and fourth steps, the microfinance programme carefully identifies the poorest and the destitute who are economically inactive and directs a part of the *zakah* fund towards meeting their basic necessities as donation. It also seeks to provide a safety net and skills training to economically inactive people, utilizing community held physical assets under *waqf*. In the fifth and sixth steps, the beneficiaries graduate with improved skills and managerial acumen and they are placed into groups with mutual guarantee under the concept of *kafalah*. In the seventh step, financing is provided on the basis of *qard hasan* to the group and also to individuals backed by guarantee under the concept of *kafalah*. When the group members pay back, they will be eligible to receive higher levels of financing. Additional guarantee against default by the group is provided by the *zakah* fund and the actual defaulting accounts are paid off with *zakah* funds. This is the distinct feature of this model. In the eighth and ninth steps, group members are encouraged to save under appropriate microsavings schemes and they are also encouraged to form a *takaful* fund to provide micro insurance against unforeseen risks and uncertainties resulting in loss of livelihood, sickness and so on.

8.8   Poverty alleviation strategies

A general financing architecture of Islamic microfinance is delineated in Figure 8.4 incorporating the poverty hierarchy. As can be seen in the figure, the bottom of the poverty hierarchy consists of the vulnerable poor whose income is usually below the poverty line due to several factors, such as disabilities, old aged household head, unemployment or having many young children. This group of people need financial aid mainly for consumption purposes and IMFIs can support them by using the funds of *zakat, waqf* and *sadaqah*. Once their immediate needs are met, they can be offered microcredit schemes.

The second layer of the poverty hierarchy consists of the labouring poor who use their physical labour to generate income. Their earnings basically come from subsistence activities like farming, fishing, etc. For this group, microcredit schemes are more suitable. *Qard hasan, murabahah*, *bay bithaman ajil* and *bay salam* can be offered to this group of people based on their abilities and skills.

Figure 8.4 Poverty hierarchy layers and Islamic microfinance mechanism

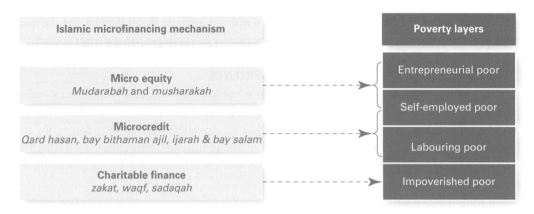

The self employed poor, who make up the third layer of the poverty hierarchy, usually provide wages for themselves by consuming the products that they can produce. This group of people are also eligible for microcredit, but after a few cycles of microcredit facilities or by enhancing their entrepreneurial skills, equity financing schemes can be extended to help them get better returns.

The entrepreneurial poor, who are at the top of the poverty hierarchy, are mostly self employed and able to create employment for others but on a small scale. Their income level is generally low due to lack of capital. Since they have the ability to manage business, PLS schemes such as *mudarabah* and *musharakah* (M&M) can be offered without requiring tangible collateral or guarantee (Rosly, 2005). *Mudarabah* schemes seek for business skills and *shari'ah* compliant business proposals. After completion of a certain number of business cycle(s) under *mudarabah,* a *mudarib* can join *musharakah* scheme with capital contribution. When the *mudarib* is able to pay a portion of the borrowed capital, s(he) can be engaged in the diminishing *musharakah (musharakah mutanaqisah)* scheme to acquire an asset. Through these practices, a *mudarib* can pay back the total price of the asset to the financial organization after a certain period of time. Thus, a *mudarib* can later be the sole owner of a business as shown in Figure 8.5.

Figure 8.5 Poverty alleviation using *musharakah mutanaqisah* mode of microfinancing

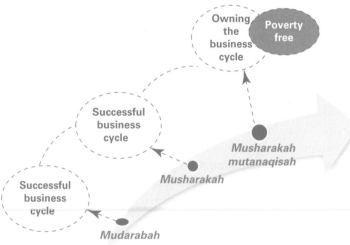

8.9   Similarities and differences between conventional and Islamic microfinance

Based on discussions earlier, we can see that MFIs and IMFIs do have similar features. Firstly, both types of MFIs provide financial services on a small scale. Although there is no general consensus in determining the threshold for the classification of the size of the loan (due to the variability of funding as well as the diverse exchange rates), any loan of less than $100 is categorized as a small loan (Aubuchon and Sengupta, 2008). The loan structures offered normally require the repayments to be made on weekly basis within a short time period to prevent a high rate of default.

Secondly, both MFIs are devoted to serving those in society who live below either the minimum level of consumption or the poverty line (Ruit and May, 2009). Although the World Bank has established an international poverty line threshold as those households living below $1, the threshold is not applicable for all countries due to the variation in the methods for measuring poverty levels (Hagenaars and Vos, 1988).

Thirdly, neither MFI requires collateral, which tends to be a condition of most banks' operation as a sort of insurance against the debtor defaulting. Since those with lower incomes tend not to be able to provide collateral (Cull, Dermigüç-Kunt and Murdoch, 2009), this group is overlooked by the commercial banks. However, in the attempt to accommodate their needs for credit, many MFIs apply joint liability lending (Karlan and Goldberg, 2011), whereby a group of people provide peer group support and share the responsibility to repay the loan.

Those main characteristics of conventional MFIs are also applicable to IMFIs. However, the distinctive features of IMFIs are their moral and ethical attributes, which are dictated by the Islamic principles regarding business transactions. Table 8.3 presents a summary of the major differences between them in their respective operational functions and with regards to their clients.

Table 8.3 Summary of differences between Islamic MFIs and conventional MFIs

Item	Islamic MFIs	Conventional MFIs
Operational functions		
Sources of funds	external funds, clients' savings, Islamic charitable sources (*waqf* and *zakat*)	external funds, clients' savings, interest from loans
Assets (modes of financing)	profit sharing based equity and debt-based instruments	interest based
Target for financing	poorest can be included by integrating *zakat* with microfinancing	poorest and vulnerable are often left out
Funds transfer	in the form of cash, goods or assets	in the form of cash
Deductions of funds at inception of contract	no deductions of funds at inception	part of the funds deducted at inception
Target group	family empowerment	women empowerment
Work incentives of employees	financial and religious incentives	financial incentives
Dealing with default	group/centre/spouse provide guarantee and non-payment of loans is considered a sin in Islamic ideology	group/centre pressure and threats
Social development programme	religious (includes behaviour, ethics and social development)	secular (or un-Islamic) behavioural, ethical and social development

Funds are important to enable both MFIs to operate and discharge their key responsibilities to the entrepreneurial poor. Conventional MFIs get their funds from interest bearing loans, foreign donors, central banks and governments. Islamic MFIs are also funded from these sources, with the exception of interest bearing loans, but in addition they get their funds from other sources. These include equity finance products applied in the finance of microenterprises and Islamic charitable sources such as *waqf, zakat* and *sadaqah* whose funds can be channelled to the poorest within a particular community. This takes care of the social financial mediation role of the IMFIs.

In terms of modes of financing, conventional MFIs are interest based while IMFIs use Islamic financial instruments that are either equity based or debt based. These sustainable financial instruments are based on *shari'ah* principles which include the prohibition of usury and interest (*riba*), avoidance of unlawful gain, prevention of risk and uncertainty in transactions (*gharar)* and promotion of religiously permitted activities (*halal*). The economic substance of those principles is to promote the welfare of society and eliminate excessive inequality (El-Gamal, 2006; Karim *et al.*, 2008). Hence, the ethical justification for the prohibition of *riba, maysir* and *gharar* is three pronged: all three are exploitative, unfair and unproductive (Warde, 2000) instruments. Various financial instruments can be used to finance different kinds of enterprises (remember the discussion on the various models of Islamic finance mentioned earlier). While a profit sharing mode may be used for a microenterprise where the micro entrepreneur and the MFI share the profit, *salam* and *parallel salam* may be more appropriate for micro farming. In order to combat the ordeal of unemployment, a *mudarabah* trust financing may be used.

With respect to the target of microfinancing, IMFIs serve all segments of the poor population including those who are in extreme poverty. If you recall the poverty alleviation strategies based on the poverty hierarchy discussed earlier, the integration of *zakat* with microfinance facilitates the provision of grants to the poor from the *zakat* funds for consumption and *qard hasan* for their entrepreneurial needs. In contrast, the poorest are often completely excluded from the microfinance net within the framework of conventional MFIs as they are deemed to be highly unsustainable and also have high tendency of defaulting on repayments.

In conventional MFIs, once a loan has been approved, a part of the principal amount (cash) is deducted by the institution for various purposes, such as the group and emergency funds, but the beneficiary still pays interest on the total amount approved. Moreover, once cash from the loan is received, the beneficiary may divert the funds to non-productive means. In contrast, IMFIs seldom transfer cash to beneficiary and instead transfer goods or assets needed by the beneficiaries. This precludes diversion of the funds to non-productive means.

Although both groups provide guarantee of repayment of the loans, there are some differences between the two frameworks. Group guarantee in the repayment of the loans to IMFIs takes the form of *kafalah*, which is based on *shari'ah* conditions and requirements. There may be an agreement among the members of a group that in the event of any default in the repayment in accordance with the instalments from a member, other members agree to help. The simple way of going about this is for the group to give such a member who is facing the problem of default payment *qard hasan*, which is interest free, to pay his or her instalments.

The majority of MFIs' clients are women as this is considered as the best means of empowering them, believing it will help to raise their income level and earn them more respect in society. However, recent research suggests that men, more often than not, encourage women to take credit facilities and at the end of the day, the men spend the money. This creates problems within the family because the women are responsible for the repayment of the instalments as they were the ones given the credit facilities.

On the other hand, the objective of targeting women by IMFIs differs from that of MFIs. Women are the target of IMFIs' credit facilities mainly because of their ease of availability for weekly meetings and for participating in social and religious development programmes. The target group of IMFIs is the family, and therefore both the women and their spouses sign the contract with the IMFIs and are made equally liable for repayment of the instalments.

The work incentive of MFIs' staff is mainly in the form of salaries. Conversely, the incentives of the staff of IMFIs are not just to earn a living but to also perform socio-religious duty of alleviating poverty within society through facilitating access to credit facilities. This additional incentive gives the staff more zeal to work efficiently towards the achievement of the vision and mission of the IMFIs.

The social development programmes of conventional MFIs are secular and in some cases go against the ideals of Islam. For instance, from the perspective of income generation for the programme, there are generally no restrictions on the type of sectors conventional MFIs invests in. Conversely, IMFIs put in place social development programmes where the ethical, social and behavioural aspects of Islamic ideals are brought to the fore. The Islamic content is introduced into the programme and members feel comfortable in adapting to them as they consider them as part of their beliefs and acts of worship. This also helps inculcate the idea of fellowship and comradeship among beneficiaries, who are morally compelled to repay their instalments regularly and when due.

In conventional MFIs, group and centre pressure is used to deal with arrears and default and if such pressures do not work, the MFIs resort to threats and sale of assets which may be too harsh for low income individuals within a developing society. In contrast, IMFIs have more sustainable and reasonable ways to deal with defaults and arrears. Under the *kafalah* group guarantee system, the group may provide *qard hasan* to a defaulting member to help the unfortunate member to settle the arrears in the event of default. This is motivated by the spirit of fellowship. Since it is also considered a sin in Islam to refuse to pay back a loan, this motivates members to fulfil their obligations and the member's spouse may also assist in paying off the arrears.

8.10 Microfinance activities in different regions

Islamic microfinance experiments in Muslim societies are still small in number and more importantly, these institutions are not integrated into the formal financial systems, with the notable exception of Indonesia. In most cases, these experimental projects were initiated by international donor agencies, religious or political groups and only very few involvement of Islamic banks in the practice of microfinance.

IMFIs display wide variations in the models, instruments and operational mechanisms and as such score better than their conventional counterparts in terms of richness and variety. However, at the present time, they still lag far behind their conventional counterparts in terms of reach, penetration and financial prowess. Similar to their conventional counterparts, IMFIs also use group financing as a substitute to collateral, they have a high concentration of women beneficiaries and their activities are aimed at alleviation of poverty in all its forms. The following are IMFIs experience in different regions.

8.10.1 THE MIDDLE EAST AND NORTH AFRICA (MENA)

a) IDB in Saudi Arabia

The IDB has for more than 20 years been at the forefront of the international development of Islamic microfinance by taking several initiatives to develop the Islamic microfinance sector. Its Access to Finance Team provides funding for various Islamic microfinance projects worldwide, particularly to help reduce the high cost associated with microfinancing and to foster financial sustainability for programmes that are over reliant on grants and/or with high financing costs, while its Islamic Financial Services Department offers technical assistance to regulators, capital market authorities and governments. Its research arm, Islamic Research and Training Institution (IRTI), pursues robust research and evaluation agenda by collaborating with the World Bank, CGAP, universities and other institutions.

b) Al-Amal *and* Hodeidah *in Yemen*

Founded in 2008, Al-Amal was one of the first IMFIs in the MENA region. Al-Amal won CGAP's Islamic Microfinance Challenge 2010 for proposing an *ijarah* (leasing) product, funded through the bank's own *shari'ah* compliant investments. Another important microfinance programme is the Hodeidah Microfinance Program which predominantly uses group and graduated financing methods that was successfully pioneered by Grameen Bank but unlike Grameen, it uses *murabahah* mode for financing.

c) Jabal Al Hoss Sanadiq *in Syria*

The *Jabal Al Hoss Sanadiq* (village banks) in Syria is an excellent model worth considering for replication. Its ownership structure is based on *musharakah* and it is wholly owned and managed by the poor themselves. Its funding is supported by the UNDP in the form of matching grants equal to the minimum share capital of village fund. Financial management of the funds are based on standardized by-laws and statutes and it established the Sanadiq Apex Fund for liquidity exchange and refinancing purposes. It offers financing products based on *mudarabah* and the net profits are shared among members. It has a project management team responsible for creating awareness of microfinance practices and also training of committee members.

d) Mu'assasat Bayt Al-Mal *in Lebanon*

The *Mu'assasat Bayt Al-Mal* in Lebanon is an affiliate of a political party, the Hezbollah, and comprises the Hasan Loan Institution (*Al-Qard Al-Hasan*) and its sister organization called Al-Yusor for Finance and Investment (*Yusor lil-Istismar wal Tamweel*). The former provides *qard-hasan* financing while the latter provides financing on a profit loss sharing mode. The uniqueness of the *Mu'assasat Bayt Al-Mal* is its emphasis on voluntarism. It has maintained a very close relationship with the people and is seen as a very respectable organization with volunteers entirely taking care of collection and disbursal of funds. It has a network of donors with complete confidence in the activities of the Institution and also enjoys high repayment rate. Financing is backed by collateral in the form of capital assets, land, gold, guarantor and bank guarantee.

8.10.2 SOUTH ASIA

a) Islami Bank Bangladesh Limited in Bangladesh

Islami Bank Bangladesh Limited (IBBL) is considered a ground breaking institution not only due to it being the first and largest formal Islamic microfinance provider but also its success in integrating a poverty alleviation platform into regular commercial banking operations. IDB and other GCC based institutions owned 66 per cent of shares in this bank. Its two main Islamic microfinance programmes are the Rural Development Scheme (RDS) and the Urban Poor Development Scheme (UPDS) which were established in 1995 and 2012, respectively. Its RDS clients comprise of more financially solvent poor and the aim of the scheme is to enable them to transit to the Small Medium Enterprise (SME) investment programme. It offers its clients small business investment facilities based mainly on *bay-muajjal* and *ijarah* and occasionally based on *musharakah* and *bay-salam*. It also offers *qard hasan* on an *ad hoc* basis for construction of tube wells for underground water access, latrines and other facilities that will help improve quality of life. It adopts the Grameen Bank model and each microfinance collective consists of 10-40 clients subdivided into two to eight groups of five members each. All its clients are required to have a *mudarabah* savings account with IBBL.

b) Akhuwat, Al Huda CIBE, Wasil Foundation and Islamic Relief in Pakistan

The market leader of Islamic microfinance in Pakistan is Akhuwat. Its operation is entirely funded by charity and it is dominant in the Punjab area. It offers only one product based on *qard Hassan* with different amounts, repayment schedules, and eligibility tailored to meet the needs of a range of beneficiaries through the following schemes: family enterprise loans, liberation loans, education loans, health loans, emergency loans, housing loans, marriage loans and mutual support fund. To keep the operations sustainable, it expects recipients to donate whatever amount they can afford every month to the organization and all meetings with clients take place in the local mosque.

Another important IMFIs is the Wasil Foundation. One of its innovative products is the agricultural financing package offered to smallholder farmers based on *salam* and *ijarah*. The Lahore based Al Huda Center for Islamic Banking Excellence (Al Huda CIBE) is also a significant IMFIs. It supports the industry by offering *shari'ah* compliance consultancy services and training workshops.

Islamic Relief Pakistan (IRP) is one of operation centres of the widely known Birmingham based international NGO, Islamic Relief Worldwide. IRP's Islamic microfinance programme has existed for more than ten years and its activities are funded by a succession of grants. Its main programme is the Small Scale Business Development (SSBD) and its financing products are classified into productive purposes or social purposes based on *murabahah* and *qard hassan*. The former financing supports entrepreneurial or income generation activities while the latter supports advancement of assets needed to improve quality of health, such as an indoor toilet or a room addition or home refurbishment.

8.10.3 SOUTH-EAST ASIA

a) Baytul Maal wat Tamwil *in Indonesia*

IMFIs in Indonesia can be categorized into the microfinance divisions of Islamic banks, the Islamic rural banks (BPRS), which is a subcategory of the rural banks (BPR), and the Islamic financial cooperatives which are generally referred to as *Baytul Maal wat Tamwil* (BMT). The BMTs are the largest, oldest, and most prominent IMFI in Indonesia with a large network of over two thousand institutions serving millions of poor Indonesian Muslims. They are backed by Islamic organizations, such as Nahdatul Ulama and Muhamadiyah. Despite having 2.2 million members, BMT's total holdings are small, with 550 branches and cumulative balance sheet assets of $800 million. Streams of charitable funds (e.g. *waqf, zakat* and *sadaqat*) are channelled into a stream for social (non-productive) financing purposes. Members' savings provide the liquidity needed for productive microfinancing and SME clients. *Zakah* funds are also an integral part of the BMTs. Unlike many single-product (*murabahah* or *qard-hasan* based), Islamic microfinance programmes and projects in other regions, the financing portfolios of Indonesian IMFIs are reasonably balanced with an array of products, based on *mudarabah, musharakah, murabahah, ijarah* and *qard hasan*.

b) *Tabung Haji, Amanah Ikhtiar Malaysia and Bantuan Rakyat 1 Malaysia in Malaysia*

Tabung Haji was established with the aim of financing Hajj related expenditure of poor Malaysian farmers who used to sell their only source of livelihood, agricultural land, for the purpose. Tabung Haji was primarily a savings and investments institution and has since grown into a large specialized finance house.

Amanah Ikhtiar Malaysia (AIM) was established in 1987 and is currently Malaysia's largest microfinance provider. A little over 300 000 households have received financing from AIM, which focuses on *shari'ah* compliant entrepreneurial loans and insurance. In 2014, the Malaysian government's Bantuan Rakyat 1 Malaysia (BR1M) or 1 Malaysia Public Relief programme was launched as an initiative to help low income earners lessen their financial burden. This initiative has also included micro-*takaful* products i-BR1M scheme to earners who received below $1119 and $839 monthly household income (Takaful Ikhlas, 2014).

8.10.4 AFRICA

Islamic microfinance program in sub-Saharan Africa, specifically in Northern Mali, was borne out of a development project initiated by the GTZ (German Technical Cooperation) and KfW (German Financial Cooperation) to help people in the former civil war areas of Timbuktu to have access to financial services. Although the idea was initially to introduce western banking, it was strongly opposed by leaders of the tribes as interest charges are seen as 'ungodly and immoral' and they prefer one that respect religious rules for financial services. Hence, Azaouad Finances plc, which operates based on profit–loss sharing was established to cater to the needs of small traders. With regards to micro-*takaful,* it was developed to provide *shari'ah*-based protection to the blue-collared, underprivileged individuals at an affordable cost.

Summary

Islamic microfinance remains a scattered industry, with a mix of small scale experiments and more established institutions. The bold revival of Islamic finance services in the 20th century in a formalized form brought with it Islamic microfinance schemes. *Shari'ah* scholars have structured Islamic financial products to suit the requirements of modern microenterprises and microcredit schemes. This makes the case for a distinct system of microfinance that may be radically different from the conventional practice of microfinance as mostly practiced in non-Muslim communities. To this end, there are a number of operational and functional differences between IMFIs and the conventional MFIs.

One of the distinctive characteristics of the IMFI is risk sharing. The moral economy of Islam is that the IMFIs and their customers should both bear the risk of the venture due to the inability of either party to control the venture's success or failure, and the determination of the *ex-ante* fixed rate of return is strictly prohibited. Since the rate of return for any venture is uncertain, IMFIs adopt a return bearing contract and apply PLS based on a formula that reflects their level of participation in a contract/project. The major types of contracts are *mudarabah* and *musharakah*. An IMFI's PLS differs from that of a conventional MFI, which receives consecutive payments during the loan tenure, so its profitability is not affected by the level of a project's rate of return. However, IMFIs under the PLS approach, posit that the physical investment is part of the institution and therefore, their profitability is directly linked to the rate of return of project. As a consequence, the creditors and borrowers both share any profit as well as any loss that might occur.

While there is agreement on the potential of microfinance to alleviate poverty, there is to date no systematic collation of information on best practices and models that others can emulate. Similarly, there is no database either at national or regional levels that will aid researchers to undertake studies that will help to identify profiles of potential beneficiaries and issues needing attention. Hence, there is a dire need for an institution that can act as a research and development centre for Islamic microfinance. The Islamic Development Bank may be the best institution to do this as it has both financial and human resources (expertise) to develop this important area in Islamic economics.

Key terms and concepts

bay muajjal-murabahah	micro entrepreneurship	parallel salam
credit union	micro-takaful	Rotating Savings and Credit
green revolution	mudarabah muqayyadah	Association (ROSCA)
microcredit	mudarabah mutlaqah	salam
microenterprise	musharakah mutanaqisah	waqf

Questions

1. Define microfinance and explain its role and objectives.

2. What are factors that may affect the impact of microfinance?

3. Describe the historical development of microfinancing.

4. What is the Islamic view on poverty?

5. Explain the Islamic prescriptions on how to solve and combat problems related to poverty.

6. Discuss the historical development of Islamic microfinance institutions.

7. Elaborate on the components of Islamic microfinance.

8. Explain the various Islamic microfinance products available to beneficiaries and clients.

9. Distinguish between *takaful* and micro-*takaful*.

10. Explain the following microfinance models:
    a) *bay muajjal-murabahah*
    b) *musharakah mutanaqisah*
    c) *mudarabah muqayyadah*
    d) *mudarabah mutlaqah*
    e) *salam* and *parallel salam*
    f) *qard hasan*

11. Explain poverty alleviation strategies that can be adopted by IMFIs to address the different groups of poor people.

12. Compare and contrast between conventional and Islamic microfinance.

13. Discuss the microfinance models adopted in the following regions:
    a) MENA region   b) South Asia
    c) South-East Asia d) Africa

References and further readings

Ahamed-Meera, A.K.M. and Abdul Razak, D. (2009), 'Home financing through the musharakah mutanaqisah contracts: Some practical issues', *Journal of King Abdul Aziz University: Islamic Economics*, 22(1), pp. 3-27.

Ahamed-Meera, A.K.M. and Abdul Razak, D. (2005), 'Islamic home financing through musharakah mutanaqisah and al-bay' bithaman ajil contracts: A comparative analysis, *Review of Islamic Economics*, 9(2), pp. 5-30.

Ahmed, H. (2004), *Role of zakah and awqaf in poverty alleviation, Occasional Paper No. 8*. Islamic Research and Training Institute, Jedddah.

Ahmed, H. (2007), *Waqf-Based Microfinance: Realizing the Social Role of Islamic Finance*. International Seminar on Integrating Awqaf in the Islamic Financial Sector, Singapore.

Akhter, W., Akhtar, N. and Jafri, K.A. (2011), Islamic microfinance and poverty alleviation – a case of Pakistan, *International Journal of Research in Computer Application and Management*, 1(4) (June), pp. 24-27.

Allen and Overy (2009), *Islamic Microfinance Report*, International Development Law Organization.

Al-Zamzami, A. and Grace, L. (2001), *Islamic banking principles applied to microfinance. Case study: Hodeidah microfinance program, Yemen*. In Series, U.S.L.A. (ed.), UNCDF Special Unit for Microfinance SUM.

Amanah Ikhtiar Malaysia (2010), *History*, Laman web rasmi Amanah Ikhtiar Malaysia Ibu Pejabat AIM, Kuala Lumpur, Malaysia. www.aim.gov.my/~cms/englishversion/AboutUs/History.htm, accessed 15 July 2018.

Angelucci, M., Karlan, D.S. and Zinman, J. (2013), *Win some lose some? Evidence from a randomized microcredit program placement experiment by Compartamos Banco*, Institute for the Study of Labor (IZA), pp. 7439-7471.

Armendáriz, B. and Morduch, J. (2010), *The Economics of Microfinance*, 2nd ed., MIT Press, Massachusetts, USA.

Aubuchon, C.P. and Sengupta, R. (2008), 'The microfinance revolution: an overview', *Federal Reserve Bank of St. Louis Review*, 90(1), pp. 9-30.

Blanco-Oliver, A., Irimia-Dieguez, A. and Reguera-Alvarado, N. (2016), 'Prediction-oriented PLS path modeling in microfinance research', *Journal of Business Research*, 69(10), pp. 4643-4649.

Briney, A. and Winter, C. (2010), Green revolution: history and overview of the green revolution, www.thoughtco.com/green-revolution-overview-1434948, accessed 14 June 2018.

CGAP (2009), The history of microfinance, www.globalenvision.org/library/4/1051/, accessed 9 May 2018.

Chapra, U. (2008), *Innovation and Authenticity in Islamic Finance*, Eighth Harvard University Forum on Islamic Finance: Innovation and Authenticity, Harvard Law School Islamic Legal Studies Program, Cambridge, USA.

Çizakça, M. (1998), 'Awqaf in history and implications for modern Islamic economies', *Islamic Economic Studies*, 6, pp. 43-70.

Çizakça, M. (2000), *A History of Philanthropic Foundations: The Islamic World from the Seventh Century to the Past*, Boğaziçi University Press, Boğaziçi.

Cornford, R. (2001), 'Microcredit', 'microfinance' or 'access to financial services' What do Pacific people need?, unpan1.un.org/intradoc/groups/public/documents/APCITY/UNPAN006911.pdf, accessed 14 June 2018.

Cull, R., Dermigüç-Kunt, A. and Murdoch, J. (2009), 'Microfinance meets the market', in Watkins, T.A. and Hicks, K. (eds), *Moving Beyond Storytelling: Emerging Research in Microfinance*, Emerald Group Publishing Limited, Bingley, UK, pp. 1-30.

Dar, H.A. and Presley, J.R. (2003), 'Islamic banking', in Mullineux, A.W. and Murinde, V. (eds), *Handbook of International Banking*, Edward Elgar, Cheltenham, UK, pp. 191-206.

Edwards, M. and Hulme, D. (1995), 'NGO performance and accountability: Introduction and overview', in Edwards, M. and Hulme, D. (eds), *Non-Governmental Organisations – Performance and Accountability: Beyond the Magic Bullet*, Earthscan Publication Limited, London, pp. 3-16.

El-Gamal, M.A. (2006), *Islamic Finance: Law, Economic and Practice*, Cambridge University Press, New York, USA.

El-Gamal, M., El-Komi, M., Karlan, D. and Osman, A. (2014), 'Bank-insured RoSCA for microfinance: Experimental evidence in poor Egyptian villages', *Journal of Economic Behavior & Organization*,103, Supplement, July, pp. S56-S73.

Ganlea, J.K., Afriyie, K. and Segbefia, A.Y. (2015), 'Microcredit: Empowerment and disempowerment of rural women in Ghana', *World Development*, pp. 335-345.

Hagenaars, A. and Vos, K.D. (1988), 'The definition and measurement of poverty', *The Journal of Human Resources*, 23(2), pp. 211-221.

Harriss-White, B. and Harriss, J. (2007), *Green revolution and after: the 'North Arcot papers' and long term studies of the political economy of rural development in South India*, QEH Working Paper Series.

Henry, C. M. and Wilson, R. (2004), 'Introduction', in Henry, C.M. and Wilson, R. (eds.), *The Politics of Islamic Finance*, Edinburgh University Press Ltd, Edinburgh, pp. 1-15.

Imady, O. and Seibel, H.D. (2003), 'Sanduq: a microfinance innovation in Jabal al-Hoss, Syria', *Nenaraca Newsletter.*, Amman, Jordan.

Iqbal, M. and Molyneux, P. (2005), *Thirty Years of Islamic Banking: History, Performance and Prospects*, Palgrave Macmillan, Basingstoke.

Iqbal, Z. and Mirakhor, A. (2011), *An Introduction to Islamic Finance: Theory and Practice*, 2nd ed., John Wiley and Sons, Singapore.

Islahi, A.A. (1997), Post independence India's contribution to Islamic economics, Jeddah, *MPRA Paper No. 18514*.

Ismail, R. (2001), 'Economic and social impact of Amanah Ikhtiar Malaysia (AIM) scheme: A case study in Kedah and Trengganu', *Humanomics*, 17(1/2), pp. 141-155.

Kaleem, A. and Ahmed, S. (2010), 'The Qur'an and poverty alleviation: A theoretical model for charity-based Islamic Microfinance Institutions (MFIs)', *Nonprofit and Voluntary Sector Quarterly*, 39(3), pp. 409-428.

Karim, N., Tarazi, M. and Reille, X. (2008), 'Islamic microfinance: an emerging market niche', *CGAP Focus Note*, No. 49.

Karlan, D. and Goldberg, N. (2011), 'Microfinance evaluation strategies: Notes on methodology and findings', in Armendáriz, B. and Labie, M. (eds.), *The Handbook of Microfinance*, World Scientific Publishing Co. Pte. Ltd, Singapore, pp. 17-58.

Khan, A.A. and Phillips, I. (2010), 'The influence of faith on Islamic microfinance programmes', *Islamic Relief*, February.

Khan, J.A. and Nisar, S. (2004), 'Collateral (Al-Rahm) as practiced by Muslims funds of North India', *Islamic Economics*, 17(1), pp. 17-34.

Kroessin, R. (2012), *An Exploratory Study of the Discourse of Islam and Development: The Case of the Islami Bank Bangladesh*, thesis, University of Birmingham.

Kustin, B. (2015), *Islamic (Micro)Finance: Culture, Context, Promise, Challenges, Financial Services for the Poor*, August 2015, Bill & Melinda Gates Foundation.

Memon, N.A. (2007), 'Islamic banking: Present and future challenges', *Journal of Management and Social Science*, 3(1) (Spring), pp. 1-10.

Obaidullah, M. (2008), *Role of Microfinance in Poverty Alleviation: Lessons from Experiences in Selected IDB Member Countries*, Islamic Research and Training Institute, Jeddah.

Robinson, M.S. (2005), 'Commercial microfinance: Past, present and future', in Swain, R.B. and Liljefrost, E. (eds), *The Democratisation of Finance: Future Directions for Microfinance*, The Collegium for Development Studies, Uppsala, pp. 5-11.

Rosly, S.A. (2005), *Critical Issues on Islamic Banking and Financial Markets: Islamic Economics, Banking and Finance, Investments, Takaful and Financial Planning*, Authorhouse Publisher, Indiana, USA.

Ruit, C.V.D. and May, J. (2009), 'Triangulating qualitative and quantitative approaches to the measurement of poverty: A case study in Limpopo Province, South Africa', *Institute of Development Studies Journal*, 34(4), pp. 21-33.

Sadeq, A.M. (2002), 'Waqf, perpetual charity and poverty alleviation', *International Journal of Social Economics*, 29(1), pp. 135-151.

Schreiner, M. and Woller, G. (2003), 'Microenterprise development programs in the United States and in the developing countries', *World Development*, 31(9), pp. 1567-1580.

Seibel, H.D. (2005), *'Does history matter? The old and the new world of microfinance in Europe and Asia': From moneylenders to microfinance: Southeast Asia's credit revolution in institutional, economic and cultural perspective - an interdisciplinary workshop*. Singapore.

Takaful Ikhlas (2014), *Smaller i-BRIM gains for takaful players*, www.takaful-ikhlas.com.my/media-centre/news-events/smaller-i-brim-gains-takaful-players, accessed 18 June 2018.

Warde, I. (2000), *Islamic Finance in the Global Economy*, Edinburgh University Press, Edinburgh.

Management and governance of financial institutions and markets

PART III

9 Financial reporting of Islamic banks

Learning Objectives

Upon completion of this chapter you should be able to:

- identify users of Islamic banks' reports and demand for information

- understand the nature and significance of the basic financial statements of conventional financial institutions

- understand the nature and significance of the basic financial statements of Islamic financial institutions

- distinguish between financial reporting of conventional and Islamic financial institutions

- understand the different tools for evaluating bank performance

- perform ratio analysis and other relevant calculations

9.1   Introduction

Islamic Financial Institutions (IFIs) including Islamic banks play an integral part as intermediaries in mobilizing funds from the surplus units to the deficit units, ensuring that the industry runs smoothly and efficiently in supporting the national economy. Islamic banks' surplus units represent pools of funds generated through people's (e.g. employees, entrepreneurs, workers, students and pensioners) savings and investments. These pools of funds represent sources of funds for Islamic banks which are then channelled to other people, businesses and governments who needed them in the form of home financing, car financing, trade financing and equity financing. Besides an intermediary role, Islamic banks also provide other banking services such as payments, depositing and lending services, investment services and e-banking.

In this chapter, we will focus on financial reporting by IFIs with particular focus on Islamic banks.[1] We will first identify the stakeholders of Islamic banks and their information needs. Then we will turn our attention to the basic financial statements of Islamic banks, the typical components therein, comparing the similarities and differences in the financial statements between Islamic and conventional banks, as well as briefly look at the accounting standards that Islamic banks must adhere to when preparing those financial statements. The last

---

[1]Sometimes the two terms may be used interchangeably as the most dominant Islamic financial institutions at present are Islamic banks.

part of this chapter is concerned with calculations of returns for sources and uses of banks' funds and the common financial ratios used in evaluating performance of Islamic banks.

9.2 Users of IFI reports and their demand for information

The growth of Islamic banking and finance suggests that there are many parties interested in the industry. The various interested parties who are formally or informally involved with and/or who are directly or indirectly affected by any industry are referred to as *stakeholders.* In the banking sector, the common stakeholders are *customers and depositors, regulators, investors, shareholders, taxpayers, politicians, internal and external auditors, the directors and employees of the banks, and the public.* The same groups of stakeholders also exist in the case of Islamic banking but with the addition of the *shari'ah* supervisory board, which is a unique feature in Islamic banking.

All stakeholders share a common interest in the proper functioning of the banking system. In the case of investors, customers, depositors, shareholders, debt holders and employees, their interest may be more towards the effective governance and management of the financial system. It is also important to recognize that the relative power among stakeholders can vary, leading to the advancement of some interests at the expense of others. For instance, the relative power of regulatory bodies and politicians will be heightened during a banking crisis while the power of shareholders, directors and staff will be weakened. Regardless of the state of their power, they all need information to help in drawing policies and assessing the banks' performance when making saving, investment, borrowing and career decisions. The bottom line is, they all need financial reports to aid in decision making.

So who are the users of Islamic banks' reports? According to the Statement of Financial Accounting 1 (SFA 1) issued by the Accounting and Auditing Organization for Islamic Financial Institutions (AAOIFI), there are seven main categories of users of Islamic banks' reports. They include *equity holders, investment accounts holders, other depositors, current and saving account holders, others who transact business with Islamic banks and those who are not equity or account holders, zakat agencies* (in case there is no legal obligation for its payment) and *regulatory agencies.* Although not necessarily a regulatory agency, another important group of users of Islamic banks' reports is the *shari'ah* supervisory board. Another group of users is the employees of the Islamic banks. Figure 9.1 illustrates the nine major groups of users of Islamic banks' reports.

Figure 9.1 Major users of Islamic banks' reports

Equity holders

Investment accounts holders

Zakah agencies

Other depositors

Major users of an Islamic financial institution's financial reports

Employees

Others who transact business with the Islamic bank

Regulatory agencies

Shari'ah supervisory boards

Current and saving accounts holders

There are three groups of users that are unique to the Islamic finance industry: investment account holders (IAHs), *zakat* agencies and the *shari'ah* supervisory boards (SSB), and the rest are common for both conventional and Islamic banks. Nevertheless, the type of information needed differs to some extent from users of reports of conventional banks because of the differences in the underlying principles which we have discussed in previous chapters. The following are some examples of the information needs of various groups of users of Islamic banks' reports:

9.2.1   EQUITY HOLDERS

Equity holders provide the capital needed to operate the business and they expect a return from their investments. They appoint board of directors for governing the bank, a *shari'ah* supervisory board (SSB) to ensure that the banking business operates within the confines of the *shari'ah* and an external auditor to verify that the financial statements show a true and fair view based on accounting standards and other regulatory requirements as well as assessing the internal control of the banks. Thus, they will be interested in the various financial statements and reports by the boards of directors, external auditor and the SSB, as well as other non-financial information such as the banks' strategies in contributing to the communities.

9.2.2   INVESTMENT ACCOUNT HOLDERS

Investment account holders put their money into the bank on partnership (*mudarabah*) or an equity participation basis (*musharakah*), but they are not the true owners of the bank and hence do not have the same rights as the equity holders. Unlike conventional banks where the contractual relationship is manifested in a borrower–lender or debtor–creditor kind of relationship, which gives less consideration to the outcome of the utilization of the fund or money, the operations of Islamic banks depend on the following relationships:

- If the relationship is based on *mudarabah* (partnership), then the financier or capital owner (*rab al-mal*) is entitled to assess and supervise activities of the *mudarib* (manager or entrepreneur) and ensure that the contractual limitations, if any, are observed. Thus, they will need information on the profitability of the venture and the amount of effort contributed by the *mudarib* in achieving the goal.
- If the relationship is based on *wakil* (agency), the principal is absolutely entitled to observe investment operations that are conducted based on the appointment of an agent, especially in view of the fact that the agent's remuneration would not be affected by the outcome of investment. There is thus a need for the principal to be aware of various products, services and circumstances surrounding those products and services to assist them in evaluating management's performance. Figure 9.2 illustrates the difference in the contractual relationship of the conventional and Islamic bank with investors, equity holders and customers.

9.2.3   *SHARI'AH* SUPERVISORY BOARD (SSB)

Members of the *shari'ah* boards are responsible for the supervision and guidance of the activities of the banks especially in terms of ensuring that the business operations and new product development activities are in conformance to *shari'ah*. Hence, they need information from the *shari'ah* audit and *shari'ah* review teams, internal and external auditors as well as management in order to provide *fatawa* and endorse the *shari'ah* legitimacy of products, services and operations. According the central bank of Malaysia, *shari'ah* audit refers to:

> periodical assessment conducted from time to time, to provide an independent assessment and objective assurance designed to add value and improve the degree of compliance in relation to the IFI's business operations, with the main objective of ensuring a sound and effective internal control system for Shariah compliance (BNM 2011, p. 23).

Figure 9.2   Difference in the contractual relationship of Islamic and conventional banks

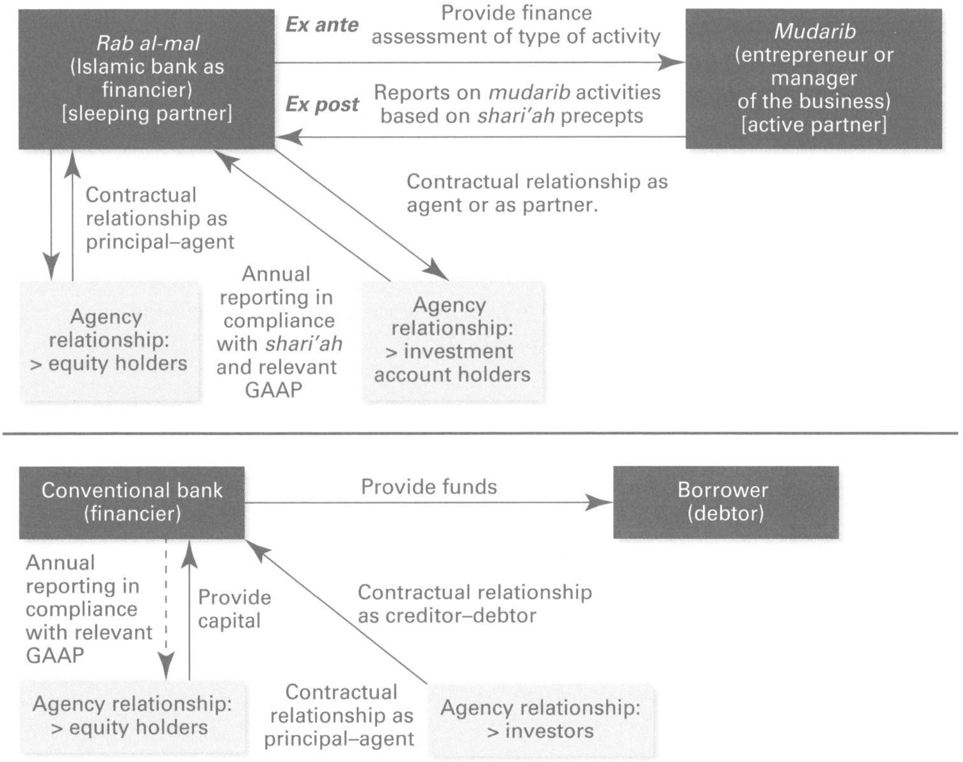

Shari'ah auditors will report the outcome of the *shari'ah* audit not only to the SSB or *Shari'ah* Committee but also the bank's audit committee. Their role is akin to the internal auditor but with wider scope to include chequeing compliance to *shari'ah* auditing standards. On the other hand, a *shari'ah* review involves reviewing various aspects of the business operations on a regular basis to ensure compliance with *shari'ah* rules and principles (*fatawa*) as decided by the SSB (or *Shari'ah* Committee). This function is conducted by those with background in *shari'ah* and they report to the board management and the SSB. The outcome of the *shari'ah* audit and *shari'ah* review will aid the SSB to form and express an opinion on the extent the IFI comply with *shari'ah* in the SSB Report included the bank's annual report.

9.2.4   ZAKAT AGENCIES
Every Muslim is required to pay *zakat* (alms) of 2.5 per cent of their net wealth each year to the eight types of beneficiaries mentioned in the *Qur'an* either directly or through the *zakat* agencies who will collect/receive the funds and distribute them to the beneficiaries. In some countries, banks pay *zakat* on behalf of the shareholders and depositors to the *zakat* agencies while in other countries the onus of paying *zakat* falls on the individuals themselves and not the banks. Therefore, *zakat* agencies are interested in the financial information to anticipate how much funds they can expect.

9.2.5   CURRENT AND SAVING ACCOUNTS HOLDERS
The contract for savings and demand deposits is based on *wadiah* (trust or safekeeping or guaranteed saving), an agency form of contract. Nevertheless, they still need transparent information on how their funds are being utilized and managed and whether they are in accordance with *shari'ah* precepts.

9.2.6 REGULATORY AGENCIES

Regulatory agencies include the central bank, financial stability board and the accounting and auditing standard boards. They are particularly interested in the financial statements to ensure that the banks have conducted their business in accordance with the rules and regulations. Also, the financial statements will indicate on the financial stability and riskiness of the bank.

9.2.7 THE PUBLIC/OTHERS

The public includes potential depositors, investors, customers, members of the media who provide financial related information to their readers and viewers, ratings agency representatives, financial advisers on investments, etc. They all rely on credible disclosures from banks to help make various types of decisions.

9.2.8 EMPLOYEES

Employees are interested to know the profitability of the bank, which influences their job security. Also they are interested to know if their employer is behaving ethically, to give confidence and pride in working in such an organization.

According to SFA 1 para 28 by AAOIFI, the common information needs of user groups specified earlier can be summarized as follows:

(i) To assist in evaluating the bank's compliance with the principles of *shari'ah* in all of its financial and other dealings.

(ii) To assist in evaluating the bank's ability in:
- using the economic resources available in a manner that safeguards these resources while increasing their value, at reasonable rates
- carrying out its social responsibilities and in particular those that have been specified by Islam, including the good use of available resources, the protection of the rights of others and the prevention of corruption on earth
- providing for the economic needs of those who deal with the bank
- maintaining liquidity at appropriate levels

(iii) To assist those employed by the bank in evaluating their relationship and future with the Islamic bank, including the bank's ability to safeguard and develop their rights and develop their managerial and productive skills and capabilities.

9.3 Basic financial statements of conventional and Islamic banks

Banks publish financial statements to provide information about the financial position, performance and changes in financial position of the banks to enable their shareholders and stakeholders to assess stewardship and management performance in order to make economic and other types of decisions. In the case of Islamic banks, financial statements along with other information in the notes to the accounts, assist users of financial statements in predicting the Islamic bank's future performance and in particular, their timing and certainty and in assessing the degree of compliance of the Islamic banks with the prescribed *shari'ah* requirements.

In preparing the financial statements, banks need to follow the mandatory requirements for standardized presentation using formats prescribed by the International Financial Reporting Standards (IFRS) of the International Accounting Standards Board (IASB). However, in the case of Islamic banks, they have the option to either follow the IFRS or the Financial Accounting Standards (FAS) by AAOIFI.

The accounting standards relevant to help shareholders and other stakeholders to make economic decisions are IAS 1: Presentation of Financial Statements by IASB, and FAS 1: General Presentation and Disclosure in the

Financial Statements of Islamic Banks and Financial Institutions by AAOIFI. Both standards require the disclosure and presentation of four financial statements to achieve fair presentation.

IAS 1 states that fair representation requires the faithful representation of the effects of transactions, other events and conditions in accordance with the definitions and recognition criteria for assets, liabilities, income and expenses set out in its conceptual framework. Similarly, AAOIFI argues that in compliance with Islamic teaching, recognition, measurement and recording of transactions and the fair presentation of rights and obligations are essential requirement as mentioned in various verses of the *Qur'an*, such as this one:

> *Woe to those that deal in fraud – those who, when they have to receive by measure from men, exact full measure, but when they have to give by measure or weight to men, give less than due* (Al-Mutafiffin, 83:1-3).[2]

The four financial statements required to achieve fair presentation are the following:

(i)   Statement of Financial Position (Balance Sheet)
(ii) Statement of Comprehensive Income (Income Statement)
(iii) Statement of Changes in Equity
(iv) Statement of Cash Flow

Each statement must be supported by appropriate explanatory notes and narrative reports: (i) to explain what has been achieved in the current year and (ii) to assist existing and potential depositors, investors and others to make economic decisions. Due to some underlying differences between Islamic and conventional banks, AAOIFI's FAS 1 requires four further statements to be disclosed in order to fairly comply with its framework. They are the Statement of Changes in Restricted Investment, Statement of Sources and Uses of *Zakat* Funds, Statement of Sources and Uses of *Qard* Fund, and any statements, reports and other data which assist in providing information required by users of financial statements as specified in the *Statement of Objectives*. Table 9.1 summarizes the differences in IAS 1 and FAS 1 in terms of preparation of financial statements by Islamic and conventional banks.

Table 9.1 Required financial statements for banks

Aspects	Islamic banks	Conventional banks
Accounting standards	IFRS or FAS	IFRS
Financial statements required	Statement of Financial Position (Balance Sheet)	Statement of Financial Position (Balance Sheet)
	Statement of Comprehensive Income (Income Statement)	Statement of Comprehensive Income (Income Statement)
	Statement of Cash Flows	Statement of Cash Flows
	Statement of Changes in Owners' Equity (Statement of Retained Earnings)	Statement of Changes in Owners' Equity (Statement of Retained Earnings)
	Notes to the Financial Statements	Notes to the Financial Statements
	Statement of Changes in Restricted Investment	
	Statement of Sources and Uses of *Zakat* and Charity Fund (if bank assumes the responsibility for the collection and distribution of *zakat*)	
	Statement of Sources and Uses of *Qard* Fund	
	Any statements, reports and other data which assist in providing information required by users of financial statements as specified in the *Statement of Objectives* (FAS 1, para 2)	

[2]www.wright-house.com/religions/islam/Quran/83-defrauding.php, accessed 30 May 2018.

9.3.1   STATEMENT OF FINANCIAL POSITION OR BALANCE SHEET

The Statement of Financial Position or Balance Sheet represents the state of wealth of banks at a particular point in time, usually at the end of the financial year. The Statement of Financial Position information is normally reported quarterly to shareholders and other stakeholders. It shows the values of all the banks' sources and uses of funds. These funds are categorized into assets, liabilities and equity. The total balance of each of those categories will satisfy the balanced nature of the financial position as depicted in the following equation:

$$Assets = Liabilities + Capital\ (Equity\ or\ net\ worth)$$

You may be more familiar with the assets, liabilities and equity in non-financial companies in your accounting courses, hence it is vital to understand the differences in the case of financial institutions, especially Islamic banks as their products and services take more forms depending on the different contracts in order to be *shari'ah* compliant, as discussed in Chapter 4. Table 9.2 presents a simple Statement of Financial Position of a conventional commercial and investment bank and Islamic bank. It can be seen that there are some differences in the assets, liabilities and equity items. We will now look at the differences in more detail.

a) Conventional and investment banks

In the case of conventional banks, their sources of funds come from the following:

- general public (retail deposits)
- companies (small, medium and large corporate deposits)
- other banks (interbank deposits)
- debt issues (bonds and loans)
- equity issues (shares)
- savings of past profits (retained earnings)

The first four items above are classified as *liabilities* (debt) and the last two items are classified as *capital* (equity). These funds are then transformed into financial and, to a lesser extent, real assets which consist of the following:

- cash
- liquid assets (securities)
- short term money market instruments such as Treasury Bills (easy to liquidate quickly when there is cash shortage)
- loans (short, medium and long term)
- other investments
- fixed assets (computers, branch network, premises)

However, there are some differences in the components of the Statement of Financial Position of investment banks. On the liabilities side, there is *commercial paper*, which comprises short term negotiable debt instruments issued by banks to raise unsecured funding and are traded in the money market. The other item is *trading liabilities*, which includes activities such as trading securities and derivatives dealings and brokerage. *Collateralized securities* are secured borrowing transactions and securities sold under agreement to repurchase. The remaining items on the liabilities side and the capital component are the same as in commercial banks. On the assets side of investment banks, there is an item called *trading assets* which refers to banks' activities related to securities brokerage, trading and underwriting, and derivatives dealing and brokerage. Another item is *securities financing transactions* which refers to securities held as collateral that the bank can sell or re-pledge. The item, *investment securities*, refers to securities owned by the bank for non-trading purposes. The other items on the assets side are similar to commercial banks.

Table 9.2 Stylized Statement of Financial Position of conventional and Islamic banks

Commercial bank	Investment bank	Islamic bank
Assets	**Assets**	**Assets**
Cash Liquid assets Money market instruments	Cash Trading assets Securities financing transactions(receivables) Investment securities	Cash and cash equivalent Short term trade financing/Sales receivables: *Murabahah* (cost-plus or mark-up) *Bay 'salam* (forward sale)
Loans	Loans, notes and mortgages	Services: *Ju'alah* (reward or commission) *Wakalah* (agency) *Kafalah* (guarantee)
Other investments	Other investments	Medium term investments/ *Mudarabah* financing: *Ijarah* (leasing) *Ijarah muntahiya bil tamlik* (financial lease) *Istisna'* (manufacture sale)
		Mudarabah investment (profit–loss sharing)
		Musharakah investment (partnership)
Fixed assets	Fixed assets Other assets	Fixed assets Other assets
Total assets	**Total assets**	**Total assets**
Liabilities	**Liabilities**	**Liabilities**
Deposits: retail Deposits: commercial Deposits: interbank	Commercial Papers Trading liabilities Collateralized securities Deposits Other payables	Demand deposits (current account) Saving deposits Interbank deposits **Payables** *Salam* (sale) *Istisna'* (manufacture) *Zakat* Taxes
Debt issues	Long term borrowing	Unrestricted investment accounts (URIA) Special investment account (SGIA)
Equity	**Equity**	**Equity**
Paid up capital Retained earnings Other reserves	Paid up capital Retained earnings Other reserves	Paid up capital Retained earnings Profit equalization reserve (PER) Investment risk reserve (IRR) Other reserves
Total liabilities and equity	**Total liabilities and equity**	**Total liabilities, profit sharing investment accounts and equity**

b) Islamic banks

The activities of Islamic banks are typically a hybrid between a conventional commercial bank and an investment bank, thus resembling a *universal bank* which offers a full range of banking and investment services. Furthermore, unlike conventional banks where the typical relationship is that of lender–borrower, Islamic banks enter into different types of contractual relationships. Accordingly, the components of the Statement of Financial Position of Islamic banks are expected, to some extent, to be different. It will be helpful to refer to Chapter 4 to recall the various contracts.

The sources of funds or liabilities of Islamic banks comprise the following:

- current accounts or demand deposits (based on *wadiah* or *mudarabah*)
- savings account or savings deposits (based on *wadiah* or *mudarabah* or *wakalah*)
- deposits of other banks or interbank deposits (based on *mudarabah*)
- payables (based on *salam, istisna'*)
- other payables (*zakat*, taxes)
- unrestricted investment accounts (URIA) or also known as general investment accounts (GIA) (based on *mudarabah* or *musharakah*)
- restricted investment accounts (RIA) or also known as specific investment account (SIA) (based on *mudarabah* or *musharakah*)
- equity issues (shares)
- savings of past profits (retained earnings)
- PER or profit equalization reserve
- IRR or investment risk reserve
- other reserves

The first three items (i.e. demand, saving and interbank deposits) are known as *transaction deposits* which are risk free and often yield no return (unless they are based on *mudarabah* or *wakalah).* They are often based on the principle of *wadiah* (trust or safekeeping) which is an agency current contract for the purpose of protecting and safekeeping the depositors' assets and providing them with accounting services as well as access to the payments system. Although they typically would not receive any returns, most Islamic banks do offer some return to entice depositors to keep their surplus funds in the bank. We will look later on in this chapter at the calculation Islamic banks may use in rewarding returns for such depositors. If they are based on *mudarabah* or *wakalah* contracts, then some returns can be expected from the deposits.

The next two items are related to payables, i.e. indebtedness of Islamic banks. This includes *salam* payable (prepaid sales), *istisna'* payable (deferred delivery), *zakat* payable (if the bank is responsible), and taxes payable. Other payables include cheques, credit cards, etc.

A major portion of an Islamic bank's liabilities is in the form of investment accounts, which are not really liabilities in the normal sense but a form of equity investment based on the principle of *mudarabah* or *musharakah* (profit–loss sharing). They are often referred to as *profit sharing investment accounts* (PSIA). These investment accounts carry the risks of capital loss and returns that are variable. This makes it different from conventional banks which promise a fixed return and no loss of capital. Figure 9.3 shows the classification of PSIA.

Figure 9.3 Classification of profit sharing investment account (PSIA)

PSIA can be further classified into *restricted investment account* (RIA) and *unrestricted investment account* (URIA). RIA, also known as *specific investment account* (SIA), refers to an Islamic investment account which is subject to certain restrictions being imposed on the bank by the account holder with respect to purpose, geographical distribution, and/or types of transactions, when investing the account holder's funds. As such, Islamic banks cannot commingle such funds with the unrestricted investment accounts. RIA or SIA is an off-balance sheet item which means that it will not appear on the bank's balance sheet. The asset allocation and the term of the investment are all specified in the *mudarabah* or *musharakah* contract, including the percentage of profit which the bank as a *mudarib* will receive as a management fee, and in the case of *musharakah* as returns from investment through joint venture. The contract is normally for a specified term and the assets of the *mudarabah* or *musharakah* fund do not usually have maturities that exceed that term. However, the contract typically spans several financial periods of the bank and requires interim profit calculations. The RIA account holder is allowed to withdraw the funds before the end of the contract term as long as advance notice is given, but s(he) will need to forego any accrued undistributed profit.

On the other hand, URIA are investment accounts that are not subject to any restrictions and the account holder authorizes the bank to invest the funds in any manner the bank deems appropriate. Thus, the bank can commingle the funds with those of the RIA holders or with other sources of funds available to the bank such as funds from current accounts. URIAs are offered in different forms and they are often linked to a pre-agreed period of maturity. One form of URIA is the *general investment account* (GIA). For such accounts, the profits and returns are distributed between the GIA holders and the bank according to a predetermined ratio. Just like the RIA holders, the GIA holders may also withdraw the funds before the end of the contract term as long as s(he) provides an ample notice period and foregoes some share of her/his profit. Typically, the amount of profit forgone depends on the notice period given by the GIA holder to the bank. The shorter the notice period given, the higher the amount of profit that the GIA holder will have to forego since a larger proportion (sometimes as much as 40 per cent) of the invested funds will be treated by the bank as unremunerated current account. The reason why the bank treats early withdrawal as such is because it needs to hold liquid assets (cash and cash equivalents) that have very low or no yield in order to honour the withdrawal obligations at very short notice. In this way, the bank hopes to discourage early withdrawals.

Another type of URIA is *special unrestricted investment account* (SUIA). They are usually customized for high net worth individuals or institutional clients. They resemble specialized funds to finance different asset classes. They also operate under *mudarabah* contract, but the modes of investment and distribution of profits are customized to suit the needs of clients and the distribution of profits are negotiated separately for each account, with the yield directly related to the success of a particular project.

The last three items are classified as equity or shareholders' funds. *Paid-up capital* refers to the permanent, ultimate, or basic resource for the survival of an Islamic bank and this cannot be reduced without a court order. The shareholders' identities and their interests are recorded in the members' register and share certificates are issued as evidence of interest in the Islamic banks.

Reserves are accumulated surpluses set aside from either capital or revenue. *Capital reserves* arise from share transactions, fixed assets revaluation or any decision to prohibit distribution through dividends. They comprise the following: *share premiums* (excess of price over par value); capital reserves arising from consolidation; unrealized surplus on revaluation of fixed assets (revaluation reserves); and amounts, which are prohibited from being distributed by the articles of association of the Islamic bank entity (special reserves). *Revenue reserves* are appropriations of operating profits that are made either by the board or by law to be unavailable for current or normal distribution. They comprise *statutory reserves* and *financing loss reserves*. The former may be required under various laws while the latter is an amount set aside from earnings for the purpose of potential bad debts.

For example, suppose that an Islamic bank suspects that £1 million worth of its financing might prove to be bad debts that will have to be written off (valued at zero) in the future. The bank can set aside £1 million of its earnings and put it into its financing loss reserves account, which will increase the Islamic bank's capital but reduce its reported earnings by £1 million. When the Islamic bank eventually determines that the £1 million financing will never be paid back, it will formally write it off, thus reducing the value of its capital and assets by £1 million, but the reported earnings will not be affected because they were reduced earlier when the Islamic bank set aside £1 million of earnings as financing loss reserves. These items may be available for distribution by special board resolutions.

One unique feature of Islamic bank's reserves is the profit equalization reserve (*PER*) which is the amount appropriated out of the *mudarabah* income by the bank before allocating the share of the *mudarib*. It is aimed at maintaining a specified level of return on investment (ROI) for the IAHs, especially the URIAHs. The share to be appropriated is based on a specific percentage decided by the central bank or any relevant authority, including the accounting profession who may not approve such practice of income smoothing. Thus, it represents a measure of stabilization over different financial periods, formed for the purpose of increasing owners' equity. The *investment risk reserve* (*IRR*) refers to the amount appropriated out of the investment account holders after allocating the *mudarib* share to cushion against future losses that IAHs may incur. The IRR reserve is based on the amount deemed prudent by the management of the Islamic bank. Table 9.3 lists the major differences between the two types of reserves.

Table 9.3 Major differences between PER and IRR

	Profit equalization reserve (PER)	**Investment risk reserve (IRR)**
Source	*mudaraba* income	IAH income
Stage of appropriation	before *mudarib* share is allocated	after *mudarib* share is allocated
Purpose/use	profit stabilization/smoothing	cushion against future losses
Ultimate beneficiary	IAHs and *mudarib*	IAHs

On the asset side, there is a diversified portfolio of heterogeneous asset classes with a wide spectrum of risk and maturity profile. They include the following:

- cash
- short term asset backed trade financing (*bay 'salam, murabahah*)
- medium term investments (*ijarah, istisna', ijarah muntahiya bil tamlik*)
- profit–loss sharing investments (*mudarabah*)
- equity partnership investments (*musharakah*)
- services (*ju'alah, wakalah, kafalah*)
- fixed assets (computers, branch network, premises)

The second item, trade financing, such as *murabahah* (cost-plus or mark-up) and *bay 'salam* (forward sale), is arranged by the bank using its skills, market knowledge and customer base to finance trading activities as well as provide short term funds to meet working capital needs. For medium term investments, the bank has several choices to invest the funds, such as in *ijarah* (leasing), *istisna'* (manufacturing sale) and *ijarah muntahiya bil tamlik* (financial lease). In the case of *ijarah*, banks incur overheads resulting from the purchase of asset and keeping ownership until their disposal and also being responsible for maintenance and other costs over the life of the contract. As for *istisna'*, the bank in its position as manufacturer, must assume liability for the ownership risk prior to delivering the object of the *istisna'* to the buyer as well as risk of theft or abnormal damage. For *ijarah muntahiya bil tamlik,* the bank will buy an asset and lease it out to the customer requiring it based on an agreed rental fee, including providing an option for the customer to acquire ownership at the end of a specified period.

Mudarabah investment involves the bank supplying the money to another party who has management expertise to undertake a specific business with the bank acting as financier and the customer as entrepreneur. *Musharakah* investment is a joint enterprise or partnership structure with profit/loss sharing implications. The profits for both instruments will be shared at a pre-agreed ratio and the loss will be borne solely by the *mudarib* in the case of *mudarabah*, while the loss will depend on the ratio of capital contribution in the case of *musharakah*.

As for banking services, there are a number of services provided by Islamic banks such as *ju'alah*, whereby a commission or reward is made upon completion of a task, *wakalah* where power of attorney is given to the agent to act on behalf of the principal for a fee, and *kafalah* which is a suretyship for a debt obligation by charging a commission.

Table 9.4 presents a summary of stylized Statement of Financial Position for conventional and Islamic banks by highlighting the major differences as discussed earlier. As can be seen, on the assets side, the portfolio of

Table 9.4 Comparison of stylized Statement of Financial Position for Islamic and conventional banks

Islamic banks	Conventional banks
Assets	**Assets**
Cash and cash equivalents	Cash and cash equivalents
Sales receivables (*bay'*)	Investment in securities
Investment in securities	Loan and advances
Investment in leased assets (*mudarabah*)	Investment in subsidiaries
Investment in real estates(*mudarabah*)	Fixed assets
Investment in subsidiaries	Other assets
Equity investment in capital ventures (*mudarabah*)	
Equity financing (*musharakah*)	
Fixed assets	
Other assets	
Liabilities	**Liabilities**
Deposits	Deposits
Other liabilities	Other liabilities
***Profit Sharing Investment Accounts* (PSIA)**	
Unrestricted investment account (URIA)	
Special investment account (SIA)	
Owners' equity	**Owners' equity**
Equity	Equity
Retained earnings	Retained earnings
Profit equalization reserve	Loan loss reserve
Investment risk reserve	

Islamic banks is composed of various finance contracts (or modes of financing) many of which are based on trading (*bay'* and *murabahah*) and profit and loss sharing principles (*musharakah* and *mudarabah*). Thus, unlike the case in conventional banking, the customer–banker relationship in Islamic banking is not a mere debtor–creditor relationship, but can take various forms. One of the major differences between an Islamic bank and a conventional Islamic bank is that the former mobilizes funds on a profit and loss sharing basis, while there is no similar concept on the liabilities side in conventional banks. On the liabilities side of conventional banks, deposit funds are mobilized on a time deposit basis whereby fixed (predetermined) interest rates are contractually guaranteed. Furthermore, Islamic banks have a unique item between the liabilities and equity called PSIAs, which does not exist in conventional banks as they are only engaged in liability with fixed ROIs. Another unique feature in the equity section of Islamic banks which again is not featured in conventional bank is the PER, which is a form of income smoothing as Islamic banks cannot promise fixed returns.

Figures 9.4 and 9.5 show examples of the Statement of Financial Position of Islamic banks prepared and presented based on IFRS and FAS, respectively.

9.3.2 COMPREHENSIVE INCOME STATEMENT

The Income Statement reports a bank's financial performance over a specific financial period. Financial performance is assessed by giving a summary of how the business incurs its revenues and expenses through both operating and non-operating activities. The Statement of Income includes all recognized gains and losses in the period including those that were previously recognized in equity. The *costs* that are derived from the liabilities side of the Statement of Financial Position relate to payments that banks have to undertake such as returns for depositors, dividends to shareholders, taxes payable and provision for loan loss. Also, banks incur staffing and other operating costs. The *revenues* are generated from the assets side of the Statement of Financial Position such as interest earned on loans (only in the case of conventional banks) and other fees and commissions. Thus the relationship between costs, revenues and profits is as follows:

Bank profit = Revenues – Expenses (or costs)

Figure 9.4   Statement of Financial Position of Al Rayan Bank as at 31 Dec 2016 (IFRS)

	NOTE	2016 £'000s	2015 £'000s
Assets			
Cash		**2 412**	1 807
Commodity Murabaha and Wakala receivables and cash deposits with banks	13	**217 297**	140 573
Net investment in Consumer Finance	14	**43**	95
Net investment in Home Purchase Plans	14	**637 093**	452 787
Net investment in Commercial Property Finance	14	**394 243**	273 276
Investment securities – Sukuk	15	**166 962**	120 934
Property and equipment	16	**6 431**	5 990
Intangible assets	17	**935**	622
Other assets	18	**4 178**	3 455
Deferred tax asset	28	**6 097**	4 781
Total assets		**1 435 691**	1 004 320
Liabilities and equity			
Liabilities			
Deposits from banks	19	**83 571**	155 717
Deposits from customers	20	**1 222 853**	730 713
Other liabilities	21	**5 982**	4 433
Total liabilities		**1 312 407**	890 863
Equity			
Called up share capital	23	**121 219**	121 219
Share premium		**54 807**	54 807
Fair value reserve		**1 980**	1 654
Retained deficit		**(54 817)**	(64 299)
Profit stabilisation reserve		**95**	76
Total equity		**123 284**	113 457
Total equity and liabilities		**1 435 691**	1 004 320

Source: Al Rayan Annual Report 2016, www.alrayanbank.co.uk/media/339335/al-rayan-bank-annual-report-and-financial-statements-2016-170420.pdf

IAS 1 and FAS 1 allow financial institutions to choose the format relevant to their operations. Hence, a statement presenting line items with costs analyzed according to function, e.g. cost of sales, distribution costs and administration expenses, is often used. FAS 1 specifically requires the format and the classification of the financial statements to have clear presentation of their content, and the terminology used to express the content of the financial statements should enable their users to understand and comprehend the information.

Since the costs and revenues are derived from the components of the Statement of Financial Position, any difference in their structure will also affect the costs and revenues reported in the Comprehensive Income Statement, as we will see in the case for conventional and Islamic banks.

a) Conventional banks

The main source of income or revenues for conventional banks is *interest income* from loans to households and other borrowers, securities and deposits lent out to other institutions. *Interest expense* is the sum of interest paid to all depositors, short term borrowing and long term debt. The difference between interest income and interest expense is the net interest income (NII). Provision for loan losses (PLL) is the amount

Figure 9.5 Statement of Financial Position of Al Baraka Banking Group as at 31 Dec 2016 (FAS)

	Notes	2016 US$ '000	2015 US$ '000
ASSETS			
Cash and balances with banks	3	5 073 418	5 373 409
Receivables	4	11 423 448	11 959 052
Mudaraba and Musharaka financing	5	1 582 396	1 558 593
Investments	6	2 629 131	3 105 750
Ijarah Muntahia Bittamleek	7	1 830 339	1 734 457
Property and equipment	8	417 295	444 608
Other assets	9	469 238	442 332
TOTAL ASSETS		23 425 265	24 618 201
LIABILITIES, EQUITY OF INVESTMENT ACCOUNTHOLDERS AND OWNERS' EQUITY			
LIABILITIES			
Customer current and other accounts		4 983 772	4 841 099
Due to banks		918 395	808 268
Long term financing	10	1 381 256	1 497 208
Other liabilities	11	856 467	862 444
Total liabilities		8 139 890	8 009 019
EQUITY OF INVESTMENT ACCOUNTHOLDERS	12	13 276 794	14 514 599
OWNERS' EQUITY	13		
Share capital		1 149 218	1 115 746
Treasury shares		(9 588)	(8 464)
Share premium		18 574	17 662
Reserves		181 971	165 459
Cumulative changes in fair values		41 271	38 529
Foreign currency translations		(666 719)	(461 948)
Retained earnings		497 374	433 631
Proposed appropriations		68 857	55 787
Equity attributable to parent's shareholders		1 280 958	1 356 402
Non-controlling interest		727 623	738 181
Total owners' equity		2 008 581	2 094 583
TOTAL LIABILITIES, EQUITY OF INVESTMENT ACCOUNTHOLDERS AND OWNERS' EQUITY		23 425 265	24 618 201

Source: Al Baraka Banking Group Annual Report 2016, www.albaraka.com/default.asp?action=article&id=55

charged against NII to absorb expected losses and the difference between NII and PLL is the *net interest income after PLL.*

Non-interest income refers to fee income, commissions and trading income including gains/losses from trading securities and foreign transactions. *Non-interest expense* includes salaries, fringe benefits to employees, property and equipment expenses. The difference between non-interest income and non-interest expense is the *net non-interest income.*

When we add the *net interest income after PLL* and *net non-interest income,* this will give us the item called *pre-tax net operating profit.* We then either add or subtract the item *securities gained or losses* which may arise from the difference in prices when selling the securities. The difference between *pre-tax net operating profit* and *securities gained or losses*, is the *profit before taxes.* Then we subtract *taxes* to give us *the net profit.* Finally, the *retained profit*, which will be transferred to the Statement of Financial Position, is equal to *net profit* minus *cash dividends.* Table 9.5 presents a simplified Comprehensive Income Statement for a conventional bank.

Table 9.5 Simplified Comprehensive Income Statement of conventional bank

a	Interest income
b	Interest expense
c = a − b	Net interest income (NII or spread)
d	Provision for loan losses (PLL)
e = c − d	Net interest income after PLL
f	Non-interest income
g	Non-interest expense
h = f − g	Net non-interest income
i = e + h	Pre-tax net operating profit
j	Securities gains (losses)
k = i +/− j	Profit before taxes
l	Taxes
m = k − l	Net profit
n	Cash dividends
p = m − n	Retained profits

In the case of conventional investment banks, their revenues are derived from four main sources: *trading and principal investments* (e.g. equity and equity derivatives trading, debt derivatives, mortgages, foreign exchange, government and agency obligations), *investment banking* (M&A advisory services), *asset management* (managing funds as agent), *portfolio service fees and commissions* (brokerage, financing services) and *interest income* (wholesale lending). The bulk of the costs will be *interest expenses* and *staff costs*.

b) Islamic banks

An Islamic bank's earnings performance is also represented by its Income Statement. The amounts reported in the Income Statement are driven by management decisions on available total assets and the level of restricted or unrestricted funds to total liabilities. Hence, the Income Statement of Islamic banks also present a picture of risk management successes or failures for a specific period of time. Strong, steady earnings are a reflection of good management while weak, fluctuating earnings are an indicator of poor management. Table 9.6 presents a simplified Comprehensive Income Statement for an Islamic bank.

Table 9.6 Simplified Comprehensive Income Statement of an Islamic bank

a	Income from financing activities
b	Income from investment activities
c = a + b	Net income from financing and investment activities
d	Return on URIA before share of *mudarib*
e	Bank's share as *mudarib*
f = d − e	Return on URIA before *zakat*
g	Bank's share in income from investment (as *mudarib* and fund owner)
h	Bank's income from its own investments
i	Bank's share in restricted investment (RIA) profit as *mudarib*
j	Bank's fees as an investment agent for restricted investment (RIA)
k	Revenue from banking services
l	Other revenues
m = g + h + I + j + k + l	Total bank revenue
n	Administrative and general expenditures
p	Depreciation
q = m − n − p	Net income(loss) before *zakat* and tax
r	Provision for *zakat* and tax
s = q − r	Net income
t	Profit equalization reserves
u = s − t	Net distributable income

It is obvious that the nature of revenues and expenses in the Income Statement is to some extent different from that of conventional banks. Unlike conventional banks, which derived their revenues mainly based on interest income from lending activities, the bulk of the income or *revenues* of Islamic banks is derived from financing and investment activities. The income received from earning (invested) assets, i.e. those on which an Islamic bank receives profit or sharing profits, is known as *financing income*. Such income is derived from *hibah* (gift), financing, advances and other loans, investment securities and money on call and deposits with financial institutions. These incomes are added up to give *net income from financing and investing activities*.

The next part deals with the returns from profit–loss sharing investments (PSIA) and the bank's own investments. The value for this item depends upon the Islamic bank's composition and value of assets capable of producing profits (earning assets). For example, an Islamic bank with a high proportion of fixed assets like furniture and fixtures will have a lower proportion of assets on which to earn profit. Also, for any given proportion of earning assets, an Islamic bank that has a higher proportion of its assets in equity financing compared to an Islamic bank with a higher portion of its assets in sales receivables will report greater total financing income. The reason for this is that equity financing is riskier than the inventories that Islamic banks can hold as sales receivables; consequently, equity financing often provide a higher return or higher profit, than sales receivables.

The fourth item in the statement related to PSIA is the *return from URIA before share of mudarib* from which the *bank's share as mudarib* is deducted to give *return on URIA before zakat*. The next four items comprise the *bank's share in income from investment as mudarib and fund owner, bank's income from own investment, bank's share in restricted investment (RIA) as mudarib, bank's fees as investment agent for restricted investment (RIA)*, followed by *revenue from banking services* in the form of commission and fees and other revenues. The sum of the six items gives the *total bank revenue*. Other operating expenses, such as administrative expenses and depreciation, are deducted from the total bank revenue to give *net income (loss) before zakat and tax. Provision for zakat and tax* is deducted from *net income (loss) before zakat and tax* to give *net income. Profit equalization reserve* is then deducted from the *net income* to give the *net distributable income* which will then be distributed among the depositors and shareholders. Figures 9.6 and 9.7 present Income Statements of an Islamic bank using IFRS and the other using FAS, respectively.

Figure 9.6   Statement of Comprehensive Income of Al Rayan Bank for the period ending 31 Dec 2016 (IFRS)

	NOTE	2016 £'000s	2015 £'000s
Income receivable from Islamic financing transactions	6	41 081	28 762
Returns payable to customers and banks	6	(15 672)	(8 004)
Net income from Islamic financing transactions	6	25 409	20 758
Fee and commission income	7	693	548
Fee and commission expense	7	(117)	(88)
Net fee and commission income	7	576	460
Gain on Sukuk disposal	6	880	34
Foreign exchange income	6	393	10
		1 273	44
Operating income		27 258	21 262
Net (impairment) / credit on financial assets	14	(449)	(557)
Personnel expenses	9	(9 308)	(7 242)
General and administrative expenses		(8 229)	(6 678)
Depreciation	16	(678)	(357)
Amortisation	17	(409)	(224)
Total operating expenses		(19 073)	(15 058)
Profit before income tax		8 185	6 204
Income tax credit	11	1 316	4 068
Profit for the year		9 501	10 272
Other comprehensive income			
Items that are or may be reclassified to profit or loss			
Change in fair value of investment securities taken to equity		326	74
Other comprehensive income for the year		326	74
Total comprehensive income for the year		9 827	10 346

Source: Al Rayan Annual Report 2016, www.alrayanbank.co.uk/media/339335/al-rayan-bank-annual-report-and-financial-statements-2016-170420.pdf

Figure 9.7   Consolidated Statement of Income of Al Baraka Banking Group for the period ending 31 Dec 2016 (FAS)

	Notes	2016 US$ '000	2015 US$ '000
INCOME			
Net income from jointly financed contracts and investments	14	1 336 569	1 223 215
Return on equity of investment accountholders before Group's share as a Mudarib		(1 114 019)	(1 026 367)
Group's share as a Mudarib	15	396 762	345 415
Return on equity of investment accountholders		(717 257)	(680 952)
Group's share of income from equity of investment accountholders (as a Mudarib and Rabalmal)		619 312	542 263
Mudarib share for managing off-balance sheet equity of investment accountholders		5 022	5 583
Net income from self financed contracts and investments	14	285 499	272 941
Other fees and commission income	16	176 837	200 513
Other operating income	17	78 859	34 794
		1 165 529	1 056 094
Profit paid on long term financing	18	(91 370)	(56 541)
TOTAL OPERATING INCOME		1 074 159	999 553
OPERATING EXPENSES			
Staff expenses		325 501	298 927
Depreciation and amortisation	19	44 579	50 054
Other operating expenses	20	197 136	186 890
TOTAL OPERATING EXPENSES		567 216	535 871
NET OPERATING INCOME FOR THE YEAR BEFORE PROVISIONS AND IMPAIRMENT AND TAXATION		506 943	463 682
Provisions and impairment	21	(122 154)	(58 371)
NET INCOME BEFORE TAXATION		384 789	405 311
Taxation		(117 153)	(119 125)
NET INCOME FOR THE YEAR		267 636	286 186
Attributable to:			
Equity holders of the parent		151 545	162 741
Non-controlling interest		116 091	123 445
		267 636	286 186
Basic and diluted earnings per share - US cents	22	13.29	14.27

Source: Al Baraka Banking Group Annual Report 2016, www.albaraka.com/default.asp?action=article&id=55

9.3.3   STATEMENT OF CASH FLOWS

The Statement of Cash Flows, also known as Funds Flow Statement, indicates how changes in the Statement of Financial Position and Comprehensive Income Statement affect cash and its equivalent. Cash flow information provides users of financial statements with a basis to assess the ability of the entity to generate cash and cash equivalents and the needs of the entity to utilize those cash flows effectively.

The cash flows are differentiated in terms of *operating, investing* and *financing* activities. IAS 1 and IAS 7 set out the requirements for the presentation and disclosure of cash flow information, and in the case of Islamic banks, FAS 1. The statement represents all of an entity's receipts and cash payments. Figures 9.8 and 9.9 illustrate the Statement of Cash Flows for Islamic banks using IFRS and FAS.

9.3.4   STATEMENT OF CHANGES IN EQUITY (OR RETAINED EARNINGS)

Both IAS 1 and FAS 1 require preparers to disclose a statement called the Statement of Changes in Equity. The statement is designed to show comprehensive income for the period and the effects of any prior period adjustments, reconciling the movement in equity from the beginning to the end of the period. The statement can also show how a period's profits are divided between dividends for shareholders and retained earnings, which are shown on the Statement of Financial Position to accumulate under owners' equity. Figures 9.10 and 9.11 illustrate the Statement of Changes in Equity for Islamic banks using IFRS and FAS.

9.3.5   OTHER TYPES OF FINANCIAL STATEMENTS

As mentioned earlier, FAS 1 also requires IFIs to produce four other financial statements if they are applicable and important for users of financial reports: (i) Statement of Changes in Restricted Investment, (ii) Statement of

Figure 9.8 Statement of Cash Flows of Al Rayan Bank (IFRS)

	NOTE	2016 £'000s	2015 £'000s
Cash flows from operating activities			
Profit for the year		**8 185**	6 204
Adjustments for:			
Depreciation	16	**678**	357
Amortisation	17	**409**	224
Gain on disposal of Sukuk	6	**(880)**	(34)
Impairment charge and write off on financial assets		**496**	557
Change in Commodity Murabaha and Wakala receivables		**(21 353)**	32 021
Change in investment in Consumer Finance		**52**	55
Change in investment in Home Purchase Plans		**(120 967)**	(141 755)
Change in investment in Commercial Property Finance		**(184 306)**	(134 067)
Change in other assets		**(723)**	(1 210)
Change in deposits from banks		**(72 145)**	123 988
Change in deposits from customers		**492 140**	220 910
Change in other liabilities		**1 549**	1 102
Net cash from operating activities		**103 135**	108 352
Cash flows from investing activities			
Purchase of investment securities - Sukuk		**(44 821)**	(11 467)
Purchase of property and equipment	16	**(1 118)**	(6 085)
Purchase of intangible assets	17	**(721)**	(489)
Net cash used in investing activities		**(46 662)**	(18 041)
Net change in cash and cash equivalents		**56 473**	90 311
Foreign exchange gains		**393**	10
Cash and cash equivalents at 1 January		**102 486**	12 165
Cash and cash equivalents at 31 December	12	**159 352**	102 486

Source: Al Rayan Annual Report 2016, www.alrayanbank.co.uk/media/339335/al-rayan-bank-annual-report-and-financial-statements-2016-170420.pdf

Sources and Uses of *Zakat* and Charity Funds, (iii) Statement of Sources and Uses of *Qard* fund, and (iv) any statements, reports and other data which assist in providing information required by users of financial statements as specified in the *Statement of Objectives*. These statements are often disclosed in the notes to the accounts.

a) Statement of changes in restricted investment

Since bank does not have the right to use or dispose of restricted investments except within the conditions of the contract between the Islamic bank and RIAHs, they cannot be considered as assets of the Islamic bank. As such, they are not reflected on the bank's Statement of Financial Position and instead it is a requirement to provide a Statement of Changes in Restricted Investments and their Equivalent in the annual report of the IFIs.

b) Statement of sources and uses of zakat and charity funds

When an Islamic bank is responsible for the collection and distribution of *zakat*, then this means that the bank acts as a fiduciary of that fund. Hence, it needs to establish a Statement of Sources and Uses of *Zakat* and Charity Funds. The basic elements of this financial statement include *sources of zakat and charity funds* and *uses of zakat and charity funds* during a period and the fund balance as of a given date. Based on the first *Zakat*

Figure 9.9   Consolidated Statement of Cash Flows of Al Baraka Banking Group (FAS 1)

	Notes	2016 US$ '000	2015 US$ '000
OPERATING ACTIVITIES			
Net income before taxation		384 789	405 311
Adjustments for:			
Depreciation and amortisation	19	44 579	50 054
Depreciation on Ijarah Muntahia Bittamleek	14.4	238 315	191 729
Unrealised gain on equity and debt-type instruments at fair value through statement of income	14.3	(152)	(145)
Gain on sale of property and equipment	17	(14 804)	(10 502)
(Gain) loss on sale of investment in real estate	14.3	(5 502)	1 332
Gain on sale of equity type instruments at fair value through equity	14.3	(3 585)	(1 509)
Gain on sale equity and debt-type instruments at fair value through statement of income	14.3	(667)	(1 636)
Gain from associates	14.3	(2 059)	(652)
Provisions and impairment	21	122 154	58 371
Operating profit before changes in operating assets and liabilities		763 068	692 353
Net changes in operating assets and liabilities:			
Reserves with central banks		859 261	(804 579)
Receivables		443 093	(18 818)
Mudaraba and Musharaka financing		(40 793)	(10 608)
Ijarah Muntahia Bittamleek		(334 197)	(431 386)
Other assets		(24 167)	3 510
Customer current and other accounts		142 675	331 783
Due to banks		110 126	(403 225)
Other liabilities		10 143	(25 342)
Equity of investment accountholders		(1 238 504)	378 244
Taxation paid		(147 598)	(104 730)
Net cash from (used in) operating activities		543 107	(392 798)
INVESTING ACTIVITIES			
Net purchase of investments		495 992	(514 289)
Net purchase of property and equipment		2 890	(57 424)
Dividends received from associates		2 329	2 068
(Purchase) disposal of investment in associate		(14 587)	3 556
Net cash from (used in) investing activities		486 624	(566 089)
FINANCING ACTIVITIES			
Long term financing		(115 952)	841 539
Dividends paid to equity holders of the parent		(22 143)	(32 816)
Net movement in treasury shares		(212)	171
Net changes in non-controlling interest		(9 018)	(33 494)
Net cash (used in) from financing activities		(147 325)	775 400
Foreign currency translation adjustments		(323 137)	(258 945)
NET CHANGES IN CASH AND CASH EQUIVALENTS		559 269	(442 432)
Cash and cash equivalents at 1 January		2 292 689	2 735 121
CASH AND CASH EQUIVALENTS AT 31 DECEMBER	23	2 851 958	2 292 689

Source: Al Baraka Banking Group Annual Report 2016, www.albaraka.com/default.asp?action=article&id=55

Conference held in Kuwait in 1984, a resolution was passed on four cases when the bank is required to satisfy its *zakat* obligation on behalf of its owners: (i) when the law requires the bank to satisfy the *zakat* obligation as an entity; (ii) when the bank is required by its charter or by-laws to satisfy the *zakat* obligation as an entity; (iii) when the general meeting of shareholders passes a resolution requiring the bank to satisfy the *zakat* obligation as an entity; and (iv) when individual owners authorize the bank to act as their agent in satisfying the *zakat* obligation. For instance, holders of investment accounts and other accounts as well as other parties may ask the Islamic bank to act as an agent in meeting the zakat obligation based on their interest in the bank. In addition, the bank may also receive charitable contributions from owners, depositors and others for distribution on their behalf.

Hence, if the Islamic bank is subject to *zakat*, the amount will be determined based on the bank's net assets and this total amount would then be divided between owners to enable each owner to meet his/her religious obligation personally.

Figure 9.10 Statement of Changes in Equity of Al Rayan Bank for the year ending 31 Dec 2016 (IFRS)

	Share Capital	Share Premium Account	Fair Value Reserve	Retained Deficit	Profit Stabilisation Rerserve	Toatl
	£'000s	£'000s	£'000s	£'000s	£'000s	£'000s
Balance at 1 January 2015	121 219	54 807	1 580	(74 545)	51	103 112
Profit for the year	-	-	-	10 272	-	10 272
Other comprehensive income	-	-	108	-	-	108
Reclassification of fair value reserve to profit & loss			(34)			(34)
Transfer to profit stabilisation reserve	-	-	-	(25)	25	-
Issue of ordinary share capital	-	-	-	-	-	-
Balance at 31 December 2015	**121 219**	**54 807**	**1 654**	**(64 298)**	**76**	**113 458**
Balance at 1 January 2016	121 219	54 807	1 654	(64 299)	76	113 457
Profit for the year	-	-	-	9 501	-	9 501
Other comprehensive income	-	-	1 206		-	1 206
Reclassification of fair value reserve to profit & loss			(880)			(880)
Transfer to profit stabilisation reserve	-	-	-	(19)	19	-
Issue of ordinary share capital	-	-	-	-	-	-
Balance at 31 December 2016	**121 219**	**54 807**	**1 980**	**(54 816)**	**95**	**123 285**

Source: Al Rayan Annual Report 2016, www.alrayanbank.co.uk/media/339335/al-rayan-bank-annual-report-and-financial-statements-2016-170420.pdf

Figure 9.11 Consolidated statement of changes in equity of Al Baraka Banking Group for the year ending 31 Dec 2016 (FAS)

| | Attributable to equity shareholders of the parent | | | | | | | | | | | | |
| | | | | Reserves | | Cumulative changes in fair values | | Foreign | | | | Non-controlling | Total owners' |
	Share capital US$'000	Treasury shares US$'000	Share premium US$'000	Statutory reserve US$'000	Other reserves US$'000	Investments US$'000	Property and equipment US$'000	currency translations US$'000	Retained earnings US$'000	Proposed appropriations US$'000	Total US$'000	interest US$'000	equity US$'000
Balance at 1 January 2016	1 115 746	(8 464)	17 662	124 585	40 874	2 229	36 300	(461 948)	433 631	55 787	1 356 402	738 181	2 094 583
Dividends paid	-	-	-	-	-	-	-	-	172	(22 315)	(22 143)	-	(22 143)
Bonus shares issued (note 13)	33 472	-	-	-	-	-	-	-	-	(33 472)	-	-	-
Movement in treasury shares	-	(1 124)	912	-	-	-	-	-	-	-	(212)	-	(212)
Net movement in cumulative change in fair value for investments	-	-	-	-	-	2 742	-	-	-	-	2 742	579	3 321
Net movement in other reserves	-	-	-	-	1 357	-	-	-	-	-	1 357	156	1 513
Foreign currency translation	-	-	-	-	-	-	-	(204 771)	-	-	(204 771)	(118 366)	(323 137)
Net income for the year	-	-	-	-	-	-	-	-	151 545	-	151 545	116 091	267 636
Transfer to statutory reserve	-	-	-	15 155	-	-	-	-	(15 155)	-	-		
Proposed dividends	-	-	-	-	-	-	-	-	(11 396)	11 396	-		
Proposed bonus shares	-	-	-	-	-	-	-	-	(57 461)	57 461	-		
Dividends of subsidiaries	-	-	-	-	-	-	-	-	-	-	-	(31 424)	(31 424)
Zakah paid on behalf of shareholders (Note 13)	-	-	-	-	-	-	-	-	(3 962)	-	(3 962)	-	(3 962)
Net movement in non-controlling interest	-	-	-	-	-	-	-	-	-	-	-	22 406	22 406
Balance at 31 December 2016	1 149 218	(9 588)	18 574	139 740	42 231	4 971	36 300	(666 719)	497 374	68 857	1 280 958	727 623	2 008 581

Source: Al Baraka Banking Group Annual Report 2016, www.albaraka.com/default.asp?action=article&id=55

c) Statement of Sources and Uses of Qard Funds

The Statement of Sources of *Qard* Funds represents the gross increase in funds available for lending during the period covered by the statement. The sources of such increase may come from *external sources* such as funds provided by the bank from current accounts at the bank, funds provided to the fund by owners of the Islamic bank and proceeds of prohibited earnings which the Islamic bank may make available to the fund on a temporary basis until such proceeds are properly disposed of. It may also come from *internal sources*, which include collections of loans during the period or funds deposited in the fund by individuals on a temporary or permanent basis. *Uses of Qard fund* represent the amount of gross decrease in funds available for lending during the period covered by the statement. Uses include new loans granted during the period, reimbursement of funds made available to the fund by the Islamic bank from current accounts and/or prohibited earnings, if any, and repayment of funds previously provided to the fund by individuals on a temporary basis. Fund balance in the *Qard* fund refers to the outstanding collectable loans and the other funds not loaned or used for other purposes.

9.4 Determining returns for assets and liabilities

Now that we understand the various Islamic banks' financial statements and their components, especially the Statement of Financial Position and Income Statement, we now turn our attention on how the rate of returns or the profits are determined. Before we proceed, let us recall a few points. Firstly, the sources of funds for banks are their liabilities and uses of the funds are their assets. Secondly, unlike conventional banks, the liabilities of Islamic banks consist of deposits and investments, and there is no promise of fixed returns in order to avoid *riba*. However, to entice depositors and investors, some form of return or reward is provided depending on the nature of contract. Thirdly, the assets of Islamic banks comprise of various modes of financing to avoid *riba*: *trading, profit–loss sharing, partnership, equity financing and banking services*. They generate returns to the banks and based on the nature of the contract, banks are entitled to all or some portion of the returns depending on their role. In the following sections, we will consider how Islamic banks work out the returns for themselves and for their depositors and investors.

9.4.1 RETURNS TO DEPOSITORS AND INVESTORS (BANK'S LIABILITIES)

As discussed earlier, an Islamic bank's liabilities mainly consist of deposits and investments. Figure 9.12 illustrates the various forms of liabilities and types of returns.

Figure 9.12   Islamic banks' liabilities and types of returns

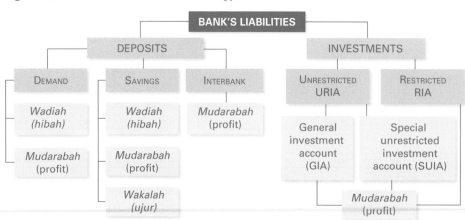

a) Demand deposits (current accounts)

Islamic banks can provide a facility for current accounts, which is also known as demand deposits accounts to individuals, societies, associations and institutions. They can be in the form of *wadiah* (guaranteed saving, i.e. the depositors are guaranteed repayment of their funds) current account or *mudarabah* (profit–loss sharing) current account.

(I) **WADIAH CURRENT ACCOUNT** These accounts are based on the principle of *wadiah* (safekeeping) whereby depositors give consent to the Islamic bank to deal with the whole or any part of money outstanding in their account in the manner that the bank deems fit and is not against *shari'ah*, provided the bank guarantees payment of the whole sum or any part thereof outstanding in the customer's account when demanded. The bank may provide a return in the form of a gift (*hibah*) to the current account holder as a token of appreciation for keeping their money with the Islamic bank. Another type of *wadiah* current account is where deposits can be withdrawn at any time and the bank pays no return, but is allowed to use these deposits profitably at its own risk. If there is profit, the bank has the discretion to give out part of the portion to the depositor on the basis of gift (*hibah*). Figure 9.13 illustrates the mechanics of *hibah* payment for *wadiah* current account.

Figure 9.13 *Hibah* payment method for *wadiah* current account

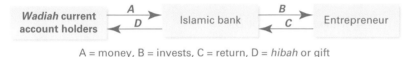

A = money, B = invests, C = return, D = *hibah* or gift

As shown in Figure 9.13, the bank receives money from the *wadiah* current account holder (A), which it then invests in a *shari'ah* compliant investment (B). When the bank receives income from its investment (C), it has the discretion to pay *wadiah* current account holders as a gift (*hibah*) as token of appreciation. The method and frequency for payment of *hibah* are at the discretion of each Islamic bank and the previous month's *hibah* rate may be displayed in the Islamic bank's premises.

An example of an Islamic bank's *hibah* rate on *wadiah* current account may be shown as follows: 1.00 per cent p.a. on any amount up to £2000, or 1.25 per cent p.a. above £2000 and 0.00 per cent below £2000, etc. Islamic banks can use either of the following formula for calculating the *hibah* amount payable to the *wadiah* current account holders:

Simple formula:

$$Hibah = P \times T \times HR$$

Where: P = Balance at the end of the period (day or months)

$$T = \frac{\text{Number of days}}{365} \text{ or } \frac{1}{365} \text{ if computed daily}$$

HR = *Hibah* rate given (determined in the previous month)

Note: If it is leap year, use 366 instead or 365.

Accumulated Daily Average (ADA) formula:

$$Hibah = \left(\frac{ADA\ balance \times HR}{365} \right)$$

$$where\ ADA\ balance = \left(\frac{Sum\ of\ end\ of\ day\ balances}{Number\ of\ days\ deposited} \right)$$

(II) MUDARABAH CURRENT ACCOUNT Besides current accounts based on *wadiah* or safekeeping, Islamic banks may also offer another form of current account based on the principle of *mudarabah*. For *mudarabah* current accounts, the depositor and the bank will agree upon the profit sharing ratio (PSR) between them at the time the deposit is accepted. The bank has discretion to pay a higher return than the contracted profit sharing to its *mudarabah* current account depositors as long as it is from the bank's shareholders' fund or from its PER. Any dividends paid in excess of the agreed sharing ratio will be treated as *hibah* or gift from the bank to its *mudarabah* current account depositors. However, the bank cannot pay less that the agreed profit sharing as a minimum.

The mechanics are the same as in Figure 9.13 except that in (D), the returns gained from the investment will be the profit to be shared with depositors based on the PSR rather than *hibah* as in the case of *wadiah* current account. The calculation of the profit rate (e.g. single rate or multi-tier) quoted is determined monthly based on the profit distribution table. Any losses will be borne by the depositor, except in cases where there is evidence of negligence by the Islamic bank in managing the depositor's funds. The method and frequency for payment of dividends shall be at the discretion of each Islamic bank. Profit payable to the depositors is determined based on the *net rate of return* derived from the distribution table. Islamic banks can use either of the following formula to calculate the profit amount payable to the depositor:

Simple formula:

$$Dividend = P \times T \times DR$$

Where:

P = balance at the end of the day or total monthly balances (average method)

$T = \dfrac{\text{Number of days}}{365}$ or $\dfrac{1}{365}$ if computed daily

DR = profit rate quoted or indicative profit rate

Note: If leap year, use 366 instead of 365.

Accumulated Daily Average (ADA) formula:

$$Dividend = \left(\frac{ADA\ balance \times DR}{365} \right)$$

Where:

$$ADA\ balance = \left(\frac{Sum\ of\ end\ of\ day\ balances}{Number\ of\ days\ deposited} \right)$$

b) Saving deposits

Islamic banks may accept an application to open a savings account subject to the applicant meeting all the requirements of each Islamic bank. The initial amount of deposit required to open the savings account shall be at the discretion of each Islamic bank or as predetermined by the central bank from time to time. The savings account is available to everyone. There are three types of saving accounts: *wadiah saving account, mudarabah saving account* and *wakalah saving account*.

(I) WADIAH SAVING ACCOUNT *Wadiah* saving account is similar to *wadiah* current account, whereby account holders deposit their surplus funds with an Islamic bank for the purpose of accumulating them over a period of time for safekeeping. The depositor grants the Islamic bank permission to utilize the money for whatever purpose permitted by *shari'ah* with a guarantee that it will be returned as and when requested by the customer. The bank can pool and utilize the funds and may at its discretion give *hibah* to the depositor especially when the bank gains high profit from its financing projects. However, in the event of a loss, the bank need not give any *hibah* to the depositor and the depositors' money in custody will not be reduced despite the loss.

Therefore, both the Islamic bank and customer equally benefits because: (i) customers may enjoy *hibah*, which is given by the Islamic bank for their money being in safe custody while not having to bear any investment risk; (ii) the rate or amount of *hibah* solely depends on the Islamic bank's discretion and it usually gives away competitive *hibah* for profitable investments in order to attract customers; (iii) the Islamic bank is not obliged to pay anything to customers if there is no profit from investment, thus the bank will not be in a disadvantaged position; and (iv) there is no *riba* involved in this account.

Islamic banks can use either of the earlier formula used for *wadiah* current account to calculate *hibah* amount payable to *wadiah* saving account holders. The method and frequency for payment are at the discretion of each Islamic bank. The returns or *hibah* rate vary from time to time and also differ from one bank to another. For example, an Islamic bank *hibah* rate on such account may be: 0.9 per cent p.a. for £1000-£5000, or 1.06 per cent p.a. up to £10 000, or 1.22 per cent p.a. for £10 000 and above.

(II) *MUDARABAH* SAVING ACCOUNT Islamic banks may also offer a saving account based on the principle of *mudarabah* (trustee profit sharing). Similar to *mudarabah* current account, the PSR will be agreed at the time of accepting the deposit and can be changed provided the account holder consents to the change. Any profit above the computed dividend amount (based on the agreed sharing ratio) shall be treated as *hibah*. Islamic banks may also, at their discretion, pay higher profits (but not lower) than the contracted PSR provided this comes from the Islamic bank's shareholders' fund or PERs.

The mechanics of the *mudarabah* saving account is similar to the *wadiah* current account, except that in step (D) in Figure 9.13, the returns gained from the bank's investment will be shared with the depositors as a profit. The method used in determining the profit rate (e.g. single rate or multi-tier) is discretionary and the calculation of the dividend rate quoted is determined monthly based on the *net rate of return* derived from the profit distribution table. However, if an Islamic bank uses the weightage formula in determining the distribution of the profit rate, this shall be at the discretion of each Islamic bank, but within the range stipulated by the central bank. Any losses will be borne by the depositor, except in cases where there is evidence of negligence by the Islamic bank in managing the depositor's funds. The method and frequency for payment of dividends shall be at the discretion of each Islamic bank and can be calculated using either of the earlier formula for *mudarabah* current account.

(III) *WAKALAH* SAVING ACCOUNT Islamic banks also offer a saving account based on the principle of *al-wakalah* (agency) whereby the bank acts as representative (*wakil*) to the depositors in managing funds. As illustrated in Figure 9.14, depositors appoint the bank as their service agent to keep their deposit and allow the agent to manage and make use of the deposit in any form, as long as it is acceptable and complies with *shari'ah* (A). Islamic banks then charge an agency fee or *ajr*, which means wage or commission imposed on a delivered service, and also provide rewards to consumers with *hibah* as a token of appreciation for permission to utilize their deposits (B). Islamic banks then allow the *mudarib* to utilize the funds for business and investment activities (C) and if there is any profit from the joint venture, it shall be shared with the Islamic bank and any loss will be borne by the *mudarib* (D).

Figure 9.14 *Ajr* payment method for *wakalah* saving account

A = money, B = *ajr* and reward, C = invests, D = return

c) *Interbank deposit*

This deposit allows Islamic banks with excess funds to channel them to other Islamic banks that face liquidity problem. Based on the principle of *mudarabah*, a deficit Islamic bank (DIB) can obtain funds invested by a surplus rich Islamic bank (SIB) based on a pre-agreed ratio. Therefore, it provides Islamic banks with the facility for funding and adjusting portfolios over the short term when market sources invest and square their short term funds. Hence, the participating Islamic banks would be able to match the funding requirements effectively and efficiently, and also promote stability in the Islamic banking system.

The period of investment can be from overnight to 12 months. The return can be based on the *gross profit rate per annum* of the investee bank. Upon maturity, DIB is liable to pay the principal invested together with the dividend derived from the use of the fund. The PSR is negotiable among both parties. The SIB at the time of negotiation would not know what the return would be, as the actual return will be crystallized towards the end of the investment period. The principal invested is repaid at the end of the period, together with a share of the profit arising from the use of the fund by the DIB. The following formula is used to calculate the profit element paid to SIB:

$$X = \frac{Prt(k)}{365}$$

Where:

X = amount of profit to be paid to the SIB
P = principal investment
r = rate of gross profit (in per cent p.a.) before distribution for investment of the DIB
t = number of days invested
k = PSR

(d) Investment deposits

Islamic banks accept investment deposits from customers for a specified period on the principle of *mudarabah*. The Islamic bank acts as the *mudarib* (agent) and the depositor as the provider of capital (*rabbul mal*) and they agree among other things, on the distribution of profits, if any, generated by the bank from the investment of the funds. The ratio of distribution may vary from time to time and in the event of loss in the investment, the depositor bears all the losses. The depositor does not participate in the management of the funds. Such PSIA can be divided into three types: *general investment accounts (GIA), special investment accounts (SGIA)* and *specific investment account (restricted) (RIA)*.

(I) GENERAL INVESTMENT ACCOUNT (GIA) This account provides absolute freedom to the Islamic bank as *mudarib* (active partner) to manage the investment of the capital. Therefore, Islamic banks will decide what is appropriate without the *rabbul mal* (account holder) laying down any restrictions as to where, how and for what purposes the fund should be invested. Under this arrangement, an Islamic bank can commingle the GIA account holders' funds with excess shareholders' funds and other funds that the Islamic bank has the right to use.

The period for GIA deposits can be less than one month and up to a period of 60 months or any other period permitted by the central bank. The minimum amount is at the discretion of each Islamic bank and all funds channelled into this account shall be deposited in a central pool, to be invested in short, medium or long term investments. GIA certificates would be issued to GIA account holders stating the amount and the tenure of the investment or the Islamic bank may require a minimum period of notification before a withdrawal is made. The investment would be automatically renewed if the account holders do not terminate their GIA upon expiry of the investment. The conditions of this account differ from those of savings accounts by virtue of: (i) higher fixed minimum amount of deposit; (ii) longer duration of deposits; and (iii) the depositor may lose some or all his funds in the event of the Islamic bank making a loss.

Figure 9.15 shows the mechanics of *mudarabah* GIA. Both the GIA holder (*rabbul mal*) and the Islamic bank (*mudarib*) agree to form a *mudarabah* contract with the former contributing the capital. They agree on the distribution of profit that y per cent and x per cent go to the *rabbul mal* and *mudarib*, respectively. The *mudarib* then invests in a project and the profit will be distributed based on the pre-agreed ratio. Any losses will be borne solely by the *rabbul mal*.

Figure 9.15 Modus operandi of *mudarabah* GIA

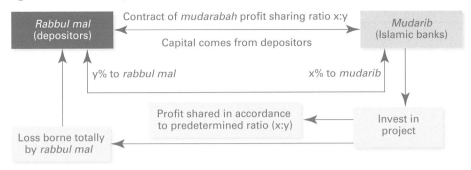

Islamic banks distribute the profit to depositors depending on the PSR, which will remain fixed until maturity of the deposit. The bank may at its discretion pay higher dividends than the contracted PSR, provided it comes from the Islamic bank's shareholders' fund or PER. The profit payable to the depositors is determined based on the *actual net rate of return* or *average actual net rate of return.*

Under the *actual net rate of return* method, profit payable to the depositor is accrued on a monthly basis and is determined based on the actual net rate of return, which is the rate directly taken from the monthly distribution table. The accrued profit is paid to the depositors, unless the depositors withdraw their deposits before maturity. Losses, if any, will be borne by the depositors, except in cases where there is evidence of negligence by the Islamic bank in managing the depositor's funds.

Under the *average actual net rate of return* method, the bank does not accrue the profit payable to depositors on a monthly basis, but instead will pay at maturity of the deposits. The amount is derived from the average actual net rate of return of each deposit based on its respective tenure. For example, the profit payable to three month GIA depositors is calculated based on the average of three months actual rate while the amount payable to six month GIA depositors is derived from the average of six months actual rate. The payment of profit in respect of deposits exceeding 12 months will be paid six months after the date of deposits. Thereafter, payment of profit will be paid every six months until maturity. Where the last period to maturity is less than six months, payment of profit will be based on the balance of the number of months to maturity and/or the total profit payable less the total interim profit paid. Hence:

Profit payable on maturity = Total profit payable − Total interim profit paid

On the maturity date, the profit is computed using the following formula:

$$Profit = \frac{P \times T \times DR}{1200} \ or \ \frac{P \times T \times DR}{365 \times 100}$$

Where:
  P = Amount of deposit (principal)
  T = Period, using number of complete months, i.e.:
      (i)   from deposit/interim profit date to maturity date or
      (ii) for interim profit – six months
  DR = profit rate quoted/indicative profit rate

In the event that the deposit is withdrawn before maturity, the profit is computed based on the number of months for which the money was deposited. Table 9.7 shows some examples of the return rate of *al-mudarabah* GIA.

(II) SPECIAL UNRESTRICTED INVESTMENT ACCOUNTS (SUIA) They also operate under the *mudarabah* principle whereby the funds, either short term or long term, are managed separately and the utilization of the funds is identified

Table 9.7 The returns of *al mudarabah* GIA

Maturity	Profit sharing ratio	Rate of return p.a.
1 month	65:35	3.18%
6 months	62:38	3.51%
12 months	58:42	3.73%
16 months	56:44	3.74%
20 months	54:46	3.74%
24 months	53:47	3.91%
25 months	53:47	3.90%
33 months	53:47	3.90%
34 months	53:47	3.89%
36 months	53:47	3.99%

and matched with specific funds. SUIA holders may stipulate that the Islamic bank will only invest the funds in specific projects or in projects within a specific sector. The operations of the SUIA must be agreed upon by all parties involved in the contract.

Islamic banks normally accept funds with some minimum amount and this is more suitable for high net worth customers. Subject to the minimum tenure, SUIA does not have a predetermined investment account period. Profit is paid upon its realization, liquidation or maturity, and computed using either of the following formulas:

$$Profit = \frac{P \times T \times DR}{365}$$

Where:

P = Amount of deposit (principal)

T = Period, using number of days:

    (i)   from deposit date or last interim profit date to maturity date or

    (ii)   for interim profit, 1 month minimum (at the discretion of the bank)

DR = Profit rate quoted or indicative profit rate

Or alternatively:

$$Profit = P \times k$$

Where:

P = Profit realized

k = PSR

In addition, it is at the Islamic bank's discretion whether to allow the depositor to withdraw before maturity and to distribute any share of the profit.

(III) SPECIFIC INVESTMENT ACCOUNT OR RESTRICTED INVESTMENT ACCOUNT (RIA) The SIA holder creates a contract with Islamic banks to invest his funds, which are restricted for a certain purpose; hence it is also known as restricted investment account (RIA). The restrictions imposed include where and how the funds should be invested and the banks may also be restricted from commingling their own funds with that of RIA funds. Therefore, the Islamic bank may utilize their funds based on a two-tier *mudharabah*, where the Islamic bank invests its depositors' money in established companies and investments. Under this model, the investor or depositor (*rabbul mal*) places money in the Islamic bank who will act as an investment manager (*mudarib*) and simultaneously becomes an investor (*rabbul mal*) by investing the investment fund in selected *shari'ah* compliant companies and investment funds, with all of the selected companies becoming *mudarib*. Through this model, the Islamic bank's main business is to obtain funds from the public on the basis of *mudarabah* and to supply funds to entrepreneurs also on the *mudarabah* basis. There is usually a minimum acceptance of deposits. The gross income comprises the share in the actual profits of the fund users, in accordance with an agreed ratio of profit sharing (e.g. Islamic bank 20: customer 80) and the actual income, after deducting the expenses incurred in managing the funds, is distributed in accordance with the predetermined PSR.

In order to attract public attention to invest in one of these accounts, Islamic banks will draw their *indicative rate of return*, which is based on prediction in accordance with the Islamic bank's previous performance. Hence, the Islamic bank is not obliged to pay out the profit based on the indicative rate but instead the *effective rate* or the actual rate of return at the time of maturity based on the actual amount of profit to be distributed to investors.

The profit rate of the special investment account is determined based on the PSR. Weightage used to determine the distribution of return of the various PSRs is at the discretion of each Islamic bank, subject to the range regulated by the central bank. The profit on maturity is computed using the following formula:

$$Profit = \frac{P \times T \times DR}{36\,500}$$

Where:

P = Amount of deposit (principal)

T = Period, using number of days:

    (i)   From deposit date or last interim profit date to maturity date; or

    (ii) For interim profit, 1 month (at the discretion of the bank)

$$DR = \frac{profit\ rate\ quoted}{indicative\ profit\ rate}$$

To calculate the indicative rate of returns, the Islamic bank may use a simplified formula as follows:

Profit = Rate of Return (ROR) $\times$ Profit Sharing Ratio (PSR) divided by 100
          = one year profit rate

For example, the rate of return (ROR) for the year is 3 per cent and the customer will be given 70 per cent predetermined PSR. Hence:

$$Profit = 3 \times \left(\frac{70}{100}\right) = 2.10$$

Thus, the 2.10 per cent in the above calculation is only an *indicative rate based* on the previous ROR, and it will be highlighted by the Islamic bank to attract public confidence on its financial performance. Table 9.8 provides an example of indicative ROR for RIA.

Table 9.8 PSR and indicative ROR for RIA

Period	Profit sharing ratio (PSR)	Rate of return (ROR) p.a.
1 month	66:34	3.13%
3 months	67:33	3.34%
6 months	64:36	3.51%
9 months	62:38	3.64%
12 months	62:38	3.87%
15 months	60:40	3.89%
18 months	58:42	3.91%
21 months	55:45	3.84%
24 months	55:45	3.95%
36 months	55:45	4.05%
48 months	55:45	4.15%
60 months and above	55:45	4.26%

9.4.2   PROFIT EQUALIZATION RESERVE (PER)

Recall that one unique feature of Islamic banks is the PER which is set up to enable the banks to mitigate the undesirable fluctuations of income and to remain competitive, particularly in terms of deposit rates. Islamic banks are allowed to make monthly provisions of up to 15 per cent of the gross income plus net trading income, other income and irregular income up to a maximum accumulated PER of 30 per cent of the bank's equity shareholders' funds. The calculation for the PER is given in the following formula:

*Profit equalization reserve (**maximum monthly provision**)*
$$= (15\% \times gross\ income) + net\ trading\ income + other\ income + irregular\ income$$

9.4.3   NET DISTRIBUTABLE INCOME IN THE INCOME STATEMENT

The last item in an Islamic bank's Income Statement is the net distributable income. The net distributable income attributable to the depositors is calculated based on two steps. Firstly, it involves calculating the *weighted average rate of return* (WAR) of each asset based on the income generated by all Islamic banking assets. Thus, the WAR per annum of each asset is derived from the following formula:

$$WAR = \left(\frac{income}{average\ daily\ amount\ of\ asset}\right) \times \left(\frac{365}{number\ of\ days\ for\ the\ month}\right) \times 100\%$$

The second step involves finding the WAR based on net income which is derived after making relevant allowances (such as general allowance, specific allowance, impairment loss and provisions for commitment and contingencies), PER, direct expenses, other expenses and income attributable to Islamic bank and various depositors before arriving at the net income. The WAR of net income therefore represents the percentage of income attributable to funds other than specific investment deposits (SID) and Islamic banking capital funds (IBCF) or shareholders' funds (SHF) which can be calculated using the following formula:

$$WAR\ of\ net\ income = \left(\frac{net\ income}{average\ daily\ amount\ of\ (total\ funds - SID - IBCF\ (or\ SHF))}\right)$$
$$\times \left(\frac{365}{number\ of\ days\ for\ the\ month}\right) \times 100\%$$

Total funds in the above formula refers to the total amount of deposits accepted, amount due to other financial institutions, bank's shareholders' funds, converted funds (i.e. placement of conventional funds in bank's operations) and other funds. The WAR of the net distributable income shows the percentage of income over other deposits or funds that are not included in the calculation of income attributable to the depositors. Islamic banks can then form a distribution table for each current, savings and general investment deposit. Table 9.9 is a template showing distribution of the income for each type of deposits: average daily amount of deposit (ADA) [column 2], weightage [column 3], weighted average daily amount (WADA) [column 4], distributable profit [columns 5 and 6], and depositors' [columns 7-9] and Islamic bank's [columns 10-12] portion of distributable profit. The table sets out the distribution of the net distributable income calculated for demand, savings and general investment deposits according to their structures (*mudarabah* or non-*mudarabah*), maturities and the pre-agreed PSRs between the bank and depositors.

The distributable profit for *mudarabah* and non-*mudarabah* deposits are calculated first before it can be distributed to other depositors and shareholders, using the following formula:

Distributable profit for mudarabah deposit

$$= \left(\frac{Total\ average\ daily\ amount\ of\ mudarabah\ deposits}{Total\ average\ daily\ amount\ of\ deposits}\right)$$
$$\times Total\ distributable\ profit$$

Table 9.9 Template of Distribution table for different types of deposits

Types of deposit	ADA	Weightage	WADA	Distributable profit		Depositor			Islamic bank		
	($)		($)	($)	(%)	PSR	($)	(%)	PSR	($)	(%)
Non-*mudarabah:*											
Wadish CA											
Wadiah SA											
Mudarabah:											
CA											
SA											
GIA											
1-month											
2-month											
⋮ ⋮	⋮ ⋮	⋮ ⋮	⋮ ⋮	⋮ ⋮	⋮ ⋮	⋮ ⋮	⋮ ⋮	⋮ ⋮	⋮ ⋮	⋮ ⋮	⋮ ⋮
12-month											
15-month											
⋮ ⋮	⋮ ⋮	⋮ ⋮	⋮ ⋮	⋮ ⋮	⋮ ⋮	⋮ ⋮	⋮ ⋮	⋮ ⋮	⋮ ⋮	⋮ ⋮	⋮ ⋮
60-month											
SGIA											

The profit distribution for each category of deposit (*mudarabah* and non-*mudarabah*: Column 5) can be calculated by using the following formula:

Distributable profit for type of mudarabah deposit

$$= \left(\frac{WADA}{\textit{Total weighted average daily amount of mudarabah deposits}} \right)$$
$$\times \textit{Distributable profit of mudarabah deposit}$$

From the above formula, the percentage of distributable profit for each type of deposits per annum (column 6) (referred to it as gross ROR) is calculated based on the following formula:

Gross rate of return

$$= \left(\frac{\textit{Distributable profit}}{\textit{Average daily amount of deposits}} \right) \times \left(\frac{365}{\textit{number of days for the month}} \right) \times 100\%$$

The distributable profits are distributed to the depositors and the bank's shareholders according to the PSR of the respective deposit types and tenures. However, the total amount of depositors' (column 8) and Islamic banks' (column 11) profit portions must be equal to the total distributable profit (column 5). In percentage form (columns 9 and 12), the distributable profit to depositors and Islamic banks per annum (or known as net ROR) can be derived as follows:

$$\textit{Net rate of return} = \textit{Gross rate} \times PSR$$

Note that the preceding calculation is only applicable for unrestricted funds. For restricted funds, all income and expenses reported in each fund's financial statement are disclosed as in the template of Table 9.9, clearly identifying and matching with the utilization of the specific funds. But, for the unrestricted funds, the attributable income can be derived from:

Income attributable to shareholder

> = (*Shareholder funds/total unrestricted funds*)
>
> × (*net gross income after special investment deposits*
>
> − *income solely belonging to the Islamic bank*)
>
> + *other income solely belonging to the Islamic bank*

9.4.4 ZAKAT DISTRIBUTION

Zakat, the third pillar of Islam, must be paid on all wealth that gives a financial return. The obligation applies when it reaches a threshold called the *nisab. Zakat* provision is calculated based on 2.5 per cent of the *net invested funds* or *net assets method.* Using the **net assets method**, the *zakat* base is determined as follows:

> **Zakat base**
>
> = *Assets subject to zakat*
>
> − *liabilities that are due to be paid during the year ending on the date of the statement of the financial position*
>
> + *equity of unrestricted investment accounts*
>
> + *minority interest + equity owned by government*
>
> + *equity owned by endowment funds + equity owned by charities*
>
> + *equity belonging to non-profit organizations excluding those that are owned by individuals*

Assets subject to *zakat* include cash and cash equivalents, receivables net of provisions for doubtful debts, assets acquired for trading (example, inventory, marketable securities, real estate, etc.), and financing assets, i.e. those assets where the net provisions may fall in value or are non-collectable (example, *mudarabah, musharakah, salam* and *istisna'a,* etc.). Funds used to acquire fixed assets relating to financing assets are deducted. Assets acquired for trading are measured at their cash equivalent value on the date on which the *zakat* is due. Using the **net invested funds method**, the *zakat* base is determined as follows:

> **Zakat base**
>
> = *Paid-up capital + reserves + provision not deducted from assets + retained earnings*
> + *net income*
> + *liabilities that are not due to be paid during the year ending on the date of the statement of financial position*
> − (*net fixed assets + investments not acquired for trading, e.g. real estate for rent + accumulated losses*)

The two methods are strictly equivalent provided their items are classified and valued consistently with due consideration given to the different valuation bases.

9.5 Evaluating the performance of Islamic banks

Banks play an important role in the economy, as they help to facilitate the flow of money from the surplus units to the deficit units, which in turn help to spur economic growth. Hence, it is not surprising that any problems in the banking system will have significant impact on the economy, as we have seen in the recent financial crisis. Since then, many studies have been conducted comparing the performance of conventional and Islamic banks (see for example, Olson and Zoubi, 2008; Beck, Demirgüç-Kunt and Merrouche, 2013). Results suggest that Islamic banks are less likely to disintermediate[3] during crises as they are better capitalized and have higher asset quality (Beck *et al.*, 2013). In other words, an equity based system can absorb banking crisis better.

Based on the structure of the Statement of Financial Position we discussed earlier, it is clear that funds available for an Islamic bank to fund its activities comes from general depositors, investors (restricted and unrestricted), liabilities (e.g. *murabahah* and *wakalah* payables, *sukuk*, current accounts and other liabilities) and owners' capital (share capital and reserves) while funds in conventional banks are only from depositors, liabilities and equity. The difference in the structure is illustrated in Figure 9.16. It is not surprising that the typical Islamic bank's biggest funding comes from long term investors (51 per cent) whereas customers' deposits are the main source for a typical conventional bank (68 per cent). Also, notice that the equity (19 per cent) of Islamic banks is also higher than conventional banks (14 per cent).

Figure 9.16   **Breakdown of equity and liabilities of a typical Islamic and conventional bank**

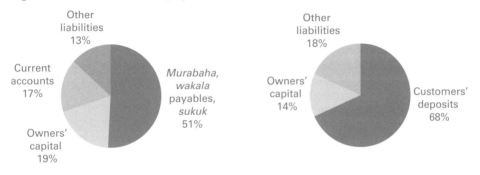

Islamic Bank – equity and liabilities   **Conventional Bank – equity and liabilities**

Similarly, the assets of Islamic banks are composed of various modes of financing, while assets of conventional banks are mainly loans. Figure 9.17 presents the breakdown of the assets components of an Islamic and conventional bank. It is clear that the assets in Islamic banks have wider spread of financial instruments such as *murabahah, mudarabah* and *ijarah* compared to the assets of conventional banks where the majority are interest based loans (58 per cent) and cash accounts (16 per cent).

Given the significant changes in the financial sector in terms of regulations and operating environment characterized by intense competition, pressure to reduce control costs, effective risk management while maximizing revenues and shareholders' wealth, assessment of bank performance is vital to signal of any potential problems early. Furthermore, given the different structure and dual objectives of Islamic banks, analyzing their performance may help ensure their sustainability in this sector.

In the following sections, we will discuss the various tools available to assess banks' performance. The most common tool is *financial ratio analysis* which helps in assessing past and current trends and also determining future estimates of bank performance in various aspects such as profitability, asset quality, capital adequacy, efficiency and solvency. Another tool often used is the *CAMELS* rating model which stand for **C**apital adequacy, **A**sset quality, **M**anagement quality, **E**arnings quality, **L**iquidity and **S**ensitivity to market risk. Over recent years, the *EAGLES* framework, which stands for **E**arnings ability, **A**sset quality, **G**rowth, **L**iquidity, **E**fficiency and **S**trategic management, has been introduced by researchers. Another development in narrative reporting is greater emphasis being given to *key performance indicators* (KPIs), which include both financial and non-financial information to enable bank's management to monitor and review their strategies. We will now consider each of these tools.

---

[3]This generally refers to the act of removing funds from the intermediary financial institutions to invest directly or to divert funds from low income yield savings to invest directly in high income yield financial instruments.

Figure 9.17   Breakdown of assets components of a typical Islamic and conventional bank

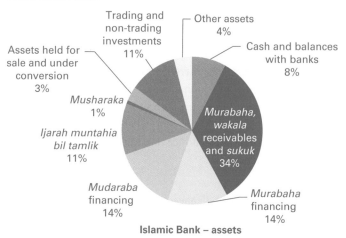

Islamic Bank – assets

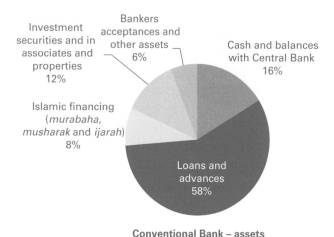

Conventional Bank – assets

9.5.1   FINANCIAL RATIO ANALYSIS

Financial ratio analysis is the most widely used tool in assessing performance of any type of business entity. The numbers are mainly extracted from the two most important financial statements, the Statement of Financial Position or Balance Sheet, and the Statement of Comprehensive Income or the Income Statement. It is best to compare the ratio figures over two periods or longer to get a better sense of the performance trend of the bank. Similarly, comparison of performance can be made across a number of banks or with the industry benchmark to get a sense of the relative position of a bank's performance against its selected competitors or against the whole industry.

The various ratios can be classified into a number of aspects for assessing performance. For the banking sector, they can be classified into five main groups: *profitability and sustainability, efficiency and productivity, portfolio quality, growth and outreach* and *financial structure*. Figure 9.18 presents the classification of financial ratios relevant to the banking industry.

a) Profitability and sustainability

This set of ratios reflects the ability of Islamic banks to continue operating in the future. The *rabbul mal* and shareholders are interested in banks which have good sustainability potential. Some of the basic profitability/ sustainability ratios include the following:

Figure 9.18 Classification of ratios for evaluating performance of banks

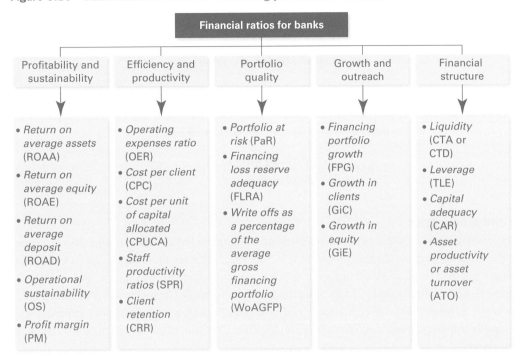

(I) RETURN ON AVERAGE ASSETS (ROAA) This measures the net operating income as a percentage of average total assets. It reveals how much net income is generated per £1 of assets held by the bank. The higher the ratio, the better, as it indicates that the bank is able to mobilize its assets to generate income.

$$ROAA = \frac{Net\ operating\ income}{Average\ total\ assets}$$

(II) RETURN ON AVERAGE EQUITY (ROAE) This is the most important ratio of bank's profitability and growth potential. It is the rate of return to shareholders or the percentage return on each £1 of equity invested in the bank. A higher ratio indicates ability to provide higher returns to equity contributors or shareholders. It must be borne in mind that in a dual objective (social and profitable) organization such an Islamic bank, the high returns will also be paid as profit or *hibah* to the depositors and others.

$$ROAE = \frac{Net\ operating\ income}{Average\ total\ equity}$$

(III) RETURN ON AVERAGE DEPOSIT (ROAD) This measures the net operating income as a percentage of average total deposits. It reveals how well the Islamic bank uses its deposits to generate profit, i.e. how much profit the bank can generate for every £1 of deposits held. The higher the ratio, the better the bank is able to generate profits from the deposits.

$$ROAD = \frac{Net\ operating\ income}{Average\ total\ deposits}$$

(IV) OPERATIONAL SUSTAINABILITY (OS) Operational sustainability is also known as *operational self-sufficiency*. This is measured as the ratio between operating income and the operating and financial expenses. If the ratio is greater than 100 per cent, it means that the Islamic bank is able to cover all of its costs through its own operations without having to rely on other contributions to survive.

$$OS = \frac{Net\ operating\ income}{Operating\ and\ financial\ expenses}$$

(V) PROFIT MARGIN (PM) This measures net operating income as a percentage of total income. This ratio shows how much of the income earned goes to the bottom line. In other words, it indicates how much income remains after deducting all expenses for every £1 of income earned. Hence, a higher ratio is better.

$$PM = \frac{Net\ operating\ income}{Total\ income}$$

b) Efficiency and productivity

This group of ratios measure the efficiency of management in utilizing the bank's funds in generating income. They require close scrutiny because the most important factors that influence these ratios can be controlled directly by management. In a competitive environment, efficiency and productivity are important means to gain a competitive edge. Hence, decisions about financing methods, financing terms (financing size, maturities, etc.), and markets in which to operate also affect efficiency and productivity. Staffing, administrative expenses and client base are equally important variables. There are many efficiency indicators but five of the most common ratios will be considered.

(I) OPERATING EXPENSES RATIO (OER) AND PORTFOLIO YIELD (PY) OER is operating expenses as a percentage of average portfolios. It reveals how much the bank spends to maintain its outstanding financing portfolio. This ratio goes hand in hand with PY which is the percentage of financial income to average portfolio. It allows the user to easily compare the expenses of the Islamic bank with its revenue. For instance, if the portfolio yield is 50 per cent, then the Islamic bank must strive for the operating expense ratio to be lower than 50 per cent.

$$OER = \frac{Operating\ expenses}{Average\ financing\ portfolio}$$

$$PY = \frac{Financial\ income}{Average\ financing\ portfolio}$$

(II) COST PER CLIENT (CPC) This figure shows how much it costs the Islamic bank to serve clients. It simply requires dividing operating expenses by the average number of clients for the period. The lower the ratio the better, as it indicates that the bank is efficient in controlling its operating costs.

$$CPC = \frac{Operating\ expenses}{Average\ number\ of\ clients}$$

(III) COST PER UNIT OF CAPITAL ALLOCATED (CPUCA) This shows how much it costs the Islamic bank to service £1 of financing. It is calculated by dividing operating expenses by the value of financing allocated in the period. The lower the ratio the better, as it indicates that the bank is efficient in controlling the cost of financing. The cost per unit of capital allocated should fall as the bank grows.

$$CPUCA = \frac{Operating\ expenses}{Total\ financing}$$

(IV) STAFF PRODUCTIVITY RATIO (SPR) Staff productivity is a vital ratio for all banks, as staff constitute the largest operating expense. Two ratios can be calculated for this purpose: (i) *the number of active clients served by each member of staff*, and (ii) *how much financing is managed by each member of staff*. Higher ratios signal bank's staff efficiency.

$$SPR = \frac{Number\ of\ active\ clients}{Number\ of\ staff}$$

$$SPR = \frac{Total\ financing}{Number\ of\ staff}$$

(V) CLIENT RETENTION RATIO (CRR) It is generally more expensive to get new clients than to retain existing ones. New clients must be sought out and require greater monitoring. Furthermore, new clients usually have smaller than average financing and therefore generate less financial income. Hence, it is in the interest of Islamic banks to focus on retaining good clients as it costs less to retain a customer than it does to replace a customer. This ratio is calculated by dividing the number of clients who left during the year by the total number of clients at the end of the year. The lower the ratio, the better is the retention rate.

$$CRR = \frac{Number\ of\ clients\ who\ left\ during\ the\ year}{Total\ number\ of\ clients\ at\ the\ end\ of\ the\ year}$$

c) Portfolio quality

The financing portfolio is the engine that drives a financial institution. The product availability, quality and price are important in running a successful Islamic bank. Since an Islamic bank receives revenue over a period of time rather than a lump sum at the time of 'sale' (financing disbursement), the bank must continue to track the quality of the financing to ensure that it is able to collect the revenue due long after the 'sale' of the financing is complete. High quality financing means low defaulting. The following ratios indicate how well credit risks are being managed and how the Islamic bank's profitability is being affected by losses.

(I) PORTFOLIO AT RISK (PAR) It is now standard practice to calculate the *portfolio at risk* as any late payment will put the entire financing balance at risk. Although most formal reporting of defaulting does not occur until 30, 60, 90, 120 or 180 days, even the minimum 30 days is indicative of either a problem with administration with the collections or with the collection itself. Also, if the financing maturities are short and payments are frequent (weekly or bi-weekly), then financing that past 30 days could mean two to four payments being late, which is obviously very serious. Portfolio at Risk (PaR) is calculated by dividing the outstanding balance of all loans with arrears over 30 days by the outstanding gross portfolio at a certain date. Since the ratio is often used to measure loans affected by arrears of more than 60, 90, 120 and 180 days, the number of days must be clearly stated (for example PaR30). If the PaR moves from past 30 days to 180 days, this clearly suggests that the bank is inefficient in pursuing defaulting clients and its earnings will be at risk.

$$PaR30 = \frac{Outstanding\ loan\ balance\ past\ 30\ days}{Outstanding\ loan\ portfolio}$$

(II) FINANCING LOSS RESERVE ADEQUACY (FLRA) Besides PaR, Islamic banks should have a policy on creating a financing loss reserve such that the size of this reserve is directly related to the portfolio at risk. Central banks have developed standards for such reserves. The requirement is based on the estimated risk of not receiving the full amount of the financing. For example, financings that passed the 30 days threshold may have a 10 per cent risk of default, while financings past 100 days or more may have a 75 per cent risk of default. For each period, the Islamic bank sets aside funds in the form of a *financing loss reserve* which reflects the current PaR. It is important for management to monitor the adequacy of the financing loss reserve. It is measured by the amount of actual financing loss reserves divided by the required or suggested financing loss reserves.

$$FLRA = \frac{(Actual\ financing - loss\ reserves)}{(Required\ financing - loss\ reserves)}$$

(III) WRITE OFFS OF THE AVERAGE GROSS FINANCING PORTFOLIO (WOAGFP) This ratio indicates the amount of financings which were restated from 'at risk' to uncollectable during the period. Write offs pose the greatest risk to any bank because they are financings that the bank has determined as uncollectable, which may not only cause the bank to lose financial income on a written off financing, but also the financing principal that is outstanding. However, it should be noted that the amount written off is an accounting procedure and not an operational decision. Accordingly, the bank should not cease attempts to collect the full amount of the financings. Financings may still be recovered through collection procedures long after they are taken off the books, so it is important for management to monitor how successful they have been in recovering the written off financings. Such recoveries will help minimize the effect of previously written off financings. Large write offs reflect poor management procedures for client selection and financing approvals, or for the collection of defaulting financings.

$$WoAGFP = \frac{(Write\ offs\ of\ uncollectable\ financing - loss\ reserves)}{Average\ gross\ financing\ portfolio}$$

d) Growth and outreach

Growth is an important target to monitor, as new clients are the basis for revenue and asset growth. In general, growth can be calculated by dividing the difference in the amount at the beginning and at the end by the initial amount. There are three key areas of growth that management should monitor.

(I) FINANCING PORTFOLIO GROWTH (FPG) Financing activities are the engine of revenue growth. Therefore, it is important for an Islamic bank to exhibit long term growth of its financing portfolio. A positive figure indicates growth while a negative figure suggests a decline.

$$FPG = \frac{(Financing\ portfolio\ at\ end\ of\ period - Initial\ financing\ portfolio)}{Initial\ financing\ portfolio}$$

(II) GROWTH IN CLIENTS (GIC) This is a good indicator of future revenues. As the number of clients increase, the financing portfolio and revenues will also increase. Net growth equals new clients minus the clients who have left the bank. Client withdrawal is critical in assessing client satisfaction and loyalty.

$$GiC = \frac{(Total\ clients\ at\ end\ of\ period - Initial\ number\ of\ clients)}{Initial\ number\ of\ clients}$$

(III) GROWTH IN EQUITY (GIE) This is the foundation for future asset growth. It also reveals the efficiency of the bank in transferring revenues to equity, thereby enabling the institution to grow.

$$GiE = \frac{(Total\ equity\ at\ end\ of\ period - Initial\ equity)}{Initial\ equity}$$

e) Financial structure

The basis of financial intermediation is the ability to manage assets (the use of funds) and liabilities (the source of funds). Asset/liability management is required at several levels:

(i) *liquidity management,* as the bank must also make sure that it has sufficient funds available to meet any short term obligations, i.e. sufficient liquidity

(ii) *leverage,* as the bank seeks to acquire funds to increase its assets which in turn may increase revenue. Increased revenue usually leads to increased net profit, which is vital for commercial institutions with shareholders. However, acquiring too much funds may put the bank at risk as it may be unable to repay its liabilities in times of trouble

(iii) *asset management,* as funds should be used to create assets that produce the most revenue, i.e. most productive assets

(iv) *profit management,* as the bank must make sure that its use of funds will generate more revenue than the cost of funds

(v) *equity management,* as this maintains the quality of capital.

In short, this final group of ratios focuses on liquidity, solvency, capital adequacy and asset productivity.

(I) LIQUIDITY RATIO Lack of cash is a primary reason for the failure of most banks. Hence, liquidity ratio gauges the risk of insufficient reserves of liquid assets (cash) in response to withdrawal demands of deposit consumers. There are two measures:

$$Cash\ to\ assets\ (CTA) = \frac{Total\ cash}{Total\ assets}$$

$$Cash\ to\ deposits\ (CTD) = \frac{Total\ cash}{Total\ deposits}$$

(II) LEVERAGE RATIO The leverage ratio shows the relationship between liabilities and equity. Liabilities must be repaid, whereas equity may be used for any purpose. It is important that the bank leverages its equity, but it should not take on so many liabilities that it might be unable to pay them back in the future.

$$Total\ liabilities\ to\ equity\ (TLE) = \frac{Total\ liabilities}{Total\ equity}$$

(III) CAPITAL ADEQUACY RATIO (CAR) One of the major concerns for banks is having enough capital. This is assessed based on what is known as the capital adequacy ratio, where the bank's capital is expressed as a percentage of a bank's risk weighted credit exposures. To ensure that banks are able to absorb losses rather than becoming insolvent, banking regulators set a minimum capital adequacy ratio that banks should follow. This will help in protecting depositors, as well as promoting the stability and efficiency of financial systems around the world. The capital adequacy ratio is calculated as follows:

$$CAR = \frac{(Tier\ 1\ capital\ +\ Tier\ 2\ capital)}{Risk\ weighted\ assets}$$

As can be seen in the above equation, a bank's capital is classified as Tier 1 and Tier 2. Tier 1 capital is the sum of a bank's equity capital, its disclosed reserves and its non-redeemable, non-cumulative preferred stock. These items can absorb losses without requiring the bank to cease trading. On the other hand, Tier 2 capital is treated as supplementary capital and it includes items such as revaluation reserves, undisclosed reserves, hybrid instruments and subordinated term debt. As for the denominator, the bank's risk weighted assets include all assets that it holds that are systematically weighted for credit risk. The weighting scale differs based on asset classes and typically cash would have a weight of 0 per cent, while loans of increasing credit risk would carry weights of 20 per cent, 50 per cent or 100 per cent. The target for the bank is to meet the minimum threshold set by the regulator. If the CAR is higher than the minimum threshold, this means that the bank is safe.

(IV) ASSET PRODUCTIVITY OR ASSET TURNOVER (ATO) This ratio highlights the extent of efficiency of the bank based on its asset structure. Generally, financings are the most lucrative account on the Balance Sheet because they generate a high rate of financial income. Hence, banks wish to maintain a high percentage of its assets in the financing portfolio, in order to be productive and profitable.

$$ATO = \frac{Net\ income}{Total\ assets}$$

9.5.2 CAMELS RATING FRAMEWORK

CAMELS stand for **C**apital adequacy, **A**sset quality, **M**anagement, **E**arning, **L**iquidity and **S**ensitivity to market risk. CAMELS rating system is to be evaluated on the scale of one to five rating in ascending order. However, the six categories do not receive equal weighting in determining the composite rating. A composite rating of 3 indicates that the bank has some problems that need to be corrected, while a rating of 4 or 5 signifies that there is a reasonable chance that the bank might fail in the near term as a result of its problems. Table 9.10 presents the description and meaning of the CAMELS rating system.

Table 9.10 Composite range of CAMELS rating

Rating	Composite range	Description	Meaning
1	1.00–1.49	strong	• basically sound in every respect • findings are of minor nature and can be handled routinely • resistant to external economic and financial disturbances • no cause for supervisory concern
2	1.5–2.49	satisfactory	• fundamentally sound • finding are of minor nature and can be handled routinely • stable and can withstand business fluctuations well • supervisory concerns are limited to extent that findings are corrected
3	2.50–3.49	fair	• financial, operational or compliance weaknesses ranging from moderately severe to unsatisfactory • vulnerable to the onset of adverse business conditions • could easily deteriorate if actions are not effective in correcting weaknesses • supervisory concern and more than normal supervision needed to address deficiencies
4	3.50–4.49	marginal	• immoderate volume of serious financial weaknesses • unsafe and unsafe conditions may exist which are not being satisfactory addressed • without corrections, these conditions could develop further and impair future viability • high potential for failure • close supervision surveillance and a definite plan for correcting deficiencies
5	4.50–5.00	unsatisfactory	• high immediate or near term probability failure • severity of weaknesses is so critical that urgent aid from stockholders or other financial sources is necessary • without immediate corrective actions, will likely require liquidation, merger or acquisition

Capital adequacy determines the ability of the bank to meet with its obligations on time and other risks such as operational risk, credit risk, etc. Better capitalized banks will be less adversely affected by a systemic bank crisis. It is measured by the ratio of total capital to risk weighted assets (CAR). The higher the value of this ratio, the lower the risk associated with the bank. BASEL III requires banks to maintain a value in the range of 8 per cent to 10.5 per cent. In other words, CAR of less than the 8 per cent benchmark should be of concern to the bank.

Asset quality refers to the quality of bank's assets, specifically, loans given to customers in the case of conventional banks, as they will generate earnings and also affect both cost and economies of scale for the banks. Asset quality and loan quality are often used interchangeably. However, in the case of Islamic banks, asset quality of banks refers to the various modes of financing and investment instead of loans. Low quality assets have higher possibility to become non-performing assets, usually in the form of bad debts that are in default or are near to being in default. There is no specific standard on the length of default to be considered as non-performing assets or loans, but most banks use three months as the threshold. It can be calculated by dividing net non-performing assets (total non-performing assets minus the provision for non-performing assets) by total advances and then multiply by 100 to get a percentage figure. A low asset quality ratio indicates good bank performance.

Management capability is not a straight forward assessment as it tends to be based more on qualitative rather than quantitative factors. Nevertheless, one quantitative measure that is often adopted is *management expenses to total deposits*; a low ratio indicates that management has good ability in handling the costs of the bank operations.

Earnings are important for banks in order to stay in the market for a longer period of time, to satisfy shareholder and to protect and improve its capital. ROAA and ROAE are the two important measures for banks. ROAA avoids the volatility of earnings linked with unusual items, and measures the profitability of the bank; a higher ratio indicates greater profitability. ROAE shows the efficiency of the bank in utilizing its own capital; a high ratio indicates efficient utilization of equity.

Liquidity management is an important aspect of banks, as they need to ensure that they have the ability to convert their financial assets into cash in a rapid manner or in a quick succession to service financial obligations when they become due or on demand from depositors.

Sensitivity to market risk refers to the extent to which the bank's earnings and capital can be adversely affected by changes in exchange rate, interest rate, equity price or commodity price although most consider changes in interest rates as market risk.

Table 9.11 shows the rating guideline when conducting CAMELS ratio analysis.

Table 9.11 CAMELS ratio analysis and rating guideline

	Component	Ratio	Weight[4]	1	2	3	4	5
C	Capital adequacy	CAR = (Tier I[1]+Tier II[2]) / Risk weighted Assets*100	20%	> 11%	8% – 11%	4% – 8%	1% – 4%	< 1%
A	Asset quality	(Total non-performing assets – provision for non-performing assets) / Advances *100	20%	< 1.5%	1.5% – 3.5%	3.5% – 7%	7% – 9.5%	> 9.5%
M	Management	Administrative expenses / Total earning *100	25%	< 25%	30% – 26%	38% – 31%	45% – 39%	> 46%
E	Earnings (ROAA)	NPBT[3] / Average total assets	15%	> 1.5%	1.25% – 1.5%	1% – 1.25%	0.75% – 1%	< 0.75%
	Earnings (ROAE)	NP / Average equity capital	22%	> 22%	17% – 22%	10% – 17%	7% – 10%	< 7%
L	Liquidity (L1)	Advances / Deposits	10%	< 60%	60% – 65%	65% – 70%	70% – 80%	> 80%
	Liquidity (L2)	Circulating Assets / Total assets	10%	< 60%	60% – 65%	65% – 70%	70% – 80%	> 80%
S	Sensitivity	Total securities / Total assets	10%	> 80%	70% – 80%	65% – 70%	60% – 65%	< 60%

Notes: [1]Tier I Capital = common stock + preferred stock + retain earnings. [2]Tier II Capital = undisclosed reserves + subordinate term debt + general provision, revaluation reserves. [3]NPBT: Net Profit before Tax. [4]The weight is just a guideline to be decided by management. For earnings and liquidity, there are two measures, and management can decide which measure to use, so this column adds up to more than 100 per cent in this table.

9.5.3 EAGLES FRAMEWORK

While the CAMELS rating has long been a popular tool used for assessing bank performance, more recently researchers have introduced the EAGLES framework. The key success factors for evaluating banks based on this framework are **E**arnings ability, **A**sset quality, **G**rowth, **L**iquidity, **E**fficiency and **S**trategic management.

Earnings ability is assessed by two measures namely *return on average assets (ROAA)* and *return on average shareholders' funds or equity (ROAE)*. As for *asset quality,* it is assessed based on the ratio of *gross impairment to total loans;* and the higher the value of this ratio, the lower would be the asset quality.

Growth, which can be assessed based on growth in bank's loans and advances and growth in its core deposits, is an important aspect for the bank as it reflects how well it has positioned itself in the market for long term sustainability. When the growth in core deposits is higher than growth in loans, this denotes that the bank has positioned itself in attracting more depositors which is usually by giving higher returns on those deposits. Likewise, when the growth in loans is higher than growth in core deposits, this implies that the bank has positioned itself in attracting more borrowers by charging lower lending rates. High growth in either loans or deposits must be treated with caution as both may lead to banks having low interest margins.

Another important performance measure for banks is *liquidity* because this will indicate whether the bank is able to meet cash demands for loans and deposit withdrawals as well as cover its operating expenses. Hence, banks will always need to maintain a certain level of liquid funds that it deems will be adequate to ensure that it is able to fulfil such demands. One of the most common ways to assess a bank's liquidity position is by considering its *loans to deposit ratio*. A low ratio indicates higher bank liquidity because there are less short term deposits tied up in long term loans or there are larger deposit base compared to loans given out. Although high liquidity is desirable, it may have implications for the bank's profitability, since the funds are not effectively used to generate income. Hence, it is important for banks to decide on an appropriate *loans to deposit* ratio such that it is able to meet the demands for deposit withdrawals and operating expenses without jeopardizing its opportunity to generate income from loans. In other words, a ratio that is too high or too low is not desirable for banks.

Efficiency is an important measure for banks as it indicates whether the bank has been able to generate high income at low cost. This is represented by the *cost to income ratio* and the higher the ratio, the less efficient the bank is in generating income. Hence, banks should aim for low *cost to income ratio*

Strategic management team quality is the final aspect in the EAGLES framework. To evaluate the strategic management team quality, a measure called the Strategic Response Quotient (SRQ) is used. The SRQ is determined by the *ratio of net interest income (NII)* to *net overhead expenses (OE)* as indicated in the following expression:

$$SRQ = \frac{Net\ interest\ income}{Net\ overhead\ expenses} = \frac{(Interest\ income - Interest\ expense)}{(Overhead\ expense - Non\text{-}interest\ income)}$$

The higher the SRQ value, the better is the bank's strategic management team quality, as it indicates effective management strategy in dealing with interest income and overheads. Looking at the numerator, a positive value indicates that the bank's interest income is in excess of its interest expense, hence its interest income can cover its interest expense. As for the denominator, a smaller value is desirable because it indicates that the bank is efficient in reducing the gap between its non-interest income and its overhead expenses.

Summary

In this chapter, we have examined the main financial statements and their components. We have seen the similarities and differences in the components of assets, liabilities and equity between conventional commercial and investment banks and specifically, Islamic banks. We have also seen how the standards adopted, i.e. IFRS or AAOIFI, influence the presentation and disclosure in the financial statements. AAOIFI standards prescribed more detailed disclosures than IFRS, which is not surprising due to the dual goal of business in Islam, seeking social justice and maximizing profits.

The structure of assets, liabilities and equities of Islamic banks are more complex than conventional banks, due to the different contractual relationships assumed by the banks. While the contractual relationship for conventional banks is mainly that of debtor–creditor, the case is different for Islamic banks as they may take the form of partnership or agency. The asset–liability structures of Islamic banks are better matched than conventional banks, hence this provides Islamic banks with more financial stability. We have also looked at the different liabilities of Islamic banks and considered the calculations used by banks to determine the returns to depositors and investors and *hibah*, in the case of *wadiah* contracts. The financial analysis of a bank often focuses on two things: identifying good or bad performance and determining its causes. We have considered various tools that can be used in performing this analysis and interpreting the results. The tools considered include various ratio analysis, CAMELS and EAGLES.

Key terms and concepts

actual net rate of return
ajr
asset productivity
assets quality
average actual net rate of return
CAMELS rating
capital adequacy ratio (CAR)
capital reserves
client retention ratio (CRR)
collateralized securities
cost per client (CPC)
cost per unit of capital allocated (CPUCA)
EAGLES framework
effective rate of return
fatawa
financing income
financing loss reserve adequacy (FLRA)
financing loss reserves
financing portfolio growth (FPG)
general investment account

gross profit rate per annum
growth in clients (GiC)
growth in equity (GiE)
indicative rate of return
International Financial Reporting Standards (IFRS)
investment account holder (IAH)
investment risk reserve (IRR)
liquidity management
management capability
mudarabah current account
mudarabah saving account
non-interest income
operating expenses ratio (OER)
operational sustainability (OS)
portfolio at risk (PAR)
portfolio yield (PY)
profit equalization reserve (PER)
profit sharing investment account
profit sharing ratio (PSR)
restricted investment account
return on average assets (ROAA)

return on average deposit (ROAD)
return on average equity (ROAE)
securities gains (losses)
Sensitivity to market risk
shari'ah audit
shari'ah review
shari'ah supervisory board
sources of *qard* fund
sources of *zakat* and charity funds
special unrestricted investment account
specific investment account
staff productivity ratio (SPR)
Statement of Cash Flow
Statement of Changes in Equity
Statement of Changes in Restricted Investment
Statement of Financial Position
Statement of Sources and Uses of *Qard* Fund
Statement of Sources and Uses of *Zakat* Funds

Strategic Response Quotient (SRQ)	uses of *Qard* fund	write-offs of average gross financing
trading assets	uses of *zakat* and charity Funds	portfolio (WoAGFP)
trading liabilities	*wadiah* current account	*zakat* agencies
transaction deposits	*wadiah* saving account	*zakat* base
universal bank	*wakalah* saving account	*zakat* distribution
Unrestricted Investment Account (URIA)	weighted average rate of return	*zakat* provision

Questions

1. What are the main differences between the assets and liabilities of an Islamic bank and a conventional bank?

2. Compare and contrast the Statements of Financial Position for Islamic and conventional banks.

3. Compare and contrast the Statement of Income of an Islamic and a conventional bank.

4. Discuss the differences in the contractual relationships of Islamic and conventional banks.

5. Report on the classification of profit sharing investment accounts (PSIA).

6. Define and appraise the major differences between PER and IRR.

7. Discuss the determinants of returns for assets and liabilities for an Islamic bank.

8. Explain the returns to depositors and investors for an Islamic bank.

9. Describe the *hibah* payment method for *wadiah* current account and *ajr* payment method for *wakalah* saving account.

10. Describe the *modus operandi* of *mudarabah* general investment account (GIA), and the returns of *al-mudarabah*.

11. Distinguish between special general investment accounts (SGIA) and restricted investment accounts (RIA).

12. Assess the weighted average rate of return (WAR) of net income.

13. Critically discuss the available tools for evaluating the performance of Islamic banks.

Case study

Bradford Islamic Bank (BIB) began its banking operations in 2010 to meet growing demands for Islamic banking products. It accepts deposits from high net worth and small investors to be invested on their behalf on the basis of restricted and unrestricted *mudarabah*, respectively. In both cases, the bank manages the funds as *mudarib* based on a pre-agreed share of profits. The restricted *mudarabah* investment are presented off balance sheet. Current account deposits are guaranteed by the bank, so customers receive no profit on their balances. The following are the financial details of BIB for the month ending 31 December 2016 and 31 January 2017.

Bradford Islamic Bank Statement of Financial Position as at		
Assets	31.12.2016 £000	31.1.2017 £000
Cash	256	307
Sale receivables	179 200	212 480
Less: deferred profits	−11 520	−19 968
Financing	64 000	64 000
Investments:		
Sukuk	15 360	33 393
Restricted investment accounts	35 840	77 916
Fixed assets	26 624	26 368
Total Assets	**309 760**	**394 496**
Liabilities		
Current accounts	19 200	44 800
Other liabilities	1 280	10 752
Unrestricted accounts		
Unrestricted investment accounts (URIA)	172 800	199 424
Investors share of profit	–	23 040
Shareholders' equity		
Paid up capital	102 400	102 400
Equity reserves	14 080	14 080
Total liabilities, URIA and Equity	**309 760**	**394 496**

Additional Information:

1. Investors' share of profit for the end of year 2016 was distributed to investors. The bank distributes profits monthly and investors' share is recorded in the Statement of Financial Position under Unrestricted Investment Accounts, if not collected by the end of the month.

2. Funds from bank free equity (i.e. equity minus fixed assets), current accounts and Unrestricted Investment Accounts are commingled (mixed-up) with finance sales receivables, financing and investments. Income generated by these investments during the month of January 2017 was £23 040 000.

3. The bank deducts, monthly, 5 per cent of income before distribution as PER and 10 per cent is deducted monthly, out of investors share, as IRR.

4. Disregard expenses.

5. *Mudarib's* share for managing unrestricted investment account is 20 per cent.

6. For profit distribution purposes the bank considers the balances on Balance Sheet partially invested as follows:

Free equity	100%
Current accounts	65%
Unrestricted investment accounts	85%

Required:

a) Advise how the January £23 040 000 profit will be distributed among the various funds and show the balances for each of the funds after the distribution of profits.

b) Based on your answer in part (a), calculate the PER, IRR, the bank share of income as *mudarib as* well as the investors share of the profit for January 2017.

c) Prepare the Statement of Financial Position as at 31 January 2017 after the allocation of profits.

References and further readings

Abdul Karim, M., Hassan, M.K., Hassan, T. and Mohamad, S. (2014), 'Capital adequacy and lending and deposit behaviors of conventional and Islamic banks', *Pacific-Basin Finance Journal, 28*, pp. 58–75.

Bank Negara Malaysia (BNM). (2011), *Shariah Governance Framework for Islamic Financial Institution* (SGF), BNM.

Beck, T., Demirgüç-Kunt, A. and Merrouche, O. (2013), 'Islamic vs. conventional banking: Business model, efficiency and stability', *Journal of Banking and Finance*, 37, pp. 433–447.

Ismail, A.G. (2010), *Money, Islamic Banks, and the Real Economy*, Cengage Learning EMEA, Andover.

Mollah, S., Hassan, M.K., Al Farooque, O., and Mobarek, A. (2017), 'The governance, risk-taking, and performance of Islamic banks'. *Journal of Financial Services Research*, 51(2), pp. 195–219.

Nawaz, T. and Haniffa, R. (2017), 'Determinants of financial performance of Islamic banks: an intellectual capital perspective', *Journal of Islamic Accounting and Business Research*, 8(2), pp. 130–142.

Olson, D. and Zoubi, T.A. (2008), 'Using accounting ratios to distinguish between Islamic and conventional banks in the GCC region', *The International Journal of Accounting*, 43, pp. 45–65.

Olson, D. and Zoubi, T.A. (2017), 'Convergence in bank performance for commercial and Islamic banks during and after the Global Financial Crisis', *The Quarterly Review of Economics and Finance*, 65, pp. 71–87.

10 Islamic bank financial management

Learning Objectives

Upon completion of this chapter you should be able to:

- define and discuss the function of asset–liability management

- describe the structure and management of Islamic bank liabilities

- appreciate factors affecting the choice of deposits and non-deposits source of funds

- discuss the structure and management of Islamic bank assets

- describe liquidity management and factors affecting it

- discuss the liquidity measurement framework

- describe the significance of capital management

- distinguish between regulatory and economic capital

- identify alternative views held by regulators and bankers on capital adequacy

- calculate capital ratio, risk adjusted capital ratio and capital adequacy ratio

- discuss the evolution of Basel I, Basel II and IFSB's capital adequacy standard

- discuss off balance sheet management

10.1 Introduction

Financial management plays an important function in every organization, as it helps management to monitor actual performance against planned goals and targets, regardless of whether it is for profit or non-profit. In the case of profit making entities, the role of financial management is to make decisions on how to acquire (financing decisions) and allocate funds (investment decisions), as well as how to conserve the funds (control decisions) in order to maximize profits and shareholders' wealth.

Similarly, the goal of financial management in Islamic banks is to manage assets and liabilities in a way that maximizes the banks' profits and at the same time also achieves the goals of *shari'ah*. There are five important aspects in Islamic bank management, as shown in Figure 10.1: *asset management*, *liabilities management*, *liquidity management*, *off balance sheet management* and *capital management*. In order to make financial decisions, bankers need to rely on the information in the various financial statements we discussed in Chapter 9.

Figure 10.1 Islamic bank financial management

Asset management in Islamic banks involves having a well-diversified portfolio of asset backed trading and different forms of investments with a wide spectrum of risk and maturity profile. This requires having effective policy in monitoring the interrelated performance of risk, return and maturity. In terms of *liabilities management*, Islamic banks need to acquire and manage restricted and unrestricted funds. They must introduce a policy that can effectively support the separate management of those funds and ensure effective monitoring. *Liquidity management* is related to Islamic banks holding enough cash and other liquid assets readily available to meet demands for daily withdrawals and other payments by their customers. *Capital management* involves Islamic banks keeping adequate level of capital to comply with regulatory requirements in order to maintain solvency and also cushion against losses. Hence, the more the capital the bank has, the bigger the cushion it has for absorbing losses. Finally, *off balance sheet management* involves controlling and limiting the exposures related to off balance sheet transactions. In the following sections, we will look into more detail on each aspect of financial management in Islamic banks.

10.2 Asset–liability management (ALM)

ALM is defined by Sinkey (2002) as an intermediate term (3-12 months) planning function undertaken by the bank's management to ensure that the bank moves in the direction of its long term (2-5 years) plan while maintaining the flexibility to adapt to short term (monthly) changes. In other words, it is a management tool that involves the strategic planning, implementation and control processes that affect the volume, mix, maturity, profit rate sensitivity, quality and liquidity of a bank's assets and liabilities. The primary goal of ALM is to produce high quality, stable, large, and growing flow of net interest/profit rate income (Greuning and Iqbal, 2008). This goal is accomplished by achieving the optimum combination in the level of assets, liabilities and financial risk.

As part of the planning function, the bank's management must monitor and control the levels, changes and mix of the bank's assets and liabilities in a coordinated way such that the bank's value and profits can be maximized subject to taking a certain level of risk while maintaining an appropriate level of safety. In the case of Islamic banks, this also involves consideration of the potential profit in proportion to the risk assumed that can satisfy the differing demands of participants while staying within the guidelines of *shari'ah*.

An effective liability management is when the bank is able to manage and monitor the restricted and unrestricted funds from depositors and investors at a low cost, while an effective asset management is when the bank is able to maximize the returns on its loans and investments through better screening, monitoring and choice of customers, minimizing its risk by diversifying its portfolio to avoid overinvesting in a particular sector, as well as having adequate liquidity by making the right decisions on the trade-off between profitability and liquidity (recall that the higher the amount of liquid assets and reserves the bank keep on hand, the more likely the bank will have lower income and profit because liquid assets tend to yield lower returns).

Typically, the ALM role is undertaken by the bank's asset and liability committee (ALCO) and it is considered as the most important management group and function in the bank. Besides ALM, this committee also needs to pay attention to capital management. Membership covers major areas of the organization, such as the chief executive officer (CEO), chief financial officer (CFO), treasurer and senior managers of credit, deposits and investments.

Thus, assessment of a bank's ALM requires the bank's ALCO to have a deep understanding of its assets and liabilities, as well as of its customers, economic environment and the competitive conditions of the bank. We will now look more closely at the assets and liabilities structures and factors affecting ALM.

10.3 Structure and management of Islamic bank liabilities

As discussed in Chapter 9, an Islamic bank's funding sources or liabilities consist of *deposits* and *non-deposits*. Deposits can be classified into two categories, restricted and unrestricted funds. *Restricted funds* refer to deposits where the utilization of the funds is clearly identified and they are managed separately. Specific investment deposits and profit equalization reserves (PER) fall under this category. These funds are often treated as off balance sheet items by Islamic banks. On the other hand, *unrestricted funds* are funds whereby their utilization is not identified and as such, these funds are comingled and managed on a pool basis. These unrestricted funds can be further classified into *profit related deposits* and *hibah related deposits*. The former refers to profit sharing type of deposits such as general investment deposits and *mudarabah* deposits while the latter refers to current deposits and savings deposits, where returns on the deposits are at the discretion of the bank and are given as a gift (*hibah*) to depositors. *Non-deposit items* consist of funds channelled by a surplus rich Islamic bank to a deficit Islamic bank i.e. a bank that may face short term liquidity. Figure 10.2 illustrates the components of liabilities of Islamic banks. Therefore, in managing their liabilities, Islamic banks need to manage restricted and unrestricted funds, and introduce a policy that can effectively support the separate management of funds and ensure effective monitoring.

Figure 10.2 Components of liabilities of Islamic banks

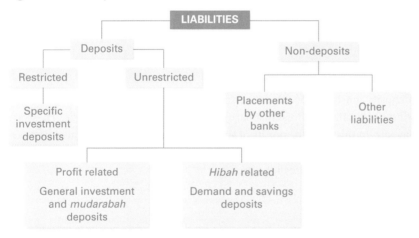

10.3.1 DEPOSITS

Deposits play a significant role in the acquisition of funding sources and Islamic banks offer customers a choice of various types of deposits. Table 10.1 presents the liabilities structure of two Islamic banks. As can be seen, more than 75 per cent of liabilities comprise of deposits from customers for both banks in the three periods with the exception for Al-Baraka in 2016 where it has fallen to 61 per cent. The next significant component is the deposits and placements of banks and other financial institutions and for both banks, this figure has steadily increased for the three periods. Other liabilities stand at about 4 per cent level for both banks for all three periods. We will look more closely at each of them and their significance.

Table 10.1 Comparison of liabilities of Islamic banks in different periods

Dubai Islamic Bank						
	2003 AED000	%	2010 AED000	%	2016 AED000	%
Liabilities						
Deposits from customers	19883	94.3	63447	79.7	122377	82.9
Deposits and placements of banks and other financial institutions	320	1.5	4409	5.5	10418	7.1
Sukuk financing instruments	-	-	4176	5.2	7695	5.2
Medium term *wakala* finance	-	-	3753	4.7	-	-
Other liabilities	858	4.1	3680	4.6	6969	4.7
Zakat and taxation	14	0.1	146	0.3	242	0.1
Total liabilities	**21075**	**100**	**79611**	**100**	**147701**	**100**

Al-Baraka Islamic Bank						
	2003 US$000	%	2010 US$000	%	2016 US$000	%
Liabilities						
Deposits from customers	736457	77.9	2906172	87.2	4983772	61.2
Deposits and placements of banks and other financial institutions	42289	4.5	424477	11.1	918395	11.3
Long term financing	-	-	-	-	1381256	17
Other liabilities	166337	17.6	490988	12.9	844418	10.4
Zakat and taxation	15	-	146	-	4315	0.1
Total liabilities	**945098**	**100**	**3821783**	**100**	**8132156**	**100**

Sources: Dubai Islamic Bank, www.dib.ae/docs/investor-relation/2003_annualreport_en.pdf, www.dib.ae/docs/investor-relation/2010_annualreport_en.pdf, www.dib.ae/docs/investor-relation/financial-statments-2016-english.pdf.

Al-Baraka Islamic Bank, www.albaraka.com/media/pdf/AnnualReports/AnualReport2004.pdf, www.albaraka.com/media/pdf/AnnualReports/AnnualReport2010_eng.pdf, www.albaraka.com/media/pdf/cc/AR16English.pdf.

a) Restricted deposits

As mentioned earlier, restricted deposits consist of specified investment deposits. Islamic banks have evolved an investment deposit with specific authorization to invest in a particular scheme or a specific trade. These are known as specified investment deposits. In this case, the profits of this specific activity are distributed between the depositor and the bank as the latter works as an agent of the investor. The bank may agree to perform this function against an agreed fee or may opt to have a share in the profit.

b) Unrestricted deposits

(I) DEMAND DEPOSITS OR CURRENT ACCOUNTS Islamic banks offer demand deposits or current accounts for their customers based on the *wadiah yad dhamanah* (safekeeping with guarantee) principle. Customers may withdraw their money anytime and the bank guarantees full return of these deposits on demand. Hence, the bank acts as custodian or guarantor of the funds deposited by customers. The bank may use these funds as a source of investment and financing for risk bearing projects. Any profits generated from such activities belong to the bank, since all risk is borne by the bank. Therefore, demand depositors are not entitled to any share in profits earned by the bank. Nevertheless, if the funds under custody of the bank suffer a loss, the bank is obliged to reimburse the funds at par value to the depositors.

From the bank's perspective, demand deposits are considered the cheapest source of funds as they are not entitled to any Islamic bank's profit. Since the bank uses demand deposits at its own risk, it is required to keep a legal reserve at the Central Bank.

(II) SAVING DEPOSITS Individuals may have surplus funds that they would like to keep somewhere safe, but at the same time have easy access to the funds whenever needed. Hence, they can use savings deposit facilities offered by Islamic banks as they can make withdrawals without having to give any notice. Generally, there are four types of savings accounts operated by Islamic banks. The first one is based on the principle of *al wadiah* (safekeeping) deposits. When accepting *al wadiah* savings deposits, Islamic banks will seek permission from depositors to use the funds, but without any risk to the depositors as they are guaranteed full return of their deposits and can make withdrawals anytime. The bank, at its discretion, may share some of the profit it makes with depositors as a gift. In other words, there is no promise of any return to depositors except at the discretion of the bank. The second type of savings deposit is based on the principle of *mudarabah* or profit sharing. Hence, for *mudarabah* savings deposits, Islamic banks will seek authorization from depositors to invest and share profits in a pre-determined ratio. The bank requests that a minimum balance is maintained during the period agreed upon for the investment. This means that the depositor is not only guaranteed full return of their deposits but will also receive some additional returns from the bank. The third type of saving deposits is based on the principle of *qard-hasan* (benevolent loan). For *qard-hasan* savings deposits, the bank assumes that depositors grant them permission to use and benefit from the money for a certain period without expecting any returns from it. The last type of savings deposit is where the bank includes the deposits into its investment pool and as such treats them as investment deposits.

(III) INVESTMENT DEPOSITS Investment deposits are also known as profit and loss sharing (PLS) accounts or participatory accounts and they operate based on the *mudarabah* principle. They are similar to term deposits in the conventional banking system but without involving interest. Investment depositors can be individuals or companies and they can choose any specified period ranging from three months, six months, a year or even longer for such deposits. Certificates will be issued to depositors confirming their subscription. Investment depositors are eligible for a share in the actual profit accruing from the bank's investment operations and there is no fixed return tied up to the face value of the certificate. They must be based on the pro-rated profit actually earned by the fund and there is no guarantee of the principal nor a rate of profit tied up with the principal. Hence, investment depositors must be aware and understand that if the investment fund earns huge profits, the return on their subscription will increase in proportion. However, if the investment fund suffers a loss, investment depositors will have to share the loss, except if the loss is caused by negligence or mismanagement, in which case the management will be liable to compensate for the loss. It is important to note that investment depositors are not allowed to make withdrawals from their accounts during this period. Such requests are only allowed under some special circumstances and depositors are required to give banks some notice period. Any amount withdrawn from the investment accounts will not be entitled to a share of the profit.

(IV) JOINT OR GENERAL INVESTMENT ACCOUNT Unlike investment deposits, which normally have a specific period, some Islamic banks offer a joint or general investment account whereby the deposits are included in an investment pool operated by the bank. This investment pool consists of investment deposits with different maturities and they are not tied to any specific investments projects. Banks use this pool of funds for financing various operations undertaken by the banks and any profits generated will be distributed on a pro-rata basis at the end of the period.

(V) LIMITED PERIOD INVESTMENT DEPOSITS Another form of investment deposits offered by Islamic banks is where the investment is for a limited period only and such deposit is known as the limited period investment deposits. The bank and the depositor enter into a contract whereby the former agrees to accept the investment for a specified period determined by mutual consent by both parties, after which the contract will terminate. Profits will be distributed at the end of each financial year.

(VI) UNLIMITED PERIOD INVESTMENT DEPOSITS As the name suggests, these investment deposits do not have any specific period. Depositors are not allowed to make any withdrawals nor increase the amount of deposits in the bank. These accounts are renewed automatically by the bank until depositors notify the bank that they wish to terminate. Normally, the banks require a notice period of three months. At the end of each financial year, profits will be calculated and distributed to depositors by the bank.

(VII) STRUCTURED TRADE DEPOSITS Besides profit related and *hibah* related deposits, Islamic banks also offer an alternative form of deposits designed to net a wider interest in generating liquidity for the bank. They are structured as a trade transaction to comply with *murabahah* principle whereby the depositor buys a commodity for spot value and sells it for deferred payment generating a profit on the sale of the commodity. By buying the commodity from the customer on a deferred payment basis will provide the bank with cash to invest in Islamic investments.

Table 10.2 provides a breakdown of deposits of a typical Islamic bank. It can be seen that investment deposits form a significant component of deposits for this bank followed by demand deposits. To help management make strategic decisions on the liabilities structure, the deposits are distinguished into *mudarabah* (profit related) and *non-mudarabah* (*hibah* related) deposits, as this helps in determining the risk profile of the Islamic bank's deposits portfolio.

Table 10.2 Breakdown of deposits in an Islamic bank

	Dubai Islamic Bank					
	2003 AED000	%	2010 AED000	%	2016 AED000	%
Deposits from customers						
Current accounts	3292	16.5	15087	23.8	29006	23.7
Savings account	3185	16.0	10047	15.8	17848	14.6
Investment deposits	13134	66.2	38124	60.1	74905	61.2
Margins	146	0.7	188	0.3	488	0.4
Profit equalization reserve	126	0.6	1	-	130	0.1
	19883	100	63447	100	122377	100

Source: Dubai Islamic Bank, www.dib.ae/docs/investor-relation/2003_annualreport_en.pdf, www.dib.ae/docs/investor-relation/2010_annualreport_en.pdf, www.dib.ae/docs/investor-relation/financial-statments-2016-english.pdf.

c) Factors affecting deposits

Given the importance of deposits for Islamic banks, management must be wary of factors that may influence deposits. Studies have shown that the decision of customers to deposit in Islamic banks is not solely driven by religious belief. Many studies have shown that savings deposits may be affected by the interest rate offered by conventional banks; when the rate of return of Islamic banks decreases below the interest rate of the conventional bank, Islamic banks' depositors tend to transfer their deposits from the Islamic banks to the conventional banks. The decision of customers to deposit in Islamic banks is also dependent on healthy financial systems, receiving economic benefits, online facilities, quick services and easily reachable locations. Thus, management must implement appropriate strategies and policies in attracting the different types of depositors that will enable the bank to have adequate resources to channel the funds for lending and investments to generate income for the bank.

10.3.2 NON-DEPOSITS

While deposits serve as a major source of funds to banks, management may face situation whereby the deposit volume is inadequate to support all loans and investments the bank would like to make. This may arise because lending and investment decisions often precede funding decisions. Therefore, management needs to seek out the lowest cost for source of borrowed funds available to meet its customers' credit needs. The alternative non-deposit sources include deposits and placements from other financial institutions, negotiable certificates of deposits, borrowings and other source of liabilities.

The demand for non-deposit funds is determined basically by the size of the gap between the institution's total credit and investment demands and its deposits and other available funds. The gap is based on the current and projected demand and investments the bank desires to make and the current and expected deposit inflows and other available funds. The size of this gap determines the need for non-deposit funds.

a) Deposits and placements of Islamic banks and other financial institutions

This serves as an important source that may help bank facing liquidity shortage. A deficit Islamic bank can obtain funds invested by a surplus rich Islamic bank to facilitate funding and adjusting its portfolios over the short term. The participating Islamic banks would be able to match their funding requirements effectively and efficiently and promote stability in the Islamic banking system. The investee banks can be other licensed banks, investment banks, central bank and other financial institutions. The period of investment ranges from overnight to 12 months and the profit sharing ratio is negotiable between both parties. The investee bank at the time of negotiation would not know what the return would be, as the actual return will be crystallized towards the end of the investment period. The principal invested shall be repaid at the end of the period together with a share of the profit arising from the use of the fund.

Table 10.3 presents the breakdown of deposits and placements. It can be seen that the use of current accounts has been declining while deposit accounts on profit sharing basis have increased.

Table 10.3 Breakdown of deposits and placement in an Islamic bank

	Dubai Islamic Bank					
	2003 AED000	%	2010 AED000	%	2016 AED000	%
Deposits and placements of banks and other financial institutions						
Current accounts	20	6.3	51	1.2	95	0.9
Deposit accounts	300	93.7	4358	98.8	10323	99.1
Total deposits and placements	**320**	**100**	**4409**	**100**	**10418**	**100**

Source: Dubai Islamic Bank, www.dib.ae/docs/investor-relation/2003_annualreport_en.pdf, www.dib.ae/docs/investor-relation/2010_annualreport_en.pdf, www.dib.ae/docs/investor-relation/financial-statments-2016-english.pdf.

b) Other liabilities

Another short term source of funds for Islamic banks includes payables and provisions. They consist of payments due to creditors, investors and other accrued expenses. Table 10.4 illustrates the breakdown of other liabilities in an Islamic bank. It can be seen that the use of payables and provisions as well as taxation have increased.

Table 10.4 Breakdown of other liabilities in an Islamic bank

	Al-Baraka Islamic Bank					
	2003 US$000	%	2010 US$000	%	2016 US$000	%
Other liabilities						
Payables	40494	24.3	208024	42.4	299433	35.5
Cash margins	52534	31.6	96835	19.7	269771	31.9
Managers' cheques	-	-	-	-	103969	12.3
Other provisions	7959	4.8	12128	2.5	11091	1.3
Current taxation	9850	5.9	52643	10.7	68055	8.1
Deferred taxation	-	-	11743	2.4	12933	1.5
Accrued expenses	8584	5.2	48779	9.9	11491	1.4
Charity fund	5636	3.4	5035	1	10658	1.3
Others	41280	24.8	55801	11.4	57017	6.7
Total of other liabilities	**166337**	**100**	**490988**	**100**	**844418**	**100**

Source: Al-Baraka Islamic Bank, www.albaraka.com/media/pdf/AnnualReports/AnualReport2004.pdf, www.albaraka.com/media/pdf/AnnualReports/AnnualReport2010_eng.pdf, www.albaraka.com/media/pdf/cc/AR16English.pdf.

c) Factors affecting choice of non-deposit funding sources

There are five main factors that affect the choice of non-deposit sources: (i) The relative costs of raising funds from each source; (ii) the risk (volatility and dependability) of each funding source; (iii) the length of time (maturity or term) for which funds are needed; (iv) the size of the institution that requires more funds; and (v) regulations limiting the use of alternative funds sources.

10.4 Structure and management of Islamic bank assets

The deposits and placements, i.e. liabilities, raised by Islamic banks would be utilized to create profit for the bank through financing and investment activities while holding some level of cash to honour the demand for withdrawals by depositors. As discussed in Chapter 9, the asset side of the bank's balance sheet comprises a diversified portfolio of heterogeneous financing and investment asset classes with a wide spectrum of risk and maturity profile.

Table 10.5 presents the asset structure of an Islamic bank. It can be seen that a large portion of the bank assets are in the form of receivables. The amount of cash and balances with banks have decreased over the years, suggesting that the bank chose to have less liquidity, which enable it to use the resource for financing and investment activities. Investment activities have also increased compared to financing activities.

Table 10.5 Assets of an Islamic bank in different periods

	Al-Baraka Islamic Bank					
	2003 US$000	%	2010 US$000	%	2016 US$000	%
Assets						
Cash and balances with banks	1 307 889	31.77	3 813 903	24.02	5 073 418	21.66
Receivables	1 741 727	42.31	8 063 331	50.78	11 423 448	48.77
Ijarah receivable	23 407	0.57	-	-	-	-
Mudarabah and *musharakah* financing	128 892	3.13	1 538 632	9.69	1 582 396	6.76
Salam financing	68,462	1.66	-	-	-	-
Investments	43 092	1.05	1 350 481	8.50	2 629 131	11.22
Investment in associates	95 743	2.33	-	-	-	-
Ijarah muntahiya bil tamlik	159 438	3.87	439 801	2.77	1 830 339	7.81
Non-trading investments	278 982	6.78	-	-	-	-
Trading securities	26 269	0.64	-	-	-	-
Property and equipment	99 721	2.42	298 852	1.88	417 295	1.78
Other assets	142 856	3.47	374 933	2.36	469 238	2.00
Total assets	**4 116 478**	**100.00**	**15 879 933**	**100.00**	**23 425 265**	**100.00**

Source: Al-Baraka Islamic Bank, www.albaraka.com/media/pdf/AnnualReports/AnualReport2004.pdf, www.albaraka.com/media/pdf/AnnualReports/AnnualReport2010_eng.pdf, www.albaraka.com/media/pdf/cc/AR16English.pdf.

10.4.1 FINANCING ACTIVITIES

Islamic banks offer a wide variety of financing activities to cater for the needs of different customers. Generally such schemes can be further classified into business, consumer and real estate financing. *Business finance* is provided to enable firms to conduct economic activities, raise short term capital (e.g. bridging and syndication financing) and improve working capital. Most trading activities and short term funds to meet working capital needs of the firms are financed through trade contracts such as *murabahah* (cost-plus) and *bay' salam* (forward sale).

Consumer financing includes all forms of instalment financing (e.g. automobile, home improvement, debt consolidation, etc.) and open-ended financing such as credit cards. Consumer financing is monitored by the central bank as it is a leading indicator of growth in the economy. *Real estate financing* includes mortgage financing and services related to it such as brokerage, appraisal, property management, etc.

10.4.2 INVESTMENT ACTIVITIES

Islamic banks have a variety of choices for investments. For medium term investments, banks can invest in *ijarah* (leasing), *ijarah muntahiya bil tamlik* (financial lease) and *istisna'* (manufacturing). *Mudarabah* (profit–loss sharing) investments involve banks providing the funds to another party, but not directly involved in managing the venture while *musharakah* (equity) investment is a joint enterprise with profit/loss implications.

10.4.3 CASH, RECEIVABLES AND FIXED ASSETS

As mentioned earlier, banks need to hold a certain level of cash to honour withdrawal demand by depositors. Receivables are amount due from financing, investment and services activities. Fixed assets include land, buildings and equipment that belong to the bank.

10.5 Liquidity management

Liquidity is a key factor in banking as banks need to ensure that it keeps enough cash and other liquid assets to meet its obligations to depositors and investors and at the same time is able to satisfy the financing demands of customers, as well as its own investing demands. This is related to what is known as *liquidity risk* i.e. inability to raise cash at a reasonable cost when it needs to do so.

Banks need to carefully plan the level of liquidity to hold, as it has implications for Islamic bank operations and, in the extreme, its viability. In determining the level of liquidity, banks need to recognize the trade-off between liquidity and profitability. Hence, banks need to calculate the opportunity cost of the amount held as liquid assets, as they are typically non-earning or low-yielding compared to investment and lending activities which may generate higher returns. In other words, poor liquidity limits an Islamic bank's flexibility and puts a brake on its ability to take advantage of new financing and investment opportunities.

Acute liquidity problems can spell serious trouble for Islamic banks especially when funds are not available to meet depositors' withdrawal demands. When this happens, the Islamic bank needs to act quickly and discreetly to meet the shortfalls. If other institutions or depositors become aware of the liquidity shortage, it could create a run on the bank leading to insolvency. Therefore, it is important that the management pays close attention to the Islamic bank's liquidity position and are aware of factors that can affect that position.

10.5.1 FACTORS AFFECTING LIQUIDITY

An Islamic bank's need for liquidity depends on internal and external factors. If the bank plans and budgets well, and is able to anticipate many of its internal liquidity needs for funding financing growth, meeting depositor demands and paying operating expenses, then it can structure its balance sheet accordingly. If the Islamic bank knows its market well, it can plan for many external events such as seasonal financing patterns, deposit run offs and business payrolls. Besides the anticipated needs, Islamic banks must also be prepared for unforeseen events such as fraud, natural disasters or equipment malfunction, which could all have serious implications on an Islamic bank's liquidity position. In short, even with the most careful planning, Islamic banks still need to maintain liquidity reserves to sustain them when the unexpected occurs. In general, three factors can influence the bank's liquidity: its *balance sheet structure, access to financial market* and *financial condition*.

a) Balance sheet structure

The liquidity position of an Islamic bank depends on how well it structures its balance sheet, i.e. how it adjusts its holdings of assets and liabilities to manage its liquidity. An Islamic bank is considered to be more liquid when more of its assets and liabilities are concentrated in categories near the top of the balance sheet. The most liquid Islamic bank, i.e. the one that can most easily handle a surprising need for funds, is the one that holds only cash which is obtained through core deposits and the owners' capital. However, such bank would not be very profitable because cash does not earn income. The challenge for Islamic bank managers is to maintain a prudent degree of liquidity while still structuring the balance sheet to earn a reasonable profit through lending and investments.

Table 10.6 illustrates the link between liquidity and balance sheet structure. The more deposits the bank holds, the more stable it is. The more cash the bank holds, the more liquid it is. The onus is on the bank's management to balance the structure of the assets and liabilities to achieve optimal benefits.

Table 10.6 Liquidity risk and balance sheet structure

	Assets	Liabilities and capital		
More liquid ↑	cash due to other banks securities financing	demand deposits savings deposits investment deposits	**core funding (deposits)**	**More stable** ↑
↓ **Less liquid**	other loans other real estate owned building and equipment	deposits and placements subordinated debt other liabilities structured deposits	**non-core funding**	↓ **Less stable**
		capital		

It is important to note that funds continually flow in and out of an Islamic bank. Inflows may come from principal and profit receipts, fee income, asset sales, deposits and other financings while outflows occur due to other expense payments, asset additions (most likely financing and investments), deposits and other financing pay downs. Even with good planning, fund inflows and outflows will rarely match due to timing differences in the flow of funds from assets and liabilities, which can leave an Islamic bank with either an excess or lack of funds. Hence, balance sheet timing differences will give rise to liquidity consequences.

Off balance sheet activities may create liquidity sources as well as potential liquidity drains. For example, if an Islamic bank has a large number of financing commitments or unused lines of financing, it may be required to make good on these obligations at short notice. On the other hand, the bank may maintain its own lines of financing with other sources such as correspondent banks or the Islamic money market. Although this is not obvious in the balance sheet, an Islamic bank with substantial financing lines may be very liquid. Nevertheless, the stability of these lines may rest on the condition and capital position of the Islamic bank. Many types of off balance sheet financing have risen over the past decade and it is important to be aware of the exposures and opportunities presented by off balance sheet activity to Islamic banks (to be discussed further in the last section of this chapter).

b) Access to financial markets

All Islamic banks have some degree of financial market access. However, smaller Islamic banks tend to have less access compared to their larger counterparts as the former may not be as well known in the markets as their larger counterparts. Thus, it has to incur cost for developing a financial track record information and making it available for the markets. This cost may be justified if the sum being raised is large. Furthermore, a significant portion of the cost of raising funds is largely fixed and this makes large transactions less expensive to complete than smaller transactions, and this may deter smaller institutions, so they make less use of financial markets than larger institutions.

c) Financial condition

An Islamic bank's financial condition is dependent on its earnings and asset quality, both of which can adversely affect liquidity. Low earnings means less cash is available to meet liquidity needs. Similarly, low quality assets or high levels of non-performing assets may damage earnings and lock an Islamic bank into assets with low marketability. Furthermore, low earnings and poor asset quality may give rise to insolvency and deter potential *rabbul mal* to provide funds.

10.5.2 LIQUIDITY MEASUREMENT FRAMEWORK

As part of its liquidity management, Islamic banks need to be aware of the maturity profiles of their assets, liabilities and off balance sheet commitments, including their forecasted position at any specific point in time. Hence, a liquidity measurement framework is developed to enable Islamic banks to match their short term liquidity requirement stemming from obligations that are maturing with those assets that are maturing. The analysis is further supported by the use of a number of ratios related to the funding structure of Islamic banks to reveal if the bank is over dependent on a particular source of funding.

Liquidity assessment is conducted in three stages. In Stage 1, the sufficiency of an Islamic bank's liquidity in the normal course of its business is being assessed based on a maturity band profile i.e. according to the period in which they are expected to mature or be called upon. The primary basis for determining the appropriate time bands is the contractual maturity. The objective of the assessment of liquidity at this stage is to arrive at a projected net maturity mismatch profile of an Islamic bank stretching from one week to five years.

In Stage 2, the assessment conducted is for the purpose of determining whether the Islamic bank has adequate liquidity surplus and reserves to withstand any sudden withdrawal shock stemming from a specific crisis affecting the Islamic bank. This involves comparing the adjusted maturity profile with the potential amount of excessive withdrawals that may occur during a crisis. Hence, the bank should aim for the available cumulative mismatch to accommodate the liquidity shocks to be beyond the compliance requirement.

In Stage 3, the focus of the assessment is on the Islamic bank's general funding structure, particularly the extent of its dependency on some markets that are known to be volatile. This involves looking at a number of ratios and complementary information on its offshore and interbank markets as well as its large customer deposits. Such information is useful in enabling the bank to gauge their liquidity risk exposure if disruptions occur in those markets.

10.6 Capital adequacy management

The banking industry is one of the most regulated sectors due to a number of reasons. Firstly, since it is one of the most leveraged industries, regulation is needed to protect against bank bankruptcy. Secondly, regulation is needed to protect depositors and consumers against losing their funds. Thirdly, regulation is needed as banking activities are closely tied to monetary, financial and economic stability.

As mentioned earlier in the chapter, besides ALM, ALCO needs to also consider the level of capital held by banks. Having adequate bank capital is important to avoid bankruptcy. Before looking at the regulations on capital adequacy, it is important to recognize the basic relationship between assets, liabilities and equity and how the structure of the balance sheet may lead to bankruptcy.

Assets	Liabilities
Assets (A)	Deposits/Debt (L)
	Capital/Equity (E)

Basic balance sheet relationship:

$$A = L + E$$
$$\text{Or net worth: } A - L = E$$

If net worth $(A - L) < E$, the firm is bankrupt.

Example:
Let us look at two scenarios of bank capital. In Case 1, the bank initially has £10 million capital while in Case 2, it has initial capital of £20 million. Assume that assets reduced by £5 million in State 1 and £15 million in State 2. It can be seen that when assets declined by £15 million in State 2, the bank that has higher capital is better able to buffer against bankruptcy.

<u>Case 1: E = 10</u>
State 0:   A = 100,   L = 90, E = 10;
State 1:   A = 95,   L = 90, E = 5; Net worth = A − L = 95 − 90 = 5
State 2:   A = 85,   L = 90, E = −5; Net worth = A − L = 85 − 90 = **(5)-Bankrupt**

<u>Case 2: E = 20</u>
State 0:   A = 100,   L = 80, E = 20;
State 1:   A = 95,   L = 80, E = 15; Net worth = A − L = 95 − 80 = 15
State 2:   A = 85,   L = 80, E = 5; Net worth = A − L = 85 − 80 = +5

It is clear from the above example the importance of capital, especially in the context of banking, because it signals to what extent the bank is safe and sound, i.e. solvent. Unlike *bank liquidity*, which is concerned with the ability of the bank to pay its obligations when they fall due, *bank solvency* is the ability of the bank to repay all its obligations ultimately. Hence, an Islamic bank must hold enough capital to cushion against losses while being able to meet the needs of its customers. Similar to bank liquidity, there is a trade-off between safety and returns because the higher the bank's capital, the lower is its return on equity (ROE). On the other hand, Islamic banks with low equity capital and high variability of operating earnings are highly vulnerable to financial distress.

Furthermore, Islamic banks with a strong capital base will be in a better position to supply financing to businesses and fund investment opportunities that will lead to growth, create employment and contribute to a stronger economy. On the other hand, a weak capital base may prevent Islamic banks from functioning effectively as risk intermediaries, due to inadequate financing and liquidity in financial markets resulting in the banks being unable to boost the productive capacity of the economy. Given the importance of financing and liquidity for the overall economy, it is not surprising that regulators are concerned about issues related to capital adequacy and capital allocation.

A strongly capitalized Islamic banking sector is also better able to promote innovation, whether in the form of new products, new services or new distribution channels, that would add value to shareholders. Moreover, Islamic bankers must vie for capital resources with a growing field of competitors to increase shareholder value. In the face of increasing competitive pressures, Islamic banks are spending more time focusing on the role of capital, capital levels, capital targets and how they relate to strategic plans and objectives.

Hence capital adequacy is a major issue for both regulators and bankers. However, they hold different views on the issue as summarized in Table 10.7. A distinction is often made between regulatory and economic capital. *Regulatory capital* is the amount of capital required by regulators. *Economic capital* is the capital that a bank believes it should hold to cover the risks it is undertaking. In the following sections, we will look into more detail at regulatory capital.

10.6.1 REGULATORY CAPITAL ADEQUACY

Regulatory capital, i.e. level of capital banks should have, was initially identified by their capital ratio, which is defined in terms of the book value of capital and assets as follows:

$$Capital\ ratio = \frac{Total\ capital}{Total\ assets}$$

Table 10.7 Alternative views on capital adequacy

Regulator	Banker
1. Concerned with the size of risk and therefore focuses on the lower end of bank's earnings.	1. Concerned with expected return to shareholders and therefore focuses on the central part of earnings distribution.
2. Perceive earnings variability in the context of the likelihood that earnings will fall to a level that capital is eliminated and the bank becoming insolvent.	2. Higher variability in earnings requires higher earnings per share to compensate shareholders for bank risk.
3. As capital is a perpetual and stable source of funds for the operations of an Islamic bank, normally regulators take the view that the amount of capital should be sufficient to support the Islamic bank. Capital planning should be an integral part of management function to maintain solvency in the long run.	3. For Islamic banks, capital should be maintained at a level sufficient to support the basic infrastructure of the business. Hence Islamic banks are encouraged to strengthen their capital positions so that fixed assets and infrastructure investments that do not directly generate cash flows could be funded through capital.

Islamic banks tend to have capital ratios in the range of 4 per cent to 10 per cent. However, deregulation in the 1970s and 1980s exposed Islamic banks to higher risk causing capital to become more important as a buffer against losses. Imposing one capital ratio to all banks was not prudent, as some banks may engage in riskier activities than others. The more the risk undertaken by banks, the more capital is needed. Since assets are a poor indicator of risk, regulators and practitioners started modifying the capital ratio to become risk adjusted capital ratio (RACR):

$$Risk\text{-}adjusted\ capital\ ratio = \frac{Total\ capital}{Risk\text{-}adjusted\ assets}$$

The risk-adjusted assets are calculated by applying risk based weights to specific assets and summing the results to derive the capital required. This was in line with the 1988 Basel Accord. There are two main components in calculating the RACR, that is, *capital base* and *total risk-adjusted assets*.

a) Capital base

Under the weight based capital standards, capital should in principle possess the following characteristics: (i) permanently available, (ii) not earmarked to any particular assets or operations, (iii) able to absorb any losses occurring in the course of on-going business; and (iv) not incurring any fixed expenses against the earnings. Based on the aforementioned criteria, capital is segregated into two tiers, namely, *Core capital (Tier 1)* and *Supplemental capital (Tier 2)*. Tier 1 or Core capital, which satisfies all the four criteria, comprises shareholders' equity capital plus disclosed reserves. Tier 2 or Supplemental capital is regarded as supplemental to Core capital as it cannot satisfy all of the four criteria. Thus, for compliance with capital adequacy requirements, the amount of Supplemental capital to be taken into calculation is limited to the amount of Core capital only. Essentially, Supplemental capital in excess of the Core capital is not eligible for the calculation of the capital adequacy ratio. Table 10.8 summarizes the components of the two classification of capital.

b) Risk-adjusted assets

The risk-adjusted assets focuses on the measurement of asset risk, which is accomplished by assigning assets and off balance sheet activities into four categories based on perceived risk weighting and summing the weighted categories to create total risk weighted assets (TRWA). Hence, the measurement of asset risk is represented in TRWA. The four weights are 0 per cent, 20 per cent, 50 per cent and 100 per cent. Table 10.9 gives the weighting scheme for calculating risk-adjusted assets for purposes of credit risk capital requirements.

Table 10.8 Components in the two classes of capital

Capital funds		
Tier 1 capital	(i)	ordinary share-up capital
	(ii)	non-cumulative perpetual preference shares
	(iii)	share premium
	(iv)	statutory reserve fund
	(v)	general reserve fund
	(vi)	retained profits as in last audited accounts less any accumulated losses, including current unaudited losses
	(vii)	after tax surplus arising from the sale of fixed assets and long term investments in the current financial year
	(viii)	current unadjusted net profits on a half yearly basis subject to certification by approved external auditors
	(ix)	minority interests consistent with the Tier 1 capital components (applicable only in the case of consolidated assessment)
Tier 2 capital (limited to no more than Tier 1 capital)	(i)	hybrid capital instruments, for example, cumulative perpetual preference shares, perpetual loan stocks and mandatory convertible loan stocks, approved by the central bank on a case-by-case basis
	(ii)	minority interests arising from the consolidation of the preference shares issued by subsidiaries (applicable only in the case of consolidated assessment)
	(iii)	subordinated term debt approved by the Central Bank (eligible amount restricted to 50 per cent of Core capital)
	(iv)	revaluation reserves of premises
	(v)	general provisions for bad and doubtful debts

Table 10.9 Components of balance sheet risk weighted asset categories

Risk category	Weights	
No default risk	0%	assets with zero or low credit risk, for example cash, claims on or guaranteed by the government, Central Bank, central governments of the Organization for Economic Cooperation and Development (OECD)
Low default risk	20%	interbank deposits, fully backed mortgage bonds, claims on or guaranteed by licensed financial institutions and non-OECD banks with a residual maturity of up to one year
Low to moderate default risk	50%	housing finance for residential purposes, municipal bonds
Moderate to high default risk	100%	all other assets including claims on the non-bank private sector, claims on commercial companies owned by the public sector, claims on non-OECD banks with a residual maturity of over one year, and investment in shares (other than those deducted from the capital bases) and fixed assets

c) Minimum capital requirements

To calculate the minimum or risk-adjusted capital ratio (RACR) for an Islamic bank, the following formula can be used:

$$RACR = Minimum\ ratio * [0.00(C_1) + 0.2(C_2) + 0.5(C_3) + 1.0(C_4)]$$

Where minimum ratio = Tier 1 or total capital minimum requirement, and

$$C_1, C_2, \ldots, C_4 = \text{the amounts held in the four asset categories.}$$

The items in the square brackets are known as the risk-adjusted assets.

Based on Basel I capital requirement, Islamic banks must hold Tier 1 capital equal to at least 4 per cent of total risk weighted assets (TRWA) and Tier 1 plus Tier 2 capital of at least equal to 8 per cent of TRWA. Table 10.10 summarizes the minimum requirement according to Basel I.

Table 10.10 Minimum capital levels

Capital	Risk adjusted assets	Total assets
Tier 1	4%	3%
Tier 1 + Tier 2 (Total capital)	8%	No requirement

Let us now look at an example of how the minimum capital requirement is calculated. Assume that the Statement of Financial Position of Bank XYZ is as follows:

Assets	£m	Liabilities	£m
Cash	5 000	Deposits and debt	95 000
Government bonds	20 000	Capital	5 000
Deposits at banks	5 000		
Loans for residential properties	10 000		
Loans to private corporations	60 000		
Total assets	**100 000**	**Total liabilities and capital**	**100 000**

Step 1: Calculate the risk weighted assets.

0% Risk weight	
Cash	5 000
Government bonds	20 000
	25 000 × 0 = 0
20% Risk weight	
Balances with banks	5 000
	5 000 × 0.2 = 1 000
50% Risk weight	
Loans for residential properties	10 000
	10 000 × 0.5 = 5 000
100% Risk weight	
Loans to private corporations	60 000
	60 000 × 1.0 = 60 000
Total risk weighted assets	***£66 000m***

Step 2: Calculate the capital ratio and the RACR.

Total Assets = £100 000m,

Total Risk Weighted Assets = £66 000m, and

Total Capital = £5000m

Therefore:

$$Capital\ ratio = \frac{\text{Total capital}}{\text{Total assets}}$$

$$= \frac{5000}{100\,000}$$

$$= 5\%$$

$$Risk\text{-}adjusted\ capital\ ratio = \frac{Total\ capital}{Total\ risk\ weighted\ assets}$$

$$= \frac{£5000}{£66\,000}$$

$$= 7.6\%$$

Step 3: Determine whether the bank meets the 8 per cent requirement.

If RACR = 8 per cent, the bank meets the minimum requirement.
If RACR < 8 per cent, the bank is undercapitalized.
If RACR > 8 per cent, the bank is overcapitalized.

Since the RACR in our example is only 7.6 per cent, the bank is slightly undercapitalized.
Note that if we used the traditional capital ratio, the capital required is only 5 per cent.

Let us look at another example.

Assume that Bank A and Bank B both have the same assets and capital value: Total assets = £100 000 and total capital = £5000. However, Bank A has relatively more risky assets and assume that its risk weighted assets is £75 000 while Bank B has relatively less risky assets and assume that its risk weighted assets is £55 000. What is the RACR for Bank A and Bank B?

Bank A (relatively more risky assets):

Total assets = £100 000, Total capital = £5000
Risk weighted assets = £75 000

$$RACR = \frac{Total\ capital}{TRWA}$$

$$= \frac{5000}{75\,000}$$

$$= 6.7\%$$

Bank B (relatively less risky assets):

Total assets = £100 000, Total capital = £5000
Risk weighted assets = £55 000

$$RACR = \frac{Total\ capital}{TRWA}$$

$$= \frac{5000}{55\,000}$$

$$= 9.1\%$$

Since the regulatory capital requirement is 8 per cent, Bank A is said to be undercapitalized (6.7 per cent), i.e. holding less capital than required by regulation. Hence, it needs to increase its capital, and can do so by issuing new shares, reducing dividends (i.e. increasing retained earnings) and reallocating assets (opt for less riskier assets).

In the case of Bank B, it is considered to be overcapitalized (9.1 per cent), i.e. holding more capital than the regulatory capital requirement. Therefore, it can reduce its capital by buying back shares, increasing dividends (i.e. decreasing retained earnings) and reallocating assets (opt for more riskier assets).

10.6.2 PROBLEMS WITH BASEL I REQUIREMENT

The Basel I requirement has serious shortcomings. Firstly, Basel I is too simplistic to adequately address the activities of more complex Islamic financial institutions (IFIs). Basel I categorizes each Islamic bank's assets into one of only four categories, each of which represents a certain risk class. Each risk class has its own risk weight that is multiplied by 8 per cent to get the minimum capital charge. This means that the whole spectrum of financing quality over which Islamic banks do much of their financing receives the same regulatory capital charge. The lack of differentiation among the degrees of risk means that the resultant capital ratios are often uninformative and/or provide misleading information for Islamic banks with risky or problematic financings or, with portfolios dominated by very safe financings.

Secondly, the limited number of risk classes not only limits the value of the capital requirement but also creates a regulatory loophole that creates incentives for Islamic banks to game the system by capital arbitrage. *Capital arbitrage* is the avoidance of certain minimum capital charges through sale or securitization of those assets for which the capital requirement that the market would impose is less than the regulatory capital charge. Clearly, the market believes that the 4 per cent capital charge on most residential mortgages (50 per cent of 8 per cent) and the 8 per cent on most credit cards (100 per cent of 8 per cent) is higher than the real risk, thus facilitating the securitization and sale of a large volume of such financings to other holders. This behaviour is perfectly understandable, and even considered as desirable in an economically efficient sense. However, this also means that Islamic banks that engage in such arbitrage will no longer retain the higher risk assets for which the regulatory capital charge and instead calibrated them to average quality assets, which is on average very low.

Thirdly, regulators are still unable to examine and evaluate the true risk position of the Islamic bank because the capital ratios of the larger Islamic banks becoming less and less meaningful. Furthermore, creditors, counterparties and investors are unable to evaluate the capital strength of individual Islamic banks from what is supposed to be risk based capital ratios because the regulations and statutory requirements tied to capital ratios are less meaningful.

In view of the aforementioned weaknesses in the Basel capital requirements, the Basel Committee issued a proposal to replace the 1988 Accord (Basel I) with a more risk sensitive framework, which is referred to as Basel II, in 1993. The standards, which are complicated and complex (251 pages), were finally completed in June 2006.[1]

10.6.3 BASEL II STANDARD

In line with developments in the conventional banking system worldwide, IFIs are also required to embrace Basel II. Basel II framework aims to further strengthen the soundness and stability of the international banking system and has a more risk sensitive capital requirement. It addresses three pillars: minimum capital requirements, supervisory review process and market discipline. Basel II provides scope for proper recognition of risks in Islamic banking products through a more risk sensitive system for risk weighting assets and stronger incentives for effective risk management (Pillar I). In addition, Basel II also suggests the appropriate balance of prudential supervision (Pillar II) and market disciplines (Pillar III) for IFIs. Hence, risk measurement becomes a crucial element for producing an effective disclosure regime that can connect market forces to official supervision.

Pillar I – minimum capital requirement – considers not only credit risk (as in Basel I) but also market and operational risk. Within this context, the Islamic Financial Services Board (IFSB) has proposed two different

---

[1] See www.bis.org/publ/bcbs107.htm, accessed 31 May 2018.

methods of fine tuning the capital charges to better reflect financial risk diversities among individual credit exposures: a *standardized* and an *internal ratings-based (IRB)* approach to credit risk. The former approach to credit risk is based on externally provided risk assessments such as the rating assignments by external credit assessment institutions, while the latter model of risk assessments is based on self-assessment.

Besides the aforementioned methods, IFIs may also use the basic indicator approach for operational risks, with respect to Pillar I of Basel II, and the various applicable measurement methods for market risks set out in the 1996 Market Risk Amendment. The operational risks include the *shari'ah* compliance risk that leads to non-recognition of income and resultant losses. By adopting Basel II, the Islamic banks' true risk can be better determined and Islamic banks can adapt the supervisory regime and enhance market discipline by encouraging sound disclosure policies.

10.6.4 CAPITAL ADEQUACY STANDARD BY ISLAMIC FINANCIAL SERVICES BOARD (IFSB) (2005)

Given the unique components in Islamic bank's balance sheet, Islamic Financial Services Board (IFSB) released an exposure draft in March 2005 focusing on the introduction of the capital adequacy standard (CAS) for IFIs. The proposal recommended a CAS based on the Basel Committee on Islamic banking supervision's documents on the: (i) International Convergence of Capital Measurement and Capital Standards: A Revised Framework, June 2004 (Basel II), and (ii) Amendment to the Capital Accord to Incorporate Market Risks, January 1996 (1996 Market Risk Amendment), with the necessary modifications and adaptations to cater for the specifications and characteristics of *shari'ah* compliant products and services.

The CAS document encompasses the minimum capital adequacy requirements based principally on the standardized approach with respect to credit risk and the basic indicator approach with regard to operational risks of the Islamic financial services (Pillar I) and the various applicable measurement methods for market risk set out in the 1996 Market Risk Amendment. The document does not address the requirements covered by Pillar II (supervisory review) and Pillar III (market discipline) of Basel II as these two issues are covered by separate standards. A typical Islamic bank model has the following balance sheet structure:

Statement of financial position

Assets	Liabilities
Banking portfolio	Deposits and debt
Trading portfolio	Reserves Equity

Liability side

- profit sharing investment accounts (PSIA): *mudarabah*
- demand deposits-*qard hasan*
- profit equalizing reserves (PER)
- investment risk reserves (IRR)

Asset side

- fixed income assets (*murabahah, istisna, salam* and *ijarah*)
- variable income assets (*mudarabah* and *musharakah)*

a) Proposed minimum capital requirements

In fulfilling the capital adequacy requirement, Islamic banks maintain the existing capital adequacy ratio (CAR) of not lower than 8 per cent for total capital. Tier 2 capital is limited to 100 per cent of the Tier 1 capital. The new framework also retains the existing definition of Tier 1 and Tier 2 as prescribed in Basel II. In the stated formula, the calculation of minimum capital adequacy requirements is based on the definition of (eligible) regulatory capital and risk weighted assets (RWA). The standard formula for *capital adequacy ratio* (CAR) is:

$$CAR = \frac{\textit{Eligible capital (definition unchanged)}}{\begin{array}{l}\textit{[Total risk − Weighted assets (Credit risk + Market risk) + Operational risks}\\ \textit{less}\\ \textit{Risk − Weighed assets funded by PSIA (Credit risk + Market risks)]}\end{array}}$$

where credit and market risks refer to both on and off balance sheet exposures, operational risks less RWA funded by PSIA balances which include PER and IRR.

The capital amount of PSIA is not guaranteed and any losses arising from investments or assets funded by PSIA are to be borne by the Investment Account Holder (IAH) except for losses arising from the bank's negligence and misconduct of its investment mandate, i.e. fiduciary risk. The capital requirement for this type of risk is dealt with under operational risks. In principle, the commercial risks on assets funded by PSIA do not represent risks for the bank's own capital and thus would not entail a regulatory capital requirement. This implies that this kind of asset would be excluded from the calculation of the denominator of the capital ratio.

However, in some jurisdictions, the regulators can also consider an extended formula to smooth income to the IAHs as part of a mechanism to minimize the withdrawal risk in overcoming concerns with systemic risk. The extended formula, known as *supervisory discretion formula*, can be written as:

$$CAR = \frac{\textit{Eligible capital (definition unchanged)}}{\begin{array}{l}\textit{\{Total risk − Weighted assets (Credit risk + Market risk) + Operational risks}\\ \textit{less}\\ \textit{(1 − α) [Risk − Weighed assets funded by PSIA (Credit risk + Market risks)]}\\ \textit{less}\\ \textit{α [Risk − Weighed assets funded by PSIA (Credit risk + Market risks)]\}}\end{array}}$$

where α = the proportion of assets funded by PSIA which is to be determined by the supervisory authorities. The value of α would not exceed 30 per cent.

The major changes proposed are in the measurement of the denominator. The denominator covers the TRWA with some adjustments. The regulatory authorities will have the option of applying two different adjustments for the risk weighting assets; option 1 using the RWA funded by PSIA or option 2 using both the RWA funded by PSIA as well as PER and IRR. In option 2, the relevant proportion of RWA funded by PER and IRR is deducted from the denominator because these reserves have the effect of reducing the *displaced commercial risk*.

The term *displaced commercial risk* refers to the risk arising from assets managed on behalf of IAH which is effectively transferred to the IFIs' own capital since the latter follows the practice of foregoing its rights to part or all of its *mudarib* share of profit, in order to offer IAH a more competitive rate of return on their funds when it considers this necessary as a result of commercial and supervisory pressure.

Subsequently, the calculation of CAR should be linked with three elements: *shari'ah* compliant instruments, provisions for operational risks and adjustment to the denominator.

Let us now look at an example in calculating CAR based on IFSB's CAS. Assume Bank XYZ has the following balance sheet:

Assets		Liabilities	
Cash	10	PSIA	40
Other assets	90	Demand deposits	55
		Equity	5
Total assets	100	Total liabilities and equity	100

Assume the following:

- total risk weighted assets = 120% of other assets = $1.2 \times 90 = 108$
- average gross income of last 3 years = 10
- operational risk capital base = average 3 year gross income $\times 0.15 = 10 \times 0.15 = 1.5$
- percentage of other assets financed by PSIA = 40/90 = 44.4%
- RWA financed by PSIA = percentage of other assets financed by PSIA $\times$ TRWA = $0.444 \times 108 = 48$

Standard formula for regulatory capital:

$$\frac{Eligible\ capital}{[\text{Total risk-weighted assets (credit and market risks)} + \text{Operational risk} - \text{risk-weighted assets funded by PSIA (credit and market risks)}]}$$

$$= \frac{5}{[108 + 1.5 - 48]}$$

$$= \frac{5}{61.5}$$

$$= 8.1\%$$

Assume Bank ABC has the following balance sheet:

Assets		Liabilities	
Cash	10	PSIA	20
Other assets	90	Demand deposits	75
		Equity	5
Total assets	100	Total liabilities and equity	100

- total risk weighted = 120% of other assets = $1.2 \times 90 = 108$
- average gross income of last 3 years = 10
- operational risk capital base = average 3 year gross income $\times 0.15 = 10 \times 0.15 = 1.5$
- percentage total assets financed by PSIA = 20/90 = 22.2%
- RWA financed by PSIA = percentage of other assets financed by PSIA $\times$ TRWA
  = $0.222 \times 108 = 24$

Standard formula for regulatory capital:

$$\frac{Eligible\ capital}{[\text{Total risk-weighted assets (credit and market risks)} + \text{Operational risk} - \text{risk-weighted assets funded by PSIA (credit and market risks)}]}$$

$$= \frac{5}{[108 + 1.5 - 24]}$$

$$= \frac{5}{85.5}$$

$$= 5.9\%$$

From the above examples, it can be seen that by sharing the risks, PSIA offsets the capital requirements of the Islamic bank's riskier assets.

10.7 Off balance sheet management

The phenomenon of globalization, institutionalization, privatization and securitization has encouraged financial innovation in the Islamic financial services industry. Off balance sheet (OBS) activities fit into the model of financial innovation which is driven by competitive, technological and regulatory forces.

Off balance sheet items are also known as *contingent liabilities* because the transaction is not complete until certain conditions or requirements are met. OBS activities involve the exchange of services with money, and such activities affect Islamic bank profits, but they do not appear on Islamic bank's balance sheets. It is critical to review these activities because they represent potential credit risk, i.e. risk that the counterparties of the transaction would not honour their obligation, and/or liquidity risk, the inability to honour withdrawal demands.

There are a number of OBS activities that banks undertake. Figure 10.3 illustrates the various types of OBS activities undertaken by Islamic banks. We will look more closely at each of them in the following sections.

Figure 10.3 Types of OBS activities by Islamic banks

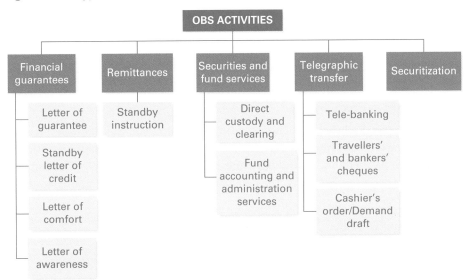

10.7.1 FINANCIAL GUARANTEES

There are several types of guarantee letters that banks provide to their customers.

a) Letter of guarantee

A letter of guarantee from an Islamic bank to a third party states that a customer who has made an order does indeed own the underlying assets and the Islamic bank will guarantee delivery if the order is assigned. There are many types of Letters of Guarantee but the underlying purpose is the same for all, i.e. a guarantee of payment to a supplier. A *Payment Guarantee* serves as a security for the supplier should the purchaser fail to meet his payment obligation on a timely basis. Letters of Guarantee may also be granted for advanced payment, retention *sukuk*, bid *sukuk*, performance *sukuk*, financing collateral and customs guarantees.

b) Standby letter of credit

The standby letter of credit is a secondary payment mechanism. An Islamic bank will issue a standby letter of credit on behalf of a customer to provide assurances of his ability to perform under the terms of a contract. The standby letter of credit assures the beneficiary of the performance of the customer's obligations. The Islamic bank is obligated to make payment to the beneficiary when presented with documents that comply with the terms of the letter of credit showing evidence that the customer has not performed its obligation. It is also issued by Islamic banks to insure the refund of advance payment, to support performance and bid obligations, and to insure completion of a sales contract. Besides that, it is often used to guarantee performance or to strengthen the credit worthiness of a customer. The financing has an expiration date.

c) Letter of comfort

A letter of comfort is essentially an instrument that is used to facilitate an action or transaction, but is constructed with the intention of not giving rise to legal obligations. In general, letters of comfort should be avoided. Officials should be aware that a letter of comfort may lead to an actual liability, either through a court finding that the party receiving the letter was entitled to rely upon its contents, or through a moral obligation for the government to make good on its assurances. It is therefore important to carefully consider who may sign letters of comfort.

d) Letter of awareness

A letter of awareness is a formal letter written to a seller, normally by a parent company, acknowledging its relationship with another group company and its awareness of a financial arrangement being made with that company. Such letters do not constitute a guarantee, but may nevertheless involve a significant moral commitment on the part of the writer.

10.7.2 REMITTANCE (STANDING INSTRUCTION)

A *standing instruction* is a remittance service by which a customer can instruct an Islamic bank to affect regular fund transfers at pre-set timings and amounts from the customer's deposit account to designated beneficiary accounts. It is like an automatic bill payment but instead of paying a bill, it puts money into our investment every month, automatically. It works best with unit trusts. The standing instruction service can be used to effect:

- repayment of financing/hire purchase instalments
- payment of bills/school fees/*takaful* contributions, etc.
- salary payments
- inter-account transfer of funds
- payment of safe deposit box rental
- inter-account transfer of SIA
- purchase of cashier's orders

10.7.3 SECURITIES AND FUND SERVICES

The services cover products such as Direct Custody and Clearing (DCC) and Fund Accounting and Administration Services.

a) Direct Custody and Clearing (DCC)

DCC is a set of services provided to investors seeking an end to end securities service solution in both the international and domestic market. The services may cover: securities settlement and clearing; safekeeping or custody; asset servicing such as corporate action processing, income collection, proxy voting; and cash management and reporting.

Securities settlement refers to the actual delivery of securities to/ from a counterparty (broker or another custodian bank or between existing clients) based on the terms of trade such as T+3 (trade date plus three working days) where trades will be settled in accordance with the relevant terms and conditions as set by the financial market. *Safekeeping of assets* are kept in book entry form and the Islamic bank will hold the securities as nominees on behalf of the client.

Corporate action management is a service which involves the timely and accurate broadcasting of a corporate action news event (e.g. dividend/interest payment, right issues, company annual or extraordinary meeting, etc.) to ensure that the shareholders are aware of their related corporate actions entitlement.

Income collection is an integral part of corporate action management and covers the timely and accurate credit of dividend/interests payments.

Proxy voting service is provided upon receipt of voting instruction from clients on a case by case basis. In providing the service, the Islamic bank will complete the proxy form and cast the votes based on their clients' instructions. The completely filled in form will then be delivered to the company or its appointed registrar.

Cash management is critical for foreign investors since trade payments are settled in local currency. In order to support this, maintaining a local currency current account is an essential component of cash management. *Reporting of cash/securities* movement is normally accomplished through telex, SWIFT or email. Islamic banks also provide a report/statement to client on the cash/securities movement which can be accessed via the electronic platform.

b) Fund accounting and administration services

This involves a range of services offered to third parties, predominantly to asset managers and fund management companies managing Islamic unit trusts and Islamic mutual funds, closed end Islamic funds, pension, retirement and provident funds. Essentially, the fund administration services cover the following: *investment accounting, portfolio valuation, net asset valuation, compliance monitoring* and *performance measurement*. Fund administration services essentially includes calculating and reporting a funds' net asset value, which encompasses tax liability (if any), recording accounting and investment transactions, and related administrative tasks for Islamic managed funds.

Investment accounting on the other hand covers the maintenance of the books and records of the fund in accordance with International Financial Reporting Standards (IFRS) or US Generally Accepted Accounting Principles (GAAP), and the Securities Commission guidelines or any local accounting guidelines that may be issued from time to time by local regulatory bodies. The *investment portfolio* may contain a variety of instruments (both OTC and exchange traded). The result of corporate actions (e.g. dividends, stock splits, etc.) will be reflected in the books and records of the fund. Periodically (usually on the valuation date), the portfolio is marked to market and, if appropriate, adjusted for foreign exchange in order to provide the basis for issuing a number of accounting statements, the most important being the calculation of the *net asset value (NAV)*. The frequency with which the NAV must be calculated depends upon both the regulatory and the business demands of the fund. Open-ended Islamic mutual funds require that NAV be calculated and published on a daily basis. A standard set of reports (known as the NAV reports) is generated which shows the current valuation, transactions, and income over the period and explains the change in value of the fund in terms of the various currency, market and income components.

In terms of *compliance monitoring*, the service is offered on a selected basis based on clients' requirements. The service helps to ensure portfolio assets conform to client's investment policies and guidelines.

10.7.4 TELEGRAPHIC TRANSFER

Telegraphic Transfer (TT) service is the fastest means for transferring money from one country to another. It is used to transfer funds (especially cash and pools of money contributed by individuals to make investments with the benefit of size or to gain tax advantages). No hard money transfer is involved in TT. The order to pay is wired to an institution's cashier to make payment to a company or individual.

a) Tele-banking

Tele-banking is a service that helps customers to access authentic, instantaneous information regarding their accounts, by using a push button telephone from any place, anytime. Customers can even leave messages to the Islamic bank. A domestic payment order sent via tele-banking is cheaper than an order made at the bank and the charge for foreign payment orders is also lower than at the branch office. Domestic payment orders and notices for collection are processed in real time. Orders accepted after the set dates are automatically processed on the next business day.

b) Travellers' cheques

Travellers' cheques are issued in fixed denominations of international currencies by certain banks. They can be cashed easily, have no specific maturity period and are a convenient means of payment for travellers. They are an ideal supplement to cards and cash. If lost or stolen, travellers' cheques are replaced as a rule within 24 hours worldwide and at no cost. Travellers' cheques do not expire and can be used anytime.

c) Cashier's order/local demand draft

A cashier's order or local demand draft can be ordered from the bank for making payments locally or for new share application subscriptions. The purchase of a cashier's order/local demand draft will be available for collection on the same day for the customer's convenience.

A *cashier's order* is a cheque issued by an Islamic bank branch and drawn on itself and is generally used within the same locality (local clearing area) to effect payment, especially if personal cheques are not acceptable or cash payment is not advisable.

A *demand draft* is an order in writing by one Islamic bank to another Islamic bank/branch requesting the Islamic bank or branch to pay a specific sum of money to a specific person upon presentation of the draft. It will specify a clearing branch where the draft can be submitted for cash. Customers can choose to bank the demand draft into any local or foreign Islamic bank for clearance. Demand drafts are valid for six months from the date of issuance.

10.7.5 SECURITIZATION

The idea behind securitization is to transform the bank's dormant illiquid assets into tradeable, negotiable and liquid assets. This is done by pooling assets of similar characteristics and selling them to third parties as security. This is useful as risks can be diversified and channelled to a wider pool of investors who are able to better match their investments with the type of risk profile. Since the year 2000, securitization has expanded exponentially for mortgages (both residential and commercial), leases and receivables from inventories, etc.

Shari'ah compliant securitization has also experienced growth in recent years. This may be attributed to the growing demand for *shari'ah* compliant financial instruments by investors and the need by banks to raise funds in a cost-effective, *shari'ah* compliant manner without affecting shareholder equity. Since securitizations are based on the performance of a set of well-defined assets, it can be used in Islamic banking.

Summary

An Islamic bank manager's role is to implement decisions that maximize the profitability of his/her institution within the confines of *shari'ah*. To achieve these aims, Islamic bank managers need to pursue strategies in various areas such as asset and liability management, liquidity management, capital management and OBS management. This chapter discusses the structure and management of each of those areas and factors affecting them. It begins by discussing asset–liability management (ALM) and the role of the asset–liabilities committee (ALCO). Another important aspect for banks is liquidity management, as decisions on the level of liquidity to hold will have implications on the bank's operations as well as its viability. Factors affecting bank's liquidity include the structure of its balance sheet, access to financial markets and the bank's financial condition. The level of a bank's capital is important, as it signals the extent the bank is solvent. A bank's capital can be classified into regulatory capital and economic capital. The regulatory capital, i.e. level of capital required by regulators, can be determined based on capital ratio and risk adjusted capital ratio (RACR) as recommended by Basel I. Due to several shortcomings in Basel I, the Basel II framework was introduced to take into account credit, operational and market risk to reflect the bank's true risk. Since the Basel Accord does not specifically apply to IFIs, the IFSB introduced the capital adequacy standard (CAS). Lastly, the various off balance sheet activities undertaken by Islamic banks have been highlighted.

Key terms and concepts

asset management
asset–liability management
bank liquidity
bank solvency
Basel I capital requirement
Basel II
business financing
capital adequacy standard
capital arbitrage
capital base
capital management
capital ratio
cashier's order
consumer financing
Core capital (Tier 1)
corporate action management
demand deposits
demand draft
deposits
deposits and placements of banks
  and other institutions
direct custody and clearing
displaced commercial risk

economic capital
fund accounting and
  administration services
general investment account
hibah related deposits
income collection
internal ratings based credit risk
investment accounting
investment deposits
letter of awareness
letter of comfort
letter of guarantee
liability management
limited period investment account
liquidity assessment
liquidity management
liquidity risk
minimum capital requirement
non-deposits
off balance sheet
off balance sheet management
Pillar I
Pillar II

Pillar III
profit related deposits
proxy voting service
real estate financing
regulatory capital
restricted funds
risk adjusted capital ratio
safekeeping of assets
savings deposit
securities settlement
securitization
standardized credit risk
standby letter of credit
standing instruction
structured trade deposits
supervisory discretion formula
Supplemental capital (Tier 2)
tele-banking
travellers' cheque
unlimited period investment
  account
unrestricted funds
wadiah yad dhamanah

Questions

1. What are the five important aspects in Islamic bank management?

2. Report on the role and primary goal of asset–liability management.

3. Describe the structure and components of Islamic banks' assets and liabilities.

4. What are the factors affecting the choice of non-deposit funding sources?

5. Islamic banks offer a wide variety of financing activities to cater for the needs of different customers. Comment on the nature of those activities.

6. Discuss the liquidity management of an Islamic bank paying more attention to the possibility of facing acute liquidity problem.

7. Report on the balance sheet structure on an Islamic bank and illustrate how it is linked to liquidity risk.

8. Summarize the main off balance sheet financing activities that an Islamic bank may be involved in.

9. Assess the capability of an Islamic bank accessing and competing in the open financial market.

10. What is capital adequacy in the banking industry? Illustrate how changes in assets of a bank may lead to bankruptcy.

11. What are the regulatory and adjusted capital adequacies?

12. Describe Core capital (Tier 1), Supplemental capital (Tier 2), and risk weighted asset categories in a bank's financial position statement.

13. Advise on the calculation of risk adjusted capital ratio for an Islamic bank.

14. Critically assess the soundness of Basel I risk requirement for Islamic banks.

15. Discuss how Basel II framework contributes to the strength and stability of Islamic financial institutions.

16. Describe capital adequacy standard as informed by the Islamic Financial Services Board.

17. What is CAR and how is it calculated?

18. What are the two factors associated with the growth of the *shari'ah* compliant securitization market?

Case Study

Select an annual report of an Islamic bank and prepare a table showing the breakdown of other liabilities of the Islamic bank. Comment on the types and proportion of each type and calculate CAR based on the standard formula for regulatory capital.

References and further readings

Abdul Rahman, A. (2010), *An Introduction to Islamic Accounting: Theory and Practice*, CERT Publications, Kuala Lumpur.

Beck, T., Demirgüç-Kunt, A. and Merrouche, O. (2013), 'Islamic vs. conventional banking: Business model, efficiency and stability', *Journal of Banking and Finance*, 37, pp. 433-447.

Greuning, H.V. and Iqbal, Z. (2008), *Risk Analysis for Islamic Banks*, The World Bank, Washington, DC.

Hassan, K., Kayed, R. and Oseni, U.A. (2013), *Introduction to Islamic Banking & Finance: Principles and Practice*, Pearson Education, Edinburgh Gate, Harlow, Essex, UK.

Ismail, A.G. (2010), *Money, Islamic Banks, and the Real Economy*, Cengage Learning EMEA, Andover.

Olson, D. and Zoubi, T.A. (2017), 'Convergence in bank performance for commercial and Islamic banks during and after the Global Financial Crisis', *The Quarterly Review of Economics and Finance*, 65, pp. 71-87.

Sinkey, J.F. Jr. (2002), *Commercial Bank Financial Management. In the Financial-Services Industry*, 6th ed., Prentice Hall, Upper Saddle River, New Jersey, USA.

11 Risk management of Islamic financial institutions

Learning Objectives

Upon completion of this chapter you should be able to:

- define risk and distinguish the terms *risk* and *uncertainty*

- explain the concept of risk–return trade-off

- discuss the principles related to the Islamic perspective of risk

- identify and explain the different types of risk faced by financial institutions

- discuss factors that may affect the financial institution's financial, operational, business and event risks exposure

- identify and explain the risks that are generic and unique to an Islamic financial institution

- define risk management and its objectives

- discuss the concept of risk management from an Islamic perspective

- identify and discuss the operational strategies according to the IFSB Guiding Principles in relation to the six categories of risk for Islamic financial institutions

- explain why it is difficult for an Islamic financial institution to manage risk

- describe the standard risk mitigating techniques adopted by Islamic financial institutions

- explain the *shari'ah* compliant risk mitigating techniques for Islamic financial institutions

11.1 Introduction

Risk has always been part of our everyday life and we are exposed to different degrees of risk from the moment we wake up until the time we get to our beds (and possibly even after that). Some risks, such as death and natural calamities, are not something that we voluntary seek or have a choice about. They are beyond our control. But there are risks that we seek and choose to undertake, such as speeding on the highway or investing in a project. These are within our control. Similarly, all organizations including financial institutions face both controllable and uncontrollable risks. Our concern in this chapter is with the former form of risks which entail both vulnerability of asset values and opportunities of income growth.

As seen in previous chapters, Islamic financial institutions have some unique features, so while they can be expected to share some risks similar to their conventional counterparts there are also risks that are unique due to their compliance with *shari'ah*. Moreover, Islamic financial institutions are constrained in utilizing some of the risk mitigation instruments that their conventional counterparts used as they are prohibited by *shari'ah*.

Therefore, in this chapter, we will define and identify the different types of risks faced by Islamic financial institutions. Then we will turn our attention to risk management processes including the guiding principles available for Islamic financial institutions. The last part of this chapter discusses issues related to risk measurement and mitigating techniques.

11.2 What is risk?

There are several possible origins of the word risk. It has been traced to the classical Greek word *rhizikón* meaning root, radical or hazard. The Latin word *resicum*, referring to something cut off, is said to be the direct formal origin for the Italian word *risico* meaning danger, Spanish *riesgo* meaning unfavourable outcome from random chance, and French *risquer* meaning hazard. Nevertheless, they all point to some form of exposure to the chance of imminent danger or loss.

In the business context, risk generally refers to a situation involving exposure to danger and the probability or threat of damage, liability, loss or any negative occurrence caused by internal or external vulnerabilities but which can be avoided through pre-emptive action. Similarly, specifically in finance and banking, risk refers to the uncertainty of future outcomes i.e. chance that the return achieved will be different from that expected. This may arise from some internal or external forces despite taking measures to minimize the difference in the expected outcomes. A *downside risk* is where the returns are below expectations while an *upside risk* is when returns exceed expectations. In short, the definitions of risk range across the spectrum, with some focusing primarily on the likelihood of bad events occurring to those that look at both upside and downside potential.

The words risk and *uncertainty* have often been used interchangeably but it is important in finance to distinguish between the two terms. The classical quote by Knight (1921) summarized the difference between risk and uncertainty as follows:

> … *Uncertainty must be taken in a sense radically distinct from the familiar notion of risk. … The essential fact is that 'risk' means in some cases a quantity susceptible of measurement, while at other times it is something distinctly not of this character; and there are far-reaching and crucial differences in the bearings of the phenomena depending on which of the two is really present and operating. … It will appear that a measurable uncertainty, or 'risk' proper, as we shall use the term, is so far different from an un-measurable one that it is not in effect an uncertainty at all. (cited in Damodaran (2008))*

From the above quote, it is clear that one of the important distinctions between risk and uncertainty is related to measurement of the uncertainty. Unlike risk where the probability of outcomes can be anticipated based on prior and current information, uncertainty refers to a situation where the probability of the outcome is not certain due to lack of information or knowledge about the present condition to define or predict the future outcome or events. Furthermore, risk can be measured and quantified through theoretical models, but it is not possible to measure uncertainty in quantitative terms since the future events are unpredictable. Moreover, risk to some extent can be controlled and minimized by taking necessary precautions while uncertainty is beyond one's control as the future is uncertain and hence steps cannot be taken to minimize the probability of negative outcomes. Table 11.1 summarizes the main differences between the two terms.

Table 11.1 Key differences between risk and uncertainty

Basis for comparison	Risk	Uncertainty
Meaning	implies a situation where the future events or outcomes are known	implies a situation where the future events or outcomes are not known
Certainty	can be measured	cannot be measured
Outcome	chances of outcomes are known	the outcome is unknown
Probabilities	assigned	not assigned
Control	controllable	uncontrollable
Minimization	yes	no

11.3   Risk–return trade-off

Risk is usually measured by the variability or volatility of outcomes, technically based on statistics such as variance or standard deviation. A high standard deviation means high risk and low standard deviation means low risk. Another important concept related to risk is what is known as the *risk–return trade-off*.

Generally, those who are willing to take higher exposure of risk (*risk takers*) can expect to get a higher return while those who prefer to stay away from high exposure of risk or willing to take low risk (*risk averse*) can expect to get lower return, as depicted in Figure 11.1.

Figure 11.1   Risk–return trade-off

The aim of risk–return trade-off is to find the balance between the desire for the lowest possible risk and the highest possible return. Determining the most appropriate risk level is not straightforward, as it depends on the *risk tolerance* of the individual or organization which may be influenced by various factors such as financial goals, amount and structure of assets, economic circumstances, etc.

Since the financial sector has its own share of risks, the decisions on how much risk to take and what type of risks to take are critical to its success in creating value for the shareholders and generating returns for other fund providers. A financial institution that protects itself from taking high risk is unlikely to generate much upside for its owners and fund providers, but it may be worse off if it exposes itself to the wrong types of risk. Hence, the essence of good management is making the right choices when it comes to dealing with different risks. In other words, a bank's business is to take calculated risks and its competitive advantage is dependent on how well it manages its risks. Furthermore, given that the risks encountered in this sector may have ripple effects on other sectors that may eventually trigger collapse in the country's economy, it is important to develop proper measures of *risk management*, which we will discuss further in a later section.

11.4   Islamic perspective of risk

Risk (*ghorm*) and uncertainties of business and investment outcomes are recognized in Islamic commercial transactions. Since one cannot predict the future with precision, variation in business outcomes constitutes risks that are unavoidable. However, one can strive to manage the risks in order to minimize adverse impacts.

The unique features of Islamic banks do not insulate them from risk. Instead, the *shari'ah* perspective on the concept of profit itself stresses that profit is a return to those who are willing to undertake risk. This is in line with the 'no risk no reward' principle (*al-riba bi daman*). The foundational *fiqh* axiom of Islamic banking of 'benefit from a certain thing is in return for the liability that accompanies that thing' (*al-kharaj bi al-daman*) and 'gain accompanies loss' (*al-ghunm bi al-ghurm*), are both related to risk. The first axiom (*al-kharaj bi al-daman*) basically means that the entitlement to the returns from an asset is intrinsically associated with the risk resulting from its possession while the second axiom (*al-ghunm bi al-ghurm*) is related to the entitlement of returns associated to the liability risk. Therefore, those who are willing to invest their deposits should also be willing to accept negative outcomes even if they expect positive returns from their investments.

11.5   Classification of risks and risk factors in financial institutions

Risks can be broadly classified into *systematic* and *unsystematic* risks, and when combined results in *total risk*. Table 11.2 presents the key differences between systematic and unsystematic risks based on a number of aspects. *Systematic risk*, which is also known as *market risk*, is associated with the uncertainty inherent to the entire market or entire segment of the market. It is also recognized as *uncontrollable risk* and *undiversifiable risk* because the effect on the overall market is a result of external or macroeconomic factors such as social, political or economic which are beyond the control of the organization and cannot be eliminated through diversification. It is sometimes referred to as *volatility risk* as the effect on the entire market leads to the fluctuation in prices arising from changes in government policy, the act of nature such as natural disaster, changes in the nation's economy, international economic components, etc.

Table 11.2 Key differences between systematic and unsystematic risks

Basis for comparison	Systematic risk	Unsystematic risk
Meaning	refers to the risk or uncertainty associated with the market or market segment as a whole	refers to the risk or uncertainty associated with a particular industry, firm or asset.
Nature of uncertainty	uncontrollable	controllable
Contributing factors	external factors	internal factors
Affects	all industries, companies and assets in the market	only specific to a particular industry, company and asset class
Types	market risk, political risk and country risk	business risk and financial risk
Protection mechanism	asset allocation	portfolio diversification

Although *systematic risk* often refers to market risk, there are two other types of risks that fall under this category: *political risk* and *country risk*. *Political risk* refers to the complications businesses and governments may face as a result of political decisions such as social policies (e.g. fiscal, monetary, trade, investment, industrial, income, labour, and developmental) or events related to political instability (e.g. terrorism, riots, coups) that alter the expected outcome and value of a given economic action (Kennedy, 1988). *Country risk* is the risk that a foreign government may default on its financial commitments arising from political, social and economic unrest. *Market risk* refers to risk that affects the bank's trading book due to changes in equity prices, interest rates, credit spreads, foreign exchange rates, commodity prices and other indicators whose values are set in a public market.

Unsystematic risk, on the other hand, is linked to the uncertainty specific to the industry, organization or asset and hence is also referred to as *specific risk*. It is also known as *controllable risk* and *diversifiable risk* as the specific effect on the industry or organization is due to internal factors which are controllable and can be minimized through diversification. It is also known as *residual risk* because the uncertainty related to the specific industry, organization or asset is after taking into considerations all measures to identify and eliminate potential threats.

Unsystematic risk can be further categorized into *business risk* and *financial risk*. *Business risk* refers to risk that affects the financial institution's performance which may arise from the nature of its business such as its rise in competition, changes in customer preferences, development of products, technological changes, etc. In contrast, *financial risk* refers to risks associated with a change in the capital structure of the financial institution and movements in the financial market.

Now that we understand the differences, let us now look more closely at the different types of risk factors classified under the three main categories: *market risk (systematic), business risk* and *financial risk (unsystematic risks)*. Figure 11.2 presents the breakdown of the types of risk exposure for financial institutions. The main source of systematic risk is market risk which is related to the potential impact of price movements on the economic value of an asset. There are four types of risks related to market risk: *interest rate risk, equity price risk, asset or commodity price risk* and *foreign exchange or currency exchange risk*.

Figure 11.2   **Classification of the different types of risk exposures for financial institutions**

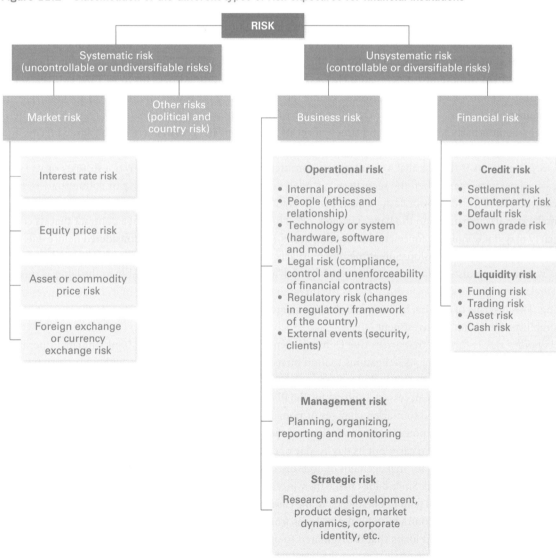

Interest rate risk is the exposure of a bank's financial conditions to movements of interest rate. *Equity price risk* refers to the exposure of a bank's financial conditions to movements of equity securities and other instruments that derive their value from a particular share, a defined portfolio of shares, or a share index. *Asset or commodity price risk* is the potential impact on the bank's financial conditions due to a change in the price of a commodity or asset. Lastly, *exchange rate or currency risk* is related to the potential impact on the bank's balance sheet due to changes in the relative value of certain foreign currencies.

In the case of unsystematic risk, the main sources are business and financial risks. Business risk factors can be further classified into *management, strategic and operational risks. Management risk* refers to the chance that the bank's *managers* will put their own interests ahead of the interest of the bank's shareholders and stakeholders (agency problem) and/or may arise due to their planning, organizing, reporting and controlling function. *Strategic risk* can be defined as the uncertainties and untapped opportunities which are embedded in the *strategy* of the bank's management and how well they succeeded in executing those strategies. They include key matters for the board such as product design, research and development, market dynamics, corporate identity, etc. which may impinge on the whole business of the bank and not just an isolated unit. *Operational risk* is the potential loss resulting from inadequate or failed *internal processes, people* (ethics and relationship), *technology or system* (hardware, software and model), *legal risk* (compliance and control including risks of unenforceability of financial contracts), *regulatory risk* (risk that arises from changes in regulatory framework of the country), or *external events* (security, clients). An example of operational risk leading to a bank's collapse is the case of Barings Bank, which was one of Britain's oldest banks. Its fall in 1995 was mainly due to failure of its internal control processes which enabled one of its traders in Singapore, Nick Leeson, to authorize his own trades and enter them into the bank's system without any supervision. He was able to hide his trading losses for more than two years. His supervisors were only aware when the losses became too huge to keep the trades and the losses a secret.

Financial risk factors can be further classified into *credit risk* and *liquidity risk. Credit risk* refers to the potential that a counterparty fails to fully and timely meet its obligations in accordance with the agreed terms and conditions of the credit contract. This includes *settlement risk, default risk, counterparty risk* and *down grade risk. Settlement risk* is the risk that a counterparty (or intermediary agent) fails to deliver a security or its value in cash as per agreement when the security was traded despite the other counterparty or counterparties have already delivered the security or cash value as per the trade agreement. *Default risk* arises when a borrower fails to make required payments to the bank. *Counterparty risk* is the risk to each party of a contract that its counterparty may not uphold its contractual obligation and this risk should be seriously considered before entering into the contractual relationship. Sometimes counterparty risk and default risk have been used interchangeably. One way to draw a distinction between the two is to look at the nature of the relationship as the latter is specifically related to borrowers. *Down grade risk* is the threat to the bank due to a lowering in its credit or investment rating. The lowering of opinion by analyst and rating agencies would send a negative signal to the market on the desirability of the bank for investment.

Liquidity risk is the risk that arises due to insufficient liquidity to cater for the bank's normal operating requirements such as meeting its obligations to fund increases in assets as they fall due without incurring unacceptable costs or losses. Hence, this includes *funding risk, asset risk, trading risk* and *cash risk. Funding risk* is the risk of inability to obtain the necessary funding for the illiquid asset positions on the expected terms and when required. *Asset risk* is related to market changes or poor investment performance of a financial asset held by banks. *Trading risk* refers to potential loss from trading the bank's spare capital. *Cash risk* arises when a bank is unable to have enough cash to carry out its day-to-day operations.

The disastrous effect of poor management of liquidity risk can be seen in the case of Northern Rock, a small bank in the north of England. Since banks make their profits from loans, it is vital that banks have surplus funds from depositors which it can lend to borrowers. In the case of Northern Rock, it only had a small depositor base and as such it struggled to continue to fund new loans from the deposits. Therefore, to obtain funds to finance its new loans, it sold the old loans that it originated to other banks and investors through what is known in the financial sector as *securitization*. This worked well when there were high demands for loans and abundant supply of credit in the financial markets. However, the market was under pressure during the financial crisis in 2007-2008. This impacted the bank badly as it was neither able to sell the loans it originated nor secure short term credits. Worse still, many of its investors withdrew their deposits, putting the bank in severe liquidity crisis. The government had to intervene by taking ownership of the bank to stop further panic in the market.

In short, financial institutions are exposed to various types of risks. However, the threat of each type of risk differs from one institution to another depending on a number of factors as shown in Table 11.3. This includes the balance sheet and income structure of the financial institution, their operational mode, types of financial contracts, types of products and services, etc.

Table 11.3 Summary of banking risk exposures

Financial risks	Operational risks	Business risks	Event risks
balance sheet structure	internal fraud	macro policy	political
income statement structure and profitability	external fraud	financial infrastructure	contagion
capital adequacy	employment practices and workplace safety	legal infrastructure	banking crisis
credit	clients, products and business services	legal liability	other exogenous risks
liquidity	damage to physical assets	regulatory compliance	
market	business disruption and system failures (technology risk)	reputational and fiduciary	
interest rate	execution, delivery and process management	country risk	
currency			

Source: Greuning and Iqbal (2008). *Risk Analysis for Islamic Banks*. Washington, DC: World Bank. © World Bank. openknowledge.worldbank.org/handle/10986/6923 License: CC BY 3.0 IGO.

11.6   Unique features of Islamic financial institutions and implications on risks

As we have seen in the previous chapter, the prohibition of interest and the use of the profit–loss sharing mode of operations by Islamic financial institutions result in their balance sheet structure to be different than their conventional counterparts, as can be seen in Table 11.4. Therefore, some the risks they face may be unique and may not apply to their conventional counterparts that rely heavily on debt instruments and returns or profits from interest.

As shown in Figure 11.3, there are six types of risks that are common to both Islamic and conventional financial institutions. However, there are six risks unique only to Islamic financial institutions. We will start by first discussing the common types of risks and their components followed by the unique risks and their components.

11.6.1 GENERIC RISKS
a) Market risk
According to the Guiding Principles of Risk Management for Islamic financial institutions (IFSB-1: 4.2), *market risk* is defined as:

> *the risk of losses in on- and off-balance sheet positions arising from movements in market prices, i.e., fluctuations in values in tradable, marketable or leaseable assets (including sukuk) and in off-balance sheet individual portfolios (e.g. restricted investment accounts).*

Table 11.4 Balance sheet structure of Islamic and conventional financial institutions

Conventional banks		Islamic banks	
Assets (uses)	**Liabilities (sources)**	**Assets (uses)**	**Liabilities (sources)**
cash and balances with other banks	interest based savings account	cash	savings account – *amanah*
loans mortgages	demand deposits	financing assets (*murabahah, istisna'a, salam, ijarah*)	demand deposits – *qard hasan*
financial leases	time deposits, certificates of deposits, etc. – fixed income liabilities	investment assets (*mudarabah* and *musharakah*)	profit sharing investment accounts (PSIA)
investment in real estate and securities	shareholders' equity and subordinated loans protect these liabilities <u>against all risks</u>	trading assets/sales receivables (*murabahah, salam, istisna'a*)	special investment accounts (*mudarabah, musharakah*)
		non-banking assets (property)	profit equalization reserve and investment risk reserve
		inventory	shareholders' equity protects these liabilities <u>only in case of fiduciary risks</u>

Figure 11.3 Generic and unique risks of Islamic financial institution

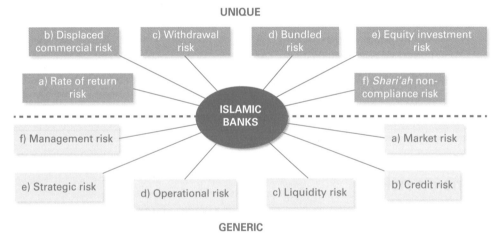

Hence, market risk for equities relates to the possibility of equity prices falling. In the case of sales receivables, market risk is related to the possibility of interest rates rising. As for transactions involving future delivery or deferred payment such as *salam* or *murabahah* and *sukuk* contracts, the market risk is related to the volatility of market values. Similarly, the market risk for *ijarah* or leasing contract and for *salam* asset relates to the market value of the leased asset and the volatility of commodity price, respectively. For international investments and cross border transactions, market risk relates to the fluctuations in currency exchange rates. However, the market risk components are slightly different for conventional and Islamic financial institutions.

(I) MARK-UP OR BENCHMARK RISK Despite not dealing with interest based instruments, Islamic financial institutions are not totally immune to *interest rate risks*. In practice, Islamic financial institutions use a benchmark rate, usually based on the London Interbank Offered Rate (LIBOR) when pricing their various financial instruments. For instance, in a *murabahah* contract, the mark-up is determined by adding a risk premium to the benchmark rate (usually based on the LIBOR) and it is fixed for the entire duration of the contract. If the benchmark rate changes, the mark-up rate on fixed income contracts cannot be adjusted causing them to be indirectly exposed to risk arising from movements in interest rate. *Mark-up risk* is also present in profit sharing modes of financing like *mudarabah* and *musharakah* and deferred sale and lease based transactions.

(II) COMMODITY/ASSET PRICE RISK Unlike the mark-up price risk which arises due to changes in the benchmark rate on financing instruments, commodity price risk arises as a result of banks holding commodities or durable assets as in the *salam, ijarah* and *mudarabah/musharakah* contracts. For example, an Islamic financial institution may be exposed to commodity risks after entering into *salam* sale contracts due to fluctuations in commodity price while holding the subject matter until it is disposed of. In the case of parallel *salam*, there is also the risk that a failure of delivery of the subject matter would leave the Islamic financial institution exposed to commodity price risks and consequently, they need to purchase a similar asset in the spot market to honour the contract. Similarly, Islamic financial institutions that are involved in buying assets that are not actively traded with the intention of selling them may be exposed to *asset price risk* attributable to changes in liquidity of the markets in which the assets are traded. Assets traded in non-liquid markets may not be realizable at prices quoted in other more active markets.

(III) EXCHANGE RATE OR CURRENCY RISK Islamic banks involved in cross border transactions and the resultant foreign currency receivables and payables are also exposed to foreign exchange risk arising from changes in foreign exchange rate. In the case of deferred trading transactions, the value of the currency in which receivables or payments are due may either depreciate or appreciate.

b) Credit risk

Credit risk is the possibility that the customer or third party of an Islamic financial institution will fail to meet obligations in accordance with the agreed terms. Although financings are the largest and most obvious source of credit risks for most Islamic financial institutions, they are increasingly facing credit risks from other financial instruments including sales receivables, trade financing, foreign exchange transactions, *sukuk,* extension of commitments and guarantees and the settlement of transactions. Two components of credit risk that are particularly significant for Islamic financial institutions are default and counterparty risks.

(I) DEFAULT RISK Defaults by customers or counter parties through financing activities of receivables and leases like *murabahah, musharakah mutanaqisah* and *ijarah*, and working capital financing transactions or projects like *salam, istisna'* or *mudarabah,* may expose Islamic financial institutions to potential loss of revenue and principal. Due to the unique characteristics of each financing instrument, such as the non-binding nature of some contracts, the commencement stage involving credit risks varies. The reason for default may be due to external systemic sources, internal financial causes or a result of moral hazard (wilful default). Therefore, credit risks are assessed separately for each financing instrument to facilitate appropriate internal controls and risk management systems.

(II) COUNTERPARTY RISK Default by a counterparty associated with trading may cause volatility in an Islamic financial institution's net cash flow or unexpected decline in total cash flow. Counterparty risks are not restricted to the adoption of profit–loss sharing modes of financing but also for non-profit–loss sharing modes of financing such as *salam, ijarah* and *istisna'a.*

In the case of *salam,* or purchase with deferred delivery contracts, counterparty risks could arise due to failure to supply or to do so on time, and failure to deliver the agreed quality or quantity. Since *salam* is an agricultural based contract, it is further exposed to systematic risk such as those caused by natural calamities. Since it involves commodities, Islamic financial institutions need to hold inventories which will further expose them to storage costs and other price related risk factors.

In a *murabahah* sale contract, Islamic financial institutions are not allowed to impose late penalty payments on the counterparty in excess of the agreed price and non-payment of dues within the stipulated time by the counterparty implies loss to an Islamic financial institution. Counterparty risk can also arise for a *murabahah* contract as some Islamic jurist consider the contract to be binding on the seller but non-binding on the client, since the order placed by the client is not a sales contract but merely a promise to buy. Therefore, the client, after putting in an order and paying the commitment fee, can rescind from the contract.

c) Liquidity risks

Liquidity risk refers to the inability of Islamic financial institutions to meet their normal operating obligations and operating needs or to fund increases in assets as they fall due. It may arise due to a number of reasons. Firstly, they lack long term funds since they mainly rely on current accounts which are callable on demand. Hence, they need to match their short term deposits with short term and low risk assets. Secondly, there is the *fiqh* restriction on the sale of existing assets which are debt in nature. Thus, securitization or raising funds by selling debt based assets is not an option for Islamic financial institutions despite debts constituting a major part of their assets. Thirdly, due to the slow development of Islamic financial instruments, Islamic financial institutions are unable to raise funds on demand when they need from the market, especially when there is no inter-Islamic bank money market. Lastly, emergency liquidity is provided by the lender of last resort (LLR) whenever financial institutions need it but in the case of Islamic financial institutions, they cannot benefit from the existing facilities as they are interest based. For instance, the closure of Ihlas Finans, an Islamic financial institution in Turkey, during the Turkey Financial Crisis 2000-2001 illustrates that Islamic financial institutions can suffer from severe liquidity crunch. Three components of liquidity risk also apply to Islamic financial institutions.

(I) FUNDING RISK This risk arises when an Islamic financial institution faces difficulties in raising cash to meet the demands to fund a portfolio of assets at appropriate maturity and rates. This is critical as it depends on depositors rather than borrowings to raise funds to support its financing, investment and trading activities.

(II) ASSET RISK It refers to the inability of Islamic financial institutions to raise cash through sale or liquidation of assets to meet their liabilities due to the absence of or inefficient inter-Islamic bank money market and also the *fiqh* restriction on sale of debt instrument or securitization.

(III) CASH RISK The risk in meeting the financial institution's expected and unexpected cash flow needs as they emerge from time to time may be attributed to mismatch between asset–liabilities and poor estimation of the level of cash liquidity to hold.

d) Operational risk

Operational risk refers to the risk of losses resulting from inadequate or failed internal controls involving processes, people and systems or from external events, which includes but is not limited to legal and regulatory risks.

(I) PEOPLE RISK – ETHICS AND MORAL HAZARD AND HUMAN RESOURCES The use of profit–loss sharing modes of financing exposes Islamic financial institutions to moral hazards and principal–agent problems. In *mudarabah* contracts, the nature is such that the Islamic financial institution bears all losses in the event of a negative outcome, and at the same time, cannot oblige users of the funds to take appropriate action to ensure better returns. Furthermore, IFIs do not have the right to monitor or participate in the project management. This could lead to the mismanagement of funds by users, exposing the Islamic financial institutions to the risk of profit–loss sharing defaults. Islamic financial institutions are only entitled to receive the principal of the financing from the entrepreneur only if profits have accrued; in the event of losses, the Islamic financial institution would not be able to recover the principal investment and potential profit share. *Mudarabah* could also expose Islamic financial institutions to principal–agent problems since Islamic financial institutions have no legal means to control the agent–entrepreneur who manages the project. The agent may decide to expand on the project and increase the consumption of non-pecuniary benefits at the expense of pecuniary returns, since the increased consumption is partly borne by the Islamic financial institutions while the benefits are entirely consumed by the agents.

Besides moral hazard, Islamic financial institutions may face operational risk due to a lack of trained personnel. Given that Islamic financial institutions are relatively new, there is a shortage of qualified professionals to manage operations, i.e. both in terms of capacity and capability.

(II) **LEGAL AND REGULATORY RISK** This may arise for various reasons. Firstly, most countries adopt either the common law or civil law and such legal systems do not have specific laws or statutes to support the unique features of Islamic products. For instance, most activities of Islamic financial institutions involves trading (*murabahah*) and investing in equities (*mudarabah* and *musharakah)*, but banking laws and regulations in most jurisdictions forbid commercial banks from undertaking such activities. Secondly, non-standardization of contracts for different Islamic products makes the process of negotiations on different aspects of the transactions more difficult and costly as well as more difficult to administer and monitor once the contract is signed. Thirdly, the absence or lack of Islamic courts that can enforce Islamic contracts increases the legal risks in terms of lawsuits or adverse judgements that can disrupt or negatively affect the operations or conditions of an Islamic bank.

(III) **TECHNOLOGY AND SYSTEM RISK** The computer software used for conventional banks may not be appropriate for Islamic banks and may give rise to system risks of developing and using informational technologies. Lack of technology increases operational risks.

e) and f) Management and strategic risks

Islamic banks are not immune from failures in governance and moral hazard, poor planning, reporting and monitoring practices. Similarly, they are exposed to strategic risks arising from lack or controversial product innovation, poor marketing and branding strategy and inappropriate portrayal of corporate identity. Such failures could have an impact upon their market position, profitability and liquidity.

11.6.2 UNIQUE RISKS

Having considered the risks that Islamic banks share in common with conventional banks, we now focused on the risks that are unique to Islamic banks.

a) Rate of return risk

Rate of return risk is the risk associated with the potential impact on the returns earned on the assets or business transactions undertaken by the Islamic financial institutions as a result of unexpected changes in the rate of returns. This uncertainty can cause a divergence from the expectations that investment account holders have on the liabilities side, and the larger the divergence, the higher the rate of return risk. In other words, this risk is generally associated with the overall balance sheet exposures where mismatches arise between assets and balances of the depositors. Returns to investors/depositors depend on the profit generated from the Islamic financial institutions' activities and the profit sharing distribution. On the liabilities side, the investment accounts are based on the *mudarabah* basis and they are utilized by the financial institution to make asset backed transaction based on either *murabahah,* where the settlement is based on a deferred basis and *ijarah,* with long term fixed rentals. These long term asset backed financial instruments are indirectly susceptible to the changes in interest rate or benchmark rate. When the benchmark rate increases, the *mudarabah* account investors will demand higher returns based on the prevailing market rates.

b) Displaced commercial risk

Displaced commercial risk refers to the risk that the bank may confront commercial pressure to pay returns that exceed the rate that has been earned on its assets financed by investment account holders (IAHs). The bank does this by foregoing part or its entire share of profit in order to retain its fund providers and dissuade them from withdrawing their funds.

Recall that returns for Islamic banks are mainly based on the fixed rates of *murabahah* assets which are shared between the banks and their IAHs. An increase in benchmark rates affect the degree of responsiveness towards movement in conventional interest rates for competitiveness which may result in IAHs having expectations of a higher rate of return. Consequently, Islamic banks may choose to give up some portion of their returns in order to pay competitive rates to IAHs to prevent them from leaving the bank. The decision of Islamic banks to waive their rights to some part or all of their *mudarib* share in profits in favour of profit–loss sharing deposit holders is a commercial decision, the basis for which needs to be subjected to clear and well defined policies and procedures approved by the Islamic bank's board of directors.

c) Withdrawal risk

The fund providers of Islamic financial institutions are of three major types: current account holders, saving account holders and profit–loss sharing deposit holders. Each group of account holders require a degree of liquidity to be maintained by the Islamic financial institution to meet cash withdrawal requests as and when they arise. Therefore, withdrawal risk for the Islamic financial institution may arise when current and saving account holders make cash withdrawal requests and repayment of the principal amounts deposited within a short period of time. In contrast, profit–loss sharing deposit holders are depositors who participate in the uncertainties of an Islamic financial institution's business and thus share in profits and bear losses arising from investments made on their behalf, to the extent of their shares. Hence, apart from general withdrawal needs, the withdrawals made by profit–loss sharing deposit holders may be the result of lower than expected or acceptable rates of return (displaced commercial risk), concerns about the financial condition of the Islamic financial institutions and non-compliance with *shari'ah* rules and principles in various contracts and activities.

In short, as fiduciary agents, Islamic financial institutions must be concerned with matching their investment policies with the risk appetites of profit–loss sharing deposit holders and shareholders. If these investment policies are not consistent with the expectations and risk appetites of profit–loss sharing deposit holders, the latter may withdraw their funds leading to a liquidity crisis for the Islamic financial institution.

d) Bundled risk

In Islamic modes of finance, it is common to find more than one risk coexisting and also the risk transformation may occur at different stages of the transaction. Consider for instance *salam* which involves selling agricultural goods in advance at a fixed price and time of delivery. Once the Islamic financial institution makes the advance payment, it will undertake *counterparty risk* concerning delivery of the commodity on time, *market risk* of the commodity arising from potential fluctuation in the price of commodity, *liquidity risk* in terms of converting the commodity into cash, *operational risk* related to logistic, etc. This is also the case for other instruments such as *istisna'a, ijarah, financial murabahah* and *musharakah/mudarabah*.

e) Equity investment risk

Equity investment generally refers to the buying and holding of shares by individuals and firms in anticipation of income in the form of dividends from profits generated from the bank's operations and also in the form of capital gain when the value of the shares rises on the stock market. In the case of unlisted companies, equity investment refers to the acquisition of equity (ownership) participation in a joint venture company or a start-up. They are sometimes known as venture capital investing and generally are considered to be of higher risk than investment in listed companies. According to IFSB-1:3.2, equity investment risk is defined as:

> the risk arising from entering into a partnership for the purpose of undertaking or participating in a particular financing or general business activity as described in the contract, and in which the provider of finance shares in the business risk.

The capital the Islamic financial institutions received from their equity investors may be used to either purchase shares in a public traded company or privately held equity. They can also be invested in a specific project, portfolio or via a pooled investment channel. This depends on whether the capital is invested through *mudarabah* or *musharakah*. As explained in Chapter 4, one distinct difference between *mudarabah* and *musharakah* is in terms of the extent of involvement of the Islamic financial institution during the contract period. In the case of *mudarabah*, the Islamic financial institution merely invests money without participating in the management of the venture. In other words, it acts as a silent partner and the other party or the *mudarib* will be fully responsible in managing the venture. In contrast, *musharakah* involves investments by the financial institution together with its partner or partners on a project. The Islamic financial institution can decide whether it is participating as a silent partner or playing an active role in the management of the project. However, note that regardless of the financing instruments, they do not promise a fixed return and in the event of a loss, they are exposed to impairment (capital impairment risk). Moreover, they are also exposed to risks associated with *mudarib* or *musharakah* partners, business activities and operations.

f) Shari'ah *non-compliance risk*

Shari'ah non-compliance risk arises from the failure of Islamic financial institutions to comply with *shari'ah* rules and principles. *Shari'ah* non-compliance risk can be found in three aspects: *non-compliant in terms of process, defects in the documentation* and *non-compliant in terms of the product.*

The basis for having an Islamic banking system is to meet the religious requirements of Muslims and fulfilling the objectives of Islamic finance, which is to achieve justice and fairness in the distribution of resources. Therefore, it is imperative to ensure acceptance, validity and enforceability of contracts from the *shari'ah* perspective as this is the aspect that distinguishes IFIs from their conventional counterparts. The inability to comply fully with *shari'ah* either knowingly or unknowingly may have financial and non-financial impact on the Islamic financial institutions. The financial impact is that the income of the Islamic financial institution is non-*halal* (not permissible) and must be removed; depositors may lose confidence and will choose to withdraw their funds, and the contracts may be invalid and may potentially lead to costly legal dispute. The non-financial impact includes impediment of Allah's blessings (*barakah*) and impairment of the bank's reputation as an Islamic financial institution.

11.7   Risk management

As we have seen in the last section, Islamic financial institutions are exposed to various generic types of risk, as are their conventional counterparts, but they also face some additional risks that are unique to the sector due to their *shari'ah* mode of business transactions. Since risks can have financial and non-financial impact on the banking business, risk management becomes an important function in the organization. So, what is risk management?

Risk management is the process of identifying, quantifying and assessing business risks in order to plan and take the necessary steps in mitigating and controlling them through regular monitoring and reporting. Hence, it is an on-going process as shown in Figure 11.4. The objectives of risk management are to reduce volatility in the outcomes, minimize or eliminate costly lower tail outcomes, maintain a certain risk profile and maximize value for the shareholders and fund providers.

Figure 11.4 **Risk management process**

A comprehensive risk management system includes maintaining a risk management review process, having appropriate limits on risk taking, developing adequate systems of risk measurement, devising a comprehensive reporting system, and implementing effective internal controls. These procedures should include among others, appropriate approval processes and limits and mechanisms designed to ensure the bank's risk management objectives are achieved.

Risk management activities take place at the strategic level by senior management and the board of directors. This includes defining the risks, formulating strategy and policies for managing the risks, as well as establishing adequate systems and controls to ensure that the risk remain within acceptable level and the returns are able to compensate for the risk taken. *Risk reviews* take place within business areas or across business lines and are often undertaken by middle management. Risks are actually created by individuals who take decisions on behalf of their organization, such as those performing front office and loan origination functions. They are thus confined to following operational procedures and guidelines set by top management.

11.7.1 RISK MANAGEMENT FROM AN ISLAMIC PERSPECTIVE

There are numerous examples of risk management in the *Qur'an*. One of the narrations in the *Qur'an* related to the need to take precautionary measure to avoid unnecessary risk is the story about the family of the Prophet Yaqub (Jacob):

> *And he said: 'O my sons! Do not enter (the capital city of Egypt) by one gate, but enter through different gates, and I cannot avail you against Allah at all. Verily, the decision rests only by Allah. In Him, I put my trust and let all those that trust, put their trust in Him alone' (Yusuf, 12:67).*[1]

Similarly in another verse, the narration in the *Qur'an* highlighted the precautionary steps to be taken to reduce the effect of the risk of famine that was anticipated in the city during the time of Prophet Yusuf (Joseph):

> *Yusuf said: 'For seven consecutive years, you shall sow as usual and that (the harvest) which you reap you shall leave it in the ears, (all) except a little of it which you may eat' (Yusuf, 12:47).*[2]

---

[1]http://www.wright-house.com/religions/islam/Quran/12-joseph.php, accessed 1 June 2018.

[2]http://www.wright-house.com/religions/islam/Quran/12-joseph.php, accessed 1 June 2018.

In short, Islam does not condone passivity and fatalism but instead expects man to consider and take steps to manage potential risk.

11.7.2 GUIDING PRINCIPLES OF RISK MANAGEMENT FOR ISLAMIC FINANCIAL INSTITUTIONS

Given the significance of the impact of risks on the financial sector, a number of regulations and guiding principles related to risk management have been put in place to guide regulators and management. As we have discussed in Chapters 9 and 10, the Basel Committee on Banking Supervision (BCBS) has set out sound practices and principles pertaining to credit, market, liquidity and operational risks for financial institutions under Basel I (capital adequacy with focus on credit risk), Basel II (focuses on risk management, especially market and operational risks, and disclosure requirements) and Basel III (focuses on improving the banking sector's ability to deal with financial stress and risk management, as well as strengthening the banks' transparency).

Since Islamic financial institutions are exposed to some unique risks, the Islamic Financial Services Board (IFSB) in 2005 issued 15 guiding principles to complement the BCBS's guidelines in order to cater for the industry specificities. IFSB-1 (General principle) states the requirement for all Islamic financial institutions to have in place a risk management framework:

> IIFS[3] shall have in place a comprehensive risk management and reporting process, including appropriate board and senior management oversight, to identify, measure, monitor, report and control relevant categories of risks and, where appropriate, to hold adequate capital against these risks. The process shall take into account appropriate steps to comply with Shari'ah rules and principles and to ensure the adequacy of relevant risk reporting to the supervisory authority (IFSB-1, 2005).

From the above quoted principle, it is clear that risk management is not only about the process but also the important role of corporate governance and *shari'ah* governance in protecting the interest of all stakeholders. We will discuss the governance issues in more detail in Chapter 12.

The remaining 14 principles are related to the recognition of six categories of risks: *credit risk, equity investment risk, market risk, liquidity risk, rate of return risk* and *operational risk*, as listed in Table 11.5. We will now look at some of the main points for operational consideration under each type of risk according to the guidelines issued by IFSB-1 (refer to IFSB website for more details).

a) Credit risk (IFSB-1:2)

Operational strategy based on the related principle includes the following:

- define and set the overall levels of *risk appetite* (the amount and type of risk that an organization is willing to take in order to meet their strategic objectives), risk diversification and asset allocation; have a list of all types of applicable and approved transactions and financings and be aware of the commencement of exposure to credit risk (2.1)
- establish policies and procedures defining eligible counterparties, have a policy for carrying out a due diligence process and engage appropriate experts to review *shari'ah* compliant (2.2)
- develop and implement appropriate risk measurement and reporting methodologies (2.3)
- define credit risk mitigating techniques, set limits on the degree of reliance and the enforceability of collateral and guarantees and establish procedures in undertaking early remedial action in the case of financial distress (2.4)

---

[3] IIFS refers to institutions offering Islamic financial services.

Table 11.5 IFSB (2005) Guiding Principles of Risk Management

2. Credit risk	
Principle 2.1	IIFS shall have in place a strategy for financing, using various instruments in compliance with *shari'ah*, whereby it recognizes the potential credit exposures that may arise at different stages of the various financing agreements.
Principle 2.2	IIFS shall carry out a due diligence review in respect of counterparties prior to deciding on the choice of an appropriate Islamic financing instrument.
Principle 2.3	IIFS shall have in place appropriate methodologies for measuring and reporting the credit risk exposures arising under each Islamic financing instrument.
Principle 2.4	IIFS shall have in place *shari'ah* compliant credit risk mitigating techniques appropriate for each Islamic financing instrument.
3. Equity investment risk	
Principle 3.1	IIFS shall have in place appropriate strategies, risk management and reporting processes in respect of the risk characteristics of equity investments, including *muḍarabah* and *musharakah* investments.
Principle 3.2	IIFS shall ensure that their valuation methodologies are appropriate and consistent, and shall assess the potential impacts of their methods on profit calculations and allocations. The methods shall be mutually agreed between the IIFS and the *mudarib* and/or *musharakah* partners.
Principle 3.3	IIFS shall define and establish the exit strategies in respect of their equity investment activities, including extension and redemption conditions for *muḍarabah* and *musharakah* investments, subject to the approval of the institution's *shari'ah* board.
4. Market risk	
Principle 4.1	IIFS shall have in place an appropriate framework for market risk management (including reporting) in respect of all assets held, including those that do not have a ready market and/or are exposed to high price volatility.
5. Liquidity risk	
Principle 5.1	IIFS shall have in place a liquidity management framework (including reporting) taking into account separately and on an overall basis their liquidity exposures in respect of each category of current accounts, unrestricted and restricted investment accounts.
Principle 5.2	IIFS shall assume liquidity risk commensurate with their ability to have sufficient recourse to *shari'ah* compliant funds to mitigate such risk.
6. Rate of return risk	
Principle 6.1	IIFS shall establish a comprehensive risk management and reporting process to assess the potential impacts of market factors affecting rates of return on assets in comparison with the expected rates of return for investment account holders (IAH).
Principle 6.2	IIFS shall have in place an appropriate framework for managing displaced commercial risk, where applicable.
7. Operational risk	
Principle 7.1	IIFS shall have in place adequate systems and controls, including Shari'ah Board/Adviser, to ensure compliance with *shari'ah* rules and principles.
Principle 7.2	IIFS shall have in place appropriate mechanisms to safeguard the interests of all fund providers. Where IAH funds are commingled with the IIFS's own funds, the IIFS shall ensure that the bases for asset, revenue, expense and profit allocations are established, applied and reported in a manner consistent with the IIFS's fiduciary responsibilities.

Source: ifsb.org/standard/ifsb1

b) Equity investment risk (IFSB-1:3)

Operational strategy based on the related principle includes the following:

● Define and set the objectives of and criteria for investments using profit sharing instruments, review the policies, procedures and have an appropriate management structure for evaluating and managing the risks involved, monitor the transformation of risks at various stages of the investment lifecycles, determine possible factors affecting the expected volume and timing of cash flow and apply risk mitigating techniques (3.1).

- Agree with partners on the appropriate valuation methods and periods for which the profit is to be calculated and allocated, have measures in place to deal with the risks associated with potential manipulation of reported results and engage independent parties to carry out audits and valuations of investments when needed (3.2).
- Establish the criteria for exit strategies (3.3).

c) Market risk (IFSB-1:4)
Operational strategy based on the related principle includes the following:

- Develop market risk strategy and establish a sound and comprehensive market risk management process and information system as well as quantify and assess market risk exposures (4.1).

d) Liquidity risk (IFSB-1:5)
Operational strategy based on the related principle includes the following:

- Maintain adequate liquidity at all times, incorporate both quantitative and qualitative factors in the policies, adhere to local requirements for liquidity management, identify any future shortfalls in liquidity, make periodical cash flow analyses and establish the maximum amounts of cumulative liquidity mismatches (5.1).
- Assess the necessity and extent of access to available funding sources, have liquidation procedures and a liquidity contingency plan addressing various stages of a liquidity crisis (5.2).

e) Rate of return risk (IFSB-1:6)
Operational strategy based on the related principle includes the following:

- Develop management processes for identification, measurement, reporting and monitoring of the risk, awareness of the factors that give rise to the risk, assess effect of dependency on current account holders' funds, employ a gapping method for allocating positions into time bands with remaining maturities or repricing dates, have effective cash flow forecasting, understand the different characteristics of balance sheet positions and employ balance sheet techniques to minimize exposures (6.1).
- Have in place a policy and framework for managing the expectations of shareholders and IAH and maintain an appropriate level of the balances of PER (6.2).

f) Operational risk (IFSB-1:7)
Operational strategy based on the related principle includes the following:

- Comply at all times with the *shari'ah* rules and principles including contract documentation, undertake a *shari'ah* compliance review (discussed in detail in the next chapter) at least annually and keep track of income not recognized as *shari'ah* compliant (7.1).
- Establish and implement a clear and formal policy for undertaking different and potentially conflicting roles in respect of managing different types of investment accounts, disclose information on a timely basis, maintain separate accounts for restricted IAH, set up separate reserves according to the accounts classes or risks, ensure that the IAH meet certain eligibility qualifications, ensure the adequacy of the quality of information when marketing an investment opportunity and ensure that the risks arising in the subsidiary and/ or special purpose vehicle are monitored and reported at the group level (7.2).

11.7.3 RISK MANAGEMENT TOOLS
The nature of risks faced by Islamic financial institutions is more complex than their conventional counterparts; hence they are more difficult to manage due to a number of reasons. Firstly, Islamic financial institutions face significant market and credit risks due to having more trading based instruments and equity financing in their

financial books. Secondly, the risks they faced are often intermingled or bundled. For instance, their leasing and trade based contracts (*murabahah, salam* and *istisna*) are exposed to both credit and market risks. Thirdly, the risks they face can transform from one type to another at different stages of the transaction. For example, it is exposed to credit risk during the transaction period of a *salam* contract but exposed to commodity risk at the conclusion stage. Lastly, the stringencies and deficiencies in the infrastructure, institutions and instruments require Islamic financial institutions to adapt the existing risk mitigation techniques or develop new ones.

While the guiding principles provide Islamic financial institutions with some broad guidance on how to manage the six different groups of risks, there are a number of techniques or tools available for their perusal in identifying and managing the risks. Figure 11.5 presents a summary of the classification of *risk mitigating techniques*. These techniques can generally be classified into two types: *standard techniques* and *shari'ah compliant techniques*. The former refers to those that can be adopted as they are consistent with the Islamic principles of finance. Some of the common techniques adopted by Islamic financial institutions include risk adjusted return on capital (RAROC), GAP analysis, risk reporting, internal and external audit and internal rating. The latter refers to newly developed or adapted techniques that are more specific to Islamic financial institutions and can be further categorized into risk avoidance *or elimination, risk absorption or management* and *risk transfer*. We will briefly discuss two of the standard techniques, namely, RAROC and GAP analysis and focus more on the *shari'ah-compliant techniques*.

Figure 11.5   Classification of risk mitigating techniques for Islamic financial institutions

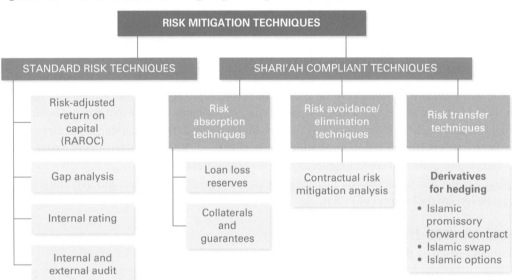

a) Standard risk techniques

(I) RISK-ADJUSTED RETURN ON CAPITAL (RAROC) Regulators have always been interested in the capital ratios of the financial institutions they oversee but it was only in the 1970s and 1980s that they started to implement explicit capital adequacy regulations (regulatory capital). However, this measure of regulatory capital does not equip bank management to anticipate potential problems and measure risk. Hence, the concept of economic capital, which is an assessment of probability of future losses, was introduced. The difference between the two concepts is that *regulatory capital* is the mandatory capital required by the regulators to be maintained and the tools used to measure them include capital ratios or risk based capital. On the other hand, *economic capital* refers to the best estimate of required capital that Islamic financial institutions use internally to manage their own risk and to allocate the cost of maintaining regulatory capital among different units within the organization.

To help their assessment, they employ risk adjusted performance metrics (RAPMs), which is based on a standard accounting performance metric (ROE) but with some adjustment to reflect economic risk. This concept, which was introduced by Bankers Trust in the late 1970s as a planning and performance tool, is commonly known as *risk-adjusted return on capital*. The formula is as follows:

$$RAROC = \frac{revenue - expenses - expected\ loss + income\ from\ capital}{capital}$$

Where:

$$revenue = \text{financing and fees income,}$$

$$expenses = \text{funding and operating costs,}$$

$$expected\ loss = \text{mean of the loss distribution from defaulting}$$
$$\text{financing or from operational risk,}$$

$$income\ from\ capital = \text{charges on risk-free rate of capital.}$$

The numerator (revenues – expenses – expected losses + income from capital) is also known as risk adjusted return.

Based on historical data of the different modes of financing for investments, the expected loss and maximum loss at certain level of confidence for a given period for different financial instruments can be estimated. Based on the result of RAROC, financial institutions can assign risk capital for different instruments accordingly (e.g. *murabahah* is considered less risky than profit sharing modes of financing such as *mudarabah* and *musharakah*).

RAROC can also be used to determine the rate of return or profit rate on different instruments *ex ante* by equating RAROCs as shown below:

$$RAROC_i = RAROC_j$$

where *i* and *j* represent different modes of financing (*mudarabah* and *musharakah*, respectively). If instrument *j* is more risky, the financial institution can ask for higher return to equate $RAROC_j$ with that of instrument *i*.

(II) GAP ANALYSIS

Income or profit gap (IGAP)

Income or profit gap is a widely used method for managing the financial institution's income sensitivity to changes in market interest rate. It is calculated by subtracting the amount of rate sensitive liabilities (RSL) from rate sensitive assets (RSA), which can be written as follows:

$$IGAP = RSA - RSL$$

Multiplying IGAP by the change in market interest rate risk (Δ_i) immediately reveals the effect on the financial institution's income (ΔI):

$$\Delta I = IGAP \times \Delta i$$

If IGAP is negative and the interest rate increases, income will decline, and if IGAP is positive and the interest rate increases, income will improve. In other words, if the financial institution has more RSL than assets, a rise in interest rate will reduce income and a decline in interest rate will raise income.

Liquidity gap (LGAP)

Liquidity gap is a widely used method for managing the financial institution's liquidity position. Liquidity gap is the difference between net liquid assets (NLA) and volatile liabilities (VL) which can be expressed as follows:

$$LGAP = NLA - VL$$

If NLA < VL, the financial institution needs to purchase funds in the market to meet shortfall in liquid assets.

Hence, it is important for the financial institution to examine the maturity profile of their assets and liabilities to identify mismatches in liquidity that require funding.

b) Shari'ah *compliant techniques*

(I) RISK ABSORPTION Some risks cannot be eliminated and transferred, so they have to be absorbed by the financial institution. This may arise due to either the complexity of the risk and difficulty in separating them from the assets, or the risks are acceptable as they are central to their business. Examples of the latter are credit and market risks which are inherent in banking and trading book activities of the banks, respectively. Some of the techniques for risk absorption include collaterals, guarantees, loan loss reserves and investment protection reserves.

Collaterals are used by banks as securities against credit loss since *ar-rahn* (asset held as security in a deferred obligation) is allowed by *shari'ah*. However, only cash, tangible assets, gold, silver and other precious commodities and shares in equities are eligible as collaterals while debt due from a third party, perishable commodities and interest based financial instruments are not allowed to be accepted as collaterals.

Commercial guarantees can supplement collateral in improving credit quality, but they have not been used by all Islamic financial institutions due to lack of *fiqh* consensus. According to *fiqh*, only a third party can provide guarantees as a benevolent act and they can charge a service fee for actual expenses incurred.

Loan loss reserves are the amount aimed at providing protection against expected credit losses as required by regulations in different jurisdictions. The effectiveness in determining the reserves depends on the credibility of the systems in place for calculating the expected losses, given that the Islamic modes of finance are diverse and heterogeneous compared to interest based credit. Besides mandatory loan reserves, some Islamic financial institutions have also established *investment protection reserves* aimed at providing protection to capital as well as investment deposits against any risk of loss including default, thereby minimizing the withdrawal risk.

(II) RISK AVOIDANCE/ELIMINATION Risk avoidance involves taking pre-emptive steps to remove moral hazards or risk prone activities. Such measures start from the contractual stage whereby all related documents are standardized in line with *shari'ah* and all processes, procedures and services rendered are endorsed and approved by the *shari'ah* board.

Thus, *contractual risk mitigation* is vital for Islamic financial institutions and the following are some ways of eliminating or reducing the risk related to counterparty default risk:

- Require up-front payment of a substantial fee to overcome risks arising from the non-binding nature of *murabahah* contract.
- Provide rebates on the remaining amount of mark-up as incentive for enhancing repayment.
- Have appropriate balance in the portfolio between fixed rate contracts that are more risky and floating rate contracts.
- For *istisna* contracts, disbursement of funds can be staggered based on different stages of the construction instead of lump sum at the beginning.
- Enforceability of *istisna'a* contracts can be enhanced by having an *al-jazaa* (a penalty clause).
- Contracting parties agree on the process to be followed in the event of disputes especially with respect to settlement of defaults.

(III) RISK TRANSFER Risk transfer involves using derivatives for hedging, selling or buying of financial claims and changing borrowing terms. As discussed in Chapter 5, derivatives are financial instruments that derive their values from the value of their underlying assets and they are of three types: *swaps, forwards/futures and options.*

Swaps refer to a bilateral contract where the parties agree to exchange a series of cash flows at fixed periodic intervals based on the underlying assets, with both parties ending up with a net financial gain. A *debt asset swap* is where debt is used as a price to buy real assets, a *liability swap* is where liabilities are swapped to minimize exposure to foreign exchange risk, and a *deposit swap* is where two banks agree to maintain mutual deposits of two currencies at an agreed exchange rate for an agreed period of time.

Futures and forward contracts, where both payments and receipts of goods/assets are prohibited by *shari'ah* except if the elements of *gharar* and *riba* are absent. In recent years, some Islamic financial institutions have used *salam and commodity futures* for public utilities as they involve a continuous supply–purchase relationship with a known but deferred price and object of sale (*bai' al-tawrid*). *Currency forwards and futures* are used by Islamic banks which have significant exposure to foreign exchange risk as required by regulators despite this being against *shari'ah*.

Options are contracts that grant the right, but not the obligation, to buy or sell an underlying asset at a set price on or before a certain date. Two variations of options that do not contradict *shari'ah* have been used by Islamic financial institutions: *bay al-tawrid with khiyar al-shart*, which is a contract where both parties are exposed to price risk, and *bay al-arbun*, which refers to down payment with an option to rescind the contract by foregoing the payment as a penalty to minimize portfolio risks known in the financial markets as the *principal protected funds* (PPFs).

Summary

The financial sector is exposed to various types of risks, some of which are easier to manage than others. The balance sheet and income structure of the financial institutions, their operational mode, types of financial contracts, and types of products and services, are some of the factors causing the threat of each type of risk to be different from one institution to another.

Islamic financial institutions share six common risks with their conventional counterparts (market, credit, liquidity, operational, strategic and management risks) but their impact may be different. For instance, the elimination of interest based transactions caused Islamic financial institutions to be considered less risky as it is less exposed to interest rate risk. On the other hand, since Islamic financial institutions do not have a large portion of their assets in fixed income or interest bearing assets compared to their conventional counterparts, they are more exposed to liquidity risk. In other words, credit risk is higher for financial institutions with high loan portfolio while those having large number of off balance sheet items are more exposed to liquidity risk. On the other hand, those with high fixed income investment will be more exposed to interest rate risk and market risk.

In a study on Islamic financial institutions in 14 countries, Ariffin, Archer and Abdel-Karim (2009) found credit risk to be the major risk faced by Islamic financial institutions, followed by liquidity risk and foreign exchange risk. Furthermore, they found *salam* and *istisna'a* contracts being perceived as riskier than *murabahah* and *ijarah* contracts by Islamic financial institutions' management while *mudarabah* and *musharakah* contracts are considered more risky than *murabahah, ijarah* and *istisna'a*. Islamic financial institutions are mainly exposed to liquidity risk due to the following reasons: (i) there is a lack of active money market for *shari'ah* compliant money market instruments; (ii) they are deprived of access to short term financing options from conventional banks as well as from central banks due to their *shari'ah* compliant status; (iii) they need to maintain a high level of cash balances out of the current account balances in order to meet customer's demand for withdrawal of deposits from their account (Iqbal and Mirakhor, 2011). Islamic financial institutions are exposed to some additional risks such as rate of return risk, displaced commercial risk, withdrawal risk, bundled risk, equity investment risk and *shari'ah* non-compliance (reputational) risk due to the differences in the financial contracts that are offered by them, their governance, liquidity structure and legal requirements.

Risk management is the process by which managers satisfy the need to manage an Islamic financial institution's risk exposure by identifying key risk factors; obtaining consistent, understandable, operational risk measures; choosing which risks to reduce and which to increase and by what means; and establishing procedures to monitor the resulting risk positions. Thus, the term risk management encompasses a wide variety of activities. It starts from the very basic process of identifying the need for risk management within an Islamic financial institution including recognizing types of risks surrounding it, measuring the risks as accurately as possible and subsequently structuring the appropriate mechanism to deal with the risks. Despite profit–loss sharing modes of financing and the elimination of interest, Islamic financial institutions are equally subjected to business risks. In some instances, the risks they are exposed to are greater than that faced by their conventional counterparts. Therefore, they are equally responsible for cultivating proper risk management cultures within their institutions. However, so far, risk management activities within Islamic financial institutions appear to be limited, due to the lack of instruments, particularly short term financial assets and derivative products and established money markets. These to some extent hinder the process of an Islamic financial institution's risk management activities. What needs to be done is to develop unique Islamic money market instruments that are *shari'ah* compliant and to induce more risk management activity among Islamic financial institutions, rather than by treating *shari'ah* principles as obstacles to effective risk management.

Key terms and concepts

al-ghunm bi al-ghurm	exchange rate or currency risk	risk averse
al-kharaj bi al-daman	financial risk	risk avoidance
al-riba bi daman	funding risk	risk management
asset or commodity price risk	income or profit gap	risk mitigating techniques
asset risk	interest rate risk	risk taker
benchmark risk	investment protection reserve	risk tolerance
bundled risk	legal risk	risk transfer
business risk	liquidity gap	risk–return trade-off
capital impairment risk	liquidity risk	securitization
cash risk	loan loss reserve	settlement risk
collateral	London Interbank Offered Rate (LIBOR)	*shari'ah* non-compliance risk
commercial guarantee	management risk	strategic risk
contractual risk mitigation	market risk	systematic risk
counterparty risk	mark-up risk	trading risk
country risk	operational risk	uncertainty
credit risk	political risk	(un)controllable risk
default risk	rate of return risk	(un)diversifiable risk
displaced commercial risk	regulatory capital	(un)Systematic risk
down grade risk	regulatory risk	upside risk
downside risk	residual risk	volatility risk
economic capital	risk absorption	withdrawal risk
equity investment risk	risk adjusted return on capital	
equity price risk	(RAROC)	

Questions

1. Define risk and distinguish between the terms risk and uncertainty.

2. Explain the concept of risk–return trade-off.

3. Discuss the principles related to the Islamic perspective of risk.

4. Identify and explain the different types of risk faced by financial institutions.

5. What are the factors that may affect a financial institution's financial, operational, business and event risks exposure?

6. Discuss the generic risks of Islamic financial institutions and their sub-components.

7. Distinguish people risk due to moral hazard and human resources.

8. Explain how legal and regulatory risk may affect Islamic financial institutions.

9. Discuss the unique risks of Islamic financial institutions.

10. What aspects may give rise to *shari'ah* compliance risk?

11. Define risk management and its objectives.

12. Discuss the Islamic perspective on risk management.

13. Identify and discuss the operational strategies related to the six categories of risk according to the IFSB Guiding principles.

14. Explain why it is difficult for Islamic financial institutions to manage their risk.

15. Discuss the risk management techniques available for Islamic financial institutions.

References and further readings

Ariffin, N.M., Archer, S. and Abdel Karim, R.A. (2009), 'Risks in Islamic banks: Evidence from empirical research', *Journal of Banking Regulation*, 10(2), pp. 153-163.

Damodaran, A (2008), *Strategic risk taking: A framework for risk management*, Wharton School Publishing.

Greuning, H.V. and Iqbal, Z. (2008), *Risk Analysis for Islamic Banks*, World Bank, Washington D.C., USA p. 65.

IFSB (2005), *Guiding Principles of Risk Management for Institutions (Other Than Insurance Institutions) Offering Only Islamic Financial Services*, Kuala Lumpur.

Iqbal, Z. and Mirakhor, A. (2011), *An introduction to Islamic Finance: Theory and Practice*, John-Wiley & Sons (Asia) Pte. Ltd, Singapore.

Kennedy, C. (1988), Political Risk Management: A Portfolio Planning Model, *Business Horizons*. 31:6, pp. 26-33.

Knight, F.H. (1921), *Risk, Uncertainty and Profit*, Hart, Schaffner and Marx, New York.

12 Regulation and supervision of Islamic financial institutions (IFIs)

Learning Objectives

Upon completion of this chapter you should be able to:

- explain the legal framework for Islamic financial institutions

- describe the contributions of the IFSB and AAOIFI to the regulatory framework for Islamic financial institutions

- discuss the dimensions in the regulatory framework that requires attention

- explain the reasons for and against the operation of Islamic windows by bank supervisors

- discuss the role of the Basel Committee and IFSB on the issue of capital adequacy

- explain the initiatives taken in responding to Basel III's liquidity requirements

- discuss the approach undertaken in the UK in developing a *shari'ah* compliant deposit facility

- critically evaluate initiatives undertaken in the reconciliation of accounting standards to enhance transparency and disclosure of Islamic financial institutions

- explain the arguments for against adoption of IFRS for Islamic financial institutions

- discuss important aspects for supervision of Islamic financial institutions

- evaluate the IFSB corporate governance framework

12.1 Introduction

Despite its relatively young existence, the Islamic financial institutions (IFIs) have developed to offer a wide range of banking and financial services that are *shari'ah* compliant. They no longer operate in parts of the world where the Islamic faith is an integral feature of the socio-economic make-up of the population and there has been increasing interest in other countries in the west to cater for the demands of an alternative form of banking and investment that are ethical and sustainable. More importantly, the integration of IFIs with international financial markets and institutions demonstrates their resilience and sustainability in the international financial system that also promises of a more inclusive and inherently stable financial system.

This is made possible through the effective roles played by various regulatory and supervisory bodies in supporting the unique requirements of Islamic banking and finance in ensuring that they remain sustainable. Therefore, in this chapter, we will look at the legal and regulatory framework, as well as the supervision and governance framework of IFIs and the issues related to the integration of *shari'ah* compliant systems within the mainstream economic system.

12.2   The legal framework

A *legal framework* refers to a set of rules, procedures, rights, duties and obligations that governs and regulates agreements, contracts, etc. that have legal implications. The financial sector is a highly regulated industry, which is understandable, as it has significant consequences for the financial and economic stability of the country. In general, the legal framework in the banking sector encompasses the legislation and guidance on the governance and supervision of banks, licensing of banks, the role of regulatory bodies and international standards, and rules related to liquidity, foreign investment requirements and liquidation regimes, among others.

In the case of IFIs, a sound legal framework is central for its existence and survival. This legal framework includes: banking laws that governs the IFIS which may be specific (e.g. the Islamic Banking Act 1983 (Malaysia)) or incorporated within the conventional banking law; the statutes related to licensing of IFIs; the relationship between IFIs with the central bank, especially in relations to statutory controls on liquidity and reserves, and dealings with other conventional financial institutions; the accounting and auditing standards that banks must adhere to; the governance framework, especially the role of the *shari'ah* supervisory board; and *shari'ah* law.

There is no one size fits all legal framework for IFIs, as they are subjected to the law of the country where they operate and also the legal tradition and view on *shari'ah* as a source of law. Hence, in developing the legal framework for IFIs, it is important to take into account the peculiarity of the jurisdiction within which they operate. According to Song and Oosthuizen (2014), the jurisdictions where IFIs operate can be classified into either *shari'ah incorporated jurisdictions*, whereby *shari'ah* is incorporated into the substantive law of the country albeit at different degrees, or *purely secular jurisdictions*, whereby *shari'ah* elements are not incorporated in the substantive laws of the country and at best only make changes to existing laws to facilitate a level playing field for the IFIs.

In *shari'ah incorporated jurisdictions*, efforts are channelled towards harmonization of *shari'ah* standards for IFIs with local standards rather than standardization. Hence, variation may still persist in such jurisdictions. For example, in jurisdictions such as Iran, Jordan, Kuwait and Iraq, only fully fledged banks and/or conventional banks that have converted to fully fledged Islamic banks are permitted to operate. In contrast, and as mentioned earlier, in *purely secular jurisdictions*, efforts are channelled towards enacting legislative changes to encourage or promote the Islamic financial industry. They can do this by either maintaining a unified set of banking laws and regulations for all banks irrespective of whether they are IFIs or conventional banks, or by having separate sets of laws and regulations for the two types of financial institutions. The advantage of a unified set of laws is avoidance of duplication of legal and regulatory provisions that are equally important for both types of financial institutions. The advantages of having separate set of laws include enhancing the transparency of IFIs and facilitating the development and growth of the sector.

Examples of the former regimes, i.e. those that make changes but still maintain a unified set of banking laws, include Singapore (e.g. amendment to the banking and tax laws in the early 2000s), the UK (e.g. Financial Services and Markets Act 2000 allowing for the establishment of Islamic banks), France (e.g. tax changes in 2008 and amendments to the French Civil 14 Code in 2009), Japan (e.g. amendments to the Asset Securitization Law in 2012), and Hong Kong (e.g. amendment to the tax law in 2013) (Song and Oosthuizen, 2014). Regimes that adopt separate sets of laws and regulations include Muslim majority countries that have recently introduced Islamic banking and finance, such as Oman, Morocco and Lebanon and those with significant experience in mature markets, such as Malaysia.

12.3   Regulatory framework

The *regulatory framework* refers to the roles and functions of the regulators in the financial sector. The main regulators who supervise this sector include the central banks or monetary authorities and the Basel Committee on Banking Supervision (BCBS). They set rules and guidelines on supervision of the industry to ensure financial stability and also decide on the accounting and auditing standards to be adopted. As discussed in earlier chapters, the Basel Committee formulates broad supervisory standards and guidelines, but they are not binding. The most significant standard is Basel III, also known as the three pillars of Basel, which address three issues: the minimum capital requirement, supervisory review process and market discipline. In most countries where IFIs operate, the default framework is the Basel Committee. Due to limitations in the regulatory framework in addressing the unique circumstances of IFIs, several jurisdictions have complemented it with the standards set by the Islamic Financial Services Board (IFSB) and the Accounting and Auditing Organization for Islamic Financial Institutions (AAOIFI) to give effect to *shari'ah* compliance. We will briefly look at the role of the two institutions before discussing dimensions in the regulatory framework that needed attention due to the unique characteristics of Islamic banking and finance.

12.3.1 THE ISLAMIC FINANCIAL SERVICES BOARD (IFSB)

The IFSB is an international standard setting body of regulatory and supervisory agencies. It was officially inaugurated on 3 November 2002 in Malaysia and began operations on 10 March 2003. As at December 2017, the IFSB has 185 members, comprising 75 regulatory and supervisory authorities, eight international intergovernmental organizations, and 102 market players (financial institutions, professional firms, industry associations and stock exchanges) operating in 57 jurisdictions (www.ifsb.org/).

Its stated mission is to promote the development of a prudent and transparent Islamic financial services industry by introducing new standards, or by adapting existing international standards to be consistent with *shari'ah* principles and recommend them for adoption. Since its inception, the IFSB has issued 27 standards, guiding principles and technical notes for the Islamic financial services industry.[1]

The end objective of the IFSB is to ensure the soundness and stability of the Islamic financial services industry, which includes Islamic banking institutions, capital market and insurance (*takaful*). Thus, the work of the IFSB complements that of the Basel Committee on Banking Supervision (BCBS), International Organization of Securities Commissions and the International Association of Insurance Supervisors.

12.3.2 ACCOUNTING AND AUDITING ORGANIZATION FOR ISLAMIC FINANCIAL
INSTITUTIONS (AAOIFI)

The AAOIFI is the leading international not-for-profit organization, established in 1991 and based in Bahrain, that is primarily responsible for development and issuance of standards for the global Islamic finance industry. As an independent international organization, AAOIFI is supported by institutional members (200 members from 45 countries, so far), including central banks, IFIs and other participants from the international Islamic banking and finance industry worldwide. It has issued a total of 100 standards in the areas of *shari'ah*, accounting, auditing, ethics and governance. In its efforts to enhance the industry's human resources base and governance structures, AAOIFI has offered professional qualification programmes.

In jurisdictions such as Bahrain, Qatar, Oman, Jordan, Syria and Sudan, AAOIFI accounting standards are mandatory regulatory requirement for IFIs to apply in preparing their financial reports. AAOIFI accounting standards have also been adopted by the IDB Group, Indonesia and Pakistan. However, in jurisdictions such as

---

[1] For details of the standards, see www.ifsb.org/background.php, accessed 1 June 2018.

Brunei, Egypt, France, Kuwait, Lebanon, Malaysia, Saudi Arabia, South Africa and UAE, AAOIFI accounting standards have been used voluntarily as basis of internal guidelines by leading IFIs.

12.3.3 DIMENSIONS IN THE REGULATORY FRAMEWORK FOR IFIs

There are several dimensions of the regulatory framework that need to take into account the unique characteristics of IFIs: licensing, capital, liquidity, deposit facility with central bank, and transparency and disclosure.

a) Licensing of Islamic financial institutions

The authority responsible for the licensing of banks in most jurisdictions is the central bank. While several elements of an appropriate licensing process are common to IFIs and conventional banks, certain modifications are needed to take into account the nature of IFIs. In countries where *shari'ah* constitutes (or is part) of the fundamental law of the country, such as in Sudan and Iran, applicants for Islamic banking licenses are required to provide information on their plans for *shari'ah* compliance. This, in turn, entails providing evidence that a robust corporate governance structure tailored to IFIs is in place. All banks in such jurisdictions are considered as fully fledged Islamic banks by virtue of the *shari'ah* constitution adopted by the state.

In countries with a parallel banking system, the application process and requirements for Islamic banking licenses vary to some extent depending on their status. For both domestic and foreign banks seeking to be fully fledge IFIs, the emphasis will be more towards *shari'ah* compliance and governance structure. On the other hand, besides providing plans on *shari'ah* compliance, conventional banks applying for license to operate Islamic banking windows need to give plans to ensure the effective segregation of funds in each window (conventional and Islamic), including through appropriate internal systems and reporting processes. However, in reality, few jurisdictions (if any) actually apply fit and proper requirements to SSB members and to staff in IFIs in charge of *shari'ah* compliance (Song and Oosthuizen, 2014). Developing and implementing these fit and proper requirements would be important for the industry.

It is worth noting that in terms of licensing, not all supervisory authorities allow the operation of Islamic windows in their jurisdictions, as they perceive that such structures carry more risks. Firstly, the commingling of funds in the Islamic windows with conventional assets and liabilities could have significant reputational risk if depositors in Islamic windows withdraw their money following leak of news and/or rumours related to the unacceptable commingling activities. Secondly, Islamic windows could hinder the establishment of effective corporate governance and risk management systems as the management and board of a conventional bank may not be sufficiently attuned to the unique risks inherent in Islamic banking activities. Hence, what may be considered as fit and proper criteria for conventional bank operating Islamic windows are unlikely to be met in their Islamic banking arm. This also poses a challenge to their *shari'ah* boards in verifying the complete segregation of assets and liabilities. Thirdly, the operation of windows could lead to regulatory arbitrage or unfair practices. For instance, given the profit and loss sharing nature of Islamic windows' accounts, banks may encourage high risk clients to get financing through their Islamic windows, as the account holders of Islamic windows will bear the losses in the case of default. Fourthly, Islamic windows may hinder effective financial oversight as it is difficult to appropriately monitor Islamic banking since their prudential ratios differ from their conventional counterparts. Similarly, it makes the preparation of proper financial statements more difficult. Fifth, the orderly resolution of a distressed conventional bank with an Islamic window may not satisfy financial stability objectives and *shari'ah* principles.

Supervisory authorities who allow the licensing of Islamic windows consider that such structure is beneficial in a number of ways. Firstly, the quality of services/products being offered may benefit from the experience of their conventional banks which subsequently may lower the cost of improvement of the services/products, which could in turn further enhance intermediation. Secondly, Islamic windows enhance competition in the market, which could result in lower cost of finance for *shari'ah* compliant products. Furthermore, opening an Islamic window could be the only feasible way in providing Islamic banking services and enhancing financial inclusion in countries with small demand for such services. Also, Islamic windows facilitate liquidity management as they usually have easy access to liquidity support from the conventional part of the bank.

b) Capital adequacy for Islamic financial institutions

Bank supervisors regard capital as a key element in the regulatory framework for financial institutions. Capital, for banks, represents its reserves and non-deposit liabilities and they are traditionally required to show a good margin of reserves in order to retain the confidence of depositors and the public. This practice was first codified in the 1988 Basel Capital Accord (Basel I) and was considered a regulatory landmark, as it had a profound influence on banking institutions around the world. It sets a minimum capital requirement of 8 per cent but this was later criticized as it focused on a single measure and taking a one size fits all approach. Hence, in the 2004 Revised Capital Framework (Basel II), the BCBS introduced three mutually reinforcing pillars: Pillar 1 which consists of minimum capital requirements; Pillar 2 addresses the concept of supervisory review; and Pillar 3 is related to market discipline. The 2011 Bank Solvency and Liquidity Rules (Basel III) issued by the BCBS build upon the Basel II three pillars approach and further strengthened the three pillars, especially Pillar 1, by enhancing the minimum capital and liquidity requirements.

Given the unique components in Islamic bank's balance sheet, IFSB released an exposure draft in March 2005 focusing on the introduction of the capital adequacy standard for IFIs, largely derived from Basel II with the necessary modifications and adaptations to cater for the specifications and characteristics of *shari'ah* compliant products and services (we have covered some of these aspects earlier in Chapter 10). Therefore, it is vital for jurisdictions where Islamic banking is present to focus on implementing the BCBS–IFSB framework. Implementation of the planning framework should start by building the capacity in managing the process effectively. Decisions on the pace of implementation would need to take into account particular characteristics of banks and banking systems, as well as supervisory constraints.

While complying with the Basel Core Principles for Effective Bank Supervision (Basel I) should be a priority for all countries, including those offering Islamic banking services, most jurisdictions would also benefit from a progressive movement towards implementing elements of Basel II and III. In general, IFIs do not face difficulties in complying with Basel III which is related to the numerator of the capital adequacy ratio (CAR), i.e. enhanced quality of capital and introduction of capital buffers. In fact, Islamic banks in many emerging market jurisdictions operate with capital buffers that are beyond the Basel minimum capital requirements. Furthermore, their capital structure is dominated by Tier I capital, particularly common equity.

However, implementation of Basel II requirements is much harder and more complex, particularly in estimating the denominator of the risk weighted assets or (CAR) accurately. Although Islamic banks use the BCBS formula in calculating CAR, they need to make substantial modifications for the recognition of risk weighted assets and sources of funds. These adjustments are essential due to the expectations for profit sharing investment accounts (PSIAs) to absorb losses of the period, thus providing the bank with an additional buffer against adverse shocks on solvency. The supervisory authorities (e.g. IFSB) in jurisdictions where Islamic banks maintained their profit equalization reserves (PER) and investment risk reserves (IRR) have the discretion to alter the denominator of the CAR formula. Hence, IFSB provides two formula to calculate CAR (refer to Chapter 10 for further discussion): (i) a *standard formula*, where all the credit and market risks associated with the assets used to fund the investment accounts are borne by the investment account holders (IAhs); and (ii) a *discretionary formula*, where a specified alpha factor is applied to reflect the extent to which investment account holders share the losses. This alpha factor, which indicates the proportion of assets funded by unrestricted investment accounts, is determined by the banking supervisory authority.

At present, the approaches to application of capital requirements vary across jurisdictions (Mejía *et al.*, 2014). In some jurisdictions like Ethiopia, Kazakhstan, UAE and the UK, the BCBS capital framework is applicable to all banks. Thus, no distinction is made between the capital requirements for Islamic banks and conventional banks. In some other jurisdictions like Bahrain, Jordan, Malaysia and Sudan, the BCBS capital framework is complemented by the pronouncements of the IFSB to cater for the unique capital structure of Islamic banking. When calculating the CAR using the discretionary formula provided by the IFSB, the alpha factor chosen by the bank supervisors of these countries vary to a large extent. For instance, the bank supervisor in Malaysia requires 100 per cent of general assets financed by investment accounts to be converted into risk weighted assets, Sudan requires 50 per cent and Bahrain and Jordan 30 per cent (Song and Oosthuizen, 2014). Although the bank supervisor does not impose any value for alpha in Turkey, a risk weight of 70 per cent is in practice applied to Islamic banking risk-sharing products.

Given the wide array of approaches to the application of capital requirements in different jurisdictions, it is difficult to make an objective comparison of CARs among Islamic banks. Therefore, to facilitate cross country comparisons and to better understand banks' capital levels, supervisory authorities should adopt IFSB standards. In determining the value of alpha as outline in the IFSB guidelines, it is important for supervisors to assess the risk profiles of Islamic banks, develop robust models, decide whether to adopt it for each individual bank or for the entire system in their jurisdiction, and to publish adequate disclosures on their approach of determining alpha.

IFIs that operate in a dual banking environments face a unique risk called displaced commercial risk (DCR), which is defined as 'the risk arising from assets managed on behalf of Investment Account Holders which is effectively transferred to the IFIs own capital because the Institution forgoes part or all of its *mudarib*'s share (profit) on such fund, when it considers this necessary as a result of commercial pressure in order to increase the return that would otherwise be payable to Investment Account Holders' (IFSB, 2005; 2-Standard para 76). Therefore, DCR is the risk that accrues to IFIs due to the commercial pressure of having to pay a competitive rate of return and absorb a portion of losses that normally would have been borne by investment account holders in order to prevent massive withdrawal of funds.

The critical role of PER and IRR in the management of DCR in IFIs cannot be underestimated, as banks normally invest these reserves to generate extra returns to investment account holders and to smooth the stream of returns on PSIA. Hence, the provisioning of those reserves (PER and IRR) is normally decided by the bank management and outlined in the contract. As a general rule, there will be no exposure to DCR when these reserves are sufficient to avert the transfer of income from shareholders to investment account holders. However, if the DCR is positive, this means that these reserves are insufficient and requires the transferring of some proportion of shareholders returns to depositors.

To account for the DCR, adjustment to the Islamic bank's CAR is required. Hence, IFSB provides two methods in dealing with this. The first method assumes that all the risks are absorbed by the bank's investment account holders alone and thus it excludes the risk weighted assets funded by the PSIA. The second method requires the inclusion of a specific proportion of the alpha[2] risk weighted assets which are financed by PSIAs in the CAR calculation. This method is more aligned with the market reality as it recognizes the inability of investment account holders to fully absorb the risk. As discussed in Chapter 10:

$$CAR = \frac{Eligible\ capital}{\begin{array}{c} Total\ RWA\ (credit + market\ risks) + operational\ risk \\ less \\ RWA\ funded\ by\ Restricted\ PSIA\ (credit + market\ risks) \\ less \\ (1-\alpha)\ (RWA\ funded\ by\ unrestricted\ PSIA\ (credit + market\ risk) \\ less \\ \alpha\ (RWA\ funded\ by\ PER\ and\ IRR\ of\ unrestricted\ PSIA\ (credit + market\ risks) \end{array}}$$

Alpha per cent is decided by the central bank and all IFIs within its jurisdiction are expected to use this value when calculating their CAR. Any change in alpha will impact the CAR. The following is an illustration of the CAR computation.

---

[2]An alpha value near zero implies an investment like product with the IAH bearing the risk while an alpha value close to one implies a deposit like product with the IAH bearing virtually no risk.

XYZ Islamic Bank	
Liabilities	
Demand deposits	200
URIAH	500
RIAH	250
PER and IRR	50
Shareholder's capital	20
Assets	
Trade financing (*murabahah*)	550
Salaam/Ijarah/Istisna'a	250
Mudarabah and *musharakah* investments	220
Total risk weighted assets	250
Risk adjusted assets financed by IAH	100
Risk adjusted assets financed by PER and IRR	10
Alpha	30%
Adjustment for market and operational risk	62.5

CAR according to the standard formula:

$$\frac{20}{250 + 62.5 - 100 - 10} = 9.88\%$$

CAR according to the supervisory discretion formula:

$$\frac{20}{250 + 62.5 - 0.7 \times 100 - 0.3 \times 10} = 8.35\%$$

If Alpha is changed to 60 per cent, the CAR according to the supervisory discretion formula would be:

$$\frac{20}{(250 + 62.5) - (0.4 \times 100 - 0.6 \times 10)} = 7.51\%$$

The above example illustrates how a change in alpha can impact the CAR. This highlights the importance of setting a value for alpha that fairly reflects the amount of DCR, taking account of the risk mitigating effects of the PER and IRR. Setting up of the right value of alpha is very important and has very significant supervisory implications. If alpha is set at zero when it should be set closer to one, means that the bank might be undercapitalized and as such, may face high risk of financial instability. On the other hand, setting alpha closer to one when it should be set closer to zero, means that the bank is required to carry excess amounts of capital which may impair its ability to compete. Therefore, the ability of the country's supervisory authority to accurately assess alpha is vital for ensuring stability and competitiveness of its IFIs as well as providing adequate incentives for IFIs to manage the DCR in respect of their PSIA.

c) Liquidity for Islamic financial institutions

One of the main innovations of Basel III was the introduction of liquidity ratios, the liquidity coverage ratio (LCR) and net stable funding ratio (NSFR). The former is designed to ensure that sufficient high quality liquid assets (HQLA), i.e. cash and assets that can be converted within 30 days with little or no loss in value, are available for one month's survival of the bank in case of a stress scenario. The latter is designed to promote resilience over longer term horizons by creating additional incentives to fund activities with more stable sources of funding on an on-going structural basis. In short, enhancement of the regulatory framework on liquidity requires effectively addressing the availability of short term funds.

Implementation of those two key elements of the liquidity framework, i.e. the LCR and the NSFR, pose significant challenges to jurisdictions with a strong presence of Islamic banking. For example, the LCR in Basel III requires banks to hold a diversified portfolio of HQLA, but in many jurisdictions the opportunity for diversification is limited to sovereign debt rather than any other HQLA. To overcome this problem, Basel III now considers *shari'ah* compliant instruments such as *sukuk* as HQLA that banks can hold.

Nevertheless, some progress has been achieved in these jurisdictions. Special liquidity management instruments have been developed including commodity *murabahah*, an instrument that has been widely used in about 45 per cent of such jurisdictions due to its reliance on existing financial infrastructure (i.e., international commodity markets). However, its usefulness may be limited due to high transaction costs, lengthy administrative process, the non-tradability of the contract, and unresolved *shari'ah* concerns (Song and Oosthuizen, 2014). Another significant progress that has been achieved in a few countries, such as Malaysia, Sudan and Bahrain, is the development of the interbank markets for Islamic banks which is made possible through *sukuk*. Interbank markets have been spreading to other countries and now operate in about 45 per cent of jurisdictions with Islamic banks. However, the development of these markets has been affected by a chronic excess of liquidity in several jurisdictions and also concerns of *shari'ah* non-compliance when Islamic banks deal with conventional banks (Song and Oosthuizen, 2014). In terms of liquidity facilities with the central bank, particularly those that would assist banks faced with liquidity shortages, progress has been limited and this may be attributed to the fact that Islamic finance transactions involving real assets are avoided by central banks. Thus, the central bank's legal and operational frameworks need reviewing to allow for the development and use of Islamic liquidity management instruments as assurance for financial stability and effective monetary policy in these jurisdictions.

d) Shari'ah *compliant deposit facility (SCF)*

Central banks play a vital role in implementing monetary policy against inflation, risks to financial instability and volatile exchange rates. They use a range of mechanisms including providing commercial banks access to the central bank's balance sheet to make cash deposits and getting returns at the prevailing central bank interest rate. These deposits are treated as a liquidity buffer asset which can be quickly liquidated by the bank when it experience an unexpected financial stress.

Such arrangements typically involve the payment and receipt of interest and as such, they cannot be used by Islamic banks as this will violate *shari'ah* principles. Hence, a *shari'ah* compliant deposit facility (SCF) by the central bank is not only important in allowing Islamic banks to conduct business on a purely *shari'ah* compliant basis, but also will allow them to comply with Basel III liquidity rules of holding a liquid asset buffer (LAB) to meet any sudden demands for liquidity they may face. To this effect, some progress has been made in some jurisdictions in developing SCF based on different models.

In the case of the UK, the government made available £200 million sovereign *sukuk* that are suitable for use by Islamic banks in 2014, but it was heavily oversubscribed. Hence, a better facility for liquidity assurance is needed, especially when Islamic banks often hold less liquid till maturity type of assets. Furthermore, the open market operation model which the Bank of England (BoE) uses to either inject or drain liquidity from the market based on the repo rate has been used by Islamic banks through a *shari'ah* compliant commercial *wa'ad* (promise) contract. Under this arrangement, the Islamic bank facing a liquidity stress would sell a *shari'ah* compliant asset, such as a *sukuk*, to the BoE who would subsequently sell the asset back to the bank at a mark-up as illustrated in Figure 12.1.

This transaction is similar to a conventional collateralized loan arrangement known as repurchase or repossession agreement (repo), and the mark-up on the sale charged by the BoE on the second transaction may be based on the conventional repo rate to make it economically equivalent. However, this *wa'ad* based model offers limited facilities for the Islamic banks and hence a more developed SCF is needed.

Figure 12.1 The *wa'ad* based liquidity support model

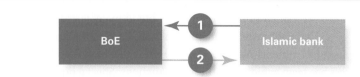

1. The Islamic bank sells security to the BoE for cash on the spot.
2. On maturity, the BoE sells the security back to the Islamic bank at a mark-up price, but under a discretionary promise rather than a contractual obligation, i.e. BoE will either promise to sell the security back to the Islamic bank, or the Islamic bank will promise to buy the security from BoE. Having this separation technically avoids what is called *bai al inah* (sale with immediate repurchase), which is not allowed under *shari'ah* principles because it is considered to be overly synthetic by some *shari'ah* scholars.

The BoE, in its attempt to design the most appropriate SCF that would allow the UK Islamic banks to hold central bank assets as part of their liquid assets buffer, conducted a survey in 2015 asking central banks in jurisdictions offering Islamic banking if they have developed any SCF and the model they used. From the survey, nine central banks indicated that they have some form of SCF such as, accepting deposits with zero return, offering emergency liquidity support in the form of *qard hasan*, and utilizing *commodity murabahah* model for purchasing an asset and then selling it at a disclosed mark-up. Figure 12.2 illustrates how the commodity murabahah deposit model works.

Figure 12.2 The commodity *murabahah* deposit model

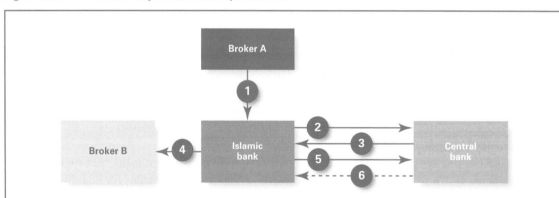

1. Broker A sells a commodity to the Islamic bank for £1 million.
2. Islamic bank sells the commodity to the central bank for £1 million, plus a mark-up (e.g. £2000), on a deferred payment basis (e.g. one week).
3. The central bank appoints the Islamic bank as agent to sell the commodities back to the market.
4. The Islamic bank sells the commodities to Broker B (must not be Broker A, to avoid *bai al inah*) at the original price of £1 million on behalf of central bank, for immediate payment.
5. The Islamic bank credits the £1 million proceeds from the sale to Broker B to the central bank.
6. On maturity (after one week), the central bank makes the deferred payment of £1 002 000 to the Islamic bank.

In addition, models such as *ju'alah* (remuneration for a specified task), *wadiah* (safe custody), and *wakalah* (agency based) fund were specifically used for deposit facilities. Upon the completion of the survey, two deposit models are favoured by the BoE: the *commodity murabahah* and the *wakalah* fund. Figure 12.3 illustrates the mechanics of the *wakalah* SCF model.

Figure 12.3   The *wakalah* SCF deposit model

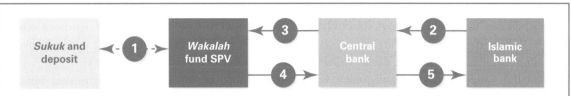

1. The Central bank establishes the facility in the first instance, by placing a deposit with the SPV which is equal to the aggregate value (at cost) of *sukuk* to be purchased for the backing fund. Upon receiving the deposit the SPV purchases a *bundle* of *sukuk* from the market.
2. The Islamic bank is invited to participate in the *wakalah* facility after paying an annual access fee.
3. The Islamic bank placed deposit which is then passed on to the SPV, on a term basis and for an expected profit rate (EPR). The Central bank reduces its own deposit in the facility by an amount corresponding to the aggregate deposits placed by the Islamic banks, to ensure the facility remains fully utilized, but it will remain a co-depositor for any residual amount. The Central bank will receive the same EPR on its deposits as the Islamic banks, meaning the SPV will not engage in any interest-based activity.
4. and 5.   On maturity of the deposit, a return is paid to all depositors (the Central bank and Islamic banks) in the facility in proportion to their holdings. This will depend on the performance of the *sukuk* portfolio, and may or may not be equal to the EPR. If, as is likely in most scenarios, the overall fund return exceeds the stated EPR, any surplus after administrative costs would be used to gradually build up a return reserve.

Responses to the first consultation from key stakeholders of the UK Islamic banks, including *shari'ah* scholars, suggest that the *wakalah* model is more *shari'ah* compliant. The BoE also share the same view, as the *wakalah* model is judged to be operationally straightforward to implement without having to make much changes to the internal systems.

In April 2017, BoE decided to establish SCF using the *wakalah* fund based model. The model would entail Islamic banks placing deposits with the BoE, and the Islamic banks would receive a return from the *wakalah* fund in lieu of *riba* earned on a non-*shari'ah* compliant deposit (Bank of England, 2017). In May 2017, BoE implemented the *wakalah* fund based model. The implementation of the model required the creation of a set of standards and internal procedures similar to those used for Sterling Monetary Framework. However, the model is structured to be consistent with the EU and Basel III liquidity rules. The service will not only be exclusive to Islamic banks, but will also be available to any other banks wishing not to engage in interest bearing activity.

The proposed SCF model by BoE is a unique approach that places all financial firms under one principles-based regulatory framework. Hence, Islamic finance institutions will not be subject to any separate rules to avoid regulatory arbitrage and the risk of parallel regulatory regimes. This is different from the two tiered Malaysian approach whereby the *Shari'ah* Advisory Council[3] supervises the operations of the Central Bank of Malaysia and also advises the directors about matters pertaining to the operational issues of Islamic banks including the appropriate SCF model, and the Securities Commission ensure compliance with the rules of *shari'ah*.

---

[3]*Shari'ah* Advisory Council whose members would be made up of Muslim religious scholars shall be established to advise the bank on the operation of its banking business. The Council shall have a minimum of three and a maximum of seven members, whose appointments shall be acceptable to the relevant government minister for a term not exceeding two years after which each member is eligible for reappointment.

e) Transparency and disclosure

As the Islamic finance sector continues to expand worldwide, the challenging question is how to account for an Islamic bank with cross borders branches and subsidiaries, diverse international stakeholders and extensive financial reporting and capital requirements. Furthermore, the accounting and reporting standards need to be aligned so as not to contravene *shari'ah*. Hence, standard setting agencies are actively trying to address the fundamental issues facing the industry.

While the IFSB provides valuable standards setting out the regulatory framework and addressing capital as well as liquidity issues which are relevant to Islamic finance, AAOIFI, on the other hand, has been actively seeking to reconcile international accounting standards with the specific Islamic accounting standards, besides providing useful guidance on *shari'ah* as well as governance standards. The efforts of both IFSB and AAOIFI facilitate the move towards greater alignment, standardization and harmonization in Islamic finance, but there is still much more to be achieved in terms of accounting.

(I) CHOICE OF ACCOUNTING STANDARD When discussing accounting practices, the two key issues are related to disclosure and measurement. Standards are set in order to provide guidance on what information IFIs need to disclose (mandatory disclosure) and how to treat and measure transactions. IFIs have a choice of which standards to follow depending on where it operates; it can adopt national Generally Accepted Accounting Practices (GAAPs), or the International Financial Reporting Standards (IFRS) issued by the International Accounting Standards Board (IASB), or Accounting Standards for Islamic Financial Institutions (ASIFIs) issued by AAOIFI. However, the majority of IFIs currently adopt IFRS, which is understandable especially for IFIs that operate beyond their own jurisdiction. In the UK, legislation requires all companies to prepare their financial statements in accordance with either IFRS (as adopted by the EU) or UK GAAP. There are no distinct accounting requirements for Islamic finance or institutions which follow *shari'ah* principles. Nonetheless, a number of UK based Islamic banks are able to meet their reporting obligations principally using IFRS.

In short, to overcome the problems of choice of accounting standards to adopt, regulators in each jurisdiction have three options: (i) fully adopt the existing IFRS (e.g. UK), (ii) harmonize IFRS to comply with *shari'ah* principles (AAOIFI), and (iii) adopt the existing IFRS for transactions commonly shared with non-Islamic banks and create new standards for the specific Islamic transactions (Malaysia). The first option, which is to apply IFRS as they are (e.g. UK Islamic banks), will compromise the position of *shari'ah* principles as the supreme reference. This option also poses the risk of preparing misinformed financial statements and presenting them to the public as a true and fair economic representation of the IFIs' performance and financial position.

The second approach is to have a separate set of standards for IFIs that represent the notable differences in transactions from their conventional non IFIs, offered by AAOIFI. However, this approach faces serious challenge with the wide spread of IFIs across different socio-economic jurisdictions, and some of them being a subsidiary of non-Islamic banks or having Islamic windows. Furthermore, there are many Islamic products and services offered by IFIs, hence creating the challenging stance of having a set of accounting standards that specifically deal with the specifications of each product and service.

Therefore, the third option has emerged in some jurisdictions such as in Malaysia and the Emirates whereby the Malaysian Accounting Standards Board (MASB) and the Emirates Certified Public Accountants agree to adopt IFRS to be applied to the transactions of IFIs that bear many similarities with non-Islamic banking transactions. As for those few areas of divergence, this can be resolved through specific guidelines within the framework of IFRSs. This option requires interested parties such as MASB to work closely with the consultative group on *shari'ah* compliant instruments and transactions set up by the IASB.

(II) ISSUES WITH IFRS Regardless of the accounting reporting framework adopted by the Islamic financial institution, i.e. IFRS, AAOIFIs FAS or national GAAP, the key issue is the ability of the framework to accommodate the underlying *shari'ah* principles. Unfortunately, the IFRS framework is built upon principles that contradict with *shari'ah* such as time value for money, substance over form, etc. Some have argued that the differences between

Islamic and conventional finance are not as significant, especially since many of the transactions are 'wrapped' to ensure *shari'ah* compliance. For example, IFRS violates *shari'ah* principles on the method of determining the fair value of a financial asset. IFRS requires discounted cash flow method that involves using the current interest rate to estimate the assets' market value. Another example is related to PER, which Islamic banks often use for income smoothing. While PER is not applicable under IFRS, the creation of such reserve might cause valuation and recognition anomalies, including how to report the residual money which constitutes a hidden reserve. In contrast, there are a number of commentators who have highlighted potential barriers that would make it potentially difficult to apply IFRS to Islamic banking and finance.

From the discussion above, it is clear that adopting IFRS raises a number of *shari'ah* compliance issues because IFRS does not fully capture the unique characteristics of Islamic financial transactions. The unique characteristics of Islamic based transactions seek different accounting treatments. These differences can be reconciled through adequate disclosure on the Islamic bank's policies, including the:

(i)   policies on portfolio diversification and investment objectives

(ii) degree of exposure to illiquid assets

(iii) main risk factors associated with the bank's investments

(iv) effectiveness of the internal controls

(v)   methodology used by the bank to calculate its ratios on performance, profitability, liquidity, investment, etc. to help investors assess how well the bank is managed

12.4   Supervision

Effective supervision requires understanding of the challenges inherent in Islamic banks. All Islamic banks can be supervised by either a supervisory authority that does not distinguish them from their conventional counterparts (e.g. Saudi Arabia, Ethiopia and the UK), or by an authority with a separate supervisory unit (e.g. Bahrain, Indonesia, Pakistan and Syria). Which method of banking supervision is appropriate for the type of banking model depends on the needs and circumstances of the country. Furthermore, an effective financial supervision system may not be achieved without an appropriate level of operational independence of the supervisory agency, a sound legal and governance framework and robust accountability practices (Viñals *et al.*, 2010).

12.4.1 RISK ASSESSMENT

Despite some supervisory authorities implementing risk based supervision on IFIs under their jurisdictions, full *shari'ah* compliance risk assessment is still required. Although there is nothing wrong in using a risk based framework such as the Capital Asset Management Earnings Liquidity Sensitivity rating system, supervisory authorities need to adapt the system to the risks associated with IFIs, particularly regarding aspects such as *shari'ah* compliance, capital adequacy and liquidity. Stress testing frameworks also need to be adapted to the main characteristics of IFIs.

12.4.2 COMPLIANCE

One method of evaluating IFIs' conduct is though assessing their compliance level. The higher the Islamic religiosity in a society, the more intensely their *shari'ah* compliance will be scrutinized by the supervisory authorities. For Islamic windows, stricter monitoring controls are needed in order to reduce the risks associated with *shari'ah* non-compliance and to enhance consumer confidence.

12.4.3 TRANSPARENCY AND DISCLOSURE REQUIREMENTS

IFIs are required to adopt appropriate guidelines to enhance transparency and disclosure requirements. In jurisdictions where both types of banks are present but *shari'ah* law is not recognized, all banks will be subject to the same reporting requirements. However, in *shari'ah* law jurisdictions where both types of banks are present, IFIs may be required to submit additional information on Islamic banking transactions to help stakeholders assess the bank's compliance with *shari'ah*.

12.4.4 ONSITE SUPERVISION

The approaches to onsite supervision are different across jurisdictions. In jurisdictions where *shari'ah* law is not recognized, all banks will be subjected to similar onsite supervision framework but with greater emphasis on operational risks. As for Islamic banks, supervisors assess whether there is a discrepancy between the facts on the ground and public representations related to *shari'ah* compliance. If a significant discrepancy is found, the supervisor has to consider its implications in relation to issues such as misselling, customer protection, governance and internal controls. In *shari'ah* law jurisdictions, it has been reported that up to 80 per cent of the resources are devoted by the supervisory authority to ensuring *shari'ah* compliance by IFIs. In such jurisdictions, the supervisory personnel are well trained and well versed in *shari'ah* law.

12.4.5 FINANCIAL SOUNDNESS INDICATORS

Any financial soundness indicators (FSIs) developed for IFIs will need to consider the unique characteristics of Islamic financial transactions and reporting. The methodology adopted in calculating the FSIs and differences from their conventional counterparts are useful to help stakeholders recognize of any underlying issues.

12.4.6 SKILL ENHANCEMENTS

There is a need for supervisory authorities in jurisdictions where IFIs operate to build expertise in the additional requirements needed to supervise IFIs, including technical assistance from international organizations such as the IFSB and other providers of technical assistance.

12.5   Corporate governance

The business model of IFIs gives rise to unique governance challenges including safeguarding the interests of investment account holders and ensuring that their transactions and products are seen as *shari'ah* compliance. Divergence of interests between shareholders and investment account holders is relatively important, to the extent it needs to be recognized in the bank's governance arrangement. The guiding principles on corporate governance of IFIs by IFSB promote addressing the following issues:

- adequate transparency in policies and reporting performance on the investment accounts
- setting up a subcommittee with the board of governance to oversee the bank's policy framework on protecting the interests of investment account holders
- setting up a SSB, comprised of qualified independent scholars appointed by shareholders, and with full mandate to approve or disapprove products and services and conduct *ex-post* reviews to ensure *shari'ah* compliance
- setting up an internal *shari'ah* review department to evaluate and report on *shari'ah* compliance
- conducting periodic *shari'ah* reviews by the SSB on policies and transactions

Summary

The uniqueness of Islamic banking and finance needs to be addressed through a regulatory regime and corporate governance framework that promotes orderly and sound development and yet is sufficiently flexible to promote innovation and the origination of various new and relevant *shari'ah* compliant financial products. Hence, the governments and legislative authorities need to find a means whereby an applicable body of law may be developed in order to provide effective legal infrastructure that will enable the industry to operate and grow in a conducive environment.

Financial regulators play important role in ensuring that the institutions they regulate, including IFIs, will stay solvent and stakeholders have access to transparent information. Remaining solvent means having adequate liquidity and this may pose an issue for Islamic banks, as they cannot hold interest bearing treasury bills or maintain deposits with central banks that pay interest like their conventional counterparts. The option of simply holding non-interest deposits with central banks will result in Islamic banks being at a competitive disadvantage and not on equal playing field with their conventional counterparts. This has led a number of central banks to offer Islamic banks liquidity facilities to support their *shari'ah* compliant products, affording them similar flexibility to other financial institutions in managing their liquidity. However, such facilities avoid the payment or receipt of interest, which is otherwise the most common basis for operating a liquidity facility. Therefore, the efforts undertaken by the Islamic Financial Services Board (IFSB) in providing guidance to regulators worldwide, including central banks, in accommodating the needs of IFIs, deserve recognition.

With regards to transparency of information, the important role played by the Accounting and Auditing Organisation for Islamic Financial Institutions (AAOIFI) in setting standards on financial reporting for IFIs cannot be underestimated. Some disclosure and measurement issues for IFIs, from an Islamic perspective, are not compatible with the widely accepted International Financial Reporting Standards (IFRS). Although the AAOIFI has issued standards related to the role of auditors in auditing financial statements of IFIs, this still poses a challenge for external auditors, as they need to provide assurance that the financial statements show a true and fair view based on accepted accounting standards. Hence, both the IFSB and AAOIFI will need to find ways of complementing the specific standards in the existing IFRS and for the audit profession to develop necessary skills in auditing IFIs.

As stakeholder interests in IFIs are distinctive from their conventional counterparts, this has implications for governance structure. The rights and obligations of the different stakeholder groups reflect two separate factors: the participatory nature of Islamic finance and the need to have a body providing *shari'ah* assurance. Hence, the conflicts of interest that may arise between shareholders and the investment *mudarabah* account holders, as well as the need for the role of the *shari'ah* supervisory board and the processes of *shari'ah* review and *shari'ah* audit, are pertinent for the industry.

Key terms and concepts

commodity *murabahah* deposit model
high quality liquid assets (HQLA)
legal framework
liquid asset buffer (LAB)

liquidity coverage ratio (LCR)
net stable funding ratio (NSFR)
profit sharing investment accounts (PSIAs)
purely secular jurisdictions

regulatory framework
shari'ah compliant deposit facility (SCF)
shari'ah incorporated jurisdictions
wakalah fund based model

Questions

1. What are the legal and regulatory frameworks for IFIs?

2. Report on the roles of the Islamic Financial Services Board (IFSB) and the Accounting and Auditing Organization for Islamic Financial Institutions (AAOIFI) with regard to the soundness and stability of the Islamic financial services industry.

3. Comment on the current debate on capital adequacy for IFIs.

4. Discuss the liquidity framework for IFIs and the SCF.

5. Assess the UK's approach in regulating the liquidity framework for IFIs.

6. Describe the *wakalah* SCF deposit model and compare its validity against commodity *murabahah* deposit mode.

7. Discuss accounting and transparency practices for IFIs.

8. An Islamic financial institution wanting to adopt IFRS faces a number of key challenges. Identify and discuss two of these challenges.

9. There are two models of supervision of IFIs in jurisdictions where both Islamic and conventional banks are present. Advise on those models.

10. Discuss the unique features associated with corporate governance in IFIs.

References and further readings

Bank of England (2017), *Islamic banks and central banking*, Topical article, Quarterly Bulletin Q3, ISSN 2399-4568, London.

Barth, J. R., Lin, C., Ma, Y., Seade, J. and Song, F. M. (2013), Do bank regulation, supervision and monitoring enhance or impede bank efficiency? *Journal of Banking & Finance*, 37(8), pp. 2879-2892.

Beck, T., Demirgüç-Kunt, A. and Merrouche, O. (2013), Islamic vs conventional banking: Business model, efficiency and stability, *Journal of Banking and Finance*, 37, pp. 433-447.

IFSB-2 (December 2005), *Capital Adequacy Standard for Institutions (other than Insurance Institutions) offering only Islamic Financial Services (IIFS)*, 2, December, KL, Malaysia. www.ifsb.org/published.php, accessed 4 June 2018.

Mejía, A.L., Aljabrin, S., Awad, R., Norat, M. and Song, I. (2014), *Regulation and Supervision of Islamic Banks*, IMF Working Paper WP/14/219; www.imf.org/en/ Publications/WP/Issues/2016/12/31/Regulation-and-Supervision-of-Islamic-Banks-42521, accessed 1 June 2018.

Grassa, R. and Matoussi, H. (2014), Corporate governance of Islamic banks: A comparative study between GCC and Southeast Asia countries, *International Journal of Islamic and Middle Eastern Finance and Management*, 7(3), pp. 346-362.

Safieddine, A. (2009), Islamic financial institutions and corporate governance: new insights for agency theory, Corporate Governance: International Review, 17, pp. 142-158.

Song, I. and Oosthuizen, C. (2014), *Islamic Banking Regulation and Supervision – Survey Results and Challenges*, IMF Working paper No. 14/220, (Washington: International Monetary Fund).

Viñals, J., Pazarbasioglu, C., Kodres, L., Narain, A. and Moretti, M. (2010), *Shaping the New Financial System: Progress and Next Steps*, IMF Staff Position Note 2010/15 (October).

Glossary

Actual net rate of return Profit payable to the depositor by Islamic banks based on the principle of the profit sharing ratio (PSR) based on profit that is accrued on a monthly basis taken directly from the monthly distribution table. Another method of distributing profit to depositor is based on *average actual net rate of return*. See ***average actual net rate of return***.

Agency cost of equity One of the principal–agent problems due to conflict of interest between shareholders and management. The former will bear costs such as contracting cost to mitigate agents from engaging in excessive consumption and other opportunistic behaviour that benefits themselves at the expense of the shareholders due to information asymmetry.

Ajr Arabic word meaning reward. In the context of Islamic finance, it refers to the agency fee or commission charged by Islamic banks for providing specific service.

Al-darurat tubeah al-mahdurat Literally means 'necessity knows no law' or 'necessity supersedes prohibition'. It is a *shari'ah* (legal) maxim or rule that justifies engaging in something unlawful due to necessity or compulsion.

Al-falah An Islamic concept of comprehensive everlasting human success, wellbeing and happiness in this world and the hereafter.

Al-ghorm bil ghonm A *shari'ah* or legal maxim stressing that risk (*ghorm*) will lead to reward or gain (*ghonm*) or simply 'no risk, no reward'. It is also expressed as *al-ghonm bi al-ghorm*.

Al-hawalah Transferring the responsibility for payment of a debt from the debtor to a third party or from one person to another.

Al-ijarah muntahiya bil tamlik Financial lease ending with ownership transfer of the leased asset to the lessee without any additional payments at the end of the lease period.

Al-kafalah A contract between two parties whereby one party agrees to discharge the liability of a third party in the case of default by the third party. As a surety, the third party will give the party that agrees to discharge liability some form of collateral and pay a small fee for the service.

Al-kharaj bi al-daman A *shari'ah* or legal maxim in Islamic banking where the entitlement to the returns from an asset is intrinsically associated with the risk resulting from its possession or benefitting from a certain thing in return for assuming liability that accompanies that thing.

Al-riba bi daman No profit without incurring cost or expenses. Similar to the no risk no reward principle.

Al-wadi'ah Deposits or safe custody contract. In Islamic banking operations, the bank has the authority to use a client's deposits in savings and current accounts with a guarantee to return it to the client when s(he) needs it.

Al-wakalah An agency contract between two parties where one party (the principal) appoints another party (agent) to act on his behalf, or the delegation of duty to another party for specific purposes under specific conditions.

American option A type of a financial derivative that gives the holder of the option (*right*) to buy or sell the underlying asset at a specified price (exercise or strike price) at any time up to the expiration date.

Anthropology The branch of social science that is concerned with man and his society.

Aqilah A joint guarantee by a group of individuals to help each other in times of disaster or misfortune.

Ar-rahn Islamic pawn broking or short term loan based on collateralization or pledging of gold items or other acceptable security for cash.

Asset backed *sukuk* A type of *sukuk* or Islamic bond which involves the actual transfer of assets to the *sukuk* holders, i.e. the *sukuk* holders actually own the asset and as a result do not have recourse to the asset but to the originator if there is a shortfall in payment.

Asset based *sukuk* A type of *sukuk* or Islamic bond where the *sukuk* holders only have beneficial ownership of the underlying asset and have recourse to the originator if there is a shortfall in payment.

Asset–liability management (ALM) An intermediate term planning function undertaken by bank management to ensure that there is no mismatch in the assets and liabilities that it holds that may affect its returns in the long run.

Asset management The management of assets held by an Islamic bank by ensuring that it has a well-diversified portfolio of asset backed trading and different forms of investments with a wide spectrum of risk and maturity profile.

Asset productivity Also known as *Asset turnover (ATO)* is a ratio that highlights the extent of efficiency of the bank based on its asset structure. It is expressed as net income over total assets. A higher ratio is preferable, as it indicates efficiency in utilizing assets to generate income.

Asset quality In the context of banking, this refers to the quality of the portfolio of loans and other financial products that provide earnings for the banks. Assets quality and *loan quality* are often used interchangeably.

Asset risk A type of market risk that may affect the Islamic bank's financial position due to a change in the price of an asset. If the risk is related to an asset in the form of a commodity held by the Islamic bank, then the risk is known as *commodity price risk*.

Average actual net rate of return Profit payable to the depositor by Islamic banks only at maturity of the deposits and the amount is determined based on the respective tenure of each deposit. See *actual net rate of return*.

Axiology Study of values and sense of goodness that drive man's behaviour.

Baitul mal State treasury bureau where all public funds are handled.

Bank based system A financial system in a country whereby the main role of allocating capital, mobilizing savings, financing and investing activities are all undertaken by banking institutions rather than through the capital market.

Bank draft A cheque issued by a bank, guaranteeing payment on behalf of a payer to the payee.

Bank financial strength rating A rating of the financial strength of the bank's asset quality based on aspects such as the banking environment, investment policies and loan administration procedures, portfolio composition and characteristics, as well as quality of forecasting, risk management practices, lending history and performance and economic values.

Bank liquidity Ability of the bank to pay its obligations when they fall due.

Bank money A medium of exchange such as *cheques*, *bills of exchange* and *bank drafts* that are used for accepting payments for goods and services or for repayment of debt or loans.

Bank solvency The ability of the bank to repay all its obligations ultimately.

Barter A trading method based solely on exchange of goods.

Basel I A set of international banking regulations put forth in 1988 by the Basel Committee on Bank Supervision (BCBS) that sets out the minimum capital requirements of financial institutions with the goal of minimizing credit risk. Primarily it focuses on Credit Risk and Risk Weighted Assets (RWA).

Basel II A set of international banking regulations put forth in 2004 by the Basel Committee on Bank Supervision (BCBS) that sets out further strengthening requirements to stabilize the international banking system. It addresses three pillars: minimum capital requirements, supervisory review process and market discipline.

Basel III A set of international banking regulations put forth in 2009 by the Basel Committee on Bank Supervision (BCBS) designed to improve the banking sector's ability to deal with financial stress and risk management, as well as strengthening the banks' transparency, following the financial crisis.

Bay al-istisna'a A sale contract to produce goods with certain specifications to be delivered at a future date.

Bay al-murabahah A cost-plus sale contract whereby the sale price includes a profit mark-up or surcharge on the stated original cost mutually agreed upon by the buyer and seller.

Bay al-salam A forward sale contract whereby payment is made in advance by the buyer for the goods or service to be supplied later by the seller.

Bay as-sarf or saraf A contract of exchange of money for money or currency trading.

Bay bithaman ajil A deferred instalment sale contract whereby the seller buys the goods required by the buyer and sells them at a mark-up price agreed upon by both parties with payments being made on an instalment basis by the buyer to the seller.

Bay muajjal-murabahah A sale contract whereby the bank sells a product required by the entrepreneur at an agreed upon fixed price on a deferred payment basis.

Benchmark risk Step undertaken to compare the bank's own risk with the average risk of other banks.

Bilateral contract A contract involving at least two parties, with one party making an offer and the other accepting the offer or a mutual consent between the parties in establishing certain rights and obligations.

Bill of exchange A written order that obliges one party to pay another party a fixed sum of money upon request or at a predetermined date. This is primarily used in international trade.

Binding contract A contract that is sound in terms of both its substance and description making it enforceable under the law. Binding contracts can be further classified as either revocable or irrevocable. A *revocable contract* is a binding contract that allows either of the parties the option to revoke (cancel) the contract at any stage while an *irrevocable contract* is a binding contract that cannot be revoked by either party at any stage once they are concluded.

Borrowers A group of individuals and institutions with financial deficit which arises from having to incur financial liabilities (debts) or as the result of not accumulating financial assets in the past.

Bundled risk A risk mitigating strategy which involves managing different risks that coexist through the different stages of the transaction from selling and time of delivery.

Business cycles The irregular periodic upward and downward trend of economic activities or outputs in a country.

Business financing A financing scheme to enable firms to conduct their economic activities, raise short term capital for their business and cover their working capital.

Business risk Unsystematic risk that affects financial performance which may arise due to competition, changes in customer preferences and loyalty, development of products, technological changes, etc.

Call option A right that grants the holder to buy an underlying asset at the exercise price within a specific period of time.

CAMELS rating A financial ratio analysis framework that helps in assessing past and current trends and also determining future estimates of bank performance in various aspects such as **Capital adequacy, Asset quality, Management quality, Earnings quality, Liquidity,** and **Sensitivity to market risk (CAMELS)**.

Capital adequacy ratio (CAR) A ratio indicating whether the bank has enough capital. It is computed based on the sum of Tier 1 (core) and Tier 2 (supplementary) capital over risk weighted assets. The target ratio is 8 per cent or higher.

Capital adequacy standard A financial standard on capital adequacy issued by the Islamic Financial Services Board (IFSB) in 2005 that is largely derived from *Basel II* with the necessary modifications and adaptations to suit Islamic financial institutions.

Capital arbitrage The avoidance of certain minimum capital charges through sale or securitization of those assets for which the capital requirement imposed by the market is less than the regulatory capital charge.

Capital base The bank's capital structure whereby it is expected to possess high quality characteristics in terms of its ability to absorb any losses occurring in the course of on-going business and not incurring any fixed expenses against the earnings. It is the numerator used for calculating *risk adjusted capital ratio*. See **risk adjusted capital ratio.**

Capital impairment risk The risk of an investment declining in value, making it worth less than what it was when first recorded leading to a decline in the bank's own capital.

Capital management An activity that involves making sure that the bank keeps an adequate level of capital to comply with regulatory requirements in order to maintain solvency and also cushion against losses.

Capital market A place where longer term *equity capital* **(shares)** and *debt capital* **(bonds)** are traded.

Capital ratio The ratio of book value of total capital to total assets, which indicates the extent to which assets are covered by capital.

Capital reserves Accumulated surplus from revenues or profit (retained earnings) and from share premium (share value that is above the issued share price).

Capitalist economy An economic system based on *laissez-faire* (market economy) with minimal governmental intervention.

Cash instrument A financial instrument that can easily be converted to cash such as short term loans and deposits and securities that can be traded in the market.

Cash risk Risk that arises when a bank does not have enough cash to carry out its day to day operations.

Cashier's order A cheque issued by a bank's branch and drawn on itself and is generally used within the same locality (local clearing area) to effect payment, especially if personal cheques are not acceptable or cash payment is not advisable.

Centralized e-money A medium of exchange that includes *debit cards, credit cards* and *charge cards* whereby currency and payments can be exchanged electronically at the point of sale instead of paper money. See *electronic money.*

Charge cards A credit card with an account that must be paid in full when a statement is issued.

Cheque An order to transfer funds from the payer's bank account to the payee's bank with both banks possibly charging a fee for the service.

Clearing house Facility provided by the central banks to aid commercial banks to offset the mutual claims of banks on one another and to make settlement on the outstanding payments.

Clearing House Interbank Payment System (CHIPS) One of the largest financial intermediaries in the world that has the capability of carrying extensive remittance information for commercial payments by cheques. Most payments over CHIPS are related to the foreign exchange and Euro-dollar markets.

Client retention ratio (CRR) A ratio indicating the bank's ability to retain good clients' or customers' loyalty. It is calculated by dividing the number of clients who left the bank during the year by the total number of clients who are still with the bank at the end of the year.

Collateral Any asset held by banks as securities against credit loss.

Collateralized securities Secured borrowing transactions whereby securities are sold under agreement to repurchase.

Command economy An economic system where the government gives orders or has ultimate power over the financial management of the state. All economic activities are administered by the central planning agency of the State. It is also known as communism.

Commercial guarantee A form of supplementary collateral to improve credit quality. Not used by all Islamic financial institutions due to lack of *shari'ah* consensus. See *collateral.*

Commodity money A medium of exchange using valuable commodities in a particular society such as salt, wheat and barley.

Commodity *murabahah* deposit model A procedure considered by the Bank of England as part of its *shari'ah* compliant deposit facility to assist Islamic banks in making cash deposits based on the *murabahah* model, getting returns without violating *shari'ah* principles and at the same time allowing banks to comply with *Basel III* liquidity rules.

Consideration According to Islamic law, the consideration in the contract is not restricted to only the monetary price and may also be in the form of another commodity.

Consumer financing All forms of instalment financing for consumers' needs such as automobile purchase, home improvement, debt consolidation, etc. and open ended financing such as credit cards.

Contract A written or spoken agreement between two or more parties.

Contract of *musharakah* An Islamic contract based on partnership. See *musharakah.*

Contractual hedging The use of financial contracts to hedge or protect against transaction exposure or loss.

Contractual risk mitigation Steps to eliminate or reduce the risk related to counterparty default.

Controller of credit It is one of the functions performed by the central bank in controlling the supply of credits by commercial banks.

Convertible bond A type of bond that gives investors the option to convert it into a fixed number of shares, thus giving them the chance to share in the upside when the company performs well in the market.

Cooperative hedging Strategic partnership among market players to overcome economic problems.

Cooperative risk sharing In a *takaful* scheme, participants or policyholders contributions are considered as donations to the common cause to assist members who suffer any loss. Hence, the indemnification component is based on mutual contribution and reciprocal donation.

Core capital (Tier 1) Components of capital required in line with the 1988 *Basel I* Accord which consist of shareholders' equity capital plus disclosed reserves.

Corporate action management A service which involves the timely and accurate broadcasting of a corporate action news event to ensure that the shareholders are aware of their related corporate actions entitlement.

Corporate credit rating Indicates the creditworthiness of the debt issuer including the risk level related to other aspects such as corporate governance and *shariʼah* quality rating, based on assessment by rating agencies such as S&P, Moody's, Fitch, MARC and IIRA.

Corporate governance quality rating Related to the standard or quality of governance of the corporate entity based on assessment on key elements of the corporate governance structures recognized at the global level, as well as best practices in the field as benchmarks for transparency, fairness, responsibility and accountability.

Cosmology A branch of knowledge related to the origin and evolution of the universe.

Cost per client (CPC) A ratio indicating how much it costs the Islamic bank to serve each client. It is computed by dividing its operating expenses by the average number of clients for the period. A lower ratio is preferable.

Cost per unit of capital allocated (CPUCA) A ratio showing how much it costs the Islamic bank to service £1 of financing. It is calculated by dividing operating expenses by the value of financing allocated in the period.

Counterparty risk The risk to each party to the contract that its counterparty may not uphold its contractual obligation and this risk should be seriously considered before entering into any contractual relationship. Sometimes counterparty risk and *default risk* have been used interchangeably, and one way to draw a distinction between the two is to look at the nature of the relationship, as the latter is specifically related to borrowers.

Country risk The risk that a foreign government may default on its financial commitments arising from political, social and economic unrest.

Coupon payment Annual interest payments that bondholders receive.

Coupon rate The rate of interest that the bond issuer must pay to the bondholder for the duration of the bond.

Credit card A medium of exchange allowing the holder to purchase goods or services on credit.

Credit default swaps (CDS) Privately negotiated contracts to protect investors against default risk on a particular debt instrument such as bonds.

Credit rating agencies Independent institutions that provide investors with an assessment of the creditworthiness of issuers of bonds and other securities in meeting their expected obligations.

Credit risk Risk or the potential that a counterparty fails to fully and timely meet its obligations in accordance with the agreed terms and conditions of the credit contract. This includes *settlement risk, default risk, counterparty risk* and *down grade risk*.

Credit union A non-profit cooperative owned by members who pool their savings and lend to each other.

Cryptocurrency A digital form of currency using encryption technique. The price is purely based on supply and demand. See *decentralized e-money*.

Currency market A place or market that deals with the trading of currencies. The main participants are commercial banks, securities dealers, hedge funds, large multinational companies, institutional investors as well as central banks.

Currency risk See *exchange rate risk*.

Currency swaps The exchange of a set of payments in one currency for a set of payments in another currency at a specified exchange rate and at specified intervals.

Custodian of cash reserves All commercial banks in most countries are required to deposit a part of their cash balances with the central bank based on a specified ratio. Hence, central banks act as custodian of cash reserves and foreign balances.

Custodian of foreign balances Foreign currencies and gold are kept by the central bank as reserve note issue and also to cater for any deficits in the balance of payment with other countries. Hence, it becomes a custodian of the nation's reserves of international currency or foreign balances.

Debit card A medium of exchange allowing the holder to transfer money electronically from their cheque or current bank account when making a payment.

Debt based instruments Financial contractual instruments such as *ijarah* and *murabahah* that pay a predetermined rate of return to investors but are *shariʼah* compliant as the return is not based on interest but as receivables.

Decentralized e-money Digital or virtual currency designed to work as a medium of exchange and it takes the form of *cryptocurrency*. The appeal of virtual currency is due to its promise of lower transaction fees than traditional online payment mechanisms. See *cryptocurrency*.

Default Risk Risk that may arise when a borrower fails to make required payments to the bank.

Deficient contract A contract that is lawful in substance but unlawful in description.

Demand deposits Current accounts provided by Islamic banks based on *wadiah* (safekeeping) or *mudarabah* (investment).

Demand draft An order in writing by one Islamic bank to another requesting it to pay a specific sum of money to a specific person upon presentation of the draft.

Deposits A sum of money paid into accounts in financial institutions by depositors for safekeeping or as investments.

Deposits and placements of banks and other institutions Also known as interbank deposit. An amount placed in the bank by other financial institutions for the purpose of settling payments and business cooperation.

Deposit taking institutions Financial institutions that are licenced to accept funds from households, businesses and government agencies. They include commercial banks and savings institutions.

Derivative instrument A financial instrument that derives its value from the characteristics of one or more underlying entities such as an asset, index or interest rate.

Derivatives A contract between two parties on agreed upon underlying instrument (like a security) or set of assets (like an index).

Dinar Islamic silver coin.

Direct custody and clearing A set of services provided to investors seeking end to end securities services solutions in both the international and domestic market.

Dirham Islamic gold coin.

Displaced commercial risk Risk that bank may confront arising from commercial pressure to pay returns that exceed the rate that it earned on its assets financed by investment account holders (IAHs).

Distributive justice Concept of justice related to fair distribution of wealth, income and economic resources as Allah has placed sufficient sustenance and provisions in the earth to cater for all human needs.

Down grade risk Risk or threat to the bank due to a lowering in its credit or investment rating, as it sends a negative signal to the market on the creditworthiness or desirability of the bank for investment. This is based on the opinion of analyst and rating agencies.

Downside risk A financial risk where the returns may be below expectations.

EAGLES framework A financial ratio analysis framework for assessing a bank's performance in various aspects such as its Earnings ability, Asset quality, Growth, Liquidity, Efficiency and Strategic management (EAGLES).

Economic capital The capital that a bank itself believes it should hold to cover the risks it is undertaking, as opposed to capital required by regulation. See *regulatory capital*.

Economic hedging A strategic arrangement by the corporate management to diversify investment without dealing with third parties or agents to achieve their purpose of hedging. It can be independent of or complementary to other hedging strategies.

Economic principles The fundamental law of economics that serves to guide decision making of consumers, producers, investors, employees and government.

Economic system A collection of economic entities like households, business firms, public institutions, and markets set up by society to deal with the allocation of resources, production and exchange of goods and services, and distribution of the resulting income and wealth.

Effective rate of return The interest rate that is actually earned or paid on an investment or loan over a given time period.

Electronic fund transfer at point of sale A real time gross settlement system in which all banking institutions initiate transfers of funds that are immediate, final and irrevocable when processed.

Electronic money Abbreviated as e-money, is the medium of exchange for the purpose of making payment transactions electronically. E-money can be either decentralized or centralized. See *de(centralized) e-money*.

Enforceable contract A contract that is valid and binding on the parties concerned according to the law. All binding contracts are enforceable contracts.

Epistemology Nature of knowledge, the rationality of belief and justification.

Equal liberty and opportunity The right of a person to have freedom and equal opportunity to combine creativity and knowledge with natural resources to generate products and services.

Equity based instruments Financial instruments such as *musharakah* and *mudarabah* whereby the financier and entrepreneur share profits based on pre-agreed ratios while losses will commensurate to their contribution (financial or physical) to the partnership.

Equity investment risk Risk related to the buying and holding of shares by individuals and firms in anticipation of income in the form of dividends from profits generated from the bank's operations and also in the form of capital gain when the value of the shares rises on the stock market.

Equity price risk A type of market risk that refers to the exposure of a bank's financial conditions to movements in the price of equity securities and other instruments that derive their value from a particular share, a defined portfolio of shares, or a share index.

European option A type of a financial derivative that gives the holder of the option the right to buy or sell the underlying asset at a specified price (exercise or strike price) only on the expiration date.

Exchange rate risk A type of market risk that is related to the potential impact on the bank's balance sheet due to changes in the relative value of certain foreign currencies. Also known as *currency risk*.

Exercise price The purchase or selling price of an underlying security.

Family *takaful* An Islamic insurance scheme that provides financial relief to the participants and/or their families in the event of misfortunes relating to the death or disability of the participants.

***Fatawa* (plural)** Singular is *fatwa*. A ruling issued by a qualified legal scholar (known as a *mufti*) in response to a specific question related to the *shari'ah*.

Financial instruments Contracts that give rise to financial assets of one entity and financial liabilities or equity instruments of another entity.

Financial intermediaries Institutions that channel funds from those having surplus to those experiencing deficit or shortage of funds.

Financial markets A place or platform that facilitates the buying and selling of financial securities (equities and bonds), commodities (precious metals, oil and gas as well as agricultural products), currencies and other fungible items of value.

Financial risk A branch of unsystematic risk that refers to risks associated with a change in the capital structure of the financial institution and movements in the financial market.

Financial system A system that facilitates the transfer of funds between the surplus units to the deficit units and it operates at three levels: micro, macro and global. See *market based* financial system and *bank based* financial system.

Financing contracts Contracts related to the creation and extension of credit facilities, financing of transactional contracts and providing channels for capital formation and resource mobilization between entrepreneurs and investors.

Financing income The income received from financing activities or earnings from investment of assets on a profit sharing basis by an Islamic bank.

Financing loss reserve adequacy (FLRA) A ratio indicating the reserve needed to protect against financing loss which is directly related to the *portfolio at risk (PaR)*. It is calculated by dividing actual financing loss reserves by required financing loss reserves.

Financing loss reserves Amounts set aside from earnings for the purpose of covering potential bad debts.

Financing portfolio growth (FPG) A ratio indicating the bank financing activities and long term growth of its financing portfolio. It is calculated by dividing the financing portfolio at end of period less the initial financing portfolio, by the initial financing portfolio. A higher ratio is preferable as it indicates growth.

Fixed rate party A person or party who intends to swap its fixed rate profits with a floating rate profit in the profit swap arrangement.

Float Cheques in the process of clearing. Until it is processed through the clearing system, the payer continues to receive credit on his account. Thus, float represents an interest free short term loan to the payer.

Floating rate party A person or party who intends to swap its floating rate profits with a fixed rate in the profit swap arrangement.

Forward contract A non-standardized agreement (flexible in terms of quantity and date of delivery) between two parties to involve in the future sale or purchase of an asset at a price agreed on the spot (*forward price*) with the underlying asset being delivered at a future date.

Forward price The price agreed upon in a forward contract. See *Forward contract*.

Fractional reserve system A system that allows an expansion in the supply of paper money without a corresponding rise in the assets (such as gold reserves) held by the bank.

Fully fledged Islamic bank A bank that fully operates based on Islamic principles and offers only *shari'ah* compliant products.

Fund accounting and administration services A range of services offered to third parties, predominantly to asset managers and fund management companies managing Islamic unit trusts and Islamic mutual funds, closed end Islamic funds, pension, retirement and provident funds.

Funding risk The risk of inability to obtain the necessary funding for an illiquid asset positions on the expected terms and when required.

Futures contract A standardized agreement between two parties to exchange a specified asset with a known standardized quantity and quality at a price agreed upon by the parties on the spot (known as *futures price or strike price*) while delivery is made at a specified future date.

Futures exchange A centralized financial market where contracting parties can trade standardized futures contracts.

Futures price See *futures contract*.

General average A concept in insurance whereby merchants whose goods were being shipped together would pay a proportionally divided premium which would be used to reimburse any merchant whose goods had to be jettisoned in order to lighten the ship and save it from total loss.

General insurance An insurance policy that protects policyholder against losses and damages other than those covered by life insurance.

General investment account (GIA) A form of *mudarabah* account that provides absolute freedom to the Islamic bank as *mudarib* (active partner) to manage the investment of the capital. Under this arrangement, an Islamic bank can commingle the GIA account holders' fund with other funds to be used by the bank for investment purposes to generate income. Also see *special unrestricted investment account (SUIA)*.

General musharakah Partnership by joint ownership (*shirkat ul-milk*).

General purchasing power Extent of power that the money owner have over the type and quantities of goods to buy, the time and place of the purchase and parties to whom s(he) chooses to deal with.

General takaful Islamic insurance involving non-life contracts of joint guarantee on a short term basis (normally one year), designed to meet the needs for protection of individuals and corporate bodies in relation to material loss or damage resulting from a catastrophe or disaster inflicted upon real estate, assets or belongings of participants.

Green revolution Reference to the harvesting success that began in Mexico as a result of modern agricultural practices.

Gross profit rate per annum The base used to calculate the return for surplus rich Islamic bank (SIB) upon maturity on its interbank deposit with the deficit Islamic bank (DIB).

Growth in clients (GiC) A ratio indicator of future revenues. It is calculated by dividing the net change in number of clients by the initial number of clients.

Growth in equity (GiE) A ratio measuring the future capital or asset growth. It is calculated by dividing the net change in equity by the initial equity at the beginning of the period.

Hadith The second source of *shari'ah* after the *Qur'an*. It is based on the sayings, approvals and actions of the Prophet Muhammad during his lifetime. It is also known as *Sunnah*.

Halal Activities that are permissible in Islam as they adhere to the *shari'ah* principles.

Haram Activities that are strictly not permissible in Islam as they are contradictory to *shari'ah* principles.

Hard commodity Natural resources that must be mined or extracted such as gold, oil and tin.

Hibah Literally means gift (also known as *hadiah*). A gift contract involves the granting of items that has value or provide some form of benefits, such as property, cash, jewellery, share certificates, etc., to another party or parties which occurs during the lifetime of the *hibah* provider. See *ajr*.

Hibah related deposits Current and savings accounts offered to depositors by Islamic banks where returns on these accounts are at the discretion of the bank and is considered as a gift (*hibah*) from the bank to the depositors. See *profit related deposits*.

High net worth individuals Bank customers who have $1 million or more of investable assets.

High quality liquid assets (HQLA) Cash and assets that can be converted within 30 days with little or no loss in value, and are available to cater for at least one month survival of the bank in case of a stress scenario.

Homo economicus An economic man, i.e. one who thinks and acts based on the potential economic outcome to fulfil his/her needs.

Homo Islamicus A God fearing Muslim man whose actions are influenced by what Allah commands.

Ibra' Offsetting of debt.

Ijab An offer that is made by one party to another.

Ijarah mawsufah al-dimmah A forward lease arrangement whereby the SPV in a *sukuk* agreement leased the assets (such as a home, office, or factory) that has not yet been constructed, for an overall term that reflects the maturity of the *sukuk*.

Ijarah thumma al-bay (AITAB). A financial lease with sale option. Under this contract, the lessee will have the option to buy the leased asset at the end of maturity of the lease. AITAB consists of two different contracts, namely, the contract of *al-ijarah* and the contract of *al-bay'*.

Ijarah wa-iqtina A lease agreement with the option for client to buy the leased asset at an agreed price from the bank at the end of the lease tenure, with rental fees previously paid constituting part of the price.

Ijma' One of the sources of *shari'ah* that is based on a consensus of Muslim scholars sharing the same opinion and applied only in the absence of an explicit answer to the issue in question.

Ijtihad One of the sources of *shari'ah* based on the efforts of individual jurists in providing independent solutions to problems on rules of behaviour which have not been addressed explicitly in the *Qur'an* and *Sunnah*.

Income collection An integral part of corporate management action in ensuring timely and accurate credit of dividend/interests payments.

Income or profit gap A widely used method for managing the financial institution's income sensitivity to changes in market interest rate. It is calculated by subtracting the amount of rate sensitive liabilities (RSL) from rate sensitive assets (RSA).

Indemnification The act of compensating for damage or loss to *takaful* participants from the pool of funds.

Indemnities Payments for claims made by *takaful* participants during the financial period.

Indicative rate of return A publicized expected rate of return used by an Islamic bank to draw public attention to invest in one of its accounts.

Inflation An economic condition when the general level of prices for goods and services is rising.

Institutional units The collective users of the facilities provided by a financial system including people, corporations and other organizations as well as government agencies.

Insurance An assurance by one party to provide a guarantee of compensation for specified loss, illness or death in return for payment of a specified premium by the insured party.

Insurance premium The fee paid by the policyholder to the insurer for agreeing to pay the policyholder a sum of money (or its equivalent) on the occurrence of a specified event.

Insured A person or entity that buys insurance. Also known as the policyholder.

Insurer The entity or party which provides insurance.

Insurer financial strength rating A rating of the insurer on its financial strength in meeting contractual obligations and this is assessed based on both qualitative (country risk of the domicile of the company and its business profile) and quantitative (strength of company's balance sheet and operating performance) factors.

Interbank market A specific money market which allows banks with excess liquidity to lend their funds to other banks experiencing shortage of funds on a short term basis (often overnight) and usually on an unsecured basis.

Interbank trading Trading of Government Investment Issue (GII) which is non-tradable in the market, but the players may exchange the papers among themselves.

Interest rate risk A type of market risk that is related to exposure of a bank's financial conditions due to movements of interest rate in the market.

Intermediation contracts Contracts that facilitate the economic agents to perform financial intermediation activities in an efficient and transparent way.

Internal ratings based credit risk (IRB) A self-assessment approach to credit risk conducted by the Islamic bank to conclude on their operational risks.

International Financial Reporting Standards (IFRS) Accounting standards issued by the International Accounting Standards Board (IASB) that banks must adhere to when preparing the financial statements.

Investment account holder (IAH) A type of investment account offered by Islamic bank for depositors. Under this account the bank manages the funds and profit will be shared based on agreed proportion, but in the case of a loss only the IAHs will bear the loss.

Investment accounting An accounting guideline that covers the maintenance of the books and records of the investment fund based on standards such as the International Financial Reporting Standards (IFRS) or US Generally Accepted Accounting Principles (GAAP) or any local GAAP.

Investment banking A financial sector that helps companies and governments raise funds in the capital market either through equity or debt, provide corporate advisory services on mergers and acquisitions, asset management as well as other securities services, e.g. brokerage, financing services and securities lending. Examples of such banks are JP Morgan, Goldman Sachs and Citi.

Investment deposits Islamic banks accept investment deposits from customers for a specified period on the principle of *mudarabah* whereby the Islamic bank acts as the *mudarib* (agent) and the depositor as the provider of capital (*rabbul mal*) and they agree among others, on the distribution of profits, if any, generated by the bank from the investment of the funds.

Investment protection reserve Amount set aside aimed at providing protection to capital as well as investment deposits against any risk of loss including default, thereby minimizing the withdrawal risk.

Investment risk reserve (IRR) The amount appropriated out of the investment account holders (IAHs) after allocating the *mudarib* share to cushion against future losses.

Irrevocable binding contract *See* ***binding contract.***

Islamic bond market An emerging innovative capital market dealing with *sukuk* instruments.

Islamic capital market A market or intermediary that facilitates the trading of *shari'ah* compliant financial equities and bonds (*sukuk*).

Islamic commercial law Law in conducting business (or *fiqh al-mu'amalat*) based on the *shari'ah* principles.

Islamic cross currency swap (ICCS) A *shari'ah* compliant bilateral contractual arrangement between two parties to exchange a series of profit and/or principal payments denominated in one currency for another series of profit and/or payments denominated in another currency, based on a notional principal amount, over an agreed period of time. The mutually agreed underlying asset used to legitimize the transactions is based on commodity *murabahah*.

Islamic economic principles *Shari'ah* guidance on the conduct of and constraints on all aspects of economic activities so that the entire pattern of production, exchange and distribution of wealth may conform to the Islamic standard of justice and equity.

Islamic economic system An economic system that deals with allocation of scarce resources, production and exchange of goods and services and distribution of resulting income and wealth based on the principles of *shari'ah*.

Islamic equity market The intermediary or place where *shari'ah* compliant shares are traded.

Islamic Exchange Traded Funds (i-ETFs) Similar to conventional ETFs except that the Islamic Benchmark Index comprises of companies which are *shari'ah* compliant as advised by the *shari'ah* adviser or *shari'ah* committee.

Islamic financial system A financial system on the flow of funds from the surplus spending unit to the deficit spending unit which is governed by a set of divine rules and regulations embodied in the *Qur'an* and *Sunnah* such as avoiding *riba* (usury or interest), *gharar* (ambiguities and uncertainties), *maysir* (gambling), *haram* (dealing in unlawful activities), and avoiding unethical or immoral transactions such as market manipulation, insider trading, short selling, etc.

Islamic foreign exchange (FX) swap A contract designed as an Islamic hedging mechanism to minimize the exposure of market participants to the volatile and fluctuating currency exchange rate in the market. To maintain absolute *shari'ah* compliance in the contract, the Fx swap generally involves the exchange and re-exchange of foreign currency. Islamic FX swaps involve two stages. The first stage involves foreign exchange of monetary currencies that occurs at the beginning and the second stage of exchange occurs at the expiry date.

Islamic Interbank Money Market (IIMM) An intermediary that provides a ready source of short term investment outlet based on *shari'ah* principles and through which Islamic banks and banks participating in the Islamic Banking Scheme (IBS) would be able to match the funding requirements effectively and efficiently.

Islamic money market The financial instruments that are part of the ***Islamic equity market*** and the ***Islamic bond market (sukuk).***

Islamic option A contract of promise to buy or sell an asset at a predetermined price within a stipulated period of time and used as a kind of risk management technique where the buyer tries to avoid or eliminate future market volatility. There are mixed opinions on the permissibility of this instrument from an Islamic perspective.

Islamic options futures (IOFS) A *shari'ah* compliant contract under which one party has the option to sell a commodity at specific price and at a specific date in the future.

Islamic principle of consumption Guideline based on *shari'ah* principles related to consumption such as avoiding consuming alcohol, pork, animals not slaughtered in the name of Allah, gambling and drugs.

Islamic principle of economic freedom Islam provides individuals the economic freedom to earn, own, enjoy and spend their wealth as they like as long as they are within the boundaries of Islamic spiritual and moral values, fulfilling mandatory obligations such as *zakat*.

Islamic principle of moderation Islam emphasizes moderation in everything an individual does and this is closely related to the issue of balance and justice. A moderate approach in balancing various concerns in any given situation and seeking the middle ground between them will often lead to the best correct action. Islam also explicitly discourages its followers from crossing the boundaries and following extreme limits in any activities.

Islamic principle of ownership Recognition and belief that the universe and everything within it belongs to God (Allah) alone and man only holds the resources as a trust for which he will be held accountable to Him.

Islamic principle of wealth Islam encourages man to utilize the resources that Allah has created and entrusted to man to create wealth as long as this is not based on exploitation of others, unlawful ways or through transgression, as guided by *shari'ah*.

Islamic profit rate swap (IPRS) A bilateral *shari'ah* compliant contract to exchange profit rates between a fixed rate party and a floating rate party or vice versa. See *fixed rate party* and *floating rate party*.

Islamic promissory forward contract (IPFC) This instrument is structured in a manner that reflects the concept of *wa'ad* (promise) in forward contracts for *salam* or *murabahah*. This is used for hedging risks associated with contracts such as commodity *murabahah*.

Islamic Real Estate Investment Trusts (i-REITs) Highly liquid asset instruments that can be sold fairly quickly to raise cash and/or to take advantage of other investment opportunities.

Islamic subsidiary An Islamic bank that is owned by its conventional bank (parent) but with separate operations and management.

Islamic window A conventional bank that also offers Islamic banking products and services as an option to its customers.

Islamic worldview A view on the existence and future of man that encompasses both the religious and worldly aspects with the ultimate aim of achieving **al-falah,** a comprehensive human success, wellbeing and happiness in this world and the hereafter.

Issue price The price featured in a *sukuk* issue or face value of conventional bond.

Issuer rating Related to the assessment of the overall financial and institutional creditworthiness of the *sukuk* issuer, which in turn would determine the potential investors' level of confidence in investing in it.

Istishan A juristic preference where a scholar or knowledge seeker (*mujtahid*) prefers one alternative over the other, despite not having an explicit argument in its favour.

Junk bond A high yield fixed income bond that carries a credit rating of BB or lower by Standard & Poor's and thus have higher default risk.

Justice in consumption Concept of justice that discourages exploitation or consumption of resources excessively to the extent of depriving others of their rights.

Justice in distribution Concept of justice that encourages economic resources and wealth to be shared or distributed within the community in a way that everyone is provided with basic necessities of life and the gulf between the rich and the poor is narrowed.

Justice in exchange Concept of justice that demands transparency, honesty and accountability between two parties involved in the exchange of goods or services.

Justice in production Concept of justice that disallowed exploitation of others in any way or form in utilizing the factors of production. Wealth should not be acquired by unfair, unlawful and fraudulent means.

Khalifa A vicegerency or stewardship role that man are expected to fulfil in this world by promoting what is good, forbidding what is wrong, establishing justice and promoting beneficence (*ihsan*), which will result in attaining high levels of good life, both individually and collectively.

Legal framework A set of rules, procedures, rights, duties and obligations that governs and regulates agreements, contracts, etc.

Legal risk Risk of potential financial or reputational loss due to non-compliance or misunderstanding of the law or regulation. This includes risks of financial contracts being unenforceable due to ambiguity of the law.

Legal tender Banknotes or coins that are legally accepted if offered as payment for services or debt.

Lender of last resort (LOLR) The central bank will assume the responsibility of providing emergency liquidity to financial institutions experiencing financial distress or difficulties. This normally involves the central bank giving cash to member banks to boost the position of their cash reserves through rediscounting of first class bills when there is a financial crisis. For Islamic financial institutions, they can only benefit from such facilities if it is in the form of interest free assets.

Lenders Those who are willing to lend their financial surplus which arises when income exceeds consumption.

Letter of awareness A formal letter written to a seller, normally by a parent company, acknowledging its relationship with another group of company and its awareness of a financial arrangement being made to that company. It does not constitute a guarantee, but may indicate significant moral commitment on the part of the writer.

Letter of comfort A formal letter that is used to facilitate an action or transaction, but is constructed with the intention of not giving rise to legal obligations.

Letter of guarantee A formal letter from an Islamic bank to a third party stating that a customer who has made an order does indeed own the underlying assets and the bank will guarantee delivery if the order is assigned.

LIBOR See *London Interbank Offered Rate (LIBOR)*.

Life Insurance A type of insurance coverage that pays out a certain amount of money to the insured or their specified beneficiaries upon a certain event affecting the individual who is insured such as death or disability.

Limited period investment account/deposit A form of investment deposits offered by Islamic banks whereby the bank and the depositor enter into a contract, with the former agreeing to accept the investment for a specified period determined by mutual consent by both parties, after which the contract will terminate and the profit will be distributed at the end of each financial year.

Liquid asset buffer (LAB) Financial requirement to comply with *Basel III* to meet any sudden demands for liquidity that banks may face.

Liquidity assessment A framework developed to enable Islamic banks to match their short term liquidity requirement stemming from obligations that are maturing with those assets that are maturing. The analysis is further supported by the use of a number of ratios related to the funding structure of Islamic banks to reveal if the bank is over dependent on a particular source of funding.

Liquidity coverage ratio (LCR) A liquidity ratio introduced by *Basel III* designed to ensure that banks have sufficient high quality liquid assets (HQLA). See high *quality liquid assets*.

Liquidity gap (LGAP) A widely used method for managing the financial institution's liquidity position. A liquidity gap is the difference between net liquid assets (NLA) and volatile liabilities (VL).

Liquidity management Actions taken to ensure that the bank holds enough cash and other liquid assets that are readily available to meet demands for daily withdrawals and other payments by their customers.

Liquidity risk Risk that arises due to insufficient liquidity to cater for the bank's normal operating requirements such as meeting its obligations to fund increases in assets as they fall due without incurring unacceptable costs or losses. This includes *funding risk*, *asset risk*, *trading risk* and *cash risk*.

Loan loss reserve The amount set aside aimed at providing protection against unexpected credit losses as required by regulations in different jurisdictions.

London Interbank Offered Rate (LIBOR) The average interest rates estimated by leading banks in London for charging the borrowers from other banks. In practice, Islamic financial institutions use a benchmark rate, usually based on the London Interbank Offered Rate (LIBOR), when pricing their various financial instruments.

Macroeconomics A discipline that studies the behaviour of the economy as a whole such as how Gross Domestic Product (GDP) is affected by changes in factors such as unemployment, national income, rate of growth and price levels.

Madhahib Islamic doctrines or school of thoughts (singular *madhahab*).

Management capability Capabilities of management to direct and control the costs of the bank operations based on qualitative rather than quantitative factors.

Management risk Risk or potential threat that the bank's managers will put their own interests ahead of the interest of the bank's shareholders and stakeholders (agency problem) when executing their planning, organizing, reporting and controlling functions.

Maqasid al-shari'ah The end objectives of *shari'ah*, which are to educate the individual, establish justice and realize benefits to the people in this world and in the hereafter. It governs every aspect of its follower's life, be it relationship with Allah or with others, including the political, economic and social institutions.

Market based system A financial system in a country whereby the main role of allocating capital, mobilizing savings, financing and investing activities are handled by market institution. Households' assets are allocated in the form of shares and bonds and businesses raise capital through IPOs (initial public offerings) and corporate equities.

Market failures An inefficient allocation of the demand for and supply of the goods and services leading to a net social welfare loss.

Market risk A type of risk that affects the bank's trading book due to changes in equity prices, interest rates, credit spreads, foreign exchange rates, commodity prices and other indicators whose values are set in a public market. See *(un)systematic risk*.

Mark-up risk The risk that the benchmark rate changes but the mark-up rate on fixed income contracts cannot be adjusted causing Islamic banks to be indirectly exposed to risk arising from movements in interest rate.

Maslahah Literally means to bring about utility and fend off damage or injury for public interest.

Maturity transformation Action taken by banks in transforming their liabilities (funds from savers/depositors) which are repayable on demand or relatively short notice into banks' assets (funds lent to borrowers) that are repayable in the medium to long term.

Maturity value The par or face value of the bond that the investor is promised to receive at the end of the period, the maturity date.

Medium of exchange An intermediary instrument used to facilitate financial transactions between parties.

Metallic money Money that replaced commodity money, which at first was full bodied money, i.e. the metallic value is equal to the face value. Later, full metallic money was replaced by minted coins for small denominations and paper notes for larger denominations as *tender money*.

Metaphysics One of the elements of worldview that deals with the ultimate reality of nature.

Microcredit Small amount of credit financing given to the poor or low income group who have no tangible collateral.

Microeconomics A discipline that studies how people and businesses make decisions regarding the allocation of resources as well as prices of goods and services.

Microenterprise A business operating on a very small scale with the support of micro enterprise based on solidarity group lending or micro credit.

Micro entrepreneurship A small business that employs fewer than ten people and is started with a small amount of investment.

Micro-*takaful* Offering protection to low income people against specific risks based on mutual risks transfer arrangement within a group.

Minimum capital requirement Also known as regulatory capital or capital adequacy whereby banks are expected to hold a minimum risk adjusted capital ratio (RACR) as required by ***Basel I***. It is calculated by multiplying Tier 1 or total capital minimum requirement by the amounts held in the four asset categories.

Mobile digital wallets Also known as e-wallets, allow the storing of multiple credit card and bank account numbers in a secured environment for making payments. It is often linked to the mobile phone.

Modern banking A business model that offers universal or full service banking such as loans, deposits, insurance, securities/investment, pensions and other financial services.

Monetary policy The macroeconomic policy and process by which the central bank, monetary authority or currency board of a country, controls the supply of money, often targeting an inflation rate or interest rate to ensure price stability and general trust in the currency.

Money A medium of exchange used to facilitate exchange of goods and services among different parties.

Money market A market or platform where monetary assets of short term nature, usually less than a year, are traded.

Muamalat Islamic commercial dealings and civil acts based on *shari'ah* principles.

***Mudarabah* current account** A current account offered by Islamic banks based on the principle of *mudarabah* where the depositor and the bank agree upon the profit sharing ratio (PSR) between them at the time the deposit is accepted.

***Mudarabah* interbank investments (MII)** A financial instrument drawn between two banks whereby a deficit Islamic banking institution, i.e. the 'investee bank', receives investment from a surplus in another Islamic banking institution, i.e. the 'investor bank'.

Mudarabah muqayyadah Restricted trust financing.

Mudarabah mutlaqah Unrestricted trust financing.

***Mudarabah* saving account** A savings account offered by Islamic banks based on the principle of *mudarabah* (trustee profit sharing). The profit sharing ratio (PSR) will be agreed at the time of accepting the deposit and can be changed provided the account holder consents to the change and any profit above the computed dividend amount (based on the agreed sharing ratio) shall be treated as *hibah* (gift).

Mudarabah takaful A *takaful* model which involves the participants acting as *rab-ul-mal* (capital provider) and the *takaful* operator as the *mudarib* (entrepreneur). Hence, any financial losses suffered from the investment and underwriting activities are to be borne solely by the *takaful* participants as the *rab-ul-mal*, provided that the losses are not attributable to the *takaful* operator's misconduct or negligence.

Municipal bonds A type of bond issued by the municipal or state government which carries a slightly higher default risk than treasury or government bonds.

Musharakah An Islamic partnership contract.

Musharakah mutanaqisah A diminishing partnership contract.

Mythological worldview Understanding of human and events based on myths or stories. See **secular worldview**.

Net stable funding ratio (NSFR) A ratio designed to promote resiliency over longer term time horizons by creating additional incentives to fund activities with more stable sources of funding on an on-going structural basis.

Non-deposits A funding source available for Islamic banks from surplus Islamic bank to an Islamic bank that may face short term liquidity deficit.

Non-deposit taking institutions Financial intermediaries consisting of contractual savings institutions such as insurance and pension funds companies and investment intermediaries such as companies offering mutual funds, financial loans, investment services and brokerage houses.

Non-interest income Fees from income, commissions and trading income including gains/losses from trading securities and foreign transactions.

Non-standardized agreements Forward contracts that are flexible in terms of quantity and date of delivery agreed by two parties who intend to involve in the future sale or purchase of an asset at a price agreed on the spot (*forward price*) but the underlying asset delivered at a future date.

Non-tradable sukuk *Sukuk* investment certificates that represent receivables of cash or goods such as *sukuk al-murabahah* and *sukuk al-salam* but they cannot be traded as they are essentially financial assets and selling them may amount to a sale of debt which is not allowed by the *shari'ah*.

Off balance sheet Assets or liabilities that are not present on the bank's Statement of Financial Position such as *specific investment account* (SIA).

Off balance sheet management Actions taken by banks in controlling and limiting exposures related to off balance sheet transactions.

Offeree The party that accepts the offer in a contract. See *offeror*.

Offeror The party that makes an offer in a contract. A minimum of two parties with one being the *offeror* and the other *offeree* is an essential component for a valid contract and the parties entering must also be legally competent or have the capacity to do so.

One stage contract A transaction that involves only one initial exchange to conclude the contract.

Open market operations Buying and selling of government securities in the open market in order to expand or contract the amount of money in the banking system to control inflation, money supply and prices.

Operating expenses ratio (OER) A ratio indicating how much the bank spends to maintain its outstanding financing portfolio. It is calculated by dividing operating expenses by the average financial portfolio.

Operating structure The functions, departmental structure, main layout and mobilization of funds adopted by the Islamic banks that adhere to *shari'ah* requirements in their operations.

Operational risk Risk of potential loss resulting from inadequate or failed internal processes, people (ethics and relationship), technology or system (hardware, software and model), *legal risk* (compliance and control including risks of unenforceability of financial contracts), *regulatory risk* (risk that arises from changes in regulatory framework of the country), or external events (security, clients).

Operational sustainability (OS) Also known as operational self-sufficiency. It is assessed based on the ratio between operating income and the operating and financial expenses. If the ratio is greater than 100 per cent, it means that the Islamic bank is able to cover all of its costs through its own operations without having to rely on other contributions to survive.

Opportunity cost The cost of sacrificing other alternatives when one alternative is chosen.

Parallel salam A contract in which the seller or the buyer in the original *salam* contract becomes a buyer or seller in another contract which entails the delivery and taking delivery of the same underlying commodity. The practice of *parallel salam* is similar to offsetting in conventional finance transactions. See *salam*.

Participants' Investment Fund (PIF) A provision from the pooled funds for family *takaful* utilized for investment purposes to generate returns.

Participants' Risk Fund (PRF) A donation from the pooled funds for family *takaful* to cover risks, managed by the *takaful* operator as an underwriting activity.

Performance fee A fee or reward that the obligator is entitled to as *mudarib* for achieving over expectation results.

Periodic distribution amounts Instalment payments made at regular intervals over more than one period.

Philosophical worldview Understanding of events or situations based on logical and rational search for answers.

Pillar I A *Basel II* framework for more effective risk management by requiring the assessment of risks in banking products through a more risk sensitive system for risk weighting assets.

Pillar II Recommendation by *Basel II* for banks to review risk through appropriate balance of prudential supervision.

Pillar III Recommendation by *Basel II* for promotion of market disciplines through regulatory disclosure requirements.

Plain vanilla swap A type of swap instrument whereby the parties specify the interest rate on the payments that are being exchanged; the type of interest payments (*fixed or variable/floating*); the amount on which the interest is paid (*notional principal*); and the time period over which the exchanges continue to be made.

Plastic cards This refers to debit card, credit card and charge card that are used for making payments for transactions instead of cash.

Political risk Risk related to changes in government or political decisions such as social policies (e.g. fiscal, monetary, trade, investment, industrial, income, labour, and developmental) or events related to political instability (e.g. terrorism, riots, coups) that alters the expected outcome and value of a given economic action.

Portfolio at risk (PAR) A ratio indicating the extent of risk of any late payment on the entire financing balance. It is calculated by dividing the outstanding balance of all loans with arrears over 30 days (or 60, 90, 120 or 180 days) by the outstanding gross portfolio as of a certain date.

Portfolio yield (PY) The percentage of financial income to average financing portfolio. The higher the percentage the better, as it indicates higher yield from the investment portfolio.

Primary market A place that provides opportunities for first time issuers of financial securities to raise capital or issue debt through underwriting and initial public offering (IPO).

Private banking Provision of high quality or bespoke financial services to wealthy or high net worth clients, both individuals and families.

Productivity The ability of a country or organization to produce goods or services based on available resources.

Profit equalization reserve (PER) A unique reserve only found in Islamic banks whereby an amount is appropriated out of the *mudarabah* income by the bank before allocating the share of the *mudarib*. It is aimed at maintaining a specified level of return on investment (ROI) for the investment account holders (IAHs), especially the unrestricted investment account holders (URIAHs).

Profit related deposits The general investment and *mudarabah* deposit accounts that are comingled and managed on a pool basis.

Profit sharing investment accounts (PSIAs) Depositors contribute to accounts for investments based on *mudarabah* contract, where investment account holders (IAHs) and Islamic banks agree to share the profit generated from assets funded by PSIA, while losses shall be borne by the IAHs.

Profit sharing ratio (PSR) The ratio for distributing profits or returns from a business venture as agreed between two or more parties.

Protection of depositor's interest A policy designed to maintain a sound banking system and to safeguard against bank failures by enabling the central bank to monitor and inspect the adequacy and soundness of commercial banks' management.

Proxy voting service A service provided upon receipt of voting instruction from clients on a case by case basis. In providing the service, the Islamic bank will complete the proxy form and cast the votes based on their clients' instructions.

Public property Natural resources such as water, minerals, forest, pasture, etc., under the guardianship and control of the State. They are considered in Islam as collective property of the community where everyone in the state shares equal rights. They can be used by members of society as long as they do not undermine the rights of other citizens. See *state property*.

Purely secular jurisdictions A legal framework in a country that clearly separates government institutions and people affairs from religious teachings. Hence, in such jurisdictions, *shari'ah* elements are not incorporated in the substantive laws of the country and at best the jurisdiction only makes changes to existing laws to facilitate a level playing field for the IFIs to operate.

Put contract A financial derivative (option) contract whereby the seller is guaranteed a minimum price or the *strike price* for an underlying asset. If the price of the underlying asset is below the strike price, a claim can be made and if the price is above the strike price, the option is not exercised.

Put option An option that grants the holder the right to sell an underlying asset at the exercise price within a specific period of time. See *put contract*.

Qabul Acceptance of an offer made by another party.

Qard ul hasanah Literally means 'beautiful loan', a terminology derived from various verses in the *Qur'an*. It is a unique contract in that the business transaction establishes a relationship between lender and borrower without any accrued tangible profits or simply interest free loans. In Islamic banking, *qard ul hasanah* may be utilized as an overdraft facility for clients who needed it.

Qiyas One of the sources of *shari'ah* based on analogical deductions to address contemporary issues which are not directly mentioned in the *Qur'an* and Sunnah, but have similar characteristics with another or earlier situation or incident in the past which is clearly based on those sources.

Qur'an The sacred book for Muslims that is revealed by Allah to the Prophet Muhammad by the Archangel Gabriel over a period of 23 years. It consists of 114 chapters (*surah*) of varying lengths touching upon all aspects of human existence, including matters of doctrine, social organization and legislation.

Rate of return risk Risk associated with the potential impact on the returns earned on the assets or business transactions undertaken by the Islamic financial institutions as a result of unexpected changes in the amount of profits generated. This uncertainty can cause a divergence from the expectations that investment account holders have on the liabilities side. The larger the divergence, the higher the rate of return risk.

Rational economic man A person who consistently thinks about how to optimize utilization and maximization of profit to fulfil his or her self-interest.

Rational person A person who systematically and purposefully thinks through what is the best action that will make him or her better off after taking into account the marginal costs and benefits.

Real estate financing Mortgage financing and services related to it such as brokerage, appraisal, property management, etc.

Real estate rating The overall rating of the developer by *sukuk* rating agencies which is assessed based on the developer's activities such as the performance of its architects, engineers, contractors and other important personnel.

Regulatory capital The amount of capital that financial institutions must hold as required by the financial regulator.

Regulatory framework The roles and functions of the regulators in the financial sector. The main regulators who supervise this sector include the central banks or monetary authorities and the Basel Committee on Banking Supervision (BCBS) who set rules and guidelines on supervision of the industry to ensure financial stability and also decide on the accounting and auditing standards to be adopted.

Regulatory risk Risk that arises from changes in the regulatory framework in a country.

Reinsurance An insurance policy that are bought by multiple insurance companies known as the reinsured in order to share the risk with a larger insurance company known as the reinsurer who agreed to insure them against the potential loss they might experience.

Religious worldview Related to a notion of a deity, divine entity or god that has set up an eternal structure of morality that must be followed, as they have long term significance for human.

Residual risk The uncertainty related to the specific industry, organization or asset after taking into considerations all measures to identify and eliminate potential threats.

Restricted funds Deposits whereby the utilization of the funds is clearly identified and are managed separately. Specific investment deposits and profit equalization reserves (PER) fall under this category and such funds are often treated as off balance sheet item by Islamic banks.

Restricted investment account (RIA) Also known as *specific investment account* (SIA). An Islamic investment account which is subject to certain restrictions being imposed on the bank by the account holder with respect to purpose, geographical distribution, and/or types of transactions, when investing the account holder's funds. As such, Islamic banks cannot commingle such funds with the unrestricted investment accounts and they do not appear on the bank's balance sheet. See *specific investment account (SIA)*.

Restricted *mudarabah* Investments accounts in Islamic banks that are presented off balance sheet.

Retakaful The Islamic alternative to reinsurance which has been structured to be *shari'ah* compliant. It involves *takaful* operators contributing an agreed amount of premium periodically to the *retakaful* company. Hence, all the underwriting risks of the *takaful* operators are insured by the *retakaful* company who plays a significant role when *takaful* operators record deficits or losses.

Return on average assets (ROAA) A ratio indicating how much net income is generated per £1 of assets held by the bank. It is calculated by dividing net operating income by average total assets.

Return on average deposit (ROAD) A ratio that indicates how well the bank uses its deposits to generate profit, i.e. how much profit the bank can generate for every £1 of deposits held. It is calculated by dividing net operating income by average total deposits.

Return on average equity (ROAE) A ratio indicating bank's profitability and growth potential. It measures the percentage return on each £1 of equity invested in the bank and is calculated by dividing net operating income by average total equity.

Revocable contract See *binding contract*.

Riba al-fadl *Fadl* literally means increase or growth. Hence, *riba al-fadl* refers to excess in counter value when two similar things are exchanged unequally.

Riba al-nasi'ah *Nasi'ah* literally means to postpone or to wait. Hence, *riba al-nasi'ah* refers to the time period that is allowed for the borrower to repay the loan in return for additional reward (premium) above the principal amount borrowed. It is also known as *riba al-duyun* (interest on loans), *riba al-jali* (obvious interest), *riba al-mubashir* (direct interest), *riba al-jahiliyyah* (interest prohibited by the *Qur'an)*.

Risk absorption Risks that cannot be eliminated and transferred will be absorbed by the financial institution. This may arise due to either the complexity of the risk and difficulty in separating them from the assets, or the risks are acceptable as they are central to their business.

Risk adjusted capital ratio (RACR) A ratio that indicates the adequacy of capital to withstand a downturn in the economy. It is calculated by applying risk based weights to specific assets and summing the results to derive the capital required. There are two main components in calculating the risk adjusted capital ratio, i.e. *capital base* divided by *total risk adjusted assets*. See *capital base* and *risk adjusted assets*.

Risk adjusted return on capital (RAROC) The amount of return on capital after adjusting for risk. It is calculated by dividing book value of total capital over risk adjusted assets.

Risk averse An investor who is reluctant to take risk and when faced with two investments opportunities with similar expected return would prefer the one with the lower risk. Also known as risk avoidance.

Risk management The process of identifying, quantifying and assessing business risks in order to plan and take the necessary steps in mitigating and controlling them through regular monitoring and reporting.

Risk mitigating techniques Techniques available for Islamic banks in order to mitigate risk. They generally fall into two types: *standard techniques* and *shariah compliant techniques*. The former refers to those that can be adopted as they are consistent with the Islamic principles of finance such as risk adjusted return on capital (RAROC), GAP analysis, risk reporting, internal and external audit and internal rating, while the latter refers to newly developed or adapted techniques that are more specific to IFIs and can be further categorized into risk avoidance or elimination, *risk absorption* or *management* and *risk transfer*.

Risk taker An investor who is willing to take higher risk exposure.

Risk tolerance The degree of variability or volatility in investment returns that an investor is willing to endure.

Risk transfer A risk management and control strategy that involves using derivatives for hedging, selling or buying of financial claims and changing contractual borrowing terms.

Risk transformation Action by banks in minimizing the risk of individual loans by diversifying their investments, pooling of risks, screening and monitoring borrowers besides holding capital and reserves as a buffer for unexpected losses.

Risk–return trade-off Risk concept whereby those who are willing to take higher exposure of risk (*risk takers*) can expect to get a higher return while those who prefer to stay away from high exposure of risk or willing to take low risk (*risk averse*).

Rotating Savings and Credit Association (ROSCA) is the simplest form and most widely used methods of informal savings whereby participants make regular contributions to a common fund which is given in whole or in part to each contributor in turn. Various types of ROSCAs exist in almost every developing country and they are known by different names: *tandas* (Mexico), *arisan* (Indonesia), *susu* (Ghana), etc.

Safekeeping of assets Assets are kept in book entry form and the Islamic bank will hold the securities as nominees on behalf of the client.

Salam Deferred delivery sale, essentially a transaction where two parties agree to carry out a sale/purchase of an underlying asset at a predetermined future date but at a price determined and fully paid today.

Salam future contract A *shari'ah* compliant sale agreement with full payment being made at the time of effecting sale between two parties for delivery of an underlying asset that is easily quantifiable and its quality determinable for delivery at a specified place at a future date.

Savings deposit Accounts that are operated by Islamic banks based on *wadiah, mudarabah* or *qard-hasan* (benevolent loan) savings deposits. In the case of *qard-hasan* savings deposit, the bank assumes that depositors grant them permission to use and benefit from it for a certain period without expecting any returns from it.
See *wadiah saving account* and *mudarabah saving account*.

Scarcity An economic concept that assume the available resources are not sufficient to fulfil human wants.

Scientific worldview A worldview that is based solely on ideas that can be tested with empirical observation and therefore, conforms to the highest levels of objectivity. This worldview detests the idea of creationism and postulate evolutionism as the foundation of reality.

Secondary market A market or platform facilitating the exchange of existing or previously issued securities (shares and debts).

Secular worldview A worldview based on a materialistic and naturalistic standpoint that rejects the supernatural and the immortality of the Creator, and the cosmos

being God's creation. This worldview can be classified into mythological, philosophical and scientific. A *mythological worldview* is based on collected myths that are deemed as being true by a particular culture, and the supernatural is often used to explain natural incidents and to explicate the nature of humanity and the universe. A *philosophical worldview* addresses all areas of existence i.e. metaphysics, epistemology and ethics, thus recognizing both idealistic and materialistic aspects of reality. See *scientific worldview*.

Secured bond A type of corporate bond where the issuer pledges a specific asset in the form of collateral on the loan. In the event of a default, the bond issuer passes the title of the asset onto the bondholders.

Securities gains (losses) The gains or losses realized when the securities held at hand and available for-sale by the bank are sold.

Securities settlement The actual delivery of securities to/from counterparty based on the terms of trade such as T+3 (trade date plus three working days).

Securitization Securitization is a financial innovation to transform the bank's dormant illiquid assets into tradable, negotiable and liquid assets by pooling assets of similar characteristics and selling them to third parties as security. Since securitizations are based on the performance of a set of well-defined assets, it is permissible in Islamic banking.

Sensitivity to market risk Risk related to the extent to which the bank's earnings and capital can be adversely affected by changes in exchange rate, interest rate, equity price or commodity price in the market.

Settlement dates Terminology used in swaps referring to the dates in which the specified payments are due.

Settlement period Terminology used in swaps referring to the period of time between the specified settlement or payment date and the transaction date.

Settlement risk Risk that a counterparty (or intermediary agent) fails to deliver a security or its value in cash as per agreement when the security was traded, despite the other counterparty or counterparties have already delivered the security or cash value as per the trade agreement.

Shari'ah Islamic canonical law, mainly based on the teachings of the Qur'an and the traditions of the Prophet (*Sunna*).

Shari'ah audit An assessment conducted to provide an independent assurance designed to add value and improve the degree of compliance in relation to the IFI's business operations, with the main objective of ensuring a sound and effective internal control system in accordance with the *shari'ah*.

Shari'ah compliant Activities, contracts or investments that are in accordance with Islamic principles.

Shari'ah compliant deposit facility (SCF) A facility created by central bank to allow Islamic banks to conduct business on a purely *shari'ah* compliant basis, but also will allow them to comply with **Basel III** liquidity rules of holding a liquid asset buffer (LAB) to meet any sudden demands for liquidity they may face.

Shari'ah filter Also known as *shari'ah* screening. The methodology applied in ensuring that the activities of the companies are *shari'ah* compliant. The screening normally involves two stages: firstly screening that the line of business or core business of the underlying company are not in non-permissible activities such as gambling, alcohol, pornography, pork, etc. and second screening based on the company's finances, i.e. whether it is involved with payments and receipts of interest.

Shari'ah governance The set of rules, practices and processes to enhance the legitimacy of products offered by the banks. It also provides confidence and satisfaction to depositors that the board is monitoring the adherence and compliance by the institution with *shari'ah* principles.

Shari'ah incorporated jurisdictions A legal framework in a country based on shari'ah principles. Hence, in *shari'ah* incorporated jurisdictions, efforts are channelled towards harmonization of *shari'ah* standards for IFIs with local standards rather than standardization. This approach is opposite to *purely secular jurisdictions*.

Shari'ah index An index of companies that are found to be compliant with the stringent rules of *shari'ah* and is monitored by a separate rating agency to help the Islamic investor community to identify and invest in businesses that are compliant with *shari'ah*.

Shari'ah non-compliance risk The risk that arises from the failure of IFIs to comply with *shari'ah* rules and principles due to process, defects in the documentation and/or non-compliant in terms of the product.

Shari'ah quality rating An independent assessment by a group of eminent *shari'ah* scholars on the *shari'ah* quality of IFIs' activities and their securities and financial products based on the *Shari'ah* Quality Rating Committee of Islamic International Rating Agency (IIRA). The rating issued ranges from AA, which denotes conforming to a very high level of standards of *shari'ah* requirements in all aspects of *shari'ah* quality analysis, to B, denoting adequate level of standards of *shari'ah* requirements but has weaknesses in some areas.

Shari'ah review A reviewing process on various aspects of the business operations conducted on a regular basis by those with background in *shari'ah* to ensure compliance with *shari'ah* rules and principles (*fatawa*) as decided by the SSB's (or *Shari'ah* Committee) of the bank. The outcome will be reported to the board management and the SSB. The outcome of the **shari'ah audit** and *shari'ah* review will aid the SSB to form and express an opinion in the SSB Report on the Islamic bank's compliance with *shari'ah* which is included in the bank's annual report.

Shari'ah supervisory board (SSB) A component of the board of governance for the Islamic bank whose membership comprises of *shari'ah* scholars i.e. those who have expertise in *fiqh muamalat* (Islamic rulings governing commercial transactions) to endorse that the activities of the Islamic banks are *shari'ah* compliant. The board reports directly to the board of directors.

Size transformation In the context of banking, this involves banks collecting their small size deposits and repackaging them into larger size loans such as mortgages.

Social welfare contracts The implicit and explicit contract between individuals and society to promote wellbeing and welfare of the underprivileged. This can be institutionalized through an intermediary.

Socialist economy An economic system, also known as socialism, that emphasizes on equitable distribution of income and wealth and lies between capitalism at one end and communism on the other hand.

Socio-economic justice An Islamic objective towards a just society which is achievable through two mechanisms: the redistribution system of wealth through *zakat*, and the prohibition of interest.

Soft commodity Agricultural or livestock products such as coffee, wheat, corn, sheep and cattle.

Sources of *qard* fund Represents the gross increase in funds available for lending on interest free basis during the period covered by the statement. The sources of such increase may come from *external sources* (e.g. depositors current accounts), from owners of the Islamic bank and from proceeds of prohibited earnings. See **Statement of Sources and Uses of Qard Fund**.

Sources of *zakah* and charity funds Represent the gross increase in funds available for distribution as *zakah* and charity to beneficiaries during the period covered by the statement.

Sovereign credit rating The credit rating of the sovereign entity or national government by taking into consideration the risk level of its regulatory, political, economic and legal environment.

Special purpose vehicle (SPV) An entity that is set up to raise financial capital through *sukuk* issuance and acts as trustee in respect of the underlying asset or activities related to the usufruct or service for the benefit of the *sukuk* holders.

Special unrestricted investment account (SUIA) An investment account that operates under the *mudarabah* principle whereby the funds, either short term or long term, are managed separately and the utilization of the funds is identified and matched with specific funds. SUIA holders may stipulate that the Islamic bank will only invest the funds in specific projects or in projects within a specific sector. The operations of the SUIA must be agreed upon by all parties involved in the contract

Specific Investment Account (SIA) The investment account holder enters into a contract with Islamic bank to invest funds which are restricted for a certain purpose, hence it is also known as restricted investment account (RIA). See **Restricted Investment Account (RIA)**.

Speculators Those who serve as the counterparty to hedgers for futures transactions and provide liquidity to the futures market.

Staff productivity ratio (SPR) A vital ratio for all banks as staff constitutes the largest operating expense. Two ratios can be calculated for this purpose: (i) the number of active clients served by each member of staff, and (ii) how much financing is managed by each member of staff. Higher ratios signal bank's staff's efficiency.

Standard of deferred payments The ability of money in maintaining its value over time, which makes it a good standard or medium suitable to be used in borrowing and lending operations where payments and receipts are made some time in the future.

Standardized credit risk Credit risk based on externally provided risk assessments such as the rating assignments by external credit assessment institutions.

Standby letter of credit A letter issued by the bank to provide assurances for various purposes on behalf of a customer especially on the ability to fulfil the terms of a contract. The bank will be responsible to make payment to the beneficiary when there is evidence that the customer has not performed its obligation in compliance to the terms of the letter of credit

Standing instruction A remittance service by which a customer can instruct an Islamic bank to affect regular fund transfers at pre-set timings and amounts from the customer's deposit account to designated beneficiary accounts.

State property This encompasses certain natural resources and other property that cannot be immediately privatized. They can be movable or immovable, and can be acquired via conquest or peaceful means. Any unclaimed, unoccupied and heirless properties, including uncultivated land, can be considered as state property. See *public property*.

Statement of Cash Flow Also known as *Funds Flow Statement*. It indicates how changes in the Statement of Financial Position and Comprehensive Income Statement affect sources and uses of cash and its equivalent.

Statement of Changes in Equity A financial statement that shows comprehensive income for the period and the effects of any prior period adjustments, reconciling the movement in equity from the beginning to the end of the period. It also shows how a period's profits are divided between dividends for shareholders and retained earnings whereby the latter amount is shown under owners' equity in the *Statement of Financial Position*.

Statement of Changes in Restricted Investment A financial statement showing only the changes in restricted investments and they are not reflected on the bank's *Statement of Financial Position.*

Statement of Financial Position Also known as balance sheet. It represents the state of wealth of banks at a particular point in time, usually at the end of the financial year. It reports quarterly to shareholders and other stakeholder the amount of assets, liabilities and equity held by the bank.

Statement of Sources and Uses of *Qard* Fund A financial statement showing the gross increase in funds available for interest free lending during the period covered by the statement. The sources of such increase may come from funds provided by the bank from current accounts, owners of the Islamic bank and proceeds from prohibited earnings which the Islamic bank may make available to the fund on a temporary basis until such proceeds are properly disposed of. See *Sources of Qard Fund*.

Store of value A necessary feature for an object to be considered as money is that it is able to be liquidated when needed and is able to maintain its value.

Strategic response quotient (SRQ) A measure on the strategic management team quality. The SRQ is determined by the ratio of net interest income (NII) to net overhead expenses (OE).

Strategic risk Risk related to uncertainties and untapped opportunities which are embedded in the strategy of the bank's management and how well they succeeded in executing those strategies.

Strike price See *futures contract*.

Structured trade deposits A type of unrestricted deposits that are structured as a trade transaction to comply with *murabahah* principle whereby the depositor buys a commodity for spot value and sells it for deferred payment generating a profit on the sale of the commodity.

Subject matter It is one of the components essential for a valid contract. Islamic law stresses on four aspects of it: existence, lawfulness, deliverability and precise determination.

Sukuk An innovative Islamic financing product similar to a bond, structured in such a way that returns can be generated to investors without infringing *shari'ah* that prohibits its *riba* or interest. Some *sukuk* are tradable while others are not. See *tradable sukuk*.

Sukuk al-ijarah The most popular type of Islamic bond structured based on a lease contract which allows for the mobilization of funds for long term infrastructure projects and also as means for securitization of tangible assets and usufruct in exchange for a rent.

Sukuk al-istisna'a A type of Islamic bond in the form of certificates of equal value whereby the holder of the *sukuk* becomes the buyer of the project under construction and the manufacturer or contractor is the obligator who agrees to complete the project by the agreed future date.

Sukuk al-istithmar A type of Islamic bond in the form of certificates of equal value that is structured by packaging the rights under *ijarah* contracts (and the relevant underlying assets), *murabahah* receivables, and/or *istisna'a* receivables (each generated by the originator), as well as shares and/or *sukuk* certificates and sold as an investment. It is used when it is not possible to identify a tangible asset for investment and if the business of the obligator is largely intangible.

Sukuk al-mudarabah A type of Islamic bond based on equity partnership whereby the holders of the *sukuk* are the silent partners who do not participate in the management of the underlying asset, business or project. The working partner is the *sukuk obligator*, and as such is entitled to a fee and/or share of the profit as spelt out in the initial contract with the investors.

Sukuk al-murabahah A type of Islamic bond in the form of certificates of equal value structured based on the *standard of deferred payment or cost-plus* that signify rights of the *sukuk* holder to share in receivables from the purchaser of the underlying *murabahah*. It is issued when it is impossible to identify a tangible or real asset for the purpose of the underlying investment.

Sukuk al-musharakah A type of Islamic bond in the form of certificates of equal value structured as joint venture whereby the *sukuk* holders (investors) are the owners of the joint venture, asset or business activity and therefore have the right to share its profits on agreed upon ratios and loss according to the individual contributions. A committee of investor representatives participates in the decision making process. It is issued when huge sums are required for mega projects. They are negotiable instruments that can be traded in the secondary market.

Sukuk al-salam A type of Islamic bond in the form of certificates of equal value structured in the form of deferred delivery. It is issued by the seller (originator) of *salam* products to raise funds needed to pay for the *salam* products to be delivered on a future date to the *sukuk* subscribers who are the buyers of the products. It is not commonly used due to its non-tradability feature.

Sukuk al-wakalah A type of Islamic bond based on an agency contract whereby the obligator will make a pool of assets or portfolio of investments as underlying assets to secure the issuance of the *sukuk,* which will be passed to the agent (*wakeel*) who will use his or her expertise to manage the resources for the best interests of the investors. It is particularly useful in situations where there is no specific tangible asset or assets.

Sukuk holders Owners of *sukuk* certificates who may receive a regular stream of income (fixed or variable) over the life of the certificate and/or with a balloon payment at maturity, depending on the structure of the *sukuk.*

Sukuk investors The subscribers of *sukuk* certificates who become *sukuk* holders and jointly owned the underlying assets with the SPV or enjoy the benefits derived from activities related to the usufruct or service.

Sukuk issuer The legal entities that develop, register and sell the *sukuk* certificates. See **sukuk obligator** and **sukuk originator**.

Sukuk obligator See *sukuk originator.*

Sukuk originator The *sukuk* originator (obligator or issuer) is the entity such as government or corporations needing the funds.

Sukuk rating The viability of the *sukuk* in the secondary market and this is assessed based on the documented terms and covenants along with the risk/return measures which would also help determine the number of potential *sukuk* subscribers.

Sukuk subscriber *Sukuk* buyer.

Supervisory discretion formula A formula used to calculate the capital adequacy ratio (CAR) and assess the withdrawal risk associated with systemic risk. See *capital adequacy ratio (CAR)*.

Supplemental capital (Tier 2) Part of capital base essential for compliance with capital adequacy requirements under *Basel II*. This includes items such as revaluation reserves, undisclosed reserves, hybrid instruments and subordinated term debt.

Swaps A derivative agreement between two parties to exchange a series of cash flows for a set period of time. The exchange normally involves one financial instrument for another for the mutual benefit of both parties.

Systematic risk See *(un)systematic risk.*

Ta'awun Mutual assistance.

Tabarru' Donation.

Takaful Islamic insurance model that complied with *shari'ah* principle whereby the participants' contributions are pooled and invested.

Takaful operator The director who manages the *takaful* funds in accordance with *shari'ah* principle on behalf of the participants who remain as the owners of the premiums.

Tawhid Islamic concept on Unity and Oneness of the Creator. It is central to the Muslim belief system reflecting the unqualified belief that all creation has only one omniscient and omnipresent Creator that is Allah, who has created and placed man in this earth as His vicegerent (*khalifa*) or trustee.

Technical provision The amount payable by *takaful* company for an immediate transfer of its obligations to a third party. Deducting technical provisions and expenses from the total premium continuation paid by the policyholders indicates the underwriting surplus.

Tele-banking A service that helps customers to access authentic, instantaneous information regarding their accounts, by using a push button telephone from any place, anytime.

Teleology Reasoning or believe of the end purpose or goal of certain event or situation.

Tender money Medium of payment accepted by law.

Theology An element of worldview that is related to the beliefs in the existence and nature of God, Prophethood, as well as God's relationship with man.

Tradable sukuk Those *sukuk* investment certificates that represent tangible assets or proportionate ownership of a business or investment portfolio that can be traded in the capital market. They include, among others, *sukuk al-ijarah, sukuk al-musharakah* and *sukuk al-mudarabah*.

On the contrary, *non-tradable sukuk* are investment certificates that represent receivables of cash or goods such as *sukuk al-murabahah* and *sukuk al-salam* and they cannot be traded as they are essentially financial assets and selling them may amount to a sale of debt which is not allowed by *shari'ah.*

Trade-off A compromising assessment between two desirable but mutually exclusive events.

Trading assets Banks' activities related to securities brokerage, trading and underwriting and derivatives dealing and brokerage.

Trading liabilities Activities related to the trading of securities, derivatives dealings and brokerage.

Trading risk Risk or potential loss from trading the bank's spare capital.

Traditional banking The business of offering loans and deposits services by banks.

Traditional economy An economic system where decisions on what, how, how much and for whom to produce are often made by the family or tribe head, according to their traditional means of production. It is also described as the economy where development of goods and services are dominated by the customs, traditions and beliefs in that area.

Transaction deposits Deposits in the bank that can be immediately transferred or withdrawn such as (i) current accounts or demand deposits, (ii) savings account or savings deposits, and (iii) deposits of other banks or interbank deposits.

Transactional contracts Agreements related to economic transactions that facilitate the exchange, sale and trade of goods and services in the real sector.

Traveller's cheque Cheques issued in fixed denominations of international currencies by certain banks. They can be cashed easily, have no specific maturity period and are a convenient means of payment for travellers.

Treasury bond A type of bond which is issued by the government and is considered as having the lowest *default risk* (of not being able to make required payments on debt obligations) as the government is reasonably expected to make good on its promised payments.

Two-tier *mudarabah* A *mudarabah* contract consisting of two contracts whereby the first tier agreement will be between the bank and the depositor(s) and the second tier agreement is between the bank and the entrepreneur where the bank acts as the financier to the entrepreneurs who seek finance from the bank on condition that profits accruing from their business will be shared between them in mutually agreed proportion.

Ummah An Arabic word referring to the creation of unity among Muslims and universal brotherhood by the ties of religion and humanity.

Uncertainty In Islamic finance and banking context, this refers to concept of *gharar* or highly speculative transactions or activities.

Underwriter An intermediary that facilitates the selling of *sukuk* and securities in a primary market or guaranteeing that it will purchase all the unsold *sukuk* or securities at its own risk.

Underwriting The act of accepting risk or liability. In the case of shares or *sukuk*, the act involves undertaking full responsibility in selling them or pledging to buy all the unsold shares or *sukuk*. In the case of *takaful* or insurance, the act involves guaranteeing payments when a loss or damage occurs. Also see *underwriter*.

Underwriting surplus The excess from the total premium paid less the total indemnities claims paid and expenses and changes in technical provisions.

Unilateral contract A contract that is initiated and concluded by a single party which involves some form of benefit being transferred to another party.

Unit of account A feature necessary for an object to be considered as money as it is used as a common denominator to measure the relative values of other goods and services.

Universal bank A bank which offers a full range of banking and investment services.

Unlimited period investment account Investment deposits that do not have any specific period and the accounts are renewed automatically by the bank until depositors notify the bank that they wish to terminate. Depositors are not allowed to make any withdrawals nor increase the amount of deposits in the bank. See *limited period investment account/deposit*.

Unrestricted funds Funds whereby their utilization is not identified and as such, these funds are commingled and managed on a pooled basis. These unrestricted funds can be further classified into *profit related deposits* and *hibah related deposits*.

Unrestricted investment accounts (URIA) Investment accounts that are not subject to any restrictions and the account holder authorizes the bank to invest the funds in any manner the bank deems appropriate. Thus, the bank can commingle the funds with those of the restricted investment account (RIA) holders or with other sources of funds available to the bank such as funds from current accounts.

Unrestricted *mudarabah* A contract in which the *rabbul mal* (principal) permits the *mudarib* (agent) to administer the *mudarabah* fund without any restriction, thus providing the *mudarib* with a wide range of business options on the basis of trust and the mudarib's business expertise.

Unsecured Bond A type of bond that is not backed by any specific assets or revenue and the issuer only promises payment in full faith. It is also known as debenture. See *secured bond*.

(Un)controllable risk *Controllable risk* is a risk where one has a choice and power to reduce or avoid the loss or damage, thus within one's control. Such risk or uncertainty is associated with a particular individual, asset, firm or industry. It is also known as *diversifiable risk* or *unsystematic risk*.

   Uncontrollable risk is a risk that one has no choice and power in preventing the loss or damage. At best one may mitigate the loss or damage through insurance and other recovery and relief resources. Such risk or uncertainty is associated with natural disasters (floods, earthquakes, storms, etc.) and events that affect the whole industry or country. It is also known as *undiversifiable risk* or *systematic risk*.

(Un)diversifiable risk See *(un)controllable risk* and *(un) systematic risk*.

(Un)systematic risk *Systematic risk*, which is also known as *market risk*, is associated with the uncertainty inherent in the entire market or entire segment of the market. It is also recognized as *uncontrollable risk* and *undiversifiable risk* because the effect on the overall market is a result of external or macroeconomic factors such as social, political or economic which are beyond the control of the organization and cannot be eliminated through diversification. It is also referred to as *volatility risk* as the effect on the entire market leads to the fluctuation in prices arising from changes in government policy, the act of nature such as natural disaster, changes in the nation's economy, international economic components, etc.

   Unsystematic risk, which is also known as *specific risk* and *residual risk*, is associated with the uncertainty that is specific to a particular asset, firm or market. It is also recognized as *controllable risk* and *diversifiable risk* because the uncertainty may be controlled or diversified by taking some precautionary actions.

Upside risk A financial risk where the returns may exceed expectations.

Uses of *qard* fund Represent the amount of gross decrease in funds available for interest free lending during the period covered by the consolidated *Statement of Sources and Uses of Qard Funds*.

Uses of *zakah* and charity funds An item in the Statement of Sources and Uses of *Zakah* and Charity Funds that represents decreases in funds due to payment for philanthropy and to charity organizations for the period.

Usufruct It is the right to use and enjoy a leased asset short of the destruction or waste of its substance. It is known as *al-manfa'ah* in Arabic.

Void contract A contract that is invalid due to any of these four key elements missing: (i) a minimum of two parties with one being the *offeror* and the other *offeree*; (ii) there must be an offer (*ijab*) and acceptance (*qabul*); (iii) existence of a subject matter; and (iv) consideration. Also, due to the descriptive elements missing.

***Wadiah* current account** A demand account based on the principle of safekeeping whereby depositors give consent to the Islamic bank to deal with the whole or any part of money outstanding in their account in the manner that the bank deems fit and is not against *shari'ah*, provided the bank guarantees payment of the whole sum or any part thereof outstanding in the customer's account when demanded.

***Wadiah* saving account** A saving account whereby account holders deposit their surplus funds with an Islamic bank for the purpose of accumulating them over a period of time for safekeeping. The bank can pool and utilize the funds and may at its discretion give depositor some return as gift (*hibah*) especially when the bank gains high profit from their financing projects.

Wadiah yad dhamanah A current or demand deposit account offered by Islamic banks for their customers based on the safekeeping with guarantee principle.

***Wakalah* fee** A management fee received by the *takaful* operator based on a pre-agreed percentage of the premium contributions paid by the *takaful* participants.

***Wakalah* fund based model** A fund established by central banks for the Islamic banks to place deposits with them and receive a return from the *wakalah* fund in lieu of *riba* earned on a non-*shari'ah* compliant deposit.

***Wakalah* saving account** A saving account offered by Islamic banks based on the principle of agency whereby the bank acts as representative (*wakil*) to the depositors in managing funds.

Wakalah takaful A business model for *takaful* based on *wakalah* principle whereby the *takaful* operator and the *takaful* participants form a principal–agent relationship whereby the former acts strictly as an agent on behalf of the latter to conduct either underwriting activities only (for general *takaful*) or both the investment and underwriting activities (for family *takaful*). The *takaful* operator will in return receive a management fee.

Wakalah-mudarabah takaful A business model for *takaful* based on both *mudarabah* and wakalah principles whereby the investors' fund and the participants' funds which are entrusted through the *wakalah* structure are segregated. It involves the principles of *tabarru'* and *qard al hassan* (benevolent loan) in delivering profitable equity and pay for agency ventures.

Wakil Shareholders' or participants agent. See ***wakalah saving account***.

Waqf Endowment funds or assets.

Waqf-wakalah-mudarabah takaful A type of business model for *takaful* based on the collective effects of *waqf-wakalah-mudarabah takaful* principles. This super-hybrid model introduces the concept of *qard hassan* (benevolent loan) to donate the funds to *waqf* (endowment) and hence eliminates 'moral hazard' associated with the sharing of surplus.

Wasiyyat A contract or will conferring a right in the substance or the usufruct of an asset after one's death.

Weighted Average Rate of Return A profitability ratio indicating the percentage of income attributable to funds other than specific investment deposits and Islamic banking capital funds or shareholders' funds. This involves calculating the return of each asset based on the income it generates.

Withdrawal risk A risk that arises when current and saving account holders make cash withdrawal requests and repayment of the principal amounts deposited within a short period of time. It may also involve withdrawals made by profit–loss sharing deposit holders because of lower than expected or acceptable rates of return.

Worldview A particular conception of the world or the philosophy of life.

Write-offs of average gross financing portfolio (WOAGFP) A ratio indicating the amount of financings which were restated from 'at risk' to 'uncollectable' that needs to be written off during the period. Large write-offs reflect poor management procedures for client selection and financing approvals, or for the collection of defaulting payments.

Writer The seller of an option. The buyer of the option is called the owner.

***Zakah* agencies** The agencies set up to collect or receive *zakat* funds from the donors and distribute them to the beneficiaries.

Zakat Alms or obligatory charity ordained by Allah to be performed by Muslims annually as an act of purifying wealth. It is the fourth pillar of the Islamic faith.

***Zakat* base** The obligation to pay the *zakah* when it reaches a threshold called the *nisab*.

***Zakat* distribution** The *zakah* funds must be distributed to the eight specified beneficiaries mentioned in the *Qur'an*: the poor and needy, *zakat* administrators, debtors, freeing the captives, Muslim reverts, those serving God's causes and the wayfarers.

Zakat* provision** The calculated amount to be taken to the *zakat* donation account based on 2.5 per cent of the ***net invested funds or ***net assets*** method.

Index